Samuel E. Wood   Ellen Green Wood   Denise Boyd

Eileen Wood   Serge Desmarais

THE WORLD OF PSYCHOLOGY

Eighth Canadian Edition

PEARSON

Toronto

Editorial Director: Claudine O'Donnell
Marketing Manager: Lisa Gillis
Program Manager: Madhu Ranadive
Project Manager: Andrea Falkenberg
Manager of Content Development: Suzanne Schaan
Developmental Editor: Martina van de Velde
Media Editor: Lila Campbell
Media Developer: Tiffany Palmer
Production Services: Cenveo® Publisher Services
Permissions Project Manager: Kathryn O'Handley
Text and Photo Permissions Research: Integra-CHI, US
Cover and Interior Design: Anthony Leung
Cover Image: ©Anthony Harvie/Stone/Getty Images Prestige

Vice-President, Cross Media and Publishing Services: Gary Bennett

Credits and acknowledgments of material borrowed from other sources and reproduced, with permission, in this textbook appear on the appropriate page within the text.

Original edition published by Pearson Education, Inc., Upper Saddle River, New Jersey, USA. Copyright © 2011 Pearson Education, Inc. This edition is authorized for sale only in Canada.

If you purchased this book outside the United States or Canada, you should be aware that it has been imported without the approval of the publisher or author.

10 9 8 7 6 5 4 3 2 1 [V0SA]

Library and Archives Canada Cataloguing in Publication

Wood, Samuel E., author
    The world of psychology / Samuel E. Wood, Ellen Green
Wood, Denise Boyd, Eileen Wood, Serge Desmarais. — Eighth
Canadian edition.

Includes bibliographical references and indexes.
ISBN 978-0-13-387025-1 (paperback)

    1. Psychology—Textbooks. I. Desmarais, Serge, 1957–, author
II. Wood, Samuel E., author III. Wood, Eileen, 1960–, author
IV. Boyd, Denise Roberts, author V. Wood, Ellen Green, author

BF121.W67 2015   150   C2015-905111-8

ISBN 978-0-13-387025-1

BRIEF CONTENTS

CONTENTS

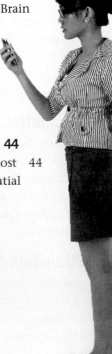

CHAPTER 4 STATES OF CONSCIOUSNESS   96

CHAPTER 9 MOTIVATION AND EMOTION 248

CHAPTER 10 SOCIAL PSYCHOLOGY 276

CHAPTER 11 PERSONALITY THEORY AND ASSESSMENT 306

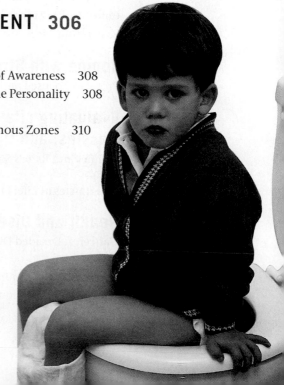

BOXES

REMEMBER IT continued

REMEMBER IT continued

TRY IT

TRY IT continued

APPLY IT

AN INVITATION TO THE STUDENT

We all learn best when we can apply new concepts to the world we know. The eighth edition of *The World of Psychology* allows you to do just that. Highly interactive and active, clearly written, and thoroughly up to date, this textbook will encourage you to think for yourself as you learn about, relate to, and apply the psychological principles that affect your life.

So that you can make the most of all the material in the following pages, this textbook package incorporates a number of helpful features and ancillary items.

A CLEAR, ENGAGING WRITING STYLE

Few texts have received such positive responses from students as *The World of Psychology*, and first and foremost is praise for its writing style. In fact, class tests of the first edition got 100 percent positive feedback at a range of schools. The style is conversational, and the text uses numerous everyday examples and real-life events to help you grasp even the most complex concepts. As well, the contents of each chapter are organized into modules to help chunk the information for easier reference.

Each chapter opens with a vignette (a dramatic real-life story or series of stories) or an activity that draws you into the topics that will be covered in the chapter and shows how psychology relates to the world around you. Each vignette or activity is memorable and directly related to the chapter's content.

You'll be especially interested in the stories and activities related to

- How Facebook and other social-networking sites affect social life.
- How you judge emotions and faces.
- How to control your dreams.
- What happens if a child is raised in the wild.

Canadian Connections introduces interesting historical or more recent Canadian news events with the goal of demonstrating how these experiences you have heard about fit within psychology. These interesting stories provide mean-

ingful real-world examples to aid in understanding the material presented in the chapters. Some *Canadian Connections* boxes highlight cutting-edge contemporary research being conducted in Canadian universities. This will give you an opportunity to see what current research is being conducted in Canada with respect to the topics you are reading about and an idea of the diverse array of research being conducted across Canada today.

INTERACT WITH YOUR TEXTBOOK

What better way to learn new material—to make it fresh, interesting, and memorable—than for you to demonstrate the principles for yourself? The unique *Try It* feature encourages you to learn by doing. This highly praised feature provides simple experiments that you can perform without elaborate equipment, usually as you read.

Knowing what to study and how to discriminate between critical points and fine or more peripheral details is a challenge for any new learner to an area. The *Learning Objectives* at the beginning of each module will help orient you to the key ideas and organize information as you read. These features follow from a substantial body of research showing that memory and comprehension can be improved by organizing information.

In addition, research has shown that checking your progress at key points as you study will also help you remember what you have read. One other way you can interact with your textbook is by taking the *Remember It* quizzes at the end of each module.

Finally, you'll have a chance to relate psychological principles to your own life in the *Apply It* section at the end of each chapter. Each *Apply It* helps you to apply psychology to your personal life and issues. Topics include

- How dangerous is it to talk on, text, or use a cellphone while driving?
- What should you consider when choosing a therapist?
- How can you improve your memory using mnemonic strategies?

SQ3R: A FORMULA FOR SUCCESS

This textbook is organized to help you maximize your learning by following five steps: Survey, Question, Read, Recite, and Review. Together, these are known as the *SQ3R method*. You will learn and remember more if, instead of simply reading each chapter, you follow these steps. Here's how they work.

Survey

First, scan the chapter you plan to read. The *chapter outline* helps you preview the content and its organization.

Read all the section headings and the *learning objectives*, which are designed to focus your attention on key information that you should learn and remember.

Glance at the illustrations and tables, including the *Review & Reflect* tables. Then read the chapter's *Summary & Review*. This survey process gives you an overview of the chapter.

Question

Before you actually read each section in the chapter, turn each topic heading into one or more questions. Some topic headings throughout the book are presented as questions. Use these questions to test yourself. Also, try creating questions of your own. For example, one topic in Chapter 1 is "The Goals of Psychology." The question is "What are the four goals of psychology?" You might add this question of your own: "What is meant by 'control' as a goal of psychology?" Asking such questions helps to focus your reading as well as encourages you to process the material more meaningfully.

Read

Read a section. After reading a section, stop. If the section is very long or if the material seems especially difficult or complex, you should stop after reading only one or two paragraphs.

Recite

After reading part or all of a section, reflect back on the learning objective for that section. Check to see if you remember and understand the material identified through each learning objective. To better grasp each topic, write a short summary of the material. If you have trouble summarizing a topic or answering the questions, scan or read the section once more before trying again.

When you have mastered one section, move on to the next. Then read and recite, answering your question or writing a brief summary as before.

Review

At the end of each module you will find a *Remember It* section that consists of a few questions about the preceding topics. Answer the questions and check your answers. If you make errors, quickly review the preceding material until you know the answers.

The *Summary & Review* section provides condensed summaries of key information in each module. You can also revisit the *Remember It* boxes to assist your review. Then confirm your understanding of the material by reviewing any sections of the text that were challenging. Finally, review the *Key Terms*. If you don't know the meaning of a key term, turn to the page listed to see the term in context; the term will also be defined in the bottom corner of that page or the opposite page. These highlighted glossary terms and definitions provide a ready reference for important key terms that appear in boldface print in the text. All definitions also appear in the end-of-text *Glossary*. Phonetic pronunciations are provided for more than 60 potentially hard-to-pronounce terms.

Then, look at the three *Thinking Critically* questions: *Evaluation, Point/Counterpoint,* and *Psychology in Your Life*. Answering these questions requires more than simple memorization. The critical thinking questions give you the chance to show that you really understand the information presented in the chapter.

Finally, spend some time reviewing the *Concept Maps* at the end of each chapter. The concept maps organize the material by module and highlight the critical information in each section. Use these maps to study and to help you make sure that you have reviewed all the key points. In addition, the concept maps show you how to link related information so that it is easier to see the relationship across the modules as well as within each module. One suggestion you could use to help you when studying is to make a template of the concept map and see how many of the boxes you can fill in. This strategy is an excellent way to assess your knowledge of the material.

Student Supplements

MyPsychLab (www.mypsychlab.com)

THE MOMENT YOU KNOW.   Educators know it. Students know it. It's that inspired moment when something that was difficult to understand suddenly makes perfect sense. Our MyLab products have been designed and refined with a single purpose in mind—to help educators create that moment of understanding with their students. The MyPsychLab Simulations present a suite of data-generating study demonstrations, self-inventories, and surveys that allow students to experience firsthand some of the main concepts covered in their Psychology textbook. Each item in the MyPsychLab Simulations generates anonymous data from introductory psychology students around the world that instructors can download and use in lecture or as homework assignments. The MyPsychLab Simulations provide opportunities for students to actively participate in doing psychology and for instructors to analyze, interpret, and discuss the results.

MyPsychLab delivers **proven results** in helping individual students succeed. It provides engaging experiences that personalize, stimulate, and measure learning for each student. And, it comes from a **trusted partner** with educational expertise and an eye on the future.

MyPsychLab can be used by itself or linked to any learning management system. To learn more about how MyPsychLab combines proven learning applications with powerful assessment, visit www.mypsychlab.com

MyPsychLab—the moment you know.

PEARSON ETEXT   Pearson eText gives students access to the text whenever and wherever they have access to the Internet. eText pages look exactly like the printed text, offering powerful new functionality for students and instructors. Users can create notes, highlight text in different colours, create bookmarks, zoom, click hyperlinked words and phrases to view definitions, and view in single-page or two-page view.

REVEL™   Designed for the way today's students read, think, and learn, REVEL is a ground-breaking immersive learning experience. It's based on a simple premise: When students are engaged deeply, they learn more and get better results.

Built in collaboration with educators and students, REVEL brings course content to life with rich media and assessments—integrated directly within the authors' narrative—that provide opportunities for students to read, learn and practice in one environment. **Learn more about REVEL** http://www.pearsonhighered.com/revel

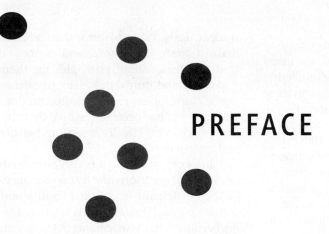

PREFACE

In preparing the eighth edition of this book, our primary goals were to introduce critical issues in psychology accurately and clearly to students, using a format that is both interesting and memorable. We present the principles of psychology using a clear and engaging writing style and a pedagogically sound learning format that is accessible and appealing to students.

Having taught thousands of students their first course in psychology, we are sensitive to the complexities of the teaching/learning process, and are acutely aware of the tremendous changes that have occurred in the field of psychology over the years. With this in mind, we sought to create a textbook that is sensitive to the changing needs of students and their professors and that will provide a context in which readers may learn about psychology's past, present, and probable future.

THE EIGHTH EDITION

Despite the overwhelming response to our first seven Canadian editions of *The World of Psychology*, we have incorporated a number of improvements into the new edition. In accordance with reviewer suggestions and the goals stated above, the eighth Canadian edition features the following elements:

- One of the comments we receive regularly about our text is that the information is laid out in an attractive and appealing way. Once again, we have tried to build on this design strength in the current revision by enhancing the visual supports. Images, graphs, drawings, and other visual supports to learning have been added, updated, and reconfigured to ensure that key ideas are accentuated. For example, some salient visual aids have been enlarged to increase their visibility and to make accompanying text easier to see.

- The modular structure introduced in our fifth edition was retained and further refined in this edition. The modular framework divides each chapter into manageable "chunks" of information that are easier for instructors to assign and for students to read. Organizing material into meaningful chunks helps improve students' memory by supporting the organization of information, and the smaller units make it easier to remember by minimizing the demands on working memory capacity—or memory span. It also allows for increased flexibility for instructors when assigning material.

- *Learning Objectives* appear at the beginning of each module, and learning objective numbers are presented with the corresponding material in the text. The goal of the learning objectives is to provide an organizer for students at the outset of each module. This will help students to understand how to read the material in each chapter by highlighting the critical information to be learned. This feature will enhance the learning experience by promoting greater memory and comprehension. Learning objectives and the corresponding summaries at the end of the chapter have been revised to ensure clear, succinct connections throughout this text.

- The concise *Concept Maps* identify the critical information in each section. These hierarchically arranged concept maps visually organize the material by module, as well as illustrate the links between topics spanning different modules.

- Canadian and international research has been updated to reflect new trends in psychology and society.

- At least one *Canadian Connections* box appears in each chapter. The function of these boxes is to highlight events past and present that show how Canadians are or have been involved in the issues being presented in the text. For example, some *Canadian Connections* boxes highlight key Canadian researchers and their most recent work, while others integrate Canadian historical events with current issues. These boxes integrate Canadian contributions and events within the broader field of psychology.

- The opening vignettes share important stories to draw attention to the practical and real-world importance of the information in the chapter. New vignettes invite students to complete activities or mini-surveys to engage them more directly in the content that will follow.

Canadian Context

Our Canadian colleagues and their students find that many introductory psychology texts target an American audience. The issues, research citations, and practical examples in these texts typically relate to U.S. events and experiences. We believe that students learn best when materials are relevant to their lives. The Canadian content in this text includes events in the media, current research, and historical references to Canadian facts and contributors. By including information that is more meaningful to Canadian students, we hope to enhance their understanding and retention of the material.

Part of the Canadian identity is our recognition of the diversity in society. To acknowledge this, we have made an effort to include the influential work of psychologists from around the world. Also, we have tried to include events and studies from different regions of Canada. We believe this added value makes *The World of Psychology*, Eighth Canadian Edition, a balanced, universal text.

A Clear, Understandable, Interesting Writing Style

First and foremost, a textbook is a teaching instrument. A good psychology text must communicate clearly to a wide audience of various ages and levels of academic ability. Our book is appealing to accomplished students, yet accessible to those whose academic skills are still developing.

We achieved this objective (we hope) by explaining concepts in much the same way as we do in our own psychology classes. Throughout the text we sought to ensure flow and continuity by using a conversational style and avoiding abrupt shifts in thought. In addition, the text is filled with everyday examples that are pertinent to students' lives.

A Series of High-Interest Features That Will Appeal to Today's Students

Every chapter opens with a vignette or activity to capture student interest and build motivation. We have also included special features:

- *Apply It* sections show the practical applications of the principles of psychology.

- *Canadian Connections* discuss Canadian news events that demonstrate concepts outlined in the text and/or highlight contemporary research being conducted in Canadian universities.

- *World of Psychology* boxes in selected chapters explore special diversity issues.

A TEXTBOOK THAT ENCOURAGES STUDENTS TO BECOME ACTIVE PARTICIPANTS IN THE LEARNING PROCESS

Reading about psychology is not enough. Students should be able to practise what they have learned, where appropriate. Many of the principles we teach can be demonstrated, often without elaborate equipment and sometimes as the student reads. What better way to teach new material and make it fresh, interesting, and memorable than to have students demonstrate principles for themselves using an important and innovative element of the book: *Try It* sections? The response to *Try It* demonstrations from professors and students has been so positive that this feature appears in every chapter. The *Try It* sections personalize psychology and make it come alive.

Student involvement is also promoted through the use of rhetorical questions and by casting the student in the role of the participant in selected studies and descriptions of real-life events. Thus, students who use *The World of Psychology* become active participants in the learning process rather than simply passive recipients of information.

An Emphasis on Critical Thinking

Thinking critically does not call for being critical of all viewpoints other than one's own. Rather, critical thinking is a process of evaluating claims, propositions, or conclusions objectively in order to determine whether they follow logically from the evidence presented. Critical thinkers are open-minded, objective, and unbiased, and they maintain a skeptical attitude that leads them to search for alternative explanations.

Critical thinking is too important to leave to chance. In addition to promoting critical thinking throughout the text, we have developed a systematic method of nurturing it. A *Thinking Critically* section at the end of each chapter features three types of questions:

1. Evaluation questions teach students to think critically as they take stock of psychological theories, techniques, approaches, perspectives, and research studies.

2. Point/counterpoint questions require students to comprehend, analyze, and formulate convincing arguments on both sides of important issues in psychology.

3. Real-life application questions allow students to apply psychological principles and concepts to their own lives and the everyday world.

Help for Students to Understand Human Diversity and More Fully Comprehend the Part Multicultural Issues Play in Contemporary Psychology

Human diversity issues are integrated throughout the book, both within the main text presentation and as highlighted special features. This form of presentation parallels the presence of diversity in Canada as a mainstream and special-interest issue. Diversity issues include cultural, gender, and age concerns in selected topic areas in each chapter. For example, in Chapter 1 we focus on the problem of bias. Later, we discuss the impact of culture on memory, the effect of personality on perception, the interpretation of emotion, and preferred forms of therapy. These, along with other segments, help to promote understanding of human diversity and how it is an integral part of our perception of the world.

Current Coverage That Preserves the Classic Contributions in Our Field

Advances in knowledge and research are occurring at an ever-increasing pace, and modern authors must keep abreast. This edition introduces students to the most up-to-date research on many topics that feature rapid change, including advanced technologies, neuropsychology, gender differences, changes in social norms, violence, aggression and stress, adolescent drug use, and new therapies.

Yet we do not value newness for its own sake. We include, as well, studies that have stood the test of time, and we explore the classic contributions to psychology in depth.

An Appreciation of Psychology's History and an Understanding That Psychology Is a Living, Growing, Evolving Science

A portion of Chapter 1 is devoted to psychology's history. But in our view, the history of psychology is best understood and appreciated in the context in which the contributions were made. Consequently, discussions of such topics as learning, memory, intelligence, emotion, and personality integrate both historical and recent research contributions to show how psychology has evolved up to the present day.

An Accurate and Thoroughly Researched Textbook That Features Original Sources

To accomplish our goal of introducing the world of psychology accurately and clearly, we have gone back to original sources and have read or reread the basic works of the major figures in psychology and the classic studies in the field. This has enabled us to write with greater clarity and assurance, without having to hedge or write tentatively when discussing what experts in the field have actually said. This book is one of the most carefully researched, up-to-date, and extensively referenced psychology textbooks available.

A Sound Pedagogical System in the Text and Learning Package

The pedagogical system in *The World of Psychology* consists of the following components:

- *Learning Objectives.* Learning objectives orient students to the critical information to be learned within each module.

- *Remember It.* There is a *Remember It* memory check at the end of every module. These checks are designed to encourage students to pause and test comprehension of material they have just read.

- *Review & Reflect Tables.* We have expanded our use of the extremely popular summary tables, called *Review & Reflect*, which are useful for reviewing and comparing various perspectives, theories, and other concepts.

- *Text-Embedded Glossary.* A text-embedded glossary provides a ready reference for important key terms that appear in boldface in the text. Definitions also appear in the *Glossary* at the back of the book. Phonetic pronunciations are provided for more than 60 potentially hard-to-pronounce terms.

- *Summary & Review.* These end-of-chapter sections provide succinct summaries for key concepts. The feature can be used both as a preview to the chapter and as a review in preparing for tests.

- *Concept Maps.* These memory aids serve two functions. First, the maps summarize the key elements of each module in an interesting, easy-to-follow visual format. Second, the maps show the relationships across modules. These links help to integrate the materials and make the flow of information more obvious.

A Complete, Coordinated Teaching Package of the Highest Quality

Instructor supplements are available for download from a password-protected section of Pearson Education Canada's online catalogue (http://catalogue.pearsoned.ca). Navigate to your book's catalogue page to view a list of those supplements that are available. See your local sales representative for details and access.

- **Instructor's Manual:** The Instructor's Resource Manual (IRM) was developed to encourage student involvement and understanding with lecture examples, demonstrations, in-class activities, critical-thinking topics, diversity issues, and guides to using other ancillary materials. Lecture Guides are included for each chapter—using the chapter outlines to integrate the suggested lecture discussions, activities, and other resources directly into the appropriate sections.

- **PowerPoint Presentation:** This slide presentation pairs key points covered in the chapter with figures from the textbook to provoke effective classroom discussion.

- **Test Item File:** This test bank in Microsoft Word format includes over 200 questions for each chapter, in multiple choice, true/false, short answer, and essay formats, each with an answer justification, page reference, difficulty rating, and type designation. This test bank is also available in a computerized testing format (see below).

- Pearson's **computerized test banks** allow instructors to filter and select questions to create quizzes, tests, or homework. Instructors can revise questions or add their own, and may be able to choose print or online options. These questions are also available in Microsoft Word format. The computerized test bank for *The World of Psychology*, Eighth Canadian Edition includes over 3600 questions in multiple-choice, true/false, and essay formats.

- **Image Library:** The image library provides you with chapter figures and tables.

MyPsychLab (www.mypsychlab.com)

THE MOMENT YOU KNOW.   Educators know it. Students know it. It's that inspired moment when something that was difficult to understand suddenly makes perfect sense. Our MyLab products have been designed and refined with a single purpose in mind—to help educators create that moment of understanding with their students.

MyPsychLab delivers **proven results** in helping individual students succeed. It provides **engaging experiences** that personalize, stimulate, and measure learning for each student. And, it comes from a **trusted partner** with educational expertise and an eye on the future.

MyPsychLab can be used by itself or linked to any learning management system. To learn more about how MyPsychLab combines proven learning applications with powerful assessment, visit www.mypsychlab.com

Included in MyPsychLab, the new **MyPsychLab Simulations** present a suite of data-generating study demonstrations, self-inventories, and surveys that allow students to experience firsthand some of the main concepts covered in their Psychology textbook. Each item in the MyPsychLab Simulations generates anonymous data from introductory psychology students around the world that instructors can download and use in lecture or as homework assignments. The MyPsychLab Simulations provide opportunities for students to actively participate in doing psychology and for instructors to analyze, interpret, and discuss the results.

PEARSON eTEXT   Pearson eText gives students access to the text whenever and wherever they have access to the Internet. eText pages look exactly like the printed text, offering powerful new functionality for students and instructors. Users can create notes, highlight text in different colours, create bookmarks, zoom, click hyperlinked words and phrases to view definitions, and view in single-page or two-page view.

peerScholar Firmly grounded in published research, peerScholar is a powerful online pedagogical tool that helps develop your students' critical and creative thinking skills. peerScholar facilitates this through the process of creation, evaluation, and reflection. Working in stages, students begin by submitting a written assignment. peerScholar then circulates their work for others to review, a process that can be anonymous or not depending on your preference. Students receive peer feedback and evaluations immediately, reinforcing their learning and driving the development of higher-order thinking skills. Students can then resubmit revised work, again depending on your preference. Contact your Pearson Representative to learn more about peerScholar and the research behind it.

Pearson's **Technology Specialists** work with faculty and campus course designers to ensure that Pearson technology products, assessment tools, and online course materials are tailored to meet your specific needs. This highly qualified team is dedicated to helping schools take full advantage of a wide range of educational resources, by assisting in the integration of a variety of instructional materials and media formats. Your local Pearson Education sales representative can provide you with more details on this service program.

REVEL™ Designed for the way today's students read, think, and learn, REVEL is a ground-breaking immersive learning experience. It's based on a simple premise: When students are engaged deeply, they learn more and get better results.

Built in collaboration with educators and students, REVEL brings course content to life with rich media and assessments—integrated directly within the authors' narrative—that provide opportunities for students to read, learn and practice in one environment. **Learn more about REVEL** http://www.pearsonhighered.com/revel

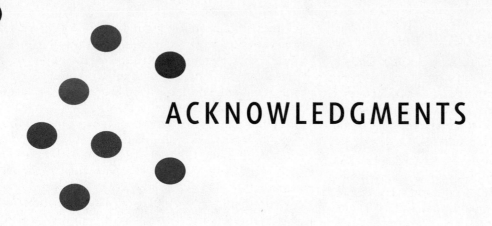

ACKNOWLEDGMENTS

We would like to thank research assistant Emily Christofides, who provided a great deal of help help during the review of the book. Also, we are indebted to an incredible group of people at Pearson Education Canada for their contributions to *The World of Psychology*. We want to thank Matthew Christian, acquisitions editor; Martina van de Velde, developmental editor; Andrea Falkenberg, project manager; and Raghavi Khullar, who provided expert assistance throughout the writing process.

ABOUT THE AUTHORS

Samuel E. Wood

Samuel E. Wood (deceased) received his doctorate from the University of Florida. He has taught at West Virginia University and the University of Missouri–St. Louis and was a member of the doctoral faculty at both universities. From 1984 to 1996, he served as president of the Higher Education Center, a consortium of 14 colleges and universities in the St. Louis area. He was a co-founder of the Higher Education Cable TV channel (HEC-TV) in St. Louis and served as its president and CEO from its founding in 1987 until 1996.

Ellen R. Green Wood

Ellen Green Wood received her doctorate in educational psychology from St. Louis University and was an adjunct professor of psychology at St. Louis Community College at Meramec. She has also taught in the clinical experiences program in education at Washington University and at the University of Missouri–St. Louis. In addition to her teaching, Dr. Wood has developed and taught seminars on critical thinking. She received the Telecourse Pioneer Award from 1982 through 1988 for her contributions to the field of distance learning.

Denise Boyd

Denise Boyd received her Ed.D. in educational psychology from the University of Houston and has been a psychology instructor in the Houston Community College System since 1988. From 1995 until 1998, she chaired the psychology, sociology, and anthropology department at Houston Community College–Central. She has co-authored three other Pearson Allyn and Bacon texts: with Helen Bee, *Lifespan Development* (Sixth Edition), *The Developing Child* (Thirteenth Edition), and *The Growing Child* (First Edition); and with Genevieve Stevens, *Current Readings in Lifespan Development*. A licensed psychologist, she has presented a number of papers at professional meetings, reporting research in child, adolescent, and adult development. She has also presented workshops for teachers whose students range from preschool to college.

Eileen Wood

Eileen Wood received her doctorate from Simon Fraser University. She is a full professor in the Department of Psychology at Wilfrid Laurier University. She conducts research in developmental and educational psychology. Her primary research interests involve studying how people acquire, maintain, and recall information, especially when technologies are involved. The impact of instructors, types of instruction, and instructional environments are also part of her research. Her secondary research interests involve gender role development and dating. Dr. Wood has authored several books, book chapters, and many articles. She was recently awarded the University Research Professor Award to pursue her research on students' use of technology in the classroom. She has also received several awards for teaching excellence. Dr. Wood primarily teaches introductory and developmental psychology at the undergraduate level and developmental psychology at the graduate level. She works collaboratively with school boards and participates in administrative boards that work toward enhancing learning for learners of all ages.

Serge Desmarais

Serge Desmarais received his Ph.D. in social psychology from the University of Waterloo. He is a full professor, a former Canada Research Chair in applied social psychology, and the current Associate Vice-President (Academic) at the University of Guelph. In this role, he oversees all aspects of the undergraduate curriculum at his university. Dr. Desmarais started teaching introductory psychology in his first academic position in 1990, and has taught this course regularly since the beginning of his career. He is the recipient of several University of Guelph teaching awards. Dr. Desmarais is an active researcher and the author of many articles and book chapters in the areas of interpersonal relations, work and pay expectations, gender issues, and the personal consequences of social media.

To Chris, for all the care, love, and support.
—S.D.

In memory of my father, who was my strongest champion,
and my family, who are my inspiration.
—E.W.

1

Do you have a Facebook account?

We're pretty sure that you do since Facebook is currently the most popular social networking site in Canada, with more than 10 million users who access Facebook every day (Oliveira, 2014). Facebook and other social media, such as Twitter, are changing the very nature of social relationships. It is estimated that nearly 90 percent of college and university students use Facebook, making it the most popular social media despite a slight drop in popularity in recent years (McDermott, 2014).

As all of you know, Facebook is used as a way of interacting with others, finding online friends, keeping friends aware of the changes in your life, showing pictures, and even starting—or ending—relationships. While popular, engaging, and convenient, Facebook is not without its problems. For instance, Facebook opens up a person's world—activities, list of friends, and personal information—to full public scrutiny (Boyd & Ellison, 2007), creating some serious concerns over issues of personal privacy (Christofides, Muise, & Desmarais, 2009). It's commonly assumed that adolescents and young people are far more likely to exchange information that may cause damaging privacy consequences, but a recent study suggests that midlife adults are equally susceptible to disclosing personal information (Christofides, Muise, & Desmarais, 2011). Other research indicates that Facebook may also cause jealousy among romantic partners and may negatively impact romantic relationships (Muise, Christofides, & Desmarais, 2009, 2014). But the potential problems associated with Facebook and other Web-based technologies do not change the fact that social media are now a significant part of everyday life—how many of us could live without them? This fact raises many important questions: Is this technology changing us? Has it become so difficult to make personal connections in our daily lives that we must use social media as a way of keeping in touch with our friends or reconnecting with people we once knew? Why is it that people are now so willing to open up their lives for the world to see, whereas only a few years ago most of us would have hidden our diaries for fear of having our perceptions, dreams, and fantasies revealed? Has technology blurred the lines between public and private life?

INTRODUCTION TO PSYCHOLOGY

©Mark Edwards/Fotolia

When you hear the word *psychology*, what is the first thing that comes to mind? Do you think about Facebook or Twitter? Probably not. However, it is exactly these simple parts of our daily lives that connect to the field of psychology, from our daily actions to the way we perceive others, to how our brain conceives of the world around us. Most people have a very poor conception of the area of psychology. They think that this field of research consists of stories about Freud, some vague understanding of psychotherapy, and perhaps some exposure to recent self-help books—likely, books about relationships and personal growth. The fact is that psychology covers more issues than you'd expect, including the everyday exchanges we have on Facebook!

There are many branches of psychology and you will be introduced to them all in this text. Psychologists specializing in the different areas of psychology look at situations from different perspectives. For example, given today's use of Facebook to connect with our friends and social network, a social psychologist might want to examine whether connecting with people online affects the quality of those relationships; do people who frequently use Facebook to keep in touch with their friends or family maintain as close a relationship with them as those who tend to meet face to face? And is it the case that examining the Facebook profile of one's dating partner increases feelings of jealousy as recent studies suggest? A personality psychologist, on the other hand, might want to find out what personal characteristics are associated with using Facebook. Are shy people more likely to prefer this means of interaction? Do very outgoing people tend to use the medium as a way to extend their social circle? Are they more likely to have lots of Facebook friends?

In contrast, a cognitive psychologist might want to investigate whether using Facebook influences the way we think, write, or communicate with others. Will the increased use of abbreviations, such as those we use when communicating with each other by text message, affect how people talk to each other? And a developmental psychologist might want to know whether children who start using Facebook early in life will develop a different understanding of themselves and the world around them—are children aware that the material they post on Facebook may be entirely accessible by anyone who has a Facebook account? (For that matter, are *you* aware of that?)

It is not possible in this brief introduction to portray the full range of research possibilities that might interest psychologists wanting to study the impact that Facebook or other online communication tools have on our lives or even to consider the ways in which these various research avenues might be investigated. This book, *The World of Psychology*, is designed to expose you to psychological research and to help clarify some of the complexities of this academic discipline and its application.

MODULE **1A** INTRODUCTION TO PSYCHOLOGY

LO 1.1 Define *psychology*.
LO 1.2 Identify and explain psychology's four primary goals.
LO 1.3 Explain what a theory is.
LO 1.4 Compare and contrast basic and applied research.

The word *psychology* conjures up images of mental disorders, abnormal behaviour, and adjustment to difficult periods of life. As we pointed out above, however, although psychologists do sometimes study the strange and unusual, they are most often interested in day-to-day events—the normal and commonplace.

Just what is psychology? Psychology has changed over the years and so has its definition. In the late 1800s, mental processes were considered to be the appropriate subject matter of psychology. Later there was a movement to restrict psychology to the study of observable behaviour alone. Today the importance of both areas is recognized, and **psychology** is now defined as the scientific study of behaviour and mental processes. **[LO 1.1]**

Before you read the next section, answer the questions in *Try It* to see how much you already know about some of the topics we will explore in *The World of Psychology*.

PSYCHOLOGY: SCIENCE OR COMMON SENSE?

Most people tend to have a vague understanding of psychology. For instance, students often begin their first course in psychology with a sense that psychology is more common sense than science. But can we make a valid claim that psychology is a science?

Let's consider your own answers to the *Try It* questions: is it possible that what you believed to be common sense may have led you astray? All the odd-numbered items are false, and all the even-numbered items are true. So common sense, on its own, will not take you very far in your study of psychology.

Many people believe that whether a field of study is a science depends on the nature of its body of knowledge. Physics, for example, is a science, and so is chemistry. But neither

TRY IT

Test Your Knowledge of Psychology

Indicate whether each statement is true or false.
1. Memory is more accurate under hypnosis.
2. All people dream during a night of normal sleep.
3. As the number of bystanders at an emergency increases, the time it takes for the victim to get help decreases.
4. There is no maternal instinct in humans.
5. Older adults tend to express less satisfaction with life in general than younger adults do.
6. Eyewitness testimony is often unreliable.
7. Children with high IQs tend to be less able physically than their peers.
8. Creativity and high intelligence do not necessarily go together.
9. When it comes to close personal relationships, opposites attract.
10. The majority of teenagers have good relationships with their parents.

qualifies as a science solely because of its subject matter. A science is a science not because of the nature of its body of knowledge, but because of the approach—the standards, methods, values, and general principles—employed in acquiring that body of knowledge. Psychology is considered a science because it uses the scientific method, which attempts to minimize biases, preconceptions, personal beliefs, and emotions (Christensen, Burke Johnson, & Turner, 2014).

THE GOALS OF PSYCHOLOGY

What are the four goals of psychology?

The goals of psychology are the description, explanation, prediction, and influence of behaviour and mental processes. **[LO 1.2]** Psychological researchers always seek to accomplish one or more of these goals when they plan and conduct their studies.

The first goal, *description*, is usually the first step in understanding any behaviour or mental process. To describe a phenomenon, we must make accurate notes about the behaviours or situations we observe. These observations become our *data*—the specific pieces of information we use in our analyses. For instance, if you are examining how two strangers from different cultures relate to each other when they meet for the first time, you need to keep accurate notes about every detail of the interaction—how long they look at each other, how far away they stand from each other, along with all other details of their behaviour. The goal of description is usually more important in a very new area of research or in the early stages of research.

The second goal, *explanation*, requires an understanding of the conditions under which a given behaviour or mental process occurs. This step certainly goes beyond description. Here, researchers try to understand the causes of the behaviour or mental process. In other words, the explanation goal allows researchers to tell "why" a given event or behaviour occurred—for example, why do strangers who meet for the first time stand far away from each other? Why does one of them smile when the other one smiles? But researchers do not reach the goal of explanation until their results have been tested, retested, and confirmed. Researchers confirm an explanation by eliminating or ruling out other, competing explanations.

The goal of *prediction* is met when researchers can specify the conditions under which a behaviour or event is likely to occur. The goal here is to understand or predict the likelihood that an event will occur under a certain set of circumstances. Researchers might ask, for example, whether the distance at which strangers stand from each other differs as a result of the culture they come from. In other words, can culture predict social distance? Is there a predictable or replicable pattern? If researchers have identified all the prior conditions required for a behaviour or event to occur, they can predict the behaviour or event.

The goal of *influence* is accomplished when researchers know how to apply a principle or change a condition to prevent unwanted occurrences or to bring about desired outcomes. The ability to influence behaviour can have positive consequences. For instance, it enables psychologists to design types of therapy to prevent anxiety attacks or depression. It also enables researchers to develop techniques that can be employed to improve one's memory.

WHAT IS A THEORY?

Any science has a well-established body of theory to guide its research, and psychology is no exception. A **theory** is a general principle or set of principles that explains how a number of separate facts are related to one another. **[LO 1.3]** In other words, a theory is an attempt to explain why something happens. It is based on evidence and attempts to predict the future occurrence of an event or action. A theory enables researchers to fit many separate facts into a larger framework; it imposes order on what otherwise would be a disconnected jumble of data. The value of a theory depends upon how well it accounts for the accumulated research findings in a given area and upon how accurately it can predict new findings.

A theory serves two important functions: (1) it organizes facts—a necessary step toward arriving at a systematic body of knowledge; and (2) it guides research. When researchers conduct a new study, they test the theory's accuracy. If the theory's predictions are supported, this new finding serves to reinforce the general principles that underlie the theory. But it is important to remember that a good theory is one that provides an explanation that is clear, comprehensive, explicit, simple, and always *falsifiable*. A falsifiable theory is scientific because it is testable and can be rejected if the predictions are not confirmed. Theories are not certainties—they are made to be tested and changed if the data do not support the theory's predictions. Researchers often use theories to generate hypotheses, as we'll discuss later in this chapter.

BASIC AND APPLIED RESEARCH

What is the difference between basic and applied research?

The two main types of research that psychologists pursue to accomplish their goals are (1) basic, or pure, research and (2) applied research. **[LO 1.4]** The purpose of **basic research** is to seek new knowledge and to explore and advance general scientific understanding. Basic research investigates such topics as the nature of memory, brain function, motivation, and emotional expression; and the causes of mental disorders such as schizophrenia, depression, sleep and eating disorders; and so on. Psychologists doing basic research usually seek to accomplish the first three goals—description, explanation, and prediction. Basic research is not intended to solve specific problems, nor is it meant to investigate ways to apply what is learned to immediate real-world problems. Yet very often the findings of basic

---

psychology: The scientific study of behaviour and mental processes.

theory: A general principle or set of principles that explains how a number of separate facts are related to one another.

basic research: Research conducted for the purpose of advancing knowledge rather than for its practical application.

research are later applied in real-world settings. For example, much basic research in neuroscience has resulted in the development of new drugs that have improved the lives of those who suffer from psychological disorders.

Applied research is conducted with the specific goal of solving practical problems and improving people's quality of life. Applied research focuses on such things as methods to improve memory or increase motivation, therapies to treat mental disorders, ways to decrease stress, and factors that improve people's job satisfaction. Applied psychologists are primarily concerned with the fourth goal of psychology—influence—because it specifies ways and means of changing behaviour. You will learn more about some fields of applied psychology at the end of this chapter.

REMEMBER IT

Introduction to Psychology

1. The orderly, systematic procedures that scientists follow in acquiring a body of knowledge are called _Scientific method_
2. The four goals of psychology are _description_, _explanation_, _prediction_, and _influence_.
3. Which of the two types of research (basic or applied) is designed to solve practical problems and improve the quality of life? _Applied_

Answers: 1. the scientific method 2. description, explanation, prediction, influence 3. applied

---

MODULE 1B DESCRIPTIVE RESEARCH METHODS

LO 1.5 Identify and compare the several types of descriptive research methods.

LO 1.6 Compare and contrast naturalistic and laboratory observations, including their advantages and limitations.

LO 1.7 Compare and contrast case studies and survey research, including their advantages and shortcomings.

LO 1.8 Explain why researchers use correlational studies.

LO 1.9 Define *correlation coefficient* and explain how to interpret it.

The goals of psychological research—description, explanation, prediction, and influence—are typically accomplished in stages. In the early stages of research, descriptive methods are usually the most appropriate since they allow researchers to identify and describe a particular phenomenon. When using **descriptive research methods**, the intent is not to identify causes of behaviour; here, the goal is only to describe a behaviour. Naturalistic observation, laboratory observation, the case study, and the survey are examples of descriptive research methods. **[LO 1.5]**

Although naturalistic observation allows researchers to study behaviour in everyday settings, observer bias may cause them to see what they expect to see.

NATURALISTIC OBSERVATION: CAUGHT IN THE ACT OF BEING THEMSELVES

What is naturalistic observation, and what are some of its advantages and limitations?

Naturalistic observation is a research method in which researchers observe and record behaviour in its natural setting without attempting to influence or control it. **[LO 1.5]** Ethologists are researchers who study the behaviour patterns of animals in their natural environment. These researchers might observe their subjects through high-powered telescopes or from blinds that they build to conceal themselves.

Often human participants are not aware that they are being observed. This can be accomplished by means of one-way mirrors, a technique researchers often use to observe children in nursery schools or special classrooms. At times, researchers may use hidden cameras or tape recorders to collect research data. The major advantage of naturalistic observation is that it allows one to study behaviour in normal settings, where it occurs more naturally and spontaneously. **[LO 1.6]** Naturalistic observation may be the only feasible way to study certain phenomena when an experiment would be impossible or unethical—for example, to learn how people react during disasters such as earthquakes or fires.

LABORATORY OBSERVATION: A MORE SCIENTIFIC LOOK AT THE PARTICIPANT

Another method of studying behaviour involves observation that takes place not in a natural setting but in the laboratory. **[LOs 1.5 & 1.6]** There, researchers can exert more control over the environment, which helps limit the effect of unexpected factors. Making observations in a laboratory may also result in the use of more precise equipment to measure responses. Much of our knowledge about sleep, for example, has been gained by laboratory observation of participants who sleep for several nights in a sleep laboratory or sleep clinic. Of course, laboratory control can have its disadvantages. For instance, researchers may lose the spontaneity that occurs when behaviours take place in a more natural setting. This disadvantage is especially relevant for human interactions that tend to be strongly affected by environmental factors.

THE CASE STUDY METHOD: STUDYING A FEW PARTICIPANTS IN DEPTH

What is the case study method, and for what purposes is it particularly well suited?

Another descriptive research method used by psychologists is the **case study**, or case history. **[LO 1.7]** In a case study, a single individual or a small number of people is studied in great depth, usually over an extended time. A case study involves observation, interviews, and sometimes psychological testing. A case study is exploratory in nature, and its purpose is to provide a detailed description of some behaviour or disorder. This method is particularly appropriate for studying people who have uncommon psychological or physiological disorders or brain injuries. Case studies often emerge in the course of treatment of these disorders. In fact, much of what we know about unusual psychological disorders comes from the in-depth analyses provided by case studies.

Although the case study has been useful in advancing knowledge in several areas of psychology, it has certain limitations. In a case study, researchers cannot establish the cause of observed behaviours. Moreover, because so few people are studied, researchers do not know how generalizable their findings are to larger groups or to different cultures. **[LO 1.7]**

SURVEY RESEARCH: THE ART OF SAMPLING AND QUESTIONING

What are the methods and purposes of survey research?

Psychologists are interested in many questions that cannot be investigated using naturalistic observation or case studies. With a **survey**, researchers use interviews and/or questionnaires to gather information about the attitudes, beliefs, experiences, or behaviours of a group of people. **[LO 1.7]** Well-designed and carefully conducted surveys have provided much of the information available to us about the incidence of drug use, about the sexual behaviour of particular segments of the population, and about the incidence of various mental disorders.

Selecting a Sample: More to Consider Than Numbers

What is a representative sample, and why is it essential in a survey?

Researchers in psychology rarely conduct experiments or surveys using all members of the group they are studying. For example, researchers studying the sexual behaviours of Canadian women do not attempt to study every woman in Canada. Instead of studying the whole **population** (the entire group of interest, or target population), they study a sample. A **sample** is a part of the population that is selected and studied

in order to reach conclusions about the entire larger population of interest.

However, researchers must ensure that the sample is representative. A **representative sample** is one that includes important subgroups in the same proportion as they are found in the larger population. That is, the representative sample should reflect the economic, ethnic, cultural, and sexual diversity of the target population.

The Use of Questionnaires

Researchers using the survey method rely on information gathered through questionnaires or interviews, or through some combination of the two. Questionnaires can be completed more quickly and less expensively than interviews.

Many people believe that a survey becomes more accurate when more people answer it. In fact, the number of people who respond to a survey is not the critical element. A researcher can generalize findings from a sample only if it is representative of the entire population of interest. For example, the readers of *Flare* or *The Hockey News* do not represent a cross-section of Canadians. So questionnaires in magazines are not scientific; neither are TV or radio phone-in surveys. Good surveys control wording, context, and format (Schwarz, 1999).

The Interview

Skilled interviewers can gather accurate information by asking well-worded questions of a carefully selected sample of participants. When respondents feel comfortable with an interviewer, they feel freer to share personal information. Imagine that you are being interviewed about a sensitive subject such as your

---

applied research: Research conducted for the purpose of solving practical problems.

descriptive research methods: Research methods that yield descriptions of behaviour rather than causal explanations.

naturalistic observation: A research method in which researchers observe and record behaviour without trying to influence or control it.

case study: An in-depth study of one or a few participants consisting of information gathered through observation, interviews, and perhaps psychological testing.

survey: A method whereby researchers use interviews and/or questionnaires to gather information about the attitudes, beliefs, experiences, or behaviours of a group of people.

population: The entire group of interest to researchers to which they wish to generalize their findings; the group from which a sample is selected.

sample: The portion of any population that is selected for study and from which generalizations are made about the larger population.

representative sample: A sample of participants selected from the larger population in such a way that important subgroups within the population are included in the sample in the same proportions as they are found in the larger population.

sexual behaviour. Will you be equally comfortable and truthful whether the interviewer is male or female? Young, middle-aged, or old? Chinese, black, francophone, or of another ethnic group? Christian, Muslim, or Jewish? The validity or truthfulness of responses can be affected by the interviewer's personal characteristics, which include gender, age, heritage, religion, social class, accent, and vocabulary.

Using the Internet for Survey Research

The internet now offers psychologists a way of soliciting participants and collecting survey responses that is fast, inexpensive, and often generates large numbers of responses (Skitka & Sargis, 2006). Some researchers are concerned that internet survey samples are often biased because they represent only the population of internet users who choose to participate in online research studies. However, some recent studies of internet samples suggest that participants in these studies tend to match very closely those in other types of studies (Gosling & Johnson, 2010).

Advantages and Disadvantages of Survey Research

If conducted properly, surveys can provide highly accurate information about large numbers of people and can show changes in attitudes and behaviour over time. Yet large-scale surveys can also be costly and time-consuming. Researchers must have expertise in many areas—selecting a representative sample, constructing questionnaires, interviewing, and analyzing data.

The major limitation of the survey is that the respondents may provide inaccurate information. Respondents may give false information because of faulty memory or a desire to please the interviewer (saying what they think the interviewer wants to hear). Respondents may have a tendency to present themselves in a good light ("the social desirability response"). They may even deliberately mislead the researcher. **[LO 1.7]**

THE CORRELATIONAL METHOD: DISCOVERING RELATIONSHIPS, NOT CAUSES

What is the correlational method, and when is it used?

Researchers are often interested in understanding the relationship between two variables (any conditions that can be manipulated, measured, or controlled). For instance, we may want to know whether there is a relationship between the amount of time students devote to studying and their grade point average. Similarly, we may want to determine whether increases in stress are associated with poorer coping or whether increased use of marijuana is associated with lower interest in school and lower grades. To answer these types of questions, researchers often use what can be considered the most powerful type of descriptive method—the **correlational method**—which is used to determine the degree of relationship (correlation) between two characteristics, events, or behaviours. **[LO 1.8]**

Correlations are not just important to scientists; they are also common in our everyday thinking. For example, you may have asked yourself whether the price of a new car relates to the social status you gain from owning it. Is it possible that as price

goes up, status does as well? When researchers conduct correlational studies, they measure two variables with accuracy, and they apply a statistical formula to obtain a correlation coefficient that estimates the strength of association between the two variables.

The Correlation Coefficient: How Variables Relate

What is a correlation coefficient?

A **correlation coefficient** is a numerical value indicating the degree and direction of the relationship between two variables. **[LO 1.9]** A correlation coefficient ranges from +1.00 (a perfect positive correlation) to 0.00 (no relationship) to −1.00 (a perfect negative correlation). The sign of a correlation coefficient (+ or −) indicates whether the two variables vary in the same or opposite directions. A positive correlation indicates that two variables vary in the same direction. In other words, an increase in the value of one variable is associated with an increase in the value of the other variable, or a decrease in the value of one variable is associated with a decrease in the value of the other. There is a positive, though weak, correlation between stress and illness, for example. When stress increases, illness is likely to increase; when stress decreases, illness tends to decrease.

A negative correlation means that an increase in the value of one variable is associated with a decrease in the value of the other variable. Think of a negative correlation as a seesaw—when one variable goes up, the other goes down. For example, there is a negative correlation between the number of cigarettes people smoke and the number of years they can expect to live. The more cigarettes people smoke, the shorter their life expectancy.

The number in a correlation coefficient indicates the relative *strength* of the relationship between two variables—the higher the number, the stronger the relationship. Examples of variables that are *not* correlated include grade point average and height, and illness and shoe size.

Correlation and Prediction

Correlations are useful in making predictions. The stronger the relationship between the variables, the better the prediction. A perfect correlation (+1.00 or −1.00) would enable you to make completely accurate predictions.

The fact that there is a correlation between two variables does not necessarily mean that one variable causes the other. Only the experimental method allows us to reach conclusions about cause and effect. When two variables such as stress and illness are correlated, we cannot conclude that stress makes people sick. It might be that illness causes stress, or that a third factor such as poverty or poor general health increases susceptibility to both illness and stress, as shown in Figure 1.1.

So, you might be thinking, if a researcher can't draw cause–effect conclusions, why do correlational studies? There are two main reasons. One reason is that it is sometimes impossible, for ethical reasons, to study variables of interest using more direct methods. Scientists can't ethically ask pregnant women to drink alcohol just so they can find out whether it causes birth defects. The only option available in such cases is the correlational

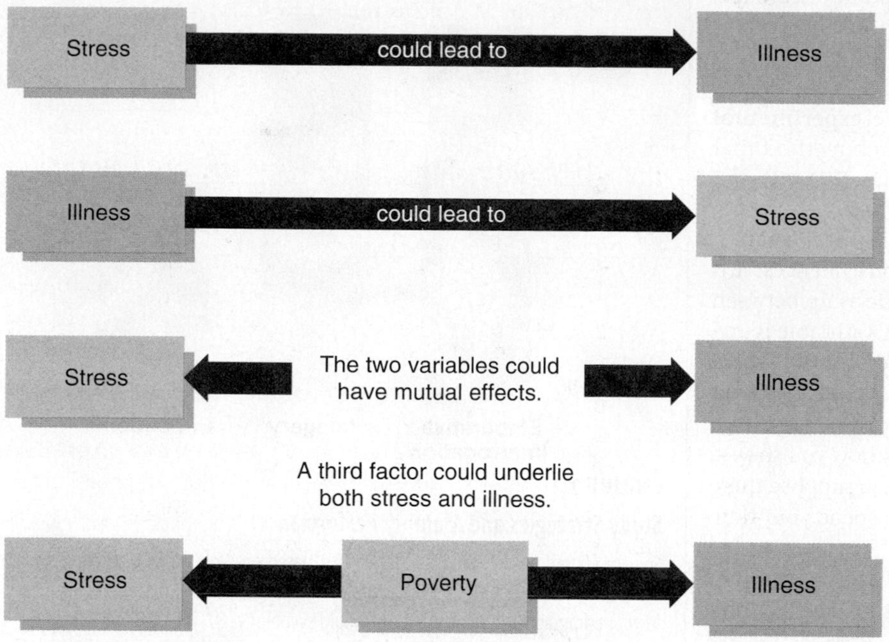

Two variables—stress and illness—are correlated.

| Stress | could lead to → | Illness |

| Illness | could lead to → | Stress |

The two variables could have mutual effects.

| Stress | ← → | Illness |

A third factor could underlie both stress and illness.

| Stress | ← Poverty → | Illness |

FIGURE 1.1

Correlation Does Not Prove Causation

A correlation between two variables does not prove that a cause–effect relationship exists between them. There is a correlation between stress and illness, but that does not mean that stress necessarily causes illness. Both stress and illness may result from another factor, such as poverty or poor general health.

method. We can ask mothers about their drinking habits and note any association with birth defects in their babies.

Another reason for using the correlational method is that many variables of interest to psychologists cannot be manipulated. We may want to know whether poverty causes health problems, but we can't assign individuals to be poor or rich so we can determine whether it causes health complications. In this case, the only option is to determine whether income and illness are correlated.

REMEMBER IT

Descriptive Research Methods

1. Much knowledge about sleep has been gained through
   a. naturalistic observation.
   b. laboratory observation.
   c. the survey.
   d. the case study.
2. The most accurate surveys are those with the largest number of respondents. (true/false)
3. A correlation coefficient shows a cause–effect relationship. (true/false)
4. Which of the following correlation coefficients indicates the strongest relationship?
   a. +.65   b. −.78   c. .00   d. +.25

Answers: 1. b 2. false 3. false 4. b

MODULE 1C THE EXPERIMENTAL METHOD: SEARCHING FOR CAUSES

LO 1.10 Define the *characteristics, process, advantages,* and *disadvantages* of experimental research.

LO 1.11 Define the following terms and explain their relationship to experimental research:
   1 *hypothesis*
   2 *independent and dependent variables*
   3 *experimental and control groups*
   4 *selection bias*
   5 *random assignment*
   6 *the placebo effect*
   7 *experimenter bias*

What is the main advantage of the experimental method?

Descriptive research methods (naturalistic observation, the case study, the survey, and even the correlation) are all well suited for satisfying the first goal of psychology—namely, description.

correlational method: A research method used to establish the relationship (correlation) between two characteristics, events, or behaviours.

correlation coefficient: A numerical value that indicates the strength and direction of the relationship between two variables; ranges from +1.00 (a perfect positive correlation) to −1.00 (a perfect negative correlation).

From descriptions, researchers may propose possible explanations for the behaviours they study. At some point researchers usually seek to determine the causes of behaviour and various other psychological phenomena.

What, for example, are the causes of depression, insomnia, stress, forgetfulness, and aggression? The **experimental method**, or the experiment, is the only research method that can be used to identify cause–effect relationships. **[LO 1.10]**

An experiment is designed to test a hypothesis. A **hypothesis** is somewhat of an educated guess; it is a testable expectation about the relationship between causes and consequences; it is a specific prediction about a cause–effect relationship between two or more conditions or variables. **[LO 1.11-1]** A variable is any condition or factor that can be manipulated, controlled, or measured. Let's consider one variable that is of great interest to you—the grade you will receive in this psychology course. Another variable that probably interests you is how you should spend your time studying for this course. Do you suppose there is a cause–effect relationship between how you spend your time studying and the grades you will receive?

The answer to that question is yes. In 1990, Vera Woloshyn and Teena Willoughby of Brock University, Eileen Wood of Wilfrid Laurier University, and Michael Pressley of the University of Notre Dame conducted an experiment to determine the impact of study strategies on learning factual material, such as that found in textbooks (Woloshyn et al., 1990). They wanted to see which of the three study strategies outlined below was most effective. Sixty students taking the introductory psychology course participated.

1. *Repetition.* Twenty students were asked to study by reading the information repeatedly, a study technique that many students prefer.

2. *Imagery.* Another 20 students were asked to generate a mental picture for each fact that they studied. This imagery method allowed them to create any mental picture as long as it contained the material to be learned.

3. *Why questions.* The last 20 students were taught how to answer "why" questions, such as "Why would that fact be true?" The questions encouraged them to draw on their own knowledge to make the facts more meaningful and hence more memorable.

In each case, all students were given the same amount of time and the same facts to study. After they had studied all the facts, students were given a memory test. The only thing that was different among the groups, then, was the type of study strategy they used.

What were the results? As you might imagine, the participants who were asked to use the more sophisticated strategies—imagery and "why" questions—remembered more than the students who simply repeated the information. However, memory performance of students using imagery was the same as that of students answering "why" questions. The researchers concluded that although many students prefer to study by repeatedly reading the material they are trying to learn, they are much better off creating mental images or answering questions (see Figure 1.2 for results). We hope that these results will guide you in studying for this and other courses.

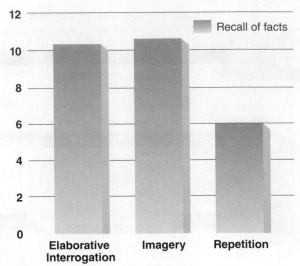

FIGURE 1.2

Study Strategies and Memory Performance

Source: (Based on Woloshyn et al., 1990.) Based on Woloshyn, V., Willoughby, T., Wood., & Pressley, M. (1990). Elaborative interrogation facilities adult learning of factual paragraphs. *Journal of Educational Psychology, 82,* 513–524.

INDEPENDENT AND DEPENDENT VARIABLES

What is the difference between the independent variable and the dependent variable?

In all experiments there are two types of variables. First, there are one or more **independent variables**—variables that the researcher manipulates in order to determine whether they cause a change in another behaviour or condition. **[LO 1.11-2]** Sometimes the independent variable is referred to as the *treatment*. In the experiment by Woloshyn et al. (1990), there was one independent variable—the study strategy that was assigned.

The second type of variable found in all experiments is the **dependent variable**. It is measured at the end of the experiment and is presumed to vary (increase or decrease) as a result of the manipulations of the independent variable or variables. **[LO 1.11-2]** The dependent variable is presumed to depend on or to be affected by changes in the independent variable. In the study by Woloshyn et al., the dependent variable was memory of the factual information tested at the end of the study.

EXPERIMENTAL AND CONTROL GROUPS: THE SAME EXCEPT FOR THE TREATMENT

How do the experimental and control groups differ?

Most experiments are conducted using two or more groups of participants. There must always be at least one **experimental group**—a group of participants who are exposed to the independent variable or the treatment. **[LO 1.11-3]** In the experiment described above, Woloshyn and colleagues used two experimental groups:

Group 2: Imagery

Group 3: "Why" questions

In most experiments it is desirable to have a **control-group**—a group that is similar to the experimental group and is used for purposes of comparison. The control group is exposed to the same experimental environment as the experimental group but is not given the treatment. **[LO 1.11-3]** The first group in the Woloshyn experiment was not exposed to the independent variable—that is, this group was not taught to use a sophisticated study strategy. Because this group was similar to the experimental group and was exposed to the same experimental environment, it should be considered a control group. At the end of an experiment, the effect on the dependent variable is measured for all groups, including the control group.

CONTROL IN THE EXPERIMENT: ATTEMPTING TO RULE OUT CHANCE

By conducting experiments in a laboratory, the experimenters can control the environmental setting to rule out other factors. For example, frustration, pain, and extreme noise or heat can change responses. Researchers carefully control the environment to ensure that these conditions are not present. They vary only the independent variables. That way, they can be reasonably certain that the manipulation of the independent variables is what causes any differences among the groups.

GENERALIZING THE EXPERIMENTAL FINDINGS: DO THE FINDINGS APPLY TO OTHER GROUPS?

What should we conclude from the Woloshyn experiment? Can we conclude that all students should use imagery or ask themselves "why" questions when studying? Before we reach such a conclusion, we should consider several factors:

- The only participants used in this experiment were introductory psychology students. Can we be sure that the same results would have occurred if individuals of other ages or groups had been used?

- The participants in this experiment were not classified according to their level of prior knowledge of the subject they were studying. Would the same results be true for both students who knew a lot in this area and those who did not?

To apply this experiment's findings to other groups, researchers would have to replicate, or repeat, the experiment using different populations of participants.

POTENTIAL PROBLEMS IN EXPERIMENTAL RESEARCH

If an experiment is properly designed and conducted, the researcher should be able to attribute changes in the dependent variable to the manipulations of the independent variable. But several factors other than the independent variables can cause changes in the dependent variable, thereby destroying the validity of the experiment. Three of these potential problems are selection bias, the placebo effect, and experimenter bias. Researchers must design experiments to control for these and other problems, which could invalidate the results.

Selection Bias: Bias from the Start

What is selection bias, and what technique do researchers use to control for it?

Selection bias occurs when participants are assigned to groups in such a way that systematic differences among the groups are present at the beginning of the experiment. **[LO 1.11-4]** If selection bias occurs, differences at the end of the experiment may not reflect the manipulation of the independent variable; rather, they may be due to pre-existing differences in the groups.

To control for selection bias, researchers must use **random assignment**. This involves selecting participants through chance (such as drawing names out of a hat) to ensure that all have an equal probability of being assigned to any of the groups. **[LO 1.11-5]** Random assignment maximizes the likelihood that the groups will be similar at the beginning of the experiment. If there had been pre-existing differences in the level of prior knowledge in the Woloshyn experiment, random assignment would have spread those differences across the groups.

experimental method: The research method whereby researchers randomly assign participants to groups and control all conditions other than one or more independent variables, which are then manipulated to determine their effect on some behaviour measured—the dependent variable in the experiment.

hypothesis: A prediction about the relationship between two or more variables.

independent variables: In an experiment, the factors or conditions that the researcher manipulates (the treatment) in order to determine their effect on another behaviour or condition, known as the *dependent variable*.

dependent variable: The variable that is measured at the end of an experiment and that is presumed to vary as a result of manipulations of the independent variable.

experimental group: In an experiment, the group of participants that is exposed to the independent variable or treatment.

control group: In an experiment, a group that is similar to the experimental group and that is exposed to the same experimental environment but is not exposed to the independent variable; used for purposes of comparison.

selection bias: The assignment of participants to experimental or control groups in such a way that systematic differences among the groups are present at the beginning of the experiment.

random assignment: In an experiment, the assignment of participants to experimental and control groups through a chance procedure, which guarantees that all participants have an equal probability of being placed in any of the groups; a control for selection bias.

REVIEW & REFLECT 1.1 RESEARCH METHODS IN PSYCHOLOGY

Method	Description	Advantages	Limitations
Naturalistic observation	Researcher observes and records behaviour in its natural setting. Participants may or may not know they are being observed.	Good source of descriptive information. Can provide basis for hypotheses to be tested later. Behaviour studied in everyday setting is more natural.	Researchers' expectations can distort observations (observer bias). Presence of researcher may influence behaviour of participants. Little or no control over conditions.
Laboratory observation	Observation under more controlled conditions where sophisticated equipment can be used to measure responses.	More control than naturalistic observation.	Possible observer bias. Behaviour of participants may be less natural than in naturalistic observation.
Case study	In-depth study of one or a few participants using observation, interviews, or psychological testing.	Source of information for rare or unusual conditions or events. Can provide basis for hypotheses to be tested later.	May not be representative of condition or event. Time-consuming. Subject to misinterpretation by researcher.
Survey	Interviews and/or questionnaires used to gather information about attitudes, beliefs, experiences, or behaviours of a group of people.	Can provide accurate information about large numbers of people.	Responses may be inaccurate. Sample may not be representative. Characteristics of interviewer may influence responses.
Correlational method	Method used to determine the relationship (correlation) between two events, characteristics, or behaviours.	Can assess strength of relationship between variables. Provides basis for prediction.	Does not demonstrate cause and effect.
Experimental method	Random assignment of participants to groups. Manipulation of independent variables and measurement of their effects on the dependent variable.	Enables identification of cause–effect relationships.	Laboratory setting may inhibit natural behaviour of participants. Findings may not be generalizable to the real world. In some cases, experiment is unethical.
Psychological tests	Tests used for measuring intelligence, scholastic achievement, aptitudes, vocational interests, personality traits, psychiatric problems.	Provide data for educational and vocational decision making, personnel selection, research, and psychological assessment.	Tests may not be reliable or valid.

placebo effect (pluh-SEE-bo): The phenomenon that occurs when a person's response to a treatment (or response to the independent variable in an experiment) is due to expectations regarding the treatment rather than to the treatment itself.

placebo: Some inert substance, such as a sugar pill or an injection of saline solution, given to the control group in an experiment as a control for the placebo effect.

experimenter bias: A phenomenon that occurs when the researcher's preconceived notions in some way influence the participants' behaviour and/or the interpretation of experimental results.

double-blind technique: An experimental procedure in which neither the participants nor the experimenters knows who is in the experimental and control groups until the results have been gathered; a control for experimenter bias.

The Placebo Effect: The Power of Suggestion (for the Participant)

What is the placebo effect, and how do researchers control for it?

Another factor that can influence the outcome of an experiment is the **placebo effect**. This occurs when the response to a treatment is due to the person's expectations rather than to the actual treatment itself. **[LO 1.11-6]** Suppose a drug is prescribed for a patient, and the patient reports improvement. The improvement could be a direct result of the drug, or it could be the result of the patient's expectation that the drug will work. Studies have shown that remarkable improvement in patients can sometimes be attributed solely to the power of suggestion—the placebo effect.

The researcher must use a control group to test whether results in an experiment are due to the treatment or to the placebo effect. So people in the control group are given a fake treatment. In drug experiments the control group is usually given a **placebo**—a harmless substance such as a sugar pill or an injection of saline solution. To control for the placebo effect, researchers do not let participants know whether they are in the *experimental* group (receiving the treatment) or in the *control* group (receiving the placebo). If getting the real drug or treatment results in a significantly greater improvement than receiving the placebo, the improvement can be attributed to the drug rather than to the power of suggestion.

But what about the expectations of those who conduct the experiments—the researchers or confederates (the experimenters or anyone else associated with the study) themselves?

Experimenter Bias: The Power of Suggestion (for the Experimenter)

What is experimenter bias, and how is it controlled?

The expectations of the experimenter are a third factor that can influence the outcome of an experiment. **Experimenter bias** occurs when researchers' preconceived notions or expectations cause them to find what they expect to find. A researcher's expectations can be communicated to the participants, perhaps unintentionally, through tone of voice, gestures, and facial expressions. [LO 1.11-7] These communications can influence the participants' behaviour. Expectations can also influence a researcher's interpretation of the experiment's results, even if no influence occurred during the experiment. When the interpretation supports the researcher's expectations in this way, it is called a *self-fulfilling prophecy*.

To control for experimenter bias, researchers must not know which participants are assigned to the experimental and control groups. The identities of both the experimental and control participants are coded, and their identities are not revealed to the researcher until after the research data are collected and recorded. (Obviously, someone assisting the researcher must know which participants are in which group.) When neither the participants nor the experimenters knows which participants are getting the treatment and which are in the control group, the **double-blind technique** is being used. The double-blind technique is the most powerful procedure for studying cause–effect relationships.

ADVANTAGES AND LIMITATIONS OF THE EXPERIMENTAL METHOD

The overwhelming advantage of the experiment is its ability to reveal cause–effect relationships. This is possible because researchers are able to exercise strict control over the experimental setting. This allows them to rule out factors other than the independent variable as possible reasons for differences in the dependent variable. But often, the more control the experimenter exercises, the more unnatural and contrived the research setting becomes, and the less generalizable the findings will be to the real world. When participants know that they are taking part in an experiment, they may behave differently than they would in a more natural setting. When a natural setting is considered to be an important factor in a study, researchers may run a field experiment (i.e., an experiment conducted in a real-life setting). The advantage of field studies is that participants behave more naturally. For example, in many field studies, the researchers cannot control for background noise, amount of sunlight, temperature, and other environmental variables. These variables are, however, assumed to be less important.

A major limitation of the experimental method is that in many areas of interest to researchers, an experiment is either unethical or impossible. Some treatments cannot be given to humans because their physical or psychological health would be endangered or their rights violated.

Review & Reflect 1.1, on the previous page, summarizes the different research methods discussed in this chapter.

REMEMBER IT

The Experimental Method

1. Which of the following statements is not true about a control group?
   a. It should be similar to the experimental group.
   b. It is exposed to the independent variable.
   c. At the end of the experiment, the effects on the dependent variable are measured for it.
   d. It is used for purposes of comparison.

2. Match the description with the appropriate term.
   _____ 1) a prediction about a relationship between two variables
   _____ 2) any condition that can be manipulated, measured, or controlled
   _____ 3) the variable measured at the end of the experiment
   _____ 4) the variable manipulated by the researcher

   a. independent variable
   b. variable
   c. hypothesis
   d. dependent variable

3. The placebo effect occurs when a participant responds according to
   a. the hypothesis.
   b. the actual treatment.
   c. how other participants behave.
   d. his or her expectations.

4. Random assignment is used to control for
   a. experimenter bias.
   b. the placebo effect.
   c. selection bias.
   d. subject bias.

Answers: 1. b   2 (1). c   (2). b   (3). d   (4). a   3. d   4. c

MODULE **1D** PARTICIPANTS IN PSYCHOLOGICAL RESEARCH

LO 1.12 Explain why psychologists use psychological tests.

LO 1.13 Compare and contrast reliability and validity, and explain how these two issues relate to psychological tests.

WORLD OF PSYCHOLOGY

Avoiding Ageism, Sexism, and Cultural Bias in Psychological Research

In planning and conducting psychological inquiries, researchers need to consider many factors besides scientific methodology. Of greatest concern is the worry about bias in psychological research. Our awareness of these biases makes us more careful when designing and interpreting studies.

For example, ageism is a continuing source of bias. This is seen in some clinicians' preferences for younger clients (Tomko & Munley, 2013) and in the fact that research papers on aging often focus on loss, deterioration, decline, and dependency, which implies that all older individuals are defined by deterioration, forgetfulness, and deficits.

Research also suggests that familiarity with clients' cultural heritage and gender issues facilitates effective counselling (Diller, 2014) and research investigations (Leung, Wang, & Deng, 2014). For instance, in one Canadian study, seven out of eight researchers were expelled from a Cree community because their research techniques were too rigid and were insensitive to traditional Cree values (Darou et al., 2000). The lack of flexibility on the part of the researchers not only had a negative impact on the community, but also had the potential to restrict their ability to investigate a unique population and, hence, to limit our understanding of this group. Greater awareness of cultural orientations, expectations, and traditions would improve both clinicians' and researchers' effectiveness when working with diverse communities.

Inequities regarding gender issues have aroused concern among psychologists and researchers in psychology (Hegarty & Pratto, 2010). Fortunately, gender bias in the selection of research participants has decreased over time, although more recent research suggests that psychological studies often treat men as the norm and women as the exception (Cundiff, 2012; Hegarty & Pratto, 2010). In addition, there is a growing body of literature that advocates a greater awareness of gender, culture, age, and sexual orientation in order to promote more effective research and counselling. ∎

HUMAN PARTICIPANTS IN PSYCHOLOGICAL RESEARCH

For practical reasons, most studies with humans in the past 40 years have used college or university students. Students are a convenient group to study, and researchers/professors often encourage their participation by offering pay or points toward a course grade. Psychology studies have also used a disproportionate number of males and whites (Cundiff, 2012; Hegarty & Pratto, 2010).

Heavy reliance on college and university students presents a problem. Students are a relatively select group in terms of age, socioeconomic status, educational level, and cultural diversity. How generalizable the findings of such studies are to the general population depends on the nature of the specific study. Studies that investigate basic psychological processes such as sensation, perception, and memory are likely to be relatively generalizable because these processes probably function in similar ways in most adults. But in research on human social behaviour, great individual and cultural variation leads to a problem in generalizing the results of studies with college and university students to other segments of the population. (See the discussion of ageism, sexism, and cultural bias in psychological research in the *World of Psychology* box above.)

PSYCHOLOGICAL TESTS: ASSESSING THE PARTICIPANT

Participants are also needed when psychologists develop and use a wide range of tests for measuring intelligence, scholastic achievement, aptitudes, creativity, vocational interests, personality traits, and psychiatric problems. Psychological tests are used in a variety of situations—in schools, in the workplace, and in therapeutic settings. Test results also provide information that can be used in educational decision making, personnel selection, and vocational guidance. But these psychological tests, and all other types of tests, are useless unless they are both reliable and valid. **[LO 1.12]**

Reliability refers to the consistency of a test. A reliable test will yield nearly the same score time after time if the same person is tested and then retested. **Validity** is the test's ability to measure what it is intended to measure. Just as a clock is a valid instrument for measuring time but not speed, so a psychological test must be able to measure accurately and adequately the specific area it is designed to measure—achievement or vocational aptitude, for example. **[LO 1.13]**

Psychologists often use testing in conjunction with their research. Tests may be administered as part of a case study. And in an experiment, the dependent variable might be the score on a psychological test. For example, an educational psychologist who is experimenting with a new educational program might use an achievement test to compare the performances of experimental and control participants.

ETHICS IN RESEARCH: FIRST AND FOREMOST

What are some ethical guidelines governing the use of human participants in research?

In 2000, the Canadian Psychological Association adopted a new set of ethical standards governing research with humans. These standards safeguard the rights of research participants while supporting the goals of scientific inquiry. Participation must be voluntary, and there must be respect for confidentiality. Moreover, participants must be free to withdraw from the study at any time and, after completing any study, they must always be debriefed about the full purpose of the study and its implications. At a more local level, colleges and universities must have ethics committees to approve any research studies proposed by professors or students.

reliability: The ability of a test to yield nearly the same scores when the same people are tested and then retested using the same test or an alternative form of the test.

validity: The ability of a test to measure what it is intended to measure.

Some studies use deception. In such studies, participants are informed that the nature of the research is different from what it actually is. This method is used when researchers believe that a participant's awareness of the true purpose of the study may affect the validity of the results. Psychologists have long debated whether studies that use deception can be justified on scientific grounds. Many psychologists believe they can be, but others are against deception in any circumstances (Kimmel, 2012). Even so, deception is used in many research studies, particularly in the field of social psychology. Today the Canadian Psychological Association's *Canadian Code of Ethics for Psychologists* (CPA, 2000) allows deception under the following circumstances:

1. if it is justified by the value of the potential findings, in circumstances where equally effective procedures that do not involve deception cannot be used;

2. if the researcher does not withhold "information about the level of risk, discomfort or inconvenience" (p. 25) that might affect their willingness to participate, *and*

3. if participants are informed as soon as possible after the experiment about the nature of the research and to clear up any misconceptions they may have had about what occurred during the study. Researchers want to erase any harmful effects of the deception and to ensure that participants understand that no other participants were actually harmed.

THE USE OF ANIMALS IN RESEARCH

Why are animals used in research?

Where would psychology be today without Pavlov's dogs, Skinner's pigeons, the ubiquitous white rat, and the many other species of animals used to advance scientific knowledge?

©Eric Esselee/Shutterstock

Most psychologists recognize that many scientific advances would not have been possible without animal research. Where do you stand on this issue?

Psychologists recognize that laboratory animals have been and still are immensely important in research; most psychologists favour their continued use. The most recent estimates

REMEMBER IT

Participants in Psychological Research

1. Which of the following groups has not been overrepresented as participants in psychological research?
   a. whites
   b. males
   c. females
   d. university students

2. Psychologists are required to debrief participants thoroughly after a research study when the study
   a. violates participants' privacy.
   b. deceives participants about the true purpose of the research.

   c. exposes participants to unreasonable risk or harm.
   d. wastes taxpayers' money on trivial questions.

3. The Canadian Psychological Association has guidelines for ethical treatment for human participants but not for animal subjects. (true/false)

4. Which of the following has not been identified as a source of bias in psychological research, according to the text?
   a. age
   b. gender
   c. race
   d. religion

suggest that animals are used in 7 to 8 percent of psychological experiments; 90 percent of the animals used have been rodents and birds, principally rats, mice, and pigeons (American Psychological Association [APA], 2006b).

Many of the marvels of modern medicine would not have been available today without the use of animals in research. Why are animals used in research? There are at least five reasons: (1) They provide a simpler model for studying processes that operate similarly in humans. (2) Researchers can exercise far more control over animal subjects and thus be more certain of a study's conclusions. (3) A wider range of medical and other manipulations can be used with animals. (4) It is easier to study the entire lifespan and multiple generations in some animal species. (5) Animals are cheaper to use and are available at the researcher's convenience. (Of course, researchers also use animals when they want to learn more about the animals themselves.)

Those conducting animal research in Canada are bound by the *Canadian Code of Ethics for Psychologists* (CPA, 2000) as well as by the ethical guidelines of the Canadian Council on Animal Care (1989). These documents support the humane treatment of animals. This means that researchers must do everything possible to minimize discomfort, pain, and illness in animal subjects. The Canadian Council on Animal Care is also responsible for regularly checking active laboratories. Furthermore, research with animals is supported only when there is a reasonable expectation that valuable knowledge will be obtained.

Nevertheless, controversy has long surrounded the use of animals in research. Animal rights advocates have been very active in their efforts to stop animal research. Some have broken into research laboratories, freed laboratory animals, destroyed research records, and wrecked laboratory equipment and other property. Many activists are also against using animals for food, clothing, or any other purpose.

MODULE 1E THE HISTORICAL PROGRESSION OF PSYCHOLOGY: EXPLORING THE DIFFERENT PERSPECTIVES

LO 1.14 Define the following early schools of psychology:

1 structuralism
2 functionalism
3 Gestalt
4 behaviourism
5 psychoanalysis
6 humanistic psychology
7 cognitive psychology

If we were to trace the development of psychology from the beginning, we would need to stretch far back to the earliest pages of recorded history, even beyond the early Greek philosophers such as Aristotle and Plato. People have always had questions about human nature and human behaviour. For centuries these questions were considered to be in the realm of philosophy.

WILHELM WUNDT: THE FOUNDING OF PSYCHOLOGY

What was Wilhelm Wundt's contribution to psychology?

It was not until experimental methods were applied to the study of psychological processes that psychology became recognized as a formal academic discipline. Three German physiologists—Ernst Weber, Gustav Fechner, and Hermann von Helmholtz—were the first to apply experimental methods to the study of psychological processes. In so doing, they profoundly influenced the early development of psychology.

Although a number of early researchers contributed to the new field of psychology, Wilhelm Wundt is generally thought of as the founder of psychology. His psychological laboratory in Leipzig, Germany, founded in 1879, is considered the "birthplace" of psychology as a formal academic discipline. However, the studies and experiments that Wundt, his associates, and his students performed in that early laboratory were very different from psychology as we know it today.

For Wundt, the subject matter of psychology was experience—the actual, immediate, conscious experiences of individuals. Wundt believed that mental experiences could be reduced to basic elements, just as the early chemists were able to describe water as composed of the basic elements of hydrogen and oxygen (H_2O). In other words, Wundt was searching for the structure of conscious experience.

Wundt and his associates conducted experiments on reaction times and on attention span. They also studied the perception of a variety of visual (sight), tactile (touch), and auditory (hearing) stimuli, including rhythm patterns.

Wundt had an important influence on Canadian psychology. Some of his students, including August Kirschmann, James Mark Baldwin, and George Humphrey, became founding members of Canada's first psychology departments. Kirschmann and Baldwin went on to teach at the University of Toronto, and Humphrey established himself at Queen's University in Kingston, Ontario (M. J. Wright & Myers, 1982).

TITCHENER AND STRUCTURALISM: PSYCHOLOGY'S BLIND ALLEY

What were the goals and methods of structuralism, the first school of psychology?

Wundt's most famous student, Edward Bradford Titchener (1867–1927), introduced psychology to North America. Although Titchener differed from Wundt on some points, he pursued similar goals. He gave the name **structuralism** to this first school of thought in psychology, which aimed at analyzing the basic elements, or the structure, of conscious mental experience. **[LO 1.14-1]**

Structuralism was most severely criticized for its primary method, introspection. Introspection relies on self-observation and is simply the reporting of any thought, idea, or feeling. Introspection was severely criticized because it was not objective, even though it involved observation, measurement, and experimentation. When different introspectionists were exposed to the same stimulus, such as the click of a metronome, they often reported different experiences. And when the same

CANADIAN CONNECTIONS

Our History Highlights

Despite the immense popularity of psychology as a field of study in today's colleges and universities, the evolution of psychology programs in Canada and the United States was fairly slow. For instance, no full psychology curriculum was developed in Canada until the 1920s.

James Mark Baldwin established the first Canadian psychology laboratory at the University of Toronto in 1889. The first psychology department was established at McGill University in 1924, soon followed by the creation of a psychology department at the University of Toronto in 1926. In the 1930s and 1940s, several other universities followed suit, such as the University of Western Ontario (1931), the University of

Manitoba (1936), the Université de Montréal (1942), the University of Saskatchewan (1947), and Dalhousie and Queen's universities (1948). The 1960s and 1970s saw the greatest growth in psychology programs as this field of research became somewhat more established within academia (M. J. Wright & Myers, 1982).

A significant milestone for the advancement of psychology in Canada was the founding of the Canadian Psychological Association in 1939. In conjunction with the American Psychological Association, the Canadian Psychological Association serves as the governing body for psychologists in Canada, providing ethical guidelines and research initiatives. ∎

---

person was exposed to exactly the same stimulus at different times, he or she often reported somewhat different experiences. Structuralism was not considered a viable school of thought for long. Later schools of thought in psychology were established partly in reaction against structuralism, which collapsed as an approach when Titchener died.

FUNCTIONALISM: THE FIRST NORTH AMERICAN SCHOOL OF PSYCHOLOGY

What was the goal of the early school of psychology known as functionalism?

As structuralism was losing its influence in the early 1900s, a new school of psychology called *functionalism* was taking shape. **Functionalism** was concerned not with the structure of consciousness but with how mental processes function— that is, with how humans and animals use mental processes in adapting to their environment. **[LO 1.14-2]**

An influential book by Charles Darwin, *On the Origin of Species by Means of Natural Selection* (1859), had a strong impact on the leading proponents of functionalism. Darwin's ideas about evolution and the continuity of species were largely responsible for the increasing use of animals in psychological experiments.

Another British thinker (and a cousin of Darwin) was Sir Francis Galton, who did pioneering work in the study of individual differences and the role of genetic inheritance in mental abilities. He also made a significant contribution in the areas of measurement and statistics.

Darwin's and Galton's ideas contributed much to the new school of functionalism. American psychologist William James (1842–1910) was an advocate of functionalism, even though he did much of his writing before this school of psychology appeared. James's best-known work is his highly regarded *Principles of Psychology*, published more than 100 years ago (1890). James taught that mental processes are fluid and that they have continuity rather than a rigid or fixed structure (which is what the structuralists had suggested). James spoke of the "stream of consciousness," which he said functioned to help humans adapt to their environment.

Functionalism broadened the scope of psychology to include the study of behaviour as well as mental processes. It also included the study of children, animals, and people who were mentally impaired. These groups had not been studied by the structuralists because they could not be trained to use introspection. Functionalists also established the subfield of applied psychology—for example, the psychology of education, the workplace, and individual differences.

GESTALT PSYCHOLOGY: THE WHOLE IS MORE THAN JUST THE SUM OF ITS PARTS

What is the emphasis of Gestalt psychology?

Several schools of thought arose in part as a reaction against structuralism. Gestalt psychology was one of these. This school appeared in Germany in 1912, at around the same time that John B. Watson was launching behaviourism (discussed next). The Gestalt psychologists objected to the central idea of structuralism—that we can best understand conscious experience by reducing it to its basic elements. **Gestalt psychology** emphasized that individuals perceive objects and patterns as whole units, and that the whole thus perceived is more than just the sum of its parts. The German word *Gestalt* roughly means "whole, form, or pattern." **[LO 1.14-3]**

The leader of the Gestalt psychologists was Max Wertheimer (1880–1943), who introduced a famous experiment demonstrating the phi phenomenon. Perhaps you have

---

structuralism: The first formal school of psychology, aimed at analyzing the basic elements, or the structure, of conscious mental experience through the use of introspection.

functionalism: An early school of psychology that was concerned with how mental processes help humans and animals adapt to their environments; developed as a reaction against structuralism.

Gestalt psychology (geh-SHTALT): The school of psychology that emphasizes that individuals perceive objects and patterns as whole units and that the perceived whole is more than just the sum of its parts.

seen flashing neon lights that you perceive as figures moving back and forth. Actually, the separate lights are being flashed on and off with precision timing: this is the phi phenomenon. We perceive wholes or patterns, not collections of separate and independent sensations. For the Gestaltists, the phi phenomenon proved that perceptions do not all arise from independent sensations, as the structuralists contended.

Other prominent Gestalt psychologists were Kurt Koffka and Wolfgang Köhler. Gestalt psychologists are still influential in the psychology of perception, which will be discussed in Chapter 3.

BEHAVIOURISM: NEVER MIND THE MIND

How did behaviourism differ from previous schools of psychology?

Psychologist John B. Watson (1878–1958) looked at the study of psychology as defined by the structuralists and functionalists and disliked virtually everything he saw. In Watson's view, the study of mental processes, the concepts of mind and consciousness, and the primary investigative technique of introspection were not scientific. Watson pointed out that each person's introspection is strictly individual. He further maintained that self-reflection and internal pondering cannot be observed, verified, understood, or communicated in objective, scientific terms. He argued that all the strictly subjective techniques and concepts in psychology must be thrown out. He did not deny the existence of conscious thought or experience. He simply did not view them as appropriate topics for psychology.

Watson proposed a radically new approach to psychology. This new school of psychology, called **behaviourism**, redefined psychology as the "science of behaviour." Behaviourism confined itself to the study of behaviour because it was observable and measurable and, therefore, objective and scientific. Behaviourism also emphasized that behaviour is determined primarily by factors in the environment. [LO 1.14-4]

B. F. Skinner: Continuing the Behaviourist Tradition

Behaviourism soon became the most influential school of thought in North American psychology. It is still a major force in modern psychology, in large part because of the profound influence of B. F. Skinner (1904–1990).

Skinner agreed with Watson that concepts such as mind, consciousness, and feelings were neither objective nor measurable and, therefore, not the appropriate subject matter of psychology. Furthermore, Skinner argued that these concepts were not needed to explain behaviour. We can explain behaviour, he maintained, by analyzing conditions that were present before the behaviour occurred and by analyzing the consequences of the behaviour.

Skinner's research on operant (i.e., deliberate) conditioning emphasized the importance of reinforcement in learning and in the shaping and maintaining of behaviour. When a behaviour is reinforced (i.e., followed by pleasant or rewarding consequences), it is more likely to be performed again. Skinner's work has had a powerful influence on modern psychology.

Behaviourism has been criticized for ignoring inner mental processes such as thoughts and feelings. Many behaviourists today do not take as extreme a view as Skinner and his colleagues did. They still emphasize the study of behaviour, but they are also willing to consider how mental processes explain behaviour.

PSYCHOANALYSIS: IT'S WHAT'S DEEP DOWN THAT COUNTS

What was the role of the unconscious in psychoanalysis, Freud's approach to psychology?

The behaviourists completely ignored unobservable mental forces in their explanations of behaviour. This is precisely where Sigmund Freud (1856–1939) looked in formulating his theory. Freud emphasized that unseen, unconscious mental forces were the key to understanding human nature and behaviour.

Freud developed a theory called **psychoanalysis**. He maintained that human mental life is like an iceberg. The smallest, visible part of the iceberg represents the conscious mental experience of the individual. But underwater, hidden from view, floats a vast store of unconscious impulses, thoughts, wishes, and desires. Although people are not aware of them directly or consciously, it is these unconscious forces that have the largest impact on behaviour. [LOs 1.14-4 & 1.14-5]

Freud believed that the unconscious acts as a storehouse for material that threatens the conscious life of the individual—for disturbing sexual and aggressive impulses as well as traumatic experiences that have been repressed, or "pushed down" to the unconscious. Once there, rather than resting quietly, the unconscious material festers and seethes.

Freud's psychological theory does not paint a very positive or hopeful picture of human nature. He believed that we do not consciously control our thoughts, feelings, and behaviours, but rather that these are determined by unconscious forces that we cannot see or control.

The overriding importance that Freud placed on sexual and aggressive impulses caused much controversy, both inside and outside the field of psychology. The most notable of Freud's famous students—Carl Jung, Alfred Adler, and Karen Horney—broke away from their mentor and developed their own theories of personality. These three are often referred to as the *neo-Freudians*.

Freud's influence on psychology is not nearly as strong as it once was (Robins, Gosling, & Craik, 1999). When people think of Freud, most imagine a psychiatrist psychoanalyzing a patient who is lying on a couch. The general public is familiar with such terms as the *unconscious, repression, rationalization*, and the *Freudian slip*. Such familiarity has made Freud a larger-than-life figure.

HUMANISTIC PSYCHOLOGY: LOOKING AT HUMAN POTENTIAL

What is the focus of humanistic psychology?

Humanistic psychology emerged in part as a reaction against behaviourism and psychoanalysis and is often labelled the "third force in psychology." **Humanistic psychology** focuses on the uniqueness of human beings and their capacity for choice, growth, and psychological health. The humanists reject the behaviourist notion that people have no free will and are shaped and controlled strictly by the environment. Humanists

REMEMBER IT

The Historical Progression of Psychology

1. Match the description with the appropriate school of psychology.

_____ 1) the scientific study of behaviour

_____ 2) the perception of whole units or patterns

_____ 3) the unconscious

_____ 4) analysis of the basic elements of conscious mental experience

_____ 5) the uniqueness of human beings and their capacity for conscious choice and growth

_____ 6) the function of conscious mental experience

_____ 7) the study of mental processes
  a. Gestalt psychology
  b. structuralism
  c. functionalism
  d. psychoanalysis

e. humanistic psychology
f. behaviourism
g. cognitive psychology

2. Match the major figures with the appropriate school of psychology.

_____ 1) James

_____ 2) Freud

_____ 3) Watson and Skinner

_____ 4) Wundt and Titchener

_____ 5) Maslow and Rogers
  a. behaviourism
  b. structuralism
  c. functionalism
  d. psychoanalysis
  e. humanistic psychology

Answers: 1 (1). f (2). a (3). d (4). b (5). e (6). c (7). g 2(1). c (2). d (3). a (4). b (5). e

---

also reject Freud's theory that people are determined and driven from within, acting and marching to the dark drums of the unconscious. **[LO 1.14-6]**

Abraham Maslow (1908–1970) and other prominent humanistic psychologists, such as Carl Rogers (1902–1987), emphasized a much more positive view of human nature. They maintained that people are innately good and possess free will. Humanists believe that people are capable of making conscious, rational choices that can lead to growth and psychological health.

Maslow proposed a theory of motivation that consists of a hierarchy of needs. He considered the need for self-actualization (developing to one's fullest potential) to be the highest need in this hierarchy. Carl Rogers developed his person-centred therapy and, with other humanists, popularized encounter groups and other techniques that are part of the human potential movement.

COGNITIVE PSYCHOLOGY: FOCUSING ON MENTAL PROCESSES

What is the focus of cognitive psychology?

Cognitive psychology is a special branch of psychology that focuses on mental processes such as memory, problem solving, concept formation, reasoning and decision making, language, and perception. **[LO 1.14-7]** Just as behaviourism developed in part as a reaction against the focus on mental processes that was characteristic of structuralism and functionalism, so cognitive psychology grew and developed partly in response to strict behaviourism (Barsalou, 2014). Ironically, several psychologists

who were behaviourists during the 1950s provided the greatest impetus to the development of cognitive psychology.

Cognitive psychologists see humans not as passive recipients who are pushed and pulled by environmental forces, but as active participants who seek out experiences, who alter and shape them, and who use mental processes to transform information in the course of their own cognitive development.

The advent of the computer provided cognitive psychologists with a new way to think of mental processes. According to the information-processing approach, our brain processes

behaviourism: The school of psychology founded by John B. Watson that views observable, measurable behaviour as the appropriate subject matter for psychology and emphasizes the role of environment as a determinant of behaviour.

psychoanalysis (SY-ko-ah-NAL-ih-sis): The term Freud used for both his theory of personality and his therapy for the treatment of psychological disorders; the unconscious is the primary focus of psychoanalytic theory.

humanistic psychology: The school of psychology that focuses on the uniqueness of human beings and their capacity for choice, growth, and psychological health.

cognitive psychology: A specialty that studies mental processes such as memory, problem solving, reasoning and decision making, language, perception, and other forms of cognition; often uses the information-processing approach.

REVIEW & REFLECT 1.2 TRADITIONAL AND MODERN SCHOOLS OF THOUGHT IN PSYCHOLOGY

School	Description
Structuralism Wilhelm Wundt Edward Titchener	The first formal school of psychology. Focuses on analyzing the basic elements or structures of conscious mental experience through the use of introspection.
Functionalism William James	The first North American school of psychology. Concerned with the study of mental processes and their role in facilitating adaptation to the environment. Broadened the scope of psychology to include the study of behaviour as well as mental processes, and the study of children, people who are mentally impaired, and animals.
Gestalt psychology Max Wertheimer Kurt Koffka Wolfgang Köhler	Emphasizes that individuals perceive objects and patterns as whole units. The perceived whole is more than just the sum of its parts and is not best understood by analysis of its elemental parts (as suggested by the structuralists).
Behaviourism John B. Watson B. F. Skinner	Views observable, measurable behaviour rather than internal mental processes as the appropriate subject matter of psychology. Stresses the roles of learning and the environment in determining behaviour.
Psychoanalysis Sigmund Freud	Emphasizes the role of unconscious mental forces and conflicts in determining behaviour.
Humanistic psychology Abraham Maslow Carl Rogers	Focuses on the uniqueness of human beings and their capacity for choice, growth, and psychological health. Called the "third force in psychology" (behaviourism and psychoanalysis being the other two forces).
Cognitive psychology	Focuses on mental processes such as memory, problem solving, reasoning, decision making, language, and perception. Uses information-processing approach.

information in sequential stages, much as a computer does. But as computers have become more sophisticated, so have cognitive theory models. For example, many contemporary researchers are examining the human memory system's capacity for *parallel processing*, the management of multiple bits of information at once, a type of information processing that is commonly used in today's computers (Bajic & Rickard, 2009; Sung, 2008).

Moreover, unlike the early behaviourists, psychologists today *can* observe some mental processes directly. Thanks to modern brain-imaging techniques, such as the PET scan, and sophisticated computer technology, researchers can observe the action (behaviour) of specific clusters of brain cells (neurons) as they carry out various mental processes (Raichle, 1994). Such mental activities as thinking, remembering, solving a problem, listening to a melody, speaking, viewing images and colours, and so on have all been "observed," and this has provided a rich field of knowledge that cognitive psychologists use in their work.

Review & Reflect 1.2 summarizes the various traditional and modern schools of thought in psychology.

MODULE 1F PSYCHOLOGY TODAY

LO 1.15 Describe the newer perspectives in modern psychology.

LO 1.16 Compare and contrast the newer perspectives in modern psychology.

LO 1.17 Identify the various fields of work available to psychologists.

CURRENT PERSPECTIVES IN PSYCHOLOGY: VIEWS ON BEHAVIOUR AND THINKING

Modern psychologists are not easily categorized by specific schools of thought. There are no structuralists roaming the halls of psychology departments, and to our knowledge there are no professors who call themselves functionalists. Today, rather than discussing schools of psychology, it is more appropriate to refer to psychological perspectives—points of view used for explaining people's behaviour and thinking, whether normal or abnormal. Psychologists need not limit themselves to only one perspective or approach.

Some take an eclectic position, choosing a combination of approaches to explain a particular behaviour or psychological problem.

Biological Perspective: It's What's Inside That Counts

What is the focus of the biological perspective?

Psychologists who adopt the **biological perspective** emphasize biological processes and heredity as the keys to understanding behaviour and thinking. **[LOs 1.15 & 1.16]** To explain thinking, emotion, and behaviour—both normal and abnormal—biologically oriented psychologists study the structures of the brain and central nervous system, the functioning of the neurons, the delicate balance of neurotransmitters and hormones, and the impact of genes. For example, we know that having too many or too few different neurotransmitters in the brain is related to various mental disorders such as schizophrenia and depression. Some drugs now being used to treat some of these disorders are designed to restore the brain's biochemical balance.

Researchers and theorists who adopt the biological perspective include physiological psychologists, psycho-biologists, and neuropsychologists. Many biological psychologists work as part of an interdisciplinary field known as *neuroscience*, which combines the work of psychologists, biologists, biochemists, and medical researchers. Many important findings in psychology have resulted from their work. In fact, neuroscience has become a driving force in biological research, not only in psychology but in other scientific areas as well.

Neuroscience—the study of brain functioning—is divided into several subfields. Most relevant to psychology are two specific areas. *Behavioural neuroscience* is now an important area of psychological research; it investigates how the brain processes activities and behaviours, including our emotions and sensations. *Cognitive neuroscience* uses new brain technology to examine the brain's cognitive functions, including memory, language, and problem solving.

Evolutionary Perspective: Adapting to the Environment

What is the focus of the evolutionary perspective?

The **evolutionary perspective** focuses on how humans have evolved and adapted behaviours required for survival in the face of various environmental pressures over the long course of evolution (Cosmides & Tooby, 2013). The basic argument of evolutionary psychology is that the adaptation of the mind has not progressed at the same rapid pace of change as that of our social circumstances. Evolutionary psychologists suggest that the human brain is still adapted to a way of life from many thousands of years ago and that it is still mostly concerned with its reproductive success. **[LOs 1.15 & 1.16]** Evolutionary psychologists study how inherited tendencies and dispositions in humans influence a wide range of behaviours such as helping behaviour, aggression, danger avoidance, and food preferences (Cosmides & Tooby, 2013). However, much of the research has focused on issues associated with human reproduction, such as the way we select mates, sexual attraction, jealousy, mate retention, and allocations of resources to parents and family (Buss, 2014).

Advocates of this perspective argue that an evolutionary perspective can be applied to any topic within the field of psychology, given that evolutionary principles are common to all humans (Cosmides & Tooby, 2000). However, this perspective has its many critics who argue that human behaviour cannot be reduced to our biology (H. Rose & Rose, 2010) and that social and cultural influences can also explain the same phenomena (Eagly & Wood, 1999). This critique is partly rooted in the sociocultural perspective.

Sociocultural Perspective: The Cultural Impact of Our World

What is the focus of the sociocultural perspective?

The **sociocultural perspective** highlights the social and cultural influences on human behaviour. In the same way that

someone who is quoted out of context is misunderstood, we may misinterpret the actions or gestures of those from other cultures if we do not understand the cultural context in which they occur. **[LOs 1.15 & 1.16]** Writers such as Kenneth Gergen and colleagues (Gergen, Gulerce, Lock, & Misra, 1996) assert that we are in "desperate need" of culturally sensitive research about people's behaviour in areas such as health, "birth control, child abuse, drug addiction, ethical and religious conflict, and the effects of technology on society" (p. 502).

PSYCHOLOGISTS AT WORK

What are some specialties in psychology, and in what settings are they employed?

In this chapter we have discussed the many fields of academic specializations within psychology. The fact is that most psychology researchers are employed in colleges and universities, where they conduct their own research and teach, or in hospitals and other health services. But what type of work can psychologists do if they are not employed in a college or university or hospital? What are their specialties, and in what settings are they employed? **[LOs 1.17]**

Although no data are available regarding the employment status of Canadian psychologists, we can use data from the United States to give us some information about where psychologists work (see Figure 1.3 on the next page). Professional psychologists have a broad number of choices of workplaces, depending on their area of expertise. Clinical psychologists make up the largest group of psychologists, followed by counselling psychologists. Both groups of professionals apply psychological principles to assist people who are dealing with psychology-related issues. *Clinical psychologists* are responsible for the diagnosis and treatment of often complex psychological disorders, whereas *counselling psychologists* tend to help those whose problems are not as severe. But do not confuse clinical psychologists and psychiatrists! Psychiatrists are physicians who have specialized in the treatment of psychiatric disorders, whereas psychologists do not study medicine.

---

biological perspective: A perspective that emphasizes biological processes and heredity as the keys to understanding behaviour.

evolutionary perspective: A perspective that focuses on how humans have evolved and adapted behaviours required for survival against various environmental pressures over the long course of evolution.

sociocultural perspective: A perspective that emphasizes social and cultural influences on human behaviour and stresses the importance of understanding those influences when we interpret the behaviour of others.

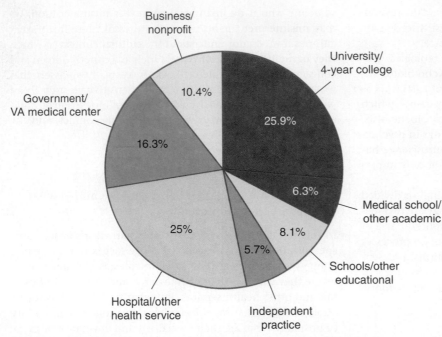

FIGURE 1.3

Where Psychologists Work

Psychologists work in a variety of settings. The largest group—about 51 percent of psychologists—work in colleges and universities and in hospitals and other health services.

Source: http://www.apa.org/careers/resources/guides/careers.aspx?item=4 From APA. (2014). Career in psychology. Retrieved from http://www.apa.org/careers/resources/guides/careers.aspx?item=4. Adapted from Michaels, D., Kohout, J., Wicherski, M., & Hart, B. (2011), 2009 Doctorate Employment Survey (Table 3). American Psychological Association.

Note: The chart represents employment settings for those with recent doctorates in psychology. Totals amount to 97 percent due to rounding and exclusion of 17 "not specified" responses. Adapted from D. Michaels, J. Kohout, M. Wicherski & B. Hart (2011), *2009 Doctorate Employment Survey* (Table 3) (PDF, 33KB).

Aside from the clinical and counselling fields, many psychologists work in education, either as school psychologists or educational psychologists. *School* and *educational psychologists* provide psychological services to students within the context of a school setting. They often work for school boards and are involved in the educational, social, linguistic, or vocational assessment of students.

Many subfields of psychology fall under the broad umbrella term of *applied psychology*. Applied psychologists use their knowledge of research methodology to examine how various aspects of human life such as emotion, motivation, social interactions, and cognitive errors affect our health, our decisions, and our work. Two related emerging fields are forensic and health psychology. There has been a recent increase of interest among college and university students in the field of forensic psychology. Much of this interest can likely be linked to popular television shows and movies that glamorize this field of work. *Forensic psychologists* apply their knowledge of psychological research to the legal system. For instance, they study issues such as the accuracy of eyewitness testimony in court cases or how to better handle hostage-taking negotiations. Some forensic psychologists work within the correctional system to diagnose and treat offenders. *Health psychologists* work in a more general field with many options—they work with patients or conduct research on the relationship between psychological processes and physical health. Some health psychologists examine the impact of stress on well-being, or how to help improve the effect of particular treatment programs. For example, health psychologists have examined how to help dieters stay on their healthy eating program, or how to help those who begin exercising persist with their new regimen. And some psychologists are specifically involved with issues of exercise and sports. *Sport psychologists* apply psychological principles to help improve the performance of athletes.

Psychologists work in a wide range of settings.

©Richard T. Nowitz/Science Source

Finally, many applied psychologists work within organizations. *Industrial* or *organizational psychologists* help businesses deal with issues such as the hiring and retention of qualified personnel, employee satisfaction, workplace violence, and occupational health. They help managers improve their leadership skills and motivate their employees. They study the difficult balance of work and family demands and also consider the negative impact of unhealthy working conditions on the work and personal lives of workers.

This section has provided only a brief overview of the many fields of work where psychologists are employed. Wherever you find human activity—the workplace, schools, hospitals, professional sport, government, and the public service—you will likely find psychologists. *Review & Reflect 1.3* outlines the modern perspectives in psychology.

REVIEW & REFLECT **1.3** MODERN PERSPECTIVES IN PSYCHOLOGY

Perspective	Emphasis
Biological	The role of biological processes and structures, as well as heredity, in explaining behaviour.
Psychoanalytic	The role of unconscious motivation and early childhood experiences in determining behaviour and thought.
Behavioural	The role of environment in shaping and controlling behaviour.
Cognitive	The importance of mental processes—perception, thinking, and memory—that underlie behaviour.
Humanistic	The importance of the individual's subjective experience as a key to understanding behaviour.
Evolutionary	The role of inherited tendencies that have proven adaptive in humans.
Sociocultural	The effect of society and culture on behaviour.

With so much information available about psychology, it is important to become a good consumer of that information. The *Apply It* box below tells you how to go about doing this.

REMEMBER IT

Psychology Today

Match the psychological perspective with its major emphasis.

_____ 1) the role of biological processes and heredity
_____ 2) the role of learning and environmental factors
_____ 3) the role of mental processes
_____ 4) the role of the unconscious and early-childhood experiences
_____ 5) the importance of the individual's own subjective experience

_____ 6) the role of social and cultural influences
_____ 7) the role of inherited tendencies that have proven adaptive in humans

a. psychoanalytical
b. biological
c. behavioural
d. cognitive
e. humanistic
f. evolutionary
g. sociocultural

Answers: 1.b 2.c 3.d 4.a 5.e 6.g 7.f

APPLY IT

Being a Good Consumer of Psychological Research

If someone asked you where to buy a car, you wouldn't send him or her to a junkyard. Similarly, in psychology you must be a wise consumer—and become a critical thinker—in order to get accurate information.

Some publications are more scientifically respectable than others—*Science News* and *Psychology Today* are more credible than the *National Enquirer* and *The Toronto Sun*. Science writers have more experience reading and understanding research and usually give more accurate reports of psychological research than general reporters do. Science writers tend to write more objectively than non-science writers and are less likely to suggest that the researchers' findings are the last word on the subject. General reporters, on the other hand, are much more likely to make sweeping statements and extreme claims such as "The most important

study of our time," "Amazing new cure," and "Dramatic new results show . . ."

To evaluate the information, James Bell suggests, you must be able to answer three key questions: "Who says so? What do they say? How do they know?" (1991, p. 36).

To critically evaluate research, you need to know who conducted the study and what methodology was used. You need a description of the participants—their number, how they were selected, whether they were human or animal, and, if they were human, information such as their age, gender, and other characteristics that are relevant to evaluating the researcher's conclusions.

Critical thinkers are those who determine whether the methodology used in the research would enable the authors to reach their conclusions, whether those conclusions are logical, whether they

are supported by the data, and whether there are alternative explanations for the findings.

Critical thinkers understand the difference between scientific and non-scientific research evidence. Testimonials and accounts of personal experience are non-scientific evidence. Testimonials appeal most often to emotions rather than to intellect.

Critical thinkers carefully consider the biases of the writers or researchers. Do they have axes to grind? Are they expressing information that can be confirmed as factual, or are they merely expressing their opinion?

Finally, critical thinkers do not accept the results of one study as definitive evidence. They want to know whether the research has been replicated and what other studies have been published on the subject. As a critical thinker, you would not modify your life on the basis of one study that you read.

THINKING CRITICALLY

Evaluation

Consider the three major forces in psychology: behaviourism, psychoanalysis, and humanistic psychology. Which do you like most? Which do you like least? Explain.

Point/Counterpoint

This chapter discussed the issue of deception in research. Prepare convincing arguments to support each of these opinions:

a. Deception is justified in research studies.

b. Deception is not justified in research studies.

Psychology in Your Life

In this chapter you've learned something about experimental research and survey research. How will this new knowledge affect the way you evaluate research studies in articles you read or in reports you hear in the future?

MyPsychLab   go to mypsychlab (access code required) to find web resources for your text that supplement the material in chapter 1.

SUMMARY & REVIEW

INTRODUCTION TO PSYCHOLOGY

What are the four goals of psychology?
The four goals of psychology are the description, explanation, prediction, and influence of behaviour and mental processes.

What is the difference between basic and applied research?
Basic research is designed to explore the fundamental aspects of life and to gain new knowledge without practical goals in mind. Applied research is conducted with the specific goal of solving practical problems and improving people's quality of life.

1B DESCRIPTIVE RESEARCH METHODS

What is naturalistic observation, and what are some of its advantages and limitations?
Naturalistic observation is a research method in which researchers observe and record behaviour in its natural setting without attempting to influence or control it. The major advantage of naturalistic observation is that it allows one to study behaviour in normal settings, where it occurs more naturally and spontaneously. Its main limitation is that it only allows a researcher to observe behaviours, without the capacity to test why they are happening as they are.

What is the case study method, and for what purposes is it particularly well suited?
The case study is an in-depth, sometimes long-term study of one or several participants through observation, interview, and sometimes psychological testing. It is particularly appropriate for studying people who have rare psychological or physiological disorders.

What are the methods and purposes of survey research?
The survey is a research method in which investigators use interviews and/or questionnaires to gather information about the attitudes, beliefs, experiences, or behaviours of a group of people.

What is a representative sample, and why is it essential in a survey?
A representative sample is a sample of participants selected from the population of interest in such a way that important subgroups within the whole population are included in the same proportions in the sample. A sample must be representative for the findings to be applied to the larger population.

What is the correlational method, and when is it used?
The correlational method is used to determine the degree of correlation or relationship between two variables. It is often used when an experimental study cannot be conducted because it is either impossible or unethical.

What is a correlation coefficient?
A correlation coefficient is a numerical value indicating the degree and direction of the relationship between two variables.

1C THE EXPERIMENTAL METHOD: SEARCHING FOR CAUSES

What is the main advantage of the experimental method?
The experimental method is the only research method that can be used to identify cause–effect relationships.

What is the difference between the independent variable and the dependent variable?
In an experiment, an independent variable is a condition or factor manipulated by the researcher to determine its effect on the dependent variable. The dependent variable, measured at the end of the experiment, is presumed to vary as a result of the manipulations of the independent variable.

How do the experimental and control groups differ?

The experimental group is exposed to the independent variable. The control group is similar to the experimental group and is exposed to the same experimental environment but is not exposed to the independent variable.

What is selection bias, and what technique do researchers use to control for it?

Selection bias occurs when there are systematic differences among the groups before the experiment begins. Random assignment—assignment of participants to groups by means of a chance procedure—maximizes the probability that groups are similar at the beginning of the experiment.

What is the placebo effect, and how do researchers control for it?

A placebo effect occurs when the response to a treatment is due to the person's expectations rather than to the treatment itself.

What is experimenter bias, and how is it controlled?

Experimenter bias occurs when the researcher's expectations affect the outcome of the experiment. It is controlled for by the use of the double-blind technique, in which neither the experimenters nor the participants knows which participants are in an experimental group and which are in a control group.

PARTICIPANTS IN PSYCHOLOGICAL RESEARCH

What are some ethical guidelines governing the use of human participants in research?

Participation in research must be strictly voluntary; there must be respect for confidentiality; participants must be free to withdraw from the study at any time; and participants must be debriefed as soon as possible after they participate.

Why are animals used in research?

Animals are used because they provide a simpler model for studying similar processes in humans; because researchers can exercise more control over animals and use a wider range of medical and other manipulations; because it is easier to study the entire lifespan (and even several generations in some species); and because animals are readily available and more economical to study.

1E THE HISTORICAL PROGRESSION OF PSYCHOLOGY: EXPLORING THE DIFFERENT PERSPECTIVES

What was Wilhelm Wundt's contribution to psychology?

Wilhelm Wundt is generally thought of as the founder of psychology. He conducted experiments in search of the basic elements of the conscious experience.

What were the goals and methods of structuralism, the first school of psychology?

Structuralism's main goal was to analyze the basic elements, or the structure, of conscious mental experience through the use of introspection.

What was the goal of the early school of psychology known as functionalism?

Functionalism was concerned with how mental processes help humans and animals adapt to their environment.

What is the emphasis of Gestalt psychology?

Gestalt psychology emphasizes that individuals perceive objects and patterns as whole units and that the perceived whole is more than just the sum of its parts.

How did behaviourism differ from previous schools of psychology?

Behaviourism, the school of psychology founded by John B. Watson, views observable, measurable behaviour as the only appropriate subject matter for psychology. Behaviourism also emphasizes that behaviour is determined primarily by factors in the environment.

What was the role of the unconscious in psychoanalysis, Freud's approach to psychology?

According to Freud's theory of psychoanalysis, our thoughts, feelings, and behaviour are determined primarily by the unconscious—the part of the mind that we cannot see and cannot control.

What is the focus of humanistic psychology?

Humanistic psychology focuses on the uniqueness of human beings and their capacity for choice, growth, and psychological health.

What is the focus of cognitive psychology?

Cognitive psychology focuses on mental processes such as memory, problem solving, concept formation, reasoning and decision making, language, and perception.

1F PSYCHOLOGY TODAY

What is the focus of the biological perspective?

The biological perspective emphasizes biological processes and heredity as the keys to understanding behaviour and thinking.

What is the focus of the evolutionary perspective?

The evolutionary perspective focuses on how humans have evolved and adapted behaviours required for survival in the face of various environmental pressures over the long course of evolution.

What is the focus of the sociocultural perspective?

The sociocultural perspective highlights the social and cultural influences on human behaviour.

What are some specialities in psychology, and in what settings are they employed?

Most psychology researchers work in colleges and universities, where they conduct research and teach. Clinical psychologists are responsible for the diagnosis and treatment of often complex psychological disorders. Counselling psychologists assist people who are dealing with psychology-related issues that are less severe. School and educational psychologists provide psychological services to students in a school setting. Forensic psychologists apply their knowledge of psychological research to the legal system. Health psychologists work with patients or conduct research on the relationship between psychological processes and physical health. Sport psychologists apply psychological principles to help improve the performance of athletes. Industrial or organizational psychologists help businesses deal with issues such as the hiring and retention of qualified personnel, employee satisfaction, workplace violence, and occupational health.

INTRODUCTION TO PSYCHOLOGY

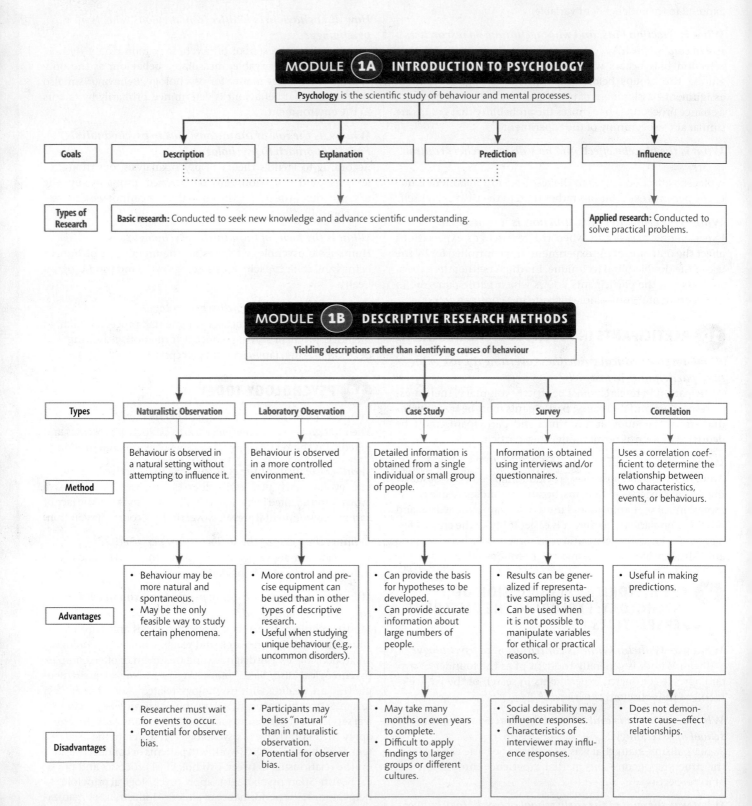

MODULE 1A INTRODUCTION TO PSYCHOLOGY

Psychology is the scientific study of behaviour and mental processes.

Goals	Description	Explanation	Prediction	Influence

Types of Research	**Basic research:** Conducted to seek new knowledge and advance scientific understanding.	**Applied research:** Conducted to solve practical problems.

MODULE 1B DESCRIPTIVE RESEARCH METHODS

Yielding descriptions rather than identifying causes of behaviour

Types	Naturalistic Observation	Laboratory Observation	Case Study	Survey	Correlation
Method	Behaviour is observed in a natural setting without attempting to influence it.	Behaviour is observed in a more controlled environment.	Detailed information is obtained from a single individual or small group of people.	Information is obtained using interviews and/or questionnaires.	Uses a correlation coefficient to determine the relationship between two characteristics, events, or behaviours.
Advantages	• Behaviour may be more natural and spontaneous. • May be the only feasible way to study certain phenomena.	• More control and precise equipment can be used than in other types of descriptive research. • Useful when studying unique behaviour (e.g., uncommon disorders).	• Can provide the basis for hypotheses to be developed. • Can provide accurate information about large numbers of people.	• Results can be generalized if representative sampling is used. • Can be used when it is not possible to manipulate variables for ethical or practical reasons.	• Useful in making predictions.
Disadvantages	• Researcher must wait for events to occur. • Potential for observer bias.	• Participants may be less "natural" than in naturalistic observation. • Potential for observer bias.	• May take many months or even years to complete. • Difficult to apply findings to larger groups or different cultures.	• Social desirability may influence responses. • Characteristics of interviewer may influence responses.	• Does not demonstrate cause–effect relationships.

Identifying cause–effect relationships

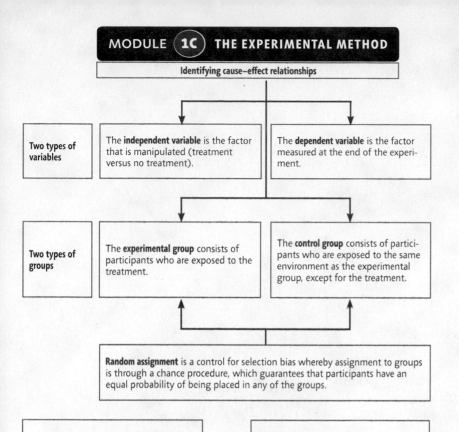

| Two types of variables | The **independent variable** is the factor that is manipulated (treatment versus no treatment). | The **dependent variable** is the factor measured at the end of the experiment. |

| Two types of groups | The **experimental group** consists of participants who are exposed to the treatment. | The **control group** consists of participants who are exposed to the same environment as the experimental group, except for the treatment. |

Random assignment is a control for selection bias whereby assignment to groups is through a chance procedure, which guarantees that participants have an equal probability of being placed in any of the groups.

Key Advantages
- Employs a high degree of control to rule out other sources of influence.
- Only research method that has the ability to reveal cause–effect relationships.

Key Disadvantages
- Generalizability issues.
- Cannot be performed in many areas of psychology due to ethical issues.
- Potential for experimenter effects and placebo effects if double-blind technique is not used.

- Researchers often use convenient samples of students. This strategy may reduce generalizability.
- Psychologists must develop tests that are reliable and valid.
- Psychologists must abide by a strict code of ethics for both human and animal research.

Wilhelm Wundt, the founder of psychology, established a laboratory in 1879 and focused on immediate, conscious experience.

Structuralism (Titchener) tried to break conscious experience down to its basic elements. Introspection was used as the primary technique.

Functionalism (James) studied the function, or purpose, of consciousness (i.e., how mental processes help one to adapt to one's environment).

Gestalt psychology (Wertheimer, Koffka, Köhler) emphasizes that individuals perceive objects and patterns as whole units, and the perceived whole is more than just the sum of its parts.

Behaviourism (Watson, Skinner) rejects the study of consciousness in favour of observable behaviour. Focuses on how behaviour is determined by factors in the environment.

Psychoanalysis (Freud) emphasizes that unconscious mental forces are the key determinants of behaviour.

Humanistic psychology (Maslow, Rogers) focuses on the uniqueness of human beings and their capacity for choice, growth, and psychological health.

Cognitive psychology focuses on mental processes such as memory, reasoning, language, and perception.

Modern psychologists need not limit themselves to only one perspective or approach.

Some perspectives in modern approaches include
- **Biological:** Emphasizes biological processes and heredity as the keys to understanding behaviour and thinking.
- **Evolutionary:** Emphasizes the role of inherited tendencies that have proven adaptive in humans.
- **Sociocultural:** Emphasizes social and cultural influences on human behaviour.

2

Recently, two Canadians became pioneers in an effort to test whether it is possible to train brains to see again, using a revolutionary eye implant device (CBC, 2014). The device, called the Argus Retinal Prosthesis System (Argus II), is comprised of a tiny video camera attached to a special set of glasses, a small computer device, and a tiny patch containing 60 electrodes which is surgically implanted to the surface of the retina (University Health Network, 2014). How does it work? The video camera records the visual information that we would normally see in our world. This information is converted into electrical impulses which are sent to the electrodes in the implant device. The implant sends signals directly to the retinal nerves and these signals are then forwarded to the brain. This is where training the brain occurs. Since the recipients of the implant have no vision or virtually no vision, their brains have to learn how to understand the information being sent to them. This requires extensive training.

The outcomes would be modest in terms of what sighted people expect to see in their everyday life. For example, one recipient learned to "see" a black and white striped pattern. This took many trials over many weeks of exposure to images on a screen that presented high black and white contrasts. Yet, for the recipient who could not see before, it was a remarkable moment to discover that she not only saw something, but also understood it was stripes. Her brain had been trained, and this was just the beginning.

Every thought we think, every emotion we feel, every sensation we experience, every decision we reach, every move we make—in short, all human behaviour—is rooted in a biological event. Therefore, we launch our exploration of psychology with the study of biology and behaviour. Our story begins where the action begins, in the smallest functional unit of the brain—the nerve cell, or neuron.

© D A Barnes/Alamy

BIOLOGY AND BEHAVIOUR

MODULE **2A** THE NEURONS AND THE NEUROTRANSMITTERS

LO 2.1 Define the function of the three types of neurons.

LO 2.2 Identify the three key structures of a neuron.

LO 2.3 Explain how neural impulses work.

LO 2.4 Contrast excitatory and inhibitory effects of neurotransmitters and how they affect behaviour.

LO 2.5 Understand the role of the following neurotransmitters: acetylcholine, dopamine, norepinephrine, epinephrine, serotonin, amino acids, and endorphins.

All our thoughts, feelings, and behaviours can be traced to the activity of specialized cells called **neurons**. These cells perform several important tasks: (1) Afferent (sensory) neurons relay messages from the sense organs and receptors—eyes, ears, nose, mouth, and skin—to the brain or spinal cord. (2) Efferent (motor) neurons convey signals from the brain and spinal cord to the glands and muscles, enabling us to move. (3) Interneurons, thousands of times more numerous than sensory or motor neurons, carry information between neurons in the brain and between neurons in the spinal cord. **[LO 2.1]**

THE NEURONS: BILLIONS OF BRAIN CELLS

Anatomy of a Neuron: Looking at Its Parts

What is a neuron, and what are its three parts?

Although no two neurons are exactly alike, nearly all are made up of three parts: cell body (soma), dendrites, and axon. **[LO 2.2]** Figure 2.1 shows the structure of a neuron. The **cell body** contains the nucleus and carries out the metabolic, or life-sustaining, functions of the neuron. Branching out from the cell body are the **dendrites**, which look much like the leafless

branches of a tree. The dendrites are the primary receivers of signals from other neurons, but the cell body can also receive the signals directly. Dendrites can also relay messages backward—from the cell body to their own branches (a process called *back propagating*). These backward messages may shape the dendrites' responses to future signals they receive (Magee & Johnston, 1997; Sejnowski, 1997).

The **axon** is the slender, tail-like extension of the neuron that sprouts into many branches, each ending in a rounded axon terminal. The axon terminals transmit signals to the dendrites or cell bodies of other neurons, and to muscles, glands, and other parts of the body. In humans, some axons are short—only thousandths of a centimetre. Others can be up to a metre long—long enough to reach from the brain to the tip of the spinal cord, or from the spinal cord to remote parts of the body.

Supporting the Neurons

Glial cells are specialized cells that hold the neurons together. They are smaller than neurons and make up more than half of the volume of the human brain. Glial cells remove waste products such as dead neurons from the brain, handle metabolic tasks, and assist in the production of myelin for cell transmission tasks. Glial cells in the spinal cord are also involved in the transmission of pain sensations from the various parts of the body to the brain.

Communication between Neurons: The Synapse

What is a synapse?

Neurons are not physically connected. The axon terminals are separated from the receiving neurons by tiny, fluid-filled gaps called *synaptic clefts*. The **synapse** is the junction where the axon terminal of a sending neuron communicates with a receiving neuron across the synaptic cleft. There may be as many as

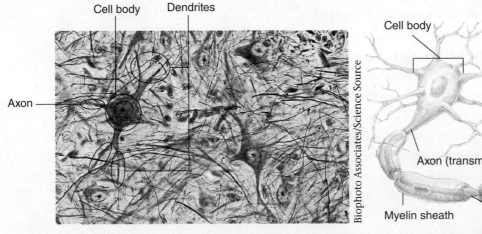

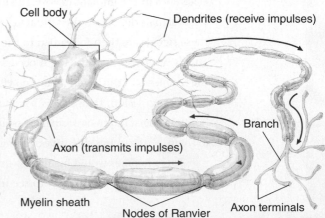

FIGURE 2.1

The Structure of a Typical Neuron

A typical neuron has three major parts: (1) a cell body, which carries out the metabolic functions of the neuron; (2) branched fibres called *dendrites*, which are the primary receivers of the impulses from other neurons; and (3) a slender, tail-like extension called an *axon*, the transmitting end of the neuron, which sprouts into many branches, each ending in an axon terminal. The photograph above shows human neurons greatly magnified.

100 trillion synapses in the human nervous system (Pakkenberg et al., 2003), with each neuron potentially connecting with thousands of other neurons (Kelner, 1997).

How big is one trillion? Numbers in the trillions are hard for us to comprehend. You know how short a time period of one second is. It takes almost 32 000 years for one trillion seconds to pass. Now try to imagine how incredibly complex your brain must be if there are between 10 trillion and 100 trillion synapses across which your neurons are passing and receiving messages.

If neurons are not physically connected, how do they communicate with one another?

The Neural Impulse: The Beginning of Thought and Action

What is the action potential?

Cells in the brain, the spinal cord, and the muscles generate electrical potentials. Every time we move a muscle, experience a sensation, or have a thought or a feeling, a small but measurable electrical impulse has occurred. How does this biological electricity work? **[LO 2.3]** Even though the impulse that travels down the axon is electrical, the axon does not transmit it the way a wire conducts an electrical current. What actually happens is that the *permeability* of the cell membrane increases. In other words, the membrane changes in a way that makes it easier for molecules to move through it and into the cell; the membrane becomes more *permeable*. This process allows *ions* (electrically charged atoms or molecules) to easily move into or out of the axon. Body fluids contain ions, some with positive electrical charges and others with negative electrical charges. Inside the axon, there are normally more negative than positive ions. When at rest (not firing), a neuron carries a negative electrical potential (or charge) relative to the fluid outside the cell. This slight negative charge is referred to as the neuron's **resting potential**.

When a neuron is sufficiently stimulated by an incoming signal, ion channels begin to open in the cell membrane, allowing positive ions to flow into the axon. This inflow of positive ions causes the membrane potential to change abruptly to a positive value (Pinel, 2000). This sudden and brief reversal of the resting potential is the **action potential**. Then the ion channels admitting positive ions close, and other ion channels open, forcing some positive ions out of the axon. As a result, the original negative charge, or resting potential, is restored. The opening and closing of ion channels progresses segment by segment down the length of the axon, causing the action potential to move along the axon (Cardoso, deMello, & Sabbatini, 2000).

The action potential operates according to the "all or none" law—a neuron either fires completely or does not fire at all. Immediately after a neuron reaches its action potential and fires, it enters a refractory period, during which it cannot fire again for one to two milliseconds. This rest period is very short. Neurons can fire up to 1000 times per second. Figure 2.2, on the next page, illustrates the movement of positive ions across the cell membrane—movement that stimulates the neuron to its action potential.

Consider this important question: if a neuron only either fires or does not fire, how can we tell the difference between a very strong and a very weak stimulus? a jarring blow and a soft touch? a blinding light and a dim one? a shout and a whisper? The answer lies in the number of neurons firing at the same time and their rate of firing (the number of times per second). A weak stimulus may cause relatively few neurons to fire; a strong stimulus may cause thousands of neurons to fire at the same time. Furthermore, a weak stimulus may cause neurons to fire very slowly; a strong stimulus may cause neurons to fire hundreds of times per second (normally the firing rate is much slower).

The most important factor in the speed of the impulse is the **myelin sheath**—a white, fatty coating wrapped around some axons that acts as insulation. If you look again at Figure 2.1, you will see that this coating has numerous gaps called *nodes of Ranvier*. These nodes cause the myelin sheath to look like links of sausage strung together. The electrical impulse is retriggered or regenerated at each node (or gap) along the axon. Thus impulses travel up to 100 times faster along axons with myelin sheaths.

NEUROTRANSMITTERS: THE CHEMICAL MESSENGERS OF THE BRAIN

What are neurotransmitters, and what role do they play in the transmission of signals from one neuron to another?

Once a neuron fires, how does it get its message to other neurons? Messages are transmitted between neurons by one

---

neurons (NEW-rons): Specialized cells that conduct impulses through the nervous system and contain three major parts—a cell body, dendrites, and an axon.

cell body: The part of the neuron that contains the nucleus and carries out the metabolic functions of the neuron.

dendrites (DEN-drytes): The branch-like extensions of a neuron that receive signals from other neurons.

axon (AK-sahn): The slender, tail-like extension of the neuron that transmits signals to the dendrites or cell body of other neurons or to the muscles, glands, or other parts of the body.

glial cells (GLEE-ul): Cells that help to make the brain more efficient by holding the neurons together, removing waste products such as dead neurons, making the myelin coating for the axons, and nourishing tasks.

synapse (SIN-aps): The junction where the axon of a sending neuron communicates with a receiving neuron across the synaptic cleft.

resting potential: The membrane potential of a neuron at rest, about 70 millivolts.

action potential: The sudden reversal of the resting potential, a reversal that initiates the firing of a neuron.

myelin sheath (MY-uh-lin): The white, fatty coating wrapped around some axons that acts as insulation and enables impulses to travel much faster.

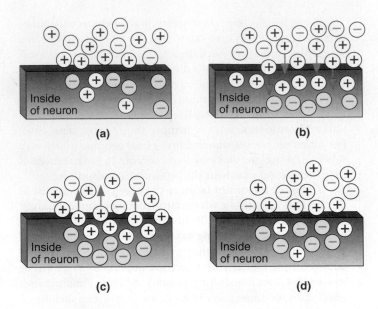

(a)

(b)

(c)

(d)

FIGURE 2.2

The Action Potential

(a) When a neuron is at rest (not firing), the inside of the neuron has a slight negative electrical charge compared to the outside; this is referred to as the neuron's *resting potential*. **(b)** When a neuron is stimulated, more positively charged particles flow into the cell, making the inside suddenly positive compared to the outside of the cell. This sudden reversal is the *action potential*. **(c)** Immediately after the neuron fires, some positive particles are actively pumped out of the cell. **(d)** The neuron returns to its resting potential and is ready to fire again if stimulated.

or more of a large group of chemical substances known as **neurotransmitters**.

Where are neurotransmitters located? Inside the axon terminal are many small, sphere-shaped containers with thin membranes, called *synaptic vesicles*, which hold the neurotransmitters. When an action potential arrives at the axon terminal, synaptic vesicles move toward the cell membrane, fuse with it, and release their neurotransmitter molecules into the synaptic cleft. This process is shown in Figure 2.3.

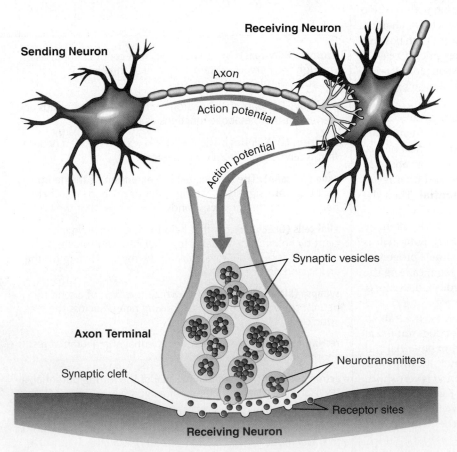

FIGURE 2.3

Synaptic Transmission

When a neuron fires, the action potential arrives at the axon terminal and triggers the release of neurotransmitters from the synaptic vesicles. Neurotransmitters flow into the synaptic cleft and move toward the receiving neuron, which has numerous receptors. The receptors bind only with neurotransmitters having distinctive molecular shapes that match theirs. Neurotransmitters influence the receiving neuron only to fire or not to fire.

The Receptor Sites: Locks for Neurotransmitter Keys

Once released, neurotransmitters do not simply flow into the synaptic cleft and stimulate all the adjacent neurons. Each neurotransmitter has a distinctive molecular shape. **Receptors** on the surfaces of dendrites and cell bodies also have distinctive shapes. Neurotransmitters can affect only those neurons that contain receptors designed to receive molecules matching their particular shape. In other words, each receptor is somewhat like a locked door that only certain neurotransmitter "keys" can unlock (Cardoso et al., 2000).

However, the binding of neurotransmitters is not as rigid as keys fitting locks. Receptors on neurons are somewhat flexible; they can expand and contract their enclosed volumes, and neurotransmitters of different types can have similar shapes. The interaction between the neurotransmitter and the receptor is controlled not by the direct influence of one on the other, but by their *mutual influence* on each other. Thus, a certain neurotransmitter may be competing for the same receptor with another neurotransmitter of a slightly different shape. The receptor will admit only one of the competing neurotransmitters—the one that fits most perfectly. This means that a neurotransmitter may be received by a receptor at one time but not at another if a better-fitting neurotransmitter molecule is present.

The Action of Neurotransmitters

When neurotransmitters enter receptor sites on the dendrites or cell bodies of receiving neurons, their action is either *excitatory* (influencing the neurons to fire) or *inhibitory* (influencing them not to fire). **[LO 2.4]** Because a single neuron may connect with thousands of other neurons at the same time, there will always be both excitatory and inhibitory influences on receiving neurons. For the neuron to fire, the excitatory influences must exceed the inhibitory influences of neurotransmitter substances by a sufficient amount (the *threshold*).

You may wonder how the synaptic vesicles can continue to pour out their neurotransmitters yet have a ready supply so that the neuron can respond to continuing stimulation. First, the cell body of the neuron is always working to manufacture more of the neurotransmitter substance. Second, unused neurotransmitter molecules in the synaptic cleft may be broken down into their components and reclaimed by the axon terminal to be recycled and used again. Third, by an important process called **reuptake**, the neurotransmitter substance may be taken back into the axon terminal, intact and ready for immediate use. This ends the neurotransmitter's excitatory or inhibitory effect on the receiving neuron.

During the last half of the twentieth century, there was considerable controversy about the nature of synaptic transmission, with some scientists arguing that transmission was primarily chemical and others arguing that it was primarily electrical. By the 1950s it seemed clear that the means of communication between neurons was chemical. Yet, at some synapses, termed *gap junctions*, electrical transmission occurs between the neurons. Although most synaptic transmission occurs chemically, (M. V. L. Bennett, 2000), electrical transmission is known to occur in the retina, the olfactory bulb (sense of smell), and the cerebral cortex.

THE VARIETY OF NEUROTRANSMITTERS: SOME EXCITE AND SOME INHIBIT

What are some of the ways in which neurotransmitters affect our behaviour, and what are some of the major neurotransmitters?

Neurotransmitters are manufactured in the brain, the spinal cord, the glands, and a few other parts of the body. Each kind of neurotransmitter affects the activity of the brain in a different way. Some neurotransmitters regulate the actions of glands and muscles; others affect learning and memory; still others promote sleep or stimulate mental and physical alertness. Some neurotransmitters orchestrate our feelings and emotions, from depression to euphoria. Others (endorphins) provide relief from pain.

To date, researchers have identified over 100 chemical substances manufactured by the body that may act as neurotransmitters (Purves et al., 2012). Neurotransmitters have two possible general effects on receiving neurons—excitatory and inhibitory. Some neurotransmitters are always excitatory; others are always inhibitory; still others can be either, depending on the receptor with which they bind.

Acetylcholine

The neurotransmitter **acetylcholine (ACh)** may produce either excitatory or inhibitory effects. **[LO 2.5]** Acetylcholine has an excitatory effect on the skeletal muscle fibres, causing them to contract so that we can move. But it has an inhibitory effect on the muscle fibres in the heart, keeping the heart from beating too fast. Differences in the receptors of the receiving neurons in skeletal and heart muscles cause these opposite effects. Acetylcholine also plays an excitatory role in stimulating the neurons involved in learning new information. So, as you are reading this text, acetylcholine is helping you understand and store the information in your memory.

---

neurotransmitters (NEW-ro-TRANS-miters): Chemicals that are released into the synaptic cleft from the axon terminal of the sending neuron, cross the synapse, and bind to appropriate receptors on the dendrites or cell body of the receiving neuron, influencing the cell either to fire or not to fire.

receptors: Sites on the dendrite or cell body of a neuron that will interact only with specific neurotransmitters.

reuptake: The process by which neurotransmitter molecules are taken from the synaptic cleft back into the axon terminal for later use, thus terminating their excitatory or inhibitory effect on the receiving neuron.

acetylcholine (ACh): A neurotransmitter that plays a role in learning, memory, and rapid eye movement (REM) sleep and causes the skeletal muscle fibres to contract.

REVIEW & REFLECT 2.1 MAJOR NEUROTRANSMITTERS AND THEIR FUNCTIONS

Neurotransmitter	Believed to Affect
Acetylcholine (ACh)	Movement, learning, memory, REM sleep
Dopamine (DA)	Learning, attention, movement, reinforcement
Norepinephrine (NE)	Eating habits, sleep
Epinephrine	Metabolism of glucose, energy release during exercise
Serotonin	Neurobiological functions such as mood, sleep, impulsivity, aggression, and appetite
GABA	Neural inhibition in the central nervous system
Endorphins	Relief from pain; feelings of pleasure and well-being

The Monoamines

An important class of neurotransmitters known as *monoamines* includes four neurotransmitters—dopamine, norepinephrine (noradrenalin), epinephrine (adrenalin), and serotonin. **[LO 2.5]** Like acetylcholine, **dopamine (DA)** produces both excitatory and inhibitory effects and is involved in several functions, including learning, attention, movement, and reinforcement. Dopamine is also important to our ability to feel pleasure (Schultz, 2006).

Norepinephrine (NE) affects eating habits (it stimulates the intake of carbohydrates) and plays a major role in alertness and wakefulness. **[LO 2.5]** *Epinephrine* (eh-peh-NEF-rin) complements norepinephrine by affecting the metabolism of glucose and causes the nutrient energy (glucose) stored in muscles to be released during strenuous exercise.

Serotonin produces inhibitory effects at most of the receptors with which it forms synapses. **[LO 2.5]** It plays an important role in regulating mood, sleep, impulsivity, aggression, and appetite (Greden, 1994). It has also been linked to depression and anxiety disorders (Dayan & Huys, 2008). Both serotonin and norepinephrine are related to positive moods, and a deficiency in them has been linked to depression. Some antidepressant drugs relieve the symptoms of depression by blocking the uptake of serotonin or norepinephrine, thus increasing the neurotransmitter's availability in the synapses.

Amino Acids

Researchers believe that some amino acids also serve as neurotransmitters. Two of particular importance—they are found more commonly than any others in the central nervous system—are *glutamate* (glutamic acid) and *GABA* (gamma-aminobutyric acid). **[LO 2.5]** Glutamate is the primary excitatory neurotransmitter in the brain (Riedel, 1996). It may be released by some 40 percent of neurons and is active in the higher brain centres that are involved in learning, thought, and emotions (Gillespie & Ressler, 2005).

GABA is the main inhibitory neurotransmitter in the brain (R. Miles, 1999) and is widely distributed throughout the central nervous system (brain and spinal cord). It is thought to facilitate the control of anxiety in humans. Tranquilizers, barbiturates, and alcohol appear to have a calming and relaxing effect because they bind with and stimulate one type of GABA receptor and thus increase GABA's anxiety-controlling effect. An abnormality in the neurons that secrete GABA is believed to be one of the causes of epilepsy, a serious neurological disorder in which neural activity can become so heightened that seizures result.

Endorphins

Over 40 years ago, researchers (Pert, Snowman, & Snyder, 1974) demonstrated that a localized region of the brain contains neurons with receptors that respond to opiates—drugs such as opium, morphine, and heroin. It is now known that the brain produces its own opiate-like substances, known as **endorphins**. Endorphins provide relief from pain or the stress of vigorous exercise and produce feelings of pleasure and well-being. **[LO 2.5]**

Generally, one single neurotransmitter is not responsible for a given mental function. Memory, for example, is modified by a collection of neurotransmitters, including acetylcholine, epinephrine, norepinephrine, and (probably) serotonin. *Review & Reflect 2.1* summarizes the major neurotransmitters and the behaviours with which they seem to be most strongly associated.

---

dopamine (DA) (DOE-pah-meen): A neurotransmitter that plays a role in learning, attention, movement, and reinforcement.

norepinephrine (NE) (nor-eh-peh-NEF-rin): A neurotransmitter affecting eating and sleeping.

serotonin: A neurotransmitter that plays an important role in regulating mood, sleep, impulsivity, aggression, and appetite.

endorphins (en-DOOR-fins): Chemicals produced naturally by the brain that reduce pain and affect mood positively.

central nervous system (CNS): The brain and the spinal cord.

spinal cord: An extension of the brain, reaching from the base of the brain through the neck and spinal column, that transmits messages between the brain and the peripheral nervous system.

REMEMBER IT

Neurons and Neurotransmitters

1. The branch-like extensions of neurons that act as the primary receivers of signals from other neurons are the
   a. dendrites.
   b. axons.
   c. glial cells.
   d. cell bodies.

2. The junction where the axon of a sending neuron communicates with a receiving neuron is called the
   a. reuptake site.
   b. receptor site.
   c. synapse.
   d. axon terminal.

3. The resting potential is the firing of a neuron that results when the charge within the neuron becomes more positive than the charge outside the cell membrane. (true/false)

4. Endorphins, norepinephrine, dopamine, and serotonin are all examples of
   a. hormones.
   b. neurotransmitters.
   c. neuropeptides.
   d. neuromodulators.

Answers: 1. a 2. c 3. false 4. b

MODULE 2B THE CENTRAL NERVOUS SYSTEM

LO 2.6 Identify the major structures of the central nervous system: brainstem, cerebellum, thalamus, hypothalamus, and limbic system.

LO 2.7 Explain the function of each of the major structures of the central nervous system.

Human functioning involves much more than the actions of individual neurons. Collections of neurons, brain structures, and organ systems must also be explored. The nervous system is divided into two parts: (1) the **central nervous system (CNS)**, which is composed of the brain and the spinal cord, and (2) the *peripheral nervous system*, which connects the central nervous system to all other parts of the body (see Figure 2.4 and Figure 2.12).

THE SPINAL CORD: AN EXTENSION OF THE BRAIN

Why is an intact spinal cord important to normal functioning?

The **spinal cord** can best be thought of as an extension of the brain. A cylinder of neural tissue about the diameter of your little finger, the spinal cord reaches from the base of the brain, through the neck, and down the hollow centre of the spinal column. The spinal cord is protected by bone and also by spinal fluid, which serves as a shock absorber. The spinal cord literally links the body with the brain. It transmits messages between the brain and the peripheral nervous system. Thus, sensory information can reach the brain, and messages from the brain can be sent to the muscles, the glands, and other parts of the body.

Although the spinal cord and the brain usually function together, the spinal cord can act without help from the brain

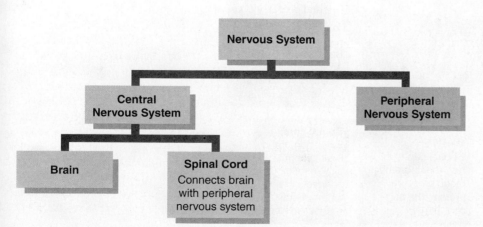

FIGURE 2.4

Divisions of the Human Nervous System

The human nervous system is divided into two parts: (1) the central nervous system, consisting of the brain and the spinal cord, and (2) the peripheral nervous system.

to protect us from injury. For example, the spinal reflex that causes you to withdraw your hand quickly from a hot stove is controlled by the spinal cord, without the initial involvement of the brain. The brain, however, quickly becomes aware and involved when the pain signal reaches it. At that point you might plunge your hand into cold water to relieve the pain.

THE BRAINSTEM: THE MOST PRIMITIVE PART OF THE BRAIN

What are the crucial functions handled by the brainstem?

The **brainstem** begins at the site where the spinal cord enlarges as it enters the skull. **[LO 2.6]** The brainstem includes the medulla, the pons, and the reticular formation, as shown in Figure 2.5. The brainstem handles functions that are vital to our physical survival; damage to it is life-threatening. **[LO 2.7]** The **medulla** is the part of the brainstem that controls heartbeat, breathing, blood pressure, coughing, and swallowing. Fortunately, the medulla handles these functions automatically, so you do not have to decide consciously to breathe or remember to keep your heart beating.

Extending through the central core of the brainstem is another important structure, the **reticular formation**, sometimes called the *reticular activating system* (RAS) (as shown in Figure 2.5). The reticular formation plays a crucial role in arousal and attention. Every day our sense organs are bombarded with stimuli, but we cannot possibly pay attention to everything we see or hear. The reticular formation screens messages entering the brain. It blocks some messages and sends others on to higher brain centres for processing.

The reticular formation also determines how alert we are. When it slows down, we doze off or go to sleep. But like an alarm clock, it can also jolt us into consciousness. Thanks to the reticular formation, important messages get through even when we are asleep. That is why parents may be able to sleep through a thunderstorm but will awaken to the slightest cry of their baby. (The next time you sleep through your alarm and are late for class, blame it on your reticular formation.)

Above the medulla and at the top of the brainstem is a bridge-like structure called the *pons* (Latin for "bridge"). The pons extends across the top front of the brainstem and connects to the left and right halves of the cerebellum. The pons plays a role in body movement and exerts an influence on sleep and dreaming.

THE CEREBELLUM: A MUST FOR GRACEFUL MOVEMENT

What are the primary functions of the cerebellum?

Cerebellum means "little cerebrum." **[LO 2.6]** With its two hemispheres, it resembles the large cerebrum, which rests above it (see Figures 2.5 & 2.7). Its main functions are to execute smooth, skilled movements and to regulate muscle tone and posture (Lalonde & Botez, 1990; Spencer, Zelaznik, Dierichsen, & Ivry, 2003). **[LO 2.7]** Although some researchers remain skeptical, some studies suggest that the cerebellum is involved in cognitive and social functions as well as motor activities (Tamminga & Vogel, 2005). The cerebellum coordinates and orchestrates

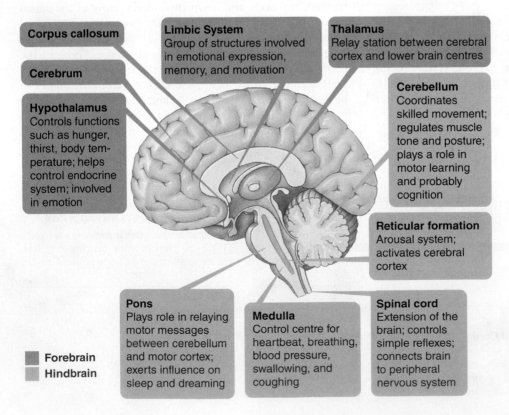

Corpus callosum

Cerebrum

Hypothalamus
Controls functions such as hunger, thirst, body temperature; helps control endocrine system; involved in emotion

Limbic System
Group of structures involved in emotional expression, memory, and motivation

Thalamus
Relay station between cerebral cortex and lower brain centres

Cerebellum
Coordinates skilled movement; regulates muscle tone and posture; plays a role in motor learning and probably cognition

Reticular formation
Arousal system; activates cerebral cortex

Pons
Plays role in relaying motor messages between cerebellum and motor cortex; exerts influence on sleep and dreaming

Medulla
Control centre for heartbeat, breathing, blood pressure, swallowing, and coughing

Spinal cord
Extension of the brain; controls simple reflexes; connects brain to peripheral nervous system

◼ Forebrain
◼ Hindbrain

FIGURE 2.5

Major Structures of the Human Brain

Some major structures of the brain are shown in the drawing, and a brief description of the function of each is provided. The brainstem contains the medulla, the reticular formation, and the pons.

The thalamus—at least one small part of it—affects our ability to learn new information, especially if it is verbal (Van Groen, Kadish, & Wyss, 2002). The thalamus also regulates sleep cycles (Saper, Scammell, & Lu, 2005). The majority of people who have had acute brain injury and remain in an unresponsive "vegetative" state have suffered significant damage to the thalamus, to the neural tissue connecting it to parts of the forebrain, or to both (D. I. Graham, Adams, Murray, & Jennett, 2005).

THE HYPOTHALAMUS: A MASTER REGULATOR

What are some of the processes regulated by the hypothalamus?

Nestled directly below the thalamus and weighing only about 56 grams, the **hypothalamus** is, for its weight, the most influential structure in the brain. **[LO 2.6]** It regulates hunger, thirst, sexual behaviour, and a wide variety of emotional behaviours. The hypothalamus also regulates internal body temperature, starting the process that causes us to perspire when we are too hot and to shiver to conserve body heat when we are too cold. And it regulates the biological clock—our body rhythms and the timing of our sleep/wakefulness cycle (Salin-Pascual, Gerashchenko, Greco, Blanco-Centurion, & Shiromani 2001; Saper et al., 2005). As small as it is, the hypothalamus maintains nearly all our bodily functions except blood pressure, heart rhythm, and breathing. **[LO 2.7]**

The physiological changes in the body that accompany strong emotion are initiated by neurons concentrated mainly in the hypothalamus. You have felt these physical changes—sweaty palms, a pounding heart, a hollow feeling in the pit of your stomach, or a lump in your throat.

©Creativa/Shutterstock

Which areas of the brain ensure that we can maintain our balance with little or no conscious effort?

the movements necessary to perform many everyday activities without studied, conscious effort. It enables you to guide food from the plate to your mouth, walk in a straight line, or touch the tip of your nose. But with a damaged cerebellum, or one that is temporarily impaired by alcohol, such simple acts may be difficult or impossible to perform.

THE THALAMUS: THE RELAY STATION BETWEEN LOWER AND HIGHER BRAIN CENTRES

What is the primary role of the thalamus?

Above the brainstem lie two extremely important structures—the thalamus and the hypothalamus (Figure 2.5). **[LO 2.6]** The **thalamus**, which looks like two egg-shaped structures, serves as the relay station for virtually all the information that flows into and out of the higher brain centres. **[LO 2.7]** This includes sensory information from all the senses except smell. Incoming sensory information from the eyes, ears, skin, and taste buds travels first to parts of the thalamus or hypothalamus and then to the area of the cortex that handles vision, hearing, touch, or taste. Pain signals connect directly with the thalamus, which sends the pain message to the appropriate sensory areas of the cerebral cortex.

brainstem: The structure that begins at the point where the spinal cord enlarges as it enters the brain; includes the medulla, the pons, and the reticular formation.

medulla (muh-DUL-uh): The part of the brainstem that controls heartbeat, breathing, blood pressure, coughing, and swallowing.

reticular formation: A structure in the brainstem that plays a crucial role in arousal and attention and screens sensory messages entering the brain.

cerebellum (sehr-uh-BELL-um): The brain structure that executes smooth, skilled body movements and regulates muscle tone and posture.

thalamus (THAL-uh-mus): The structure located above the brainstem that acts as a relay station for information flowing into or out of the higher brain centres.

hypothalamus (HY-po-THAL-uh-mus): A small but influential brain structure that controls the pituitary gland and regulates hunger, thirst, sexual behaviour, body temperature, our biological clock, and a wide variety of emotional behaviours.

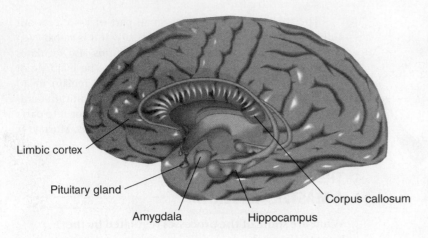

Limbic cortex

Pituitary gland

Amygdala   Hippocampus

Corpus callosum

FIGURE 2.6

The Principal Structures in the Limbic System

The amygdala plays an important role in emotion; the hippocampus is essential in the formation of conscious memory.

THE LIMBIC SYSTEM: PRIMITIVE EMOTION AND MEMORY

What is the role of the limbic system?

The **limbic system** is a group of structures deep within the brain, including the amygdala and the hippocampus, that are collectively involved in emotional expression, memory, and motivation (Figure 2.6). **[LO 2.6]** The **amygdala** plays an important role in emotion, particularly in response to unpleasant or punishing stimuli (Neugebauer, Li, Bird, & Han, 2004; LeDoux, 2000). **[LO 2.7]** It is also prominently involved in various aspects of learning, such as learned fear responses that help humans and other animals avoid dangerous situations and aversive consequences (LeDoux, 1995). Specifically, the amygdala helps us form associations between external events (including social ones) and the emotions related to those events (Aggleton, 1993). Damage to the amygdala can also impair one's ability to recognize (1) facial expressions showing fear or anger and (2) tones of voice expressing these emotions (Ariatti, Benuzzi, & Nichelli, 2008; LeDoux, 2000; S. K. Scott et al., 1997).

The **hippocampus** is another important part of the limbic system, located in the interior temporal lobes (see also Figure 2.8, on page p. 40). **[LO 2.6]** The hippocampus is absolutely essential in the formation of conscious memory (Squire, 1992). **[LO 2.7]** If your hippocampal region—the hippocampus and the underlying cortical areas—were destroyed, you would not be able to store or recall any new personal or cognitive information, such as that day's baseball score or the phone number of the person you met at dinner (Eichenbaum, 1997; Gluck & Myers, 1997; Vargha-Khadem et al., 1997). However, memories already stored before the hippocampal region was destroyed would remain intact. Research indicates there is a possibility of cell regeneration in the hippocampus in human adults (I. H. Robertson & Murre, 1999). The hippocampus also plays a role in the brain's internal representation of space in the form of neural "maps" that help us learn our way around new environments and remember where we have been (Maguire, Nannery, & Spiers, 2006; Thompson & Best, 1990; M. A. Wilson & McNaughton, 1993).

REMEMBER IT

The Central Nervous System

1. The brain and the spinal cord make up the peripheral nervous system. (true/false)
2. The hypothalamus regulates all of the following except
   a. internal body temperature.
   b. hunger and thirst.
   c. coordinated movement.
   d. sexual behaviour.
3. Match each function with the appropriate structure.
   _____ 1) connects the brain with the peripheral nervous system
   _____ 2) controls heart rate, breathing, and blood pressure
   _____ 3) consists of the medulla, the pons, and the reticular formation
   _____ 4) influences attention and arousal
   _____ 5) coordinates complex body movements
   _____ 6) serves as a relay station for sensory information flowing into the brain
      a. medulla
      b. spinal cord
      c. reticular formation
      d. thalamus
      e. cerebellum
      f. brainstem

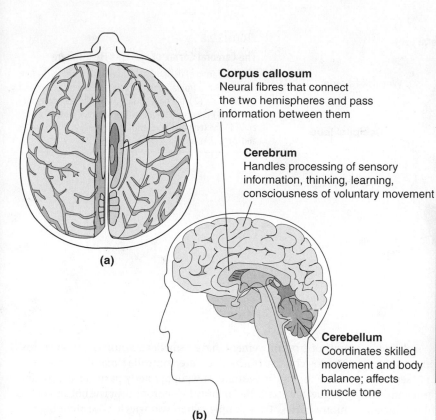

Corpus callosum
Neural fibres that connect the two hemispheres and pass information between them

Cerebrum
Handles processing of sensory information, thinking, learning, consciousness of voluntary movement

Cerebellum
Coordinates skilled movement and body balance; affects muscle tone

(a)

(b)

FIGURE 2.7

Two Views of the Cerebral Hemispheres

The two hemispheres rest side by side like two matched halves, physically connected by the corpus callosum, shown in **(a)**. An inside view of the right hemisphere of the cerebrum and cerebellum is shown in **(b)**.

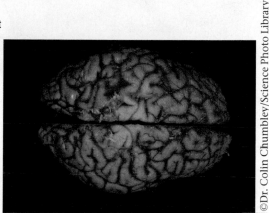

The two cerebral hemispheres show up clearly in this view looking down on an actual brain.

©Dr. Colin Chumbley/Science Photo Library

MODULE 2C THE CEREBRAL HEMISPHERES

LO 2.8   Identify and explain the function of each of the lobes of the cerebral hemisphere.

LO 2.9   Explain how damage within a lobe might affect performance and functioning in everyday life.

What are the cerebral hemispheres, the cerebral cortex, and the corpus callosum?

What functions come to mind when you think of the brain? Like most people, you probably identify this organ with logic, problem solving, language comprehension and production, and other "higher" cognitive functions. Though other parts of the brain play important roles in these functions, the cerebrum is the primary site for such functions. Indeed, the most essentially human part of our magnificent human brain is the cerebrum and its cortex.

If you could peer into your skull and look into your own brain, you would see a structure that resembles the inside of a huge walnut (Figure 2.7). Just as a walnut has two matched halves connected to each other, the **cerebrum** is composed of two **cerebral hemispheres**—a left and a right. These are physically connected at the bottom by a thick band of nerve fibres called the **corpus callosum**. This connection makes possible the transfer of information and the coordination of activity between the hemispheres. In general, the right cerebral hemisphere controls movement and feeling in the left side of the body; the left cerebral hemisphere controls the right side of the body.

The cerebral hemispheres have a thin outer covering about half a centimetre thick called the **cerebral cortex**, which

is primarily responsible for the higher mental processes of language, memory, and thinking. The presence of the cell bodies of billions of neurons in the cortex gives it a greyish appearance. Thus, the cortex is often referred to as *grey matter*. Beneath the cortex are the white myelinated axons (white matter) that connect cortex neurons with those in other brain regions. It

limbic system: A group of structures in the brain, including the amygdala and hippocampus, that are collectively involved in emotion, memory, and motivation.

amygdale (ah-MIG-da-la): A structure in the limbic system that plays an important role in emotion, particularly in response to aversive stimuli.

hippocampus (hip-po-CAM-pus): A structure in the limbic system that plays a central role in the formation of long-term memories.

cerebrum (seh-REE-brum): The largest structure of the human brain, consisting of the two cerebral hemispheres connected by the corpus callosum and covered by the cerebral cortex.

cerebral hemispheres (seh-REE-brul): The right and left halves of the cerebrum, covered by the cerebral cortex and connected by the corpus callosum.

corpus callosum (KOR-puskah-LO-sum): The thick band of nerve fibres that connects the two cerebral hemispheres and makes possible the transfer of information and the synchronization of activity between them.

cerebral cortex (seh-REE-brul-KOR-tex): The grey, convoluted covering of the cerebral hemispheres that is responsible for higher mental processes such as language, memory, and thinking.

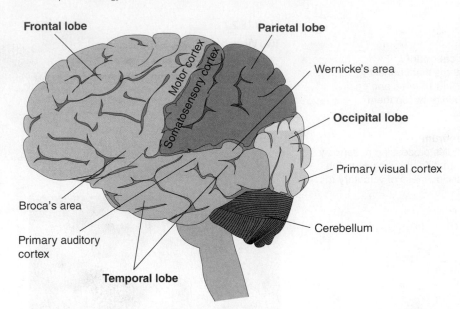

Frontal lobe

Parietal lobe

Motor cortex

Somatosensory cortex

Wernicke's area

Occipital lobe

Primary visual cortex

Cerebellum

Broca's area

Primary auditory cortex

Temporal lobe

FIGURE 2.8

The Cerebral Cortex of the Left Hemisphere

This illustration of the left cerebral hemisphere shows the four lobes: (1) the frontal lobe, including the motor cortex and Broca's area; (2) the parietal lobe, with the somatosensory cortex; (3) the occipital lobe, with the primary visual cortex; and (4) the temporal lobe, with the primary auditory cortex and Wernicke's area.

is arranged in numerous folds or wrinkles called *convolutions*. About two thirds of the cortex is hidden from view in the folds. The cerebral cortex contains three types of areas: (1) sensory input areas, where vision, hearing, touch, pressure, and temperature register; (2) motor areas, which control voluntary movement; and (3) **association areas**, which house our memories and are involved in thought, perception, and language.

THE LOBES OF THE BRAIN

In each cerebral hemisphere there are four lobes—the frontal lobe, the parietal lobe, the occipital lobe, and the temporal lobe. Find them in Figure 2.8.

The Frontal Lobes: For Moving, Speaking, and Thinking

What are some of the main areas within the frontal lobes, and what are their functions?

Of the lobes in the brain, the **frontal lobes** are by far the largest. They begin at the front of the brain and extend to the top centre of the skull. They contain the motor cortex, Broca's area, and the frontal association areas. **[LO 2.8]**

THE MOTOR CORTEX The **motor cortex** controls voluntary body movement (Figure 2.9). The right motor cortex controls movement on the left side of the body, and the left motor cortex controls movement on the right side of the body.

In 1937, Canadian neurosurgeon Wilder Penfield applied electrical stimulation to different areas of the motor cortex of conscious human patients undergoing neurosurgery. On the basis of the patients' responses, Penfield was able to "map" the motor cortex, as shown in Figure 2.9. Notice the motor homunculus, or "little man," drawn next to the cross-section of the motor cortex. The body parts are drawn in proportion to the amount of motor cortex that controls each body part. The parts of the body that are capable of the most finely coordinated movements, such as the fingers, lips, and tongue, have a larger share of the motor cortex. Areas such as the legs and the trunk, which are capable

only of gross movement, have a smaller amount of motor cortex. The lower parts of the body are controlled mainly by neurons at the top of the motor cortex; upper-body parts (face, lips, and tongue) are controlled mainly by neurons near the bottom of the motor cortex. For example, when you wiggle your right big toe, a cluster of brain cells firing at the top of the left motor cortex is chiefly responsible for producing the movement.

How accurately and completely does Penfield's map account for the control of body movement? Although it may be useful in a broad sense, more recent research has shown that there is not a one-to-one correspondence between specific points on the motor cortex and movement of particular body parts. Rather, clusters of neurons active over a wider area of the cortex are responsible for moving a body part—a finger, for example (Sanes & Donoghue, 2000). This means that there is considerable overlap in the neurons that fire to move a finger (Schieber & Hibbard, 1993).

What happens when part of the motor cortex is damaged? **[LO 2.9]** Depending on the severity of the damage, either paralysis or some impairment of coordination can result. Sometimes damage in the motor cortex causes the seizures of grand mal epilepsy. On the other hand, if an arm or leg is amputated, many of the neurons in the corresponding area of the motor cortex will eventually be dedicated to another function (D. Murray, 1995).

Evidence has come to light showing that the motor cortex also participates in learning and cognitive events (Sanes & Donoghue, 2000). **[LO 2.8]** And its *plasticity*—its ability to adapt to changes such as brain damage—is maintained throughout life. This plasticity allows synapses to strengthen and reorganize their interconnections when stimulated by experience and practice. For more information about plasticity, see Module 2F and the *Canadian Connections* box later in this chapter.

BROCA'S AREA In 1861, Paul Broca performed autopsies on two bodies—one of a person who had been totally without speech, the other of a person who had been able to say only four words (Jenkins, Jimenez-Pabon, Shaw, & Sefer, 1975). Broca found that both individuals had damage in the left hemisphere, slightly in front of the part of the motor cortex that controls movement of the jaw, lips, and tongue. Broca was among the first scientists

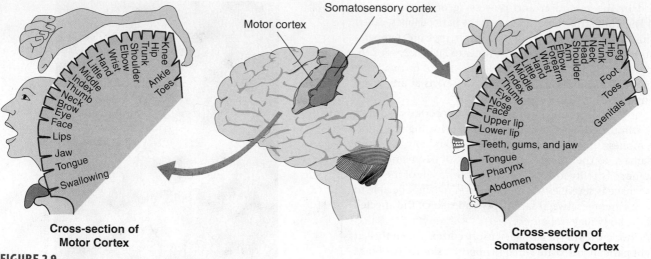

Cross-section of Motor Cortex

Cross-section of Somatosensory Cortex

FIGURE 2.9

The Motor Cortex and the Somatosensory Cortex from the Left Hemisphere

The left motor cortex controls voluntary movement in the right side of the body. [LO 2.8] The left somatosensory cortex is the site where touch, pressure, temperature, and pain sensations from the right side of the body register. The more sensitive the body parts and the more capable they are of finely coordinated movements, the greater the areas of somatosensory cortex and motor cortex dedicated to those body parts. Note what large sections of cortex serve the head, face, hands, and fingers, and what small sections serve such large areas as the trunk, arms, and legs.

to demonstrate the existence of localized functions in the cerebral cortex (Schiller, 1993). He concluded that the site of damage, now called **Broca's area**, was the part of the brain responsible for speech production (see Figure 2.8). Broca's area is involved in directing the pattern of muscle movements required to produce speech sounds. A brain-imaging study (Embick, Marantz, Miyashita, O'Neil, & Sakai, 2000) indicates that Broca's area buzzes with activity when a person knowingly makes grammatical errors, especially those involving word order. This finding confirms the existence of distinct brain structures for language knowledge and a specialization within Broca's area for grammar.

If Broca's area is damaged, **Broca's aphasia** may result. [LO 2.9] **Aphasia** is a general term for a loss or impairment of the ability to produce or use language, resulting from damage to the brain. Characteristically, patients with Broca's aphasia know what they want to say but can speak very little or not at all. If they are able to speak, their words are produced very slowly, with great effort, and are poorly articulated. Broca's aphasia, then, is a problem in producing language, not in understanding it (Maratsos & Matheny, 1994).

FRONTAL ASSOCIATION AREAS Much of the frontal lobe consists of association areas that are involved in thinking, motivation, planning for the future, impulse control, and emotional responses (Stuss, Gow, & Hetherington, 1992).

Sometimes pronounced changes in emotional responses occur when the frontal lobes are damaged. One famous case involved Phineas Gage, a 25-year-old man who was involved in an accident in which a metal rod was driven through the bottom of his left cheekbone and out through the top of his skull. The damage to the frontal lobes drastically altered impulse control and emotional responses. Using measurements from Gage's skull and modern brain-imaging techniques, researchers have been able to identify the probable location of the damage Gage's brain suffered (Damasio, Grabowski, Frank, Galaburda,

& Damasio, 1994). The photo on the next page shows the most likely trajectory of the metal rod that tore through his skull.

The Parietal Lobes: Vital to Our Sense of Touch

What are the primary functions of the parietal lobes in general and the somatosensory cortex in particular?

The **parietal lobes** lie directly behind the frontal lobes, in the top-middle portion of the brain. The parietal lobes are

association areas: Areas of the cerebral cortex that house memories and are involved in thought, perception, learning, and language.

frontal lobes: The lobes that control voluntary body movements, speech production, and such functions as thinking, motivation, planning for the future, impulse control, and emotional responses.

motor cortex: The strip of tissue at the rear of the frontal lobes that controls voluntary body movement.

Broca's area (BRO-kuz): The area in the frontal lobe, usually in the left hemisphere, that controls production of the speech sounds.

Broca's aphasia (BRO-kuz uh-FAY-zyah): An impairment in the ability to physically produce speech sounds or, in extreme cases, an inability to speak at all; caused by damage to Broca's area.

aphasia (uh-FAY-zyah): A loss or impairment of the ability to understand or communicate through the written or spoken word, resulting from damage to the brain.

parietal lobes (puh-RY-uh-tul): The lobes that contain the somatosensory cortex (where touch, pressure, temperature, and pain register) and other areas that are responsible for body awareness and spatial orientation.

involved in the reception and processing of touch stimuli. **[LO 2.8]** The front strip of brain tissue in the parietal lobes, called the **somatosensory cortex**, is where touch, pressure, temperature, and pain register in the cortex (refer to Figures 2.8 & 2.9). The somatosensory cortex also makes us aware of our body movements and the positions of our body parts at any given moment. **[LO 2.8]**

If various points on your somatosensory cortex were electrically stimulated, you would feel either a tingling sensation or a numbness in a corresponding part of your body. A person with damage to the somatosensory cortex of one hemisphere loses some sensitivity to touch on the opposite side of the body. If the damage is severe enough, the person may not be able to feel the difference between sandpaper and silk. Or the affected part of the body may feel numb.

The two halves of the somatosensory cortex (i.e., in the left and right parietal lobes) are wired to opposite sides of the body. Also, cells at the top of the somatosensory cortex govern feeling in the lower extremities of the body. When you drop a brick on your right foot, the topmost brain cells of the left somatosensory cortex fire and register the pain sensation. (Note: This is not a *Try It* exercise!) Notice in Figure 2.9 the large somatosensory areas connected to sensitive body parts such as the tongue, lips, face, and hand, particularly the thumb and index finger. Observe the small amount of cortex connected to the trunk of the body, which is a large area.

The somatosensory cortex may reorganize itself to accommodate unusual demands made upon it (Diamond, Huang, & Ebner, 1994). For example, among blind people, experienced Braille readers have a larger area of the somatosensory cortex dedicated to the fingertips they use for reading than to their other fingertips (Pascual-Leone & Torres, 1993).

Other parts of the parietal lobes are responsible for spatial orientation and sense of direction. There are association areas in the parietal lobes that house our memory of how objects feel so that we can identify objects by touch. People with damage to these areas could hold a pencil, computer mouse, or a ball in their hand but not be able to identify the item by touch alone.

somatosensory cortex (so-MAT-o-SENS-or-ee): The strip of tissue at the front of the parietal lobes where touch, pressure, temperature, and pain register in the cerebral cortex.

occipital lobes (ahk-SIP-uh-tul): The lobes that contain the primary visual cortex, where vision registers, and association areas involved in the interpretation of visual information.

primary visual cortex: The area at the rear of the occipital lobes where vision registers in the cerebral cortex.

temporal lobes: The lobes that contain the primary auditory cortex, Wernicke's area (left lobe), and association areas for interpreting auditory information.

primary auditory cortex: The part of the temporal lobes where hearing registers in the cerebral cortex.

Wernicke's area: The language area in the temporal lobe involved in comprehension of the spoken word and in formulation of coherent speech and written language.

Wernicke's aphasia: Aphasia resulting from damage to Wernicke's area; the patient's spoken language is fluent, but the content is either vague or incomprehensible to the listener.

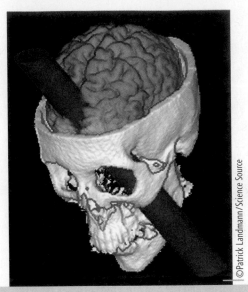

This computer-generated image shows the likely path of the bar that tore through Phineas Gage's skull.

©Patrick Landmann/Science Source

The Occipital Lobes: The Better to See You With

What are the primary functions of the occipital lobes in general and the primary visual cortex in particular?

Behind the parietal lobes at the rear of the brain lie the **occipital lobes**, which are involved in the reception and interpretation of visual information (refer to Figure 2.8). **[LO 2.8]** At the very back of the occipital lobes is the **primary visual cortex**, the site where vision registers in the cerebral cortex.

Each eye is connected to the primary visual cortex in both the right and left occipital lobes. Look straight ahead and draw an imaginary line down the middle of what you see. Everything to the left of the line is referred to as the *left visual field* and registers in the right visual cortex. Everything to the right of the line is the *right visual field* and registers in the left visual cortex. A person who sustains damage to one primary visual cortex will still have partial vision in both eyes. The association areas in the occipital lobes are involved in the interpretation of visual stimuli. The association areas hold memories of past visual experiences and enable us to recognize what is familiar among the things we see. When these areas are damaged, people can lose their ability to identify objects visually, although they are still able to identify the same objects by touch or through some other sense. **[LO 2.9]**

The Temporal Lobes: Hearing's Here

What are the major areas within the temporal lobes, and what are their functions?

The **temporal lobes**, located slightly above the ears, are involved in the reception and interpretation of auditory stimuli. **[LO 2.8]** The site in the cortex where hearing registers is known as the **primary auditory cortex**. When this area is stimulated with an electrical probe, the person hears bursts of sound. The primary auditory cortex in each temporal lobe receives sound inputs from both ears. Injury to one of these areas results in reduced hearing in both ears; the destruction of both areas causes total deafness. **[LO 2.9]**

WERNICKE'S AREA Adjacent to the primary auditory cortex in the left temporal lobe is **Wernicke's area**, which is the area involved in comprehending the spoken word and in formulating coherent written and spoken language (refer to Figure 2.8). **[LO 2.8]** In about 95 percent of people, Wernicke's area is in the left hemisphere. When you listen to someone speak, the sound registers first in the primary auditory cortex. The sound is then sent to Wernicke's area, where the speech sounds are unscrambled into meaningful patterns of words. The same areas that are active when we listen to someone speak are also active in deaf individuals when they watch a person using sign language. Wernicke's area is also involved when we select the words to use in speech and written expression (Nishimura et al., 1999).

Wernicke's aphasia is a type of aphasia resulting from damage to Wernicke's area. Although speech is fluent and words are clearly articulated, the actual message does not make sense to others (Kirshner & Jacobs, 2008; Maratsos & Matheny, 1994). The content may be vague or bizarre, it may contain inappropriate words and parts of words, or it may be gibberish containing non-existent words. Because people with Wernicke's aphasia are not aware that anything is wrong with their speech, this disorder is difficult to treat.

Another kind of aphasia is *auditory aphasia*, or *word deafness*. It can occur if there is damage to the nerves connecting the primary auditory cortex with Wernicke's area. The person is able to hear normally but may not understand spoken language—this is similar to when you hear a foreign language spoken—you hear the sounds but have no idea what the speaker is saying.

Because the left hand of a professional string player must rapidly and accurately execute fine movements and slight pressure variations, it is not surprising that these musicians have an unusually large area of the somato-sensory cortex dedicated to the fingers of that hand.

©aldegonde/Shutterstock

THE TEMPORAL ASSOCIATION AREAS The other parts of the temporal lobes consist of the association areas that house memories and are involved in the interpretation of auditory stimuli. For example, you have an association area where your memories of various sounds are stored so that you instantly recognize the sounds of running water, fire-engine sirens, barking dogs, and so on. There is also a special association area where familiar melodies are stored.

REMEMBER IT

The Cerebral Hemispheres

1. What is the thick band of fibres connecting the two cerebral hemispheres?
   a. cortex
   b. cerebrum
   c. corpus callosum
   d. motor cortex

2. The thin outer covering of the cerebrum is the
   a. cerebral cortex.
   b. myelin sheath.
   c. cortex callosum.
   d. white matter.

3. Match the lobes with the brain areas they contain.
   _____ 1) primary auditory cortex, Wernicke's area
   _____ 2) primary visual cortex
   _____ 3) motor cortex, Broca's area
   _____ 4) somatosensory cortex
      a. frontal lobes
      b. parietal lobes
      c. occipital lobes
      d. temporal lobes

4. Match the specialized area with the appropriate description of the function.
   _____ 1) site where hearing registers
   _____ 2) site where vision registers
   _____ 3) site where touch, pressure, and temperature register
   _____ 4) speech production
   _____ 5) voluntary movement
   _____ 6) formulation and understanding of the spoken and written word
   _____ 7) thinking, motivation, impulse control
      a. primary visual cortex
      b. motor cortex
      c. frontal association area
      d. primary auditory cortex
      e. somatosensory cortex
      f. Wernicke's area
      g. Broca's area

MODULE **2D** SPECIALIZATION OF THE CEREBRAL HEMISPHERES

LO 2.10 Contrast the functions of the left and right hemispheres.

The two cerebral hemispheres make different but complementary contributions to our mental and emotional life. Research has shown that some **lateralization** of the hemispheres exists—that is, each hemisphere is specialized, to some extent, for certain functions. Yet functions are usually not handled exclusively by one hemisphere; the two hemispheres always work together (Bradshaw, 1989; Efron, 1990). Much of what we know about lateralization is derived from pioneering research conducted by Doreen Kimura at the University of Western Ontario (1961, 1973). Kimura studied tasks in which different information could be presented to each of the hemispheres at the same time, thus demonstrating hemispheric specialization.

FUNCTIONS OF THE LEFT HEMISPHERE: LANGUAGE FIRST AND FOREMOST

What are the main functions of the left hemisphere?

In 95 percent of right-handers and in about 62 percent of left-handers, the **left hemisphere** handles most of the language functions, including speaking, writing, reading, and understanding the spoken word (Hellige, 1990; Long & Baynes, 2002). **[LO 2.10]** American Sign Language (ASL), which is used by people who are deaf or hard-of-hearing, is processed by both hemispheres (Neville et al., 1998). The left hemisphere is specialized for mathematical abilities, particularly calculation; it also processes information in an analytical and sequential, or step-by-step, manner (Corballis, 1989). Logic is primarily though not exclusively a left-hemisphere activity.

The left hemisphere coordinates complex movements by directly controlling the right side of the body and by indirectly controlling the movements of the left side of the body. It accomplishes this by sending orders across the corpus callosum to the right hemisphere so that the proper movements will be coordinated and executed smoothly. (Remember that the cerebellum also plays an important role in coordinating complex movements.)

FUNCTIONS OF THE RIGHT HEMISPHERE: THE LEADER IN VISUAL-SPATIAL TASKS

What are the primary functions of the right hemisphere?

The **right hemisphere** is generally considered to be better at visual-spatial relations. **[LO 2.10]** The auditory cortex in the right hemisphere appears to be far better able to process music than is the left (Zatorre, Belin, & Penhune, 2002). Artists, sculptors, architects, and household do-it-yourselfers have strong visual-spatial skills. When you put together a jigsaw puzzle, draw a picture, or assemble a piece of furniture

according to instructions, you are calling primarily on your right hemisphere.

The right hemisphere processes information holistically rather than part by part or piece by piece (Corballis, 1989). While auditory, visual, and touch stimuli register in both hemispheres, the right hemisphere appears to be more specialized for complex, perceptual tasks. Consequently, the right hemisphere is better at recognizing patterns, whether of familiar voices (Van Lancker, Cummings, Kreiman, & Dobkin, 1988), melodies and music (Springer & Deutsch, 1985; Zatorre et al., 2002), or things seen.

Although the left hemisphere is generally considered the language hemisphere, the right hemisphere makes an important contribution to how we "hear" language. According to Howard Gardner, the right hemisphere is involved "in understanding the theme or moral of a story, in grasping metaphor . . . and even in supplying the punch line for a joke" (1981, p. 74). It is the right hemisphere that is able to understand familiar idiomatic expressions such as "turning over a new leaf." If the right hemisphere is damaged, a person can understand only the literal meaning of such a statement.

To experience an effect of the specialization of the cerebral hemispheres, take the challenge in *Try It*.

Creativity and intuition are typically considered right-hemisphere specialties, but the left hemisphere shares these functions. The right hemisphere controls singing and seems to be more specialized for musical ability in untrained musicians (Kinsella, Prior, & Murray, 1988). But in trained musicians, both hemispheres play important roles in musical ability. In fact, parts of the left auditory cortex are significantly larger in musicians with perfect pitch (Schlaug, Jancke, Huang, & Steinmetz, 1995).

Patients with right-hemisphere damage may have difficulty with spatial orientation, such as in finding their way around, even in familiar surroundings. They may have attentional deficits and be unaware of objects in the left visual field—a condition called *unilateral neglect* (Deovell, Bentin, & Soroker, 2000). Patients with unilateral neglect may eat only the food on the right side of their plate, read only the words on the right half of a page, and even groom only the right half of their body (Bisiach, 1996). And remarkably, some patients may even deny that their arm on the side opposite the brain damage belongs to them (Chen-Sea, 2000; Posner, 1996).

The Right Hemisphere's Role in Emotion: Recognizing and Expressing Emotion

According to Philip Bryden and his colleagues at the University of Waterloo, the right hemisphere is also more active in recognizing and expressing emotion (Bryden & MacRae, 1988). Reading and interpreting non-verbal behaviour, such as gestures and facial expressions, is primarily a right-hemisphere task (Hauser, 1993; Kucharska-Pietura & Klimkowski, 2002). Test this for yourself in the *Try It*, below.

It is also the right hemisphere that responds to the emotional messages conveyed by another's tone of voice (Heilman, Scholes, & Watson, 1975; LeDoux, 2000). For example, say a professor sarcastically tells a student who

TRY IT

The Right Hemisphere's Role in Recognizing Emotion

Which is the happy face and which is the sad face?

Your answer probably depended on whether you are right- or left-handed. Even though these drawings are mirror images, right-handed people tend to see the face on the left as the happier face. Since the right side of the brain controls the left side of the body, you would use the left side of people's faces to make inferences about their emotional states (McGee & Skinner, 1987). Left-handers display the opposite pattern. They rely on the left side of the brain to interpret emotions, and because the left side of the brain controls the right side of the body, they usually judge the face on the right to be the happier one.

TRY IT

Testing the Hemispheres

Get a metre stick or yardstick. Try balancing it vertically on the end of your left index finger, as shown in the illustration. Then try balancing it on your right index finger. Most people are better with their dominant hand. Is this true for you?

Now try this: Begin reciting the alphabet out loud as fast as you can while balancing the stick with your left hand. Do you have less trouble this time? Why?

The right hemisphere controls the act of balancing with the left hand. However, your left hemisphere, though poor at controlling the left hand, still tries to coordinate your balancing efforts. When you distract the left hemisphere with a steady stream of talk, the right hemisphere can orchestrate more efficient balancing with your left hand, without interference.

enters the class late, "Well, I'm so glad you could come today." A student with right-hemisphere damage might respond only to the actual meaning of the words rather than to the sarcastic tone.

The right hemisphere is involved in our tone of voice and particularly in our facial expressions. The left side of the face, controlled by the right hemisphere, usually conveys stronger emotion than the right side of the face does (Sackeim, Gur, & Saucy, 1978). Laurence Miller (1988) describes the facial expressions and the voice inflections of people with right-hemisphere damage as "often strangely blank—almost robotic" (p. 39).

Evidence also continues to accumulate that brain mechanisms responsible for negative emotions are located in the right hemisphere, while those responsible for positive emotions are in the left hemisphere (Hellige, 1993). For instance, brain-imaging studies have shown that watching violent programs on television activates areas in the right hemisphere of children's brains that are not activated when they watch non-violent programs (J. Murray et al., 2006). Research also shows that patients suffering from major depression experience decreased activity in the left prefrontal cortex, where positive emotions are produced (Drevets et al., 1997). Interestingly, too, patients with brain tumours in the right hemisphere perceive their situation more negatively than those with tumours on the left side of the brain (Salo et al., 2002). By contrast, doctors' ratings of patients' quality of life do not vary according to the hemisphere in which the tumour is located.

THE SPLIT BRAIN: SEPARATE HALVES OR TWO SEPARATE BRAINS?

What is the significance of the split-brain operation?

The fact that parts of the human brain are specialized for some functions does not mean that some people are left-brained while others are right-brained. Unless the hemispheres have been surgically separated, they do not operate in isolation and cannot be educated separately. Although each has important

lateralization: The specialization of one of the cerebral hemispheres to handle a particular function.

left hemisphere: The hemisphere that controls the right side of the body, coordinates complex movements, and (in 95 percent of people) controls the production of speech and written language.

right hemisphere: The hemisphere that controls the left side of the body and, in most people, is specialized for visual-spatial perception and for understanding of non-verbal behaviour.

Left Hemisphere Right Hemisphere

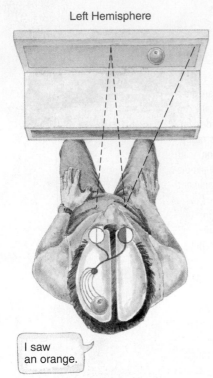
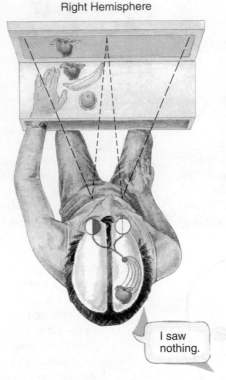

I saw
an orange.

I saw
nothing.

FIGURE 2.10

Testing a Split-Brain Person

Using special equipment, researchers are able to study the independent functioning of the hemispheres in split-brain persons. In this experiment, when a visual image (an orange) is flashed on the right side of the screen, it is transmitted to the left (talking) hemisphere. When asked what he saw, the split-brain patient replies, "I saw an orange." When an image (an apple) is flashed on the left side of the screen, it is transmitted only to the right (non-verbal) hemisphere. Because the split-brain patient's left (language) hemisphere did not receive the image, he replies, "I saw nothing." But he can pick out the apple by touch if he uses his left hand, proving that the right hemisphere "saw" the apple.
Source: (Based on Gazzaniga, 1983.)

specialized functions, the cerebral hemispheres are always in intimate and immediate contact, thanks to the corpus callosum.

In rare cases, people have been born with no corpus callosum or have had their corpus callosum severed in a drastic surgical procedure called the **split-brain operation**. Neurosurgeons Joseph Bogen and Phillip Vogel (1963) found that patients with severe epilepsy, suffering frequent grand mal seizures, could be helped by surgery that severed the corpus callosum. In this way, the pulsing waves of neural activity that occur during a seizure could be confined to one brain hemisphere.

The split-brain operation surgically separates the hemispheres, making the transfer of information between them impossible. The patient is left with two independently functioning hemispheres. In some cases the operation has been quite successful, completely eliminating seizures. And it causes no major changes in personality or cognitive functioning.

Research with split-brain patients by Roger Sperry (1964, 1966) and colleagues Michael Gazzaniga (1967, 1970, 1989) and Jerre Levy (1985) has expanded our knowledge of the unique capabilities of the individual hemispheres. Sperry (1968) found that when surgically separated, each hemisphere continued to have individual and private experiences, sensations, thoughts, and perceptions. However, most sensory experiences were shared almost simultaneously, because each ear and eye has direct sensory connections to both hemispheres.

Testing the Split-Brain Person

Sperry's research revealed some fascinating findings. In Figure 2.10, a split-brain patient sits in front of a screen that separates the right and left fields of vision. If an orange is flashed to the right field of vision, it will register in the left (verbal) hemisphere. If asked what he saw, the patient will readily reply, "I saw an orange." But suppose that an apple is flashed to the left visual field and is relayed to the right (non-verbal) hemisphere. If asked what he saw, the patient will reply, "I saw nothing."

How could the patient report that he saw the orange but not the apple? Sperry maintains that in split-brain patients, only the verbal left hemisphere can report what it sees. In these experiments, the left hemisphere does not see what is flashed to the right hemisphere, and the right hemisphere is unable to report verbally what it has viewed. But did the right hemisphere actually see the apple that was flashed in the left visual field? Yes, because with his left hand (which is controlled by the right hemisphere), the patient can pick out from behind a screen the apple or any other object shown to the right hemisphere. The right hemisphere knows and remembers what it sees just as well as it does the left; but unlike the left hemisphere, the right cannot name what it has seen. (In these experiments, images must be flashed for no more than one or two tenths of a second so that the participants do not have time to refixate their eyes and send the information to the opposite hemisphere.)

split-brain operation: An operation, performed in severe cases of epilepsy, in which the corpus callosum is cut, separating the cerebral hemispheres and usually lessening the severity and frequency of grand mal seizures.

plasticity: The ability of the brain to reorganize and compensate for brain damage.

REMEMBER IT

Specialization of the Cerebral Hemispheres

1. Match the hemisphere with the specialized abilities usually associated with it.

_____ 1) visual-spatial skills

_____ 2) speech

_____ 3) recognition and expression of emotion

_____ 4) singing

_____ 5) mathematics

      a. right hemisphere

      b. left hemisphere

2. Which of these statements is not true of the split-brain operation?

a. It is used for people suffering from severe epilepsy.

b. It provides a means of studying the functions of the individual hemispheres.

c. It causes major changes in intelligence, personality, and behaviour.

d. It makes transfer of information between the hemispheres impossible.

Answers: 1(1). a (2). b (3). a (4). a (5). b 2. c

MODULE 2E THE BRAIN ACROSS THE LIFESPAN

LO 2.11 Map out the major developmental changes of the brain across the lifespan.

LO 2.12 Understand the impact of synaptic losses across the lifespan.

LO 2.13 Understand the implications that plasticity has for recovery from brain damage.

Does the brain stop changing at any point in development?

Do you consider your brain to be fully matured? When do you think the brain reaches full maturity? The answer to this question might surprise you. In fact, the brain grows in spurts from conception until well into adulthood (Fischer & Rose, 1994). **[LO 2.11]** In childhood and adolescence, many of these spurts are correlated with major advances in physical and intellectual skills. Each growth spurt also seems to involve a different brain area. For example, the spurt that begins around age 17 and continues into the early 20s mainly affects the frontal lobes, where the abilities to plan and to control one's emotions are located. Differences between teens and adults may be due to this growth spurt.

Does the brain ever stop changing? No, the brain both gains and loses synapses throughout life. **[LO 2.12]** At some point in adulthood, losses begin to exceed gains (Huttenlocher, 1994). Brain weight begins to decline around age 30. One brain-imaging study showed that grey matter, but not white matter, is lost with normal aging in both hemispheres of the cerebellum (A. M. Sullivan, Maerz, & Madison, 2000). Age-related deficits due to the loss of grey matter are common. For example, elderly people tend to experience problems with balance. However, as

is true in childhood, intellectual and motor training can positively influence the brains of older adults.

BRAIN DAMAGE: CAUSES AND CONSEQUENCES

What must occur in the brain for there to be some recovery from brain damage?

How can a person survive such massive brain damage as in the case of Phineas Gage, while a small bullet fired into the brain in particular places can result in instant death? The precise location of a brain injury is the most important factor determining whether a person lives or dies. Had the metal rod torn through Gage's brainstem, that would have been the end of him. Brain damage has many causes. Stroke is the most common cause of injury to the adult brain, but other factors (e.g., head injuries, diseases, tumours, and the abuse of drugs) can leave people with a variety of disabilities.

Recovering from Brain Damage

It was formerly thought that once neurons are destroyed, they are gone forever. However, research indicates that the hippocampus can regenerate neurons (D. Jones, 1999); damaged neurons can sprout new dendrites and re-establish connections with other neurons to assume some of the functions of the brain cells that were lost; and axons are able to regenerate and grow (Fawcett, 1992).

Some abilities lost through brain damage can be regained if areas near the damaged site take over the lost function. The brain's ability to reorganize and to compensate for brain damage is termed **plasticity**. **[LO 2.13]** Plasticity is greatest in young children, whose hemispheres haven't yet been completely lateralized (Bach-y-Rita & Bach-y-Rita, 1990). Some individuals who have had an entire hemisphere removed early

CANADIAN CONNECTIONS

Neuroplasticity

Throughout our lives we learn new things. When exposed to new situations, we are able to create new memories, we acquire new physical skills, and, in general, we agree that we "change." But what exactly do we mean by "change"? Neuroscientists such as Bryan Kolb and his colleagues at the University of Lethbridge in Alberta investigate how the structures of the brain change in response to the wide array of experiences we have in our lives (Kolb & Gibb, 2007; Mychasiuk, Gibb, & Kolb, 2012).

The ability of the nervous system to reorganize and change its function is referred to as *plasticity* (Kolb, Gibb, & Robinson, 2003), and "the logical place to look for plastic changes is at the junctions between neurons, that is, at synapses" (p. 1). **[LO 2.13]** In particular, since we know that about 95 percent of cell synapses are found on their dendrites, examining the length of dendrites can provide a good estimate of the number of synapses. Both reductions and increases in synapses indicate change. Variables such as prenatal and postnatal experiences, genetic factors, psychoactive drugs, diet, disease, injury, and gonadal hormones have all been identified as important contributors to neural change (Kolb, Mychasiuk, Williams, & Gibb, 2011). For example, Kolb and his colleagues manipulated the environment of pregnant animals to see if there was any long-term impact on their offspring (Kolb et al., 2003; Kolb & Gibb, 2007). When pregnant animals were housed in a complex, stimulating environment, their offspring had increased dendritic length. Interestingly, these increases in dendritic length were evident when the offspring became adults, demonstrating the potential long-term implications of early (prenatal) experience.

The work of Kolb and his colleagues has also demonstrated that plastic changes can be both quantitative (change in number) and qualitative (Kolb et al., 2003; Kolb & Gibb, 2007). For example, when groups of juvenile, adult, or old animals were exposed to complex environments, all the groups showed increases in dendritic

Bryan Kolb

length; however, the changes in neural structures were not the same across age. The younger animals showed greater dendritic length but less density. Additionally, Kolb and his colleagues have demonstrated that all neural functions may not recover equally from brain damage (Kolb et al., 2011; Kolb & Gibb, 2007). Kolb's work opens the door for many questions ranging from understanding more precisely what plasticity is, to the impacts of plasticity on behaviour over the lifespan (Kolb et al., 2003; Kolb & Gibb, 2007; Kolb et al., 2011). ■

in life because of uncontrollable epilepsy have been able to lead near-normal intellectual lives (Bower, 1988). For more information about plasticity, see *Canadian Connections* above.

REMEMBER IT

The Brain across the Lifespan

1. The brain grows in _____.
2. _____ is the most common cause of injury to the adult brain.
3. The ability of the brain to adapt and change is known as _____.
4. Plasticity of the brain increases with age. (true/false)

Answers: 1. spurts 2. Stroke 3. plasticity 4. false

MODULE **2F** DISCOVERING THE BRAIN'S MYSTERIES

LO 2.14 Identify tools used to study the brain, including the electroencephalograph, computerized axial tomography, magnetic resonance imaging, and positron emission tomography.
LO 2.15 Understand the kind of information that can be gained from each tool used to study the brain.

What are some methods that researchers have used to learn about brain function?

Today, researchers are unlocking the mysteries of the human brain using electrical stimulation, the electroencephalograph (EEG), the microelectrode, and scanning devices such as computerized axial tomography (CT scan), magnetic resonance

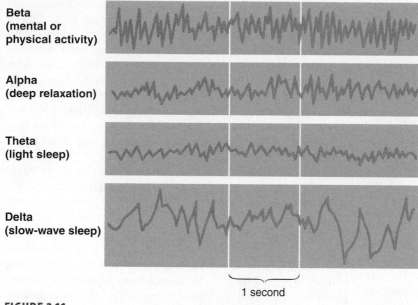

Beta
(mental or
physical activity)

Alpha
(deep relaxation)

Theta
(light sleep)

Delta
(slow-wave sleep)

1 second

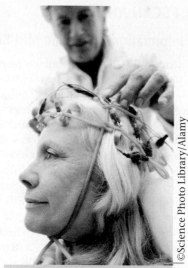

The electroencephalograph (EEG) uses electrodes placed on the scalp to amplify and record electrical activity in the brain.

©Science Photo Library/Alamy

FIGURE 2.11

EEG Patterns Associated with Various Waking and Sleeping States

EEG patterns vary according to the level of brain activity monitored. Beta waves occur when a person is mentally or physically active.

imaging (MRI), positron emission tomography (PET scan), functional MRI, and others.

THE EEG AND THE MICROELECTRODE

What is the electroencephalogram (EEG), and what are the four brainwave patterns it reveals?

In 1924, Austrian psychiatrist Hans Berger invented the electroencephalograph, a machine that amplifies a million times the electrical activity occurring in the brain. **[LO 2.14]** This electrical activity, detected by electrodes placed at various points on the scalp, produces a record of brainwave activity called an **electroencephalogram (EEG)**. The EEG measures four types of waves. **Beta waves** are associated with mental or physical activity, **alpha waves** with deep relaxation, **theta waves** with light sleep, and **delta waves** with deep sleep. Figure 2.11 shows the various brainwave patterns and their associated psychological states.

A computerized version of the EEG shows the different levels of electrical activity occurring every millisecond on the surface of the brain (Gevins, Leong, Smith, Le, & Du, 1995). It can show an epileptic seizure in progress and can be used to study neural activity in people with learning disabilities, schizophrenia, Alzheimer's disease, sleep disorders, and other neurological problems.

While the EEG is able to detect electrical activity in different areas of the brain, it cannot reveal what is happening in individual neurons. **[LO 2.15]** Microelectrodes can. A **microelectrode** is a wire so small it can be inserted into a single neuron without damaging it. Microelectrodes can be

used to monitor the electrical activity of a single neuron or to stimulate activity within it. Researchers have used microelectrodes to discover the exact functions of single cells within the primary visual cortex and the primary auditory cortex.

electroencephalogram (EEG) (ee-lek-tro-en-SEFF-uh-lo-gram): The record made by an electroencephalograph of an individual's brainwave activity.

beta wave (BAY-tuh): The brainwave of 13 or more cycles per second that occurs when an individual is alert and mentally or physically active.

alpha wave: The brainwave of 8 to 12 cycles per second that occurs when an individual is awake but deeply relaxed, usually with the eyes closed.

theta wave: A slow brainwave that occurs during light sleep, in trances, and in the state just before deep sleep or just before wakening.

delta wave: The slowest brainwave, having a frequency of 1 to 3 cycles per second and associated with slow-wave (deep) sleep.

microelectrode: An electrical wire so small that it can be used either to monitor the electrical activity of a single neuron or to stimulate activity within it.

THE CT SCAN AND MRI

What Information Do CT and MRI Scans Give Us?

The patient undergoing a **CT scan** (computerized axial tomography) is placed inside a large, doughnut-shaped structure. **[LO 2.14]** An X-ray tube then circles the patient's entire head and shoots pencil-thin X-rays through the brain. A series of computerized cross-sectional images results; these images reveal the structures within the brain (or other parts of the body) as well as abnormalities and injuries, including tumours and old or recent strokes. **[LO 2.15]**

Another technique, **MRI** (magnetic resonance imaging), produces clearer and more detailed images than the CT scan without exposing patients to the hazards of X-ray photography (Potts, Davidson, & Krishman, 1993). **[LO 2.14]** MRI is a powerful diagnostic tool that can be used to find abnormalities in the central nervous system and in other systems of the body. **[LO 2.15]**

Although the CT scan and MRI do a remarkable job of showing what the brain looks like both inside and out, they cannot reveal what the brain is doing. But other technologies can.

THE PET SCAN, THE FUNCTIONAL MRI, AND OTHER IMAGING TECHNIQUES

What Information can We Learn from PET Scans, Functional MRI Techniques, and Other Similar Imaging Tools?

The **PET scan** (positron emission tomography) is a powerful instrument for identifying malfunctions that cause physical and psychological disorders and also for studying normal brain activity. **[LO 2.14]** The PET scan can map the patterns of blood flow, oxygen use, and consumption of glucose (the food of the brain).

It can also show the action of drugs and other biochemical substances in the brain and other bodily organs (Farde, 1996). **[LO 2.15]**

The patient undergoing a PET scan either is injected with radioactive glucose or inhales oxygen laced with low-level radioactivity. The more active any part of the brain is, the more oxygen and glucose it consumes. The PET scan produces a computerized image in colours that vary with the amount of radioactive substance left behind as the brain uses different levels of oxygen or glucose. The PET scan detects *changes* in blood flow and in oxygen and glucose consumption as they occur in the various brain areas.

Functional magnetic resonance imaging (fMRI) can image both brain structure and brain activity. **[LO 2.14]** How does it work? It has been known for some time that more active brain areas require more oxygen, and, consequently, more blood is distributed to those regions. For example, suppose a given part of the brain is involved in reading. Whenever you read (this passage, for example), the neurons in that part of your brain will require more oxygen. fMRI magnets allow researchers to examine these kinds of changes in the flow of oxygen within the brain. **[LO 2.15]**

This technique has several advantages over PET. It requires nothing (radioactive or otherwise) to be injected into participants. Its ability to image precise locations of activity clearly is better than that of PET, and it can detect changes that take place in less than a second compared with around a minute for PET ("Brain imaging and psychiatry—Part 1," 1997).

Still other imaging devices are available. SQUID (superconducting quantum interference device) shows brain activity by measuring the magnetic changes produced by the electric current that neurons discharge when they fire. Another imaging technology, MEG (magnetoencephalography), also measures such magnetic changes and shows neural activity within the brain as rapidly as it occurs, much faster than PET or fMRI (Clarke & Braginski, 2006).

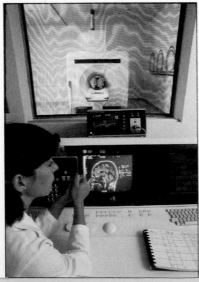

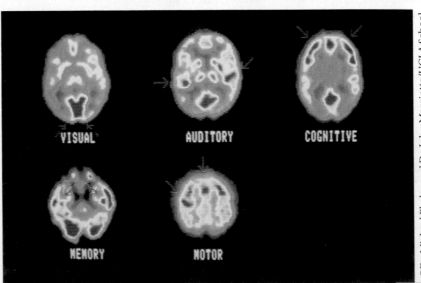

MRI (left) is a powerful tool for revealing what the brain looks like. Unlike PET scans (right), however, it cannot show us what the brain is doing. PET scans show activity in specific areas of the brain.

REMEMBER IT

Discovering the Brain's Mysteries

1. The CT scan and MRI are used to produce images of the _____ of the brain.
2. The _____ reveals the electrical activity of the brain by producing a record of brainwaves.
3. An imaging technique called _____ reveals both brain structure and brain activity.
4. Match the brainwave pattern with the state associated with it.

_____ 1) slow-wave (deep) sleep

_____ 2) deep relaxation while awake

_____ 3) physical or mental activity

_____ 4) light sleep

    a. beta wave

    b. delta wave

    c. alpha wave

    d. theta wave

Answers: 1. structures   2. electroencephalograph   3. fMRI   4(1) b   (2) c   (3) a   (4) d

MODULE 2G THE PERIPHERAL NERVOUS SYSTEM

LO 2.16 Identify and explain the function of the two components of the peripheral nervous system.

LO 2.17 Explain the function of the sympathetic and parasympathetic nervous systems.

What is the peripheral nervous system?

What makes your heart pound and your palms sweat when you watch a scary movie? It is your **peripheral nervous system (PNS)**. The peripheral nervous system is made up of all the nerves that connect the central nervous system to the rest of the body. Without the peripheral nervous system, the brain and spinal cord, encased in their bone coverings, would be isolated and unable to send information to or receive information from other parts of the body. The peripheral nervous system has two subdivisions—the somatic nervous system (SNS) and the autonomic nervous system (ANS). **[LO 2.16]** Figure 2.12, on the next page, shows the subdivisions within the peripheral nervous system.

THE SOMATIC NERVOUS SYSTEM

The somatic nervous system consists of all the *sensory* nerves, which transmit information from the sense receptors—eyes, ears, nose, tongue, and skin—to the central nervous system; and all the *motor* nerves, which relay messages from the central nervous system to all the skeletal muscles of the body. In short, the nerves of the somatic nervous system make it possible for us to sense our environment and to move, and they are primarily under our conscious control. **[LO 2.16]**

THE AUTONOMIC NERVOUS SYSTEM

What are the roles of the sympathetic and parasympathetic nervous systems?

The word *autonomic* is sometimes misread by students as *automatic*. That is not a bad synonym because the autonomic

nervous system operates quite well automatically, without our being conscious of it. It transmits messages between the central nervous system and the glands, the cardiac (heart) muscle, and the smooth muscles (such as those in the large arteries, the gastrointestinal system, and the small blood vessels), which are not normally under voluntary control.

The autonomic nervous system is further divided into two parts—the sympathetic and the parasympathetic nervous systems. Any time you are under stress or faced with an emergency, the **sympathetic nervous system** automatically mobilizes the body's resources, preparing you for action. This physiological arousal produced by the sympathetic nervous system is called the *fight-or-flight response*. If an ominous-looking stranger started following you and quickened his pace as you turned down a dark, deserted street, your sympathetic nervous system would automatically get to work. Your heart would begin to pound, your pulse rate would increase rapidly, your breathing would quicken, and your digestive system would nearly shut down. The blood flow to your skeletal muscles would be

CT scan: A brain-scanning technique involving a rotating X-ray scanner and a high-speed computer analysis that produces slice-by-slice, cross-sectional images of the structure of the brain.

MRI: A diagnostic scanning technique that produces high-resolution images of the structures of the brain.

PET scan: A brain-imaging technique that reveals activity in various parts of the brain on the basis of the amount of oxygen and glucose consumed.

peripheral nervous system (PNS) (peh-RIF-er-ul): The nerves connecting the central nervous system to the rest of the body; has two subdivisions–the autonomic and the somatic nervous systems.

sympathetic nervous system: The division of the autonomic nervous system that mobilizes the body's resources during stress, emergencies, or heavy exertion, preparing the body for action.

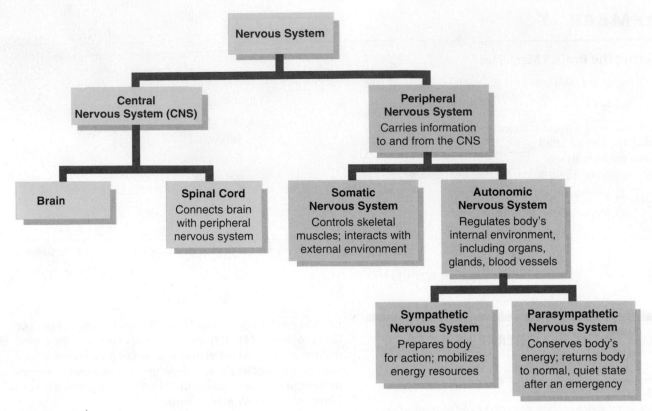

FIGURE 2.12

The Human Nervous System

The nervous system is divided into two parts: the central nervous system and the peripheral nervous system. The diagram shows the relationships among the parts of the nervous system and provides a brief description of the functions of those parts.

enhanced, and all of your bodily resources would be made ready to handle the emergency—RUN!

But once the emergency is over, something must happen to bring these heightened bodily functions back to normal. The **parasympathetic nervous system** is responsible for this. As a result of its action, your heart stops pounding and slows to normal, your pulse rate and breathing slow down, and the digestive system resumes its normal functioning. As you can see in Figure 2.13, the sympathetic and parasympathetic branches act as opposing but complementary forces in the autonomic nervous system. Their balanced functioning is essential for our health and survival.

REMEMBER IT

The Peripheral Nervous System

1. The _____ nervous system connects the brain and spinal cord to the rest of the body.
2. The _____ nervous system mobilizes the body's resources during times of stress.
3. The _____ nervous system restores the body's functions to normal once a crisis has passed.

Answers: 1. peripheral 2. sympathetic 3. parasympathetic

MODULE 2H THE ENDOCRINE SYSTEM

LO 2.18 Identify the components of the endocrine system.
LO 2.19 Understand the role of glands and hormones within the endocrine system

What is the endocrine system, and what are some of the glands within it?

We have seen how chemical substances called neurotransmitters influence the 100 billion or so neurons in the nervous system. There is another system that stimulates and regulates important functions in the body by means of chemical substances. The **endocrine system** is a series of ductless glands, found in various parts of the body, that manufacture and secrete chemicals known as *hormones* (from the Greek word for "excite"). **[LO 2.18]** Hormones are manufactured and released in one part of the body but have an effect on other parts of the body. They are released into the bloodstream and travel throughout the circulatory system, but each hormone performs its assigned job only when it connects with the body cells having receptors for it. **[LO 2.19]** Some neurotransmitters act as hormones as well— norepinephrine and vasopressin, to name two (Bergland, 1985). Figure 2.14 shows the glands in the endocrine system and their locations in the body.

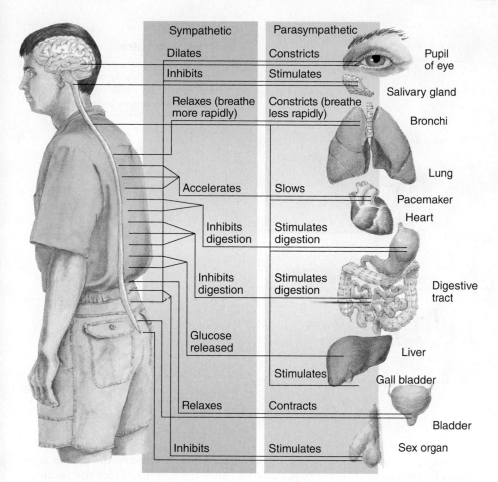

Sympathetic	Parasympathetic	
Dilates	Constricts	Pupil of eye
Inhibits	Stimulates	Salivary gland
Relaxes (breathe more rapidly)	Constricts (breathe less rapidly)	Bronchi
		Lung
Accelerates	Slows	Pacemaker Heart
Inhibits digestion	Stimulates digestion	
Inhibits digestion	Stimulates digestion	Digestive tract
Glucose released		Liver
	Stimulates	Gall bladder
Relaxes	Contracts	Bladder
Inhibits	Stimulates	Sex organ

FIGURE 2.13

The Autonomic Nervous System

The autonomic nervous system consists of (1) the sympathetic nervous system, which mobilizes the body's resources during emergencies or during stress, and (2) the parasympathetic nervous system, which is associated with relaxation and which brings the heightened bodily responses back to normal after an emergency. **[LO 2.17]** This diagram shows the opposite effects of the sympathetic and parasympathetic nervous systems on various parts of the body.

THE PITUITARY GLAND

The **pituitary gland** rests in the brain just below the hypothalamus and is controlled by it (see Figure 2.14). The pituitary is considered to be the "master gland" of the body because it releases the hormones that "turn on," or activate, the other glands in the endocrine system—a big job for a tiny structure about the size of a pea. **[LO 2.19]** The pituitary also produces the hormone that is responsible for body growth (Howard et al., 1996). Too little of this powerful substance will make a person a dwarf, whereas too much will produce a giant.

THE THYROID GLAND

The thyroid gland rests in the front lower part of the neck just below the voice box (larynx). The thyroid produces the important hormone thyroxine, which regulates the rate at which food is metabolized, or transformed into energy. **[LO 2.19]** Too much thyroxine can result in hyperthyroidism, a condition in which people are nervous and excitable, find it hard to be still and relax, and are usually thin. Hypothyroidism, an underproduction of thyroxine, has just the opposite effect. An adult with hypothyroidism may feel sluggish, lack energy, and be overweight.

THE ADRENAL GLANDS

Lower in the body are the two **adrenal glands**, which rest just above the kidneys, as shown in Figure 2.14. The adrenal glands produce epinephrine and norepinephrine, two hormones that activate the sympathetic nervous system. **[LO 2.19]** The adrenal glands release the corticoids, which control the body's salt balance, and also release small amounts of the sex hormones.

THE PANCREAS

Curving around between the small intestine and the stomach is the pancreas (see Figure 2.14). The pancreas regulates the body's

parasympathetic nervous system: The division of the autonomic nervous system that is associated with relaxation and the conservation of energy and that brings the heightened bodily responses back to normal after an emergency.

endocrine system (EN-duh-krin): A system of ductless glands in various parts of the body that manufacture and secrete hormones into the bloodstream or lymph fluids, thus affecting cells in other parts of the body.

hormones: Substances manufactured and released in one part of the body that affect other parts of the body.

pituitary gland: The endocrine gland located in the brain and often called the "master gland," which releases hormones that control other endocrine glands and also releases a growth hormone.

adrenal glands (ah-DREE-nal): A pair of endocrine glands that release hormones that prepare the body for emergencies and stressful situations and also release small amounts of the sex hormones.

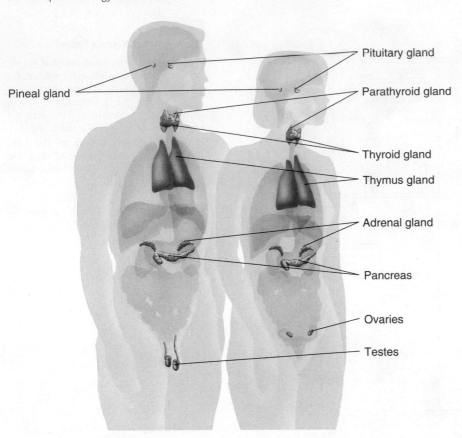

FIGURE 2.14

The Endocrine System

The endocrine system is a series of glands that manufacture and secrete hormones. The hormones travel through the circulatory system and have important effects on many bodily functions.

Pituitary gland

Pineal gland

Parathyroid gland

Thyroid gland

Thymus gland

Adrenal gland

Pancreas

Ovaries

Testes

blood sugar levels by releasing the hormones insulin and glucagon into the bloodstream. **[LO 2.19]** The pancreas also produces digestive enzymes. In people with diabetes, too little insulin is produced. Without insulin to break down the sugars we ingest, the level of blood sugar can get dangerously high. In hypoglycemia, the opposite effect occurs—too much insulin is produced, resulting in low blood sugar.

THE SEX GLANDS

The gonads are the sex glands—the ovaries in females and the testes in males (see Figure 2.14). Activated by the pituitary gland, the gonads release sex hormones that make reproduction possible and that are responsible for the secondary sex characteristics—pubic and underarm hair in both sexes, breasts in females, and facial hair and a deepened voice in males. **[LO 2.19]**

Androgens, the male sex hormones, influence sexual motivation. Estrogen and progesterone, the female sex hormones, help regulate the menstrual cycle. Although both males and females have androgens and estrogens, males have considerably more androgens and females have considerably more estrogens.

REMEMBER IT

The Endocrine System

1. The endocrine glands secrete _____ directly into the _____.
   a. hormones; bloodstream
   b. enzymes; digestive tract
   c. enzymes; bloodstream
   d. hormones; digestive tract

2. Match the endocrine gland with the appropriate description.
   _____ 1) keeps the body's metabolism in balance
   _____ 2) acts as a master gland that activates the other glands
   _____ 3) regulates blood sugar

   _____ 4) makes reproduction possible
   _____ 5) releases hormones that prepare the body for emergencies
   a. pituitary gland
   b. adrenal glands
   c. gonads
   d. thyroid gland
   e. pancreas

3. Sex hormones are produced by both the _____ and the _____.

APPLY IT

Handedness: Does It Make a Difference?

Are you a "lefty" or a "righty"? Have you ever wondered why? If you are left-handed, you share the hand preference of notable historical figures such as Alexander the Great, Michelangelo, Leonardo da Vinci, Albert Einstein, and Joan of Arc. Among left-handers of more recent times are Celine Dion, Jim Carrey, and Wayne Gretzky.

Several studies suggest that approximately 90 percent of the world's population are right-handed (Bryden, Roy, McManus, & Bulman-Fleming, 1997; Coren & Porac, 1977; Johnston, Nicholls, Shah, & Shields, 2009). Left-handedness occurs more often in males than in females. People who are left-handed are generally also left-footed, and to a lesser extent left-eyed and left-eared as well. There is a difference in the motor control provided by the two hemispheres of the brain. Thus, in a person whose left hand is dominant, the right hemisphere provides superior motor control for that hand (Coren, 1989; Coren & Halpern, 1991).

A number of physiological differences between right-handed and left-handed people have been identified. On average, the corpus callosum of left-handers is 11 percent larger and contains up to 2.5 million more nerve fibres than that of right-handers (Witelson, 1985, 1990). In about 60 percent of left-handers, language functions are controlled by the left hemisphere; in 25–27 percent, by the right hemisphere; and in about 15 percent, by both hemispheres. In general, left-handers appear to be less lateralized than right-handers, meaning that the two sides of the brain are less specialized (Hellige et al., 1994; Knecht et al., 2000). The literature is mixed in defining whether these differences result in advantages or disadvantages (Johnston et al., 2009).

Scholars and scientists have long wondered why such a small percentage of humans are left-handed. It used to be believed that cultural forces that shape child-rearing practices were responsible for the large right-handed majority (Provins, 1997). There is some evidence to support this view. For instance, in cultures where the belief in right-handedness as "normal" is very strong, there is a great deal of pressure on children to adopt a right-hand preference. As a result, there are lower proportions of left-handers in these cultures than in cultures where it is widely believed that forcing children to be right-handed is detrimental to their development (F. R. Wilson, 1998). However, even in very tolerant cultures, right-handedness predominates. Why?

Some researchers propose that handedness is determined by genetics (Annett, 1985; Levy & Nagylaki, 1972). Archaeological studies of ancient skeletons show that the proportions of left- and right-handers in the human population have been about the same for several thousand years (Steele & Mays, 1995). Furthermore, studies examining ancient artwork and tools in locations all over the world also show that humans have been predominantly right-handed for thousands of years (F. R. Wilson, 1998). Consistent with the genetic hypothesis, handedness appears early in human life. For example, babies almost always point with their right hands (Butterworth, Franco, McKenzie, Graupner, & Todd, 2002). These findings tend to support a genetic explanation for handedness.

Some neuroscientists believe that the predominance of right-handedness is just one manifestation of a general "rightward bias" in the human nervous system. Even infants are more likely to attend to an object that appears in the right visual field than one that appears in the left (Butterworth et al., 2002). In addition, more than half of left-handers demonstrate right-side dominance in motor skills that do not involve the hands (D. C. Bourassa, McManus, & Bryden, 1996). These findings suggest that a biologically based and species-wide rightward bias may be a more powerful influence on hand preference than one's own individual heredity.

THINKING CRITICALLY

Evaluation

Using your knowledge about how the human brain has been studied in the past and today, point out the advantages and the disadvantages of the older investigative methods: the case study, the autopsy, and the study of people with brain injuries or who have had brain surgery (including the split-brain operation). Follow the same procedure to discuss the more modern techniques: EEG, CT scan, PET scan, and fMRI.

Point/Counterpoint

A continuing controversial issue is whether animals should be used in biopsychological research. Review the chapter and find each occasion in which animals were used to advance our knowledge of the brain. Using what you have read in this chapter and any other information you have acquired, prepare arguments to support each of the following positions:

a. The use of animals in research projects is ethical and justifiable because of the possible benefits to humankind.

b. The use of animals in research projects is not ethical or justifiable on the grounds of possible benefits to humankind.

Psychology in Your Life

How would your life change if you had a massive stroke in your left hemisphere? How would it change if the stroke were in your right hemisphere? Which stroke would be more tragic for you, and why?

go to mypsychlab (access code required) to find web resources for your text that supplement the material in chapter 2.

SUMMARY & REVIEW

THE NEURONS AND THE NEUROTRANSMITTERS

What is a neuron, and what are its three parts?
A neuron is a specialized cell that conducts messages through the nervous system. Its three main parts are the cell body, dendrites, and axon.

What is a synapse?
A synapse is the junction where the axon terminal of the sending neuron communicates with the receiving neuron across the synaptic cleft.

What is the action potential?
The action potential is the firing of a neuron that results when the charge within the neuron becomes more positive than the charge outside the cell's membrane.

What are neurotransmitters, and what role do they play in the transmission of signals from one neuron to another?
Neurotransmitters are chemicals released into the synaptic cleft from the axon terminal of the sending neuron. They cross the synapse and bind to receptor sites on the receiving neuron, influencing the cell to fire or not to fire. Neurotransmitters regulate the actions of our glands and muscles, affect learning and memory, promote sleep, stimulate mental and physical alertness, and influence our moods and emotions, from depression to euphoria.

What are some of the ways in which neurotransmitters affect our behaviour, and what are some of the major transmitters?
Neurotransmitters affect how we learn, move, feel, and react to our world. Although many chemicals function as neurotransmitters, some of the major ones are Acetylcholine, monoamines (including dopamine, norepinephrine, and seratonin), amino acids (including glutamate and and GABA), and endorphins.

2B THE CENTRAL NERVOUS SYSTEM

Why is an intact spinal cord important to normal functioning?
The spinal cord provides the link between the body and the brain. The spinal cord also has reflexes which help us to avoid injury.

What are the crucial functions handled by the brainstem?
The brainstem contains (1) the medulla, which controls heartbeat, breathing, blood pressure, coughing, and swallowing; (2) the reticular formation, which plays a crucial role in arousal and attention and screens messages coming into the brain; and (3) the pons, which plays a role in body movement and exerts an influence on sleep and dreaming.

What are the primary functions of the cerebellum?
The main functions of the cerebellum are to execute smooth, skilled movements and to regulate muscle tone and posture.

What is the primary role of the thalamus?
The thalamus acts as a relay station for information flowing into or out of the higher brain centres.

What are some of the processes regulated by the hypothalamus?
The hypothalamus controls the pituitary gland and regulates hunger, thirst, sexual behaviour, body temperature, our biological clock, and a variety of emotional behaviours.

What is the role of the limbic system?
The limbic system is a group of structures in the brain, including the amygdala and the hippocampus, that are collectively involved in emotion, memory, and motivation.

THE CEREBRAL HEMISPHERES

What are the cerebral hemispheres, the cerebral cortex, and the corpus callosum?
The cerebral hemispheres are the two halves of the cerebrum, connected by the corpus callosum and covered by the cerebral cortex, which is responsible for higher mental processes such as language, memory, and thinking.

What are some of the main areas within the frontal lobes, and what are their functions?
The frontal lobes contain (1) the motor cortex, which controls voluntary motor activity; (2) Broca's area, which functions in speech production; and (3) the frontal association areas, which are involved in thinking, motivation, planning for the future, impulse control, and emotional responses.

What are the primary functions of the parietal lobes in general and the somatosensory cortex in particular?
The parietal lobes are involved in the reception and processing of touch stimuli. They contain the somatosensory cortex, where touch, pressure, temperature, and pain register.

What are the primary functions of the occipital lobes in general and the primary visual cortex in particular?
The occipital lobes are involved in the reception and interpretation of visual information. They contain the primary visual cortex, where vision registers in the cerebral cortex.

What are the major areas within the temporal lobes, and what are their functions?
The temporal lobes contain (1) the primary auditory cortex, where hearing registers in the cortex; (2) Wernicke's area, which is

involved in comprehending the spoken word and in formulating coherent speech and written language; and (3) association areas, where memories are stored and auditory stimuli are interpreted.

2D SPECIALIZATION OF THE CEREBRAL HEMISPHERES

What are the main functions of the left hemisphere?
The left hemisphere controls the right side of the body, coordinates complex movements, and handles most of the language functions, including speaking, writing, reading, and understanding the spoken word.

What are the primary functions of the right hemisphere?
The right hemisphere controls the left side of the body; it is specialized for visual-spatial perception, singing, reading, and non-verbal behaviour; and it is more active in the recognition and expression of emotion.

What is the significance of the split-brain operation?
Research following split brain surgeries has allowed us to understand the unique roles of the two hemispheres.

2E THE BRAIN ACROSS THE LIFESPAN

Does the brain stop changing at any point in development?
The brain constantly changes. Early in development (from conception to adulthood), there are growth spurts. Changes later in life are less dramatic, but synapses continue to be lost and gained. The brain's ability to reorganize and to compensate is termed *plasticity*.

What must occur in the brain for there to be some recovery from brain damage?
Plasticity allows the brain to reorganize and reallocate existing neuronal resources to areas that are damaged. In addition, regeneration of neurons or dendrites may assist recovery.

2F DISCOVERING THE BRAIN'S MYSTERIES

What are some methods that researchers have used to learn about brain function?
Researchers have learned about brain function from studies using the EEG, microelectrodes, the CT scan, fMRI, MRI, and the PET scan.

What is the electroencephalogram (EEG), and what are the four brainwave patterns it reveals?
The EEG measures electrical activity in the brain. The four brain waves it measures are alpha, beta, delta, and theta waves.

What information do CT and MRI scans give us?
These scans can be used to detect abnormalities and injuries to the CNS and other parts of the body.

What information can we learn from PET scans and functional MRI techniques and other similar imaging tools?
These scans can be used to map normal activity in the brain as well as to identify problem areas or malfunctions.

2G THE PERIPHERAL NERVOUS SYSTEM

What is the peripheral nervous system?
The peripheral nervous system (PNS) connects the central nervous system (CNS) to the rest of the body. It has two subdivisions: (1) the somatic nervous system (SNS), which consists of the nerves that make it possible for us to sense and move, and (2) the autonomic nervous system (ANS).

What are the roles of the sympathetic and parasympathetic nervous systems?
The autonomic nervous system has two parts: (1) the sympathetic nervous system, which mobilizes the body's resources during emergencies or during stress, and (2) the parasympathetic nervous system, which is associated with relaxation and brings the heightened bodily responses back to normal after an emergency.

2H THE ENDOCRINE SYSTEM

What is the endocrine system, and what are some of the glands within it?
The endocrine system is a system of glands in various parts of the body that manufacture hormones and secrete them into the bloodstream. The hormones affect cells in other parts of the body. The pituitary gland releases hormones that control other glands in the endocrine system and also releases a growth hormone. The thyroid gland produces thyroxine, which regulates metabolism. The adrenal glands release epinephrine and norepinephrine, which prepare the body for emergencies and stressful situations, and also release small amounts of the sex hormones. The pancreas produces insulin and regulates blood sugar. The gonads are the sex glands, which produce the sex hormones and make reproduction possible.

BIOLOGY AND BEHAVIOUR

MODULE 2A THE NEURONS AND THE NEUROTRANSMITTERS

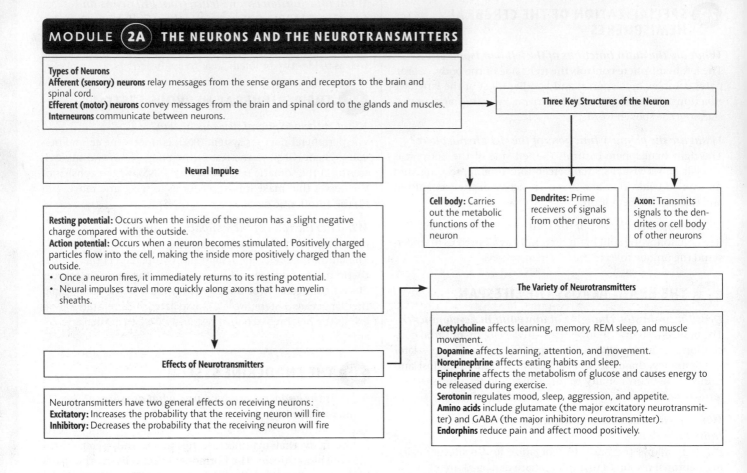

Types of Neurons
Afferent (sensory) neurons relay messages from the sense organs and receptors to the brain and spinal cord.
Efferent (motor) neurons convey messages from the brain and spinal cord to the glands and muscles.
Interneurons communicate between neurons.

Three Key Structures of the Neuron

Cell body: Carries out the metabolic functions of the neuron

Dendrites: Prime receivers of signals from other neurons

Axon: Transmits signals to the dendrites or cell body of other neurons

Neural Impulse

Resting potential: Occurs when the inside of the neuron has a slight negative charge compared with the outside.
Action potential: Occurs when a neuron becomes stimulated. Positively charged particles flow into the cell, making the inside more positively charged than the outside.
• Once a neuron fires, it immediately returns to its resting potential.
• Neural impulses travel more quickly along axons that have myelin sheaths.

Effects of Neurotransmitters

Neurotransmitters have two general effects on receiving neurons:
Excitatory: Increases the probability that the receiving neuron will fire
Inhibitory: Decreases the probability that the receiving neuron will fire

The Variety of Neurotransmitters

Acetylcholine affects learning, memory, REM sleep, and muscle movement.
Dopamine affects learning, attention, and movement.
Norepinephrine affects eating habits and sleep.
Epinephrine affects the metabolism of glucose and causes energy to be released during exercise.
Serotonin regulates mood, sleep, aggression, and appetite.
Amino acids include glutamate (the major excitatory neurotransmitter) and GABA (the major inhibitory neurotransmitter).
Endorphins reduce pain and affect mood positively.

MODULE 2B THE CENTRAL NERVOUS SYSTEM

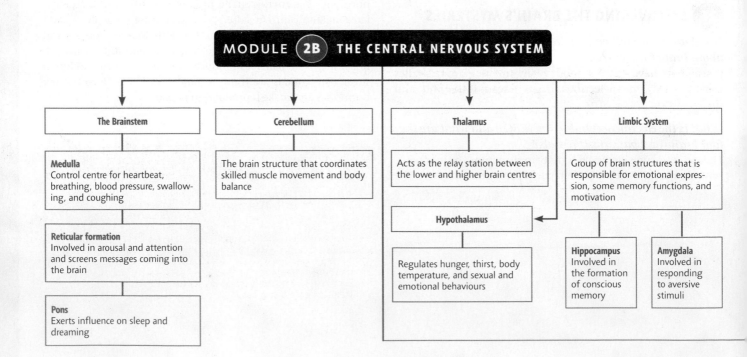

The Brainstem

Medulla
Control centre for heartbeat, breathing, blood pressure, swallowing, and coughing

Reticular formation
Involved in arousal and attention and screens messages coming into the brain

Pons
Exerts influence on sleep and dreaming

Cerebellum
The brain structure that coordinates skilled muscle movement and body balance

Thalamus
Acts as the relay station between the lower and higher brain centres

Hypothalamus
Regulates hunger, thirst, body temperature, and sexual and emotional behaviours

Limbic System
Group of brain structures that is responsible for emotional expression, some memory functions, and motivation

Hippocampus
Involved in the formation of conscious memory

Amygdala
Involved in responding to aversive stimuli

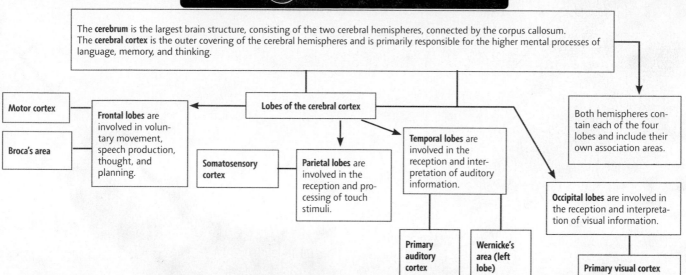

MODULE 2C THE CEREBRAL HEMISPHERES

The **cerebrum** is the largest brain structure, consisting of the two cerebral hemispheres, connected by the corpus callosum.
The **cerebral cortex** is the outer covering of the cerebral hemispheres and is primarily responsible for the higher mental processes of language, memory, and thinking.

Lobes of the cerebral cortex

Motor cortex

Broca's area

Frontal lobes are involved in voluntary movement, speech production, thought, and planning.

Somatosensory cortex

Parietal lobes are involved in the reception and processing of touch stimuli.

Temporal lobes are involved in the reception and interpretation of auditory information.

Both hemispheres contain each of the four lobes and include their own association areas.

Occipital lobes are involved in the reception and interpretation of visual information.

Primary auditory cortex

Wernicke's area (left lobe)

Primary visual cortex

MODULE 2D SPECIALIZATION OF THE CEREBRAL HEMISPHERES

Left hemisphere: Handles most language functions (e.g., speaking, reading, and writing), mathematical ability, logical and sequential processing of information, and coordinating complex movements.
Right hemisphere: Visual-spatial relations; recognizing patterns; holistic processing of information; creativity; recognition and expression of emotions.

MODULE 2E THE BRAIN ACROSS THE LIFESPAN

The brain develops through growth spurts, and gains and losses of synapses; plasticity allows for reorganization and recovery.

MODULE 2F DISCOVERING THE BRAIN'S MYSTERIES

- **Electroencephalogram (EEG)** reveals electrical activity of the brain by recording four types of brain waves.
- **Computerized axial tomography (CT) scan** produces cross-sectional X-ray images that reveal the structures within the brain.
- **Magnetic resonance imaging (MRI)** produces high-resolution images of the structures of the brain without use of X-rays.
- **Positron emission tomography (PET) scan** produces images of brain activity by injecting radioactive glucose and measuring the amount of oxygen and glucose consumed.

MODULE 2G THE PERIPHERAL NERVOUS SYSTEM

Peripheral nervous system contains two major divisions—the somatic and autonomic nervous systems, which connect the central nervous system (CNS) to the rest of the body.

Somatic nervous system relays information from sense receptors to the CNS and from the CNS to all the skeletal muscles of the body (primarily under conscious control).

Autonomic nervous system regulates the body's internal functions (involuntary control) and has two parts.

- **Sympathetic nervous system** increases arousal; mobilizes body for action.
- **Parasympathetic nervous system** decreases arousal; conserves body's energy.

MODULE 2H THE ENDOCRINE SYSTEM

Glands manufacture and secrete hormones. Hormones travel through the circulatory system via the bloodstream, and affect bodily functions.
- **Pituitary gland** is the master gland. It releases hormones that activate other glands within the endocrine system.
- **Thyroid gland** produces a hormone that regulates metabolism.
- **Pancreas** releases hormones that regulate the body's blood sugar levels.
- **Adrenal glands** produce hormones that activate the sympathetic nervous system.
- **Sex glands** enable reproduction and stimulate the development of secondary sex characteristics.

3

When Helen Keller (1880–1968) was only 19 months old, she was struck with a serious illness that left her totally blind and deaf. Her sensory world was limited to only three avenues— taste, smell, and touch. The overwhelming reality of her world was permanent darkness and silence. Only the most rudimentary communication with her parents was possible (she could spit out food she disliked). As Helen grew from infancy into early childhood, her frustration gave way to explosive tantrums. The Keller family needed help!

When Helen was six years old, her father learned of an institution that had achieved success in teaching people with physical disabilities. So he and the family took Helen there, and they met Anne Sullivan, a talented young teacher who agreed to tutor Helen. Anne used a manual alphabet to slowly spell out the names of objects with her fingers in the palm of Helen's hand to teach Helen that everything has a name—a fundamental requirement for communication.

Progress was slow at first. But then one day, as Anne poured water over one of Helen's hands and spelled out w-a-t-e-r in her other hand, a look of surprise and delight lit up Helen's face. That look told Anne that she had gotten through at last. Helen quickly learned to use her fingers to write the names for virtually everything and everyone around—Mama, Papa, Anne, and, of course, Helen.

And Helen didn't stop there. She learned to read and write in Braille. She also learned how to understand much of what others were saying by using her thumb to sense the vibrations coming from a speaker's vocal cords and her forefinger to interpret lip movements. With her other three fingers, she could "see" facial expressions. And, of course, Helen could recognize and identify anyone she knew by the feel of the person's face. Remarkably, Helen learned to speak, an amazing achievement for one who had not been able to hear during the critical years of language development. At 20, Helen enrolled in college and graduated with honours, thanks to the daily help of her tutor and companion, Anne Sullivan.

SENSATION AND PERCEPTION

What is the difference between sensation and perception?

As the story of Helen Keller illustrates, sensation and perception are intimately related to everyday experience, but they are not the same. **[LO 3.1] Sensation** is the process by which the senses detect visual, auditory, and other sensory stimuli and transmit them to the brain. **Perception** is the process by which sensory information is actively organized and interpreted by the brain. Sensation furnishes the raw material of sensory experience; perception provides the finished product. Young Helen could sense her teacher's fingers tracing letters in her hand, but she could not perceive their symbolic character until her sudden revelation about the spelling of *water*.

In this chapter we will explore the five primary senses—vision, hearing, smell, taste, and touch—and some of the secondary ones, such as balance and pain. You will learn how the senses detect sensory information and how this information is actively organized and interpreted by the brain. We begin with a closer look at sensation.

MODULE **3A** **SENSATION: THE SENSORY WORLD**

LO 3.1 Identify and understand the difference between sensation and perception.

LO 3.2 Define and explain each of the following measures of the senses: absolute threshold, difference threshold, and signal detection theory.

LO 3.3 Understand how sensory stimuli come to be experienced as sensations.

Our senses serve as ports of entry for all information about our world. Yet it is amazing how little of this sensory world we actually sense. For example, we see only a thin slice of the vast spectrum of electromagnetic energy. With the unaided eye we cannot see microwaves, X-rays, or ultraviolet light. We are unable to hear the ultrasonic sound of a dog whistle, and our ears can detect a scant 20 percent of the sounds that a dolphin or bat can hear; nor can we see the outline of a warm-blooded animal from its infrared heat pattern at night, though rattlesnakes and other pit vipers can. Yet all of these sensory stimuli exist in the real, physical world.

Whichever of our senses we select for comparison, humans are not at the top of the list for quality or sensitivity. Nevertheless, humans have remarkable sensory and perceptual abilities.

THE ABSOLUTE AND DIFFERENCE THRESHOLDS: TO SENSE OR NOT TO SENSE

What is the difference between the absolute threshold and the difference threshold?

What is the softest sound you can hear, the dimmest light you can see, the most diluted substance you can taste? Researchers in sensory psychology have performed many experiments over the years to answer these questions. Their research has established measures for the senses known as *absolute thresholds*. Just as the threshold of a doorway is the dividing point between being outside a room and being inside it, the **absolute threshold** of a sense marks the difference between not being able to perceive a stimulus (e.g., see a light) and being just barely able to perceive it. **[LO 3.2]** Psychologists have arbitrarily defined this absolute threshold as the minimum amount of sensory stimulation that can be detected 50 percent of the time. For example, the absolute thresholds established for the five primary senses in humans are equivalent to the following: (1) for vision, a candle flame 48 kilometres away on a clear night; (2) for hearing, a watch ticking 6 metres away; (3) for taste, 1 teaspoon of sugar dissolved in 9 litres of water; (4) for smell, a single drop of perfume in a three-room house; and (5) for touch, a bee's wing falling a distance of 1 centimetre onto your cheek.

If you are listening to music, the very fact that you can hear it means that the absolute threshold has been crossed. But how much must the volume be turned up or down for you to notice a difference? Or, if you are carrying a load of books, how much weight must be added or subtracted for you to be able to sense that your load is heavier or lighter? The **difference threshold** is a measure of the smallest increase or decrease in a physical stimulus that is required to produce the **just noticeable difference (JND)**. **[LO 3.2]** The just noticeable difference is the smallest change in sensation that we are able to detect 50 percent of the time. If you were holding a 2-kilogram weight and 500 grams were added, you could easily tell the difference. But if you were holding 50 kilograms and one additional 500-gram weight were added, you could not sense the difference. Why not? After all, the weight added was the same.

More than 150 years ago, Ernst Weber (1795–1878) observed that the just noticeable difference for all our senses depends on a proportion or percentage of change rather than on a fixed amount of change. This observation became known as **Weber's law**. A weight we are holding must increase or decrease by 2 percent for us to notice the difference. The difference threshold is not the same for all the senses. We need a very large (20 percent) difference to detect some changes in taste. In contrast, if you were listening to music, you would notice a difference if a tone changed in pitch by only 0.33 percent. According to Weber's law, the greater the original stimulus, the more it must be increased or decreased for the difference to be noticeable.

Aren't some people more sensitive to sensory changes than others? As you might suspect, Weber's law best applies to people with average sensitivities and to sensory stimuli that are neither very strong (loud thunder) nor very weak (a faint whisper). For instance, expert wine tasters would know if a particular vintage was a little too sweet, even if its sweetness varied by only a fraction of the 20 percent necessary for changes in taste.

Furthermore, people who have lost one sensory ability often gain greater sensitivity in others. One study found that children with early onset blindness were more capable of correctly labelling 25 common odours than were children with sight, whereas another found that students who were congenitally deaf possessed motion-perception abilities superior to those of students who could hear (Bavelier et al., 2000).

Moreover, students who are deaf appear to be more easily distracted by visual stimuli than are their counterparts who can hear (Dye, Hauser, & Bavelier, 2008).

SIGNAL DETECTION THEORY

You may have realized that the classic methods for measuring sensory thresholds have a serious limitation. They focus exclusively on the physical stimulus—how strong or weak it is or how much the stimulus must change for the difference to be noticed. But there is significant variation among individuals in sensory sensitivities; and within the same individual, sensory capabilities vary both across time and according to the conditions. Factors that affect a person's ability to detect a sensory signal are (besides the strength of the stimulus) the motivation to detect it, previous experience, the expectation that it will occur, and the level of alertness (or fatigue).

Another approach takes into account these factors. **Signal detection theory** suggests that detecting a sensory stimulus involves both noticing a stimulus against background "noise" and deciding whether the stimulus is actually present. **[LO 3.2]** Deciding whether a stimulus is present depends partly on the probability that the stimulus will occur and partly on the potential gain or loss associated with deciding that it is present or absent.

Suppose you were given the description of a cousin you had never seen before and were asked to pick her up at the gate when her plane arrived at the airport. Your task would be to scan a sea of faces for someone fitting the description and then to decide which of the several people who fit the description is actually your cousin. All the other faces and objects in your field of vision would be considered background noise. How certain you felt before you would be willing to approach someone would depend on several factors—for example, the embarrassment you might feel approaching the wrong person as opposed to the distress you would feel if you failed to find your cousin.

Signal detection theory has special relevance to people in many occupations—air traffic controllers, police officers, military personnel on guard duty, medical professionals, and poultry inspectors, to name a few. Whether these professionals detect certain stimuli can have important consequences for the health and welfare of us all (Swets, 1992, 1998).

TRANSDUCTION AND ADAPTATION: TRANSFORMING SENSORY STIMULI INTO NEURAL IMPULSES

How are sensory stimuli in the environment experienced as sensations?

You may be surprised to learn that our eyes do not actually see; nor do our ears hear. Our sense organs provide only the beginning point of sensation, which must be completed by the brain. As you learned in Chapter 2, specific clusters of neurons in specialized parts of the brain must be stimulated for us to see, hear, taste, and so on. The brain itself cannot respond directly to light, sound waves, odours, and tastes. How, then, does it get the message? The answer involves the sensory receptors.

The body's sense organs are equipped with specialized cells called **sensory receptors**, which detect and respond to one type of stimuli—light, sound waves, odours, and so on. Through a process known as **transduction**, the receptors change the sensory stimulation into neural impulses. **[LO 3.3]** The neural impulses are then transmitted to their own special locations in the brain, such as the primary visual cortex for vision and the primary auditory cortex for hearing. We experience a sensation only when the appropriate part of the brain is stimulated. Our sense receptors provide the essential links between the physical sensory world and the brain.

After a time, the sensory receptors grow accustomed to constant, unchanging levels of stimuli—sights, sounds, smells—so that we notice them less and less, or not at all. For example, smokers become accustomed to the smell of cigarette smoke in their homes and on their clothing. This process is known as **sensory adaptation** (see *Try It* on the next page). Even though it reduces our sensory awareness, sensory adaptation allows us to shift our attention to what is most important at any given moment. However, sensory adaptation is not likely to occur in the presence of very strong stimuli—the smell of ammonia, an ear-splitting sound, or the taste of rancid food!

sensation: The process through which the senses pick up visual, auditory, and other sensory stimuli and transmit them to the brain.

perception: The process by which sensory information is actively organized and interpreted by the brain.

absolute threshold: The minimum amount of sensory stimulation that can be detected 50 percent of the time.

difference threshold: The smallest increase or decrease in a physical stimulus required to produce a difference in sensation that is noticeable 50 percent of the time (the just noticeable difference).

just noticeable difference (JND): The smallest change in sensation that we are able to detect 50 percent of the time.

Weber's law: The law stating that the just noticeable difference for all our senses depends on a proportion or percentage of change in a stimulus rather than on a fixed amount of change.

signal detection theory: The view that detection of a sensory stimulus involves both discriminating a stimulus from background "noise" and deciding whether the stimulus is actually present.

sensory receptors: Specialized cells in each sense organ that detect and respond to sensory stimuli—light, sound, odours, etc.—and transduce (convert) the stimuli into neural impulses.

transduction: The process by which sensory receptors convert sensory stimulation—light, sound, odours, etc.—into neural impulses.

sensory adaptation: The process of becoming less sensitive to an unchanging sensory stimulus over time.

TRY IT

Sensory Adaptation

Take three large cereal bowls or small mixing bowls. Fill one with very cold water, another with hot water (*not* boiling or scalding), and the third with lukewarm water. Hold your left hand in the cold water and your right hand in the hot water for at least 1 minute. Then quickly plunge both hands into the lukewarm water at the same time.

Why do you experience the illusion that the lukewarm water feels simultaneously warmer and colder than its actual temperature? The answer is adaptation. You perceive the lukewarm water as warm on your cold-adapted left hand and as cold on your warm-adapted right hand. This illustrates that our perceptions of sensory stimuli are relative and are affected by differences between stimuli we are already adapted to and new stimuli.

REMEMBER IT

Sensation

1. The process through which the senses detect sensory information and transmit it to the brain is called (sensation/perception).
2. The point at which you can barely sense a stimulus 50 percent of the time is called the (absolute/difference) threshold.
3. Which of the following is not true of sensory receptors?
   a. They are specialized to detect certain sensory stimuli.
   b. They transduce sensory stimuli into neural impulses.
   c. They are located in the brain.
   d. They provide the link between the physical sensory world and the brain.
4. Each morning when Jackie goes to work at the dry cleaner, she smells the strong odour of cleaning fluid. After she is there for a few minutes, she is no longer aware of it. What accounts for this?
   a. signal detection theory
   b. sensory adaptation
   c. transduction
   d. the just noticeable difference

Answers: 1. sensation 2. absolute 3. c 4. b

People who swim in icy water experience a degree of sensory adaptation, which helps their bodies adjust to the frigid temperature. What other examples of sensory adaptation can you think of?

©Seppo Hinkula/Alamy

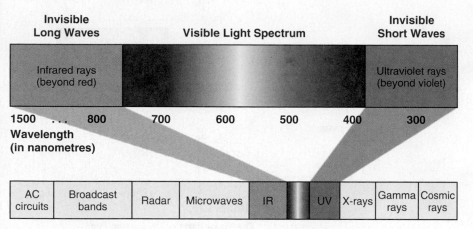

Infrared rays
(beyond red)

Ultraviolet rays
(beyond violet)

| 1500 | ... | 800 | 700 | 600 | 500 | 400 | 300 |

Wavelength
(in nanometres)

| AC circuits | Broadcast bands | Radar | Microwaves | IR | | UV | X-rays | Gamma rays | Cosmic rays |

FIGURE 3.1

The Electromagnetic Spectrum

The electromagnetic spectrum is composed of waves ranging in wavelength from many kilometres long (radio and other broadcast bands) to only 0.25 trillionths of a centimetre (cosmic rays). Our eyes can perceive only a very thin band of electromagnetic waves, known as the visible spectrum.

MODULE **3B** VISION

LO 3.4 Identify and describe the major structures of the eye.
LO 3.5 Compare the function of rods and cones.
LO 3.6 Define and compare the two theories of colour vision.
LO 3.7 Explain the relative contributions of the two theories of colour vision.
LO 3.8 Define *colour blindness*.

For most of us, vision is our most valued sensory experience, and it is the sense that has been the most investigated. But before looking at how we see, consider *what* we see. We cannot see any object unless light is reflected from it or given off by it.

LIGHT: WHAT WE SEE

Light, one form of electromagnetic rays, is made up of tiny light particles called *photons*, which travel in waves. The vast majority of these waves are either too long or too short for humans and other animals to see. Our eyes can respond only to a very narrow band of electromagnetic waves, a band called the **visible spectrum** (see Figure 3.1).

The length of a light wave determines the colour we perceive. The shortest light waves we can see appear violet, and the longest ones we can see appear red. *What* we see is confined to the visible spectrum, but *how* we see depends on the many parts of the eye and brain that bring us the world of sight.

THE EYE: WINDOW TO THE VISUAL SENSORY WORLD

Our eyes are our most important sensory connections to the world. Look at the parts of the eye (Figure 3.2), and read in the text the role each part plays in vision.

The Cornea, the Iris, and the Pupil: Up Front in the Eye

How do the cornea, the iris, and the pupil function in vision?

The globe-shaped human eyeball measures about 2.2 centimetres in diameter. **[LO 3.4]** Bulging from its front surface is the **cornea**—the tough, transparent, protective layer covering the front of the eye. The cornea performs the first step in vision by bending the light rays inward. It herds the light rays through the pupil—the small, dark opening in the centre of the iris.

The iris is the circular, coloured part of the eye. Two muscles in the iris dilate and contract the pupil, thus regulating the amount of light entering the eye. Although the pupil never closes completely, in very bright light it can contract to the size of the head of a pin; in very dim light it can dilate to the size of a pencil eraser. We have no control over the dilation and contraction of our pupils; the motion is a reflex.

From Lens to Retina: Focusing Images

What are the lens and the retina?

Suspended just behind the iris and the pupil, the **lens** is composed of many thin layers and looks like a transparent disc. **[LO 3.4]** The lens performs the task of focusing on viewed objects. It flattens as it focuses on objects viewed at a distance; it bulges in the centre as it focuses on close objects. This flattening and bulging action is referred to as **accommodation**. As we grow older, the lens loses some elasticity—that is, it loses the ability to change its shape to accommodate for near vision, a condition called *presbyopia* ("old eyes"). This is why many people over 40 must hold a book or newspaper at arm's length or use reading glasses to magnify the print.

---

visible spectrum: The narrow band of electromagnetic rays that are visible to the human eye.

cornea (KOR-nee-uh): The transparent covering of the coloured part of the eye that bends light rays inward through the pupil.

lens: The transparent structure behind the iris that changes in shape as it focuses images on the retina.

accommodation: The changing in shape of the lens as it focuses objects on the retina; it becomes flatter for far objects and more spherical for near objects.

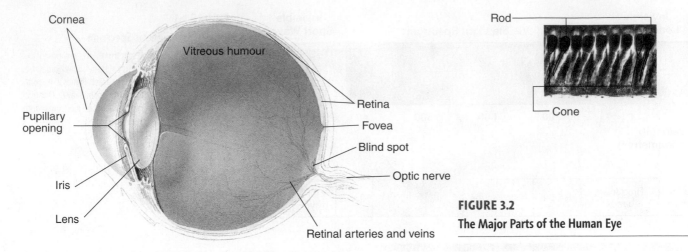

FIGURE 3.2
The Major Parts of the Human Eye

The lens focuses the image we see onto the **retina**—a membrane about the size of a small postage stamp and as thin as onion skin. The retina contains the sensory receptors for vision. The image projected onto the retina is upside down and reversed left to right. You can demonstrate this for yourself in *Try It*.

In some people, the distance through the eyeball (from the lens to the retina) is either too short or too long for proper focusing (Figure 3.3). Nearsightedness (myopia) occurs when the lens focuses images of distant objects in front of, rather than on, the retina. A person with this condition will be able to see near objects clearly, but distant images will be blurred. Farsightedness (hyperopia) occurs when the focal image is longer than the eye can handle, as if the image should focus behind the retina. The individual is able to see far objects clearly, but close objects are blurred. Both conditions are correctable with eyeglasses or contact lenses, or by surgical procedures.

The Rods and Cones: Receptors for Light and Colour

What roles do the rods and cones play in vision?

At the back of the retina is a layer of light-sensitive receptor cells—the **rods** and the **cones**. Named for their shapes, the rods look like slender cylinders, and the cones are shorter and more rounded. There are about 91 million rods and 4.5 million cones in each retina (Purves, Augustine, Fitzpatrick, et al., 2001). The cones are the receptor cells that enable us to see colour and fine detail in adequate light, but they do not function in very dim light. **[LO 3.5]** By contrast, the rods respond to black and white; while they encode all other visible wavelengths, they do so in shades of grey instead of in colour. **[LO 3.5]** The rods are extremely sensitive, allowing the eye to see in very dim light and therefore providing for night vision. Changes in a chemical called *rhodospin*, found in the rods, enable us to adapt to the darkness of a movie theatre or to the brightness of a beach on a sunny day.

At the centre of the retina is the **fovea**, a small area about the size of the period at the end of this sentence (see Figure 3.2). When you look directly at an object, the image of the object is focused on the centre of your fovea. The clearest point of your vision, the fovea is the part of the retina that you use for fine detail work. The fovea contains no rods but has some 30 000 cones tightly packed together (Beatty, 1995). Cones are most densely packed at the centre of the fovea, and their density decreases sharply just a few degrees beyond the fovea's centre and levels off more gradually to the periphery of the retina (Abramov & Gordon, 1994; Farah, 2000).

TRY IT

How the Retina Works

Take an ordinary teaspoon—one in which you can see your reflection. Looking at the bottom (the convex surface) of the spoon, you will see a large image of your face, an image that is right side up—the way the image enters the eye. Turn the spoon over and look in the inside (the concave surface) and you will see your face upside down and reversed left to right—the way the image appears on the retina. The brain, however, perceives images right side up.

In normal vision, an image is focused on the retina.

In nearsightedness (myopia), the image is focused in front of the retina.

In farsightedness (hyperopia), the image is focused behind the retina.

FIGURE 3.3
Normal Vision, Nearsightedness, and Farsightedness

From the Retina to the Brain: From Visual Sensation to Visual Perception

What path does the neural impulse take from the retina to the visual cortex?

Before light rays reach the sensory receptors on the rods and cones, they pass through four layers of tissue, each of which contains specialized neurons—*ganglion cells, amacrine cells, bipolar cells,* and *horizontal cells*—none of which are capable of responding directly to the light rays (see the inset in Figure 3.4 on the next page). When the light rays reach the sensory receptors (the rods and cones), the receptors transduce them, that is, change them into neural impulses. The impulses are then transmitted to the bipolar, amacrine, and horizontal cells, which carry them to the ganglion cells. The approximately one million axon-like extensions of the ganglion cells are bundled together in a pencil-sized cable that extends through the wall of the retina and leaves the eye on its way to the brain. Where the cable runs through the retinal wall, there can be no rods or cones, and so we are blind in that spot in each eye. Find your own blind spot by performing the following *Try It.*

After the cable leaves the retinal wall, it becomes known as the **optic nerve.** The optic nerves from both eyes come together at the optic chiasm, a point where some of the nerve fibres cross to the opposite side of the brain. The visual information from the left visual field is received by the right hemisphere and the visual information from the right hemisphere is received by the left hemisphere. This crossing over is important because it

Find Your Blind Spot

To locate your blind spot, hold this book at arm's length. Close your right eye and look directly at the magician's eyes. Now slowly bring the book closer, keeping your eye fixed on the magician. When the rabbit disappears, you have found the blind spot in your left eye.

You might wonder why the blind spot in each eye is not perceived as a black hole in each visual field. The reason is that we usually have both eyes open, and each eye provides a slightly different view. The right eye can see the tiny area that is blind to the left eye, and vice versa.

allows visual information from a single eye to be represented on the visual cortex of both hemispheres of the brain. It also plays an important part in depth perception.

From the optic chiasm, the optic nerve travels to the thalamus. There the optic nerve synapses with neural fibres that transmit the impulses to the primary visual cortex. About one quarter of the primary visual cortex is dedicated exclusively to analyzing input from the fovea, which, as we have seen, is a very small but extremely important part of the retina.

The Primary Visual Cortex: Getting the Big Picture

By inserting tiny electrodes into single cells in the visual cortexes of cats, Hubel and Wiesel (1959) were able to determine what was happening in individual cells when cats were

retina: The tissue at the back of the eye that contains the rods and the cones and onto which the image is projected.

rods: The light-sensitive receptors in the retina that provide vision in dim light in black, white, and shades of grey.

cones: The receptor cells in the retina that enable us to see colour and fine detail in adequate light but that do not function in dim light.

fovea (FO-vee-uh): A small area of the retina that provides the clearest and sharpest vision because it has the largest concentration of cones.

optic nerve: The nerve that carries visual information from the retina to the brain.

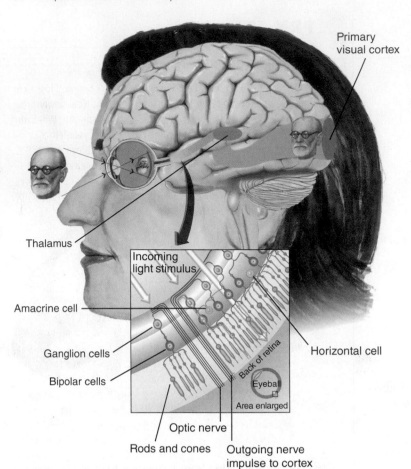

Primary visual cortex

Thalamus

Amacrine cell

Ganglion cells

Bipolar cells

Incoming light stimulus

Horizontal cell

Back of retina

Eyeball

Area enlarged

Optic nerve

Rods and cones

Outgoing nerve impulse to cortex

FIGURE 3.4

From Retinal Image to Meaningful Information

Because of the way the lens alters slight rays in order to produce a clear image, images are upside down on the retina. The brain's visual processing system takes the upside-down retinal image and flips it so it is properly oriented.

exposed to different kinds of visual stimuli. They discovered that each neuron responded only to specific patterns. Some neurons responded only to lines and angles, while others fired only when cats saw lines of specific lengths. Neurons of this type are known as **feature detectors**, and they are already coded at birth to make their unique responses. Yet we see whole images, not collections of isolated features, because visual perceptions are complete only when the visual cortex transmits the millions of pieces of visual information it receives to other areas of the brain, where they are combined and assembled into whole visual images (Perry & Zeki, 2000; Self & Zeki, 2005).

COLOUR VISION: A MULTICOLOURED WORLD

What are the three dimensions that combine to provide the colours we experience?

Some light waves striking an object are absorbed by it, and others are reflected from it. We see only the wavelengths that are reflected, not those that are absorbed. Our everyday visual experience goes far beyond the colours in the rainbow. We detect thousands of subtle colour shadings. What enables us to make these fine colour distinctions? Researchers have identified three dimensions that combine to provide the rich world of colour we experience: (1) **Hue**, which is the chief dimension, refers to the actual colour we view—red, green, and so forth. (2) **Saturation** refers to

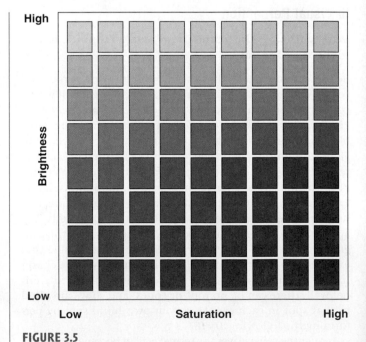

High

Brightness

Low

Low   Saturation   High

FIGURE 3.5

Hue, Saturation, and Brightness

Three dimensions combine to produce the rich world of colour we experience. They are (1) hue, the actual colour we see (blue, green, and so on); (2) saturation, the purity of a colour; and (3) brightness, the intensity of the light energy reflected from a surface. The colours shown here are of the same hue but differ in saturation and brightness.

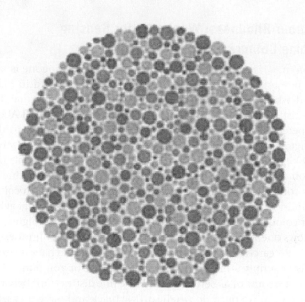

FIGURE 3.6

The Ishihara Colour Blindness Test

The Ishihara colour blindness test uses an array of dots, with some dots of specified colours making a pattern—like the dots here, which make the number 5. In this example a person with red-green colour blindness will see a 2 rather than the 5.

the purity of a colour. A colour becomes less saturated, or less pure, as other wavelengths of light are mixed with it. (3) **Brightness** refers to the intensity of the light energy we perceive, and corresponds to the amplitude (magnitude) of the light wave. Figure 3.5 illustrates the dimensions of hue, saturation, and brightness.

Theories of Colour Vision: How We Sense Colour

What two major theories attempt to explain colour vision?

Two major theories have been offered to explain colour vision. **[LO 3.6]** Both were formulated before the development of laboratory technology capable of testing them. The **trichromatic theory**, first proposed by the English scholar Thomas Young in 1802, was modified by Hermann von Helmholtz about 50 years later. This theory states that there are three kinds of cones in the retina and that each kind makes its maximum chemical response to one of three colours—blue, green, or red, as shown in Figure 3.6. Research in the 1950s and 1960s by Nobel Prize winner George Wald (1964; Wald, Brown, & Smith, 1954) supports the trichromatic theory. Wald discovered that even though all cones have basically the same structure, the retina does indeed contain three kinds of cones. Subsequent research demonstrated that each cone is particularly sensitive to one of the three colours—blue, green, or red (Roorda & Williams, 1999).

The other major attempt to explain colour vision is the **opponent-process theory**, first proposed by physiologist Ewald Hering in 1878 and revised in 1957 by Leo Hurvich and Dorothea Jameson. **[LO 3.6]** According to this theory, three classes of cells respond by increasing or decreasing their rate of firing when different colours are present. The red/green cells increase their firing rate when red is present and decrease it when green is present. The yellow/blue cells increase to yellow and decrease to blue. Another type of cell increases to white light and decreases to the absence of light. Think of the opponent-process theory as opposing pairs of cells on a seesaw. As one of this pair goes up, the other goes down. The relative firing rates of the three pairs of cells transmit colour information to the brain.

If you look long enough at one colour in the opponent-process pair (red/green, yellow/blue, black/white) and then look at a white surface, your brain will give you the sensation of the opposite colour—a negative **afterimage**. After you have stared at one colour in an opponent-process pair, the cell responding to that colour tires and the opponent cell begins to fire, producing the afterimage. Demonstrate this for yourself in *Try It*, on the next page.

But which theory of colour vision is correct? It turns out that both have merit because each explains a different phase of colour processing. **[LO 3.7]** The trichromatic theory is consistent with what happens with the cones, and the opponent-process theory is consistent with what happens in the ganglion cells. Researchers believe that colour processing starts at the level of the retina, continues through the bipolar and ganglion cells, and is completed in the colour detectors in the visual cortex (Masland, 1996; Sokolov, 2000).

feature detectors: Neurons in the brain that respond only to specific visual patterns (e.g., lines or angles).

hue: The property of light commonly referred to as "colour" (red, blue, green, and so on), determined primarily by the wavelength of light reflected from a surface.

saturation: The degree to which light waves producing a colour are of the same wavelength; the purity of a colour.

brightness: The dimension of visual sensation that is dependent on the intensity of light reflected from a surface and that corresponds to the amplitude of the light wave.

trichromatic theory: The theory of colour vision suggesting that there are three types of cones, which are maximally sensitive to red, green, or blue, and that varying levels of activity in these receptors can produce all of the colours.

opponent-process theory: The theory that certain cells in the visual system increase their firing rate to signal one colour and decrease their firing rate to signal the opposing colour (red/green, yellow/blue, white/black).

afterimage: The visual sensation that remains after a stimulus is withdrawn.

TRY IT

Testing the Opponent-Process Theory

Stare at the dot in the green and black flag for about one minute. Then shift your gaze to the dot in the white space. You will see the Canadian flag in its true colours—the opponent-process colours of red and white.

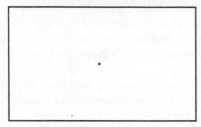

On the top, a hot air balloon is shown as it would appear to a person with normal colour vision; on the bottom, the same balloon is shown as it would appear to a person with red-green colour blindness.

©Robert Harbison

Colour Blindness: Weakness for Sensing Some Colours

You may have wondered what it means when someone is said to be "colour blind." Does that person see the world in black and white? Generally no—**colour blindness** is the inability to distinguish certain colours from one another. **[LO 3.8]** About 8 percent of males experience some kind of difficulty in distinguishing colours, most commonly red from green (Mather, 2006). (The second picture in *Try It* shows how a hot air balloon would look to someone with red-green colour blindness.) By contrast, fewer than 1 percent of females suffer from colour blindness (this sex difference is explained by the fact that genes for colour vision are carried on the X chromosome). Figure 3.6 shows one way that people can be tested for colour blindness.

Research has shown that colour blindness can have degrees; it isn't simply a matter of either you have it or you don't. And why are some of us better able to make fine distinctions between colours, as we must do when sorting black and navy socks, for example? These differences appear to be related to the number of colour-vision genes individuals have. Researchers have found that, in people with normal colour vision, the X chromosomes may contain as few as two or as many as nine genes for colour perception (Neitz & Neitz, 1995). Those who have more genes appear to be better able to make very fine distinctions between colours.

REMEMBER IT

Vision

1. Match the parts of the eye with their descriptions.
   - _____ 1) the coloured part of the eye
   - _____ 2) the opening in the iris that dilates and constricts
   - _____ 3) the transparent covering of the iris
   - _____ 4) the transparent structure that focuses an inverted image on the retina
   - _____ 5) the thin, photosensitive membrane at the back of the eye on which the lens focuses an inverted image
     - a. retina
     - b. cornea
     - c. pupil
     - d. iris
     - e. lens

2. The receptor cells in the retina that enable us to see in dim light are the (cones/rods); the cells that enable us to see colour and sharp images are the (cones/rods).

3. Most people who are colour blind see no colour at all. (true/false)

4. The optic nerve carries neural impulses from the retina to the _____, from which the impulses are passed on to the _____.

Answers: 1 (1). d (2). c (3). b (4). e (5). a 2. rods; cones 3. false 4. thalamus, primary visual cortex.

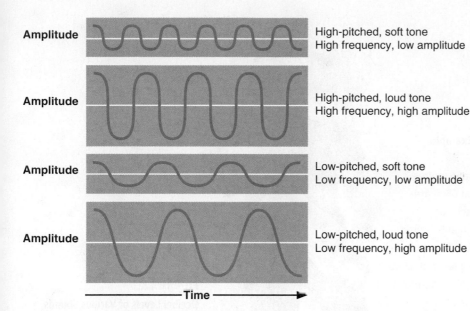

Amplitude — High-pitched, soft tone
High frequency, low amplitude

Amplitude — High-pitched, loud tone
High frequency, high amplitude

Amplitude — Low-pitched, soft tone
Low frequency, low amplitude

Amplitude — Low-pitched, loud tone
Low frequency, high amplitude

Time ⟶

FIGURE 3.7

The Frequency and Amplitude of a Sound Wave

The frequency of a sound wave—the number of cycles completed per second—determines the pitch (high or low) of the sound. Loudness (soft or loud tone) is determined by amplitude—the energy or height of the sound wave.

MODULE 3C HEARING

LO 3.9 Identify and define the major structures used for hearing.

LO 3.10 Compare and contrast the two theories of hearing.

Many years ago the frightening science fiction movie *Alien* was advertised this way: "In space no one can hear you scream." Although the movie was fiction, the statement is true. Light can travel through the vast nothingness of space, a vacuum, but sound cannot. In the following section, you will learn why.

SOUND: WHAT WE HEAR

What determines the pitch and the loudness of sound, and how is each quality measured?

Sound requires a medium through which to move, such as air, water, or a solid object. This was first demonstrated in 1660 by Robert Boyle, who suspended a ringing pocket watch by a thread inside a specially designed jar. When Boyle pumped all the air out of the jar, he could no longer hear the watch ringing. But when he pumped the air back into the jar, he could again hear the watch ringing.

If you have ever attended a very loud concert, you not only heard but actually felt the mechanical vibrations. The pulsating speakers may have caused the floor, your seat, the walls, and the air around you to shake or vibrate. You were feeling the moving air molecules being pushed toward you in waves as the speakers blasted their vibrations outward.

Frequency is an important characteristic of sound and is determined by the number of cycles (or vibrations) completed by a sound wave in one second. The unit used to measure frequency, or cycles per second, is the hertz (Hz). The pitch—how high or low the sound—is chiefly determined by frequency: the higher the frequency (the more vibrations per second), the higher the sound.

The human ear can hear sound frequencies from low bass tones of around 20 Hz up to high-pitched sounds of about 20 000 Hz. Amazingly, dolphins can respond to sounds up to 100 000 Hz.

The loudness (tone) of a sound is determined largely by its **amplitude**. Amplitude depends on the energy (magnitude or intensity) of the sound wave. Loudness is determined mainly by the force or pressure with which the air molecules are moving. Figure 3.7 shows how sound waves vary in frequency and amplitude. We can measure the pressure level (loudness) of sounds using a unit called the *bel*, named for the Canadian inventor Alexander Graham Bell. Because the bel is a rather large unit, we usually express the measure in tenths of a bel, or **decibels (dB)**. The threshold of human hearing is set at 0 dB, which does not mean the absence of sound but the softest sound that can be heard in a very quiet setting. Each increase of 10 decibels makes a sound 10 times louder. A whisper is about 20 decibels and a normal conversation, around 60 decibels. Figure 3.8 shows the comparative decibel levels for a variety of sounds.

If pitch and loudness were the only perceptual dimensions of sound, we could not tell the difference between two instruments if both were playing exactly the same note at the same

colour blindness: The inability to distinguish some or all colours in vision, resulting from a defect in the cones.

frequency: Measured in the unit *hertz*, the number of sound waves or cycles per second, determining the pitch of the sound.

amplitude: Measured in decibels, the magnitude or intensity of a sound wave, determining the loudness of the sound; in vision, the magnitude or intensity of a light wave that affects the brightness of a stimulus.

decibels (dB) (DES-ih-bels): A unit of measurement of the intensity or loudness of sound based on the amplitude of the sound wave.

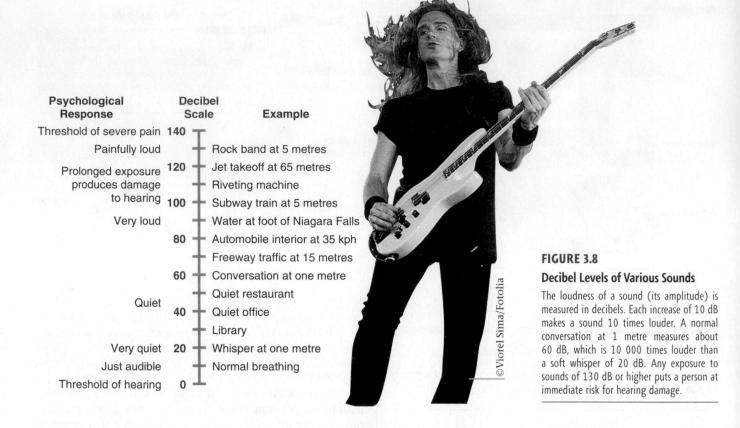

Psychological Response	Decibel Scale	Example
Threshold of severe pain	140	
Painfully loud		Rock band at 5 metres
	120	Jet takeoff at 65 metres
Prolonged exposure produces damage to hearing		Riveting machine
	100	Subway train at 5 metres
Very loud		Water at foot of Niagara Falls
	80	Automobile interior at 35 kph
		Freeway traffic at 15 metres
	60	Conversation at one metre
		Quiet restaurant
Quiet	40	Quiet office
		Library
Very quiet	20	Whisper at one metre
Just audible		Normal breathing
Threshold of hearing	0	

©Viorel Sima/Fotolia

FIGURE 3.8

Decibel Levels of Various Sounds

The loudness of a sound (its amplitude) is measured in decibels. Each increase of 10 dB makes a sound 10 times louder. A normal conversation at 1 metre measures about 60 dB, which is 10 000 times louder than a soft whisper of 20 dB. Any exposure to sounds of 130 dB or higher puts a person at immediate risk for hearing damage.

decibel level. A third characteristic of sound, **timbre**, is the distinct quality of a sound that distinguishes it from other sounds of the same pitch and loudness. Unlike the pure sound of a tuning fork, which has only one frequency, most sounds we hear consist of several different frequencies. The frequencies that form the sound pattern above any tone a musical instrument is playing are called *overtones*, or *harmonics*. Overtones are not actually heard as tones, but they give musical instruments their characteristic quality of sound, or timbre. The rich, full sound of a French horn is due to the large number of overtones present above the note being played. The almost pure sound of the flute is produced because relatively few overtones are generated above the notes sounded on that instrument.

THE EAR: MORE TO IT THAN MEETS THE EYE

How do the outer, middle, and inner ears function in hearing?

The part of the body that we call the ear plays only a minor role in **audition** (the process of hearing) in humans. In fact, if your visible outer ears were cut off, your hearing would suffer very little (Warren, 1999). Let us travel more deeply within the ear and learn how each part contributes to our ability to hear.

The Structure of the Ear: The Outer, Middle, and Inner Ears

The oddly shaped, curved flap of cartilage and skin called the *pinna* is the visible part of the **outer ear** (see Figure 3.9). **[LO 3.9]** Inside the ear, your auditory canal is about 2.5 centimetres

long. Its entrance is lined with hairs. At the end of the auditory canal is the eardrum (the tympanic membrane), a thin, flexible membrane about a centimetre in diameter. The eardrum moves in response to the sound waves that strike it.

It marks the transition to the **middle ear**. Inside the middle ear's chamber are the *ossicles*, the three smallest bones in your body, each "about the size of a grain of rice" (Strome & Vernick, 1989). Named for their shapes, the three connected ossicles—the hammer, the anvil, and the stirrup—link the eardrum to the oval window. The ossicles amplify the sound some 22 times (von Békésy, 1957).

The **inner ear** begins at the inner side of the oval window in the base of the **cochlea**, a fluid-filled, snail-shaped, bony chamber. When the stirrup pushes against the oval window, it sets up vibrations that move the fluid in the cochlea back and forth in waves. The movement of the fluid sets in motion the thin *basilar membrane*, which runs through the cochlea. Attached to the basilar membrane are about 15 000 sensory receptors called **hair cells**, each with a bundle of tiny hairs protruding from it. The tiny hair bundles are pushed and pulled by the motion of the fluid inside the cochlea. This produces an electrical impulse, which is transmitted to the brain by way of the auditory nerve.

Having two ears, one on either side of the head, enables us to determine the direction from which sounds are coming. Unless a sound is directly above, below, in front of, or behind us, it reaches one ear slightly before it reaches the other (Spitzer & Semple, 1991). The brain detects differences as small as 1/10 000 of a second and interprets them, telling us the direction of the sound (Rosenzweig, 1961). The

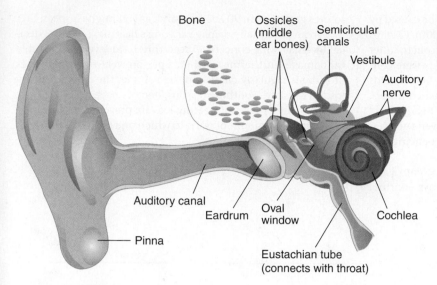

Bone   Ossicles (middle ear bones)   Semicircular canals   Vestibule   Auditory nerve   Auditory canal   Eardrum   Oval window   Cochlea   Pinna   Eustachian tube (connects with throat)

FIGURE 3.9

Anatomy of the Human Ear

Sound waves pass through the auditory canal to the eardrum, causing it to vibrate and set in motion the ossicles in the middle ear. When the stirrup pushes against the oval window, it sets up vibrations in the inner ear. This moves the fluid in the cochlea back and forth and sets the hair cells in motion, causing a message to be sent to the brain via the auditory nerve.

source of a sound may also be determined by the difference in intensity of the sound reaching each ear (Middlebrooks & Green, 1991).

THEORIES OF HEARING: HOW HEARING WORKS

What two major theories attempt to explain hearing?

In the 1860s, Hermann von Helmholtz helped develop **place theory**, one of the two major theories of hearing. **[LO 3.10]** This theory holds that each individual pitch we hear is determined by the particular spot or place along the basilar membrane that vibrates the most. By observing the living basilar membrane, researchers verified that different locations do indeed vibrate in response to differently pitched sounds (Ruggero, 1992). Even so, place theory cannot really explain how we perceive frequencies below 150 Hz.

Another attempt to explain hearing is **frequency theory**. **[LO 3.10]** According to this theory, the hair-cell receptors vibrate the same number of times per second as the sounds that reach them. Thus, a tone of 500 Hz would stimulate the hair cells to vibrate 500 times per second as well. Frequency theory seems valid for low- and medium-pitched tones, but not for high-frequency tones because individual neurons cannot fire more than about 1000 times per second. Therefore, they could not signal to the brain the higher-pitched tones from 1000 to 20 000 Hz.

Today, we believe that frequency theory best explains how we perceive low frequencies and that place theory best explains how we perceive the remaining frequencies.

HEARING LOSS: KINDS AND CAUSES

What are some major causes of hearing loss?

Hearing loss and deafness can be caused by disease, birth defects, injury, excessive noise, and old age. *Conductive* hearing loss, or conduction deafness, is usually caused by disease or injury to the eardrum or the bones of the middle ear, with the result that sound waves cannot be conducted to the cochlea.

The vast majority of conductive hearing losses can be repaired medically or surgically. And, in rare cases, people can be fitted with a hearing aid that bypasses the middle ear and uses bone conduction to reach the cochlea.

Many people over the age of 60 (more men than women) suffer from *sensorineural* hearing loss, which involves damage either to the cochlea or to the auditory nerve. In cases where damage to the cochlea is not too severe, conventional hearing aids may be fitted to reduce the hearing loss (Bramblett, 1997; Korczak, Kurtzberg, & Stapells, 2005). But hearing aids are useless if the damage is to the auditory nerve that connects the cochlea to the brain.

timbre (TAM-burr): The distinctive quality of a sound that distinguishes it from other sounds of the same pitch and loudness.

audition: The sensation of hearing; the process of hearing.

outer ear: The visible part of the ear, consisting of the pinna and the auditory canal.

middle ear: The portion of the ear containing the ossicles, which connect the eardrum to the oval window and amplify the vibrations as they travel to the inner ear.

inner ear: The innermost portion of the ear, containing the cochlea, the vestibular sacs, and the semicircular canals.

cochlea (KOK-lee-uh): The snail-shaped, fluid-filled organ in the inner ear that contains the hair cells (the sound receptors).

hair cells: Sensory receptors for hearing, found in the cochlea.

place theory: The theory that sounds of different frequencies or pitch cause maximum activation of hair cells at certain locations along the basilar membrane.

frequency theory: The theory that hair-cell receptors vibrate the same number of times as the sounds that reach them, thereby accounting for the way variations in pitch are transmitted to the brain.

Many cases of hearing loss in adults appear to be caused by lifelong exposure to excessive noise (Rabinowitz, 2000). Perhaps this is why the Mabaan people of the Sudan don't seem to suffer much hearing loss as they age. When hearing tests were conducted on the Mabaan, it was found that some 80-year-olds could hear as well as 20-year-olds in industrialized countries. The Mabaan pride themselves on their sensitive hearing and consider it important never to raise their voices. Even their festivals and celebrations are quiet affairs, featuring dancing and soft singing (W. I. Bennett, 1990).

Noise-induced hearing loss is not just a problem of the elderly. Children's hearing can be damaged by toys emitting sounds greater than 90 decibels, and, as you might suspect, fireworks can potentially damage anyone's hearing. Likewise, decibel levels at some concerts exceed threshold levels for possible ear damage. Furthermore, when a person wearing headphones or earbuds regularly cranks up the volume, the risk of hearing loss is increased. For these reasons, doctors have noted that the vast majority of cases of hearing loss are preventable simply by managing the amount of noise to which one is exposed (Daniel, 2007; Rabinowitz, 2000).

REMEMBER IT

Hearing

1. Pitch is chiefly determined by _____; loudness is chiefly determined by _____.
   a. amplitude; frequency
   b. wavelength; frequency
   c. intensity; amplitude
   d. frequency; amplitude

2. Pitch is measured in (hertz/decibels); loudness is measured in (decibels/hertz).

3. Match the part of the ear with the structures it contains.
   _____ 1) ossicles
   _____ 2) pinna, auditory canal
   _____ 3) cochlea, hair cells
      a. outer ear
      b. middle ear
      c. inner ear

4. The two major theories that attempt to explain hearing are
   a. conduction theory and place theory.
   b. hair-cell theory and frequency theory.
   c. place theory and frequency theory.
   d. conduction theory and hair-cell theory.

Answers: 1. d 2. hertz; decibels (1). b (2). a (3). c 4. c

MODULE **3D** SMELL AND TASTE

LO 3.11 Define *olfaction* and *gustation*.
LO 3.12 Identify the structures and the role of the structures used for smell and taste.

SMELL: SENSING SCENTS

Consider what it would be like to live in a world without smell. "Not really so bad," you might say. "Although I could not smell flowers, perfume, or my favourite foods, I would never again have to endure the foul odours of life. It's a trade-off, so what's the difference?"

The difference is large indeed. Your ability to detect odours close at hand and at a distance is an aid to survival. You smell smoke and can escape before the flames of a fire envelop you. Your nose broadcasts an odour alarm to the brain when certain poisonous gases or noxious fumes are present. But the survival value of odour detection in humans does not stop there. Smell, aided by taste, is the last line of defence—your final chance to avoid putting spoiled food or drink into your body.

It is well known that odours alone have a powerful ability to call forth old memories and rekindle strong emotional feelings, even decades after events in our lives. This is not surprising when we consider that the olfactory system sends information to the limbic system, an area in the brain that plays an important role in emotions and memories as well (Horvitz, 1997). Indeed, brain-imaging studies of human olfactory functioning have established key connections among smell, emotion, and memory (Hertz, 2004; Pause & Krauel, 2000; Zald & Pardo, 2000).

Did you know that the human olfactory system is capable of sensing and distinguishing 10 000 different odours? The process of sensing odours is the same in every individual, but there are large differences in sensitivity to smells. For example, perfumers and whisky blenders can distinguish subtle variations in odours that are indistinguishable to the average person (Dobb, 1989). Young people are more sensitive to odours than older people are, and non-smokers are more sensitive than smokers (Boyce & Shone, 2006; Danielides et al., 2009).

The Mechanics of Smell: How the Nose Knows

What path does a smell message take on its journey from the nose to the brain?

Olfaction—the sense of smell—is a chemical sense. **[LOs 3.11 & 3.12]** We cannot smell a substance unless some of its molecules vaporize—pass from a solid or liquid into a gaseous state. Heat speeds up the evaporation of molecules, which is why food that is cooking has a stronger and more distinct odour than uncooked food. When odour molecules vaporize, they become airborne and make their way up our nostrils to the **olfactory epithelium**. The olfactory epithelium consists of two patches of tissue, one at the top of each nasal cavity, that together contain about 10 million olfactory neurons—the receptor cells for smell. Each of these neurons contains only one of the 1000 different types of odour receptors (Bargmann, 1996). The intensity of the smell stimulus—how strong or weak it is—is apparently determined by the number of olfactory neurons firing at the same time (Freeman, 1991). Figure 3.10 shows a diagram of the human olfactory system.

The olfactory neurons are special types of neurons that come into direct contact with sensory stimuli and reach directly into the brain. Unlike all other neurons, olfactory neurons have a short lifespan—between 30 days and 1 year—and are continuously being replaced (Bensafi et al., 2004;

©Ermolaev Alexandr Alexandrovich/Fotolia

Odours have a powerful ability to evoke memories and stir up emotions.

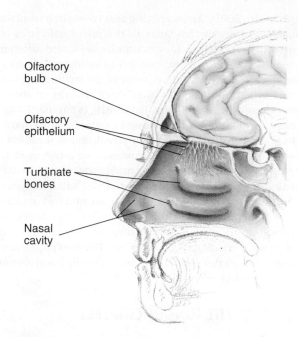

FIGURE 3.10

The Olfactory Sense

Odour molecules travel up the nostrils to the olfactory epithelium, which contains the receptor cells for smell. Olfactory receptors are special neurons with axons that form the olfactory nerve. The olfactory nerve relays smell messages to the olfactory bulbs and on to other parts of the brain.

Buck, 1996). The axons of the olfactory receptor cells relay smell messages directly to the olfactory bulbs—two brain structures the size of matchsticks that rest above the nasal cavities (see Figure 3.10). From the **olfactory bulbs**, messages are relayed to different parts of the brain.

Pheromones

Many animals excrete chemicals called **pheromones**, which can have a powerful effect on the behaviour of other members of the same species (e.g., Vander Meer & Alonso, 2002). Animals use pheromones to mark off territories, signal sexual receptivity, and sense the presence of predators or danger (Brechbuhl, Klaey & Broillet, 2008; Sullivan, Maerz, & Madison, 2002).

Humans emit and respond to pheromones. For example, the human pheromone *androsterone* causes changes in physiological functions such as heart rate and mood states (De Bortoli,

olfaction (ol-FAK-shun): The sensation of smell; the process of smell.

olfactory epithelium: A patch of tissue at the top of each nasal cavity that contains about 10 million receptors for smell.

olfactory bulbs: Two matchstick-sized structures above the nasal cavities, where smell sensations first register in the brain.

pheromones: Chemicals excreted by humans and animals that act as signals to and elicit certain patterns of behaviour from members of the same species.

Tifner, & Zanin, 2001). An interesting area of research involves *menstrual synchrony*, the tendency of the menstrual cycles of women who live together to synchronize with one another over time. In one study of women living in college dormitories, researchers found that 38 percent of the roommate pairs developed synchronous cycles after three months of living together (Morofushi, Shinohoara, Funabashi, & Kimura, 2000). Roommates who synchronized showed greater olfactory sensitivity to androsterone than did non-synchronized dormitory residents. Researchers have also demonstrated a rise in male testosterone levels when exposed to pheromones from ovulating females (Grammer as cited in Holden, 1996; Miller & Maner, 2010). For example, in one study young men who had used an inhalant to sniff pheromones found in female vaginal secretion only showed an increase of testosterone in their saliva when exposed to women's ovulatory secretions. The men apparently recognized, though not consciously, which of the women were most likely to be fertile.

TASTE: WHAT THE TONGUE CAN TELL

What are the five primary taste sensations, and how are they detected?

Psychology textbooks have long maintained that **gustation**, the sense of taste, produces four distinct kinds of sensations—sweet, sour, salty, and bitter. [LO 3.11] This is true. But research also suggests that there is a fifth taste sensation in humans (Herness, 2000). The fifth taste sensation, called *umami*, is a response to the chemical glutamate, which is widely used in the form of monosodium glutamate as a flavouring in Asian foods (Matsunami, Montmayeur, & Buck, 2000). Many protein-rich foods, such as meat, milk, aged cheese, and seafood, contain glutamate. All five taste sensations can be detected on all locations of the tongue. Indeed, even a person with no tongue could taste to some extent, thanks to taste receptors found in the palate, in the mucous lining of the cheeks and lips, and in parts of the throat, including the tonsils.

When we say that a food tastes good or bad, we are actually referring to **flavour**—the combined sensory experience of taste, smell, and touch. As we taste, we feel the texture and temperature of foods we put in our mouths. But most of the pleasure we attribute to our sense of taste is actually due to smell, which comes from odour molecules forced up the nasal cavity by the action of the tongue, cheeks, and throat when we chew and swallow. Can you identify some common foods by taste alone? See *Try It* on this page.

When tastes are mixed, the specialized receptors for each type of flavour are activated and send separate messages to the brain (Frank, Formaker, & Hettinger, 2003; Sugita & Shiba, 2005). In other words, your brain perceives the two distinctive flavours present in sweet and sour sauce quite separately. This analytical quality of the sense of taste prevents your being fooled into eating spoiled or poisoned food when the characteristic taste of either is combined with some kind of pleasant flavour.

The Taste Receptors: Taste Detectors

If you look at your tongue in the mirror, you will see many small bumps called *papillae*. [LO 3.12] There are four different types of

TRY IT

Taste Test

Cover your eyes and hold your nose tightly. Ask a friend to feed you small pieces of food with a similar texture, such as raw potato, apple, and even onion. See if you can identify the food by taste alone. Most people cannot.

papillae, and three of them contain taste buds, which cluster around the cracks and crevices between the papillae. Each of the **taste buds** is composed of 60 to 100 receptor cells, which resemble the petals of a flower. The lifespan of the receptor cells for taste is very short, only about 10 days, and they are continually replaced.

Researchers, using videomicroscopy, have actually counted the number of taste buds on the tongues of different individuals (I. J. Miller & Reedy, 1990). Not surprisingly, people with a reduced ability to taste (non-tasters) had the smallest number of taste buds per square centimetre—an average of 96. Medium tasters averaged nearly twice as many taste buds (184), and supertasters had more than four times as many taste buds (425). But the fact that supertasters do not taste all substances with greater intensity suggests that the number of taste buds alone does not explain general taste sensitivity. In fact, the three groups (non-tasters, medium tasters, and supertasters) differ on taste sensitivity for certain sweet and bitter substances (Yackinous & Guinard, 2002). Non-tasters are unable to taste some sweet and bitter compounds, but they do taste most other substances, although with less sensitivity. Supertasters, on the other hand, taste certain sweet and bitter compounds with much greater intensity. For example, supertasters are particularly sensitive to the chemical that gives fruits and vegetables a bitter taste, and thus they tend to eat less salad than medium and non-tasters do (Yackinous & Guinard, 2002). Researchers are currently investigating links between taste sensitivity, eating behaviours, and health status variables, such as obesity.

REMEMBER IT

Smell and Taste

1. The olfactory, or smell, receptors are located in the
- **a.** olfactory tract.
- **b.** olfactory nerve.
- **c.** olfactory epithelium.
- **d.** olfactory bulbs.

2. The five primary taste sensations are _____, _____, _____, _____, and _____.

3. Our ability to identify foods with similar texture is most influenced by our sense of (taste/smell).

3. Each (papilla/taste bud) contains from 60 to 100 receptor cells.

Answers: 1. c   *2.* sweet, salty, sour, bitter, and umami   *3.* smell   *4.* taste bud

---

MODULE **3E**

THE SKIN SENSES: INFORMATION FROM OUR NATURAL CLOTHING

LO 3.13 Explain how the skin provides sensory information.
LO 3.14 Explain the gate-control theory.
LO 3.15 Explain the role of endorphins.

Our skin is the largest organ of the body. It performs many important biological functions while also yielding much of what we know as sensual pleasure. Your skin can detect heat, cold, pressure, pain, and a vast range of touch sensations—caresses, pinches, punches, pats, rubs, scratches, and the feel of many different textures, from silk to sandpaper.

THE MECHANISM OF TOUCH: HOW TOUCH WORKS

How does the skin provide sensory information?

Tactile information is conveyed to the brain when an object touches and depresses the skin, stimulating one or more of the several distinct types of receptors in the nerve endings. **[LO 3.13]** These sensitive nerve endings in the skin send the touch message through nerve connections to the spinal cord. The message travels up the spinal cord and through the brainstem and the midbrain, finally reaching the brain's somatosensory cortex. (Remember from Chapter 2 that the somatosensory cortex is the strip of tissue at the front of the parietal lobes, where touch, pressure, temperature, and pain register.) Only then do we become aware of where and how hard we have been touched. If we examine the skin from the outermost to the deepest layer, we find a variety of nerve endings that differ markedly in appearance. Most or all of these nerve endings appear to respond in some degree to all different types of tactile stimulation.

In the 1890s, one of the most prominent researchers of the tactile sense, Max von Frey, discovered the two-point threshold, which measures how far apart two points must be before we feel them as two separate touches. Demonstrate the two-point threshold yourself in *Try It*.

Figure 3.11 illustrates two-point thresholds for different body parts, showing the actual distance apart at which two-point discriminations can be made by most people.

TRY IT

Testing the Two-Point Threshold

Have someone touch the middle of your back with two toothpicks held about four centimetres apart. Do you feel one point or two? How far apart do the toothpicks have to be before you perceive them as two separate touch sensations? How far apart do they have to be on your face? on your hands? on your fingers? on your toes? Which of these body parts are the most sensitive? Which are the least sensitive?

---

gustation: The sensation of taste.

flavour: The combined sensory experience of taste, smell, and touch.

taste buds: The structures that are composed of 60 to 100 sensory receptors for taste.

tactile: Pertaining to the sense of touch.

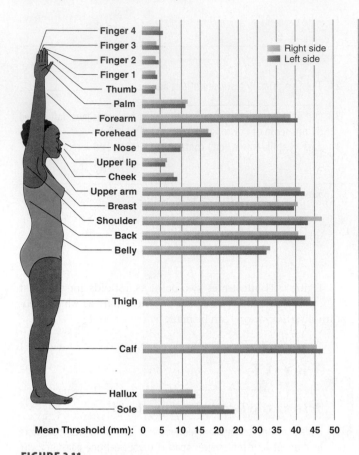

FIGURE 3.11

The Two-Point Threshold

The two-point threshold measures how far apart two points must be to be felt as two separate touches. The drawing shows the average two-point thresholds for different parts of the body. The shortest bars on the graph indicate the greatest sensitivity; the longest bars, the least sensitivity. The thumb and fingers, being the most sensitive body parts, have the lowest two-point thresholds (less than 5 mm). The calves, being the least sensitive body parts, have two-point thresholds of about 45 mm.
Source: (After Weinstein, 1968.) Intensive and extensive aspects of tactile sensitivity as a function of body part, sex and laterality. In D.R. Kenshalo (Ed.). The skin senses. Springfield, IL: Charles C. Thomas.

PAIN: PHYSICAL HURTS

What beneficial purpose does pain serve?

Although our sense of touch brings us a great deal of pleasure, it delivers pain as well. Pain motivates us to tend to injuries, to restrict activity, and to seek medical help. Pain also teaches us to avoid pain-producing circumstances in the future.

Chronic pain, however, persists long after it serves any useful function and is a serious medical problem for many Canadians. The three major types of chronic pain are low back pain, headache, and arthritic pain. For its victims, chronic pain is like a fire alarm that no one can turn off.

The Gate-Control Theory: Conducting Pains Great and Small

What is the gate-control theory of pain?

Pain is probably the least understood of all the sensations. We are not certain how pain works, but one major theory seeks to explain it—the **gate-control theory** of McGill researchers Melzack and Wall (1965, 1983). **[LO 3.14]** Melzack and Wall contend that there is an area in the spinal cord that can act as a "gate" and either inhibit pain messages or transmit them to the brain. Only so many messages can go through the gate at any one time. We feel pain when pain messages carried by the small, slow-conducting nerve fibres reach the gate and cause it to open. Large, fast-conducting nerve fibres carry other sensory messages from the body; these can effectively tie up traffic at the gate so that it will close and keep many of the pain messages from getting through.

What is the first thing you do when you stub your toe or pound your finger with a hammer? If you rub or apply gentle pressure to the injury, you are stimulating the large, fast-conducting nerve fibres to send their message to the spinal gate first; this blocks some of the pain messages from the slower nerve fibres. Applying ice, heat, or electrical stimulation to the painful area also stimulates the large nerve fibres and closes the spinal gate.

The gate-control theory also accounts for the fact that psychological factors, both cognitive and emotional, can influence the perception of pain (Dickenson, 2002). Melzack and Wall (1965, 1983) contend that messages from the brain to the spinal cord can inhibit the transmission of pain messages at the spinal gate and thereby affect the perception of pain. This may explain why some people can undergo surgery under hypnosis and feel little or no pain, and why athletes injured during games are so distracted that they often do not experience pain until some time after the injury.

Endorphins: Our Own Natural Pain Relievers

What are endorphins?

Throughout the world, people spend more effort and money trying to get rid of pain than for any other medical purpose.

Our body produces its own natural painkillers, the **endorphins**, which block pain and produce a feeling of well-being (Hendler & Fenton, 1979). **[LO 3.15]** Endorphins are released when we are injured, when we experience stress or extreme pain, and when we laugh, cry, or exercise (Terman, Shavit, Lewis, Cannon, & Liebeskind, 1984). "Runner's high" and an elevated mood after exercising are often attributed to an increase in endorphin levels (Goldberg, 1988). More recent findings suggest that the release of endorphins that occurs during acupuncture treatments may be one of the factors involved in the favourable response of some individuals to these treatments for conditions such as chronic back pain (Cabýoglu, Ergene, & Tan, 2006).

Some people release endorphins even when they only *think* they are receiving pain medication but are being given, instead, a placebo in the form of a sugar pill or an injection of saline solution (Zubieta et al., 2005). Imaging studies confirm that placebo administration causes a reduction of activity in the regions of the brain that are associated with pain perception (Price, Finniss, & Benedetti, 2008).

Why? When patients believe that they have received a drug for pain, apparently that belief stimulates the release of natural pain relievers, the endorphins. The next time you experience pain, you may want to try some other pain-controlling techniques in *Try It.*

The experience of pain is affected by cultural background, and this influence extends even to childbirth, which is endured more stoically by women in some cultures.

TRY IT

Controlling Pain

If you experience pain, you can try any of the following techniques for controlling it:

- Distraction can be particularly effective for controlling brief or mild pain. Generally, activities or thoughts that require a great deal of attention will provide more relief than passive distractions.

- Counter-irritation—stimulating or irritating one area of the body to mask or diminish pain in another area—can be accomplished with ice packs, heat, massage, mustard packs, or electrical stimulation.

- Relaxation techniques are useful for reducing the stress and muscular tension that usually accompany pain.

- Positive thoughts can help you cope with pain, whereas negative thoughts tend to increase your anxiety.

- Attention and sympathy from family members and friends should be kept at a moderate level; too much attention may prove to be so reinforcing that it serves to prolong pain.

REMEMBER IT

The Skin Senses

1. Each skin receptor responds only to touch, pressure, warmth, or cold. (true/false)
2. The two-point threshold varies for different body parts. (true/false)
3. People would be better off if they could not feel pain. (true/false)

Answers: 1. false 2. true 3. false

©Debby Rogow/PhotoEdit Inc.

MODULE **3F** THE SPATIAL ORIENTATION SENSES

LO 3.16 Identify the kinds of information provided by the kinesthetic sense.

LO 3.17 Describe the vestibular sense.

What would it be like if you could not sense how high to raise a hammer in order to hit a nail? How would you keep from falling if you couldn't sense whether you were standing up straight or leaning to one side? Fortunately, the kinesthetic and vestibular senses keep you apprised of exactly where all parts of your body are and how the location of your body is related to your physical environment.

THE KINESTHETIC SENSE: KEEPING TRACK OF OUR BODY PARTS

What kind of information does the kinesthetic sense provide, and how is this sensory information detected?

The **kinesthetic sense** provides information about (1) the position of the body parts in relation to one another and (2) the movement in various body parts. **[LO 3.16]** This information is detected by receptors in the joints, ligaments, and muscles. The other senses, especially vision, provide additional information about body position and movement, but our kinesthetic sense works well on its own. Thanks to our kinesthetic sense, we are able to perform smooth and skilled body movements without visual feedback or a studied, conscious effort. A companion sense, the vestibular sense, involves equilibrium, or the sense of balance.

THE VESTIBULAR SENSE: SENSING UP AND DOWN AND CHANGES IN SPEED

What is the vestibular sense, and where are its sensory receptors located?

Our **vestibular sense** detects movement and provides information about where we are in space. **[LO 3.17]** The vestibular sense organs are located in the semicircular canals and the

gate-control theory: The theory that the pain signals transmitted by slow-firing nerve fibres can be blocked at the spinal gate if fast-firing fibres get their message to the spinal cord first or if the brain itself inhibits the transmission of the pain messages.

endorphins (en-DOR-fins): Chemicals produced naturally by the pituitary gland that reduce pain and affect mood positively.

kinesthetic sense: The sense that provides information about the position of body parts and about body movement, detected by sensory receptors in the joints, ligaments, and muscles.

vestibular sense (ves-TIB-yu-ler): The sense that provides information about movement and our orientation in space through sensory receptors in the semicircular canals and the vestibular sacs, which detect changes in the movement and orientation of the head.

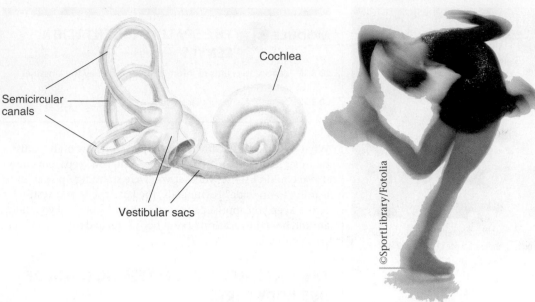

Cochlea

Semicircular canals

Vestibular sacs

FIGURE 3.12

Sensing Balance and Movement

We sense the rotation of the head in any direction because the movement (as during the figure skater's spin on the right) sends fluid coursing through the tubelike semicircular canals in the inner ear. The moving fluid bends the hair-cell receptors, which in turn send the message to the brain.

©SportLibrary/Fotolia

vestibular sacs in the inner ear. The **semicircular canals** sense the rotation of your head, such as when you are turning your head from side to side or when you are spinning around (Figure 3.12). The tubelike canals are filled with fluid; rotating movements of the head in any direction send this fluid coursing through them. In the canals, the moving fluid bends the hair cells, which act as receptors and send neural impulses to the brain. Because there are three canals, each positioned on a different plane, the hair cells in one canal will bend more than the hair cells in the other canals, depending on the direction of rotation.

The semicircular canals and the vestibular sacs signal only *changes* in motion or orientation. If you were blindfolded and had no visual or other external cues, you would not be able to sense motion once your speed reached a constant rate. For example, in an airplane you feel the takeoff and landing or sudden changes in speed. But once the pilot levels off and maintains about the same speed, your vestibular organs do not signal to the brain that you are moving, even if you are travelling hundreds of kilometres per hour.

REMEMBER IT

The Spatial Orientation Senses

1. The (kinesthetic/vestibular) sense provides information about the position of our body parts in relation to one another and about movement in those body parts.
2. The receptors for the (kinesthetic/vestibular) sense are located in the semicircular canals and vestibular sacs in the (middle ear/inner ear).

Answers: 1. kinesthetic   2. vestibular; inner ear

MODULE **3G** PERCEPTION: WAYS OF PERCEIVING

LO 3.18 Identify and explain the four Gestalt principles of grouping.
LO 3.19 Identify the four types of constancies.
LO 3.20 Define *binocular depth cues*.
LO 3.21 Identify and give an example of the seven monocular depth cues.
LO 3.22 Define *motion perception*.

In the first part of this chapter, you learned how the senses detect visual, auditory, and other sensory information and transmit it to the brain. Now we will explore *perception*—the process by which this sensory information is actively organized and interpreted by the brain. We *sense* sounds in hertz and decibels, but we *perceive* melodies. We *sense* light of certain wavelengths and intensities, but we *perceive* a multicoloured world of objects and people. Sensations are the raw materials of human experiences; perceptions are the finished products.

Are our perceptions random and haphazard in nature, or do our brains provide us with rules for interpreting sensory experiences? Researchers addressing this question have found a few principles that appear to govern perceptions in all human beings.

THE GESTALT PRINCIPLES OF PERCEPTUAL ORGANIZATION

What are the Gestalt principles of perceptual organization?

The Gestalt psychologists maintained that we cannot understand our perceptual world by breaking down experiences into tiny parts and analyzing them separately. When sensory elements are brought together, something new is formed. They insisted that the whole is more than just the sum of its parts. The German word *Gestalt* has no exact English equivalent, but it roughly refers to the whole form, pattern, or configuration that we perceive.

How do we organize the world of sights, sounds, and other sensory stimuli in order to perceive the way we do? The Gestalt psychologists argued that we organize our sensory experience according to certain basic principles of perceptual organization. These principles include the figure–ground relationship and principles of perceptual grouping.

Figure and Ground: One Stands Out

The **figure–ground** relationship is the most fundamental principle of perceptual organization and is, therefore, the best place to start analyzing how we perceive. As you view your world, some objects (the figure) seem to stand out from the background (the ground).

Figure–ground perception is not limited to vision. If you listen to a symphony orchestra or a rock band, the melody line tends to stand out as figure, while the chords and the rest of the accompaniment are heard as ground. An itch or a pain would immediately get your attention, while the remaining tactile stimuli you feel would fade to ground.

How can we be sure that knowing the difference between figure and ground is a result of our perceptual system, and that the difference isn't part of the sensory stimulus itself? The best proof is represented by reversible figures, where figure and ground seem to shift back and forth between two equal possibilities, as shown in Figure 3.13.

Sometimes a figure or an object blends so well with its background that we can hardly see it. When there are no sharp lines of contrast between a figure and its background, a figure is camouflaged. For many animals, camouflage provides protection from predators.

Gestalt Principles of Grouping: Perceptual Arrangements

The Gestalt psychologists believed that when we see figures or hear sounds, we organize them according to the simplest, most basic arrangement possible. They proposed the following principles of grouping: similarity, proximity, continuity, and closure (Wertheimer, 1958). **[LO 3.18]**

SIMILARITY We tend to group visual, auditory, and other stimuli according to the principle of *similarity*. Objects that have similar characteristics are perceived as a unit. In Figure 3.14(a), dots of a similar colour are perceived as belonging together to form horizontal rows (on the left) and vertical columns (on the right). When we listen to music, we group the instruments and perceive them as units—the violins, trumpets, and so on—on the basis of similarity in sound.

PROXIMITY Objects that are close together in space or time are usually perceived as belonging together, because of a principle of grouping called *proximity*. Because of their spacing, the lines in Figure 3.14(b) are perceived as four pairs of lines rather than as eight separate lines. Musical notes sounded close together in time are perceived as belonging together to produce musical phrases.

CONTINUITY The principle of *continuity* suggests that we perceive figures or objects as belonging together if they appear to form a continuous pattern, as in Figure 3.14(c). When two singers sing or two instruments are played in harmony, we perceive the notes in the melody line as belonging together, and the notes in the harmony line as belonging together, even if they converge on the same note and then cross over.

CLOSURE The principle of *closure* addresses our tendency to complete figures with gaps in them. Even though parts of the figure in Figure 3.14(d) are missing, we use closure and perceive them as a triangle. If you were listening to your favourite song on the radio and interference periodically interrupted it, you would fill in the gaps to perceive the whole song.

PERCEPTUAL CONSTANCY

What is perceptual constancy, and what are its four types?

As we view people and objects from different angles and distances and under different lighting conditions, we tend to see them as maintaining the same size, shape, brightness, and colour. We call this phenomenon **perceptual constancy**. **[LO 3.19]**

Size Constancy: When Smaller Means Farther Away

When you say goodbye to friends and watch them walk away, the image they cast on your retina grows smaller and smaller

FIGURE 3.13
Reversing Figure and Ground

In this illustration, you can see a white vase against a black background or two black faces in profile on a white background. Exactly the same visual stimulus produces two opposite figure–ground perceptions.

semicircular canals: Three fluid-filled tubular canals in the inner ear that provide information about rotating head movements.

***Gestalt* (geh-SHTALT):** A German word roughly meaning "form" or "pattern."

figure–ground: A principle of perceptual organization whereby the visual field is perceived in terms of an object (figure) standing out against a background (ground).

perceptual constancy: The tendency to perceive objects as maintaining stable properties, such as size, shape, and brightness, despite differences in distance, viewing angle, and lighting.

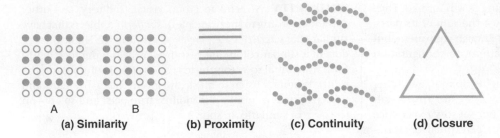

FIGURE 3.14
Gestalt Principles of Grouping
Gestalt psychologists proposed four principles of perceptual grouping: similarity, proximity, continuity, and closure.

(a) Similarity   (b) Proximity   (c) Continuity   (d) Closure

until they finally disappear in the distance. But the shrinking-size information that the retina sends to your brain (the sensation) does not fool the perceptual system. As objects or people move farther away from us, we continue to perceive them as about the same size.

This perceptual phenomenon is known as **size constancy**. We do not make a literal interpretation about the size of objects from the **retinal image**—the image projected onto the retina of objects in the visual field. If we did, we would believe that objects we see become larger as they approach us and smaller as they move away from us.

Shape Constancy: Seeing Round as Round from Any Angle

The shape or image of an object projected onto the retina changes according to the angle from which we view it. But our perceptual ability gives us **shape constancy**—the tendency to perceive objects as having a stable or unchanging shape regardless of changes in the retinal image resulting from differences in viewing angle. In other words, we perceive a door as rectangular and a plate as round from whatever angle we view them (Figure 3.15).

Brightness Constancy: Perceiving Brightness in Sunlight and Shadow

We normally see objects as maintaining a constant level of brightness regardless of differences in lighting conditions—a phenomenon known as **brightness constancy**. Nearly all objects reflect some part of the light that falls upon them, and we know that white objects reflect more light than black objects do. However, a black asphalt driveway actually reflects more light at noon in bright sunlight than a white shirt reflects indoors at night in dim lighting. Nevertheless, the driveway still looks black and the shirt still looks white. Why? We learn to infer the brightness of objects by comparing them with the brightness of all other objects viewed at the same time.

Colour Constancy: When Colours Stay the Same in Sunlight or Shadow

Colours can change considerably under different lighting conditions. But when objects are familiar to us, they appear to look about the same colour under different conditions of illumination. This is called **colour constancy**. Like brightness constancy, colour constancy depends on the comparisons we make between differently coloured objects we view at the same time (Brou, Sciascia, Linden, & Lettvin, 1986).

Imagine what a strange world you would live in if it were not for the perceptual constancies. Fortunately, the perceptual constancies, provide a stable perceptual world.

DEPTH PERCEPTION: WHAT'S UP CLOSE AND WHAT'S FAR AWAY

Depth perception is the ability to perceive the visual world in three dimensions and to judge distances accurately. We judge how far away objects and other people are. We climb and

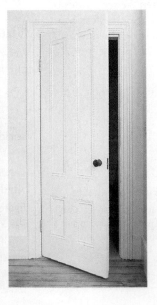

FIGURE 3.15
Shape Constancy
The door projects very different images on the retina when viewed from different angles. But because of shape constancy, we continue to perceive the door as rectangular.

descend stairs without stumbling, and perform other visual tasks requiring depth perception.

Depth perception captures three dimensions, yet each eye is able to provide us with only two dimensions. The images cast upon the retina do not contain depth; they are flat, just like a photograph. How, then, do we perceive depth so vividly?

Binocular Depth Cues: The Cues Only Two Eyes Reveal

What are the binocular depth cues?

Some cues to depth perception depend on our two eyes working together. **[LO 3.20]** These are called **binocular depth cues**, and they include convergence and binocular disparity. **Convergence** occurs when our eyes turn inward as we focus on nearby objects—the closer the object, the greater the convergence. Hold the tip of your finger about 30 centimetres in front of your nose and focus on it. Now slowly begin moving your finger toward your nose. Your eyes will turn inward so much that they virtually cross when the tip of your finger meets the tip of your nose. Many psychologists believe that the tension of the eye muscles as they converge conveys information to the brain that serves as a cue for distance and depth perception.

Fortunately, our eyes are just far enough apart, about 6 centimetres or so, to give each eye a slightly different view of the objects we focus on and, consequently, a slightly different retinal image. The difference between the two retinal images, known as **binocular disparity** (or *retinal disparity*), provides an important cue for depth and distance. The farther away from us are the objects we view (up to 6 metres or so), the less is the disparity or difference between the two retinal images. The brain integrates these two slightly different retinal images and gives us the perception of three dimensions (H. Wallach, 1985). Ordinarily we are not aware that each eye provides a slightly different view of the objects we see. You can prove this for yourself in *Try It*.

Convergence and binocular disparity provide depth or distance cues only for nearby objects. Fortunately, each eye by itself provides cues for objects at greater distances.

Monocular Depth Cues: The Cues One Eye Can Detect

What are the seven monocular depth cues?

Close one eye and you will see that you can still perceive depth. The visual depth cues perceived by one eye alone are called **monocular depth cues**. The following is a description of seven monocular depth cues, many of which artists use to give the illusion of depth to their paintings. (See Figure 3.16 for examples of each.) **[LO 3.21]**

- *Interposition.* When one object partially blocks our view of another, we perceive the partially blocked object as farther away.

- *Linear perspective.* Linear perspective is a depth cue in which parallel lines that are known to be the same distance apart appear to grow closer together or converge as they recede into the distance.

TRY IT

Testing Binocular Disparity

Hold your forefinger or a pencil at arm's length straight in front of you. Close your left eye and focus on the pencil. Now quickly close your right eye at the same time that you open your left eye. Repeat this procedure, closing one eye just as you open the other. The pencil will appear to move from side to side in front of your face.

Now slowly bring the pencil closer and closer until it almost reaches your nose. The closer you bring the pencil, the more it appears to move from side to side. This is because there is progressively more disparity between the two retinal images as we view objects closer and closer.

---

size constancy: The tendency to perceive objects as the same size regardless of changes in the retinal image.

retinal image: The image of objects in the visual field projected onto the retina.

shape constancy: The tendency to perceive objects as having a stable or unchanging shape regardless of differences in viewing angle.

brightness constancy: The tendency to see objects as maintaining the same brightness regardless of differences in lighting conditions.

colour constancy: The tendency to see objects as maintaining about the same colour regardless of differences in lighting conditions.

depth perception: The ability to see in three dimensions and to estimate distance.

binocular depth cues: Depth cues that depend on two eyes working together; convergence and binocular disparity.

convergence: A binocular depth cue in which the eyes turn inward as they focus on nearby objects—the closer an object, the greater the convergence.

binocular disparity: A binocular depth cue resulting from differences between the two retinal images cast by objects at distances up to about six metres.

monocular depth cues (mah-NOK-yu-ler): Depth cues that can be perceived by only one eye.

Interposition
When one object partially blocks your view of another, you perceive the partially blocked object as being farther away.

©Kent Meireis/The Image Works

Linear Perspective
Parallel lines are the same distance apart but appear to grow closer together, or converge, as they recede into the distance.

©Oksana Shufrych/Shutterstock

Relative Size
Larger objects are perceived as being closer to the viewer, and smaller objects as being farther away.

©ortodoxphoto/fotolia

Texture Gradient
Objects close to you appear to have sharply defined features, and similar objects farther away appear less well defined, or fuzzier in texture.

©romaneau/fotolia

Atmospheric Perspective
Objects in the distance have a bluish tint and appear more blurred than do objects close at hand (sometimes called *aerial perspective*).

©tlorna/fotolia

Shadow or Shading
When light falls on objects, they cast shadows, which add to the perception of depth.

©dotshock/Shutterstock

Motion Parallax
When you ride in a moving train and look out the window, the objects you see outside appear to be moving in the opposite direction and at different speeds; those closest to you appear to be moving faster than those in the distance.

©marekuliasz/shutterstock

FIGURE 3.16
Monocular Depth Cues

- *Relative size.* Larger objects are perceived as being closer to us, and smaller objects as being farther away.

- *Texture gradient.* Texture gradient is a depth cue in which near objects appear to have a sharply defined texture, while similar objects appear progressively smoother and fuzzier as they recede into the distance.

- *Atmospheric perspective.* Atmospheric perspective, sometimes called *aerial perspective*, is a depth cue in which objects in the distance have a bluish tint and appear more blurred than objects close at hand.

- *Shadow or shading.* When light falls on objects, shadows are cast. We can distinguish bulges from indentions by the shadows they cast.

- *Motion parallax.* When we ride in a moving vehicle and look out the side window, the objects we see outside appear to be moving in the opposite direction. The objects also seem to be moving at different speeds—those closest to us appear to be moving faster than objects in the distance. Objects very far away, such as the moon and

the sun, appear to move in the same direction as we are moving.

Figure 3.17 summarizes the binocular and monocular depth cues.

Motion Perception

Imagine you're sitting in a bus looking through the window at another bus parked parallel to the one in which you are sitting. Suddenly, you sense your bus moving; then, you realize that it is not your bus that moved but the one next to it. In other words, your ability to perceive the motion of objects has been fooled in some way. This example illustrates the complexity of motion perception, a process that is primarily visual but that also involves auditory and kinesthetic cues. **[LO 3.22]** False motion perceptions are common, so much so that researchers use the terms **real motion** to refer to perceptions of motion tied to movements of real objects through space and **apparent motion** for perceptions of motion that seem to be psychologically constructed in response to various kinds of stimuli.

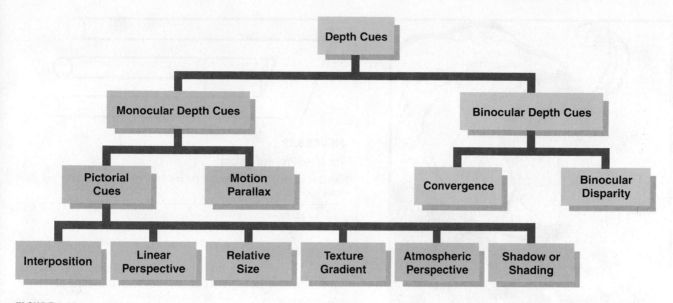

FIGURE 3.17

Binocular and Monocular Depth Cues

Depth cues that require two eyes working together are binocular; those that require only one eye are monocular.

REAL MOTION Research indicates that motion detection is caused by brain mechanisms linked to the retina, the edges of which appear to be especially sensitive to motion, just as the fovea is specialized for detail and colour (Bach & Hoffman, 2000). However, if you walk across a room with your eyes fixed on an object—your sofa, for example—the object will move across your retina. So, movement of an image across the retina isn't sufficient for motion detection. Your own kinesthetic sense contributes to judgments of motion. Generally, you know whether you're moving or not. But have you ever watched a train go by while sitting still? It's not unusual to have the feeling that your head is moving as you watch the railroad cars whiz by. So, your kinesthetic sense is also linked to your perceptions of movement outside your own body. Brain-imaging studies show that such stimuli activate the vestibular cortex, just as real body movements do (Nishiike, Nakagawa, Tonoike, Takeda, & Kubo, 2001).

James Gibson (1994) argued that our perceptions of motion appear to be based on fundamental, but frequently changing, assumptions about stability. Our brains seem to search for some stimulus in the environment to serve as the assumed reference point for stability. Once the stable reference point is chosen, all objects that move relative to that reference point are judged to be in motion. For example, in the bus situation, your brain assumes that the other bus is stable, and when the motion sensors linked to your retina detect movement, it concludes that your bus is moving. In the train situation, your brain assumes that the train is stable, and so your head must be moving. And when you're driving a car, you sense the car to be in motion relative to the outside environment. But your brain uses the inside of the car as the stable point of reference for your own movements. Only your movements in relation to the seat, steering wheel, and so on are sensed as motion by your brain.

APPARENT MOTION In one type of apparent motion study, several stationary lights in a dark room are flashed on and off in sequence, causing participants to perceive a single light is moving from one spot to the next. This type of apparent motion, called the **phi phenomenon**, was first discussed by Max Wertheimer (1912), one of the founders of Gestalt psychology. How many neon signs have you seen that caused you to perceive motion? The neon lights don't move; they simply flash on and off in a particular sequence. When you watch a motion picture, you are also perceiving this kind of apparent motion, often called *stroboscopic motion*.

The fact that the eyes are never really completely still also contributes to perceptions of apparent motion. For instance, if you stare at a single unmoving light in a dark room for a few seconds, the light will appear to begin moving, a phenomenon called the **autokinetic illusion**. However, if you look away from

real motion: Perceptions of motion tied to movements of real objects through space.

apparent motion: Perceptions of motion that seem to be psychologically constructed in response to various kinds of stimuli.

phi phenomenon: Apparent motion that occurs when several stationary lights in a dark room are flashed on and off in sequence, causing the perception that a single light is moving from one spot to the next.

autokinetic illusion: Apparent motion caused by the movement of the eyes rather than the movement of the objects being viewed.

FIGURE 3.18
Old Woman/Young Woman by E. G. Boring
The most famous ambiguous figure can be seen alternately as a young woman or an old woman, depending on where your eyes fixate.
Source: From Hill, W. E. (William Ely), 1887–1962, My wife and my mother-in-law.

the light and then return to watching it, it will again appear to be stable. Two lights placed close to one another will appear to move together, as if they are linked by an invisible string. What is really happening is that your eyes, not the lights, are moving. Because of the darkness of the room, the brain has no stable visual reference point to use in deciding whether the lights are actually moving or not (J. Gibson, 1994). But when the room is lit up, the brain immediately "fixes" the error because it has a stable visible background for the lights.

EXTRAORDINARY PERCEPTIONS   We perceive ambiguous figures, impossible figures, and illusions as well.

Ambiguous Figures: More Than One Way to See Them

When we are faced for the first time with the ambiguous figure, we have no experience to call on. Our perceptual system is puzzled and tries to work its way out of the quandary by seeing the ambiguous figure first one way and then another, but not both at once. We never get closure with ambiguous figures, which seem to jump back and forth beyond our control.

In some ambiguous figures, two different objects or figures are seen alternately. The best known of these, *Old Woman/Young Woman*, by E. G. Boring, is shown in Figure 3.18. If you direct your gaze to the left of the drawing, you are likely to see an attractive young woman, her face turned away. But the young woman disappears when you suddenly perceive the image of the old woman. Such examples of object ambiguity offer striking evidence that our perceptions are more than the mere sum

FIGURE 3.19
The Three-Pronged Trident
This is an impossible figure because the middle prong appears to be in two places at the same time.

of sensory parts. It is hard to believe that the same drawing (the same sum of sensory parts) can convey such dramatically different perceptions.

Impossible Figures: This Can't Be

At first glance, the pictures of impossible figures do not seem so unusual—not until we examine them more closely. Would you invest your money in a company that manufactured three-pronged tridents as shown in Figure 3.19? Such an object could not be made as pictured because the middle prong appears to be in two different places at the same time.

Illusions: False Perceptions

An **illusion** is a false perception or a misperception of an actual stimulus in the environment. We can misperceive size, shape, or the relationship of one element to another. For example, recent research conducted at McMaster University examines temporal illusions. Interestingly, these illusions appear to be predicted by personality. For more information on these illusions, read the Canadian Connections Box. Many illusions studied to date are visual illusions. We need not pay to see illusions performed by magicians: illusions occur naturally and we see them all the time. An oar in the water appears to be bent where it meets the water. The moon looks much larger at the horizon than it does overhead. Why? One explanation of the moon illusion involves relative size. The suggestion is that the moon looks very large on the horizon because it is viewed in comparison to trees, buildings, and other objects. When viewed overhead, the moon cannot be compared with other objects, and it appears smaller.

THE MÜLLER-LYER ILLUSION   Look at Figure 3.20(a), on page 88. Which of the vertical lines is longer? Actually, they are the same length. The same is true of the arrows in Figure 3.20(b). British psychologist R. L. Gregory (1978) has suggested that the Müller-Lyer illusion is actually a misapplication of size constancy. When two lines are the same length, the line we perceive to be farther away will look longer.

THE PONZO ILLUSION   The Ponzo illusion also plays an interesting trick. Look at Figure 3.21. Which obstruction on the railway tracks looks larger? You have undoubtedly

CANADIAN CONNECTIONS

The Effects of Narcissism on the Perception of Self-produced Actions and Effects

Flick the light switch and the light goes on. Press the doorbell and it rings. Turn the key and the car starts. Every day we engage in actions that change something in our environment. One important aspect of these actions is that we feel control over them and the consequences they produce. When the light comes on, for example, we just "know" it was our flicking of the switch that caused it—we don't act surprised to see the room illuminated. This sense of control over our own actions is called the Sense of Agency (SoA). One way that researchers study SoA is to perform experiments in which individual participants are asked to make an action like a simple key press, which is followed a couple of hundred milliseconds later by a tone. After the tone, researchers ask the participant to rate how long they think the interval between their key press and the tone was, in milliseconds. Interestingly, people in this task fall prey to an illusion whereby they perceive the interval as shorter than it really is. That is, the brain seems to bind the perceived time of the key press and the perceived time of the tone together. If the participant's finger is mechanically pushed onto the key, this binding is not present. In view of this dependency on specifically intentional acts, such binding has been termed "intentional binding." It is a robust and reliable illusion surrounding the production of intentional actions. But is this illusion the same for everyone? In a recent study, researchers asked whether specific personality traits might change the degree to which intentional binding occurs. Narcissism is a personality trait associated with a grandiose sense of self and beliefs about the self as an effective, powerful actor. Researchers tested whether individuals with different levels of narcissism (as measured on a scale called the Narcissistic Personality Inventory, or NPI) displayed different degrees of intentional binding. Researchers predicted that those lower in narcissism would feel less agency than those higher in narcissism, and would consequently

show less binding than those higher in narcissism. This is exactly what they found! Individuals who scored low on the NPI showed weaker intentional binding than individuals with medium to high levels of narcissism (Hascalovitz & Obhi, 2015). These results were the first to show that a low level temporal illusion surrounding voluntary action differs across individuals with different personality profiles. ■

Sukhvinder Obhi

Dr. Sukhvinder S. Obhi

guessed by now, contrary to your perceptions, that A and B are the same size. Again, our perceptions of size and distance, which we trust and which are normally accurate in informing us about the real world, can be wrong. If we saw two obstructions on real railway tracks identical to the ones in the illusion, the one that looked larger would indeed be larger. So the Ponzo illusion is not a natural illusion but rather a contrived one. In fact, all these illusions are really misapplications of principles that nearly always work properly in our normal everyday experience.

CULTURAL DIFFERENCES IN VISUAL ILLUSIONS Note that our susceptibility to visual illusions is not necessarily inborn. Several studies have examined the influence of culture or experience on people's perceptions of visual illusions. M. H. Segall, Campbell, and Herskovitz (1966) tested 1848 adults and children from 15 different countries and found "marked differ-

ences in illusion susceptibility across cultural groups" (p. 137). People from all cultures showed some tendency to see the illusions but experienced different perceptions. Zulus from Africa who had round houses and saw few corners of any kind were not as fooled by the Müller-Lyer illusion. In similar research, D. M. Pedersen and Wheeler (1983) studied Native American responses to the Müller-Lyer illusion among Navajos and found that those who had lived in round houses, like the Zulus, tended not to see the illusion.

illusion: A false perception of actual stimuli involving a misperception of size, shape, or the relationship of one element to another.

(a)

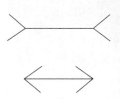

(b)

FIGURE 3.20

The Müller-Lyer Illusion

Although the two vertical lines in **(a)** are the same length, the line on the left seems to project forward and appears closer than the line on the right, which seems to recede. The two horizontal lines in **(b)** are identical in length. When two lines are the same length, the one perceived as farther away will appear longer.

Source: Based on Gregory, R.L. (1978). Eye and brain: The psychology of seeing (3rd ed.). New York: McGraw-Hill.

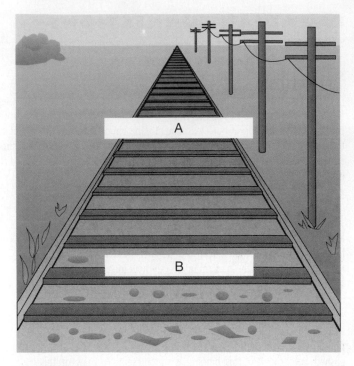

FIGURE 3.21

The Ponzo Illusion

The two white bars superimposed on the railway track are actually identical in length. Because A appears farther away than B, we perceive it as longer.

REMEMBER IT

Perception

1. Camouflage blurs the distinction between
   a. sensation and perception.
   b. figure and ground.
   c. continuation and closure.
   d. proximity and similarity.

2. Which of the perceptual constancies cause us to perceive objects as being different from the retinal image they project?
   a. brightness constancy and colour constancy
   b. colour constancy and shape constancy
   c. shape constancy and size constancy
   d. colour constancy and size constancy

3. Match the appropriate monocular depth cue with each example.

_____ 1) one building partly blocking another
_____ 2) railway tracks converging in the distance
_____ 3) closer objects appearing to move faster than far objects
_____ 4) far objects looking smaller than near objects
   a. motion parallax
   b. linear perspective
   c. interposition
   d. relative size

4. An illusion is
   a. an imaginary sensation.
   b. an impossible figure.
   c. a misperception of a real stimulus.
   d. a figure—ground reversal.

Answers: 1. b 2. c 3 (1). c (2). b (3). a (4). d 4. c

MODULE 3H ADDITIONAL INFLUENCES ON PERCEPTION

LO 3.23 Compare and contrast bottom-up and top-down processing.

Why don't all people perceive sights, sounds, odours, and events in the same way? The reason is that our perceptions involve more than just the sensory stimuli themselves.

BOTTOM-UP AND TOP-DOWN PROCESSING

In what types of situations do we rely more on bottom-up or top-down processing?

Psychologists distinguish between two distinct information-processing techniques that we use in recognizing patterns—bottom-up processing and top-down processing. **[LO 3.23]** **Bottom-up processing** begins with the individual components of a stimulus that are detected by the sensory receptors. The information is then transmitted to areas in the brain where it is combined and assembled into the whole patterns that we perceive.

In **top-down processing**, on the other hand, past experience and knowledge of the context plays a role in forming our perceptions. In other words, what we perceive is more than the sum of the individual elements taken in by our sensory receptors. If you have ever tried to decipher a prescription written by your doctor (bottom-up processing), you may have been amazed that your pharmacist could fill it. But prior knowledge and experience enabled the pharmacist to use top-down processing.

Of course, we use both bottom-up and top-down processing when we form perceptions. In situations unfamiliar to us, we are likely to use bottom-up processing. In familiar situations, where we have some prior knowledge and experience, we tend to use top-down processing.

PERCEPTUAL SET

The **perceptual set**—what you expect to perceive—determines, to a large extent, what you actually see, hear, feel, taste, and smell. If you were served raspberry sherbet that was coloured green, would it still taste like raspberry, or might it taste more like lime? People often bend reality to meet their expectations. Thus, perceptual set results from top-down processing.

ATTENTION

Often linking sensations to meanings requires very little mental effort. For instance, when you are reading familiar words, the sensation of seeing the word and the perception of its meaning occur almost simultaneously (Heil, Rokle, & Pecchinenda, 2004). Similarly, when you are driving, perceiving that the other objects on the road are cars takes very little mental effort because you are so familiar with them. In other words, these are *automatic* (non-effortful) mental processes. However, more mental effort is required to determine which cars we should watch most closely. When we engage in this kind of mental effort, the process of *attention* is at work. **Attention** is defined as

When you look at this photograph, you can easily notice the gorilla-costumed figure. However, this photo is actually a frame from a video used in Simons's inattentional blindness studies. Participants see the video after being told to keep track of how many times the basketball is passed from one person to another. Under these conditions, participants typically fail to notice when the gorilla-costumed figure enters the scene. You can view clips from Simons's videos at http://viscog.beckman.illinois.edu/flashmovie/15.php.

Simons, D.J., & Chabris, C.F. (1999). Gorillas in our midst: Sustained inattentional blindness for dynamic events. Perception, 28, 1059–1074.

the process of sorting through sensations and selecting some of them for further processing. Without attention, perception of all but the most familiar sensations would be impossible.

Of course, we cannot pay attention to everything at once. It is important to realize that attention carries certain perceptual costs. Research examining the phenomenon of **inattentional blindness** has helped to illustrate these costs (Bressan & Pizzighello, 2008; Mack, 2003; Mack & Rock, 1998; Simons & Rensink, 2005). Inattentional blindness occurs when we shift our attention from one object to another and fail to

---

bottom-up processing: Information processing in which individual components or bits of data are combined until a complete perception is formed.

top-down processing: Application of previous experience and conceptual knowledge to first recognize the whole of a perception and thus easily identify the simpler elements of that whole.

perceptual set: An example of top-down processing where individuals' expectations affect their perceptions.

attention: The process of sorting sensations and selecting some for further processing.

inattentional blindness: The phenomenon in which we shift our focus from one object to another and, in the process, fail to notice changes in objects to which we are not directly paying attention.

notice changes in objects to which we are not paying attention (Woodman & Luck, 2003). For example, Daniel Simons and colleagues (e.g., Simons & Chabris, 1999) showed participants a videotape of a basketball game in which one team wore white uniforms and the other team wore black uniforms (see the photo on this page). Participants were instructed to count how many times the ball was passed from one player to another, either on the white team or on the black team. Under such conditions, about one third of participants typically failed to later recall the appearance on the screen of even extremely incongruent stimuli (for example, a man dressed in a gorilla costume). The inattentional blindness happens even when the incongruous stimulus is present on the screen for a long period of time. Simons's research helps us understand why we sometimes exclaim, "Where did that car come from?" when a car we had been ignoring suddenly swerves into our path. Read the *Apply It* feature at the end of this chapter to learn about the possible dangers of talking on a cellphone while driving.

Although attending to a stimulus is associated with deficits in the ability to attend to other stimuli, attention is clearly not an all-or-nothing process. We can, and often do, process more than one stimulus at a time. For example, listeners who were presented with different verbal messages in either ear could remember the content of only the message to which the experimenter directed their attention (e.g., "Pay attention to the message in your left ear") (Cherry, 1953). Nevertheless, they were able to remember many things about the unattended message, such as whether it had been delivered by a male or a female.

APPLY IT

How Dangerous Is It to Talk, Text, or Use a Cellphone While Driving?

When you read about the research demonstrating inattentional blindness, does it raise your level of concern about the possible dangers of driving while talking on a cellphone? Interestingly, surveys suggest that we are more concerned about other drivers' cellphone use than our own (Troglauer, Hels, & Christens, 2006). Nevertheless, research clearly shows that talking on a cellphone, or engaging in other kinds of attention-demanding tasks (for example, eating, reading [including maps or the GPS], or using other mobile devices), results in potentially dangerous changes in our behind-the-wheel behaviour.

Behavioural Effects of Cellphone Use

Most experiments examining cellphone use while driving take place in laboratories in which participants use driving simulators. Experimental group participants talk on the cellphone while driving, but those in the control groups do not. Studies of this type show that cellphone use affects drivers' behaviour in a variety of ways (Drews, Pasupathi, & Strayer, 2008):

- Drivers slow down when talking on the phone.
- Drivers have slower reaction times when engaged in phone conversations.

- Drivers who talk on a cellphone often fail to stay within the boundaries of the lane in which they are driving.
- Drivers using cellphones sometimes stop at green lights but drive through red lights and stop signs.

These effects have been observed just as often in studies using hands-free phones as conventional hand-held models (Strayer & Drews, 2004). However, one study suggested that hands-free phone use gave drivers a false sense of safety (P. Langer, Holzner, Magnet, & Kopp, 2005). Thus, experimental studies show definitively that, on average, cellphone use impairs driving ability. (Klauer et al., 2014). Motor vehicle accident statistics support experimental findings with 80 percent of collisions and 65 percent of near-crashes being attributed to inattention when driving (National Highway Traffic Safety Administration (NHTSA), 2010).

Compensating for the Effects of Cellphone Use

Despite the clear findings of these studies, other research suggests that there are several factors that help drivers compensate for the distractions associated with cellphone use (Charlton,

2009; Hunton & Rose, 2005; Pöysti, Rajalin, & Summala, 2005; Shinar, Tractinsky, & Compton, 2005). Here are a couple of them:

- Reducing other distractions, such as turning off the radio, helps drivers keep their minds on driving while also talking on the phone.
- Some drivers end a cellphone call with "I'll call you back later when I'm not driving" when they realize that the attentional demands of a specific conversation are incompatible with those of driving.

These findings show that drivers are well aware of the potentially risk-enhancing effects of behaviour changes caused by distractions. As a result, they actively work to manage the number of demands on their attention while driving.

It's about Attention

You may know from personal experience that attention-demanding tasks impair driving behaviours. Studies of youth show that 21 percent of distracted drivers aged 15–19 years were distracted by the use of cell phones (NHTSA, 2013). In addition, 25 percent of teenage drivers reported responding to a text message at least once every time they drive, while 20 percent of teenage drivers and 10 percent of parents admitted to having had a texting conversation spanning multiple texts during driving (University of Michigan Transportation Research Institute, 2012). Clearly, talking and texting are common distractions. The take-away message from this chapter's discussion of inattentional blindness is clear. When drivers pay attention to anything that is not relevant to the task of operating a vehicle, they limit their ability to focus on driving. Consequently, the goal of anyone who is operating a vehicle ought to be to minimize distractions to as great a degree as possible:

- If possible, drivers should pull off the road to talk or text on their cellphones.
- Changing radio stations, scrolling through music selections, reading map instructions and other distractions should be postponed until drivers are stopped at a red light or stop sign.

- Whenever passengers are distracting them, drivers should politely request that they refrain from talking.

By taking these measures, drivers will reduce their risk of missing important cues such as traffic lights and decrease the likelihood that they will, at best, get a traffic ticket or, at worst, cause an accident.

THINKING CRITICALLY

Evaluation

Using what you have learned about the factors that contribute to hearing loss, prepare a statement indicating what the government should do to control noise pollution, even to the extent of banning certain noise hazards. Consider the workplace, the home, toys, machinery, rock concerts, and so on.

Point/Counterpoint

Much commercial advertising is aimed at providing products that reduce or eliminate pain. Prepare a sound, logical argument supporting one of the following positions:

a. Pain is valuable and necessary.
b. Pain is not necessary.

Psychology in Your Life

Vision and hearing are generally believed to be the two most highly prized senses. How would your life change if you lost your sight? How would your life change if you lost your hearing? Which sense would you find more traumatic to lose? Why?

MyPsychLab   go to mypsychlab (access code required) to find web resources for your text that supplement the material in chapter 3.

SUMMARY & REVIEW

What is the difference between sensation and perception?
Sensation is the process through which the senses pick up sensory stimuli and transmit them to the brain. Perception is the process by which this sensory information is actively organized and interpreted by the brain.

Sensory receptors detect and respond to stimuli (e.g., light, sound waves, odours). Through transduction, the receptors change the sensory stimulation into neural impulses that are transmitted to the brain. We experience a sensation only when the appropriate part of the brain is stimulated.

SENSATION: THE SENSORY WORLD

What is the difference between the absolute threshold and the difference threshold?
The absolute threshold is the minimum amount of sensory stimulation that can be detected 50 percent of the time. The difference threshold is a measure of the smallest increase or decrease in a physical stimulus that can be detected 50 percent of the time.

How are sensory stimuli in the environment experienced as sensations?

VISION

How do the cornea, the iris, and the pupil function in vision?
The cornea bends light rays inward through the pupil—the small, dark opening in the eye. The iris dilates and contracts the pupil to regulate the amount of light entering the eye.

What are the lens and the retina?
The lens changes its shape as it focuses images of objects from varying distances on the retina, a thin membrane containing the sensory receptors for vision.

What roles do the rods and cones play in vision?
The cones detect colour, provide our sharpest vision, and function best in high illumination. The rods enable us to see in dim light. Rods respond to black and white, and they encode all other visible wavelengths in shades of grey.

What path does the neural impulse take from the retina to the visual cortex?
The neural impulses are carried by ganglion cells that extend through the wall of the retina and become the optic nerve. The impulses cross the optic chasm and travel to the visual cortex.

What are the three dimensions that combine to provide the colours we experience?
The three dimensions are hue, saturation, and brightness.

What two major theories attempt to explain colour vision?
Two major theories that attempt to explain colour vision are the trichromatic theory and the opponent-process theory.

 **HEARING**

What determines the pitch and the loudness of sound, and how is each quality measured?
The pitch of a sound is determined by frequency, which is measured in hertz. The loudness of a sound is determined largely by the amplitude of the sound wave and is measured in decibels.

How do the outer, middle, and inner ears function in hearing?
Sound waves enter the pinna, the visible part of the outer ear, and travel to the end of the auditory canal, causing the eardrum to vibrate. This sets in motion the ossicles in the middle ear, which amplify the sound waves. The vibration of the oval window causes activity in the inner ear, setting in motion the fluid in the cochlea and moving the hair-cell receptors, which transduce the vibrations into neural impulses. The auditory nerve carries the neural impulses to the brain.

What two major theories attempt to explain hearing?
Two major theories that attempt to explain hearing are place theory and frequency theory.

What are some major causes of hearing loss?
Many things can contribute to hearing loss, including disease, birth defects, injury, excessive noise, and old age.

 **SMELL AND TASTE**

What path does a smell message take on its journey from the nose to the brain?
The act of smelling begins when odour molecules reach the smell receptors in the olfactory epithelium at the top of the nasal cavity. The axons of these receptors form the olfactory nerve, which relays the smell message to the olfactory bulbs. From there the smell message travels to other parts of the brain.

What are the five primary taste sensations, and how are they detected?
The primary taste sensations are sweet, sour, salty, bitter, and umami. The receptor cells for taste are found in the taste buds on the papillae of the tongue and in other parts of the mouth and throat.

 THE SKIN SENSES : INFORMATION FROM OUR NATURAL CLOTHING

How does the skin provide sensory information?
Nerve endings in the skin (the sensory receptors) respond to different kinds of stimulation, including heat and cold, pressure, pain, and a vast range of touch sensations. The neural impulses ultimately register in the somatosensory cortex.

What beneficial purpose does pain serve?
Pain motivates us to tend to injuries, to restrict activity, and to seek medical help. Pain also teaches us to avoid pain-producing circumstances in the future.

What is the gate-control theory of pain?
Melzack and Wall's gate-control theory holds that pain signals transmitted by slow-conducting fibres can be blocked at the spinal gate (1) if fast-conducting fibres get their message to the gate first or (2) if the brain itself inhibits their transmission.

What are endorphins?
Endorphins, released when we are stressed or injured, are the body's natural painkillers; they block pain and produce a feeling of well-being.

 THE SPATIAL ORIENTATION SENSES

What kind of information does the kinesthetic sense provide, and how is this sensory information detected?
The kinesthetic sense provides information about the position of body parts and movement in those body parts. The position or motion is detected by sensory receptors in the joints, ligaments, and muscles.

What is the vestibular sense, and where are its sensory receptors located?
The vestibular sense provides information about movement and our orientation in space. Sensory receptors in the semicircular canals and in the vestibular sacs detect changes in the movement and orientation of the head.

 PERCEPTION: WAYS OF PERCEIVING

What are the Gestalt principles of perceptual organization?
Gestalt principles of perceptual organization include the figure–ground relationship and four principles of perceptual grouping—similarity, proximity, continuity, and closure.

What is perceptual constancy, and what are its four types?

Perceptual constancy is the tendency to perceive objects as maintaining the same size, shape, brightness, and colour despite changes in lighting conditions or changes in the retinal image that result when objects are viewed from different angles and distances.

What are the binocular depth cues?

The binocular depth cues are convergence and binocular (or retinal) disparity; they depend on two eyes working together for depth perception.

What are the seven monocular depth cues?

The monocular depth cues—those that can be perceived by one eye—comprise interposition, linear perspective, relative size,

texture gradient, atmospheric perspective, shadow or shading, and motion parallax.

3H ADDITIONAL INFLUENCES ON PERCEPTION

In what types of situations do we rely more on bottom-up or top-down processing?

We use bottom-up processing more in unfamiliar situations; we use top-down processing more in situations in which we have some prior knowledge and experience.

SENSATION AND PERCEPTION

MODULE 3A SENSATION

Sensation is the process through which the senses detect visual, auditory, and other sensory stimuli and transmit them to the brain.

Transduction is the process by which sensory receptors convert sensory stimulation into neural impulses.

Measurement of the Senses
Absolute threshold: The minimum intensity of sensory stimulation required for a person to be able to detect it 50 percent of the time.
Difference threshold: The smallest increase or decrease in a physical stimulus required to produce a difference in sensation that is noticeable 50 percent of the time.
Signal detection theory: Detection of a stimulus involves both distinguishing the sensory stimulus from background "noise" and deciding that the stimulus is present.

MODULE 3B VISION

Major Structures of the Eye
Cornea: The transparent, protective outer covering of the eye; bends light rays inward.
Iris: The circular, coloured part of the eye. Two muscles in the iris regulate the amount of light entering the eye by dilating and contracting the pupil.
Pupil: The dark opening in the centre of the iris through which light passes.
Lens: The transparent structure behind the iris that focuses images on the retina.
Retina: The tissue at the back of the eye that contains the visual receptors.
Fovea: A small area of the retina that contains only cones and provides the sharpest, clearest vision.

The Visual Receptor Cells
Rods: The light-sensitive receptors that respond to black and white; provide for night vision and seeing in dim light.
Cones: The receptors that enable us to see colour and fine detail; do not function in dim light.

The Two Theories That Explain Colour Vision
Trichromatic theory states that colour vision is a function of three types of cones, which are maximally sensitive to red, green, or blue.
Opponent-process theory states that cells in the visual system increase or decrease their rate of firing when opposing colours are present.

Nearsightedness versus Farsightedness
• Hyperopia, or farsightedness, occurs when the lens focuses the image behind the retina (close objects appear blurred).
• Myopia, or nearsightedness, occurs when the lens focuses the image in front of the retina (distant objects appear blurred).

MODULE 3C HEARING

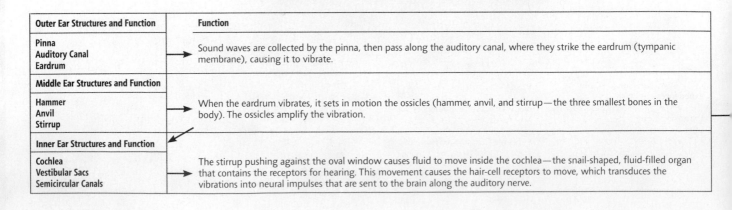

Outer Ear Structures and Function	Function
Pinna Auditory Canal Eardrum	Sound waves are collected by the pinna, then pass along the auditory canal, where they strike the eardrum (tympanic membrane), causing it to vibrate.
Middle Ear Structures and Function	
Hammer Anvil Stirrup	When the eardrum vibrates, it sets in motion the ossicles (hammer, anvil, and stirrup—the three smallest bones in the body). The ossicles amplify the vibration.
Inner Ear Structures and Function	
Cochlea Vestibular Sacs Semicircular Canals	The stirrup pushing against the oval window causes fluid to move inside the cochlea—the snail-shaped, fluid-filled organ that contains the receptors for hearing. This movement causes the hair-cell receptors to move, which transduces the vibrations into neural impulses that are sent to the brain along the auditory nerve.

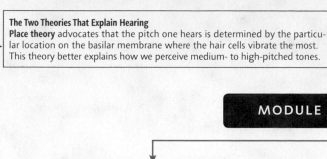

The Two Theories That Explain Hearing
Place theory advocates that the pitch one hears is determined by the particular location on the basilar membrane where the hair cells vibrate the most. This theory better explains how we perceive medium- to high-pitched tones.

Frequency theory posits that hair-cell receptors vibrate the same number of times per second as the sounds that reach them. This theory better explains how we perceive low-pitched tones.

MODULE 3D SMELL AND TASTE

Smell
Olfaction refers to the sensation of smell.
- Odour molecules first reach the smell receptors in the olfactory epithelium, located at the top of each nasal cavity.
- Smell messages are then routed to the two olfactory bulbs located above the nasal cavities, which relay the messages to different areas of the brain.

Taste
Gustation refers to the sensation of taste.
- The sensory receptors for taste are found within the taste buds. Receptor cells have a very short lifespan, continually being replaced every 10 days or so.
- The actual number of taste buds affects our taste ability, with supertasters having over four times as many taste buds as those with a reduced taste ability.

MODULE 3E THE SKIN SENSES

Tactile
- The skin is the largest sensory organ.
- Different parts of the body vary in their sensitivity to touch, with the thumb and fingers being the most sensitive and the calves the least.

Pain
Gate-control theory suggests that neural mechanisms in the spinal cord act as a gate that either inhibits pain messages or transmits them to the brain.

MODULE 3F THE SPATIAL ORIENTATION SENSES

Kinesthetic Sense
Provides information about positioning of body parts and about body-part movement. Receptors in the joints, ligaments, and muscles detect changes.

Vestibular Sense
Vestibular sense: Detects changes in motion (sense of balance) and provides information about one's orientation in space.
Semicircular canals and vestibular sacs: Provide information on head movements. Each canal is filled with fluid that moves whenever the head rotates, which causes the hair-cell receptors located within to bend, triggering neural impulses to be sent to the brain.

Endorphins
- Chemicals produced naturally by the brain that block pain and produce feelings of well-being.
- Injury, stress, acupuncture, and exercise are some factors that stimulate the release of endorphins.

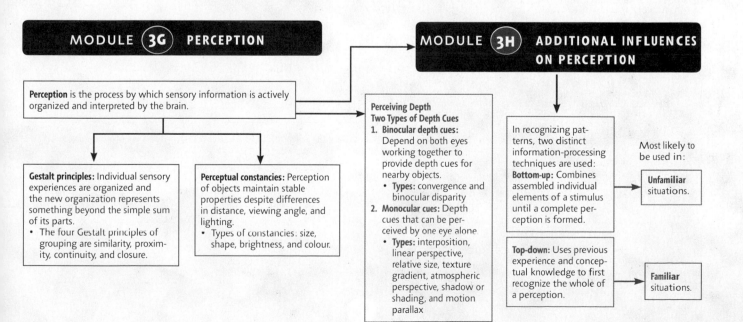

MODULE 3G PERCEPTION

MODULE 3H ADDITIONAL INFLUENCES ON PERCEPTION

Perception is the process by which sensory information is actively organized and interpreted by the brain.

Gestalt principles: Individual sensory experiences are organized and the new organization represents something beyond the simple sum of its parts.
- The four Gestalt principles of grouping are similarity, proximity, continuity, and closure.

Perceptual constancies: Perception of objects maintain stable properties despite differences in distance, viewing angle, and lighting.
- Types of constancies: size, shape, brightness, and colour.

Perceiving Depth
Two Types of Depth Cues
1. **Binocular depth cues:** Depend on both eyes working together to provide depth cues for nearby objects.
   - **Types:** convergence and binocular disparity
2. **Monocular cues:** Depth cues that can be perceived by one eye alone.
   - **Types:** interposition, linear perspective, relative size, texture gradient, atmospheric perspective, shadow or shading, and motion parallax

In recognizing patterns, two distinct information-processing techniques are used:
Bottom-up: Combines assembled individual elements of a stimulus until a complete perception is formed.

Top-down: Uses previous experience and conceptual knowledge to first recognize the whole of a perception.

Most likely to be used in:

Unfamiliar situations.

Familiar situations.

4

Have you ever awakened in the midst of a dream that was so good that you wished it could continue?

If so, then you might be interested to learn the steps involved in a technique that researchers have devised to study the controllability of dreams. Here are the steps:

1. Relax.
2. Close your eyes and focus on an imaginary spot in your field of vision.
3. Focus on your intention to control your dream.
4. Tell yourself that you're going to dream about whatever you want.
5. Imagine yourself having the dream that you are trying to create.
6. Repeat the steps until you fall asleep.

As you will learn later in the chapter, dreams may indeed be, at least to some degree, under conscious control. But what do we mean when we say "conscious" control? It stands to reason that psychologists need a working definition of *consciousness* before they can understand the processes, such as dreaming, that modify it. Thus, we begin our exploration of phenomena such as biological rhythms, sleep, meditation, and the brain's response to mind-altering substances with a discussion of states of awareness.

©Andrea Zanchi/E+/Getty Images

STATES OF CONSCIOUSNESS

Let's start with an important but complex question: "What does being *conscious* really mean?" Is consciousness nothing more than simply being awake? For example, have you driven to school only to realize that you have no recollection of the details of the drive? Certainly, you were awake, even aware enough to drive—so were you really conscious? Given the importance of our state of consciousness, it is surprising that our ability to define and explain consciousness is still imprecise. But we should not be surprised by how difficult it is to capture the meaning of *consciousness*—writers, philosophers, biologists, and psychologists have struggled for years to come up with a definition that fully captures the meaning of the term.

Early psychologists held widely varying views of the nature of consciousness. William James (1890) likened consciousness to a flowing stream that can be influenced by the level of attention one exerts on a specific issue, thought, or activity. Sigmund Freud (1900/1953a) emphasized the notion that not all actions or thoughts are necessarily driven by consciousness and that unconscious thoughts, emotions, or wishes can also influence a person's actions. Recently, psychologists have begun to examine the subjective experience of consciousness with objective observations of the brain through computerized axial tomography (CT scan) and the electroencephalograph (EEG) under states such as sleep, hypnosis, and the like (Dehaene, 2014).

For our purposes, we will define **consciousness** as it connects to our awareness. Consciousness is therefore defined as our awareness at any given time—our thoughts, feelings, sensations, and perceptions of the external environment. But this awareness can also vary in degree or focus. Consciousness is not an "all or nothing" process; we drift in and out of consciousness rapidly as the degree of focus we place on one event or thought comes and goes as quickly as we shift our attention to other issues.

Clearly, there are times during which we place all our attention on a specific issue. This is what happens when we are fully absorbed and our thoughts are fixed on the details of what we are concentrating on, whether it is our studies, a new skill, or a basketball game on TV. Other forms of attention are less effortful; for example, when we are daydreaming. And, of course, attention is even less effortful when we sleep. We will now explore the various states of consciousness and examine the many ways in which consciousness may be altered. Ordinary waking consciousness can be altered by substances—alcohol or drugs, for example—and by focused concentration such as in meditation and hypnosis. This chapter will explore these altered states of consciousness.

The most fundamental altered state is one in which we spend about one third of our lives, the one we visit for several hours nearly every night—sleep.

MODULE **4A** CIRCADIAN RHYTHMS: OUR 24-HOUR HIGHS AND LOWS

LO 4.1 Define *circadian rhythms* and explain how they influence sleep.

LO 4.2 Explain the importance of the suprachiasmatic nucleus.

LO 4.3 Describe the problems associated with shift work.

What is a circadian rhythm, and which rhythms are most relevant to the study of sleep?

Do you notice changes in the way you feel throughout the day—fluctuations in your energy level, mood, or efficiency? These daily fluctuations, called **circadian rhythms**, are controlled largely by the brain and play a critical role in the timing of life-sustaining processes in virtually all organisms, from humans and other vertebrates to plants, and even single-cell life forms (Rea, Bierman, Figueiro, & Bullough, 2000). Blood pressure, heart rate, appetite, secretion of hormones and digestive enzymes, sensory acuity, elimination, and even our body's responses to medication all follow circadian rhythms (Morofushi, Shionohara, & Kimura, 2001). Moreover, the circadian timing system is involved in the 24-hour variation of virtually every physiological and psychological variable researchers have studied (Kunz & Herrmann, 2000). **[LO 4.1]**

Sleep is mostly influenced by two important factors that vary according to circadian patterns—alertness and body temperature. Normal human body temperature can range from a low of about 36.1 degrees Celsius between 4:00 and 5:00 a.m. to a high of about 37 degrees Celsius between 5:00 and 8:00 p.m. People sleep best when their body temperature is lowest, and they are most alert when their body temperature is at its daily high point (Monk, 2012). Alertness also follows a circadian rhythm, one that is quite separate from the sleep/wakefulness rhythm (Monk, 2012). For most of us, alertness decreases between 2:00 and 5:00 p.m. and between 2:00 and 7:00 a.m. (Mitler, Aldrich, Koob, & Zarcone, 1994; Webb, 1995). During the afternoon decrease in alertness, body temperature also dips.

Note that circadian rhythms are not the only types of biological rhythms that influence our lives. In nature, rhythms occur at very short or much longer regular intervals and are influenced by a variety of factors, including the moon, the seasons, and various biological factors. Aside from circadian rhythms, ultradian and infradian rhythms are most relevant to human life. *Ultradian rhythms* are biological patterns that occur more than once a day. Hunger patterns, for example, occur several times a day at roughly regular intervals. Eyeblinks and heartbeats are other examples of ultradian patterns. By contrast, *infradian rhythms* have a cycle that exceeds a 24-hour pattern. The female menstrual cycle is an example of an infradian rhythm.

THE SUPRACHIASMATIC NUCLEUS: THE BODY'S TIMEKEEPER

What is the suprachiasmatic nucleus?

So, what part of our brain acts as a biological clock? Studies suggest that it is a tiny piece of brain tissue smaller than the head of a pin located in the hypothalamus called the **suprachiasmatic nucleus (SCN)** located in the brain's hypothalamus (Buhr & Takahashi, 2013). The suprachiasmatic nucleus responds to the amount of light, particularly sunlight (Wright et al., 2013), reaching the eye and then transferred via the optic nerve. **[LO 4.2]** Specialized cells in the retina, called *photoreceptors*, respond to the amount of light reaching the eye and relay this information via the optic nerve to the suprachiasmatic nucleus.

The SCN acts on this information by signalling the pineal gland, located in the centre of the brain. In response, the pineal gland secretes the hormone melatonin from dusk until shortly before dawn but does not secrete it during daylight (Cajochen, Chellappa, & Schmidt, 2010). Melatonin induces sleep, perhaps through its ability to keep all of the body's tissues aware of both the time of day and the time of year (Benarroch, 2008).

But light is not the only factor that influences our biological clock. In normal circumstances, external stimuli—day and night, alarm clocks, job or school demands—cause us to modify our biological clock to a 24-hour schedule. Circadian rhythms are slightly disrupted each year when daylight saving time begins and ends. An even greater disruption occurs when people fly across a number of time zones or when they work rotating shifts.

JET LAG: WHERE AM I AND WHAT TIME IS IT?

Suppose you fly from Toronto to Paris, and the plane lands at midnight Toronto time, about the time you usually go to sleep. When it is midnight in Toronto, it is 6:00 a.m. in Paris, almost time to get up. Everything in Paris, including the clocks and the sun, tells you it is early morning, but you still feel as though it is midnight. You are experiencing jet lag.

The problem is not simply the result of losing a night's sleep. You are fighting your own biological clock, which is synchronized with your usual time zone and not the time zone you are visiting (Sack, 2009). It is difficult to sleep when your biological clock is telling you to wake up and feel alert. It is even harder to remain awake and alert when your internal clock is telling you to sleep. Travellers can prevent jet lag to some degree by slowly advancing their sleep schedules about an hour a day for several days before they leave home (Eastman, Gazda, Burgess, Crowley, & Fogg, 2005). Exposure to bright sunlight during the early morning and avoidance of bright lights during the evening may be an effective strategy to restore regular circadian rhythms (Serkh & Forger, 2014). Of course, such strategies can't be employed by all travellers, especially those who travel long distances within relatively short time spans. For instance, a flight attendant might cross several time zones within a period of just a couple of days. For these travellers, exposure to bright sunlight during the early morning hours and avoidance of bright lights during the evening, along with melatonin supplements, may restore circadian rhythms (Sack et al., 2007). However, chronic jet lag, such as that experienced by many airline pilots and flight attendants, can produce memory deficits that may be permanent (Gibson et al., 2010).

SHIFT WORK: WORKING DAY AND NIGHT

What are some problems experienced by employees who work rotating shifts?

According to Statistics Canada (2008), over 4 million workers aged 19 to 64 worked something other than a regular day shift in 2005. Of these shift workers, about 3.3 million worked full-time. Rotating shifts and irregular schedules were the most common types of shift work, accounting for 2.3 million full-time workers. Service workers, including those employed in

What are the physical and psychological effects of disturbing the normal sleep/wakefulness cycle when a person works the night shift?

©Reza Estakhrian/The Image Bank/Getty Images

sales, health care, and police and fire departments, are more likely to do shift work. When people must work at night, they experience a disruption in the rhythms of many bodily functions that are normally synchronized for daytime, which can cause a variety of physical and psychological problems. **[LO 4.3]**

The 2008 report by Statistics Canada indicates that shift workers are more likely to cut back on sleep, to spend less time with their spouse, and to worry about not spending enough time with family, compared with regular day workers. Other studies indicate that shift workers average two to four hours less sleep per night than non-shift workers of the same age, and also report more gastrointestinal and cardiovascular problems, use more prescription drugs, have more emotional exhaustion and mood problems, and have higher divorce rates than non-shift workers (Vogel et al., 2012). People who work on permanent afternoon shifts also suffer the negative consequences associated with shift work (Barnes-Farrell et al., 2008). The negative impact of shift work may last for months or even years after shift work ends (Rouch, Wild, Ansiau, & Marquié, 2005).

consciousness: The continuous stream of thoughts, feelings, sensations, and perceptions of which we are aware from moment to moment.

altered states of consciousness: Mental states other than ordinary waking consciousness, such as sleep, meditation, hypnosis, or a drug-induced state.

circadian rhythms (sur-KAY-dee-un): Within each 24-hour period, the regular fluctuations from high to low points of a bodily function, such as sleep/wakefulness.

suprachiasmatic nucleus (SCN): A tiny structure in the brain's hypothalamus that controls the timing of circadian rhythms; often referred to as the *biological clock*.

What about performance on the job? Alertness and performance deteriorate if people work during **subjective night**, when their biological clock is telling them to go to sleep (Mullins, Cortina, Drake, & Dalal, 2014). During subjective night, energy and efficiency reach their lowest point, reaction time is slowest, productivity is diminished and, in the long run, job stress increases (Jamal, 2004).

Aside from the psychological and performance-related effects of shift work, much recent research has shown that shift work significantly increases the risk of physical injury (Wong, McLeod, & Demers, 2011). Many air, rail, marine, and highway accidents have occurred when the shift workers in charge suffered sleep loss and fatigue because of the disruption of their circadian rhythms (Philip et al., 2014). University of British Columbia psychologist Stanley Coren has demonstrated that even the one-hour sleep loss we experience when we put our clocks forward in the spring for daylight saving time is associated with a significant increase in traffic accidents and deaths (Coren, 1996a, 1996b, 1997).

Can anything be done to make shift rotation less disruptive? While all forms of shift work are problematic, it appears that rotating shifts, simultaneous use of timed bright light and light-blocking glasses, as well as health-related strategies such as increased physical activity and a healthy diet, all have positive impacts on the health of shift workers (Neil-Sztramko, Pahwa, Demers, & Gotay, 2014). Other studies have shown that brief nap periods during each shift to help sleepy workers adjust to rotating shifts (Ruggiero, 2014) or having a night shift that does not encompass the entire night period (Hossain et al., 2004). Others are investigating the use of a new wakefulness drug called modafinil, which helps people remain alert without the side effects of stimulants (Roth, 2012).

Light exposure is another important factor in understanding the effects of shift work. Some researchers have used a device called a *light mask* to reset shift workers' biological clocks. These masks allow researchers to control the amount of light to which the closed eyelids of research participants are exposed. The findings of studies using light masks suggest that exposing participants to bright light during the last four hours of sleep is an effective treatment for the kinds of sleep problems experienced by shift workers (R. J. Cole, Smith, Alcala, Elliott, & Kripke, 2002).

REMEMBER IT

Circadian Rhythms

1. Which of the following best defines *consciousness*?
   a. awareness
   b. wakefulness
   c. receptiveness
   d. rationality

2. The two circadian rhythms most relevant to the study of sleep are the sleep/wakefulness cycle and
   a. blood pressure.
   b. secretion of hormones.
   c. body temperature.
   d. heart rate.

3. We sleep best when our body temperature is at the low point in our 24-hour cycle. (true/false)

4. Which is not characteristic of people who work rotating shifts?
   a. disturbed sleep
   b. digestive problems
   c. increased efficiency and alertness during subjective night
   d. greater use of caffeine, alcohol, and sleeping pills

Answers: 1. a 2. c 3. true 4. c

MODULE **4B** **SLEEP: THAT MYSTERIOUS ONE THIRD OF OUR LIVES**

LO 4.4 Define and compare *NREM* and *REM sleep*.
LO 4.5 Describe the pattern of sleep cycles.
LO 4.6 Explain how age influences sleep.
LO 4.7 Define *larks* and *owls* and describe their different sleep patterns.
LO 4.8 Describe the function of sleep and how sleep deprivation affects functioning.
LO 4.9 Compare REM and NREM dreams.

Over a lifetime, a person spends about 25 years sleeping. For decades, sleep researchers argued about the function of sleep. Some believed sleep simply served a restorative function; others argued that sleep evolved to keep animals out of harm's way. But neither of these theories alone accounts for many of the research findings about sleep. For example, if you miss a night's sleep, why are you very sleepy during the middle of the night but less so the next day? Today most sleep researchers believe that sleep should be viewed as a circadian rhythm that, in part, serves to restore energy and consolidate memory (Diekelmann & Born, 2010). This view accommodates the variety of findings about sleep that we will explore in the following pages.

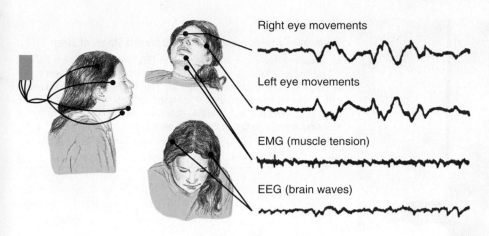

Right eye movements

Left eye movements

EMG (muscle tension)

EEG (brain waves)

FIGURE 4.1

How Researchers Study Sleeping Participants

Researchers study participants in a sleep laboratory or sleep clinic by taping electrodes to the participant's head to monitor brainwave activity, eye movements, and muscle tension.

Source: After Dement, W.C. (1974). Some must watch while some must sleep. San Francisco: W.H. Freeman.

NREM AND REM SLEEP: WATCHING THE EYES

Before the 1950s there was no scientific understanding of what goes on during the state of consciousness we call sleep. Then, in the 1950s, several universities set up sleep laboratories where people's brainwaves, eye movements, chin-muscle tension, heart rate, and respiration rate were monitored through a night of sleep. From the data they gathered, researchers discovered that there are two major categories of sleep: NREM (non-rapid eye movement) sleep and REM (rapid eye movement) sleep. Figure 4.1 shows a sleep research participant whose brain activity, eye movement, and chin-muscle activity are being recorded.

NREM Sleep: From Light to Deep Sleep in Stages

How does a sleeper act physically during NREM sleep?

NREM sleep (pronounced NON-rem) is the sleep in which there is no rapid eye movement. It is often called *quiet sleep* because heart rate and respiration are slow and regular, there is little body movement, and blood pressure and brain activity are at their lowest points of the 24-hour period. **[LO 4.4]**

There are four stages of NREM sleep, with Stage 1 being the lightest sleep and Stage 4 being the deepest. We pass gradually rather than abruptly from one stage to the next. Each stage can be identified by its brainwave pattern, as shown in Figure 4.2, on the next page. Growth hormone is secreted mainly during Stage 3 and Stage 4 sleep (Feinberg, 2000).

REM Sleep: Rapid Eye Movement and Dreams

How does the body respond physically during REM sleep?

Most of us envision sleep as a time of deep relaxation and calm. But **REM sleep**, sometimes called *active sleep*, is anything but calm, and it constitutes 20 to 25 percent of a normal night's sleep in adults. During the REM state, there is intense brain activity, and our body reacts as if to a daytime emergency. Epinephrine (adrenalin) shoots into the system, blood pressure rises, heart rate and respiration become faster and irregular, and brain temperature increases (J. M. Krueger & Takahashi, 1997). In contrast to this storm of internal activity, there is an external calm during REM sleep. The large muscles of the body—arms, legs, trunk—become paralyzed (Chase & Morales, 1990). And if you awaken during REM sleep, you may not go back into this kind of sleep for at least 30 minutes. This is why most people have experienced the disappointment of waking up in the middle of a wonderful dream and then trying to get back to sleep quickly and into the dream again but being unable to do so.

If you observe a sleeper during the REM state, you can see the eyes darting around under the eyelids. Eugene Azerinsky discovered these bursts of rapid eye movement in 1952. Five years later, William Dement and Nathaniel Kleitman made the connection between rapid eye movement and dreaming. It is during REM periods that most of our vivid dreams occur. When awakened from REM sleep, 80 percent of people report dreaming (Carskadon & Dement, 1989), and reports of visual imagery are more frequent than if someone is awakened from any other stages of sleep (Desseilles et al., 2011).

subjective night: The time during a 24-hour period when people's body temperature is lowest and their biological clock tells them to go to sleep.

NREM sleep (NON-rem): Non-rapid eye movement sleep, consisting of the four sleep stages and characterized by slow, regular respiration and heart rate, an absence of rapid eye movement, and blood pressure and brain activity that are at a 24-hour low point.

REM sleep: Sleep characterized by rapid eye movement, paralysis of large muscles, fast and irregular heart rate and respiration rate, increased brainwave activity, and vivid dreams.

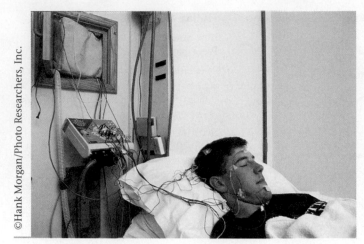

FIGURE 4.2

Brainwave Patterns Associated with Different Stages of Sleep

By monitoring brainwave activity with the EEG throughout a night's sleep, researchers have identified the brainwave patterns associated with different stages of sleep. As sleepers progress through the four NREM stages, the brainwave pattern changes from faster, low-voltage waves in Stages 1 and 2 to the slower, larger delta waves in Stages 3 and 4. Notice that the brainwave activity during REM sleep is similar to that of the subject when awake.

Source: After Hobson, J.A. (1989). Sleep. New York: Scientific American Library. Holt, Henry & Company, Inc. The Macmillan Group.

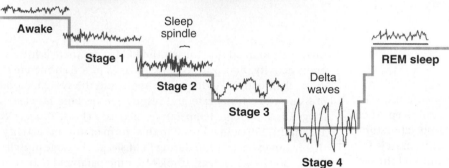

SLEEP CYCLES: THE NIGHTLY PATTERN OF SLEEP

What is the progression of NREM stages and REM sleep that a person goes through in a typical night of sleep?

Many people are surprised to learn that sleep follows a fairly predictable pattern each night. We sleep in cycles. During each **sleep cycle**, which lasts about 90 minutes, we have one or more stages of NREM sleep followed by a period of REM sleep. Let us go through a typical night of sleep for a young adult (see Figure 4.3). **[LO 4.5]**

The first sleep cycle begins with a few minutes in Stage 1 sleep, sometimes called *light sleep*. Stage 1 is actually a transition stage between waking and sleeping. Then sleepers descend into Stage 2 sleep, in which they are somewhat more deeply asleep and harder to awaken. About 50 percent of the total night's sleep is spent in Stage 2 sleep. Next, sleepers enter Stage 3 sleep, the beginning of **slow-wave sleep** (or *deep sleep*). As sleep gradually becomes deeper, brain activity slows and more **delta waves** (*slow waves*) appear in the EEG. When there are more than 50 percent delta waves on the EEG, people are said to be in **Stage 4 sleep**, the deepest sleep, when people are hardest to awaken

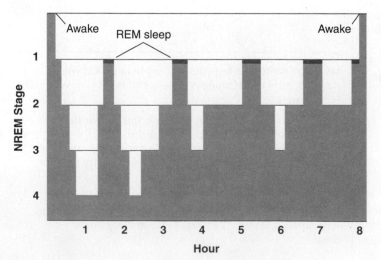

FIGURE 4.3

The Typical Composition of Sleep Cycles for Young Adults

A typical night's sleep for young adults consists of about five sleep cycles of about 90 minutes each. Stage 4 sleep occurs during the first two sleep cycles. People spend progressively more time in REM sleep with each succeeding 90-minute cycle.

Source: After Hartmann, E. (1967). The biology of dreaming. Springfield, IL: Charles C. Thomas.

(Traub & Whittington, 2014). Perhaps you have taken an afternoon nap and awakened confused, not knowing whether it was morning or night, a weekday or a weekend. If so, you probably awakened during Stage 4 sleep.

After about 40 minutes in Stage 4 sleep, brain activity increases and the delta waves begin to disappear from the EEG. Sleepers make an ascent back through Stage 3 and Stage 2 sleep, then enter the first REM period of the night, which lasts 10 or 15 minutes. At the end of this REM period, the first sleep cycle is complete, and the second sleep cycle begins. Unless people awaken after the first sleep cycle, they go directly from REM sleep into Stage 2 sleep. They then follow the same progression as in the first sleep cycle, through Stages 3 and 4 and back again into REM sleep.

After the first two sleep cycles of about 90 minutes each (three hours in total), the sleep pattern changes and sleepers usually get no more Stage 4 sleep. From this point on, during each 90-minute sleep cycle, people alternate mainly between Stage 2 and REM sleep for the remainder of the night. With each sleep cycle, the REM periods (the "dreaming times") get progressively longer. By the end of the night, REM periods may be 30 to 40 minutes long. In a night, most people sleep about five sleep cycles (7.5 to 8 hours) and get about 1.5 hours of slow-wave sleep and 1.5 hours of REM sleep.

INDIVIDUAL DIFFERENCES IN SLEEP PATTERNS: HOW WE DIFFER

There are great individual variations in sleep patterns. The major factor contributing to these variations is age.

The Older We Get, the Less We Sleep

How do sleep patterns change over the lifespan?

Which age group sleeps the greatest number of hours per day? Most people think it's teenagers, but infants and young children have the longest sleep time and highest percentage of REM and deep sleep. Children in middle childhood, between age six and puberty, are the champion sleepers and wakers. **[LO 4.6]** They fall asleep easily, sleep soundly for 8.5 to 9 hours at night, and feel awake and alert during the day. Between puberty and the end of adolescence, teenagers average about 7.6 hours of sleep, with older teens getting less than 7 hours of sleep per day (National Sleep Foundation, 2006). But regardless of their age, most teens would need about two hours more to be as alert as they should for school (National Sleep Foundation, 2006).

As people age, they usually experience a decrease in quality and quantity of sleep (Wolkove, Elkholy, Baltzan, & Palayew, 2007). Some researchers hypothesize that the decline is due to a reduction in the need for sleep that is a part of the natural aging process (Klerman & Dijk, 2008). Even among older people, those who are above the age of 75 report worse sleep than those between 65 and 74 (C. S. McCrea et al., 2008). Older people have more difficulty falling asleep, and they typically have lighter sleep and more and longer awakenings than younger people (Tel, 2013). They spend more time awake in bed but less time asleep, averaging about 6.5 hours of sleep (Prinz, Vitiello, Raskind, & Thorpy, 1990). **[LO 4.6]**

Their percentage of REM sleep, however, stays about the same (Floyd et al., 2007).

Larks and Owls: Early to Rise and Late to Bed

Some people awaken early every morning and leap out of bed with enthusiasm, eager to start the day. Others fumble for the alarm clock and push in the snooze button to get a few more precious minutes of sleep. Sleep researchers have names for these two types—*larks* and *owls*—and there is a physical explanation for the differences in how they feel. **[LO 4.7]** About 25 percent of people are larks—people whose body temperature rises rapidly after they awaken and stays high until about 7:30 p.m. Larks turn in early and have the fewest sleep problems. Then there are the 25 percent who are owls and the 50 percent who are somewhere in between. The body temperature of an owl rises gradually throughout the day, peaking in the afternoon and not dropping until later in the evening. It is not surprising that larks have more difficulty than owls in adapting to night shifts. They are sleepier during their subjective night and are more likely to complain of difficulty sleeping (Vetter, Juda, & Roenneberg, 2012). Differences in one or more of the genes that run the biological clock are responsible, in part, for the differences between larks and owls (Barclay, Eley, Buysse, Archer, & Gregory, 2010).

REM SLEEP: A PART OF SLEEP THAT WE SHOULD NOT DO WITHOUT

Sleep Deprivation: How Does It Affect Us?

What is the longest you have ever stayed awake—one day, two days, three days, or four days? According to the *Guinness Book of World Records*, Californian Robert McDonald stayed awake 453 hours and 40 minutes (almost 19 days) in a 1986 rocking-chair marathon. Unlike McDonald, most of us have missed no more than a few consecutive nights of sleep, perhaps while studying for final exams. If you have ever missed two or three nights of sleep, you may remember having experienced difficulty concentrating, lapses in attention, and general irritability. After 60 hours without sleep, some people have minor hallucinations. Even the rather small amount of sleep deprivation associated with delaying your bedtime on weekends leads to decreases in cognitive performance on Monday morning (Chee et al., 2008). Most people who try to stay awake for long periods of time will have

---

sleep cycle: A cycle of sleep lasting about 90 minutes and including one or more stages of NREM sleep followed by a period of REM sleep.

slow-wave sleep: Stage 3 and 4 sleep; deep sleep.

delta waves: The slowest brainwaves, having a frequency of 1 to 3 cycles per second and associated with slow-wave (deep) sleep.

Stage 4 sleep: The deepest NREM stage of sleep, characterized by an EEG pattern of more than 50 percent delta waves.

microsleeps, two- to three-second lapses from wakefulness into sleep. You may have experienced a microsleep if you have ever caught yourself nodding off for a few seconds in class or on a long automobile trip.

Researchers have known for some time that sleep deprivation impairs a variety of cognitive functions, such as the retrieval of recently learned information from memory, in both children and adults (Sadeh, Gruber, & Raviv, 2003). But do not despair if you are one of these people who tends to wake up often during the night, as this will not reduce your alertness the next day. **[LO 4.8]**

When people are deprived of REM sleep as a result of general sleep loss, illness, or too much alcohol (or other drugs), their bodies will make up for the loss by getting an increased amount of REM sleep after the deprivation (Suchecki, Tiba, & Machado, 2012). This increase in the percentage of REM sleep to make up for REM deprivation is called a **REM rebound.** Because the intensity of REM sleep is increased during a REM rebound, nightmares often occur. But why do we need REM sleep?

The Function of REM Sleep: Necessary, but Why?

The fact that newborns have such a high percentage of REM sleep has led to the conclusion that REM sleep is necessary for maturation of the brain in infants.

Recent research has shown that REM sleep aids in information processing, helping people sift through daily experiences in order to organize and store in memory information that is relevant to them (M. Walker & Stickgold, 2006). **[LO 4.8]** Karni and colleagues (Karni, Tanne, Rubenstein, Askenasy, & Sagi, 1994) found that research participants learning a new perceptual skill showed an improvement in performance, with no additional practice, 8 to 10 hours later if they had a normal night's sleep or if only their NREM sleep was disturbed. Performance did not improve, however, in those who were deprived of REM sleep. Naps that are long enough to include both slow-wave and REM sleep also appear to enhance learning (Nishida, Pearsall, Buckner, & Walker, 2008).

DREAMING: MYSTERIOUS MENTAL ACTIVITY WHILE WE SLEEP

How do REM and NREM dreams differ?

Whether or not you remember them when you wake up, all of us have dreams during a regular night's sleep. Not surprisingly, people have always been fascinated by dreams. The vivid dreams we remember and talk about are **REM dreams**—the type that occur almost continuously during each REM period. But people also have **NREM dreams,** which occur during NREM sleep (Foulkes, 1996). REM dreams have a storylike or surreal quality and are more visual, vivid, emotional, and likely to include aggressive behaviour perpetrated by and against the dreamer than NREM dreams do (McNamara, McLaren, & Durso, 2007). **[LO 4.9]**

Have you ever heard that an entire dream takes place in an instant? Do you find that hard to believe? In fact, it is not

What do we dream about? REM dreams have a storylike quality and are more visual, vivid, and emotional than NREM dreams.

true. Sleep researchers have discovered that it takes about as long to dream a dream as it would to experience the same thing in real life (Kleitman, 1960). Let's take a closer look at the dream state.

Dream Memories: We Remember Only a Few

Very few dreams are memorable enough to be retained very long—roughly 10 minutes—and what tends to stand out are those parts that are bizarre or emotional. Sleep researchers have learned that sleepers have the best recall of a dream if they are awakened during the dream; the more time that passes after the dream ends, the poorer the recall (Kleitman, 1960). Perhaps the reason for the quick loss of memory is that human brain chemistry during sleep appears to differ from that in the waking state and does not facilitate the storing of memories (Hobson et al., 2000). Research now suggests that different neurotransmitters are dominant in the cortex during wakefulness and during REM sleep (Gottesmann, 2000, 2008); this difference may explain why we are anchored in reality when awake and more likely to have impulsive thoughts and show intense brain activity when dreaming.

The Content of Dreams: Bizarre or Commonplace?

In general, what have researchers found regarding the content of dreams?

What do we dream about? Do your dreams often seem very strange? This isn't really surprising. Because dreams are notoriously hard to remember, the features that stand out tend to be those that are bizarre or emotional. Indeed, individuals who suffer from delusional disorders, such as schizophrenia, report more bizarre dreams than do individuals without such disorders (van der Kloet, Merckelbach, Giesbrecht, & Lynn, 2012; D. Watson, 2001). However, researchers don't know whether the dreams of people with these mental illnesses really are more bizarre or if their disorders cause them to focus more on the dreams' bizarre qualities.

TRY IT

What's in Your Dreams?

Read this list of 20 common dream themes. Check each one you have dreamed about.

_____ Being chased or pursued, not physically injured
_____ Sexual experiences
_____ Falling
_____ School, teachers, studying
_____ Arriving too late (e.g., missing a train)
_____ Being on the verge of falling
_____ Trying repeatedly to do something
_____ A person now alive as dead (death of a loved one)
_____ Flying or soaring through the air
_____ Vividly sensing a presence in the room
_____ Failing an examination
_____ Being physically attacked (beaten, stabbed, raped)
_____ Being frozen with fright
_____ A person now dead as alive
_____ Being a child again
_____ Being killed
_____ Insects or spiders

_____ Swimming
_____ Being nude in public
_____ Being inappropriately dressed

©Minerva Studio/Fotolia

TABLE 4.1 Common Dream Themes

These are the most common dream themes reported by 1348 Canadian university students and the percentage of students having each type of dream.

Type of Dream	Percentage of Students
Chased or pursued, not physically injured	82
Sexual experiences	77
Falling	74
School, teachers, studying	67
Arriving too late, e.g., missing a train	60
Being on the verge of falling	58
Trying repeatedly to do something	54
A person now alive as dead	54
Flying or soaring through the air	48
Vividly sensing a presence in the room	48
Failing an examination	45
Physically attacked (beaten, stabbed, raped)	42
Being frozen with fright	41
A person now dead as alive	38
Being a child again	37
Being killed	35
Insects or spiders	34
Swimming	34
Being nude in public	33
Being inappropriately dressed	33

Source: Based on Nielsen et al., 2003. Based on Nielsen,T.A; Zadrs,A.L; Simard,V; Saucier,S; Stenstrom,P; Smith,C; & Kuiken,D. (2003). The typical dreams of Canadian university students. Dreaming, 13(4), 211–235.

Table 4.1 reports the results of a study that lists the most common dream themes among 1348 Canadians enrolled in first-year university. Compare the results of your dream themes in _Try It_ with the results of the study shown in Table 4.1.

Some people are troubled by unpleasant recurring dreams. The two most common themes involve falling or being chased, threatened, or attacked (Nielsen et al., 2003). Recent research suggests that dream themes differ somewhat for women and men (Schredl & Reinhard, 2008). Aggressive themes as well as references to tool usage and street scenes are more frequent for men, whereas women's dreams include more frequent references to clothing, friendly interactions, and animals.

Is there anything that can be done to prevent frightening recurring dreams? Doing so may be important since people who have such dreams seem to experience a greater number

microsleeps: Momentary lapses from wakefulness into sleep, usually occurring when one has been sleep-deprived.

REM rebound: The increased amount of REM sleep that occurs after REM deprivation; often associated with unpleasant dreams or nightmares.

REM dreams: The type of dream that occurs almost continuously during each REM period; more vivid, visual, emotional, and bizarre than NREM dreams, with a surreal, storylike quality.

NREM dreams: Mental activity occurring during NREM sleep that is more thoughtlike in quality than are REM dreams.

of minor physical complaints, greater stress, and more anxiety and depression than other people do (Soffer-Dudek, Shalev, Shiber, & Shahar, 2011). As you learned at the beginning of the chapter, researchers have devised procedures designed to control dreams, so you won't be surprised to learn that some people have been taught to deliberately control dream content in order to stop unwanted, recurrent dreams. Some researchers (Laberge, 2014) argue that dreaming while exerting control over one's dreams, called **lucid dreams**, is a learnable skill that can be perfected with regular practice. Research suggests that individuals who are good at controlling their thoughts when awake are also successful at lucid dreaming (Blagrove & Hartnell, 2000).

Interpreting Dreams: Are There Hidden Meanings in Our Dreams?

Sigmund Freud believed that dreams function to satisfy unconscious sexual and aggressive wishes. Because such wishes are unacceptable to the dreamer, they have to be disguised and therefore appear in dreams in symbolic form. Freud (1900/1953a) asserted that objects like sticks, umbrellas, tree trunks, and guns symbolize the male sex organ; objects like chests, cupboards, and boxes represent the female sex organ. Freud differentiated between the manifest content of the dream—the dream as recalled by the dreamer—and the underlying meaning of the dream, called the latent content, which he considered more significant.

In recent years there has been a major shift away from the Freudian interpretation of dreams. The greater focus now is on the manifest content—the actual dream itself—rather than on the search for symbols that can be decoded to reveal some inner conflict. The symbols in dreams, when analyzed, are now perceived as being specific to the individual rather than as having standard or universal meanings for all dreamers.

J. Allan Hobson (1988) rejects the notion that nature would equip us with a capability and a need to dream dreams that only a specialist could interpret. Hobson and McCarley (1977) advanced the activation-synthesis hypothesis of dreaming. This hypothesis suggests that dreams are simply the brain's attempt to make sense of the random firing of brain cells during REM sleep.

However, contemporary research on dreams now contradicts the view that the content of dreams emerges from random signals. Brain-imaging studies suggest that several brain structures such as the hypocampus and the amygdala play important roles in dream activity (Nielsen & Stenstrom, 2005). Studies of dream content also confirm that the content of dreams generally shows a good deal of continuity with the overall concerns of dreamers (Domhoff, 2005).

REMEMBER IT

Sleep

1. State the type of sleep—NREM or REM—that corresponds to each characteristic.
   _____ 1) paralysis of large muscles
   _____ 2) slow, regular respiration and heart rate
   _____ 3) rapid eye movement
   _____ 4) penile erection and vaginal swelling
   _____ 5) vivid dreams
       a. REM
       b. NREM

2. Match the age group with the appropriate description of sleep.
   _____ 1) have most difficulty sleeping; most awakenings
   _____ 2) sleep best at night; feel best during day
   _____ 3) have highest percentage of REM and deep sleep
   _____ 4) are usually sleepy during the day regardless of the amount of sleep at night
       a. infancy and early childhood
       b. middle childhood
       c. adolescence
       d. old age

3. Which type of sleep seems to aid in learning and memory in humans and other animals?
   a. Stage 1
   b. Stage 2
   c. Stages 3 and 4
   d. REM sleep

4. Compared with REM dreams, NREM dreams are
   a. more emotional.
   b. more visual.
   c. more thoughtlike.
   d. more confusing.

Answers: 1 (1). a (2). b (3). a (4). a (5). a 2 (1). d (2). b (3). a (4). c 3. d 4. c

LO 4.10 Describe the factors that influence how much sleep we need.

LO 4.11 Define *parasomnia*.

LO 4.12 Describe and compare the different types of parasomnia.

LO 4.13 Describe and compare the different types of major sleep disorder.

VARIATIONS IN SLEEP

What factors influence our sleep needs?

Perhaps you have wondered how much sleep you need in order to feel good, and perhaps you are hoping to find the answer in this chapter. When it comes to sleep, the expression "one size fits all" does *not* apply. Although adults average about 7.5 hours of sleep daily, with an extra hour on weekends, this is too much for some people and too little for others. *Short sleepers* are the 20 percent who require fewer than six hours; *long sleepers* are the 10 percent who require more than nine. There seems to be a limit below which most of us cannot go. In one study, not a single participant could get by with less than 4.5 hours of sleep. It seems that 6.5 hours is the minimum for most people. **[LO 4.10]**

What accounts for the large variation in the need for sleep? Genetics appears to play a part. **[LO 4.10]** Identical twins, for example, have strikingly similar sleep patterns compared with fraternal twins (Genderson et al., 2013). But genetics aside, people need more sleep when they are depressed, under stress, or experiencing significant life changes such as changing jobs or schools. Increases in mental, physical, or emotional effort also increase our need for sleep (Hartmann, 1973). Contrary to popular opinion, the amount of activity required in an occupation does not affect the amount of sleep a person needs. **[LO 4.10]**

Do most people sleep enough? The answer is no, according to data from a number of North American studies. In fact, more than 36 percent of the population is chronically sleep deprived (Ferrara & De Gennaro, 2001). This pattern may be even worse for adolescents. A 2006 Canadian study revealed that 70 percent of the students in the sample were mildly to severely sleep deprived (E. S. Gibson et al., 2006). The National Sleep Foundation in the United States recommends between eight and nine hours of sleep for most teens and young and middle-aged adults (National Sleep Foundation, 2006).

PARASOMNIAS: UNUSUAL BEHAVIOURS DURING SLEEP

So far our discussion has centred on a typical night for a typical sleeper. While the exact numbers are difficult to confirm, it is estimated that as many as 20 percent of North Americans have sleep disturbances (NINDS, 2014). Sleep problems range from mild to severe and from problems that affect only sleep to those that affect a person's entire life.

Parasomnias are sleep disturbances in which behaviours and physiological states that normally occur only in the waking state take place during sleep or during the transition from

©Esbin Anderson/ The Image Works

How much sleep does the average person need? Probably more than he or she gets. And a temporary increase in mental activity can increase the need for sleep. Because sleep plays such an important role in our cognitive and emotional well-being, researchers have devoted much attention to the impact of sleep disorders.

sleep to wakefulness (Schenk & Mahowald, 2000). **[LO 4.11]** Sleepwalking and sleep terrors are two parasomnias that occur during Stage 4 sleep and in which the sleeper does not come to full consciousness (Ackroyd, D'Cruz, & Sharp, 2007).

Sleepwalking and Sleep Terrors

What are the characteristics of sleepwalking and sleep terrors?

Sleepwalking (**somnambulism**) and sleep terrors are parasomnias that often run in families (Dement, 1974). Typically, there is no memory of the episode the following day (Moldofsky, Gilbert, Lue, & MacLean, 1995). Most cases begin in childhood and are attributed primarily to a delayed development of the nervous system (Nevsimalova et al., 2013). The disturbances are usually outgrown by adolescence, and treatment is generally not advised. If the problems persist, however, or develop later in

lucid dreams: Dreams during which the dreamer is aware of dreaming; the dreamer is often able to influence the content of a lucid dream while it is in progress.

parasomnias: Sleep disturbances in which behaviours and physiological states that normally occur only in the waking state take place during sleep or the transition from sleep to wakefulness (e.g., sleepwalking, sleep terrors).

somnambulism (som-NAM-bue-lism): Sleepwalking that occurs during a partial arousal from Stage 4 sleep.

adulthood, the origin is thought to be psychological, and treatment is recommended.

Cartoonists often depict sleepwalkers groping about with their eyes closed and their arms extended forward as if to feel their way about. Actually, sleepwalkers have their eyes open with a blank stare, and rather than walking normally, they shuffle about. Their coordination is poor, and if they talk, their speech is usually unintelligible. **[LO 4.12]**

If an EEG recording were made during a sleepwalking episode, it would show a combination of delta waves, indicating deep sleep, and alpha and beta waves, signalling the waking state. Sleepwalkers are awake enough to carry out activities that do not require their full attention, but asleep enough not to remember having done so the following day. Sleepwalkers may get up and roam through the house or simply stand for a short time and then go back to bed (Modi, Camacho, & Valerio, 2014). Occasionally they get dressed, eat a snack, or go to the bathroom. The most important concern in sleepwalking is safety. Because of their reduced alertness and coordination, sleepwalkers are at risk of hurting themselves. They have been known to walk out of windows, accidentally run into objects, or fall down (Sheth, 2005).

Finally, let us dispel a myth about sleepwalking. You may have heard that it is dangerous to awaken a sleepwalker. This piece of conventional wisdom is not true. It may, in fact, be somewhat difficult to wake someone who is sleepwalking, but once woken up, the person may simply be confused or disoriented for a short time.

What is a sleep terror?

Sleep terrors usually begin with a piercing scream. The sleeper springs up in a state of panic—eyes open, perspiring, breathing rapidly, with the heart pounding at two to four times the normal rate (Haupt, Sheldon, & Loghmanee, 2013). Episodes usually last from five to 15 minutes, and then the person falls back to sleep. **[LO 4.12]** If not awakened during a night terror, children usually have no memory of the episode the next morning. If awakened, however, they may recall a single frightening image (Stores, 2009). Up to 5 percent of children have sleep terrors (M. Anderson, 2011), but only about 1 percent of adults experience them (Partinen, Hublin, Kaprio, Koskenvuo, & Guilleminault, 1994). Parents should not be unduly alarmed by sleep terrors in young children, but episodes that continue through adolescence into adulthood are more serious (Horne, 1992). Sleep terrors in adults often indicate extreme anxiety or other psychological problems.

Nightmares: The Worst of Dreams

How do nightmares differ from sleep terrors?

Nightmares are very frightening dreams that occur during REM sleep and are likely to be remembered in vivid detail. **[LO 4.12]** The most common themes are being chased, threatened, or attacked. Nightmares can be a reaction to traumatic life experiences (Krakow & Zadra, 2006), and are more frequent at times of high fever, anxiety, and emotional upheaval. REM rebound during drug withdrawal or after long periods without sleep can also produce nightmares. Whereas sleep terrors occur early in the night during Stage 4 sleep, anxiety nightmares occur toward morning, when the REM periods are longest.

Sleeptalking (Somniloquy): Might We Reveal Secrets?

Do you sometimes talk in your sleep? Are you afraid that you might confess to something embarrassing, or reveal some deep, dark secret? Relax. Sleeptalkers rarely reply to questions, and they usually mumble words or phrases that make no sense to the listener. **[LO 4.12]** Sleeptaking can occur during any sleep stage and is more frequent in children than in adults (Ackroyd, D'Cruz, & Sharp, 2007). There is no evidence at all that sleeptalking is related to a physical or psychological disturbance—not even to a guilty conscience.

MAJOR SLEEP DISORDERS

Some sleep disorders can be so debilitating that they affect a person's entire life. These disorders are narcolepsy, sleep apnea, and insomnia.

Narcolepsy: Sudden Attacks of REM Sleep

What are the major symptoms of narcolepsy?

Narcolepsy is an incurable sleep disorder characterized by excessive daytime sleepiness and uncontrollable attacks of REM sleep, usually lasting 10 to 20 minutes (Mahowald, 2011). **[LO 4.13]** People with narcolepsy are often unfairly stigmatized as lazy, depressed, and uninterested in their work.

Anything that causes an ordinary person to be tired can trigger a sleep attack in a narcoleptic—a heavy meal, sunbathing at the beach, or a boring lecture. A sleep attack can also be brought on by any situation that is exciting (narcoleptic attacks often occur during lovemaking) or that causes a strong emotion, such as anger or laughter. Narcolepsy is a physiological

Mable, a dog who suffers from narcolepsy, is shown here while experiencing a narcoleptic sleep attack. Much has been learned about narcolepsy through research with dogs.

©Barcroft Media/Getty Images

REMEMBER IT

Variations in Sleep and Sleep Disorders

1. Which factor least affects the amount of sleep people need?
   a. their heredity
   b. their emotional state
   c. the amount of stress in their lives
   d. the amount of physical activity required in their occupation

2. Which is not a characteristic common to sleepwalking and sleep terrors in children?
   a. They occur during partial arousals from Stage 4 sleep.
   b. Episodes are usually forgotten the next morning.
   c. The disturbances occur most often in children.
   d. The disturbances indicate a psychological problem that should be treated by a mental health professional.

3. Match the disorder with the description or associated symptom.
   _____ 1) sleep attacks during the day
   _____ 2) cessation of breathing during sleep; loud snoring
   _____ 3) difficulty falling or staying asleep
   _____ 4) a very frightening REM dream
   _____ 5) partial awakening from Stage 4 sleep in a panic state related to a frightening dream image
   a. narcolepsy
   b. sleep apnea
   c. sleep terror
   d. insomnia
   e. nightmare

Answers: 1. d   2. d   3 (1). a (2) b (3) d (4) e (5) c

---

disorder caused by an abnormality in the part of the brain that regulates sleep, and it appears to have a strong genetic component (Sakurai, 2013).

Sleep Apnea: Can't Sleep and Breathe at the Same Time

What is sleep apnea?

Sleep apnea consists of periods during sleep when breathing stops and the individual must awaken briefly to breathe. Recent research suggests that 3.4 percent of Canadian adults—mostly obese men—have been professionally diagnosed with sleep apnea, while an additional 23.4 percent are at high risk for this sleep disorder (Evans et al., 2010). The major symptoms of sleep apnea are excessive daytime sleepiness and extremely loud snoring (as loud as a jackhammer), often accompanied by snorts, gasps, and choking noises. **[LO 4.13]**

In very severe cases, apnea may last throughout the night, with as many as 800 partial awakenings to gasp for air. Alcohol and sedative drugs aggravate the condition (Riemann et al., 2010). Severe sleep apnea can lead to chronic high blood pressure, heart problems, and even death (Lavie et al., 1995). Physicians sometimes treat sleep apnea by surgically modifying the upper airway. When this surgery is effective, patients not only sleep better, but also exhibit higher levels of performance on tests of verbal learning and memory (Dahlöf et al., 2002).

Insomnia: When You Can't Fall Asleep

What is insomnia?

People with **insomnia** suffer distress and impairment in daytime functioning owing to difficulty falling or staying asleep or to experiencing sleep that is light, restless, or of poor quality. **[LO 4.13]** The rates of insomnia in Canada are quite alarming, with more than 3.3 million Canadians (13.4 percent of the population aged 15 or older) dealing with the disorder (Tjepkema, 2005b). Temporary insomnia, lasting three weeks or less, can result from jet lag, emotional highs or lows, or a brief illness or injury that interferes with sleep. Much more serious is chronic insomnia, which lasts for months or even years (Singareddy et al., 2012).

Chronic insomnia may begin as a reaction to a psychological or medical problem but persist long after the problem has been resolved.

In *Apply It* at the end of this chapter, we examine some ways to overcome insomnia.

---

sleep terrors: Sleep disturbances in which a person partially awakens from Stage 4 sleep with a scream, in a dazed, groggy, and panicky state, and with a racing heart.

nightmares: Very frightening dreams occurring during REM sleep.

narcolepsy (NAR-co-lep-see): A serious sleep disorder characterized by excessive daytime sleepiness and sudden, uncontrollable attacks of REM sleep.

sleep apnea: A sleep disorder characterized by periods when breathing stops during sleep and the person must awaken briefly to breathe; major symptoms are excessive daytime sleepiness and loud snoring.

insomnia: A sleep disorder characterized by difficulty falling or staying asleep, or by light, restless, or poor sleep; causes distress and impaired daytime functioning.

MODULE **4D** **ALTERING CONSCIOUSNESS THROUGH CONCENTRATION AND SUGGESTION**

LO 4.14 Define *meditation* and describe its purpose.
LO 4.15 Define *hypnosis* and describe its use.

Sleep is an altered state of consciousness and a necessary one. We must sleep. But there are other, voluntary forms of altered consciousness. Meditation and hypnosis are two of these.

MEDITATION: EXPANDED CONSCIOUSNESS OR RELAXATION?

For what purposes is meditation used?

Meditation is a group of techniques that involve focusing attention on an object, a word, one's breathing, or body movement to block out all distractions and achieve an altered state of consciousness. **[LO 4.14]** Some forms of meditation—yoga, Zen, and transcendental meditation (TM)—have their roots in Eastern religions and are practised by followers of those religions to attain a higher state of spirituality. Others use these approaches to increase relaxation, reduce arousal, or expand consciousness. Brain-imaging studies support the conclusion that meditation, in addition to being relaxing, induces an altered state of consciousness (Raffone & Srinivasan, 2010). Recent research has shown that, in addition to having a range of positive health effects such as stress reduction (Travis et al., 2009) and lowering blood pressure and cholesterol levels (Seeman, Dubin, & Seeman, 2003), meditation may also alter brain structure (Fox et al., 2014). Regular meditation also helps individuals, even those who are severely depressed, learn to control their emotions (L. Butler et al., 2008). **[LO 4.14]**

Some meditators sit in a comfortable chair with eyes closed, both feet flat on the floor, and hands in the lap or simply resting on the arms of the chair. They might begin meditation by relaxing their muscles from the feet up to achieve a deep state of relaxation. Other people concentrate on their breathing—slowly, rhythmically, in and out. In transcendental meditation, the meditator is given a mantra, a word (such as *om*) assigned by the teacher. The meditator repeats the mantra over and over during meditation to block out unwanted thoughts and facilitate the meditative state. Dr. Herbert Benson (1975) suggests that any word or sound will do. Moreover, he asserts that the benefits of meditation can be achieved through simple relaxation techniques. Do *Try It* to experience Benson's relaxation response.

HYPNOSIS: LOOK INTO MY EYES

What is hypnosis, and when is it most useful?

Have you ever been hypnotized? Many people are fascinated by this unusual, somewhat mysterious phenomenon. Other people doubt that it even exists.

Hypnosis is a trancelike state of concentrated and focused attention, heightened suggestibility, and diminished response

TRY IT

Relaxing through Meditation

Find a quiet place and sit in a comfortable position.

1. Close your eyes.
2. Relax all your muscles deeply. Begin with your feet and move slowly upward, relaxing the muscles in your legs, buttocks, abdomen, chest, shoulders, neck, and finally your face. Allow your whole body to remain in this deeply relaxed state.
3. Now concentrate on your breathing, and breathe in and out through your nose. Each time you breathe out, silently say the word *om* to yourself.
4. Repeat this process for 20 minutes. (You can open your eyes to look at your watch periodically, but don't use an alarm.) When you are finished, remain seated for a few minutes—first with your eyes closed, and then with them open.

Benson recommends that you maintain a passive attitude. Don't try to force yourself to relax. Just let it happen. If a distracting thought comes to mind, ignore it and just repeat *om* each time you exhale. It is best to practise this exercise once or twice each day, but not within two hours of your last meal. Digestion interferes with the relaxation response.

to external stimuli. In the hypnotic state, people suspend their usual rational and logical ways of thinking and perceiving and allow themselves to experience distortions in perceptions, memories, and thinking. Under hypnosis, people may experience positive hallucinations in which they see, hear, touch, smell, or taste things that are not present in the environment; or they may have negative hallucinations and fail to perceive those things that are present. **[LO 4.15]**

About 80 to 95 percent of people are hypnotizable to some degree, but only 5 percent can reach the deepest levels of trance (Lynn & Kirsch, 2015). The ability to become completely absorbed in imaginative activities is characteristic of highly hypnotizable people.

Hypnosis: Separating Fact from Fiction

Although hypnosis has been studied extensively, many misconceptions remain. Here are the facts:

- Hypnotized subjects *are* aware of what is going on during hypnosis.
- Individuals will *not* violate their moral values under hypnosis.
- Individuals *cannot* demonstrate superhuman strength or perform amazing feats because they are hypnotized.
- Memory is *not* more accurate under hypnosis.
- Hypnotized individuals will *not* reveal embarrassing secrets.
- Hypnotized individuals will *not* relive events as they believe the events should have occurred (i.e., rather than as they actually took place in childhood).

A hypnotized person is in a state of heightened suggestibility. The hypnotherapist may therefore be able to help the woman control chronic pain or postsurgery pain.

©Todd Keith/E+/Getty Images

- Hypnotized individuals are *not* under the complete control of the hypnotist.

- The hypnotized person's responses are often automatic and involuntary (Bowers & Woody, 1996).

Medical Uses of Hypnosis:
It's Not Just Entertainment

Hypnosis has come a long way from the days when it was used mainly by entertainers. It is now recognized as a viable technique to be used in medicine, dentistry, and psychotherapy (Weisberg, 2008). Hypnosis is accepted by the American Medical Association, the American Psychological Association, and the American Psychiatric Association. Hypnosis has been particularly helpful in the control of pain (Uman, Chambers, McGrath, & Kisely, 2008), especially in the management of pain and other side effects associated with cancer care (Montgomery et al., 2014). **[LO 4.15]**. However, hypnosis has been only moderately effective in controlling weight (Hartmann, 2010) and virtually useless in reducing smoking (Green, Lynn, & Montgomery, 2008).

Critics' Explanations of Hypnosis:
Is It Really What It Seems?

Because there is no reliable way to determine whether a person is truly hypnotized, some critics offer other explanations for behaviour occurring during this state. One explanation is that people are simply acting out the role suggested by the hypnotist (Spanos, 1991). Although some people who declare that they are hypnotized may be role-playing, this theory does not adequately explain how people can undergo surgery with hypnosis rather than a general anaesthetic (Tefikow et al., 2013). This may be why some researchers have argued that hypnosis does indeed affect our ability to control behaviours. Former University of Waterloo researcher Ken Bowers proposed that the hypnotist's suggestions weaken the executive function of the brain and that the hypnotized person's responses are automatic and involuntary (Bowers, 1992; Bowers & Woody, 1996). Even though researchers still have theoretical differences, hypnosis is being increasingly used in clinical practice.

REMEMBER IT

Altering Consciousness through Concentration and Suggestion

1. Which is not a proposed use of meditation?
   a. to promote relaxation
   b. to substitute for anaesthesia during surgery
   c. to bring a person to a higher level of spirituality
   d. to alter consciousness
2. A special mantra is used in transcendental meditation. (true/false)
3. Which of the following statements is true of people under hypnosis?
   a. They will often violate their moral code.
   b. They are much stronger than in the normal waking state.
   c. They can be made to experience distortions in their perceptions.
   d. Their memory is more accurate than during the normal waking state.
4. For a moderately hypnotizable person, which use of hypnosis would probably be most successful?
   a. for relief from pain
   b. for surgery instead of a general anaesthetic
   c. for treating drug addiction
   d. for improving memory

Answers: 1. b   2. true   3. c   4. a

meditation: A group of techniques that involve focusing attention on an object, a word, one's breathing, or body movement in order to block out all distractions and achieve an altered state of consciousness.

hypnosis: A trancelike state of concentrated, focused attention, heightened suggestibility, and diminished response to external stimuli.

MODULE 4E ALTERED STATES OF CONSCIOUSNESS AND PSYCHOACTIVE DRUGS

LO 4.16 Define *psychoactive drugs*.

LO 4.17 Describe and contrast drug dependence and drug tolerance.

LO 4.18 Explain what factors influence the addictive potential of a drug.

LO 4.19 Identify the most common types of stimulants and describe their effects.

LO 4.20 Identify the most common types of hallucinogens and describe their effects.

LO 4.21 Describe the effects of marijuana.

LO 4.22 Identify the three most common types of depressants and describe their effects.

The altered states of consciousness we have examined thus far are natural ones. We will now explore the effect of psychoactive drugs. A **psychoactive drug** is any substance that alters mood, perception, or thought. Some of these drugs are legal, but most are not. **[LO 4.16]** When these drugs are approved for medical use only, they are called *controlled substances*.

In Canada, there is considerable concern about the sale and use of illicit drugs. But in terms of damage to users, harm to society, and numbers of addicts, alcohol and tobacco are the most serious problem drugs by far. According to a report from the Canadian Centre on Substance Abuse (Rehm, Baliunas, et al., 2006), tobacco and alcohol combined account for 79.3 percent of the $39.8 billion lost annually to the Canadian economy as a result of substance abuse.

Why do so many Canadians use psychoactive drugs? There are many reasons for taking drugs, and users often do not recognize their real motives. Some people take drugs to cope with or relieve anxiety, depression, or boredom (T. B. Baker, 1988). But regardless of the motive for taking drugs, doing so creates the same subjective sense of physical pleasure that results from the drug's effect on the brain's reward system. The pleasure response begins when the drug triggers a surge of dopamine molecules into a part of the brain's limbic system known as the *nucleus accumbens* (Koob & Le Moal, 2008). Thus, it isn't surprising that researchers have found that a surge of dopamine is involved in the rewarding and motivational effects produced by most psychoactive drugs (Blum et al., 2013).

Peer influence is the factor most highly correlated with adolescents' use of illicit drugs, cigarettes, and alcohol. The earlier that adolescents start using drugs, the more likely they are to progress to more serious drug addictions (McGorry, Purcell, Goldstone, & Amminger, 2011). Moreover, adolescents who use drugs seek out peers who also use and, in turn, are influenced by those peers (Brook, Pahl, & Rubenstone, 2008). Research also suggests that parental drug attitudes and sibling drug use also have a significant impact on the likelihood of illicit drug use as well as on the use of cigarettes and alcohol (Bahr, Hoffmann, & Yang, 2005). Table 4.2 summarizes the risk factors and protective factors associated with adolescent drug use and abuse.

TABLE 4.2 Risk Factors and Protective Factors for Adolescent Drug Use and Abuse

	Risk Factors	Protective Factors
Peer influences	Peers use and encourage use Peers provide substances	Peers are not users
Educational variables	Poor school performance Low educational aspirations	Good grades High educational aspirations
Social/family variables	Family conflict Family alcohol and/or drug abuse Lack of religious commitment	Positive family relationships Perceived sanctions against drug use Involvement in religious community
Environmental variables	Extreme poverty Neighbourhood disorganization Availability of drugs	
Psychological/behavioural variables	Low self-esteem Antisocial behaviour Need for excitement Poor impulse control Stressful life events Depression Anxiety Apathy and pessimism Alienation and rebelliousness	Self-acceptance Law abidance Perceived future opportunities

Sources: Adapted from de Wit, 2009; Hawkins, Catalano, & Miller, 1992; Koob & Le Moal, 2008; Newcomb, 1997; Newcomb & Felix-Ortiz, 1992.

DRUG DEPENDENCE: SLAVE TO A SUBSTANCE

What is the difference between physical and psychological drug dependence?

The effects of drugs are not always predictable. Some drugs create a physical or chemical dependence; others create a psychological dependence. **Physical drug dependence** comes about as a result of the body's natural ability to protect itself against harmful substances by developing a **drug tolerance**. This means that the user becomes progressively less affected by the drug and must take larger doses to get the same effect or same high (Koob, 2008). Tolerance grows because the brain adapts to the presence of the drug by responding less intensely to it. The various bodily processes adjust in order to continue to function with the drug in the system. **[LO 4.17]**

Once drug tolerance is established, a person cannot function normally without the drug. If the drug is taken away, the user begins to suffer withdrawal symptoms. The **withdrawal symptoms**, both physical and psychological, are usually the exact opposite of the effects produced by the drug. For example, withdrawal from stimulants leaves a person exhausted and depressed; withdrawal from tranquilizers leaves a person nervous and agitated.

If physical dependence alone explained drug addiction, there would be no problem with drugs long thought to be physically non-addictive. Once the period of physical withdrawal was over, the desire for the drug would end along with the withdrawal symptoms. But this is not the case—there is more to drug addiction than physical dependence. **Psychological drug dependence** is a craving or irresistible urge for the drug's pleasurable effects, and it is more difficult to combat than physical dependence (Sinha, 2014).

Four factors influence the addictive potential of a drug: (1) how quickly the effects of the drug are felt; (2) how pleasurable the drug's effects are; (3) how long the pleasurable effects last; and (4) how much discomfort is experienced when the drug is discontinued (Medzerian, 1991). **[LO 4.18]** With the most addictive drugs, the pleasurable effects are felt almost immediately but are short-lived. For example, the intensely pleasurable effects of crack cocaine are felt in seven seconds but last only about five minutes. Because the discomfort is intense after the pleasurable effects wear off, the user is highly motivated to continue taking the drug. With any drug, the abuse potential is higher if the drug is injected rather than taken orally, and higher still if it is smoked rather than injected.

Psychoactive drugs alter consciousness in a variety of ways. Let's consider the various alterations produced by the major categories of drugs: stimulants, hallucinogens (or psychedelics), and depressants.

STIMULANTS: SPEEDING UP THE NERVOUS SYSTEM

How do stimulants affect the user?

Stimulants, often called **uppers**, speed up the central nervous system, suppress appetite, and can make a person feel more awake, alert, and energetic. Stimulants increase pulse, blood pressure, and respiration rate; they also reduce cerebral blood flow (Flavel, White, & Todd, 2012). **[LO 4.19]** In higher doses, they make people feel nervous, jittery, and restless, and they can also cause shaking or trembling and interfere with sleep.

No stimulant actually delivers energy to the body. Instead, a stimulant forces the body to use some of its stored-up energy sooner and in greater amounts than it would naturally. When the stimulant's effect wears off, the body's natural energy is depleted. This leaves the person feeling exhausted and depressed.

There are *legal* stimulants such as caffeine and nicotine, *controlled* stimulants such as amphetamines, and *illegal* stimulants such as cocaine.

Caffeine: The Most Widely Used Drug

Caffeine is the world's most widely used drug. If you cannot start your day without a cup of coffee (or two, or more), you may be addicted to it. Coffee, tea, cola, chocolate, along with many energy drinks and more than 100 prescription and over-the-counter drugs, contain caffeine. They provide a mild jolt to the nervous system, at least temporarily. Caffeine makes us more mentally alert and can help us stay awake (Wesensten et al., 2002). **[LO 4.19]** Many people use caffeine to lift their mood, but recent research suggests that, other than its negative impact on sleep, there is little cause for concern regarding its typical use in the general population (Wesensten, 2014).

Nicotine: A Deadly Poison

Nicotine is a poison so strong that the body must develop a tolerance for it almost immediately—in only hours, in contrast to days or weeks for heroin and usually months for alcohol. **[LO 4.19]** It is estimated that 16.7 percent of Canadians smoke and that nearly half of them have tried to quit in the past year (PROPEL Centre for Population Health Impact, 2012). Despite the fact that the number of Canadian smokers has decreased steadily in the past 40 years and is at an all-time low, 37 000

---

psychoactive drug: A drug that alters normal mental functioning—mood, perception, or thought; if used medically, called a *controlled substance*.

physical drug dependence: A compulsive pattern of drug use in which the user develops a drug tolerance coupled with unpleasant withdrawal symptoms when the drug is discontinued.

drug tolerance: A condition in which the user becomes progressively less affected by the drug so that larger and larger doses are necessary to achieve or maintain the same effect.

withdrawal symptoms: The physical and psychological symptoms (usually the opposite of those produced by the drug) that occur when a regularly used drug is discontinued and that terminate when the drug is taken again.

psychological drug dependence: A craving or irresistible urge for a drug's pleasurable effects.

stimulants: A category of drugs that speed up activity in the central nervous system, suppress appetite, and cause a person to feel more awake, alert, and energetic.

uppers: A slang term for stimulants.

Canadians die each year from cigarette smoking (Baliunas et al., 2007)—roughly five times the number of deaths caused by car accidents, suicides, drug abuse, murder, and AIDS combined. The many health problems associated with smoking are discussed in Chapter 12.

Amphetamines: Energy to Burn—at a Price

What effects do amphetamines have on the user?

Amphetamines form a class of stimulants that increase arousal, relieve fatigue, suppress appetite, and give a rush of energy. In low to moderate doses, these stimulants may temporarily improve athletic and intellectual performance. A person who takes amphetamines becomes more alert and energetic, experiences mild euphoria, and usually becomes more talkative, animated, and restless. **[LO 4.19]**

In high doses—100 milligrams or more—amphetamines can cause confused and disorganized behaviour, extreme fear and suspiciousness, delusions and hallucinations, aggressiveness and antisocial behaviour, and even manic behaviour and paranoia (Petit, Karila, Chalmin, & Lejoyeux, 2012). One powerful amphetamine, known as *methamphetamine* ("crank" or "speed"), now comes in a smokable form, "ice," which is highly addictive and can be fatal.

Withdrawal from amphetamines leaves a person physically exhausted, sleeping for 10 to 15 hours or more. The user awakens in a stupor, extremely depressed and intensely hungry. Victims of fatal overdoses of stimulants usually have multiple hemorrhages in the brain.

Cocaine: Snorting White Powder, Smoking Crack

How does cocaine affect the user?

Cocaine, a stimulant derived from coca leaves, can be sniffed (snorted) as a white powder, injected intravenously, or smoked in the form of **crack**. The rush of well-being is dramatically intense and powerful, but it is just as dramatically short-lived. In the case of cocaine, the euphoria lasts no more than 30 to 45 minutes; with crack, the effect lasts no more than five to 10 minutes (Wise & Kiyatkin, 2011). **[LO 4.19]** In both cases, the euphoria is followed by an equally intense **crash** that is marked by depression, anxiety, agitation, and a powerful craving for more of the drug (Shorter, Domingo, & Kosten, 2014). Chronic cocaine use can also result in holes in the nasal septum (the ridge of cartilage running down the middle of the nose) and in the palate (the roof of the mouth) (Greenfield & Hennessy, 2008).

Cocaine stimulates the reward or "pleasure" pathways in the brain, which use the neurotransmitter dopamine (Landry, 1997). With continued use, the reward systems fail to function normally and the user becomes incapable of feeling any pleasure except from the drug (Shorter, Domingo, & Kosten, 2014). Animal researchers have shown that animals addicted to multiple substances prefer cocaine when offered a choice of drugs (Manzardo, Stein, & Belluzi, 2002) and will lose interest in everything else—food, water, sex—in order to continually

self-administer cocaine. The main withdrawal symptoms are psychological—the inability to feel pleasure and the craving for more cocaine (Edge & Gold, 2011).

Cocaine constricts the blood vessels, raises blood pressure, speeds up the heart, quickens respiration, and can even cause epileptic seizures in people who have no history of epilepsy (Pascual-Leone, Dhuna, Altafullah, & Anderson, 1990). Over time, or even quickly in high doses, cocaine can cause heart palpitations, an irregular heartbeat, and heart attacks (Furlanello et al., 2012). Recent studies (Health Canada, 2012) suggest that cocaine use has remained low in Canada over the past 10 years, with just over 1 percent of Canadians reporting cocaine use in the past year. The cheapest and perhaps the most dangerous form of cocaine, **crack**, can produce a powerful dependency in several weeks (Canadian Centre on Substance Abuse, 2006).

HALLUCINOGENS: SEEING, HEARING, AND FEELING WHAT IS NOT THERE

What are the main effects of hallucinogens, and what are three psychoactive drugs in this class?

The **hallucinogens**, or *psychedelics*, are drugs that can alter and distort perceptions of time and space, alter mood, and produce feelings of unreality. **[LO 4.20]** Hallucinogens have been used for recreation and in religious rituals and ceremonies in diverse cultures since ancient times. As the name implies, hallucinogens also cause **hallucinations**, sensations that have no basis in external reality (Halberstadt, 2015).

Rather than producing a relatively predictable effect like most other drugs, hallucinogens usually magnify the mood or the frame of mind of the user at the time the drug is taken. And contrary to the belief of some, hallucinogens may actually reduce rather than enhance creative thinking (M. Bourassa & Vaugeois, 2001). The hallucinogens we will discuss are LSD, ecstasy, and marijuana.

LSD: Mind Altering, Not Mind Expanding

LSD, sometimes referred to simply as *acid*, is the acronym for *lysergic acid diethylamide*. **[LO 4.20]** The average LSD "trip" lasts 10 to 12 hours and usually produces extreme perceptual changes—visual hallucinations and distortions. Emotions can become very intense and unstable, ranging from euphoria to anxiety, panic, and depression (Weaver & Schnoll, 2008). LSD sometimes causes "bad trips," which can leave the user in a state of terror. Some bad LSD trips have ended in accidents, death, or suicide. Sometimes a person who has taken LSD in the past experiences a **flashback**—a brief, sudden recurrence of a trip. Flashbacks can occur as many as five years after LSD use (American Psychiatric Association, 1994).

Ecstasy: The Arrival of Designer Drugs

Ecstasy (MDMA) is a designer drug—a laboratory creation—that is a cross between a hallucinogen and an amphetamine. **[LO 4.20]** The drug's main appeal is its psychological effect—users of MDMA describe a wonderfully pleasant state

Marijuana, the most widely used illicit drug in North America, has been associated with loss of motivation, general apathy, and decline in school performance.

©sturti/Getty Images

of consciousness, in which even the most backward, bashful, self-conscious people shed their inhibitions (Canadian Public Health Association, n.d.). However, research suggests that there is a price to be paid for entering this "joyous" state. MDMA is known to impair a variety of cognitive functions, including memory, sustained attention, analytical thinking, and self-control (Weaver & Schnoll, 2008). Early animal studies suggested that MDMA may cause irreversible destruction of serotonin, but recent research argues that the impact on humans may not be adequately predicted from animal models (Green, King, Shortall, & Fone, 2012). Ecstasy can also impair cognitive functions such as attention, analytical thinking, and self-control (National Institute on Drug Abuse, 2001). Rates of use among Canadians have remained constant since 2004, with 0.7 percent of Canadians reporting having used ecstasy in the past year (Health Canada, 2012).

Marijuana: More Harmful Than We Once Believed

What are some harmful effects associated with heavy marijuana use?

Marijuana is the most widely used illicit substance used by Canadians aged 15 or older (Health Canada, 2012). Marijuana tends to produce a feeling of well-being, promote relaxation, and lower inhibitions and anxiety. The user may experience giddiness; an increased sensitivity to sights, sounds, and touch; and perceptual distortions and hallucinations such as a "slowing" of time. **[LO 4.21]**

THC (**tetrahydrocannabinol**), the ingredient in marijuana (and in hashish) that produces the high, remains in the body for days or even weeks (Julien, 1995). **[LO 4.21]** A person who smokes even one marijuana cigarette, or "joint," every few weeks is never completely free of THC. Marijuana impairs

attention and coordination and slows reaction time; these effects make operating complex machinery such as an automobile dangerous, even after the feeling of intoxication has passed.

amphetamines: A class of central nervous system stimulants that increase arousal, relieve fatigue, and suppress appetite.

cocaine: A stimulant that produces a feeling of euphoria.

crack: The most potent, inexpensive, and addictive form of cocaine, and the form that is smoked.

crash: The feelings of depression, exhaustion, irritability, and anxiety that occur following an amphetamine, cocaine, or crack high.

hallucinogens (hal-LOO-sin-o-jenz): A category of drugs, sometimes called *psychedelics*, that alter perception and mood and can cause hallucinations.

hallucinations: Sensory perceptions in the absence of any external sensory stimulus; imaginary sensations.

LSD: Lysergic acid diethylamide, a powerful hallucinogen with unpredictable effects ranging from perceptual changes and vivid hallucinations to states of panic and terror.

flashback: The brief recurrence of effects a person has experienced while taking LSD or other hallucinogens, occurring suddenly and without warning at a later time.

ecstasy: MDMA, a designer drug that is a hallucinogen-amphetamine and can produce permanent damage of the serotonin-releasing neurons.

marijuana: A hallucinogen with effects ranging from relaxation and giddiness to perceptual distortions and hallucinations.

THC (tetrahydrocannabinol): The principal psychoactive ingredient in marijuana and hashish.

CANADIAN CONNECTIONS

The Dangers of Prescription Drugs

In this chapter, we have paid much attention to some of the potentially negative consequences associated with drug use. Few would praise the positive effects of cigarettes or heroin given our knowledge of the addictive and dangerous qualities of these drugs. What often tends to be overlooked, however, are the possible negative consequences of many prescription drugs.

Statistics on the use of prescription drugs are rather astounding. In 2008, prescription drug sales in Canada reached $21.4 billion, up $1.2 billion from the previous year. Put another way, Canadians are currently "popping pills at a rate of almost $60 million a day" (Picard, 2009).

While the sheer volume of prescription drugs purchased in Canada is surprising in itself, recent research suggests that a high percentage of these legally purchased drugs are diverted into the illicit market for use and abuse (Haydon, Monga, Rehm, Adlaf, & Fischer, 2005). Seniors and women have been the primary focus of research in Canada on prescription drug abuse, but more studies have begun to examine the use of prescription drug use among adolescents and young adults (Adlaf & Paglia, 2004; S. E. McCabe et al., 2011).

With Canada ranking in the top 10 percent of countries in the use of prescribed and addictive drugs such as barbiturates (e.g., Valium®), muscle relaxants, and stimulants (International Narcotics Control Board, 2004), the possibility that these drugs are diverted for non-prescription use is fairly high. When prescription drugs become available on the street they are sold for 15 to 50 times the pharmacy prices. With such high profits to be made from selling these prescribed drugs on the street, the appeal of using various illegal strategies to obtain them, such as robbery or fake prescriptions, and then to resell them illegally should not be surprising. ∎

Marijuana can interfere with concentration, logical thinking, and the ability to form new memories. It can produce fragmentation in thought, as well as confusion in remembering recent occurrences (Dougherty et al., 2013). **[LO 4.21]** Many of the receptor sites for marijuana are in the hippocampus, which explains why memory is affected (Wells & Ott, 2011). Chronic use of marijuana has been associated with loss of motivation, general apathy, and decline in school performance—referred to as *amotivational syndrome* (Andreasen & Black, 1991).

Surprisingly, recent studies have shown that marijuana does not increase rates of lung cancer (Tashkin, 2006). However, marijuana abuse affects the reproductive system in males, causing a 44 percent reduction in testosterone levels (Toson, 2011) and a substantial reduction in sperm count and testosterone levels (Gordon, Conley, & Gordon, 2013). In women, failure to ovulate and other menstrual irregularities have been associated with heavy marijuana smoking (Di Blasio, Vignali, & Gentilini, 2013).

Marijuana shows some promise as a treatment for certain medical conditions. For instance, marijuana is being prescribed by doctors to treat the eye disease glaucoma (Restak, 1993) and to control nausea and stimulate appetite in patients receiving chemotherapy for cancer or AIDS (Fackelmann, 1997). **[LO 4.21]** But there is a continuing controversy over whether marijuana should be legalized, either for medical purposes or for recreational consumption. According to recent polls, over 65 percent of Canadians would like to see possession of small amounts of marijuana decriminalized, and 40 percent would support the legalization of marijuana (Vandaelle, 2012). Despite this apparent public support, the political debate about the medical and recreational use of marijuana will continue in the years to come.

DEPRESSANTS: SLOWING DOWN THE NERVOUS SYSTEM

What are some of the effects of depressants, and what drugs make up this category?

Depressants (sometimes called **downers**) decrease activity in the central nervous system, slow down bodily functions, and reduce sensitivity to outside stimulation. **[LO 4.22]** Within this category of drugs are the sedative–hypnotics (alcohol, barbiturates, and minor tranquilizers) and the narcotics, or opiates.

Alcohol: The Nation's Number-One Drug Problem

Even though **alcohol** is a depressant, the first few drinks seem to relax and enliven at the same time. But the more alcohol a person consumes, the more the central nervous system is depressed (Knapp, Ciraulo, & Kramzler, 2008). **[LO 4.22]** As drinking increases, the symptoms of drunkenness mount—slurred speech, poor coordination, staggering. Men tend to become more aggressive (Pihl, Lau, & Assaad, 1997) and more sexually aroused (Roehrich & Kinder, 1991) but less able to perform sexually (Crowe & George, 1989). Alcohol also decreases the ability to form new memories (Kirchner & Sayette, 2003; Ray & Bates, 2006). Too much alcohol can cause a person to lose consciousness, and extremely large amounts can kill. Deaths due to extreme consumption of alcohol, usually over a short period of time, are quite common both in Canada and the United States (A. Cohen, 1997). Table 4.3 shows the effects of various blood alcohol levels.

Barbiturates: Sedatives That Can Kill in Overdose

Barbiturates (sometimes called *downers*) depress the central nervous system and, depending on the dose, can act as a sedative or a sleeping pill. Phenobarbital is an example. People who abuse barbiturates become drowsy and confused. **[LO 4.22]** Their thinking and judgment suffer, and their coordination and reflexes are affected (Löscher & Rogawski, 2012). Barbiturates can kill if taken in overdose, and a lethal dose can be as little as only three times the prescribed dose. The popular **minor tranquilizers**, the benzodiazepines, came on the scene in the early 1960s and are sold under the brand names Valium®, Librium®, Dalmane®, and, more recently, Xanax® (also used as an antidepressant). Excessive use of tranquilizers is associated with both temporary and permanent impairment

TABLE 4.3   Behavioural Effects Associated with Different Blood Alcohol Levels

Blood Alcohol Level (in milligrams of alcohol per millilitre of blood)	Behavioural Effects
0.05	Alertness is lowered, judgment is impaired, inhibitions are lowered, and the user relaxes and feels good.
0.10	Reaction is slowed, motor functions are impaired, and the user is less cautious.
0.15	Reaction time is slowed markedly; the user may stagger, slur speech, and act impulsively.
0.20	Perceptual and motor capabilities are markedly depressed; the user shows obvious intoxication.
0.25	Motor functions and sensory perceptions are severely distorted; the user may see double and fall asleep.
0.30	The user is conscious but in a stupor and not able to comprehend events in the environment.
0.35	The user is completely anaesthetized.
0.40–0.80	The user is unconscious.
	Respiration and heartbeat stop; the user dies (blood level of 0.40 causes death for 50 percent of people; death comes by 0.80 for the rest).

Sources: Adapted from Hawkins et al., 1992; Newcomb, 1997; Newcomb & Felix-Ortiz, 1992.

of memory (Paraherakis, Charney, & Gill, 2001). Alcohol and benzodiazepines, when taken together, are a potentially fatal combination.

Narcotics: Drugs from the Opium Poppy

What are the general effects of narcotics, and what are several drugs in this category?

The word *narcotic* comes from a Greek word meaning "stupor." **Narcotics** produce both a pain-relieving and a calming effect. All narcotics originate from opium, a dark, gummy substance derived from the opium poppy. **[LO 4.22]** Opium affects mainly the brain and the bowel. It paralyzes the intestinal muscles, which is why it is used medically to treat diarrhea. Because opium suppresses the cough centre, it is used in some cough medicines. Both morphine and codeine, two drugs prescribed for pain, are natural constituents of opium. OxyContin® and Vicodin® are two highly prescribed forms of these drugs that are also highly addictive. Due to its highly addictive potential, the Canadian manufacturers of OxyContin® pulled it off the market in February 2012 and replaced it with a less addictive version of the drug called OxyNEO®.

Perhaps the most highly addictive narcotic derived from morphine is **heroin**. Heroin addicts describe a sudden "rush," or euphoria, followed by drowsiness, inactivity, and impaired concentration. Withdrawal symptoms begin about 6 to 24 hours after use, and the addict becomes physically sick (American Psychiatric Association, 1994). Nausea, diarrhea, depression, stomach cramps, insomnia, and pain grow worse and worse until they become intolerable—unless the person gets another fix. Heroin use has fluctuated over time, with higher rates in the 1990s and decreasing rates currently (Johnston, O'Malley, Bachman, & Schulenberg, 2011).

Review & Reflect 4.1, on the next page, provides a summary of the effects and withdrawal symptoms of the major psychoactive drugs.

HOW DRUGS AFFECT THE BRAIN

Did you know that all kinds of physical pleasure have the same neurological basis? Whether derived from sex, food, a psychoactive chemical, or any other source, a subjective sense of physical pleasure results from the stimulus's effect on the brain's reward system. These sources of pleasure increase the availability of the neurotransmitter dopamine in a part of the brain's limbic system known as the *nucleus accumbens*. The stimulation of the nucleus accumbens by dopamine plays an important role in reinforcement and reward (Koob & Le Moal, 2008).

There is now ample evidence that dopamine is involved in the rewarding and motivational effects produced by a long list of drugs, including alcohol, amphetamines, cocaine (Landry, 1997), marijuana, heroin (Tanda, Pontieri, & Di Chiara, 1997), and nicotine (Pich et al., 1997). Amphetamines, alcohol, and nicotine stimulate the release of dopamine, whereas both

depressants: Drugs that decrease activity in the central nervous system, slow down bodily functions, and reduce sensitivity to outside stimulation.

downers: A slang term for depressants.

alcohol: A central nervous system depressant.

barbiturates: A class of addictive central nervous system depressants used as sedatives, sleeping pills, and anaesthetics; in overdose can cause coma or death.

minor tranquilizers: Central nervous system depressants that calm the user (e.g., Valium®, Librium®, Dalmane®, Xanax®).

narcotics: Derived from the opium poppy, a class of depressant drugs that have pain-relieving and calming effects.

heroin: A highly addictive, partly synthetic narcotic derived from morphine.

REVIEW & REFLECT 4.1 WITHDRAWAL SYMPTOMS OF SOME PSYCHOACTIVE DRUGS

Psychoactive Drug	Effects	Withdrawal Symptoms
Stimulants		
Tobacco (nicotine)	Effects range from alertness to calmness; lowers appetite for carbohydrates; increases pulse rate and other metabolic processes.	Irritability, anxiety, increased appetite
Caffeine	Produces wakefulness and alertness; increases metabolism but slows reaction time.	Headache, depression
Amphetamines	Increase metabolism and alertness; elevate mood, cause wakefulness, suppress appetite.	Fatigue, increased appetite, depression, long periods of sleep, irritability
Cocaine	Brings on euphoric mood, energy boost, feeling of excitement; suppresses appetite.	Depression, fatigue, increased appetite, long periods of sleep, irritability
Hallucinogens		
Marijuana	Generally produces euphoria, relaxation; affects ability to store new memories.	Anxiety, difficulty sleeping, decreased appetite, hyperactivity
LSD	Produces excited exhilaration, hallucinations; experiences perceived as insightful and profound.	
Depressants		
Alcohol	First few drinks stimulate and enliven while lowering anxiety and inhibitions; higher doses have a sedative effect, slowing reaction time, impairing motor control and perceptual ability.	Tremors, nausea, sweating, depression, weakness, irritability, and, in some cases, hallucinations
Tranquilizers (e.g., Valium®, Xanax®)	Lower anxiety, have calming and sedative effect, decrease muscular tension.	Restlessness, anxiety, irritability, muscle tension, difficulty sleeping
Barbiturates (e.g., phenobarbital)	Promote sleep, have calming and sedative effect, decrease muscular tension, impair coordination and reflexes.	Sleeplessness, anxiety; sudden withdrawal can cause seizures, cardiovascular collapse, and death
Narcotics		
Opium, morphine, heroin	Produce euphoria, relax muscles, suppress pain, cause constipation.	Anxiety, restlessness, diarrhea, nausea, muscle spasms, chills and sweating, runny nose

cocaine and amphetamines slow the reuptake of dopamine at the synapses, and thus increase and prolong its reinforcing effects (Volkow, Wang, Fischman, et al., 1997; Volkow, Wang, Fowler, et al. 1997).

Opiates such as morphine and heroin mimic the effects of the brain's own endorphins, which make us feel good, and have analgesic, or pain-relieving, properties.

Alcohol, barbiturates, and benzodiazepines (which include Valium® and Librium®) act upon GABA receptors (Sulzer, 2011). GABA is primarily an inhibitory neurotransmitter that slows down the central nervous system. Thus, stimulating the release of GABA by ingesting alcohol or tranquilizers has a calming and sedating effect. If enough GABA is released, it can shut down the brain. This is why the combination of alcohol and tranquilizers is potentially so deadly.

Unfortunately, most addicts experience a virtually irresistible compulsion to use drugs and are apparently unable to consider the likely consequences of their acts—the loss of the love and respect of family and friends, of money, of jobs, of health, and even of their lives (Leshner, 1999).

REMEMBER IT

Altered States of Consciousness and Psychoactive Drugs

1. Which of the following does not necessarily occur with drug tolerance?
  a. The body adjusts to functioning with the drug in the system.
  b. The person needs larger and larger doses of the drug to get the desired effect.
  c. The user becomes progressively less affected by the drug.
  d. The user develops a craving for the pleasurable effects of the drug.

2. Match the stimulant with the appropriate description.
  _____ 1) responsible for the most deaths
  _____ 2) used to increase arousal, relieve fatigue, and suppress appetite
  _____ 3) found in coffee, tea, chocolate, and colas
  _____ 4) snorted or injected
  _____ 5) most dangerous, potent, and addictive form of cocaine
    a. caffeine
    b. cigarettes

c. amphetamines
d. crack
e. cocaine

3. Decreased activity in the central nervous system is the chief effect of
  a. stimulants.
  b. depressants.
  c. hallucinogens.
  d. narcotics.

4. Narcotics have
  a. pain-relieving effects.
  b. stimulating effects.
  c. energizing effects.
  d. perception-altering effects.

Answers: 1. d 2 (1). b (2). c (3). a (4). e (5). d 3. b 4. a

APPLY IT

How to Get a Good Night's Sleep

How would you describe your own sleep habits? Could they stand a bit of improvement? Given that we live in a world filled with endless stimulations—watching TV or YouTube, keeping in touch with your friends on Facebook, or just hanging out with friends at late hours—it isn't surprising that we do not get enough sleep. This situation is even worse for adolescents who attend college or university. To assist you in getting enough sleep, here is a list of tips compiled by researchers at the Mayo Clinic (2006). You will find the full article at http://mayoclinic.com. Here are a few highlights:

- Keep a regular schedule that includes fairly consistent times for going to bed and getting up.
- Avoid eating or drinking to excess just before going to bed.
- Limit your intake of nicotine and caffeine throughout the day.
- Get regular exercise.
- Maintain a comfortable temperature and light level in the place where you sleep.
- Do not nap during the day.
- Make your bed as comfortable as possible.
- Establish a going-to-bed routine that relaxes you.
- Do not lie in bed awake for more than 30 minutes. Get up and do something until you feel sleepy enough to go back to bed.
- Don't push yourself to stay awake beyond the point at which you begin to feel sleepy.
- Avoid resorting to sleep medications unless absolutely necessary.

THINKING CRITICALLY

Evaluation

The famous sleep researcher Wilse Webb wrote a book called *Sleep, the Gentle Tyrant.* From what you have learned about sleep, explain why this is or is not a fitting title.

Point/Counterpoint

You hear much debate about the pros and cons of legalizing drugs. Present the most convincing argument possible to support each of these positions:
a. Illicit drugs should be legalized.
b. Illicit drugs should not be legalized.

Psychology in Your Life

You have been asked to make a presentation to Grade 7 and 8 students about the dangers of drugs. What are the most persuasive general arguments you can give to convince them not to get involved with drugs? What are some convincing, specific arguments against using each of these drugs: alcohol, marijuana, cigarettes, and cocaine?

SUMMARY & REVIEW

CIRCADIAN RHYTHMS: OUR 24-HOUR HIGHS AND LOWS

What is a circadian rhythm, and which rhythms are most relevant to the study of sleep?
A circadian rhythm is the regular fluctuation in certain body functions from a high point to a low point within a 24-hour period. Two rhythms that are highly relevant to sleep are the sleep/wakefulness cycle and body temperature.

What is the suprachiasmatic nucleus?
The suprachiasmatic nucleus is the body's biological clock, which regulates circadian rhythms and signals the pineal gland to secrete or suppress secretion of melatonin.

What are some problems experienced by employees who work rotating shifts?
People working rotating shifts experience a disruption in their circadian rhythms that causes sleep difficulties, digestive problems, and lowered alertness, efficiency, productivity, and safety during subjective night.

SLEEP: THAT MYSTERIOUS ONE THIRD OF OUR LIVES

How does a sleeper act physically during NREM sleep?
During NREM sleep, heart rate and respiration are slow and regular, blood pressure and brain activity are at a 24-hour low point, and there is little body movement and no rapid eye movement.

How does the body respond physically during REM sleep?
During REM sleep, the large muscles of the body are paralyzed, respiration and heart rates are fast and irregular, brain activity increases, and the sleeper has rapid eye movement and vivid dreams.

What is the progression of NREM stages and REM sleep that a person goes through in a typical night of sleep?
During a typical night, a person sleeps in sleep cycles, each lasting about 90 minutes. The first sleep cycle contains Stages 1, 2, 3, and 4, and REM sleep; the second contains Stages 2, 3, and 4, and REM sleep. In the remaining sleep cycles, the sleeper alternates mainly between Stage 2 and REM sleep, with each sleep cycle having progressively longer REM periods.

How do sleep patterns change over the lifespan?
Overall, the older we are the less sleep we get. Infants and young children have the longest sleep time and highest percentage of REM and deep sleep. Research also suggests that teens would benefit from sleeping longer than the 7 hours of sleep they get, on average. As people age, they usually experience a decrease in quality and quantity of sleep.

How do REM and NREM dreams differ?
REM sleep is characterized by high levels of brain activity and increases in blood pressure and heart rate. It is during REM periods that most of our vivid dreams occur. By contrast, NREM sleep is associated with no rapid eye movement. It is often called *quiet sleep* because heart rate and respiration are slow and regular, there is little body movement, and blood pressure and brain activity are at their lowest points of the 24-hour period.

In general, what have researchers found regarding the content of dreams?
Dreams usually reflect the dreamer's preoccupations in waking life. Dreams tend to have commonplace settings, be more unpleasant than pleasant, and be less emotional and bizarre than people remember them to be.

 VARIATIONS IN SLEEP AND SLEEP DISORDERS

What factors influence our sleep needs?
Much of the variability in sleep is due to genetics. However, people tend to need more sleep when they are depressed, under stress, or are experiencing significant life changes. Increases in mental, physical, or emotional effort also increase our need for sleep.

What are the characteristics of sleepwalking and sleep terrors?
Sleepwalking and sleep terrors occur during a partial arousal from slow-wave sleep, and the person does not come to full consciousness. Episodes are rarely recalled. These disorders are typically found in children and outgrown by adolescence, and they tend to run in families.

What is a sleep terror?
A sleep terror is a parasomnia in which the sleeper awakens from Stage 4 sleep with a scream, in a dazed, groggy, and panicky state, and with a racing heart.

How do nightmares differ from sleep terrors?
Nightmares are frightening dreams occurring during REM sleep and remembered in vivid detail. Sleep terrors occur during Stage 4 sleep, are rarely remembered, and often involve a single, frightening dream image.

What are the major symptoms of narcolepsy?

Narcolepsy is a condition characterized by excessive daytime sleepiness and uncontrollable attacks of REM sleep, usually lasting 10 to 20 minutes.

What is sleep apnea?

Sleep apnea is a serious sleep disorder in which breathing stops during sleep and the person must awaken briefly to breathe. Its major symptoms are excessive daytime sleepiness and loud snoring.

What is insomnia?

Insomnia is characterized by difficulty falling or staying asleep or experiencing sleep that is light, restless, or of a poor quality.

ALTERING CONSCIOUSNESS THROUGH CONCENTRATION AND SUGGESTION

For what purposes is meditation used?

Meditation is used by some to promote relaxation and reduce arousal, and by others to expand consciousness or attain a higher level of spirituality.

What is hypnosis, and when is it most useful?

Hypnosis, which has been used most successfully for the control of pain, is a trancelike state of consciousness characterized by focused attention, heightened suggestibility, and diminished response to external stimuli.

ALTERED STATES OF CONSCIOUSNESS AND PSYCHOACTIVE DRUGS

What is the difference between physical and psychological drug dependence?

With physical drug dependence, the user develops a drug tolerance so that larger and larger doses are needed to get the same effect. Withdrawal symptoms appear when the drug is discontinued and disappear when the drug is taken again. Psychological drug dependence involves an intense craving for the drug.

How do stimulants affect the user?

Stimulants speed up activity in the central nervous system, suppress appetite, and make a person feel more awake, alert, and energetic.

What effects do amphetamines have on the user?

Amphetamines increase arousal, relieve fatigue, and suppress the appetite; with continued use they result in exhaustion, depression, and agitation.

How does cocaine affect the user?

Cocaine creates a rush of well-being that is dramatically intense and powerful, but it is just as dramatically short-lived. The positive effect lasts no more than 45 minutes and is followed by an equally intense crash that is marked by depression, anxiety, agitation, and a powerful craving for more of the drug.

What are the main effects of hallucinogens, and what are three psychoactive drugs in this class?

Hallucinogens—LSD, ecstasy, and marijuana—can alter perception of time and space, mood, and cause hallucinations.

What are some harmful effects associated with heavy marijuana use?

Heavy use of marijuana can interfere with concentration, logical thinking, and the ability to form new memories. It can also result in loss of motivation and general apathy.

What are some of the effects of depressants, and what drugs make up this category?

Depressants decrease activity in the central nervous system, slow down body functions, and reduce sensitivity to outside stimulation. Depressants include sedative–hypnotics (alcohol, barbiturates, and minor tranquilizers) and narcotics (opiates).

What are the general effects of narcotics, and what are several drugs in this category?

Narcotics, which include opium, codeine, morphine, and heroin, have both pain-relieving and calming effects.

STATES OF CONSCIOUSNESS

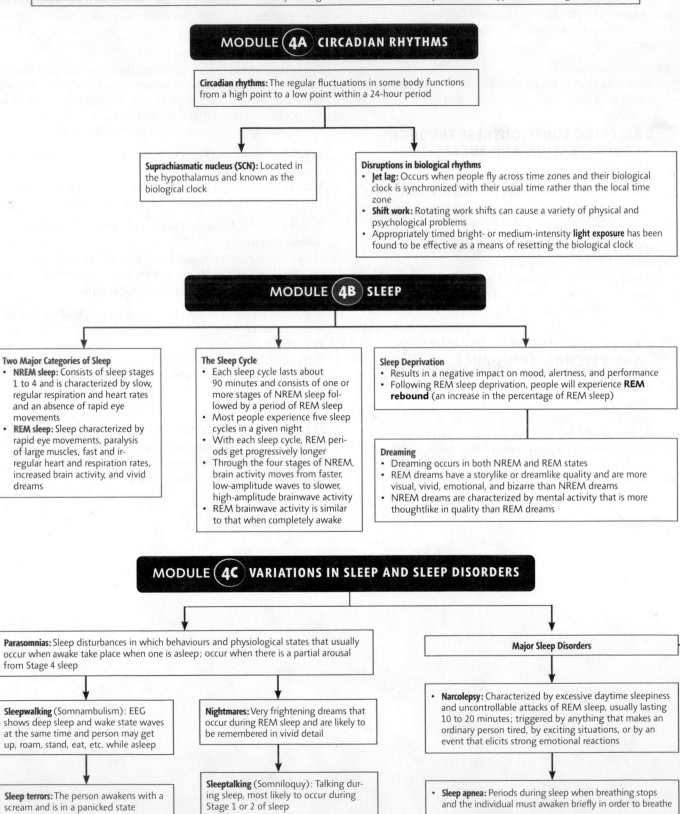

Consciousness: Continuous stream of thoughts, feelings, sensations, and perceptions of which we are aware from moment to moment
Altered state of consciousness: A mental state other than ordinary waking consciousness, such as sleep, meditation, hypnosis, or a drug-induced state

MODULE 4A CIRCADIAN RHYTHMS

Circadian rhythms: The regular fluctuations in some body functions from a high point to a low point within a 24-hour period

Suprachiasmatic nucleus (SCN): Located in the hypothalamus and known as the biological clock

Disruptions in biological rhythms
- **Jet lag:** Occurs when people fly across time zones and their biological clock is synchronized with their usual time rather than the local time zone
- **Shift work:** Rotating work shifts can cause a variety of physical and psychological problems
- Appropriately timed bright- or medium-intensity **light exposure** has been found to be effective as a means of resetting the biological clock

MODULE 4B SLEEP

Two Major Categories of Sleep
- **NREM sleep:** Consists of sleep stages 1 to 4 and is characterized by slow, regular respiration and heart rates and an absence of rapid eye movements
- **REM sleep:** Sleep characterized by rapid eye movements, paralysis of large muscles, fast and irregular heart and respiration rates, increased brain activity, and vivid dreams

The Sleep Cycle
- Each sleep cycle lasts about 90 minutes and consists of one or more stages of NREM sleep followed by a period of REM sleep
- Most people experience five sleep cycles in a given night
- With each sleep cycle, REM periods get progressively longer
- Through the four stages of NREM, brain activity moves from faster, low-amplitude waves to slower, high-amplitude brainwave activity
- REM brainwave activity is similar to that when completely awake

Sleep Deprivation
- Results in a negative impact on mood, alertness, and performance
- Following REM sleep deprivation, people will experience **REM rebound** (an increase in the percentage of REM sleep)

Dreaming
- Dreaming occurs in both NREM and REM states
- REM dreams have a storylike or dreamlike quality and are more visual, vivid, emotional, and bizarre than NREM dreams
- NREM dreams are characterized by mental activity that is more thoughtlike in quality than REM dreams

MODULE 4C VARIATIONS IN SLEEP AND SLEEP DISORDERS

Parasomnias: Sleep disturbances in which behaviours and physiological states that usually occur when awake take place when one is asleep; occur when there is a partial arousal from Stage 4 sleep

Major Sleep Disorders

Sleepwalking (Somnambulism): EEG shows deep sleep and wake state waves at the same time and person may get up, roam, stand, eat, etc. while asleep

Nightmares: Very frightening dreams that occur during REM sleep and are likely to be remembered in vivid detail

- **Narcolepsy:** Characterized by excessive daytime sleepiness and uncontrollable attacks of REM sleep, usually lasting 10 to 20 minutes; triggered by anything that makes an ordinary person tired, by exciting situations, or by an event that elicits strong emotional reactions

Sleep terrors: The person awakens with a scream and is in a panicked state

Sleeptalking (Somniloquy): Talking during sleep, most likely to occur during Stage 1 or 2 of sleep

- **Sleep apnea:** Periods during sleep when breathing stops and the individual must awaken briefly in order to breathe

MODULE (4D) ALTERING CONSCIOUSNESS THROUGH CONCENTRATION AND SUGGESTION

Meditation: A group of techniques used to block out all distractions and achieve an altered state of consciousness

Hypnosis: A trancelike state of concentrated and focused attention, heightened suggestibility, and diminished response to external stimuli

Used by some to increase relaxation, reduce arousal, expand consciousness, or attain a higher state of spirituality

Has been used successfully for the control of pain, a variety of disorders, and certain medical conditions

Although most people are hypnotizable to some degree, only 5 percent can reach the deepest level of trance

MODULE (4E) ALTERED STATES OF CONSCIOUSNESS AND PSYCHOACTIVE DRUGS

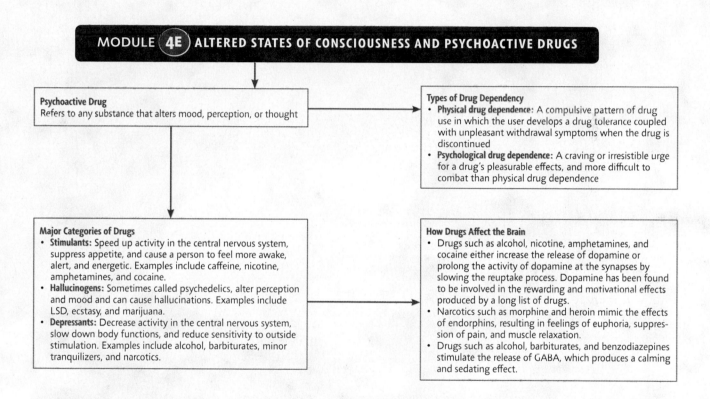

Psychoactive Drug
Refers to any substance that alters mood, perception, or thought

Types of Drug Dependency
- **Physical drug dependence:** A compulsive pattern of drug use in which the user develops a drug tolerance coupled with unpleasant withdrawal symptoms when the drug is discontinued
- **Psychological drug dependence:** A craving or irresistible urge for a drug's pleasurable effects, and more difficult to combat than physical drug dependence

Major Categories of Drugs
- **Stimulants:** Speed up activity in the central nervous system, suppress appetite, and cause a person to feel more awake, alert, and energetic. Examples include caffeine, nicotine, amphetamines, and cocaine.
- **Hallucinogens:** Sometimes called psychedelics, alter perception and mood and can cause hallucinations. Examples include LSD, ecstasy, and marijuana.
- **Depressants:** Decrease activity in the central nervous system, slow down body functions, and reduce sensitivity to outside stimulation. Examples include alcohol, barbiturates, minor tranquilizers, and narcotics.

How Drugs Affect the Brain
- Drugs such as alcohol, nicotine, amphetamines, and cocaine either increase the release of dopamine or prolong the activity of dopamine at the synapses by slowing the reuptake process. Dopamine has been found to be involved in the rewarding and motivational effects produced by a long list of drugs.
- Narcotics such as morphine and heroin mimic the effects of endorphins, resulting in feelings of euphoria, suppression of pain, and muscle relaxation.
- Drugs such as alcohol, barbiturates, and benzodiazepines stimulate the release of GABA, which produces a calming and sedating effect.

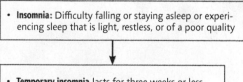

- **Insomnia:** Difficulty falling or staying asleep or experiencing sleep that is light, restless, or of a poor quality

- **Temporary insomnia** lasts for three weeks or less
- **Chronic insomnia** lasts for months or years

5

On an episode of a popular cable television comedy program, the hosts offered $100 to any studio audience member who would eat an entire stick of butter. As you would probably predict, they had no trouble finding a volunteer; we all know that the expectation of some kind of a payoff influences our behaviour. But do all rewards influence behaviour in the same way? Would the hosts have been successful if they had offered $1 instead of $100? Not likely—the reward would have to be worth completing the task. In addition, what if there was only a 75 percent chance that the audience member would actually receive the $100 after eating the stick of butter—would this affect his or her willingness to participate?

The predictability of an expected reward does matter, but not in the way that you might think. To find out what we mean, estimate the likelihood that each behaviour in the accompanying chart will actually yield its associated payoff. Use a scale of 0 to 10, with 0 = no chance at all and 10 = absolute certainty that the behaviour, if executed correctly, will lead to the payoff. For example, how likely is it that you will find a TV program you want to watch when you channel-surf? Is there no chance (0)? Some chance (5)? Will you definitely find a program (10)? Make your estimations for this and the other items listed in the chart.

Chances are good that your ratings for some behaviours were higher than for others; for example, the likelihood that you would get money from an ATM was probably rated higher than the likelihood that you would win the lottery. But now take a moment to think about which of these behaviours you could get so involved in that you continue them for much longer than you originally intended. The chances are good that you don't see yourself repetitively punching in your PIN at an ATM or baking cookies for hours on end, even if these have a high probability of paying off. On the other hand, who hasn't wasted time channel-surfing or playing video games? And how many people regularly buy lottery tickets despite having never won any money? In this way, everyday experience confirms an important principle that you will read about in this chapter: unpredictable rewards usually influence behavioural changes (what psychologists call *learning*) more strongly than predictable rewards do.

Behaviour	Potential Payoff	Probability of Payoff
Channel-surfing	Find a program you want to watch	0 ←——→ 10
Using an ATM	Get cash	0 ←——→ 10
Playing a video game	Beat opponent or your own past performance	0 ←——→ 10
Baking cookies according to a recipe	Cookies turn out as expected	0 ←——→ 10
Buying lottery tickets	Win money	0 ←——→ 10

LEARNING

MODULE **5A** CLASSICAL CONDITIONING

LO 5.1 Define *learning* and *classical conditioning*.

LO 5.2 Define and explain each of the key elements of classical conditioning, including *US, UR, CS,* and *CR*.

LO 5.3 Understand how basic principles such as extinction, spontaneous recovery, generalization, discrimination, and higher-order conditioning function within classical conditioning.

LO 5.4 Apply classical conditioning theory in a real-world context.

LO 5.5 Identify and explain the factors that influence classical conditioning.

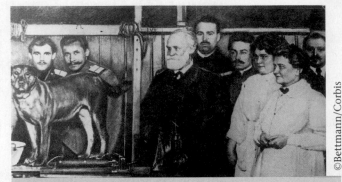

©Bettmann/Corbis

Ivan Pavlov (1849–1936) earned fame by studying the conditioned reflex in dogs.

Psychologists define **learning** as a relatively permanent change in behaviour, knowledge, capability, or attitude that is acquired through experience and cannot be attributed to illness, injury, or maturation. **[LO 5.1]** Several parts of this definition warrant further explanation. First, defining learning as a "relatively permanent change" excludes temporary changes in our behaviour or attitudes that could result from illness, fatigue, or fluctuations in mood. Second, by referring to changes that are "acquired through experience," we exclude some relatively permanent, readily observable changes in behaviour that occur as a result of brain injury or certain diseases. Moreover, there are observable changes as we grow and mature that have nothing to do with learning. For example, a young male at puberty does not *learn* to speak in a deeper voice; rather, his voice changes to a lower pitch as a result of maturation.

Learning is an important topic in the field of psychology, and available evidence suggests that we learn through many different avenues. This chapter explores three basic forms of learning: classical conditioning, operant conditioning, and observational/cognitive learning.

Classical conditioning is one of the simplest forms of learning, yet it has a powerful effect on our attitudes, likes and dislikes, and emotional responses. In classical conditioning, an association is learned between one stimulus and another. **[LO 5.1]** A **stimulus** is any event or object in the environment to which an organism responds. We have all learned to respond in specific ways to a variety of words and symbols; for example, Santa Claus, Canada Revenue Agency, the Montreal Canadiens, and the HST are just sounds and symbols; but they tend to evoke strong emotional responses because of their associations.

The explanation for these feelings is simple—learning by association (associative learning). We associate one thing with another—a positive or a negative attitude with a name, a particular gesture, a style of dress, or a manner of speaking. Our lives are profoundly influenced by the associations we learn through classical conditioning, which is sometimes referred to as *respondent conditioning*, or *Pavlovian conditioning*.

PAVLOV AND CLASSICAL CONDITIONING

What was Pavlov's major contribution to psychology?

Ivan Pavlov (1849–1936) organized and directed research in physiology at the Institute of Experimental Medicine in St. Petersburg, Russia, from 1891 until his death 45 years later. For his classic experiments on the physiology of digestion, he won a Nobel Prize in 1904. Pavlov's study of the conditioned reflex in dogs brought him fame, and he pursued this research from about 1898 until the end of his career. Pavlov's contribution to psychology came about quite by accident. To conduct his study of the salivary response, Pavlov made a small incision in the side of each experimental dog's mouth. Then he attached a tube so that the flow of saliva could be diverted from the animal's mouth, through the tube, and into a container, where the saliva was collected and measured.

The purpose of this was to collect the saliva that the dogs secreted naturally in response to food placed in the mouth. But Pavlov noticed that in many cases, the dogs began to salivate even before the food was presented. Pavlov observed drops of saliva collecting in the container when the dogs heard the footsteps of the laboratory assistants coming to feed them. And he observed saliva collecting when the dogs heard only their feeding dishes rattling, when they saw the attendant who fed them, and at the mere sight of their food. How could an involuntary response such as salivation come to be associated with the sights and sounds accompanying the act of feeding? Pavlov spent the rest of his life studying this question. The type of learning that he studied is known today as *classical conditioning*.

Pavlov was a meticulous researcher; he wanted an experimental environment in which he could carefully control all the factors that could affect the dogs during the experiments. To accomplish this, he planned and built a laboratory at the institute specifically for his purposes.

The dogs were isolated inside soundproof cubicles and placed in harnesses that restrained their movements. From an adjoining cubicle, the experimenter observed the dogs through a one-way mirror. Food and other stimuli could be presented and the flow of saliva measured by remote control (Figure 5.1). What did Pavlov and his colleagues learn?

THE ELEMENTS AND PROCESSES IN CLASSICAL CONDITIONING

The Reflex: We Can't Help It

Reflexes are involuntary responses to a particular stimulus. Two examples are the eyeblink response to a puff of air and salivation when food is placed in the mouth. There are two kinds

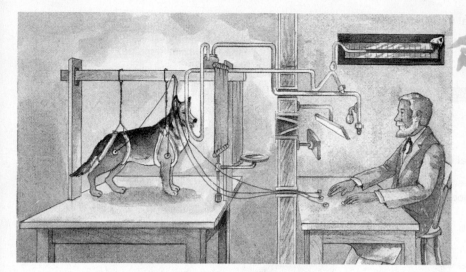

FIGURE 5.1

The Experimental Apparatus Used in Pavlov's Classical Conditioning Studies

In Pavlov's classical conditioning studies, the dog was restrained in a harness in the cubicle and isolated from all distractions. An experimenter observed the dog through a one-way mirror and, by remote control, presented the dog with food and other conditioning stimuli. A tube carried the saliva from the dog's mouth to a container, where it was measured.

of reflexes—conditioned and unconditioned. Think of the term *conditioned* as meaning "learned" and the term *unconditioned* as meaning "unlearned." Salivation in response to food is called an *unconditioned reflex* because this behaviour is an inborn, automatic, unlearned response to a particular stimulus. Unconditioned reflexes are built into the nervous system.

When Pavlov observed that his dogs salivated at the sight of food or the sound of the rattling of their feeding dishes, he realized that this salivation reflex was the result of learning. He called these learned involuntary responses **conditioned reflexes**.

The Conditioned and Unconditioned Stimulus and Response

How is classical conditioning accomplished?

Pavlov continued to investigate the circumstances under which a conditioned reflex is formed. He used tones, bells, buzzers, lights, geometric shapes, electric shocks, and metronomes in his conditioning experiments. In a typical experiment, food powder was placed in the dog's mouth, causing salivation. Dogs do not need to be conditioned to salivate in response to food, so salivation in response to food is an unlearned or **unconditioned response (UR)**. Any stimulus, such as food, that without learning will automatically elicit, or bring forth, an unconditioned response is called an **unconditioned stimulus (US)**. [LO 5.2]

Remember that a reflex is made up of both a stimulus and a response. Following is a list of some common unconditioned reflexes, showing their two components—the unconditioned stimulus and the unconditioned response:

Unconditioned Reflexes

Unconditioned Stimulus (US)	Unconditioned Response (UR)
food	salivation
onion juice	tears
heat	perspiration
loud noise	startle
light in eye	contraction of pupil
puff of air in eye	blink
touching a hot stove	hand withdrawal

Pavlov demonstrated that dogs could be conditioned to salivate in response to a variety of stimuli that had never before been associated with food. During the conditioning, or acquisition, process, the researcher would present a neutral stimulus such as a musical tone shortly before placing food powder in the dog's mouth. The food powder would cause the dog to salivate. After pairing the tone and food many times—usually 20 or more—Pavlov (1960) found that the tone alone would elicit salivation (p. 385). Because dogs do not naturally salivate in response to musical tones, he concluded that this salivation was a learned response. Pavlov called the tone the *learned* or **conditioned stimulus (CS)**,

learning: A relatively permanent change in behaviour, knowledge, capability, or attitude that is acquired through experience and cannot be attributed to illness, injury, or maturation.

classical conditioning: A process through which a response previously made only to a specific stimulus is made to another stimulus that has been paired repeatedly with the original stimulus.

stimulus (STIM-yu-lus): Any event or object in the environment to which an organism responds; plural is *stimuli*.

reflexes: Inborn, unlearned, automatic responses to certain environmental stimuli (e.g., swallowing, coughing, blinking, sucking, grasping).

conditioned reflexes: Learned reflexes, as opposed to naturally occurring ones.

unconditioned response (UR): A response that is invariably elicited by the unconditioned stimulus without prior learning.

unconditioned stimulus (US): A stimulus that elicits a specific response without prior learning.

conditioned stimulus (CS): A neutral stimulus that, after repeated pairing with an unconditioned stimulus, becomes associated with it and elicits a conditioned response.

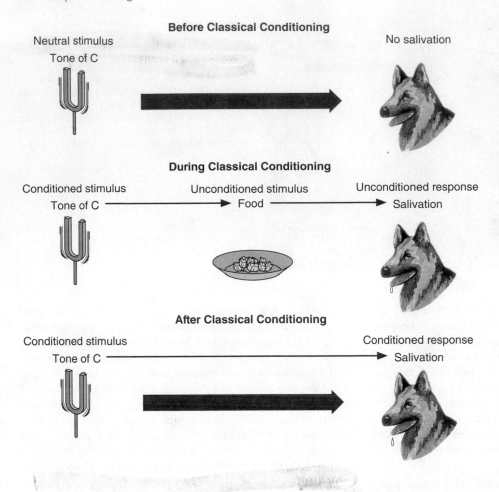

Before Classical Conditioning

Neutral stimulus
Tone of C

No salivation

During Classical Conditioning

Conditioned stimulus	Unconditioned stimulus	Unconditioned response
Tone of C	Food	Salivation

After Classical Conditioning

Conditioned stimulus
Tone of C

Conditioned response
Salivation

FIGURE 5.2

Classically Conditioning a Salivation Response

A neutral stimulus (a tone) elicits no salivation until it is repeatedly paired with the unconditioned stimulus (food). After many pairings, the neutral stimulus (now called *conditioned stimulus*) alone produces salivation. Classical conditioning has occurred.

and salivation to the tone the *learned* or **conditioned response (CR)** (Figure 5.2). **[LO 5.2]**

The conditioned stimulus can also be thought of as a signal indicating that the unconditioned stimulus will follow (Schreurs, 1989). In Pavlov's experiment, the tone became a signal that food would follow shortly. So the signal (conditioned stimulus) gives advance warning, and a person or animal is prepared with the proper response (conditioned response) even before the unconditioned stimulus arrives.

Extinction and Spontaneous Recovery: Gone but Not Forgotten

How does extinction occur in classical conditioning?

After conditioning an animal to salivate to a tone, what happens when you continue to sound the tone but no longer pair it with food? Pavlov found that salivation to the tone without the food became weaker and weaker and then finally disappeared altogether—a process known as **extinction**.

By *extinction*, we do not mean that the conditioned response has been completely erased or forgotten. Rather, the animal learns that the tone is no longer a signal that food will follow shortly, and the old conditioned response is gradually inhibited or suppressed. **[LO 5.3]** Animals are better able to adapt to a changing environment if they have the ability

to discard conditioned responses that are no longer useful or needed.

How did Pavlov determine whether the conditioned response, once extinguished, had been inhibited rather than permanently erased or forgotten? If, after the response had been extinguished, the dog was allowed to rest and was then brought back to the laboratory, Pavlov found that the dog would again salivate to the tone. He called this recurrence **spontaneous recovery**. The spontaneously recovered response, however, was weaker and shorter in duration than the original conditioned response. Figure 5.3 illustrates the processes of extinction and spontaneous recovery. **[LO 5.3]**

Generalization: Responding to Similarities

What is generalization?

Assume that you have conditioned a dog to salivate when it hears the tone middle C on the piano. If in your experiment you accidentally played the tone D or E, would that note produce salivation? Or would the dog not salivate to this slightly different tone? Pavlov found that a tone similar to the original conditioned stimulus produced the conditioned response, a phenomenon called **generalization**. **[LO 5.3]** Salivation decreases the further the new tone is away from the original tone. Eventually the tone will be so different that the dog will not salivate at all (Figure 5.4).

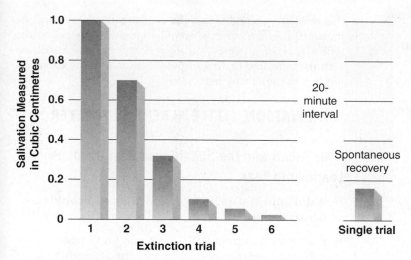

FIGURE 5.3

Extinction of a Classically Conditioned Response

When a classically conditioned stimulus (the tone) was presented in a series of trials without the unconditioned stimulus (the food), Pavlov's dogs salivated less and less until there was virtually no salivation. But after a 20-minute rest, with one sound of the tone, the conditioned response would reappear in a weakened form (producing only a small amount of salivation), a phenomenon Pavlov called *spontaneous recovery*.

Source: (Data from Pavlov, 1960, p. 58.) Data from Pavlov, I.P. (1960). Conditioned reflexes: An investigation of the physiological activity of the cerebral cortex (G. V. Anrep, Trans.). New York: Dover. (Original translation published 1927). p. 58.

It is easy to see the impact of generalization in our everyday experience. Suppose that as a child you had been bitten by a large grey dog. To experience fear in the future, you would not need to see exactly the same dog or another of the same breed or colour coming toward you: your original fear would probably generalize to all large dogs of any description. Because of generalization, we do not need to learn a conditioned response to every stimulus. Rather, we learn to approach or avoid a range of stimuli similar to the one that produced the original conditioned response. **[LO 5.3]**

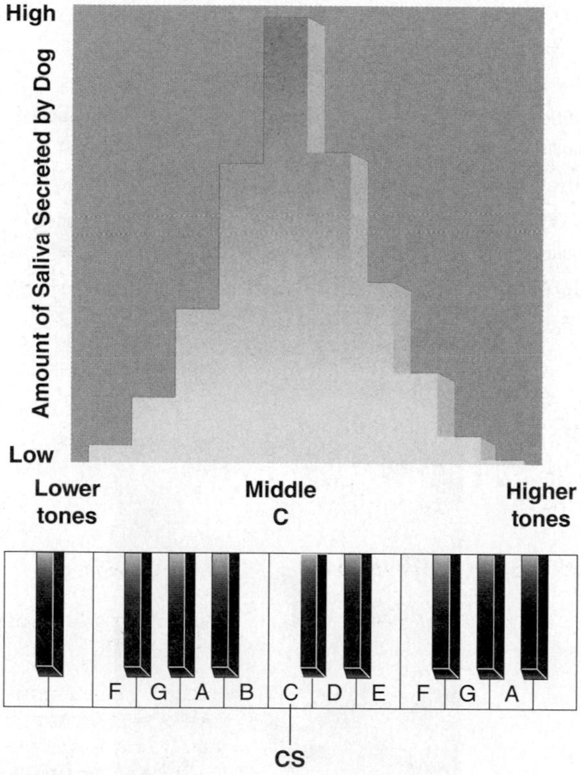

Discrimination: Learning That They're Not All Alike

What is discrimination in classical conditioning?

We must learn not only to generalize, but also to distinguish between similar stimuli. Using the previous example of a dog being conditioned to a musical tone, we can trace the process of discrimination: **[LO 5.3]**

Step 1: The dog is conditioned to the tone C.

Step 2: Generalization occurs, and the dog salivates to a range of musical tones above and below tone C. The dog salivates less and less as the note moves away from C.

Step 3: The original tone C is repeatedly paired with food, but when neighbouring tones are sounded, they are

conditioned response (CR): A response that comes to be elicited by a conditioned stimulus as a result of its repeated pairing with an unconditioned stimulus.

extinction: The weakening and often eventual disappearance of a learned response (in classical conditioning, the conditioned response is weakened by repeated presentation of the conditioned stimulus without the unconditioned stimulus).

spontaneous recovery: The reappearance of an extinguished response (in a weaker form) when an organism is exposed to the original conditioned stimulus following a rest period.

generalization: In classical conditioning, the tendency to make a conditioned response to a stimulus that is similar to the original conditioned stimulus; in operant conditioning, the tendency to make the learned response to a stimulus that is similar to the one for which it was originally reinforced.

discrimination: The learned ability to distinguish between similar stimuli so that the conditioned response occurs only to the original conditioned stimulus but not to similar stimuli.

FIGURE 5.4

Generalization in Classical Conditioning

Because of the phenomenon of generalization, a dog conditioned to salivate to middle C (the CS) on the piano also salivates to similar tones—but less and less so as the tone moves away from middle C.

A child attacked by a dog can easily develop a long-lasting fear of all dogs, through the process of generalization.

not followed with food. The dog is being conditioned to discriminate. Gradually, the salivation response to the neighbouring tones is extinguished, while salivation to the original tone C is strengthened:

Conditioned Stimulus	Conditioned Response
Tone C	More salivation
Tones A, B, D, E	Progressively less salivation

Step 4:   Eventually, discrimination is achieved:

Conditioned Stimulus	Conditioned Response
Tone C	Stronger salivation response
Tones A, B, D, E	No salivation

Like generalization, discrimination has survival value. Discriminating between the odours of fresh and spoiled milk will spare you an upset stomach. Knowing the difference between a rattlesnake and a garter snake could save your life. **[LO 5.4]**

Higher-Order Conditioning

Classical conditioning would be somewhat limited in its effect on behaviour if a conditioned response could be produced in only two ways: (1) by the pairing of a conditioned stimulus with an unconditioned stimulus or (2) through generalization. Fortunately, classical conditioning can occur in another way—through higher-order conditioning. **Higher-order conditioning** takes place when a neutral stimulus is paired with an existing conditioned stimulus, becomes associated with it, and gains the power to elicit the same conditioned response. **[LO 5.3]** Suppose

that after Pavlov conditioned the dogs to salivate to a tone, he presented a light (a neutral stimulus) immediately before the tone a number of times. The light would become associated with the tone, and the dogs would learn to give the salivation response to the light alone.

JOHN WATSON, LITTLE ALBERT, AND PETER

Little Albert and the Conditioned Fear Response: Learning to Fear

How did John Watson demonstrate that fear could be classically conditioned?

In 1919, John B. Watson (1878–1958) and his laboratory assistant, Rosalie Rayner, conducted a now-famous study to prove that fear could be classically conditioned. The participant in the study, known as "Little Albert," was a healthy and emotionally stable infant. When tested, he showed no fear except of the loud noise Watson made by striking a hammer against a steel bar. In this classic experiment, Watson tested whether he could condition 11-month-old Albert to fear a white rat by causing Albert to associate the rat with a loud noise.

In the laboratory, Rayner presented Little Albert with a white rat. As Albert reached for the rat, Watson struck a steel bar with a hammer just behind Albert's head. This procedure was repeated, and Albert "jumped violently, fell forward and began to whimper" (J. B. Watson & Rayner, 1920, p. 4). A week later, the rat was paired with the loud noise five more times. Then at the sight of the white rat alone, Albert began to cry.

Conditioned Stimulus	Unconditioned Stimulus	Unconditioned Response
white rat	loud noise	fear reaction
Conditioned Stimulus		**Conditioned Response**
white rat		fear reaction

John B. Watson

PhotoSynthesis Archives

Little Albert demonstrates that his fear of the white rat has generalized to a rabbit.

When Albert returned to the laboratory five days later, his fear had generalized to a rabbit and (to a lesser degree) to a dog, a seal coat, Watson's hair, and a Santa Claus mask. When he made his final visit to the laboratory 30 days later, his fears remained, although they were somewhat less intense. The researchers concluded that conditioned fears "persist and modify personality throughout life" (J. B. Watson & Rayner, 1920, p. 12). **[LO 5.4]**

Although Watson had formulated techniques for removing conditioned fears, Albert and his family moved away before those techniques could be tried on him. (Since Watson knew that Albert would leave the area before receiving the fear-removal techniques, he showed a disregard for the child's welfare. Fortunately, the American Psychological Association [APA] and the Canadian Psychological Association [CPA] now have strict ethical standards for research involving humans and animals to ensure their well-being.) Some of Watson's ideas for removing fears were excellent and laid the groundwork for therapies that are used today.

Removing Peter's Fears: The Triumph of Candy and Patience

Three years after the experiment with Little Albert, Watson and colleague Mary Cover Jones (1924) found three-year-old Peter, who, like Albert, was afraid of white rats. He was also afraid of rabbits, a fur coat, feathers, cotton, and a fur rug. Peter's fear of the rabbit was his strongest fear, and this became the target of these two researchers' fear-removal techniques.

Peter was brought into the laboratory, seated comfortably in a high chair, and given candy to eat. A white rabbit in a wire cage was brought into the room but kept far enough away from Peter so that it would not upset him. Over the course of 38 therapy sessions, the rabbit was brought closer and closer to Peter, who continued to enjoy his candy. Occasionally, some of Peter's friends were brought into the laboratory to play with the rabbit (at a safe distance) so that Peter could see first-hand that the rabbit did no harm. Toward the end of the therapy, the rabbit was taken out of the cage and eventually put in Peter's lap. By the final session, Peter had grown fond of the rabbit. Moreover, he had lost all fear of the fur coat, cotton, and feathers, and he could tolerate the white rats and the fur rug.

FACTORS INFLUENCING CLASSICAL CONDITIONING

What are four factors that influence classical conditioning?

Four major factors affect the strength of a classically conditioned response and the length of time required for conditioning. **[LO 5.5]**

1. *The number of pairings of the conditioned stimulus and the unconditioned stimulus.* The number of pairings required varies considerably, depending on the individual characteristics of the person or animal being conditioned. Generally, the greater the number of pairings, the stronger the conditioned response.

2. *The intensity of the unconditioned stimulus.* If a conditioned stimulus is paired with a very strong unconditioned stimulus, the conditioned response will be stronger and will be acquired more rapidly than if it is paired with a weaker unconditioned stimulus (Gormezano, 1984). Striking the steel bar with the hammer produced stronger and faster conditioning in Little Albert than would have occurred if Watson had merely clapped his hands behind Albert's head.

3. *How reliably the conditioned stimulus predicts the unconditioned stimulus.* Robert Rescorla (1967, 1968) has shown that classical conditioning does not occur automatically just because a neutral stimulus is repeatedly paired with an unconditioned stimulus. The neutral stimulus must also reliably predict the occurrence of the unconditioned stimulus. A smoke alarm that never goes off except in response to a fire will elicit more fear than one that occasionally gives false alarms. A tone that is *always* followed by food will elicit more salivation than one that is followed by food only some of the time.

4. *The temporal relationship between the conditioned stimulus and the unconditioned stimulus.* Conditioning takes place fastest if the conditioned stimulus occurs shortly before the unconditioned stimulus. It takes place more slowly or not at all when the two stimuli occur at the same time. Conditioning rarely takes place when the conditioned stimulus follows the unconditioned stimulus (Spetch, Wilkie, & Pinel, 1981; Spooner & Kellogg, 1947).

The ideal time between the presentation of the conditioned and the unconditioned stimulus is about half a second, but this varies according to the type of response being conditioned and the nature and intensity of the conditioned and unconditioned stimulus (E. A. Wasserman & Miller, 1997). Age may also affect the optimal time interval (P. R. Solomon,

---

higher-order conditioning: Occurs when a neutral stimulus is paired with an existing conditioned stimulus, becomes associated with it, and gains the power to elicit the same conditioned response.

REMEMBER IT

Classical Conditioning

1. The gradual weakening and disappearance of a conditioned response—when the conditioned stimulus is presented repeatedly without the unconditioned stimulus—is termed
   a. generalization.
   b. discrimination.
   c. extinction.
   d. spontaneous recovery.

2. Five-year-old Jesse was bitten by his neighbour's collie. He won't go near that dog but seems to have no fear of other dogs, even other collies. Which process accounts for his behaviour?
   a. generalization
   b. discrimination
   c. extinction
   d. spontaneous recovery

3. Albert's fear of the white rat transferred to the rabbit, dog, seal coat, and mask. What process did this demonstrate?
   a. generalization
   b. discrimination
   c. extinction
   d. spontaneous recovery

4. Which of the following does not increase the strength of the conditioned response in classical conditioning?
   a. more pairings of the conditioned with the unconditioned stimulus
   b. presenting the conditioned stimulus a considerable time before the unconditioned stimulus
   c. increasing the intensity of the unconditioned stimulus
   d. always following the conditioned stimulus with the unconditioned stimulus

Answers: 1. c 2. b 3. a 4. b

Blanchard, Levine, Velazquez, & Groccia-Ellison, 1991). In general, if the conditioned stimulus occurs too long before the unconditioned stimulus, an association between the two will not form. One notable exception to this general principle relates to the conditioning of taste aversions.

CONTEMPORARY VIEWS OF CLASSICAL CONDITIONING

Which aspect of the classical conditioning process is most important? Pavlov believed that the critical element in classical conditioning was the repeated pairing of the conditioned stimulus and the unconditioned stimulus, with only a brief interval between the two. Beginning in the late 1960s, though, researchers began to discover exceptions to some of the general principles Pavlov had identified.

The Cognitive Perspective

Psychologist Robert Rescorla (1967, 1968, 1988; Rescorla & Wagner, 1972) demonstrated that the critical element in classical conditioning is not the repeated pairing of the conditioned stimulus and the unconditioned stimulus (Rescorla, 2008). Rather, the important factor is whether the conditioned stimulus provides information that enables the organism to reliably *predict* the occurrence of the unconditioned stimulus. Using rats as his subjects, Rescorla used a tone as the conditioned stimulus and a shock as the unconditioned stimulus. For one group of rats, the tone and shock were paired 20 times—with the shock always occurring during the tone. The other group of rats also received the shock 20 times while the tone was sounding, but this group also received 20 shocks that were not paired with the tone. Only the first group, for which the tone was a reliable predictor of the shock, developed the conditioned response to the tone. For the second group, the tone provided no additional information about the shock because the shock was just as likely to occur without the tone as with it.

Biological Predisposition

You might be surprised to learn that genetics plays a role in classical conditioning. For instance, a single gene seems to underlie the ability of a mouse to quickly learn to avoid a potentially harmful stimulus such as an electric shock (Mathur, Graybeal, Feyder, Davis, & Holmes, 2009). Mice with this gene require only one trial to learn to avoid the stimulus, whereas those who lack the gene require more trials or fail to acquire the avoidance response at all. Thus, many contemporary researchers claim that *biological predispositions*, or the degree to which genes prepare animals and humans to acquire or resist acquiring classically conditioned responses, are an important factor in the conditioning process.

One important finding concerns the tendency of humans to acquire conditioned fears of some objects more easily than they do of others. For example, think back to Watson's Little Albert experiment. Do you think Watson could just as easily have conditioned a fear response to a flower or a piece of ribbon? Probably not. Research has shown that humans are more easily conditioned to fear stimuli that can have very real negative effects on their well-being, such as snakes (Mineka & Oehlberg, 2008). Moreover, fear of snakes and other potentially threatening animals is just as common in apes and monkeys as in humans, suggesting a biological predisposition to develop these fearful responses.

According to Martin Seligman (1972), most common fears "are related to the survival of the human species through the long course of evolution" (p. 455). Seligman (1970) suggested that humans and other animals are prepared to associate only certain stimuli with particular consequences. One example of this preparedness is the tendency to develop a **taste aversion**—the intense dislike and/or avoidance of a particular food that has been associated with nausea or discomfort. For example, experiencing nausea after eating, say, a hot dog can be enough to condition a long-lasting taste aversion to hot dogs.

In a classic study of taste aversion, Garcia and Koelling (1966) exposed rats to a three-way conditioned stimulus: a bright light, a clicking noise, and flavoured water. They measured how much flavoured and unflavoured water the rats would consume. For one group of rats, the unconditioned stimulus involved being exposed to either X-rays or lithium chloride, both of which produce nausea and vomiting several hours after exposure. A second group of rats received electric shock to their feet as the unconditioned stimulus. The group of rats that were made ill associated the flavoured water with the nausea and avoided it at all times. These rats would drink unflavoured water even when the bright light and the clicking sound were present—so *only the flavoured water served as a conditioned stimulus*. The rats who received the electric shock, however, continued to prefer the flavoured water over unflavoured water, but they would not drink at all when the bright light or clicking noise were present. This second group associated the electric shock *only* with the light and sound, not with the presence or absence of flavouring.

Garcia and Koelling's research established two exceptions to traditional ideas of classical conditioning. First, the finding that rats formed an association between nausea and flavoured water ingested several hours earlier contradicted the principle that the conditioned stimulus must be presented shortly before the unconditioned stimulus. Second, the finding that the groups of rats formed different associations (i.e., one group associated electric shock *only* with noise and light and the other associated nausea *only* with the flavoured water) suggested that animals may be biologically predisposed to make certain associations when faced with one stimulus and other associations when faced with other stimuli. Therefore, associations between *any* two stimuli may not be readily conditioned.

Other research on conditioned taste aversions has led to the solution of practical problems such as helping cancer patients. One unfortunate result of radiation therapy and chemotherapy is that patients often associate nausea with the foods they ate several hours before treatment (Bovbjerg et al., 1992). As a result, they often develop taste aversions to the foods they normally eat—even favourite foods. This can lead to

a loss of appetite and weight at a time when good nutrition is particularly important.

Bernstein and colleagues (Bernstein, Webster, & Bernstein, 1982; Bernstein, 1985) devised a technique to help patients avoid developing aversions to desirable foods. A group of cancer patients were fed a novel-tasting, maple-flavoured ice cream before chemotherapy. The nausea caused by the treatment resulted in a taste aversion to the ice cream. It was found that when an unusual or unfamiliar food became the "scapegoat" or target for taste aversion, other foods in the patient's diet were often protected, and the patient continued to eat them regularly. To address conditioned food aversions, researchers also have identified drugs and natural plant-based alternatives to reduce nausea during treatment (Kamen, Tejani, Chandwani, Janelsins, Peoples, Roscoe, & Morrow, 2014).

CLASSICAL CONDITIONING IN EVERYDAY LIFE

What types of responses can be learned through classical conditioning?

Do certain songs have special meaning because they remind you of a current or past love? Do you find the scent of a certain perfume or aftershave pleasant or unpleasant because it reminds you of a particular person? Many of our emotional responses, whether positive or negative, result from classical conditioning (often higher-order conditioning). Classical conditioning is an important, even essential, learning capacity for humans. Indeed, some research suggests that the inability to acquire classically conditioned responses may be one of the first signs of Alzheimer's disease, and may appear prior to any memory loss (Woodruff-Pak, 2001). **[LO 5.4]**

Fear Responses

Fears and phobias largely result from classical conditioning. For example, many people who have had painful dental work develop a dental phobia. Not only do they come to fear the dentist's drill, but they also develop anxiety in response to a wide range of environmental stimuli associated with it—the dental chair, the waiting room, or even the building where the dentist's office is located.

Drug Use

Through classical conditioning, environmental cues associated with drug use can become conditioned stimuli and later produce the conditioned responses of drug craving (M. Field & Duka, 2002; Childs & Wit, 2011). The conditioned stimuli associated with drugs become powerful, often irresistible forces that lead individuals to seek out and use those substances (Porrino & Lyons, 2000). For example, why do many drug addicts treated for overdoses in hospital emergency rooms report that they had taken only their usual dose but were *not* in their usual drug-taking environment when they overdosed?

All drugs produce characteristic physiological effects. As a person continues to use a drug, the body makes adjustments to

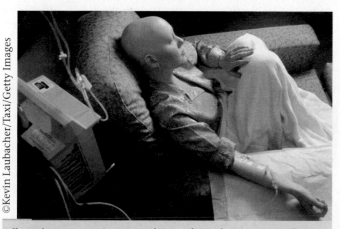

Chemotherapy treatments can result in conditioned taste aversions, but providing patients with a "scapegoat" target for the taste aversion can help them maintain a proper diet.

taste aversion: The dislike and/or avoidance of a particular food that has been associated with nausea or discomfort.

Classical conditioning helps explain why certain environmental cues or social situations can lead to continued drug use.

decrease the drug's effects. These adjustments enable the body to *tolerate* the drug. Over time a **drug tolerance** develops—that is, the user becomes progressively less affected by the drug and must take higher and higher doses to maintain the same effects.

If drug tolerance were solely a physiological phenomenon, it wouldn't make any difference where or in what circumstances

the addict took the drug. But it does make a difference. In many cases, addicts suffer overdoses (some of them fatal) in unfamiliar surroundings—a hotel room, for example—not in a place where they habitually take the drug. Why should the same amount of a drug produce stronger physiological effects in an unfamiliar environment than in a familiar one? The answer involves classical conditioning.

Here is how the process works. Environmental cues associated with the setting where drugs are usually taken—the familiar surroundings, sights, sounds, odours, and drug paraphernalia, along with the familiar drug-use ritual—can act as conditioned stimuli that become associated with the unconditioned stimulus, which is the drug itself (Dworkin, 1993; M. Field & Duka, 2002; Siegel, Hinson, Krank, & McCully, 1982). These environmental cues come to signal to the user that the drug is on the way, and initiate the compensatory mechanisms. In other words, these cues stimulate physiological effects that are primarily the opposite of the physiological effects of the drug. When the user takes the usual dose of the drug in unfamiliar surroundings, the environmental cues that initiate these protective mechanisms are not present. Consequently, the effects of the drugs are more powerful—sometimes even fatal. Drug counsellors therefore strongly urge recovering addicts to avoid any cues (people, places, and things) associated with their past drug use. Relapse is far more common in those who do not avoid such associated environmental cues.

ADVERTISING When business people wine and dine customers, they are hoping they and their product or service will elicit the same positive response as the pleasant setting and fine food. Advertisers are trying to classically condition us when they show us their products along with great-looking models or celebrities or in situations where people are enjoying themselves. The advertisers are relying on the probability that if the "neutral" product is associated with people, objects, or situations that we particularly like, then in time the product will elicit a similarly positive response. Pavlov found that presenting the tone slightly before the food was the most efficient way to condition salivation. Television advertisements, too, are most effective when the products are presented *before* the beautiful people or situations are shown (van den Hout & Merckelbach, 1991). You might want to see just how much the principles of classical conditioning are applied in advertising by doing *Try It*.

spare me the guilt chip.

Katy Perry

Classical conditioning has proved to be a highly effective tool for advertising. Here a relatively new and neutral product is paired with an image of an attractive and popular celebrity.

TRY IT

Classical Conditioning in Commercials

Some commercials simply give information about a product or place of business. Others are designed to classically condition the viewer to form a positive association. One night while you are watching TV, keep a record of the commercials you see. What proportion rely on classical conditioning? What are the kinds of cues (people, objects, or situations) with which the products are to be associated? Are the products introduced slightly before, during, or after these cues?

SEXUAL AROUSAL Classical conditioning also may serve a vital role in sexual arousal (Pfaus, Kippen, & Coria-Avila, 2003; Parada, Abdul-Ahad, Censi, Sparks, & Pfaus, 2011). Recent Canadian research has used animal models to demonstrate how environmental cues (such as specific places), smells, and other artifacts (for example, clothing) become associated with sexual experiences and subsequently come to have an important role in successful sexual experiences. For more information about classical conditioning and sexual arousal, see the *Canadian Connections* box.

CANADIAN CONNECTIONS

Sexual Arousal and Classical Conditioning

We are all familiar with things in the environment that can promote sexual arousal; for example, some people are aroused by erotic images, or scents, or sensuous touch, or some combination of these. In extreme cases, erotic interest and satisfaction may require the presence of an inanimate object such as underclothing, leather, or high-heeled shoes. This psychological condition is known as a *paraphilia or fetish*.

Can classical conditioning help explain how these preferences develop? Research conducted by James Pfaus and his colleagues at Concordia University uses animal models to help us understand how the environment and sexual arousal are linked in humans (e.g., Pfaus, 2007; Pfaus, Erickson & Talianakis, 2013). In one study, young male rats were introduced to clothing as part of their first sexual experiences. Specifically, the male rats were each given a small jacket to wear just before being placed in a chamber with a sexually receptive female rat. Over the next few days, the male rats were given several opportunities to mate—each time dressed in their jackets before gaining access to the female. Would the jackets prove important for sexual arousal after consistently being paired with the mating opportunity?

To find the answer, half of the males that had worn the jackets were each placed in a chamber with a receptive female, but this time without their jackets on. The other half continued to wear their jackets when they were placed with a female. The group that no longer wore their jackets took a much longer time to begin trying to copulate and a much longer time to ejaculate than did their jacketed counterparts. Clearly, the jackets had become an important part of the rats' sexual experience. Jackets had become a conditioned stimulus for sexual arousal, and without them, the rats' sexual performance suffered.

James Pfaus

Pfaus suggests that these findings indicate how elements in the environment paired with early sexual experiences might account for the development of fetishes or other preferences for sexual arousal. ∎

REMEMBER IT

Classical Conditioning

1. According to Rescorla, the most critical element in classical conditioning is _____.
2. Garcia and Koelling's research suggests that classical conditioning is influenced by _____.
3. Conditioning of a _____ contradicts the general principle of classical conditioning that the unconditioned stimulus should occur immediately after the conditioned stimulus and the two should be paired repeatedly.
4. Classical conditioning can help to explain drug overdose as both the drug and the _____ in which drugs are taken appear to be important.

Answers: 1. prediction 2. biological predispositions 3. taste aversion 4. environment

drug tolerance: A condition in which the user becomes progressively less affected by a drug so that larger and larger doses are necessary to achieve or maintain the same effect.

MODULE **5B** OPERANT CONDITIONING

LO 5.6 Define *operant conditioning*.

LO 5.7 Define and explain each of the key elements of operant conditioning, including *reinforcers/reinforcement* and *punishers/punishment*.

LO 5.8 Understand how basic principles such as shaping, extinction, spontaneous recovery, generalization, and discrimination function within operant conditioning.

LO 5.9 Explain how different reinforcement schedules impact on learning.

LO 5.10 Understand the strengths and weaknesses associated with punishment.

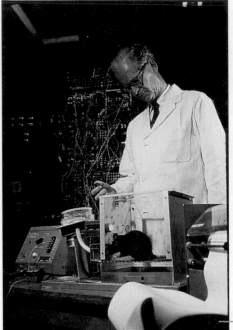

B. F. Skinner shapes a rat's bar-pressing behaviour in a Skinner box.

SKINNER AND OPERANT CONDITIONING

How are responses acquired through operant conditioning?

Recall that in classical conditioning, the organism does not learn a new response. Rather, it learns to make an old or existing response to a new stimulus. Classically conditioned responses are involuntary or reflexive, and in most cases the person or animal cannot help but respond in expected ways.

Let's now examine a method for conditioning *voluntary* responses, known as **operant conditioning**. Operant conditioning does not begin, as does classical conditioning, with the presentation of a stimulus to elicit a response. Rather, the response comes first, and the consequence tends to modify this response in the future. In operant conditioning, the consequences of behaviour are manipulated to increase or decrease the frequency of a response or to shape an entirely new response. **[LO 5.6]** Behaviour that is reinforced—followed by rewarding consequences—tends to be repeated. A **reinforcer** is anything that strengthens a response or increases the probability that the response will occur. Behaviour that is ignored or punished is less likely to be repeated. **[LO 5.7]**

Operant conditioning permits the learning of a wide range of new responses. A simple response can be operantly conditioned if we merely wait for it to appear and then reinforce it. But this can be time-consuming. We can speed the process up with a technique called *shaping*. Shaping can also be used to condition responses that would never occur naturally.

Shaping Behaviour: Just a Little Bit at a Time

How is shaping used to condition a response?

Shaping is a technique that was employed by B. F. Skinner. Skinner is seen by many as the great authority on operant conditioning, which is particularly useful in conditioning complex behaviours. In shaping, rather than waiting for the desired response to occur and then reinforcing it, we reinforce any movement in the direction of the desired response, gradually guiding the responses closer and closer to the ultimate goal. **[LO 5.8]**

Skinner designed a soundproof operant-conditioning apparatus, commonly called a **Skinner box**, with which

he conducted his experiments. One type of Skinner box is equipped with a lever or bar that a rat presses to gain a reward of food pellets or water from a dispenser. A complete record of the animal's bar-pressing responses is registered on a device called a *cumulative recorder*, also invented by Skinner.

Rats in a Skinner box are conditioned through the use of shaping to press a bar for rewards. A rat may be rewarded first for simply turning toward the bar. Once this behaviour is established, the next reward comes only when the rat moves closer to the bar. Each step closer to the bar is rewarded. Next, the rat may touch the bar and receive a reward; finally, the rat is rewarded only when it presses the bar.

Shaping—rewarding gradual **successive approximations** toward the terminal or desired response—has been used effectively to condition complex behaviours in people as well as in non-human animals. **[LO 5.8]** Parents may use shaping to help their children develop good table manners, praising them each time they show gradual improvements. Teachers often use shaping with disruptive children, rewarding them at first for very short periods of good behaviour and then gradually expecting them to work productively for longer and longer periods. Through shaping, circus animals have learned to perform a wide range of amazing feats, and pigeons have learned to bowl and play table tennis. You might even want to try shaping your own behaviour using the next *Try It*.

Superstitious Behaviour: Mistaking a Coincidence for a Cause

Sometimes a rewarding event follows a response but is not caused by or connected with it. Superstitious behaviour occurs when an individual believes that a connection exists between an act and its consequences although, in fact, there is no relationship between the two.

A gambler in Windsor, Ontario, blows on the dice just before he rolls them and wins $1000. On the next roll, he follows the same ritual and wins again. Although this rewarding event follows the ritual of blowing on the dice, the connection between the two is accidental. Nevertheless, the gambler will probably persist in this superstitious behaviour at least as long as his winning streak continues. Some professional athletes have been known to carry superstitious behaviour to remarkable extremes. For example, hockey goaltender Patrick Roy had a warm-up routine that included standing in front of the net and imagining it shrinking. Roy never stepped on the blue line or red line, and he talked to the goalposts during the game (Murdoch, 2005).

Extinction: Withholding Reinforcers

How does extinction occur in operant conditioning?

We have seen that responses followed by reinforcers tend to be repeated. What happens when reinforcement is no longer available? A rat in a Skinner box will eventually stop pressing a bar when it is no longer rewarded with food pellets. In operant conditioning, extinction occurs when reinforcers are withheld. **[LO 5.8]**

In humans and other animals, extinction can lead to frustration or even rage. Consider a child having a temper tantrum. If whining and loud demands do not bring the reinforcer, the child may progress to kicking and screaming. If a vending machine takes your coins but fails to deliver candy or pop, your button-pushing or lever-pulling behaviour may become erratic and more forceful. You might even shake the machine or kick it before giving up. Not getting what we expect makes us angry.

The process of spontaneous recovery, which we discussed in relation to classical conditioning, also occurs in operant conditioning. A rat whose bar pressing has been extinguished may again press the bar a few times when returned to the Skinner box after a period of rest.

Generalization and Discrimination

Skinner conducted many of his experiments with pigeons placed in a Skinner box specially designed for them. The box contained small, illuminated disks that the pigeons could peck to receive bits of grain from a food tray. Skinner found that generalization occurs in operant conditioning. A pigeon rewarded for pecking at a yellow disk is likely to peck at another disk similar in colour. The less similar a disk is to the original colour, the lower the rate of pecking will be. **[LO 5.8]**

Discrimination in operant conditioning involves learning to distinguish between a stimulus that has been reinforced and other stimuli that may be very similar. **[LO 5.8]** We learn discrimination when our response to the original stimulus is reinforced but responses to similar stimuli are not reinforced. For example, to encourage discrimination, a researcher would reward the pigeon for pecking at the yellow disk but not for pecking at the orange or red disk.

TRY IT

Can You Modify Your Own Behaviour?

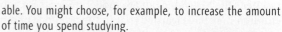

Use conditioning to modify your own behaviour.

1. *Identify the target behaviour*. It must be both observable and measurable. You might choose, for example, to increase the amount of time you spend studying.
2. *Gather and record baseline data*. Keep a daily record of how much time you spend on the target behaviour for about a week. Also note where the behaviour takes place and what cues (or temptations) in the environment precede any slacking off from the target behaviour.
3. *Plan your behaviour modification program*. Formulate a plan and set goals to either decrease or increase the target behaviour.
4. *Choose your reinforcers*. Any activity you enjoy more can be used to reinforce any activity you enjoy less. For example, you could reward yourself with a game of basketball after a specified period of studying.
5. *Set the reinforcement conditions and begin recording and reinforcing your progress*. Be careful not to set your reinforcement goals so high that it becomes nearly impossible to earn a reward; remember Skinner's concept of shaping—rewarding small steps to reach a desired outcome. Be perfectly honest with yourself and claim a reward only when the goals are met. Chart your progress as you work toward gaining more and more control over the target behaviour.

Certain cues come to be associated with reinforcement or punishment. For example, children are more likely to ask their parents for a treat when the parents are smiling than when they are frowning. The stimulus that signals whether a certain

operant conditioning: A type of learning in which the consequences of behaviour tend to modify that behaviour in the future (behaviour that is reinforced tends to be repeated; behaviour that is ignored or punished is less likely to be repeated).

reinforcer: Anything that strengthens a response or increases the probability that it will occur.

shaping: Gradually moulding a desired behaviour by reinforcing responses that become progressively closer to it; reinforcing successive approximations of the desired response.

Skinner box: Invented by B. F. Skinner for conducting experiments in operant conditioning; a soundproof chamber with a device for delivering food and either a bar for rats to press or a disk for pigeons to peck.

successive approximations: A series of gradual training steps, with each step becoming more like the final desired response.

response or behaviour is likely to be rewarded, ignored, or punished is called a **discriminative stimulus**. If a pigeon's peck at a lighted disk results in a reward but a peck at an unlighted disk does not, the pigeon will soon be pecking at the lighted disk but not at the unlighted one. The presence or absence of the discriminative stimulus, in this case the lighted disk, will control whether or not the pecking takes place.

We may wonder why children sometimes misbehave with a grandparent but not with a parent, or why they make one teacher's life miserable but are model students for another. The children may have learned that in the presence of some people (the discriminative stimuli), misbehaviour will almost certainly lead to punishment, whereas in the presence of certain other people it may even be rewarded.

REINFORCEMENT: WHAT'S THE PAYOFF?

Positive and Negative Reinforcement: Adding the Good, Taking Away the Bad

What are the goals of both positive and negative reinforcement, and how are the goals accomplished for each?

Reinforcement is a key concept in operant conditioning, and may be defined as any event that increases the probability of the response that it follows. There are two types of reinforcement: positive and negative. **[LO 5.7]** These terms are used in their mathematical sense in operant conditioning. Thus, *positive* is equivalent to *added*, and *negative* is equivalent to *subtracted* or *removed*.

Positive reinforcement refers to any *positive* consequence that, if applied after a response, increases the probability of that response. We know that many people will work hard for a raise or a promotion, that salespeople will increase their efforts to get awards and bonuses, that students will study to get good grades, and that children will throw temper tantrums to get candy or ice cream. In these examples, raises, promotions, awards, bonuses, good grades, candy, and ice cream are positive reinforcers.

Negative reinforcement involves learning a behaviour in order to make something unpleasant go away. When people find that a response successfully ends an aversive condition, they are likely to repeat it. People will turn on their air conditioner to terminate the heat, and they will get out of bed to turn off a faucet to avoid listening to the annoying "drip, drip, drip." For many students, studying with classmates (learned behaviour) reduces test anxiety (removed consequence). Thus, for these students, test anxiety is an important source of negative reinforcement, one that encourages them to engage in effective study behaviours. In these instances, negative reinforcement involves putting an end to the heat, the dripping faucet, and anxiety.

Responses that end discomfort and responses that are followed by rewards are likely to be strengthened or repeated because *both* lead to a more favourable outcome. Some behaviours are influenced by a combination of positive and negative reinforcement. If you eat a plateful of rather disgusting leftovers to relieve intense hunger, then eating probably has been negatively reinforced. You are eating solely to remove hunger, a negative reinforcer. But if your hunger is relieved by a gourmet dinner at a fine restaurant, both positive and negative reinforcement will have played a role. Your hunger has been removed, and the delicious dinner has been a reward in itself.

Do the *Try It* to see how your behaviour is influenced by positive and negative reinforcers in everyday life.

Primary and Secondary Reinforcers: The Unlearned and the Learned

A **primary reinforcer** is one that fulfills a basic physical need for survival and does not depend on learning. Food, water, sleep, and termination of pain are examples of primary reinforcers. And sex too is a powerful reinforcer. Fortunately, learning does not depend solely on primary reinforcers. If that were the case, we would need to be hungry, thirsty, or sex-starved before we would respond at all. Much observed behaviour in humans is in response to secondary rather than primary reinforcers. A **secondary reinforcer** is acquired or learned by association with other reinforcers. Some secondary reinforcers (money, for example) can be exchanged at a later time for other reinforcers. Praise, good grades, awards, bonuses, applause, and signals of approval such as a smile or a kind word are all examples of secondary reinforcers. **[LO 5.7]**

Attention is a secondary reinforcer of great general worth. To obtain the reinforcers we seek from other people, we must first get their attention. Children vie for the attention of parents because they represent the main source of a child's reinforcers. But often parents reward children with attention for misbehaviour and ignore their good behaviour. When this happens, misbehaviour is strengthened, and good behaviour may be extinguished for lack of reinforcement.

Schedules of Reinforcement: When Will I Get My Reinforcers?

What are the four major schedules of reinforcement, and which schedule yields the highest response rate and the greatest resistance to extinction?

In conditioning the bar-pressing response in rats, every time the rat pressed the bar, the experimenter reinforced the response with a food pellet. Reinforcing every correct response, known as **continuous reinforcement**, is the most efficient way to condition a new response. **[LO 5.9]** However, after a response has been conditioned, partial or intermittent reinforcement is more effective if we want to maintain or increase the rate of response (Nation & Woods, 1980). **Partial reinforcement** is operating when some but not all of an organism's responses are reinforced. In real life, reinforcement is almost never continuous. Partial reinforcement is the rule.

Partial reinforcement may be administered according to different **schedules of reinforcement**. Different schedules produce distinct rates and patterns of responses, as well as varying degrees of resistance to extinction when reinforcement is discontinued. Although several varieties of reinforcement

TRY IT

Reinforcement in Everyday Life

In a chart, list all of your behaviours during the course of a day that have been influenced by either positive or negative reinforcement. Also list the behaviours that have been influenced by a combination of the two. During that day, were more behaviours positively or negatively reinforced?

Behaviour	Positive Reinforcement	Negative Reinforcement	Combination
Ate breakfast			
Attended class			
Totals			

schedules are possible, the two basic types are the ratio and interval schedules. Ratio schedules require that a certain *number of responses* be made before one of the responses is reinforced. With interval schedules, a given *amount of time* must pass before a reinforcer is administered. These schedules are further subdivided into fixed and variable categories.

Following are descriptions of the four most basic schedules of reinforcement: the fixed-ratio schedule, the variable-ratio schedule, the fixed-interval schedule, and the variable-interval schedule. **[LO 5.9]**

THE FIXED-RATIO SCHEDULE On a **fixed-ratio schedule**, a reinforcer is administered after a fixed number of non-reinforced correct responses. If the fixed ratio is set at 30 responses (FR–30), a reinforcer is given after 30 correct responses. Examples of this schedule are factory workers whose payment depends on the

Migrant farm workers are paid according to a fixed-ratio schedule. Since their earnings depend on the number of bushels of tomatoes they pick, they are motivated to work quickly.

©Chris Thomaidis/The Image Bank/Getty Images

number of units produced and farm workers who are paid by the basket for the fruit they pick.

The fixed-ratio schedule is a very effective way to maintain a high response rate, because the number of reinforcers received depends directly on the response rate. The faster people respond, the more reinforcers they earn. When large ratios are used, people and animals tend to pause after each reinforcement but then return to the characteristic high rate of responding.

THE VARIABLE-RATIO SCHEDULE Pauses after reinforcement do not occur when the variable-ratio schedule is used. On a **variable-ratio schedule**, a reinforcer is administered on the basis of an average ratio after a varying number of non-reinforced correct responses. With a variable ratio of 30 responses (VR–30), you might be reinforced one time after 10 responses, another after 50, another after 30, and so on. You cannot predict exactly which responses will be reinforced, but in this example, reinforcement would average 1 in 30.

Variable-ratio schedules result in higher, more stable rates of responding than fixed-ratio schedules do. B. F. Skinner (1953) reports that on this schedule "a pigeon may respond as rapidly

discriminative stimulus: A stimulus that signals whether a certain response or behaviour is likely to be followed by reward or punishment.

reinforcement: An event that follows a response and increases the strength of the response and/or the likelihood that it will be repeated.

positive reinforcement: A reward or pleasant consequence that follows a response and increases the probability that the response will be repeated.

negative reinforcement: The termination of an unpleasant stimulus after a response in order to increase the probability that the response will be repeated.

primary reinforcer: A reinforcer that fulfills a basic physical need for survival and does not depend on learning (e.g., food, water, sleep, termination of pain).

secondary reinforcer: A neutral stimulus that becomes reinforcing after repeated pairing with other reinforcers.

continuous reinforcement: Reinforcement that is administered after every desired or correct response; the most effective method of conditioning a new response.

partial reinforcement: A pattern of reinforcement in which some portion, rather than 100 percent, of the correct responses are reinforced.

schedules of reinforcement: Systematic programs for administering reinforcement that have a predictable effect on behaviour.

fixed-ratio schedule: A schedule in which a reinforcer is administered after a fixed number of non-reinforced correct responses.

variable-ratio schedule: A schedule in which a reinforcer is administered on the basis of an average ratio after a varying number of non-reinforced correct responses.

©Misko Kordic/Fotolia

Gamblers receive payoffs according to a variable-ratio schedule. They cannot predict when they will be reinforced, so they are highly motivated to keep playing.

as five times per second and maintain this rate for many hours" (p. 104). According to Skinner (1988), the variable-ratio schedule is useful because "it maintains behavior against extinction when reinforcers occur only infrequently. The behavior of the dedicated artist, writer, businessman, or scientist is sustained by an occasional, unpredictable reinforcement" (p. 174).

An insurance salesperson working on a variable-ratio schedule may sell policies to two clients in a row, but then may have to contact 20 more prospects before making another sale. The best example of the seemingly addictive power of the variable-ratio schedule is the gambling casino. Slot machines, roulette wheels, and most other games of chance pay on this schedule. The variable-ratio schedule, in general, produces the highest response rate and the most resistance to extinction.

THE FIXED-INTERVAL SCHEDULE   On a **fixed-interval schedule**, a specific time interval must pass before a response is reinforced. For example, on a 60-second fixed-interval schedule (FI–60), a reinforcer is given for the first correct response that occurs 60 seconds after the last reinforced response. People working on salary are reinforced on the fixed-interval schedule.

Unlike ratio schedules, reinforcement on interval schedules does not depend on the number of responses made, only on the one correct response made after the time interval has passed. Characteristic of the fixed-interval schedule is a pause or a sharp decline in responding immediately after each reinforcement and a rapid acceleration in responding just before the next reinforcer is due.

As an example of this schedule, think of a psychology test as a reinforcer (that's a joke, isn't it?) and studying for the test as the desired response. Suppose you have four tests scheduled during the semester. Your study responses will probably drop to zero immediately after the first test, gradually accelerate, and perhaps reach a frenzied peak just before the next scheduled exam; then your study responses will immediately drop to zero again, and so on. As you may have guessed, the fixed-interval schedule produces the lowest response rate.

THE VARIABLE-INTERVAL SCHEDULE   Variable-interval schedules eliminate the pause after reinforcement that is typical of the fixed-interval schedule. On a **variable-interval schedule**, a reinforcer is administered on the basis of an average time after the first correct response following a varying time of non-reinforced responses. Rather than reinforcing a response every 60 seconds, for example, a reinforcer might be given after a 30-second interval, with others following after 90-, 45-, and 75-second intervals. But the average time elapsing between reinforcers would be 60 seconds (VI–60). Although this schedule maintains remarkably stable and uniform rates of responding, the response rate is typically lower than that of the ratio schedules because reinforcement is not tied directly to the *number* of responses made. Random drug testing in the workplace is an excellent example of the variable-interval schedule that appears to be quite effective.

Review & Reflect 5.1 summarizes the characteristics of the four schedules of reinforcement.

The Effect of Continuous and Partial Reinforcement on Extinction

What is the partial-reinforcement effect?

One way to understand extinction in operant conditioning is to consider how consistently a response is followed by reinforcement. On a continuous schedule, a reinforcer is expected without fail after each correct response. When a reinforcer is withheld, it is noticed immediately. But on a partial-reinforcement schedule, a reinforcer is not expected after every response. Thus, no immediate difference is apparent between the partial-reinforcement schedule and the onset of extinction. **[LO 5.8 & 5.9]**

When you put money in a vending machine and pull the lever but no candy or pop appears, you know immediately that something is wrong with the machine. But if you are playing a broken slot machine, you could have many non-reinforced responses before suspecting that the machine is malfunctioning.

REVIEW & REFLECT 5.1 REINFORCEMENT SCHEDULES COMPARED TO RESPONSE RATE, PATTERN OF RESPONSES, AND RESISTANCE TO EXTINCTION

Schedule of Reinforcement	Response Rate	Pattern of Responses	Resistance to Extinction
Fixed-ratio	Very high	Steady response with low ratio	The higher the ratio, the more resistant to extinction
		Brief pause after each reinforcement with very high ratio	
Variable-ratio	Highest	Constant response pattern, no pauses	Most resistant to extinction
Fixed-interval	Lowest	Long pause after reinforcement followed by gradual acceleration	The longer the interval, the more resistant to extinction
Variable-interval	Moderate	Stable, uniform response	More resistant to extinction than fixed-interval schedule with same average interval

Partial reinforcement results in a greater resistance to extinction than does continuous reinforcement (Lerman, Iwata, Shore, & Kahng, 1996). This result is known as the **partial-reinforcement effect**. There is an inverse relationship between the percentage of responses that have been reinforced and resistance to extinction—that is, the lower the percentage of responses that are reinforced, the longer extinction will take when reinforcement is withheld (Weinstock, 1954). The strongest resistance to extinction that we can find on record occurred in one experiment in which pigeons were conditioned to peck at a disk. According to Holland and Skinner (1961), "After the response had been maintained on a fixed ratio of 900 and reinforcement was then discontinued, the pigeon emitted 73,000 responses during the first . . . 2 hours of extinction" (p. 124).

Parents often wonder why their children continue to nag to get what they want, even though the parents *usually* do not give in to the nagging. Unwittingly, the parents are reinforcing their children's nagging on a variable-ratio schedule, which results in the most persistent behaviour. For this reason experts always caution parents to be consistent. If parents *never* reward nagging, the behaviour will extinguish; if they give in occasionally, it will persist and be extremely hard to extinguish.

FACTORS INFLUENCING OPERANT CONDITIONING

What three factors, in addition to the schedule of reinforcement, influence operant conditioning?

We know that responses are acquired more quickly with continuous rather than partial reinforcement, and that the schedule of reinforcement influences both response rates and resistance to extinction. Several other factors affect how quickly a response is acquired, the response rate, and the resistance to extinction.

The first factor is the *magnitude of reinforcement*. In general, as the magnitude of reinforcement increases, acquisition of a response is faster, the rate of responding is higher, and resistance to extinction is greater (K. N. Clayton, 1964). For example, in studies examining the influence of cash incentives on drug addicts' ability to abstain from taking the drug, researchers have found that the greater the amount of the incentive, the more likely the addicts are to abstain over extended periods of time (Dallery, Silverman, Chutuape, Bigelow, & Sitzer, 2001; Katz et al., 2002).

The second factor affecting operant conditioning is the *immediacy of reinforcement*. In general, responses are conditioned more effectively when reinforcement is immediate. As a rule, the longer the delay in reinforcement, the more slowly the response will be acquired (Church, 1989; Mazur, 1993; and see Figure 5.5, on the next page). One reason overweight people have difficulty changing their eating habits is because of the long delay between their behaviour change and the rewarding consequences of weight loss and better health.

The third factor influencing conditioning is the *level of motivation* of the learner. If you are highly motivated to learn

fixed-interval schedule: A schedule in which a reinforcer is administered following the first correct response after a fixed period of time has elapsed.

variable-interval schedule: A schedule in which a reinforcer is administered on the basis of an average time after the first correct response following a varying time of non-reinforcement.

partial-reinforcement effect: The greater resistance to extinction that occurs when a portion, rather than 100 percent, of the correct responses have been reinforced.

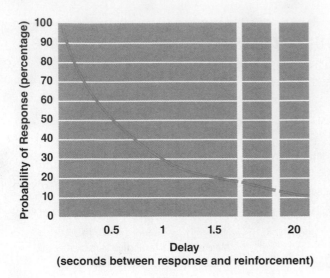

FIGURE 5.5

The Effect of Delay in Reinforcement on Conditioning of a Response

In general, responses are conditioned more effectively when reinforcement is immediate. The longer the delay in reinforcement, the lower the probability that a response will be acquired.

to play tennis, you will learn faster and practise more than if you have no interest in the game. Skinner found that when food is the reinforcer, a hungry animal will learn faster than a full animal. To maximize motivation, he used rats that had been deprived of food for 24 hours and pigeons that were maintained at 75 to 80 percent of their normal body weight.

PUNISHMENT: LESS IS BEST!

How does punishment differ from negative reinforcement?

Punishment is the opposite of reinforcement. Punishment lowers the probability of a response. **[LOs 5.7 & 5.10]** It can be accomplished by the addition of an unpleasant stimulus or by the removal of a pleasant stimulus. The added unpleasant stimulus might be a scolding, criticism, a disapproving look, a fine, or a prison sentence. The removal of a pleasant stimulus might involve withholding affection and attention, suspending a driver's licence, or taking away a privilege such as watching television.

It is common to confuse negative reinforcement and punishment. Unlike punishment, negative reinforcement increases the probability of a desired response by removing an unpleasant stimulus when the correct response is made (see *Review & Reflect 5.2*). "Grounding" can be used in either punishment or negative reinforcement. When a teenager fails to clean her room after many requests to do so, her parents could ground her for the weekend—a punishment. An alternative approach would be to use negative reinforcement—tell her she

is grounded *until* her room is clean. Which approach is likely to be more effective?

The Disadvantages of Punishment: Its Downside

What are some disadvantages of punishment?

Skinner always argued that punishment does not extinguish an undesirable behaviour; rather, it suppresses that behaviour when the punishing agent is present—the behaviour is likely to continue when the threat of punishment is removed and in settings where punishment is unlikely. **[LO 5.10]** There is ample empirical support for Skinner's argument. If punishment (imprisonment, fines, and so on) did extinguish criminal behaviour, there would be fewer repeat offenders in our criminal justice system.

Another problem with punishment is that it indicates which behaviours are unacceptable but does not help people develop more appropriate behaviours. If punishment is used, it should be administered in conjunction with reinforcement or rewards for appropriate behaviour.

Controlling behaviour by punishment has a number of other potential disadvantages. A person who is severely punished often becomes fearful and feels angry and hostile toward the punisher. These reactions may be accompanied by a desire to avoid or escape from the punisher and the punishing situation, or to find a way to retaliate.

Punishment frequently leads to aggression. Those who administer physical punishment may become models of aggressive behaviour—people who demonstrate aggression as a way of solving problems and discharging anger. Children of abusive, punishing parents are at greater risk than other children of becoming aggressive and abusive themselves (Huesmann, Moise-Titus, Podolski, & Eron, 2003; Widom, 1989).

Alternatives to Punishment: There's More Than One Way to Change Behaviour

Many psychologists believe that *removing the rewarding consequences of undesirable behaviour* is the best way to extinguish a problem behaviour. According to this view, parents should extinguish a child's temper tantrums not by punishment, but by *never* giving in to the child's demands during a tantrum. A parent might best extinguish problem behaviour that is performed merely to get attention by ignoring it and giving attention to more appropriate behaviour. Sometimes, simply explaining why certain behaviours are not appropriate is all that is required to extinguish the behaviour.

Using positive reinforcement such as praise will make good behaviour more rewarding for children. This approach brings with it the attention that children want and need—attention that too often is given only when they misbehave. And as we saw in our earlier example of grounding, negative reinforcement can often be more effective than punishment in bringing about desired outcomes.

Review & Reflect 5.2 summarizes the differences between reinforcement and punishment.

REVIEW & REFLECT **5.2** THE EFFECTS OF REINFORCEMENT AND PUNISHMENT

Reinforcement (increases or strengthens a particular behaviour)	Punishment (decreases or suppresses a particular behaviour)
Adding a Positive (positive reinforcement)	*Adding a Negative*
Presenting food, money, praise, attention, or other rewards	Delivering a pain-producing or otherwise aversive stimulus such as a spanking or an electric shock
Subtracting a Negative (negative reinforcement)	*Subtracting a Positive*
Removing or terminating some pain-producing or otherwise aversive stimulus, such as electric shock	Removing some pleasant stimulus or taking away privileges such as TV watching or use of automobile

Source: Wood, Samuel e.; Wood, Ellen Green; Boyd, Denise, The World of Psychology, 7th Ed., ©2011, pp.169, 174, 191. Reprinted and Electronically reproduced by permission of Pearson Education, Inc., New York, NY.

Making Punishment More Effective: Some Suggestions

What three factors increase the effectiveness of punishment?

When punishment is perceived to be necessary (e.g., to stop destructive behaviour), how can we be sure that it will be effective? Research has revealed several factors that influence the effectiveness of punishment: its *timing*, its *intensity*, and the *consistency* of its application (Parke, 1977). **[LO 5.10]**

1. Punishment is most effective when it is applied during the misbehaviour or as soon afterward as possible. Interrupting the problem behaviour is most effective because it abruptly halts the rewarding aspects of the misbehaviour. The longer the delay between the response and the punishment, the less effective the punishment will be in suppressing the response (Azrin & Holz, 1966; Camp, Raymond, & Church, 1967). If the punishment is delayed, the punisher should remind the perpetrator of the incident and explain why the behaviour was inappropriate.

2. Ideally, punishment should be the minimum necessary to suppress the problem behaviour. Unnecessarily severe punishment is likely to be accompanied by the negative side effects mentioned earlier. But if the initial punishment is too mild, it will have no effect. What if the intensity of the punishment is gradually increased? The perpetrator will gradually adapt to it, and the unwanted behaviour will persist (Azrin & Holz, 1966; R. L. Solomon, 1964). At a minimum, if a behaviour is to be suppressed, the punishment must be more punishing than the misbehaviour is rewarding. In human terms, a $2 speeding ticket would not be much of a deterrent; a $200 ticket is more likely to suppress the urge to speed.

3. To be effective, punishment must be applied consistently. For example, a parent cannot ignore an act of misbehaviour one day and punish the same act the next. There should also be consistency between different people administering the punishment. Both parents ought to react to the same misbehaviour in a consistent manner.

An undesired response will be suppressed more effectively when the probability of punishment is high. Few people would speed while observing a police car in the rear-view mirror.

4. Punishment should not be administered in anger. The purpose of punishment must always be clearly understood: it is not to vent anger but rather to modify behaviour. Also, punishment meted out in anger is likely to be more intense than necessary to bring about the desired result.

ESCAPE AND AVOIDANCE LEARNING

Learning to perform a behaviour because it terminates an aversive event is called *escape learning*, and it reflects the power of negative reinforcement. Running away from a punishing situation and taking a painkiller to relieve a pounding headache are examples of escape behaviour. In these situations, the aversive event has begun and an attempt is being made to escape it.

Avoidance learning depends on two types of conditioning. First, through classical conditioning, an event or condition comes to signal an aversive state. Drinking and driving may be associated with automobile accidents and death. Then, because of such associations, people may engage in behaviours to avoid the anticipated aversive consequences. Making it a practice to avoid driving with people who have had too much to drink is sensible avoidance behaviour.

Many avoidance behaviours are maladaptive, however, and occur in response to phobias. Students who have had a

punishment: The removal of a pleasant stimulus or the application of an unpleasant stimulus, both of which tend to suppress a response.

avoidance learning: Learning to avoid events or conditions associated with dreaded or aversive outcomes.

bad experience speaking in front of a class may begin to fear any situation that involves speaking before a group. Such students may avoid taking classes that require class presentations, or avoid taking leadership roles that require public speaking. Avoiding such situations prevents them from suffering the perceived dreaded consequences. But the avoidance behaviour is negatively reinforced and thus strengthened through operant conditioning. Maladaptive avoidance behaviours are very difficult to extinguish because people never give themselves a chance to learn that the dreaded consequences probably will not occur or are greatly exaggerated.

LEARNED HELPLESSNESS

It is fortunate that we (like other animals) can easily learn to escape and avoid punishing or aversive situations. Research on learned helplessness, however, suggests that if we are exposed to repeated aversive events that we can neither escape nor avoid, we may learn to do nothing—simply to sit or stand helplessly and suffer the punishment. **Learned helplessness** is a passive resignation to aversive conditions learned by repeated exposure to aversive events that are inescapable and unavoidable.

The initial experiment on learned helplessness was conducted by Overmeier and Seligman (1967), who used dogs as their subjects. Dogs in the experimental group were strapped, one at a time, into a harness from which they could not escape, and were exposed to electric shocks. Later, these same dogs were placed in a shuttle box with two experimental compartments separated by a low barrier. The dogs then experienced a series of trials in which a warning signal was followed by an electric shock. The floor on one side was electrified, and the dogs should have learned quickly to escape the electric shocks simply by jumping the barrier. Surprisingly, the dogs did not do so; they simply suffered as many shocks as the experimenter chose to deliver, *as if* they could not escape.

Another group of dogs, the control group, had not previously experienced the inescapable shock, and they behaved in an entirely different manner. They quickly learned to escape the shock by jumping the barrier when the warning signal sounded. Seligman reported that the dogs experiencing the inescapable shock were less active, had less appetite, and showed other depression-like symptoms (Seligman, 1990).

REMEMBER IT

Operant Conditioning

1. Which of the following processes occurs in operant conditioning when reinforcers are withheld?
   a. generalization
   b. discrimination
   c. spontaneous recovery
   a. extinction

2. Jennifer and Ashley are both employed raking leaves. Jennifer is paid $1 for each bag of leaves she rakes; Ashley is paid $4 per hour. Jennifer is paid according to the _____ schedule; Ashley is paid according to the _____ schedule.
   a. fixed-interval; fixed-ratio
   b. variable-ratio; fixed-interval
   c. variable-ratio; variable-interval
   d. fixed-ratio; fixed-interval

3. Which schedule of reinforcement yields the highest response rate and the greatest resistance to extinction?
   a. variable-ratio
   b. fixed-ratio
   c. variable-interval
   d. fixed-interval

4. Which of the following is not presented in the text as one of the major factors influencing the effectiveness of punishment?
   a. timing
   b. consistency
   c. intensity
   d. frequency

Answers: 1. d 2. d 3. a 4. d

MODULE 5C COMPARING CLASSICAL AND OPERANT CONDITIONING

LO 5.11 Compare and contrast the similarities and differences between classical and operant conditioning and the factors that influence them.

What processes are comparable in classical and operant conditioning?

The processes of generalization, discrimination, extinction, and spontaneous recovery occur in both classical and operant conditioning. **[LO 5.11]** Both types of conditioning depend on *associative learning*. But in classical conditioning, the association is formed between two stimuli—for example, a tone and food, a white rat and a loud noise, or a product and a celebrity. In operant conditioning, the association is established between a response and its consequences—studying hard and a high test grade, good table manners and praise from a parent, or (in the world of rats and pigeons) bar pressing and food or disk pecking and food.

In classical conditioning, the focus is on what precedes the response. Pavlov focused on what led up to the salivation in his dogs, not on what happened after they salivated. In operant conditioning, the focus is on what follows the response. If a rat's bar pressing or your studying is followed by a reinforcer, that response is more likely to occur in the future.

Generally, in classical conditioning, the subject is passive and responds to the environment rather than acting upon it.

In operant conditioning, the subject is active and *operates* on the environment. Children *do* something to get their parents' attention or their praise. *Review & Reflect 5.3* highlights the major differences between classical and operant conditioning.

Exceptions can be found to most general principles. Research in biofeedback indicates that internal responses, once believed to be completely involuntary, can be brought under a person's voluntary control.

REVIEW & REFLECT 5.3 CLASSICAL AND OPERANT CONDITIONING COMPARED

Characteristics	Classical Conditioning	Operant Conditioning
Type of association	Between two stimuli	Between a response and its consequence
State of subject	Passive	Active
Focus of attention	On what precedes response	On what follows response
Type of response typically involved	Involuntary or reflexive response	Voluntary response
Bodily response typically involved	Internal responses: emotional and glandular reactions; movement and verbal responses	External responses: muscular and skeletal
Range of responses	Relatively simple	Simple to highly complex
Responses learned	Emotional reactions: fears, likes, dislikes	Goal-oriented responses

Source: Wood, Samuel e.; Wood, Ellen Green; Boyd, Denise, The World of Psychology, 7th Ed., ©2011, pp. 169, 174, 191. Reprinted and Electronically reproduced by permission of Pearson Education, Inc., New York, NY.

REMEMBER IT

Comparing Classical and Operant Conditioning

1. Which of the following is not true of classical conditioning?
   a. An association is made between two stimuli.
   b. The participant is active.
   c. Responses are involuntary.
   d. The range of responses is relatively simple.

2. Both classical and operant conditioning rely upon _____ learning.

3. Recall what you have learned about classical and operant conditioning. Which of the following is descriptive of operant conditioning?
   a. An association is formed between a response and its consequence.
   b. The responses acquired are usually emotional reactions.
   c. The subject is usually passive.
   d. The response acquired is usually an involuntary or reflexive response.

Answers: 1. b 2. associative. 3. a

MODULE 5D BEHAVIOUR MODIFICATION: CHANGING OUR ACT

LO 5.12 Define *behaviour modification* and *token economy*.
LO 5.13 Apply behaviour modification in a real-world context.

What is behaviour modification?

Behaviour modification is a method of changing behaviour through a systematic program based on the principles of learning—classical conditioning, operant conditioning, or observational learning (which we will discuss soon). Most behaviour

learned helplessness: The learned response of resigning oneself passively to aversive conditions, rather than taking action to change, escape, or avoid them; learned through repeated exposure to inescapable or unavoidable aversive events.

behaviour modification: The systematic application of the learning principles of operant conditioning, classical conditioning, or observational learning to individuals or groups in order to eliminate undesirable behaviour and/or encourage desirable behaviour.

modification programs use the principles of operant conditioning. **[LO 5.12]**

Many institutions—schools, mental health care hospitals, homes for young offenders, prisons—have used behaviour modification programs with varying degrees of success. **[LO 5.13]** Institutions lend themselves well to such techniques because they provide a restricted environment where the consequences of behaviour can be more strictly controlled. Some institutions, such as prisons or mental health care hospitals, use **token economies**—programs that motivate socially desirable behaviour by reinforcing it with tokens. **[LO 5.12]** The tokens (poker chips or coupons) may later be exchanged for desired goods like candy or cigarettes and privileges such as weekend passes, free time, or participation in desired activities. People in the program know in advance exactly what behaviours will be reinforced and how they will be reinforced. Token economies have been used effectively in mental health care hospitals to encourage patients to attend to grooming, to interact with other patients, and to carry out housekeeping tasks (Ayllon & Azrin, 1965, 1968). **[LO 5.13]** Although the positive behaviours generally stop when the tokens are discontinued, this does not mean that the programs are not worthwhile. After all, most people who are employed would probably quit their jobs if they were no longer paid.

Classroom teachers have used behaviour modification to modify undesirable behaviour and to encourage learning. "Time out" is a useful technique in which a child who is misbehaving is removed for a short time from sources of positive reinforcement. (Remember that according to operant conditioning, a behaviour that is no longer reinforced will be extinguished.)

Some research indicates, however, that it may be unwise to reward students for participating in learning activities they already enjoy. Reinforcement in such cases may lessen students' natural interest in the tasks so that when reinforcers are withdrawn, that interest may disappear (Deci, 1975; Lepper, Greene, & Nisbett, 1973).

Behaviour modification has been used successfully in business and industry to increase profits and to modify employee behaviour in health, safety, and learning. To reduce costs associated with automobile accidents and auto theft, automobile insurance companies attempt to modify the behaviour of their policy holders. They offer incentives in the form of reduced insurance premiums for installing airbags and burglar alarm systems. To encourage their employees to take company-approved college and university courses, many companies offer tuition reimbursement contingent on course grades. Many companies also promote sales by giving salespeople special bonuses, awards, trips, and other prizes for increasing sales.

One of the most successful applications of behaviour modification has been in the treatment of psychological problems ranging from phobias to addictive behaviours. In this context, behaviour modification is called *behaviour therapy*. This kind of therapy is discussed in Chapter 14.

You can learn how to use behaviour modification in shaping your own behaviour in the *Apply It* box at the end of this chapter.

REMEMBER IT

Behaviour Modification

1. Applying the principles of learning to eliminate undesirable behaviour and/or encourage desirable behaviour is called (operant conditioning/behaviour modification).

2. In token economies, tokens
   a. represent desired goods or privileges.
   b. are earned.
   c. are contingent on behaviours specified before the program is initiated.
   d. all of the above

Answers: 1. behaviour modification   2. d

MODULE 5E COGNITIVE LEARNING

LO 5.14 Define *cognitive learning/observational learning*.
LO 5.15 Understand the role of observational modelling.

So far, we have explored relatively simple types of learning. In classical and operant conditioning, learning is defined in terms of observable or measurable changes in behaviour. Early behaviourists believed that learning through operant and classical conditioning could be explained without reference to internal mental processes. Today, psychologists acknowledge the role of mental processes. They have broadened the study of learning to include such **cognitive processes** as thinking, knowing, problem solving, remembering, and forming mental representations. **[LO 5.14]** Here we will focus on observational learning and the work of the Canadian researcher Albert Bandura.

OBSERVATIONAL LEARNING: WATCHING AND LEARNING

What is observational learning?

In our exploration of operant conditioning, you read how people and other animals learn by directly experiencing the consequences, positive or negative, of their behaviour. But must we experience rewards and punishments directly in order to learn? No, according to Albert Bandura (1986), who contends that many of our behaviours or responses are acquired through observational learning. **Observational learning**, sometimes called **modelling**, is learning that results when we observe the behaviour of others and the consequences of that behaviour. **[LO 5.15]**

The person who demonstrates a behaviour or whose behaviour is imitated is called the **model**. Parents, movie stars, and sports personalities are often powerful models. The effectiveness of a model is related to his or her status, competence, and power. Other important factors are the age, sex, attractiveness, and ethnic status of the model. Whether or not learned behaviour is actually performed depends largely on whether the observed models are rewarded or punished for their behaviour and whether the individual expects to be rewarded for the behaviour (Bandura, 1969, 1977). Research has also shown that observational learning is improved when several sessions of observation (watching the behaviour) precede attempts to perform the behaviour and are then repeated in the early stages of practising it (Weeks & Anderson, 2000).

We use observational learning to acquire new responses or to strengthen or weaken existing responses. Consider your native language or accent, attitudes, gestures, personality traits, good habits (or bad habits, for that matter), moral values, food preferences, and so on. Do you share any of these with your parents? While you were growing up, their example probably influenced your behaviour for better or worse. Look around the classroom and observe the clothes, hairstyles, and verbal patterns of the other students. Most people have been greatly influenced by observing others.

Observational learning is particularly useful when we find ourselves in unusual situations. Picture yourself as a guest at an elaborate dinner with the prime minister. More pieces of silverware surround the plate than you have ever seen before. Which fork should be used for what? How should you proceed? You might decide to take your cue from the other guests—observational learning.

Inhibitions can be weakened or lost as a result of our observation of the behaviour of others. Adolescents can lose whatever resistance they may have to drinking, drug use, or sexual activity by seeing or hearing about peers engaging in these behaviours. With peer pressure, there is often an overwhelming tendency to conform to the behaviour and accept the values of the peer group. But inhibitions can also be strengthened through observational learning. A person does not need to experience the unfortunate consequences of dangerous behaviour to avoid it.

Fears, too, can be acquired through observational learning. A parent with an extreme fear of the dentist or of thunderstorms might serve as a model for these fears in a child. Conversely, children who see "a parent or peer behaving non-fearfully in a potential fear-producing situation may be 'immunized' to feeling fear when confronting a similar frightening situation at a later time" (Basic Behavioral Science Task Force of the National Advisory Mental Health Council, 1996, p. 139). Note too that observational learning is not restricted to humans, as it has been shown by research on monkeys (Cook, Mineka, Wolkenstein, & Laitsch, 1985), octopuses (Fiorito & Scotto, 1992), and pigeons (Alderks, 1986).

Learning Aggression: Copying What We See

Albert Bandura suspected that aggressive behaviour is particularly subject to observational learning and that aggression and violence on television and in cartoons tend to increase

TRY IT

Learning in Everyday Life

Think about everything you did yesterday from the time you woke up until the time you went to sleep. List 10 behaviours in a chart and indicate whether observational learning (OL), operant conditioning (OC), and/or classical conditioning (CC) played some role in the acquisition of each one. Remember, a behaviour may originally have been learned by some combination of the three types of learning and then been maintained by one or more of the types.

You probably learned to brush your teeth through a combination of observational learning (watching a parent demonstrate) and operant conditioning (being praised as your technique improved—that is, shaping). Now the behaviour is maintained through operant conditioning, specifically negative reinforcement (getting rid of the terrible taste in your mouth). Avoiding cavities and the scorn of everyone around you is an extra bonus.

Which kind of learning has the most Xs on your chart?

Behaviour	Acquired through:			Maintained through:		
	OL	**OC**	**CC**	**OL**	**OC**	**CC**
Brushing teeth	X	X	X			

aggression in children. His pioneering work has greatly influenced current thinking on these issues. In several classic experiments, Bandura demonstrated how children are influenced by exposure to aggressive models. **[LO 5.15]**

One study (Bandura, Ross, & Ross, 1961) involved three groups of preschool children. Children in one group individually observed an adult model punching, kicking, and hitting an inflated plastic Bobo doll (a large, plastic doll that is weighted at the bottom so that it doesn't fall over) with a mallet, while uttering aggressive words such as "Sock him in the nose," "Throw him in the air," "Kick him," and "Pow" (p. 576). Children in the second group observed a non-aggressive model who ignored the Bobo doll and sat quietly assembling Tinkertoys. Children in the control group were placed in the same setting as those in the two other groups, but with no adult present. Later, each

token economies: Behavioural techniques used to encourage desirable behaviours by reinforcing them with tokens that can be exchanged later for desired objects, activities, and/or privileges.

cognitive processes (COG-nuh-tiv): Mental processes such as thinking, knowing, problem solving, and remembering.

observational learning: Learning by observing the behaviour of others and the consequences of that behaviour; learning by imitation.

modelling: Another name for observational learning.

model: The individual who demonstrates a behaviour or serves as an example in observational learning.

Television portrayals of violence as an acceptable way to solve problems tend to encourage aggressive behaviour in children.

©Chris Stein/Digital Vision/Getty Images

child was observed through a one-way mirror. Participants exposed to the aggressive model imitated much of the aggression and also engaged in significantly more non-imitative aggression than either of the other groups. Participants in the second group, who had observed the non-aggressive model, showed less aggressive behaviour than the control group did.

A further study (Bandura, Ross, & Ross, 1963) compared the degree of aggression in children following exposure to (1) a live aggressive model, (2) a filmed version of the episode, and (3) a film depicting an aggressive cartoon character using the same aggressive behaviours in a fantasylike setting. A control group was not exposed to any of the three situations of aggression. The groups exposed to aggressive models used significantly more aggression than the control group. The researchers concluded that "of the three experimental conditions, exposure to humans on film portraying aggression was the most influential in eliciting and shaping aggressive behaviour" (p. 7).

Bandura's research provided the impetus for studying the effects of violence and aggression in entertainment media. Many studies have demonstrated the negative impact of television violence and playing violent video games (e.g., C. A. Anderson & Bushman, 2001). In addition, the effects of media violence are evident whether the violence is presented in music, music videos, advertising, or on the internet (Villani, 2001).

But, you might argue, if televised violence is followed by appropriate consequences, such as an arrest, it may actually teach children not to engage in aggression. However, experimental research has demonstrated that children do not process information about consequences in the same ways as adults do (Krcmar & Cooke, 2001). Observing consequences for aggressive acts does seem to help preschoolers learn that violence is morally unacceptable. By contrast, school-aged children appear to judge the rightness or wrongness of an act of violence on the basis of provocation; that is, they believe that violence

demonstrated in the context of retaliation is morally acceptable even if it is punished by an authority figure.

Remarkably, too, evidence shows that the effects of childhood exposure to violence persist well into the adult years (Huesman, Moise-Titus, Podolski, & Eron, 2003). Brain-imaging studies suggest that these long-term effects may be the result of patterns of neural activation that underlie emotionally laden behavioural scripts that children learn while watching violent programming (J. Murray et al., 2006).

A number of studies have shown that playing violent games increases feelings of hostility and decreases sensitivity to violent images (Arriaga, Esteyes, Carneiro, & Monteiro, 2006; Carnagey & Anderson, 2005; Greitemeyer, 2014). Researchers have also found that such games influence the physiological correlates of hostile emotions and aggressive behaviour. These correlates include particular patterns of brain activation, hormonal secretions, and vital functions such as heart rate and respiration (Brady & Matthews, 2006; Hébert, Béland, Dionne-Fournelle, Crête, & Lupien, 2005; Wang & Perry, 2006; Weber, Ritterfeld, & Mathiak, 2006). Research has also consistently shown that individuals with aggressive behavioural histories more strongly prefer and are more emotionally responsive to violent games than are their non-aggressive peers (C. A. Anderson & Dill, 2000).

But just as children imitate the aggressive behaviour they observe on television, they also imitate the prosocial, or helping, behaviour they see there. Programs such as *Sesame Street* have been found to have a positive influence on children. Like television, video games can be used to teach positive messages and skills.

Many avenues of learning are available to humans and other animals. Luckily, people's capacity to learn seems practically unlimited. Certainly, advances in civilization could not have been achieved without the ability to learn. Many positive outcomes follow from learning; see the *Apply It* box for one that might help you with your school work!

REMEMBER IT

Cognitive Learning

1. Grant has been afraid of mice for as long as he can remember, and his mother has the same paralyzing fear. Grant most likely acquired his fear through _____ learning.

2. Alexander watches his father stirring the cake mix and pouring the batter into a pan. Later, while playing in his sandbox, Alexander stirs mud in his pail and pours it in an imaginary pan to make cake for his toys. Alexander's father was _____ how to make a cake.
   a. reinforcing
   b. modelling

   c. conditioning
   d. shaping

2. Which of the following researchers is associated with observational learning?
   a. Skinner
   b. Pavlov
   c. Bandura
   d. Seligman

Answers: 1. observational 2. b 3. c

APPLY IT

How to Win the Battle against Procrastination

Do you often find yourself studying for an exam or finishing a course paper at the last minute? If so, you might want to learn how to overcome the biggest time waster of all—procrastination. Research indicates that academic procrastination arises partly out of a lack of confidence in one's ability to meet expectations (Wolters, 2003). Once procrastination has become established as a behaviour pattern, it often persists for years (D. Lee, Kelly, & Edwards, 2006). Nevertheless, anyone can overcome procrastination, and gain self-confidence in the process, by using behaviour modification techniques. Systematically apply the following suggestions to keep procrastination from interfering with your studying:

- *Identify the environmental cues that habitually interfere with your studying.* What competing interests are most likely to cause you to put off studying or to interrupt your studying—television, computer or video games, bed, visits to the refrigerator, telephone calls, friends, family members? These can be powerful distractors that consume hours of valuable study time. However, these distractors can be useful positive reinforcers to enjoy after you've finished studying.

- *Schedule your study time and reinforce yourself for adhering to your schedule.* Schedule your study time in advance so that your decisions about when to start work will not be ruled by the whim of the moment. Be as committed to that schedule as you would be to a work schedule for an employer. And be sure to schedule something you enjoy to follow the study time.

- *Get started.* The most difficult part is getting started. Give yourself an extra reward for starting on time and, perhaps, a penalty for not starting on time.

- *Use visualization.* Much procrastination results from a failure to consider its negative consequences. Visualizing the consequences of not studying can be an effective tool. Suppose you are considering going out of town with friends for the weekend instead of studying for a midterm test on Monday. Picture this! You walk into the classroom Monday morning unprepared; you know the answers to very few questions; you flunk the test. Now visualize the outcome if you stay home for the weekend and study.

- *Become better at estimating how long it takes to complete an assignment.* Estimate how long it will take to complete an assignment, and then keep track of how long it actually takes. Your estimation skills will become more accurate over time if you record and use past time taken to help with the estimate for a current task.

- *Avoid jumping to another task when you reach a difficult part of an assignment.* This procrastination tactic gives you the feeling that you are busy and accomplishing something, but it is an avoidance mechanism. Encourage yourself to stay on task even when the task is challenging.

- *Avoid preparation overkill.* Procrastinators may spend hours preparing for the task rather than performing the task itself. For example, they might gather enough library materials to write a book rather than a five-page paper. This enables them to postpone writing the paper.

- *Keep a record of the reasons you give yourself for postponing studying or completing important assignments.* This list will let you see the kinds of excuses you use for postponing your work. If a favourite rationalization is "I'll wait until I'm in the mood to do this," count the number of times in a week you are seized with the desire to study. The mood to study typically arrives after you begin, not before. Try to formulate a rebuttal for each excuse. When you find yourself using one of the excuses on the list, use your rebuttal to help you get down to the task.

Apply the steps outlined here to gain more control over your behaviour. You can also contact your student counselling services, study services, or learning centre for help. You can win the battle over procrastination.

THINKING CRITICALLY

Evaluation

Prepare statements outlining the strengths and limitations of classical conditioning, operant conditioning, and observational learning in explaining how behaviours are acquired and maintained.

Point/Counterpoint

The use of behaviour modification has been a source of controversy among psychologists and others. Prepare arguments supporting each of the following positions:

a. Behaviour modification should be used in society to shape the behaviour of others.

b. Behaviour modification should not be used in society to shape the behaviour of others.

Psychology in Your Life

Think of a friend, a family member, or a professor whose behaviour you would like to change. Using what you know about classical conditioning, operant conditioning, and observational learning, formulate a detailed plan for changing a particular behaviour of the target person.

MyPsychLab   go to mypsychlab (access code required) to find web resources for your text that supplement the material in chapter 5.

SUMMARY & REVIEW

 CLASSICAL CONDITIONING

What was Pavlov's major contribution to psychology?
Ivan Pavlov's study of the conditioned reflex provided psychology with a model of learning called *classical conditioning*.

How is classical conditioning accomplished?
During classical conditioning, a neutral stimulus (e.g., a tone) is presented shortly before an unconditioned stimulus (e.g., food) that naturally elicits, or brings forth, an unconditioned response (e.g., salivation). After repeated pairings, the conditioned stimulus (the tone) by itself will elicit the conditioned response (salivation).

How does extinction occur in classical conditioning?
If the conditioned stimulus (e.g., a tone) is presented repeatedly without the unconditioned stimulus (e.g., food), the conditioned response (e.g., salivation) will become progressively weaker and eventually disappear—a process called *extinction*.

What is generalization?
Generalization occurs when an organism makes a conditioned response to a stimulus that is similar to the original conditioned stimulus.

What is discrimination in classical conditioning?
Discrimination is the ability to distinguish between similar stimuli so that the conditioned response is made only to the original conditioned stimulus.

How did John Watson demonstrate that fear could be classically conditioned?
John Watson demonstrated that fear could be classically conditioned when, by presenting a white rat along with a loud, frightening noise, he conditioned Little Albert to fear the white rat.

What are four factors that influence classical conditioning?
Four factors influencing classical conditioning are (1) the number of pairings of the conditioned stimulus and the unconditioned stimulus, (2) the intensity of the unconditioned stimulus, (3) how reliably the conditioned stimulus predicts the unconditioned stimulus, and (4) the temporal relationship between the conditioned stimulus and the unconditioned stimulus.

What types of responses can be learned through classical conditioning?
Positive and negative emotional responses (including likes, dislikes, fears, and phobias) and conditioned drug tolerance in drug users are some types of responses acquired through classical conditioning.

5B OPERANT CONDITIONING

How are responses acquired through operant conditioning?
Operant conditioning is a method for conditioning voluntary responses. The consequences of behaviour are manipulated to shape a new response or to increase or decrease the frequency of an existing response.

How is shaping used to condition a response?
In shaping, rather than waiting for the desired response to be produced, we selectively reinforce successive approximations toward the goal response until the desired response is achieved.

How does extinction occur in operant conditioning?
In operant conditioning, extinction occurs when reinforcement is withheld.

What are the goals of both positive and negative reinforcement, and how are the goals accomplished for each?
Both positive reinforcement and negative reinforcement are used to strengthen or increase the probability of a response. With positive reinforcement, the desired response is followed by a reward; with negative reinforcement, it is followed by the termination of an aversive stimulus.

What are the four major schedules of reinforcement, and which schedule yields the highest response rate and the greatest resistance to extinction?
The four major schedules of reinforcement are the fixed-ratio, variable-ratio, fixed-interval, and variable-interval schedules. The variable-ratio schedule provides the highest response rate and the greatest resistance to extinction.

What is the partial-reinforcement effect?
The partial-reinforcement effect is the greater resistance to extinction that occurs when responses are maintained under partial reinforcement rather than under continuous reinforcement.

What three factors, in addition to the schedule of reinforcement, influence operant conditioning?
In operant conditioning, the acquisition of a response, the response rate, and the resistance to extinction are influenced by the magnitude of reinforcement, the immediacy of reinforcement, and the level of motivation of the organism.

How does punishment differ from negative reinforcement?
Punishment is used to decrease the frequency of a response; negative reinforcement is used to increase the frequency of a response.

What are some disadvantages of punishment?
Punishment generally suppresses rather than extinguishes behaviour; it does not help people develop more appropriate behaviours; and it can cause fear, anger, hostility, and aggression in the punished person.

What three factors increase the effectiveness of punishment?
Three factors that can increase the effectiveness of punishment are timing, intensity, and consistency of application.

5C COMPARING CLASSICAL AND OPERANT CONDITIONING

What processes are comparable in classical and operant conditioning?
The processes of generalization, discrimination, extinction, and spontaneous recovery occur in both classical and operant conditioning.

5D BEHAVIOUR MODIFICATION: CHANGING OUR ACT

What is behaviour modification?
Behaviour modification involves the systematic application of learning principles to individuals or groups in order to eliminate undesirable behaviour and/or encourage desirable behaviour.

5E COGNITIVE LEARNING

What is observational learning?
Observational learning is learning by observing the behaviour of others—called *models*—and the consequences of that behaviour.

CHAPTER 5 LEARNING

Learning is a relatively permanent change in behaviour, knowledge, capability, or attitude acquired through experience and not attributed to illness, injury, or maturation.

MODULE 5A CLASSICAL CONDITIONING

Classical conditioning: A type of learning in which a response previously made to one stimulus is made to another stimulus that has been repeatedly paired with the original stimulus.

Key Elements

Natural Pairing/Learning
Unconditioned stimulus (US) is a stimulus that elicits a specific response without prior learning.
Unconditioned response (UR) is a response that is elicited by the unconditioned stimulus without prior learning.

Element to Be Learned
A neutral stimulus does not naturally produce the desired UR. It is repeatedly presented with the US.

Successful Learning
After repeated pairings, the neutral stimulus elicits the desired UR and is called the conditioned stimulus (CS) because it elicits a newly learned response, which is called the conditioned response (CR).

Basic Principles

Extinction: A weakening of the newly learned CR and its eventual disappearance due to the repeated presentation of the CS without the US.
Spontaneous recovery: The reappearance of an extinguished response following re-exposure to the original CS after a rest period.
Generalization: The tendency to make a CR to a stimulus that is similar to the original CS.
Discrimination: Occurs when the CR is made to the original CS but not to other, similar stimuli.

Factors Influencing Classical Conditioning
- Number of pairings of the CS and the US
- The intensity level of the US
- How reliably the CS predicts the US
- The temporal relationship between the CS and the US

Contemporary Views of Classical Conditioning
Cognitive Perspective: Learning occurs when the CS provides information that enables the organism to reliably *predict* the occurrence of the US stimulus.
Biological Predispositions: An important factor in the conditioning process.

MODULE 5B OPERANT CONDITIONING

Operant conditioning: A type of learning in which the consequences of a behaviour tend to modify that behaviour in the future.

Key Elements

Reinforcement/reinforcers increase the likelihood that a particular response will be repeated.
Types of Reinforcers
Positive: Any positive consequence that encourages the probability of a behaviour to reoccur because the consequence is desirable.
Negative: A consequence that encourages the probability of a behaviour to reoccur because an unpleasant stimulus is terminated following a response.
Secondary reinforcer: A reinforcer acquired or learned through association with other reinforcers (e.g., money, praise).
Primary reinforcer: A type of reinforcer that is unlearned and fulfills basic survival needs (e.g., food, water).

Punishment/punishers reduce the likelihood that a particular response will be repeated; refers to the removal of a pleasant stimulus or the application of an unpleasant stimulus.

Drawbacks Associated with Punishment
- Often suppresses the behaviour only when the punishing authority is present.
- Does not help people develop more appropriate behaviours; it only indicates which behaviours are unacceptable.
- May lead to fear and hostility toward the punishing authority.
- Provides models for aggressive behaviour.

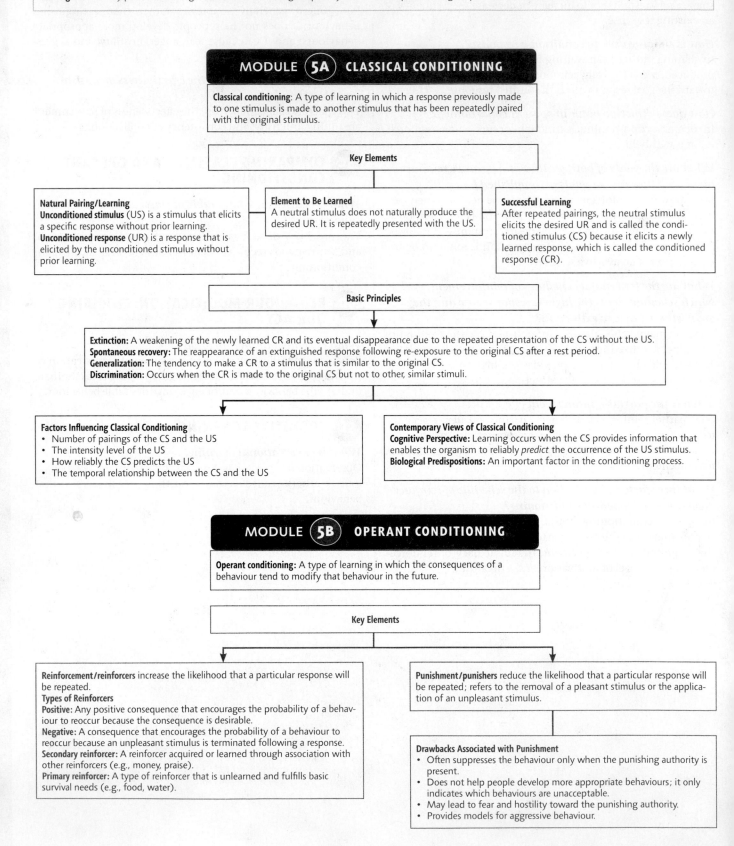

MODULE (5C) COMPARING CLASSICAL AND OPERANT CONDITIONING

Both rely on associative learning: classical conditioning depends on the relation between two stimuli; operant conditioning relies on the relation between a response and its consequence.

MODULE (5D) BEHAVIOUR MODIFICATION

Involves developing a program to change behaviour using one or more of the conditioning techniques systematically.

MODULE (5E) COGNITIVE LEARNING

Cognitive learning: Emphasizes mental processes (such as thinking, problem solving, remembering) in the study of learning.

Observational learning (modelling): Learning by observing the behaviours of others, called models, and the consequences of that behaviour.

- The effectiveness of a model is related to such factors as the model's age, sex, status, competence, and attractiveness.
- Even if a behaviour is learned, imitation of that behaviour is dependent on whether the observed models are punished or rewarded for their behaviour.
- The imitation of others' behaviour is likely to be used in unfamiliar situations where we are unsure how to act.
- Aggressive and prosocial behaviours can be learned through observation.

Basic Principles

Shaping: Involves reinforcing successive approximations of a desired response until a desired response is achieved.
Extinction: Occurs when reinforcers are withheld. Responses no longer followed by reinforcers occur less and less often and eventually stop.
Spontaneous recovery: Occurs when a response tendency that has been extinguished reappears following a period of rest.
Generalization: Occurs when the learned response is made to a stimulus that is similar to the one for which it was originally reinforced.
Discrimination: Occurs when the learned response is made to the original stimulus for which it was reinforced but not to other, similar stimuli.
Discriminative stimulus: The stimulus that signals whether a certain response or behaviour is likely to be rewarded, ignored, or punished.

Factors Influencing Operant Conditioning
- Magnitude of reinforcement
- Immediacy of reinforcement
- Learner's level of motivation

Schedules of Reinforcement
Continuous reinforcement: Administration of reinforcement after every desired response is made. Most efficient way to condition a new response.
Partial reinforcement: Administration of reinforcement after some, but not all, of the desired responses made. Results in a greater resistance to extinction. Best way to maintain a learned response.
Ratio schedules: Those based on a number of responses that must be made before a response is reinforced.
- **Fixed ratio:** Reinforcer is administered after a fixed number of non-reinforced correct responses
- **Variable ratio:** Reinforcer is given after a varying number of non-reinforced responses based on an average ratio
Interval schedules: Based on a given amount of time that must pass before the administration of a reinforcer
- **Fixed interval:** Reinforcer is given following the first correct response after a fixed period of time has elapsed
- **Variable interval:** Reinforcer is given after the first correct response following a varying time of non-reinforcement based on an average time

6

One night, psychologist Donald Thomson was a guest on an Australian talk show about eyewitness testimony. He was with other experts, including the chief of police. He argued that good eyewitnesses need to notice specific features of the face to help them identify perpetrators later. He pointed to the important features on his own face (eyes, smile, and so on). While the show was being broadcast, a woman who was watching him on the show was assaulted and raped. Later, when she regained consciousness and was interviewed by police, she clearly identified Donald Thomson as her assailant. But Donald Thomson was not the perpetrator. Fortunately for Thomson, it was a live taping that he had participated in, so he had witnesses to support his alibi—and to prove that he could not possibly have committed this crime. The ironic thing about this case is that Thomson studies the very phenomenon that led to his arrest— eyewitness testimony.

Does this case simply reflect the rare and unusual in human memory, or are memory errors common occurrences? This and many other questions you may have about memory will be answered in this chapter. We will describe three memory systems: sensory, short-term, and long-term. You will learn how much information each system holds, for how long, and in what form. You will discover why virtually everyone finds it harder to remember names than faces. Is memory like a video recorder, in which the sights and sounds we experience are captured intact and simply played back in exact detail? Or do we "reconstruct" the past when we remember, leaving out certain bits and pieces of events that actually happened and adding others that did not?

Would you like to improve your memory? You will learn some techniques that can help you study more effectively, and some mnemonic devices (memory strategies) that can be used in practical ways every day as memory aids. Read on . . . and remember.

©Radius Images/Alamy

MEMORY

MODULE 6A REMEMBERING

LO 6.1 Identify and define the three memory processes: *encoding, storage,* and *retrieval.*

LO 6.2 Define and explain the functioning of each component of the Atkinson–Shiffrin model of memory, including *sensory, short-term,* and *long-term memory.*

LO 6.3 Explain how the levels-of-processing model accounts for memory.

LO 6.4 Define and understand the types of long-term memory: *declarative* and *non-declarative.*

LO 6.5 Compare and contrast the three methods of measuring memory: recall, recognition, and relearning.

Our memory is the storehouse for everything we know. It enables us to know who and where we are when we awaken each morning. Memory provides the continuity of life—the long thread to which are tied our joys and sorrows, our knowledge and skills, our triumphs and failures, and the people and places that form our lives. Psychologists have been studying memory for more than a century. However, the need to break down the memory process into its constituent parts, necessitated by the invention of modern computers and computer programming, has opened the doors to psychologists' understanding of how the human memory system works.

THE THREE PROCESSES IN MEMORY: ENCODING, STORAGE, AND RETRIEVAL

What three processes are involved in the act of remembering?

How do our minds create memories? The act of remembering requires the successful completion of three processes: encoding, storage, and retrieval (Figure 6.1). **[LO 6.1]** The first process, **encoding**, involves transforming information into a form that can be stored in memory. For example, if you witness a car crash, you might try to form a mental picture of it to help you remember what you saw.

This sounds easier than it actually is. To ensure that we encode information appropriately we must focus our *attention*. At any given time, we are bombarded with all kinds of sensory information. Imagine yourself in your classroom,

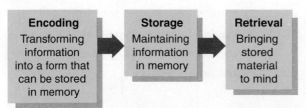

FIGURE 6.1

The Processes Required in Remembering

The act of remembering requires the successful completion of three processes: encoding, storage, and retrieval. Memory failure can result from the failure of any one of the three processes.

and recall how hard it is to focus on your instructor's voice when you can also hear overhead fans and the clicking of keyboards, or when you are distracted by how hot you feel, how uncomfortable your chair is, or how hungry or thirsty you are. All of these events compete for your attention. Because we cannot absorb every piece of information in our environment, we have to selectively attend to some information and let the other information fade into the background. **Selective attention** is the tool that allows us to eliminate interference from the relevant information.

The second memory process, **storage**, involves keeping or maintaining information in memory. **[LO 6.1]** For encoded information to be stored, some physiological change in the brain must take place—a process called **consolidation**. Consolidation involves physiological changes that require the synthesis of protein molecules (Lopez, 2000). Consolidation occurs automatically in normal circumstances. If a person loses consciousness for any reason, the process can be disrupted and a permanent memory will not form (Deutsch & Deutsch, 1966). That is why someone who has been in a serious car accident may awaken in a hospital and not remember what has happened.

The final process, **retrieval**, occurs when information stored in memory is brought to mind. **[LO 6.1]** To remember, we must perform all three of these processes—encode the information, store it, and then retrieve it. Memory failure can result from the failure of any one of the three processes.

Similar steps are required in the information processing done by computers. Information is encoded (entered in some form the computer is able to use), then stored on the hard drive or a cloud server or a DVD, and later retrieved on the screen or through the printer. You would not be able to retrieve the material if you had failed to enter it, if a power failure occurred before you could save what you had entered, or if you could not access the disk or file that contained the needed information. Of course, human memory is far more complex than even the most advanced computer systems, but computer processing provides a useful analogy for memory, provided we don't take it too literally.

INFORMATION-PROCESSING APPROACH: THE THREE MEMORY SYSTEMS

How are memories stored? Most current efforts to understand human memory have been conducted within a framework known as the **information-processing approach** (Klatzky, 1984). This approach makes use of computer science and related fields to provide models that help us understand the processes involved in memory (Kon & Plaskota, 2000). In keeping with the computer analogy, information-processing theorists sometimes apply such terms as *hardware* (e.g., brain structures that are involved in memory) and *software* (e.g., learned memory strategies) to various aspects of the human memory system. According to one widely accepted view, the *Atkinson–Shiffrin model,* there are three different, interacting memory systems: sensory, short-term, and long-term (R. C. Atkinson & Shiffrin, 1968; Broadbent, 1958; Shiffrin & Atkinson, 1969). **[LO 6.2]** Considerable research in the biology of memory lends support to the model (Squire, Knowlton, &

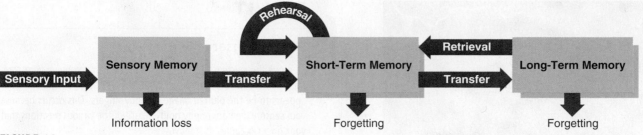

FIGURE 6.2

The Three Memory Systems

According to the Atkinson–Shiffrin model, there are three separate memory systems: sensory memory, short-term memory, and long-term memory.

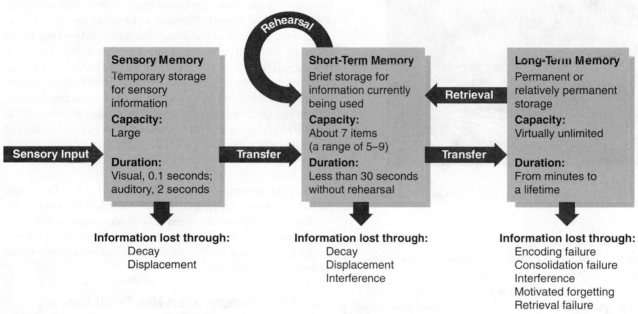

FIGURE 6.3

Characteristics of and Processes Involved in the Three Memory Systems

Musen, 1993; Suthana et al., 2011). We will examine each of these three memory systems, which are shown in Figure 6.2.

Sensory Memory: Images and Echoes

What is sensory memory?

Imagine yourself walking down a busy city street. How many separate pieces of information are you sensing? You are probably seeing, hearing, feeling, and smelling millions of tiny bits of information every minute. But how many of them do you remember? Very few, most likely. That's because, although virtually everything we see, hear, or otherwise sense is held in **sensory memory**, each piece of information is stored for only the briefest period of time. As shown in Figure 6.3, sensory memory normally holds visual images for a fraction of a second and holds sounds for about two seconds (Crowder, 1992; Klatzky, 1980). Visual sensory memory lasts just long enough

encoding: Transforming information into a form that can be stored in short-term or long-term memory.

selective attention: Focusing on one piece of information while placing other information in the background.

storage: The act of maintaining information in memory.

consolidation: The presumed process by which a permanent memory is formed; believed to involve the hippocampus.

retrieval: The act of bringing to mind material that has been stored in memory.

information-processing approach: An approach to the study of mental structures and processes that uses the computer as a model for human thinking.

sensory memory: The memory system that holds information coming in through the senses for a period ranging from a fraction of a second to several seconds.

Sensory memory holds a visual image, such as a lightning bolt, for a fraction of a second—just long enough for us to perceive a flow of movement.

©Dennis Hallinan/Alamy

to keep whatever you are viewing from disappearing when you blink your eyes. **[LO 6.2]** You can demonstrate visual sensory memory for yourself by doing the *Try It*.

For a fraction of a second, glance at the following three rows of letters and numbers and then close your eyes. How many of the items can you recall?

X B D F

M P Z G

L C N H

Most people can correctly recall only four or five of the items when they are briefly presented. Does this indicate

TRY IT

Testing Sensory Memory

To prove the existence of the visual sensory memory, move your forefinger back and forth rapidly in front of your face. You will see what appears to be the blurred image of many fingers. This occurs because your sensory memory briefly holds a trace of the various positions that your finger occupies as it moves.

that visual sensory memory can hold only four or five items at a time? To find out, researcher George Sperling (1960) briefly flashed 12 letters, as shown below, to participants. Immediately upon turning the display off, he sounded a high, medium, or low tone that signalled the participants to report *only* the top, middle, or bottom row of items. Before they heard the tone, the participants had no way of knowing which row they would have to report. Sperling found that when the participants could view the letters for 0.015 to 0.5 seconds, they could report correctly all the items in any row nearly 100 percent of the time. But the items fade from sensory memory so quickly that during the time it takes to report three or four of the items, the other eight or nine have already disappeared. Figure 6.4 shows the steps that were involved in Sperling's research study.

Sensory memory for sound is similar to that for vision. **[LO 6.2]** You have experienced auditory sensory memory when the last few words someone has spoken seem to echo briefly in your mind. Auditory sensory memory usually lasts about two seconds, compared with the fractions of a second for visual sensory memory (Klatzky, 1980).

Short-Term Memory: Short Life, Small Capacity

What are the characteristics of short-term memory?

Whatever you are thinking about right now is in your **short-term memory (STM)**. We use short-term memory when we carry on a conversation, solve a problem, or look up a telephone number and remember it just long enough to dial it. **[LO 6.2]**

Short-term memory does not hold sensory stimuli the way sensory memory does. Short-term memory usually codes

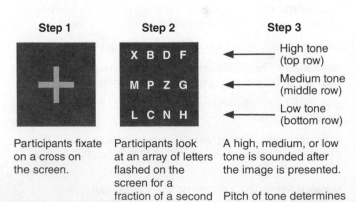

Step 1	**Step 2**	**Step 3**	**Step 4**
	X B D F ←	High tone (top row)	
	M P Z G ←	Medium tone (middle row)	"M, P, Z, G"
	L C N H ←	Low tone (bottom row)	
Participants fixate on a cross on the screen.	Participants look at an array of letters flashed on the screen for a fraction of a second (e.g. 0.5 seconds)	A high, medium, or low tone is sounded after the image is presented. Pitch of tone determines which row of letters the participants will report.	Participants report letters.

FIGURE 6.4

Sperling's Study of the Capacity of Sensory Memory

Sperling demonstrated that sensory memory holds more information than participants are able to report completely because the visual afterimage fades so quickly. Sperling proved that people could retain 12 items in sensory memory, but only long enough to report four items in the designated row.

Source: (Based on Sperling, 1960.) The information available in brief visual presentations. Psychological Monographs: General and Applied, 74 (Whole No. 498), 1-29.

information according to sound—that is, in acoustic form **[LO 6.2]** (Conrad, 1964). The letter *T* is coded as the sound "tee," not as the shape T. Short-term memory can also hold visual images, and store information in semantic form (i.e., according to meaning; Shulman, 1972).

THE CAPACITY OF SHORT-TERM MEMORY Unlike sensory memory, which can hold a vast amount of information briefly, short-term memory has a very limited capacity—about seven different items or bits of information (plus or minus two) at one time (G. A. Miller, 1956). **[LO 6.2]** Test the capacity of your short-term memory in the *Try It* below.

How well did you do in the *Try It*? Most people recall about seven items. This is just enough for phone numbers and postal codes. When short-term memory is filled to capacity, **displacement** can occur (Waugh & Norman, 1965). In displacement, each incoming item pushes out an existing item, which is then forgotten.

One way to overcome the limitation of seven or so bits of information is to use a technique that George A. Miller (1956) calls *chunking*. *Chunking* means organizing or grouping separate bits of information into larger units, or *chunks*. A chunk is an easily identifiable unit such as a syllable, a word, an acronym, or a number (Cowan, 1988). For example, the numbers 5 1 9 7 3 1 2 8 5 6 could be chunked 519 731 2856 (just like phone numbers), leaving the short-term memory with the easier task of dealing with three chunks of information instead of ten separate bits. Complete the next *Try It* and see if chunking works for you.

THE DURATION OF SHORT-TERM MEMORY Items in short-term memory are lost in less than 30 seconds, unless we repeat them over and over to ourselves, silently or out loud, to retain them. **[LO 6.2]** This process is known as **rehearsal**. We rehearse telephone numbers we have looked up to keep them in short-term memory long enough to dial the number. But short-term memory is easily disrupted. It is so fragile, in fact, that an interruption or a distraction can cause information to be lost in just a few seconds.

Researchers have tried to determine how long short-term memory lasts if rehearsal is prevented. In a series of early studies, participants were briefly shown three consonants, such as H, G, and L, and were then asked to count

TRY IT

Testing Short-Term Memory

Read aloud the digits in the first row (row "a" below) at a steady rate of about two per second. Then, from memory, write them down on a sheet of paper.

Repeat the process, row by row.

a. 3 8 7 1
b. 9 6 4 7 3
c. 1 8 3 0 5 2
d. 8 0 6 5 9 1 7
e. 5 2 9 7 3 1 2 5
f. 2 7 4 0 1 9 6 8 3
g. 3 9 1 6 5 8 4 5 1 7

TRY IT

Chunking

Read the following letters individually at the rate of about one per second and then see if you can repeat them.

N – H – L – C – B – C – P – E – I – V – C – R – R – C – M – P

Did you have difficulty? Probably, because there are 16 different letters. But now try this:

NHL CBC PEI VCR RCMP

Did you find that five chunks are easier to remember than 16 separate items?

backward by threes from a given number (738, 735, 732, and so on). After intervals lasting from three to 18 seconds, participants were instructed to stop their backward counting and recall the three letters (J. Brown, 1958; Peterson & Peterson, 1959). Following a delay of nine seconds, the participants could recall an average of only one of the three letters. After 18 seconds, there was practically no recall whatsoever. An 18-second distraction had completely erased the three letters from short-term memory.

SHORT-TERM MEMORY AS WORKING MEMORY Short-term memory is more than just a system that holds information received from sensory memory until we are able to store it in long-term memory. Alan Baddeley (1990, 1992, 1995, 1998) suggested that short-term memory is one component of a broader system of temporary storage structures and processes known as *working memory*. Simply put, working memory is the memory subsystem with which you work on information to understand it, remember it, or use it to solve a problem or to communicate with someone. More than just a temporary way station between sensory memory and long-term memory, working memory is a kind of mental workspace that temporarily holds incoming information from sensory memory or information retrieved from long-term memory in order to perform some conscious cognitive activity. **[LO 6.2]** "Without it you couldn't understand this sentence, add up a restaurant tab in your head, or find your way home. Working memory is an erasable mental blackboard that allows you to hold briefly in your mind and manipulate the information, whether it be words, menu prices, or a map of your surroundings" (Wickelgren, 1997, p. 1580). Research shows that the prefrontal cortex is the primary area responsible for

short-term memory (STM): The second stage of memory, which holds about seven (a range of five to nine) items for less than 30 seconds without rehearsal; working memory; the mental workspace we use to keep in mind tasks we are thinking about at any given moment.

displacement: The event that occurs when short-term memory is holding its maximum and each new item entering short-term memory pushes out an existing item.

rehearsal: The act of purposely repeating information to maintain it in short-term memory or to transfer it to long-term memory.

Declarative memory stores facts, information, and personal life events, such as a trip to a foreign country. Non-declarative memory encompasses motor skills, such as dance movements, which—once learned—can be carried out with little or no conscious effort.

working memory (Courtney, Ungerleider, Keil, & Haxby, 1997; Kane & Engel, 2002; Rao, Rainer, & Miller, 1997).

So just what kind of "work" goes on in working memory? One of the most important memory processes is the application of *memory strategies*. Using a memory strategy involves manipulating information in ways that make it easier to remember. We use some memory strategies almost automatically, but others require more effort. For example, sometimes we repeat information over and over again until we can recall it easily. Your teachers may have used a drill to try to cement the multiplication tables in your long-term memory. This rote rehearsal, however, is not necessarily the best way to transfer information to long-term memory (Craik & Watkins, 1973). Researchers at the University of Toronto proved just that with their **levels-of-processing model** of memory (Craik & Lockhart, 1972). They demonstrated that "shallow" processing (encoding based on superficial features of information such as the sound of a word) was less likely to lead to long-term retention than "deep" processing (encoding based on the meaning of information) **[LO 6.3]**. Retention tests showed that the deeper the level of processing, the higher the accuracy of memory. What do strategies that promote deeper processing look like? When you relate new information to the information already safely tucked away in long-term memory, you increase the chances that you will be able to retrieve the new information (Symons & Johnson, 1997; Willoughby, Wood, McDermott, & McLaren, 2000). These strategies are called *elaboration strategies*. You can check out other strategies in the *Apply It* box at the end of this chapter. Figure 6.3 summarizes the three memory systems.

Long-Term Memory: As Long as a Lifetime

What is long-term memory, and what are its subsystems?

If information is processed effectively in short-term memory, it makes its way into long-term memory. **Long-term memory (LTM)** is our vast storehouse of permanent or relatively permanent memories. **[LO 6.2]** There are no known limits to the storage capacity of long-term memory. Long-term memories last a long time, some of them for a lifetime.

When we talk about memory in everyday conversation, we are usually referring to long-term memory. Long-term memory holds all the knowledge we have accumulated, the skills we have acquired, and the memories of our past experiences. Although visual images, sounds, and odours can be stored in long-term memory, information in long-term memory is usually stored in semantic form.

THE TWO SUBSYSTEMS: DECLARATIVE MEMORY AND NON-DECLARATIVE MEMORY Two main subsystems within long-term memory are declarative memory and non-declarative memory. **[LO 6.4]**

Declarative memory (also called *explicit memory*) stores facts, information, and personal life events that can be brought to mind verbally or in the form of images. There are two types of declarative memory—episodic memory and semantic memory. **[LO 6.2]**

EPISODIC MEMORY **Episodic memory** is the part of declarative memory that contains the memory of events we have experienced personally (Wheeler, Stuss, & Tulving, 1997). Endel Tulving (1985) at the University of Toronto described it as something like a mental diary that records the episodes of our lives—the people we have known, the places we have seen, and the personal experiences we have had. According to Tulving,

> The episodic system stores and makes possible subsequent recovery of information about personal experiences from the past. It enables people to travel back in time, as it were, into their personal past, and to become consciously aware of having witnessed or participated in events and happenings at earlier times. (1989, p. 362)

SEMANTIC MEMORY **Semantic memory**, the second part of declarative memory, is our memory for general knowledge and is made up of objective facts and information. In other

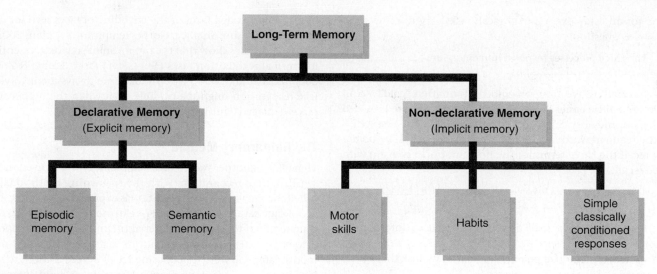

FIGURE 6.5

Subsystems of Long-Term Memory

Declarative memory can be divided into two subparts—episodic memory, which stores memories of personally experienced events, and semantic memory, which stores facts and information. Non-declarative memory consists of motor skills acquired through repetitive practice, habits, and simple classically conditioned responses.

words, semantic memory is our mental dictionary or encyclopedia of stored knowledge such as the following:

> The three memory systems are sensory, short-term, and long-term memory.

> *Dictionary* is spelled d-i-c-t-i-o-n-a-r-y.
> 10 times 10 equals 100.

As a rule, the semantic facts you have stored are not personally referenced to time and place, as episodic memories are. You probably do not remember exactly where and when you learned to spell *dictionary* or to multiply 10 times 10.

NON-DECLARATIVE MEMORY   Non-declarative memory (also called *implicit memory*) consists of motor skills, habits, and simple classically conditioned responses (Squire et al., 1993). **[LO 6.4]** Motor skills are acquired through repetitive practice and include such things as eating with a fork, riding a bicycle, and driving a car. Although acquired slowly, once learned, these skills become habit, are quite reliable, and can be remembered and carried out with little or no conscious effort. For example, you probably use the keyboard on a computer without consciously being able to name the keys in each row from left to right.

Figure 6.5 shows the subsystems of long-term memory.

MEASURING MEMORY

What are three methods of measuring retention?

Psychologists use three main methods of measuring memory: recall, recognition, and the relearning method. **[LO 6.5]**

Recall

Recall tasks are usually the most difficult. In **recall**, we must produce the required information by searching our memory

without the help of **retrieval cues**. **[LO 6.5]** Remembering someone's name, recalling items on a shopping list, memorizing a speech or a poem word for word, and remembering what you

levels-of-processing model: A single-memory-system model in which retention depends on how deeply information is processed.

long-term memory (LTM): The relatively permanent memory system with a virtually unlimited capacity.

declarative memory: The subsystem within long-term memory that stores facts, information, and personal life experiences; also called *explicit memory*.

episodic memory (ep-ih-SOD-ik): The subpart of declarative memory that contains memories of personally experienced events.

semantic memory: The subpart of declarative memory that stores general knowledge; our mental encyclopedia or dictionary.

non-declarative memory: The subsystem within long-term memory that consists of skills acquired through repetitive practice, habits, and simple classically conditioned responses; also called *implicit memory*.

recall: A measure of retention that requires one to remember material without the help of retrieval cues, as in an essay test.

retrieval cues: Any stimuli or bits of information that aid in the retrieval of particular information from long-term memory.

need for an essay exam are all recall tasks. Try to answer the following question:

> The three processes involved in memory are _____, _____, and _____.

In recalling, we must remember information "cold." Recall tasks are a little easier if cues, called *retrieval cues*, are provided to jog our memory. Such cues might consist of the first letters of the required words for fill-in-the-blank questions. If you did not recall the three terms for the first question, try again with cued recall:

> The three processes involved in memory are e_____, s_____, and r_____.

Sometimes *serial recall* is required—that is, information must be recalled in a specific order. This is the way you learned the alphabet, memorize poems, and learn any task that has to be carried out in a certain sequence.

Recognition

Recognition is exactly what the name implies: we simply recognize something as familiar—a face, a name, a taste, a melody. **[LO 6.5]** Some multiple-choice, matching, and true/false questions are examples of recognition test items (although others are not!). Consider a version of the question that was posed before:

> Which of the following is *not* one of the processes involved in memory?
>
> a. encoding
> b. assimilation
> c. storage
> d. retrieval

Was this recognition question easier than the recall version? The main difference between recall and recognition is that a recognition task does not require you to supply the information but only to recognize it when you see it. The correct answer is included along with the other items in a recognition question. Recent brain-imaging studies have discovered that the hippocampus plays an extensive role in memory tasks involving recognition but that the degree of hippocampal activity varies for different tasks. When the task is recognizing famous faces, widespread brain activity takes place in both hemispheres. Less widespread brain activity is observed during the recognition

of recently encoded faces or the encoding of faces seen for the first time (Henson, Shallice, Gorno-Tempinin, & Dolan, 2002). Although studies show that the hippocampal region is essential for normal recognition tasks (Teng, Stefanacci, Squire, & Zola, 2000; Zola et al., 2000), when short time delays are involved, face recognition might be possible even when the hippocampus is damaged (Smith et al., 2014).

The Relearning Method

There is yet another way to measure memory that is even more sensitive than recognition. With the **relearning method** (also called the *savings method*), retention is expressed as the percentage of time saved when material is relearned compared with the time required to learn the material originally. **[LO 6.5]** Suppose it took you 40 minutes to memorize a list of words, and one month later you were tested, using recall or recognition, to see how many of the words you remembered. If you could not recall or recognize a single word, would this mean that you had absolutely no memory of anything on the test? Or could it mean that the recall and the recognition methods of testing were not sensitive enough to pick up what little information you may have stored? How could we measure what is left of this former learning?

Using the relearning method, we could time how long it would take you to relearn the list of words. If it took 20 minutes to relearn the list, this would represent a 50 percent savings over the original learning time of 40 minutes. The percentage of time saved—the **savings score**—reflects how much material remains in long-term memory.

Often parents wonder if the time they spend reading to their young children or exposing them to good music has any lasting influence. Do some traces of such early exposure remain? Many years ago, H. E. Burtt (1932) carried out a unique relearning experiment on his son Benjamin to study this question.

Every day Burtt read to his son three passages from Sophocles's *Oedipus Tyrannus* in the original Greek. He would repeat the same three passages for three months and then read three new passages for the next three months. This procedure continued from the time Benjamin was 15 months until he was three years old. Nothing more was done for five years until the boy reached the age of eight. Then Burtt tested Benjamin by having him memorize some of the passages read to him originally and some similar passages that he had never heard before. It took Benjamin 27 percent fewer trials to memorize the original passages. This 27 percent savings score suggests that a considerable amount of information remained in his memory for an extended period of time—information that could not have been detected through recall or recognition tests. The study also suggests that even information we do not understand can be stored in memory. Between 15 months and three years of age, young Benjamin did not speak or understand Greek, yet much of the information remained in his memory for years.

Students demonstrate this each semester when they study for comprehensive final exams. Relearning material for the final exams takes less time than it took to learn the material originally. (We'll discuss this further in Module 6E: Forgetting.)

TRY IT

Testing the Levels-of-Processing Model

Answer *yes* or *no* to each of the following questions:

1. Is the word *LARK* in capital letters?
2. Does the word *speech* rhyme with *sleet*?
3. Would the word *park* make sense in this sentence?
   The woman passed a _____ on her way to work.
   Now continue reading.

REMEMBER IT

Basic Memory Processes and Measures of Retention

1. Match the memory system with the best description of its capacity and the duration of time it holds information.

_____ 1) sensory memory

_____ 2) short-term memory

_____ 3) long-term memory

    a. virtually unlimited capacity; long duration

    b. large capacity; short duration

    c. very limited capacity; short duration

2. Match the example with the appropriate memory system.

_____ 1) semantic memory

_____ 2) episodic memory

_____ 3) non-declarative memory

_____ 4) working memory

    a. playing tennis

    b. remembering your high school graduation

    c. deciding what you will do tomorrow

    d. naming the premiers of the provinces

3. Which subsystem of long-term memory does not require conscious awareness?

    a. episodic memory

    b. semantic memory

    c. non-declarative memory

    d. declarative memory

4. Match all examples with the corresponding method of measuring retention.

_____ 1) recognition

_____ 2) relearning

_____ 3) recall

    a. identifying a suspect in a lineup

    b. answering a fill-in-the-blank question on a test

    c. having to study less for a comprehensive final exam than for the sum of the previous exams

    d. answering questions on this *Remember It*

Answers: 1(1).b (2).c (3).a 2(1).d (2).b (3).a (4).c 3.c 4(1).a,d (2).c (3).b

---

MODULE 6B THE NATURE OF REMEMBERING

LO 6.6 Explain what is meant when memory is described as a *reconstructive process*.

LO 6.7 Define and explain what *schemas* are and do.

LO 6.8 Describe factors that can limit or enhance accuracy of eyewitness testimony.

LO 6.9 Understand the strengths and weaknesses associated with hypnosis.

MEMORY AS A PERMANENT RECORD: THE VIDEO RECORDER ANALOGY

For hundreds of years, people have speculated about the nature of memory. Aristotle suggested that the senses imprint memories in the brain like signet rings stamping impressions in wax. Freud believed that all memories are permanently preserved, with some lying deep in the unconscious. Wilder Penfield (1969), a Canadian neurosurgeon, asserted that experiences leave a "permanent imprint on the brain . . . as though a tape recorder had been receiving it all" (p. 165).

MEMORY AS A RECONSTRUCTION: PARTLY FACT AND PARTLY FICTION

What is meant by the statement "Memory is reconstructive in nature"?

Research does not suggest that memory works like a video recorder, capturing every part of an experience exactly as it

happens. Normally, what we recall is not an exact replica of an event (D. L. Schachter, Norman, & Koutstaal, 1998). Rather, it is a **reconstruction**—a piecing together of a few highlights, using information that may or may not be accurate (Loftus & Loftus, 1980). **[LO 6.6]** Even for those of us with the most accurate memories, recall is partly truth and partly fiction (Conway, Collins, Gathercole, & Anderson, 1996). We supply what we *think* are facts to flesh out or complete those fragments of our experiences that we do recall accurately. This was the finding of another pioneer in memory research, Sir Frederic Bartlett.

recognition: A measure of retention that requires one to identify material as familiar, or as having been encountered before.

relearning method: Measuring retention in terms of the percentage of time or learning trials saved in relearning material compared with the time required to learn it originally; also called the *savings method*.

savings score: The percentage of time or learning trials saved in relearning material over the amount of time or number of learning trials required for the original learning.

reconstruction: A memory that is not an exact replica of an event but one that has been pieced together from a few highlights, with the use of information that may or may not be accurate.

When people recall an event, such as a car accident, they are actually reconstructing it from memory by piecing together bits of information that may or may not be totally accurate.

Sir Frederic Bartlett

What is Bartlett's contribution to our understanding of memory?

Sir Frederic Bartlett (1886–1969) studied memory using rich and meaningful material learned and remembered under more lifelike conditions. Bartlett (1932) gave participants stories to read and drawings to study. Then, at varying time intervals, he had them reproduce the original material. Accurate reports were rare. His participants seemed to reconstruct rather than actually remember the material they had learned. They recreated the stories, making them shorter and more consistent with their own individual points of view. They rationalized puzzling features of the stories to fit their own expectations; and they often changed details and substituted more familiar objects or events. Bartlett also found that errors in memory increased with time and that his participants were not aware that they had partly remembered and partly invented. Ironically, the parts his participants had created were often the very parts that they most adamantly claimed to have remembered.

Bartlett concluded that we systematically distort the facts and the circumstances of our experiences and that we do not simply remember new experiences as isolated events. Rather, information already stored in long-term memory exerts a strong influence on how we remember new information and experiences.

Schemas and Memory

What are schemas, and how do they affect memory?

Bartlett suggested that the inaccuracies in the participants' memories reflected **schemas**—integrated frameworks of knowledge and assumptions about people, objects, and events. Schemas help us process large amounts of material by providing us with frameworks to incorporate new information and experience. They also provide association cues that can help us with retrieval. **[LO 6.7]** For example, you probably have a schema for

fast-food restaurants. You typically order at a counter, pay immediately, wait for your food, carry your food to a table, and put your tray away when you're finished. We are often made aware of our schemas when they are violated. For example, if you went into a restaurant that you expected to serve fast food, you would be surprised if someone gave you a menu and tried to seat you.

Once formed, our schemas influence what we notice and how we encode and recall information. When we encounter new information or have a new experience related to an existing schema, we try to make it "fit" that schema. To this end, we may have to distort some aspects of the information and ignore or forget other aspects. Some of the distorting and ignoring occurs as the material is being encoded; more can occur when we try to remember or reconstruct the original experience (Brewer & Nakamura, 1984).

Distortion in Memory

When we reconstruct our memories, we do not purposely try to distort the actual experience—unless, of course, we are lying. But all of us tend to omit some facts that actually occurred and to supply other details from our own imaginations. Distortion occurs when we alter the memory of an event or of our experience so that it fits our beliefs, expectations, logic, or prejudices.

The tendency toward systematic distortion of actual events has been demonstrated many times. Try your own demonstration of distortion in memory in the *Try It*.

The *Try It* shows that we are very likely to alter or distort what we see or hear to make it fit with what we believe *should* be true. Since all the words on the list are related to sleep, it seems logical that *sleep* should be one of the words. In a recent study that used word lists similar to the one in the *Try It*, Roediger and McDermott (1995) found that 40 to 55 percent of the participants "remembered" the word that was not on the list. If you "remembered" the word *sleep*, you created a false memory, which probably seemed as real to you as a true memory (Dodson & Shimamura, 2000).

Our tendency to distort makes the world more understandable and lets us organize our experiences into our existing systems of beliefs and expectations. This tendency is,

TRY IT

Testing Memory Distortion

Read this list of words aloud at a rate of about one word per second. Then close your book and write all the words you can remember.

bed	rest	awake	tired
dream	wake	snooze	doze
nap	yawn	snore	slumber

Now check your list. Did you "remember" the word *sleep*? Many people do, even though it is not one of the words on the list. *Source:* Based on Deese, 1959. Deese, J. (1959). On the prediction of occurrence of particular verbal instructions in immediate recall. Journal of Experimental psychology, 58, 17–22.

however, also frequently responsible for gross inaccuracies in what we remember. We tend to distort memories in a positive way, and this is sometimes called the *positive bias* (W. J. Wood & Conway, 2006). Bahrick, Hall, and Berger (1996) found that 89 percent of college students accurately remembered the A's they earned in high school, but only 29 percent accurately recalled the D's.

Remarkably, research suggests that memories of even the most horrific experiences can be influenced by positive bias. In several studies carried out in the 1980s, Holocaust survivors' recollections of their experiences in Nazi concentration camps were compared to reports they had given to war crimes investigators during and immediately after World War II (1939–1945). In one case, a man reported in the 1940s that he had personally witnessed prisoners being drowned by concentration camp guards. In the 1980s, however, he claimed that no such incident had occurred and even denied having given the earlier report (Baddeley, 1998). In addition, the positive bias is not a function of aging; it is present in young and old adults (Grun, Smith, & Baltes, 2005). Why are our memories subject to such positive bias? Researchers speculate that positive bias may be important to regulation of current states of emotional well-being (Kennedy, Mather, & Carstensen, 2004). In other words, our current need for emotional well-being allows us to selectively process our memories of past events and distort our memories. Some of the most dramatic examples of systematic distortion are found in eyewitness testimony.

EYEWITNESS TESTIMONY: IS IT ACCURATE?

What conditions reduce the reliability of eyewitness testimony?

When people say, "I ought to know—I saw it with my own eyes," we are likely to accept their statement almost without question. After all, seeing is believing. Or is it?

Studies on the accuracy of human memory suggest that eyewitness testimony is highly subject to error and should always be viewed with caution (Brigham, Maass, Snyder, & Spaulding, 1982; Loftus, 1993a). **[LO 6.8]** Nevertheless, eyewitness testimony does play a vital role in our justice system. Says Loftus (1984), "We can't afford to exclude it. Sometimes, as in cases of rape, it is the only evidence available, and it is often correct" (p. 24). In fact, researchers at the University of British Columbia argue that eyewitness testimony may not be as problematic as others suggest. Yuille and Tollestrup (1992) believe that in most crime incidents, the victims are involved and "invested" (unlike participants in laboratory research). Hence, their memories tend to be more accurate. **[LO 6.8]**

Fortunately, there are ways in which eyewitness mistakes can be minimized. Eyewitnesses to crimes typically identify suspects from a lineup. The composition of the lineup is important. Other subjects in a lineup must resemble the suspect in age, body build, and certainly in race. Even then, if the lineup does not contain the guilty party, eyewitnesses may identify the person who most resembles the perpetrator (Gonzalez, Ellsworth, & Pembroke, 1993). Eyewitnesses are less likely to identify the culprit incorrectly and just as likely to make a correct identification if a sequential lineup is used—that is, if the members of the lineup are viewed one after the other rather

The composition of this police lineup is consistent with research findings that suggest that all individuals in a lineup should be similar to the suspect in age, ethnicity, body build, and other physical characteristics.

©James Shaffer/PhotoEdit Inc.

than simultaneously (Loftus, 1993a). **[LO 6.8]** Some police officers and researchers prefer a "showup" to a lineup. In a showup, one suspect is presented and the witness indicates whether that person is or is not the perpetrator. There are fewer misidentifications with a showup, but also more failures to make positive identifications (Dekle, 2006; Gonzalez et al., 1993; Wells, 1993). However, Yarmey, Yarmey, and Yarmey (1996) at the University of Guelph caution that lineups may provide greater accuracy than showups when the time interval between the occurrence and identification is lengthened.

The race of the individual is also a critical concern because eyewitnesses are more likely to identify the wrong person if the person's race is different from their own (Knuycky, Kleider, & Cavrak, 2014). According to Egeth (1993), misidentifications are about 15 percent higher in cross-race than in same-race identifications.

In the case of children, fast "elimination lineups" seem to be most effective. In a Canadian study (Pozzulo & Lindsay, 1999), children were most accurate when asked to eliminate lineup members until only one suspect was left. Then the children were told about the consequences of incorrectly identifying an innocent person as a criminal. This procedure enhanced children's performance to the level of adults. It has also been used effectively with preschoolers (Pozzulo, Dempsey, & Crescini, 2009).

Questioning witnesses after a crime also can influence what they later remember. Because leading questions can substantially change a witness's memory of an event, it is critical that interviewers ask neutral questions (Leichtman & Ceci, 1995). Misleading information supplied after the event can result in erroneous recollections of the actual event, a phenomenon known as the *misinformation effect* (Loftus, 1997, 2005). Furthermore, after eyewitnesses have repeatedly recalled information, whether accurate or inaccurate, they become even

schemas: The integrated frameworks of knowledge and assumptions we have about people, objects, and events that affect how we encode and recall information.

more confident when they testify in court because the information is so easily retrieved (J. S. Shaw, 1996). Surprisingly, though, each time witnesses recount testimony, they become more susceptible to changing their testimony in response to misinformation, despite the increased feeling of confidence they gain each time they retell their story (Chan, Thomas, & Bulevich, 2009). Witnessing a crime is highly stressful. How does stress affect eyewitness accuracy? Research suggests that eyewitnesses tend to remember the central, critical details of the event even though their arousal is high. **[LO 6.8]** It is the memory of peripheral details that suffers more globally as a result of high arousal (Burke, Heuer, & Reisberg, 1992; Christianson, 1992; Wilford, Chan, & Tuhn, 2014).

When working with children, interviewers can take simple steps to increase the likelihood that children will provide better reports: **[LO 6.8]**

Do's:

- Do let the child talk more than the interviewer.

- Do ask general questions that give the child the opportunity to describe things in her or his own words (e.g., "Tell me what happened," "What else happened?" "What happened next?").

- Do use information already provided by children (e.g., "You said you were playing on the jungle gym. Tell me more about playing on the jungle gym.").

- Do give the child time to respond to your question (tolerate at least two seconds of silence before asking another question).

- Do ask simple questions that contain a single idea; for example, "Were you in the bathroom?" rather than complex questions like "Were you with R. in the bathroom when your mum came home from work?"

Don'ts:

- Don't interrupt!

- Don't use long or unusual words (e.g., *molest*, *perpetrator*, *confession*, *testimony*).

- Don't expect children to use conventional measurement systems (e.g., days of the week, height in metres); instead, let them describe in their own words using things that have meaning to them (e.g., a child could say it happened just before her birthday or describe what TV show was on when it happened).

For more information about children's eyewitness testimony and research being conducted in this area, see the *Canadian Connections* box.

Hypnosis for Eyewitnesses

Does hypnosis improve the memory of eyewitnesses?

Research suggests that under controlled laboratory conditions, people do not show improved memory under hypnosis (Buckhout, Eugenio, Licitra, Oliver, & Kramer, 1981; Erdelyi, 2010).

[LO 6.9] Hypnotized subjects may supply more information and are more confident of their recollections, but they supply more *inaccurate* information as well (Dywan & Bowers, 1983; Nogrady, McConkey, & Perry, 1985). Because subjects are much more confident of their memories after hypnosis, they become very convincing witnesses. Some critics of hypnosis are against using it as an aid for eyewitness testimony, but they believe that it can be a valuable investigative tool for police.

RECOVERING REPRESSED MEMORIES: A CONTROVERSY

Since the late 1980s, thousands of people, most of them adult women under the age of 50, have come forward claiming to have been sexually abused as children. Given the fact that childhood sexual abuse is widespread and underreported, the growing number of claims of sexual abuse, including incest, should not be surprising. But many of these new claims are controversial in that the accusers maintain that they had repressed all memory of the abuse until they underwent therapy or read a self-help book for survivors of childhood sexual abuse. Is it likely that people could endure repeated episodes of childhood sexual abuse for years, selectively repress all memories of their abuse, and then recover the repressed memories as adults? On this issue, psychologists are divided (Erdelyi, 2010).

Many psychologists are skeptical of recovered memories, claiming that the "recovered" memories are false memories created by the suggestions of therapists or others. Critics argue "that repression of truly traumatic experiences is rare" (Bowers & Farvolden, 1996, p. 355); moreover, they maintain that "when it comes to a serious trauma, intrusive thoughts and memories are the most characteristic reaction" (p. 359). According to Loftus (1993b), "the therapist convinces the patient with no memories that abuse is likely, and the patient obligingly uses reconstructive strategies to generate memories that would support that conviction" (p. 528).

Critics also charge that recovered memories of sexual abuse are suspect because of the techniques therapists usually use to uncover them: hypnosis and guided imagery. As you have learned, hypnosis does not improve the accuracy of memory, only the confidence that what one remembers is accurate.

Can merely imagining experiences lead people to believe that those experiences actually happened to them? Yes, according to some studies. Many research participants who are instructed to imagine that a fictitious event happened do, in fact, develop a false memory of the imagined event (Hyman & Pentland, 1996; Mazzoni & Memon, 2003; Worthen & Wood, 2001).

In contrast to criticism about repressed memories, Connie Kristiansen (1994) at Carleton University argues that the question is not whether repressed memory occurs, but how often it occurs. Even those who contest the existence of repressed memories (e.g., Loftus, 1993b) report finding them in some people. Kristiansen reports that false memory syndrome is not occurring in "epidemic proportions" (Hovdestad & Kristiansen, 1996). In fact, only 3.9 to 13.6 percent of individuals with recovered memories satisfy the criteria for diagnosis. Kristiansen also suggests that "repressed" memory might be better called *dissociated memory* to reflect the trauma that would lead a person to dissociate himself or herself from an event.

CANADIAN CONNECTIONS

Children as Eyewitnesses

The Badgley Report, commissioned by the federal government and released in 1984, was a catalyst for legal changes that made it possible for very young children to testify in criminal court (Committee on Sexual Offences against Children and Youth, 1984). The admission of testimony from very young children presented many challenges to courts.

Dr. Deborah Connolly (Simon Fraser University) and her colleagues conduct research that examines this very issue. One challenge concerns the kind of offence about which children testify; often, child victims report having been abused repeatedly and are asked to report particular instances of the abuse (Connolly, Price, & Gordon, 2010; Guadagno, Powell, & Wright, 2006). This complicates testimony in several forensically relevant ways. Children who are questioned suggestively about an instance of a repeated event are often more likely to report that the suggested details really had occurred than are children who are questioned about an event that was experienced only once (Connolly & Lindsay, 2001; Connolly & Price, 2006; H. L. Price & Connolly, 2004, 2007). Heightened suggestibility among repeat-event children has been observed even a year after the event (Price & Connolly, 2013). Even in the absence of suggestive questioning, children who report an instance of a repeated event are less consistent in their reports than children who report a one time event (Connolly, Price, Lavoie, & Gordon, 2008). This is particularly important because judges and jurors use consistency to judge credibility, and cases involving child victims often rely on perceptions of credibility (Connolly, Price, & Gordon, 2009, 2010). Not surprisingly, then, children who report an instance of a repeated event are seen to be less credible than children who report a unique event—even when actual accuracy is controlled (Connolly et al., 2008). Inconsistency does not occur because repeat-event children report details that never happened. In

Deborah Connolly

fact, in the absence of suggestive questioning, repeat-event children are less likely than single-event children to report details that they never experienced (Connolly & Lindsay, 2001). The problem appears to be that children have a lot of trouble isolating particular instances of repeated abuse.

Understanding factors about children (such as how anxiety might impact on children's face recognition memory; Fitzgerald, Price, & Connolly, 2012) as well as situational factors (such as how general and specific questions are ordered in interviews; Connolly & Gordon, 2014) are key to understanding what improves or detracts from the accuracy or perceived credibility of children's eyewitness testimony. ∎

The North American governing bodies for psychology (the American Psychological Association and the Canadian Psychological Association) maintain that the current evidence supports the possibility both that repressed memories exist *and* that false memories can be constructed in response to suggestions of abuse (e.g., American Psychological Association, 1994). Moreover, individuals who hold false memories are often fully convinced that they are accurate because of the details such memories contain and the strong emotions associated with them (Dodson, Koutstaal, & Schacter, 2000; Gonsalves et al., 2004; Henkel, 2004; Henkel, Franklin, & Johnson 2000; Loftus, 2004; Loftus & Bernstein, 2005; McNally et al., 2004). Thus, many experts recommend that recovered memories of abuse or violence should be verified independently before they are accepted as facts.

UNUSUAL MEMORY PHENOMENA

Flashbulb Memories: Extremely Vivid Memories

Some of you might remember exactly what you were doing and how you felt when you first heard about the tragic events of September 11, 2001. Others might recall their actions when they heard Michael Jackson had died, or when they heard

about the gunman who fatally shot a Canadian Forces member at the National War Memorial in Ottawa, before charging into the Parliament Buildings and engaging in a gunfight. This type of extremely vivid memory is called a **flashbulb memory** (Bohannon, 1988; R. Brown & Kulik, 1977; Demiray & Freund, 2015). Brown and Kulik suggest that a flashbulb memory is formed when an individual learns of an event that is highly shocking and emotional. You may have a flashbulb memory of the time you received the news of the death or serious injury of a close family member or a friend.

Pillemer (1990) argues that flashbulb memories do not constitute a completely different type of memory. Rather, he suggests, all memories can vary on the dimensions of emotion, consequentiality (the importance of the consequences of the event), and rehearsal (how often people think or talk about the event afterwards). Flashbulb memories rank high in all three dimensions and thus are extremely memorable. Others suggest that flashbulb memories may differ qualitatively

flashbulb memory: An extremely vivid memory of the conditions surrounding one's first hearing of the news of a surprising, shocking, or highly emotional event.

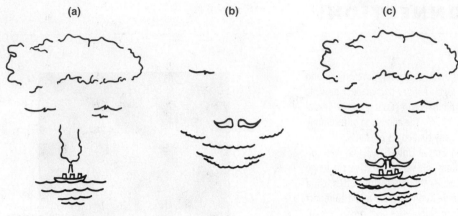

FIGURE 6.6

Test for Eidetic Imagery

Researchers test children for eidetic imagery by having them stare for 30 seconds at a picture like the one in **(a).** A few minutes later, the drawing in **(b)** is shown to the children, who are asked to report what they see. Those with eidetic imagery usually maintain that they see a face and describe the composite sketch in **(c)**. The face can be perceived only if the participant retains the image of the first picture and fuses it with the middle drawing.

Source: (Based on Haber, 1980.) Haber, R.N. (1980, November). Eidetic images are not just imaginary. Psychology Today, 72–82.

and quantitatively from typical autobiographical memories (Lanciano & Curci, 2012).

Several studies suggest that flashbulb memories may not be as accurate as people believe them to be. In an early study, Neisser and Harsch (1992) questioned first-year university students about the *Challenger* space shuttle disaster the morning after the space shuttle disintegrated while in flight. When the same students were questioned again three years later, one third gave accounts that differed markedly from those they gave initially, even though they were extremely confident of their recollections. Interestingly, research suggests that flashbulb memories tend to be forgotten at about the same rate and in the same ways as other types of memories (Curci., Luminet, Finenauer, & Gisler, 2001).

Eidetic Imagery: Almost Like "Photographic Memory"

Have you ever wished you had a photographic memory? Perhaps you have heard of someone who is able to read a page in a book and recall it word for word. More than likely, this person has developed such an enviable memory by learning and applying principles of memory improvement. Psychologists doubt that there are more than a few rare cases of truly photographic memory, which captures all the details of any experience and retains them perfectly. But some studies do show that about 5 percent of children apparently have something akin to photographic memory, which psychologists call *eidetic imagery* (Haber, 1980). **Eidetic imagery** is the ability to retain the image of a visual stimulus, such as a picture, for several minutes after it has been removed from view and to use this retained image to answer questions about the visual stimulus (see Figure 6.6).

Children with eidetic imagery generally have no better long-term memory than children without it, and virtually all children who have eidetic imagery lose it before adulthood. One exception, however, is Elizabeth, a highly intelligent teacher and a skilled artist. Elizabeth can project on her canvas an exact duplicate of a remembered scene with all its rich detail. Even more remarkable is her ability to retain visual images other than scenes and pictures: "Years after having read a poem in a foreign language, she can fetch back an image of the printed page and copy the poem from the bottom line to the top line as fast as she can write" (Stromeyer, 1970, p. 77).

REMEMBER IT

The Nature of Remembering

1. What early memory researcher found that, rather than accurately recalling information detail by detail, people often reconstruct and systematically distort facts to make them more consistent with past experiences?
   a. H. E. Burtt
   b. Frederic Bartlett
   c. Wilder Penfield
   d. William James

2. When a person uses _____ to process information, both encoding and retrieval can be affected.

3. As a rule, people's memories are more accurate under hypnosis. (true/false)

4. The ability to retain a visual image several minutes after it has been removed from view is called
   a. photographic memory.
   b. flashbulb memory.
   c. eidetic imagery.
   d. sensory memory.

MODULE **6C** FACTORS INFLUENCING RETRIEVAL

LO 6.10 Define and describe the *serial position effect*, including primacy and recency effects.

LO 6.11 Explain how the environmental context impacts on retrieval.

LO 6.12 Define *state-dependent memory*.

Researchers in psychology have identified several factors that influence memory. We can control some of these factors, but not all of them.

THE SERIAL POSITION EFFECT: TO BE REMEMBERED, BE FIRST OR LAST BUT NOT IN THE MIDDLE

What is the serial position effect?

If you were introduced to a dozen people at a party, you would most likely recall the names of the first few people you met and the last one or two, but forget most of the names in the middle. A number of studies have revealed the **serial position effect**—the finding that for information learned in sequence, recall is better for items at the beginning and the end than for items in the middle of the sequence. **[LO 6.10]**

Information at the beginning of a sequence has a fairly high probability of being recalled because there has been time to rehearse it and encode it into long-term memory. This is called the **primacy effect**. Information at the end of a sequence has an even higher probability of being recalled because it is still in short-term memory and being rehearsed and encoded at the time you need to remember it. This is known as the **recency effect**. **[LO 6.10]** The poorer recall of information in the middle of a sequence occurs because that information is no longer in short-term memory and has not yet been placed in long-term memory. The serial position effect lends strong support to the notion of separate systems for short-term and long-term memory (Glanzer & Cunitz, 1966; Postman & Phillips, 1965).

Primacy and recency effects can also have an impact on information stored for longer periods of time (Roediger, 1991). For example, children learning the alphabet are likely to remember the first and last several letters of the alphabet better than many of the letters in the middle.

ENVIRONMENTAL CONTEXT AND MEMORY

How does environmental context affect memory?

Have you ever stood in your living room and thought of something you needed from your bedroom, only to forget what it was when you went there? Did the item come to mind when you returned to the living room? Some research has revealed that we tend to recall information better when we are in the same location—the same environmental context—as when the information was originally encoded. **[LO 6.11]** Tulving and Thompson (1973) suggest that many elements of the physical setting in which we learn information are encoded along with the information and become part of the memory trace. If part or all of the original context is reinstated, it may serve as a retrieval cue. Then the information previously learned in that context may come to mind. This is known as the *encoding specificity hypothesis*.

Godden and Baddeley (1975) conducted one of the early studies of context and memory with members of a university scuba-diving club. Students memorized a list of words when they were either 3 metres underwater or on land. They were later tested for recall of the words in the same or in a different environment. The results of the study suggest that recall of information is strongly influenced by environmental context (see Figure 6.7). Words learned underwater were best recalled underwater, and words learned on land were best recalled on land. In fact, when the scuba divers learned and recalled the words in the same context, their scores were 47 percent higher than when the two contexts were different. More recent studies have found similar context effects (e.g., Bjorklund et al., 2000; Smith, Handy, Angello, & Manzano, 2014).

Odours can also supply powerful and enduring retrieval cues for memory (Ball, Shoker, & Miles, 2010). For example, experimental participants who experienced a pleasant odour during learning and again when tested five days later had greater recall than those who did not experience the odour during both learning and recall (C. Morgan, 1996).

Not all studies have found that memory is enhanced when students learn and are tested in the same environment (Fernandez & Glenberg, 1985; Saufley, Otaka, & Bavaresco, 1985). How can the discrepancy be explained? McDaniel, Anderson, Einstein, & O'Halloran (1989) reasoned that the more completely and carefully people encode material to be remembered, the less dependent they are on reinstating the original context or environment. But we have already learned that people do not always carefully encode information and events to be remembered. Consequently, authorities investigating crimes often bring eyewitnesses back to the crime scene or ask them to visualize it to help them recall more details of the crime.

THE STATE-DEPENDENT MEMORY EFFECT

What is the state-dependent memory effect?

Does our internal state (e.g., happy or sad, intoxicated or sober) influence our memory? Yes, it does. We tend to recall information better if we are in the same internal state as when the information was encoded. Psychologists call this

---

eidetic imagery (eye-DET-ik): The ability to retain the image of a visual stimulus several minutes after it has been removed from view.

serial position effect: The tendency to recall the beginning and ending items in a sequence better than the middle items.

primacy effect: The tendency to recall the first items in a sequence more readily than those in the middle of the sequence.

recency effect: The tendency to recall the last items in a sequence more readily than those in the middle of the sequence.

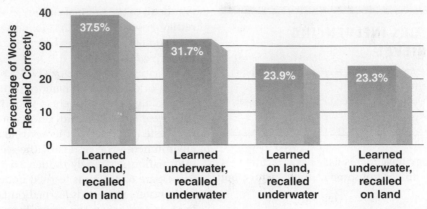

FIGURE 6.7

Context-Dependent Memory

Godden and Baddeley showed the strong influence of environmental context on recall. Scuba divers who memorized a list of words, either on land or underwater, had significantly better recall in the same physical context in which the learning had taken place.
Source: Data from Godden & Baddeley, 1975.

the **state-dependent memory effect. [LO 6.12]** Anxiety appears to affect memory more than other emotions. For example, when researchers exposed college students to spiders and/or snakes while they were learning lists of words, the students recalled more words when the creatures were also present during tests of recall (Lang, Craske, Brown, & Ghaneian, 2001).

Alcohol, Other Drugs, and Memory

Some studies have shown a state-dependent memory effect for animals (Zarrindast & Rezayof, 2004) and humans (Eich, 1980) for alcohol and drugs such as morphine, marijuana, amphetamines, and barbiturates. In one study, people learned (encoded) material while sober or intoxicated, and later were tested in either the sober or the intoxicated state. Recall was found to be best when the subjects were in the same state for both learning and testing (Weingartner, Adefris, Eich, & Murphy, 1976). As in other studies, the state-dependent memory effect was evident for recall but not for recognition.

Mood and Memory

Adults who are clinically depressed tend to recall more negative life experiences (D. M. Clark & Teasdale, 1982) and are likely to recall their parents as unloving and rejecting (Lewinsohn & Rosenbaum, 1987). Moreover, a review of 48 studies revealed a significant relationship between depression and memory impairment. But as depression lifts, the tendency toward negative recall reverses itself (Lloyd & Lishman, 1975).

REMEMBER IT

Factors Influencing Recall

1. When children learn the alphabet, they often are better at learning and recalling the first few (A, B, C, D) and last few (X, Y, Z) letters of the alphabet before learning the letters in between. This is called the
   a. primacy effect.
   b. recency effect.
   c. serial position effect.
   d. state-dependent memory effect.

2. Recall is about as good when people visualize the context in which learning occurred as it is when recall and learning occur in the same context. (true/false)

3. Which best explains why drugs such as alcohol and marijuana can interfere with recall if the drugs are taken during learning but not during retrieval?

   a. the consistency effect
   b. the state-dependent memory effect
   c. context-dependent memory
   d. consolidation failure

4. Compared with non-depressed people, depressed people tend to have
   a. more sad memories.
   b. fewer memories.
   c. more pleasant memories.
   d. memories about the same in emotional content.

MODULE (6D) BIOLOGY AND MEMORY

LO 6.13 Understand how exceptional cases of memory loss help us to understand memory processes and functioning.

LO 6.14 Understand the role of the hippocampus, prefrontal lobe, and hormones for memory.

LO 6.15 Define *anterograde amnesia* and *long-term potentiation* and explain their role in memory.

We have learned a great deal about how we remember. And we know that our vast store of information must exist physically somewhere in the brain. But where?

BRAIN DAMAGE: A CLUE TO MEMORY FORMATION

Researchers continue to find specific locations in the brain that house and mediate functions and processes in memory. One important source of information comes from people who have suffered memory loss as a result of damage to specific brain areas. **[LO 6.13]** One such person is H. M., who has had a major influence on present-day knowledge of human memory. Much of what we know about H. M. was recorded by Canadian researcher Brenda Milner.

The Case of H. M.

What has the study of H. M. revealed about the role of the hippocampus in memory?

H. M. suffered from such severe epilepsy that, out of desperation, he agreed to a radical surgical procedure. The surgeon removed the site responsible for his seizures, the medial portions of both temporal lobes—the amygdala and the *hippocampal region*, which includes the hippocampus itself and the underlying cortical areas. **[LO 6.14]** It was 1953, and H. M. was 27 years old.

After his surgery, H. M. remained intelligent and psychologically stable, and his seizures were drastically reduced. But unfortunately, the tissue cut from H. M.'s brain housed more than the site of his seizures. It also contained his ability to use working memory to store new information in long-term memory. **[LO 6.13]** Though his short-term memory was still as good as ever and he easily remembered the events of his life stored well before the operation, H. M. suffered from **anterograde amnesia**. He was not able to remember a single event that occurred from the surgery to 56 years later, when he died in 2008. As far as his conscious long-term memory was concerned, it was still 1953 and he was still 27 years old. **[LO 6.15]**

Brenda Milner, a psychologist from McGill University, was contacted to investigate this very unusual case of amnesia, and her work with H. M. provided answers to many questions regarding the location of and biological structures that support different kinds of memories.

For example, surgery affected only H. M.'s declarative, long-term memory—his ability to store facts, personal experiences, and names, faces, telephone numbers, and the like. Researchers were surprised to discover that he could still form non-declarative memories—that is, he could still acquire skills through repetitive practice, although he could not remember having done so. After the surgery, H. M. learned to play tennis and improve his game, but he had no memory of having played (Milner, 1966, 1970; Milner, Corkin, & Teuber, 1968).

H. M.'s case was one of the first indications that the hippocampal region is involved in the formation of long-term memories. **[LOs 6.13 & 6.14]** Other patients who, like H. M., have suffered similar brain damage, exhibit the same types of memory loss (Squire, 1992). Most recent research indicates that the hippocampus is critically important in forming episodic memories (Eichenbaum, 1997; Eichenbaum & Fortin, 2003; Spiers, Maguire, & Burgess, 2001). **[LO 6.14]** Semantic memory, however, depends not on the hippocampus itself, but on the other parts of the hippocampal region underlying it (Hoenig & Scheef, 2005; Vargha-Khadem et al., 1997). Consequently, many researchers argue that neurological bases for episodic and semantic memory are completely separate (e.g., Tulving, 2002).

The Case of K. C.

To support the distinction between semantic and episodic memory, Tulving (1989; Tulving, Schacter, McLachlan, & Moscovitch, 1988) cites the case of K. C., a Toronto resident who sustained a severe head injury from a motorcycle accident. K. C. suffered massive damage to his left frontal lobe and other parts of the brain. **[LO 6.13]**

K.C.'s case is remarkable in that he cannot remember, in the sense of bringing back to conscious awareness, a single thing that he has ever done or experienced. He cannot remember himself experiencing situations and participating in life's events. This total absence of personal recollections makes K. C.'s case unique; no other reports exist of amnesiac patients who have been incapable of recollecting *any* personal happenings (Tulving, 1989).

Although his episodic memory was erased, K. C.'s semantic memory was largely spared. His storehouse of knowledge from fields such as geography, history, politics, and music is still large, enabling him to answer questions about many topics. Most research supports the hypothesis that the hippocampus is especially important in forming episodic memories (Eichenbaum, 1997; Eichenbaum & Fortin, 2003; Gluck & Myers, 1997; Spiers et al., 2001). Semantic memory, however, depends not only on the hippocampus, but also on the other parts of the hippocampal region (Hoenig & Scheef, 2005; Vargha-Khadem et al., 1997). Once stored, memories can be retrieved without the involvement of the hippocampus (Gluck & Myers, 1997; J. L. McClelland, McNaughton, & O'Reilly, 1995). Consequently, many researchers argue that neurological underpinnings of episodic and semantic memories are entirely separate (e.g., Tulving, 2002).

state-dependent memory effect: The tendency to recall information better if one is in the same pharmacological or psychological (mood) state as when the information was encoded.

anterograde amnesia: The inability to form long-term memories of events occurring after brain surgery or a brain injury, although memories formed before the trauma are usually intact.

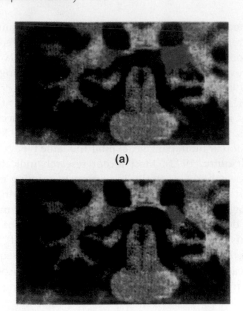

(a)

(b)

FIGURE 6.8

MRI Scans Showing the Larger Size of the Posterior Hippocampus in the Brain of an Experienced Taxi Driver

The posterior (rear) hippocampus of an experienced London taxi driver, shown in red in MRI scan **(a)**, is significantly larger than the posterior hippocampus of a research participant who was not a taxi driver, shown in red in scan **(b)**.
Source: (Adapted from Maguire et al., 2000.) Maguire, E.A., Gadian, D.G., Johnsrude, I.S., Good, C.D., Ashburner, J., Frackowiak, R.S.J., & Frith, C.D. (2000). Navigation-related structural change in the hippocampi of taxi drivers. Proceedings of the National Academy of Science, 97, 4398-4403. National Academy of Sciences. Copyright (2000) National Academy of Sciences, U.S.A.

Research with taxi drivers and other work with birds and animals suggest that the hippocampus may also support navigational skills by helping to create intricate neural spatial maps. For example, MRI scans of taxi drivers and of adults whose living did not depend on their navigational skills (Figure 6.8) revealed that the rear (posterior) region of the hippocampus was much larger in the taxi drivers (Maguire et al., 2000). In addition, the longer the time spent as a taxi driver, the greater the volume of the posterior hippocampus. Similarly, in many birds and small mammals, the volume of the hippocampus increases seasonally, as navigational skills for migration and spatial maps showing where food is hidden become critical for survival (N. S. Clayton, 1998; Colombo & Broadbent, 2000). Thus the hippocampus is important for storing and using mental maps to navigate the environment.

We have described how researchers have been able to identify some of the brain structures that play a part in memory. But what processes within these structures make new memories?

NEURONAL CHANGES IN MEMORY: BRAIN WORK

Some researchers are exploring memory more minutely by studying the actions of single neurons. Others are studying collections of neurons and their synapses as well as the neurotransmitters whose chemical action begins the process of recording and storing a memory (Kesner, 2009). The first close look at the nature of memory in single neurons was provided by Eric Kandel and his colleagues, who traced the effects of learning and memory in the sea snail *Aplysia* (Dale & Kandel, 1990; Dash, Hochner,

& Kandel, 1990). Using tiny electrodes implanted in several single neurons in the sea snail, Kandel and his fellow researchers have been able to map neural circuits that are formed and maintained as the animal learns and remembers. Furthermore, they have discovered the different types of protein synthesis that facilitate short-term and long-term memory (E. R. Kandel, Castellucci, Goelet, & Schacher, 1987; Sweatt & Kandel, 1989).

But the studies of learning and memory in *Aplysia* reflect only simple classical conditioning, which is a type of non-declarative memory. Other researchers studying mammals report that physical changes occur in the neurons and synapses in brain regions involved in declarative memory (I. Lee & Kesner, 2002).

Long-Term Potentiation: Prolonged Action at the Synapses

What is long-term potentiation, and why is it important?

As far back as 1949, Canadian psychologist Donald O. Hebb argued that the necessary neural ingredients for learning and memory must involve the enhancement of transmission at the synapses. Hebb (1949) proposed that some process must operate at the synapse to initiate and maintain the continuous and simultaneous interaction of the presynaptic (sending) neurons and the postsynaptic (receiving) neurons. Such a process, he asserted, would strengthen the synaptic connection.

A widely studied model for learning and memory at the level of the neurons is **long-term potentiation**, or LTP (Cotman & Lynch, 1989; L. Stein, Xue, & Belluzzi, 1993; Wang & Morris, 2010). Long-term potentiation meets the requirements of the mechanism Hebb described (Fischbach, 1992). To *potentiate* means to make potent or to strengthen. Long-term potentiation is a long-lasting increase in the efficiency of neural transmission at the synapses (Schuman & Madison, 1994). **[LO 6.15]** It has become the leading model for the facilitation of some types of long-term memory in mammals because it can last for days and even weeks (Bliss & Lomo, 1973; Nguyen, Abel, & Kandel, 1994). Long-term potentiation is important because it may be the basis for learning and memory at the level of the neurons.

Long-term potentiation does not take place unless *both* the presynaptic and postsynaptic neurons are activated at the same time by intense high-frequency stimulation. Also, the postsynaptic neuron must be depolarized (ready to fire) when stimulation arrives, or long-term potentiation will not occur. Increased neural activity at very fast frequencies (20–70 cycles per second) occurs at the synapses when learning and memory tasks are performed (Miltner, Braun, Arnold, Witte, & Taub, 1999). Long-term potentiation is a common occurrence in the hippocampus, which, as you have learned, is essential in the formation of declarative memories. Much of the research on long-term potentiation has been conducted in various areas of the hippocampus (Eichenbaum & Otto, 1993).

If the types of changes in synapses produced by long-term potentiation are the same neural changes that take place in learning, then blocking or interfering with long-term potentiation should likewise interfere with learning. And it does. However, controversy continues as to whether the relatively long-lasting increase in synaptic efficiency that constitutes LTP is the result of an increase in the amount of neurotransmitter released, an increase in the number of receptors at the synapses, or both (M. L. V. Bennett, 2000).

HORMONES AND MEMORY

How do memories of threatening situations compare with ordinary memories?

The strongest and most lasting memories are usually those fuelled by emotion (Cahill, Babinsky, Markowitsch, & McGaugh, 1995). When a person is emotionally aroused, the adrenal glands release the hormones epinephrine (adrenalin) and norepinephrine (noradrenalin) into the bloodstream. Long known to be involved in the fight-or-flight response, these hormones enable humans to survive, and they also imprint powerful and enduring memories of the circumstances surrounding threatening situations. [LO 6.14] Such emotionally laden memories activate the amygdala (known to play a central role in

emotion) and other parts of the memory system (Gabrieli, 1998). Emotional memories are lasting memories, and this may be the most important factor in explaining the intensity and durability of flashbulb memories.

Other hormones may have important effects on memory. Excessive levels of the stress hormone cortisol, for example, have been shown to interfere with memory in patients who suffer from diseases of the adrenal glands, the site of cortisol production (Jelicic & Bonke, 2001). Estrogen, the female sex hormone, appears to improve working memory efficiency (Dohanich, 2003). Estrogen appears to exert this effect by helping to build and maintain synapses between neurons in brain areas known to be involved in memory, such as the hippocampal region (Woolley, Weiland, McEwen, & Schwartzkroin, 1997). [LO 6.14]

REMEMBER IT

Biology and Memory

1. The hippocampus is the brain structure involved in the formation of permanent memories of
   a. motor skills.
   b. facts and personal experiences.
   c. motor skills, facts, and personal experiences.
   d. motor skills and personal experiences.

2. What is the term for the long-lasting increase in the efficiency of neural transmission at the synapses that may be the basis for learning and memory at the level of the neurons?

   a. long-term potentiation
   b. synaptic facilitation
   c. synaptic potentiation
   d. presynaptic potentiation

3. H. M. retained his ability to add to his _____ memory.

Answers: 1. b   2. a   3. non-declarative

MODULE 6E FORGETTING

LO 6.16 Identify the major causes of forgetting.

Patient: Doctor, you've got to help me. I'm sure I'm losing my memory. I hear something one minute and forget it the next. I don't know what to do!
Doctor: When did you first notice this?
Patient: Notice what?

Most of us think of forgetting as a problem to be overcome, but forgetting is not all bad. Wouldn't it be depressing if you were condemned to remember in stark detail all the bad things that ever happened to you? Forgetting clearly has its advantages.

HERMANN EBBINGHAUS AND THE FIRST EXPERIMENTAL STUDIES ON LEARNING AND MEMORY

What was Ebbinghaus's major contribution to psychology?

Hermann Ebbinghaus (1850–1909) conducted the first experimental studies on learning and memory. Ebbinghaus realized that some materials are easier than others to understand and

remember. To study memory objectively, he was faced with the task of selecting materials that would all be equally difficult to memorize. To accomplish this, he originated the use of **nonsense syllables**, which are consonant-vowel-consonant combinations that are not actual words. Examples are LEJ, XIZ, LUK, and ZOH. The use of nonsense syllables largely accomplished Ebbinghaus's goal. But did you notice that some of the syllables sound more like actual words than others and would, therefore, be easier to remember?

Ebbinghaus conducted his famous studies on memory using 2300 nonsense syllables as his material and himself as his only subject. He carried out all his experiments in the same surroundings at about the same time of day, and he kept away all possible distractions. Ebbinghaus's method was to learn lists of nonsense syllables, repeating them over and over at a constant rate of 2.5 syllables per second, marking time with a metronome or the ticking of a watch. He repeated a list until he could recall it twice without error, a point that he called *mastery*.

---

long-term potentiation: A long-lasting increase in the efficiency of neural transmission at the synapses.

nonsense syllables: Consonant-vowel-consonant combinations that do not spell a word; used to control for the meaningfulness of the material.

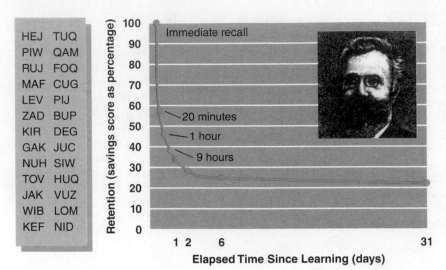

HEJ	TUQ
PIW	QAM
RUJ	FOQ
MAF	CUG
LEV	PIJ
ZAD	BUP
KIR	DEG
GAK	JUC
NUH	SIW
TOV	HUQ
JAK	VUZ
WIB	LOM
KEF	NID

FIGURE 6.9

Ebbinghaus's Curve of Forgetting

After memorizing lists of nonsense syllables similar to those on the left of the figure, Ebbinghaus measured his retention after varying intervals of time using the relearning method. Forgetting was most rapid at first, as shown by his retention of only 58 percent after 20 minutes and 44 percent after one hour. Then the rate of forgetting tapered off, with a retention of 34 percent after one day, 25 percent after six days, and 21 percent after 31 days.

Source: Data from Ebbinghaus, 1913.

Ebbinghaus recorded the amount of time or the number of learning trials it took to memorize his lists to mastery. Then, after different periods of time had passed and forgetting had occurred, he recorded the amount of time or the number of trials he needed to relearn the same list to mastery. Ebbinghaus compared the time or the trials required for relearning with those of the original learning and then computed the percentage of time saved, or *savings score*. For him, the percentage of savings represented the percentage of the original learning that remained in memory.

Ebbinghaus's famous curve of forgetting, shown in Figure 6.9, consists of savings scores at various time intervals after the original learning. What does the curve of forgetting show about how rapidly this type of material is forgotten? Forgetting begins very quickly and then gradually tapers off. Ebbinghaus found that if he retained information as long as a day or two, very little more would be forgotten even a month later. But remember, this curve of forgetting applies to nonsense syllables. The forgetting of meaningful, carefully encoded, deeply processed, or frequently rehearsed material usually occurs more slowly.

What Ebbinghaus learned about the rate of forgetting is relevant for all of us. Do you, like most students, cram before a big exam? If so, don't assume that everything you memorize on Monday can be held intact until Tuesday. Because a significant amount of forgetting can occur within the first 24 hours, it is wise to spend at least some time reviewing the material on the day of the test. The less meaningful the material is to you, the more forgetting you can expect and the more necessary a review will be.

THE CAUSES OF FORGETTING

What are seven causes of forgetting?

There are many reasons why we fail to remember. Among them are encoding failure, decay, interference (proactive and retroactive), consolidation failure, motivated forgetting, retrieval failure, and prospective forgetting.

Encoding Failure

There is a distinction between forgetting and not being able to remember. Forgetting is "the inability to recall something now that could be recalled on an earlier occasion" (Tulving,

1974, p. 74). But often when we say we cannot remember, we have not actually forgotten. Our inability to remember may be a result of **encoding failure**—the information never entered our long-term memory in the first place. **[LO 6.16]** Of the many things we encounter every day, it is sometimes surprising how little we actually encode. Can you recall accurately, or even recognize, something you have seen thousands of times before? Do the *Try It* on the opposite page to find out.

In your lifetime you have seen thousands of pennies, nickels, and dimes, but unless you are a coin collector, you probably have not encoded the details of a penny, nickel, or dime. If you did poorly on the *Try It*, you have plenty of company. Nickerson and Adams (1979) studied people's memory for pennies and reported that few people could reproduce a penny from recall. In fact, only a handful of subjects could even recognize a drawing of a real penny when it was presented along with incorrect drawings. Was the same true for you for the nickel or dime?

In preparing for tests, do you usually assume a passive role? Do you merely read and reread your textbook and notes and assume that this process will eventually result in learning? If you don't test yourself, you may find that you have been the unwitting victim of encoding failure. Textbook features such as margin questions and end-of-section tests can help you by providing structure for acquiring the information and a check that the material has been encoded.

Decay

Decay theory, probably the oldest theory of forgetting, assumes that memories, if not used, fade with time and ultimately disappear entirely. **[LO 6.16]** The term *decay* implies a physiological change in the neural trace that recorded the experience. According to this theory, the neural trace may decay or fade within seconds or days or over a much longer period of time.

Today, most psychologists accept the notion of decay, or fading of the memory trace, as a cause of forgetting in sensory and short-term memory, but not in long-term memory (see Figure 6.3 on p. 157). If there were a gradual, inevitable decay of the memory trace in long-term memory, Harry Bahrick and colleagues (Bahrick, Bahrick, & Wittlinger, 1975) would not have found that after 35 years, people recognized 90 percent of their high school classmates' names and photographs—the same percentage as for recent graduates.

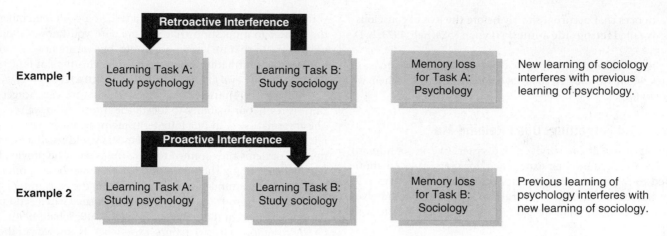

FIGURE 6.10

Retroactive and Proactive Interference

In Example 1, retroactive interference occurs when new learning hinders the ability to recall information learned previously. In Example 2, proactive interference occurs when prior learning hinders new learning.

Interference

What is interference, and how can it be minimized?

A major cause of forgetting, and one that affects us every day, is **interference**. Interference refers to those times when new information or information you have already learned interferes with what you are now learning or trying to recall (Figure 6.10). **[LO 6.16]** There are two forms of interference: proactive and retroactive (Underwood, 1964).

PROACTIVE INTERFERENCE   Laura's romance with her new boyfriend, Todd, got off to a bad start when she accidentally called him Dave, her former boyfriend's name. And how many cheques written early in January do you suppose have the wrong year? Such mistakes happen frequently, and the reason for that is proactive interference. Proactive interference occurs when information or experiences already stored in long-term memory hinder our ability to remember newer information (Underwood, 1957). When you buy a new car, it may take a while to feel comfortable with the new arrangement of the dashboard. Your memory of the old car's dashboard may at first interfere with your driving. This type of proactive interference is called *negative transfer*. One explanation for interference is that old and new responses are competing with each other (G. H. Bower, Thompson-Schill, & Tulving, 1994).

RETROACTIVE INTERFERENCE   New learning or experience that interferes with our ability to remember information previously stored is called *retroactive interference*. The more similar the new learning or experience is to the previous learning, the more interference there is. However, research shows that the effects of retroactive interference are often temporary (Lustig, Konkel, & Jacoby, 2004). In fact, after some time has passed, the old information may be better remembered than the material that was learned more recently. So the material a student learned in a previous sociology course may appear to fade when he encounters similar information presented in a somewhat different light in a psychology course, but in the long run, his sociology knowledge may outlast what he learned in psychology.

Consolidation Failure

Consolidation is the process by which encoded information is stored in memory. When a disruption in the consolidation process occurs, a permanent memory usually does not form. **Consolidation failure** can result from anything that causes a person to lose consciousness—a car accident, a blow to the head, a grand mal seizure, or an electroconvulsive shock treatment given for severe depression. **[LO 6.16]** Memory loss of the

TRY IT

Penny for Your Thoughts

On a separate sheet of paper, draw a sketch of a penny, nickel, or dime from memory using recall. In your drawing, show the direction the Queen's image is facing and the location of the date, and include all the words on the "heads" side of the coin.

Once your drawing is complete, check the accuracy of your recall by comparing your drawing to a real coin. How accurate were you?

encoding failure: Forgetting resulting from material never having been put into long-term memory.

decay theory: A theory of forgetting that holds that the memory trace, if not used, disappears with the passage of time.

interference: The cause of memory loss that occurs when information or associations stored either before or after a given memory hinder our ability to remember it.

consolidation failure: Any disruption in the consolidation process that prevents a permanent memory from forming.

experiences that occurred shortly before the loss of consciousness is called **retrograde amnesia** (Lynch & Yarnell, 1973; L. D. Stern, 1981).

We have discussed ways to avoid forgetting. But there are times when we may need to avoid remembering—when we *want* to forget.

Motivated Forgetting: Don't Remind Me

Victims of assault and survivors of disasters (natural or human) may be haunted by their experiences for years. They are motivated to forget. However, even people who have not suffered any trauma use **motivated forgetting** to protect themselves from experiences that are painful, frightening, or otherwise unpleasant.

With one form of motivated forgetting, *suppression*, a person makes a conscious, active attempt to put a painful or disturbing memory out of mind but is still aware that the painful event occurred. With another type of motivated forgetting, **repression**, unpleasant memories are literally removed from consciousness, and the person is no longer aware that the unpleasant event ever occurred (Freud, 1922). **[LO 6.16]** People who have **amnesia** (memory loss) that is not due to loss of consciousness or brain damage have actually repressed the events they no longer remember. To deal with unpleasant memories, more people probably use motivated forgetting than any other method. Humans, it seems, have a natural tendency to forget the unpleasant circumstances of life and to remember the pleasant ones (Linton, 1979; Matlin, 1989; Meltzer, 1930).

Retrieval Failure: Misplaced Memories

How many times have these experiences happened to you? You are with a friend when you meet an acquaintance, but you can't introduce the two because you cannot recall the name of your acquaintance. Or while taking a test, you can't remember the answer to a question that you are sure you know. Often we are certain that we know something, but we are not able to retrieve the information when we need it. This type of forgetting is called *retrieval failure* (Shiffrin, 1970). **[LO 6.16]**

Tulving (1974) asserts that much of what we call "forgetting" is really our inability to locate the information we seek. The information is in our long-term memory, but we cannot retrieve it. Tulving found that participants could recall a large number of items they seemed to have forgotten if he provided retrieval cues to jog their memory. For example, odours often provide potent reminders of experiences from the past, and they can serve as retrieval cues for information learned when certain odours were present (Ball, Shoker, & Miles, 2010; Schab, 1990).

A common retrieval failure experience is known as the "tip-of-the-tongue" (TOT) phenomenon (R. Brown & McNeil, 1966). You try to recall a name, a word, or some other bit of information, fully aware that you know the item almost as well as your own name. You can almost recall the word or name, and perhaps even know the number of syllables and the beginning or ending letter of the word. It is on the tip of your tongue, but it just won't quite come out.

Prospective Forgetting: Forgetting to Remember

Do you have trouble remembering appointments? Do you forget to mail birthday cards on time, pick up your clothes at the cleaners, pay your bills, or water your plants? If you do, you are not alone. In a study of everyday forgetting, Terry (1988) had 50 people keep a diary of the instances of forgetting that occurred each day. Of the 751 recorded instances of forgetting, most did not involve forgetting names, facts, or other information already known. Rather, they involved prospective memory—remembering to carry out an action in the future.

REMEMBER IT

Forgetting

1. Match the example with the appropriate cause of forgetting.
   _____ 1) encoding failure
   _____ 2) consolidation failure
   _____ 3) retrieval failure
   _____ 4) repression
   _____ 5) interference

   a. failing to remember the answer on a test until after you turn the test in
   b. forgetting a humiliating experience from childhood
   c. not being able to describe the back of a five-dollar bill
   d. calling a friend by another's name
   e. waking up in the hospital and not remembering you had an automobile accident

2. To minimize interference, it is best to follow learning with
   a. rest.
   b. recreation.
   c. sleep.
   d. unrelated study.

3. According to the text, the major cause of forgetting is interference. (true/false)

4. Who invented the nonsense syllable, conceived the relearning method for testing retention, and plotted the curve of forgetting?
   a. George Sperling
   b. H. E. Burtt
   c. Fredric Bartlett
   d. Hermann Ebbinghaus

Answers: 1(1). c (2). e (3). a (4). b (5). d 2. c 3. true 4. d

MODULE **6F** IMPROVING MEMORY

LO 6.17 Identify and define four study habits that aid memory.

LO 6.18 Compare the learning outcomes of overlearning, spaced versus massed practice, and active learning versus rereading.

STUDY HABITS THAT AID MEMORY

What are four study habits that can aid memory?

There are no magic formulas for improving your memory. Remembering is a skill and, like any other skill, requires knowledge and practice. In this section we will review how organization, overlearning, spaced practice, and active learning can improve your memory.

Organization: Everything in Its Place

A telephone directory would be of little use to you if the names and phone numbers were listed in random order. In a similar way, you are giving your memory a task it probably will not accept if you try to remember large amounts of information in a haphazard fashion. Organizing material to be learned is a tremendous aid to memory. **[LO 6.17]** You can prove this for yourself by completing *Try It.*

We tend to retrieve information from long-term memory according to the way we have organized it for storage. Almost anyone can name the months of the year in about 12 seconds, but how long would it take to recall them in alphabetical order? The same 12 items, all well known, are much harder to retrieve in alphabetical order because they are not organized that way in memory. When you study, it is helpful to organize items in some meaningful way (in alphabetical order, or according to categories, historical sequence, theories) to make retrieval easier.

Overlearning: Reviewing Again, and Again, and Again

What is overlearning, and why is it important?

Do you still remember the words to songs that were popular when you were in high school? Can you recite many of the nursery rhymes you learned as a child even though you haven't heard them in years? You probably can because of **overlearning**.

Let us say that you wanted to memorize a list of words, and you studied until you could recite the words once without error. Would this amount of study or practice be sufficient? Many studies suggest that we remember material better and longer if we overlearn it—that is, if we practise or study beyond the minimum needed to barely learn it (Ebbinghaus, 1885/1964). **[LO 6.17]** A pioneering study in overlearning by W. C. F. Krueger (1929) showed very substantial long-term gains for participants engaged in 50 percent and 100 percent overlearning. Furthermore, overlearning makes material more resistant to interference. It is perhaps your best insurance against stress-related forgetting.

The next time you study for a test, don't stop studying as soon as you think you know the material. Spend another hour or so going over it, and you will be surprised at how much more you will remember.

TRY IT

Organizing Information to Aid Memory

Have a pencil and a sheet of paper handy. Read the following list of items out loud and then write down as many as you can remember.

peas	ice cream	fish	perfume	bananas
toilet paper	onions	apples	cookies	ham
carrots	shaving cream	pie	grapes	chicken

If you organize this list, the items are much easier to remember. Now read each category heading and the items listed beneath it. Write down as many items as you can remember.

Desserts	Fruits	Vegetables	Meat	Toilet Articles
pie	bananas	carrots	chicken	perfume
ice cream	apples	onions	fish	shaving cream
cookies	grapes	peas	ham	toilet paper

Spaced Versus Massed Practice: A Little at a Time Beats All at Once

We have all tried cramming for examinations, but spacing study over several different sessions generally is more effective than **massed practice**—learning in one long practice session without rest periods, especially for challenging material (Bahrick & Phelps, 1987; Glover & Corkill, 1987; Son, 2004). **[LO 6.17]** The spacing effect applies to learning motor skills as well as to learning facts and information. All music students can tell you that it is better to practise for half an hour each day, every day, than to practise for many hours in a row once a week.

---

retrograde amnesia (RET-ro-grade): A loss of memory for events occurring during a period of time preceding a brain trauma that caused a loss of consciousness.

motivated forgetting: Forgetting through suppression or repression in order to protect oneself from material that is too painful, anxiety- or guilt-producing, or otherwise unpleasant.

repression: The act of removing unpleasant memories from one's consciousness so that one is no longer aware of the painful event.

amnesia: A partial or complete loss of memory resulting from brain trauma or psychological trauma.

overlearning: Practising or studying material beyond the point where it can be repeated once without error.

massed practice: One long learning practice session as opposed to spacing the learning in shorter practice sessions over an extended period.

You will remember more with less total study time if you space your study over several sessions. Long periods of memorizing make material particularly subject to interference and often result in fatigue and lowered concentration. Moreover, when you space your practice, you probably create a new memory that may be stored in a different place, and this increases your chances of recalling it. **[LO 6.18]**

Active Learning versus Rereading: Active Learning Wins

Many students simply read and reread their textbook and notes when they study for an exam. Research over many years shows that you will recall more if you increase the amount of active learning in your study. For example, it is better to read a page or a few paragraphs and then practise recalling what you have just read. **[LO 6.17]** Even better, you should ask yourself questions as you read, especially questions that encourage you to connect the new information you need to learn with knowledge that you already have (E. Wood, Pressley, & Winne, 1990; Willoughby et al., 2000). **[LO 6.18]** "Why" questions (e.g., Why would that fact be true?) have proved particularly useful for learning facts from text materials.

The *Apply It* box offers some useful techniques to help you remember material.

REMEMBER IT

Ways to Improve Memory

1. When you are studying for an exam, it is better to spend
   a. more time reciting than rereading.
   b. more time rereading than reciting.
   c. equal time rereading and reciting.
   d. all of the time reciting rather than rereading.

2. Being able to recite a number of nursery rhymes from childhood is probably due mainly to
   a. spaced practice.
   b. organization.

   c. mnemonics.
   d. overlearning.

3. If you were to ask yourself "why" while you study, you would be engaging in
   a. overlearning
   b. active learning
   c. spaced practice
   d. organization

Answers: 1. a   2. d   3. b

APPLY IT

Improving Memory with Mnemonic Devices

We all use external aids to remember things. Making notes, writing lists, and keeping an electronic schedule are often more reliable and accurate than trusting our own memory. What if you need information at unpredictable times, when you do not have external aids handy?

Many mnemonics, or memory devices, have been developed to aid memory. The mnemonic techniques we explore here are the first-letter technique, the method of loci, and the keyword method (see Carney, 2011; Schneider & Pressley, 1997; E. Wood, Woloshyn, & Willoughby, 1995).

The First-Letter Technique

A useful technique is to take the first letter of each item to be remembered and form a word, a phrase, or a sentence with those letters (Matlin, 1989). For example, if you had to memorize the seven colours of the visible spectrum in their proper order, you could use the first letter of

each colour to form the name Roy G. Biv. Three chunks are easier to remember than seven different ones.

Red	Orange	Yellow	Green
Blue	Indigo	Violet	

As a child taking music lessons, you may have learned the saying "*every good baby does fine*" to remember the lines of the treble clef, and *F A C E* to remember the spaces.

The Method of Loci

The method of loci is a mnemonic device you can use to remember things that need to be recalled in a specific order. The word *loci* is the plural of *locus*, which is Latin for "location" or "place."

To use the method of loci, select any familiar location for which you can form a mental map—your home, for example—and simply associate the items to be remembered with places there. You begin by picturing the

first locus, for example, your driveway; the second locus, your garage; the third locus, the walk leading to your front door; and the fourth locus, perhaps the front hall closet. You progress through your house from room to room in an orderly fashion. Then you visualize the first item or idea you want to remember in its place on the driveway, the second item in your garage, the third at your front door, and so on until you have associated each word, idea, or item you want to remember with a specific place. You will probably find it helpful to conjure up exaggerated images of the items that you place at each location, as the examples from a grocery list in Figure 6.11 illustrate.

When you want to recall the items, take an imaginary walk starting at the first place, and the first idea will pop into your mind. When you think of the second place, the second idea will come to mind, and so on through all the places you visualize.

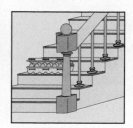

FIGURE 6.11

The Method of Loci

Begin by thinking of locations, perhaps in your home, that are in a sequence. Then visualize one of the items to be remembered in each location.
Source: Wood, Samuel e.; Wood, Ellen Green; Boyd, Denise, The World of Psychology, 7th Ed., ©2011, pp.169, 174, 191. Reprinted and Electronically reproduced by permission of Pearson Education, Inc., New York, NY.

Step 1

Step 2

FIGURE 6.12

The Keyword Method

Illustrated here are the first two steps for the keyword strategy. In Step 1, you picture something that sounds like the word you have to learn, such as "canner" for the word *canard*. In Step 2, you make an interactive image with the sound-alike picture and a picture of the real word you have to learn ("duck in a can" for *canard*).

The Keyword Method

The keyword method is used primarily to assist in vocabulary and second-language learning. It has three steps, the first two of which are illustrated in Figure 6.12. In Step 1, you take the new or foreign word that you have to remember and look for a familiar homonym (a word that sounds alike) for the whole word or part of the new word. For example, as an English speaker, I want to learn the French word for *duck* (*canard*). One homonym might be *canner* or *can*. These are good homonyms because it is easy to make a mental picture of someone making a can or just visualizing a can. In Step 2, you construct an image of the homonym (*canner/can*) and the meaning of the word (*canard = duck*). The image would be of a duck sitting in a can. Vivid images work better, so my duck is flapping his wings in the can. In Step 3 (not illustrated), you try to remember. When you see the word canard, you think of the homonym (*canner/can*) and ask yourself, "Who was in the can in my picture?" The answer is "duck." If, on the other hand, you are asked for a translation for the word *duck*, you try to imagine what the duck was doing. This gives you "canner" or "can," which acts as a cue for the word *canard*.

THINKING CRITICALLY

Evaluation

Some studies cited in this chapter involved only one or a few participants.

a. Select two of these studies and discuss the possible problems in drawing conclusions on the basis of studies using so few participants.

b. Suggest several possible explanations for the researchers' findings other than those proposed by the researchers.

c. In your view, should such studies even be mentioned in a textbook? Why or why not?

Point/Counterpoint

Using what you have learned in this chapter on memory, prepare an argument citing cases and specific examples to support each of these positions:

a. Long-term memory is a permanent record of our experiences.

b. Long-term memory is not necessarily a permanent record of our experiences.

Psychology in Your Life

Drawing upon your knowledge, formulate a plan that you can put into operation to help improve your memory and avoid the pitfalls that cause forgetting.

MyPsychLab   go to mypsychlab (access code required) to find web resources for your text that supplement the material in chapter 6.

SUMMARY & REVIEW

 REMEMBERING

What three processes are involved in the act of remembering?

Three processes involved in remembering are (1) encoding—transforming information into a form that can be stored in memory; (2) storage—maintaining information in memory; and (3) retrieval—bringing stored material to mind.

What is sensory memory?

Sensory memory holds information coming in through the senses for only a few seconds, just long enough for us to begin to process the information and send some on to short-term memory.

What are the characteristics of short-term memory?

Short-term (working) memory holds about seven unrelated items of information for less than 30 seconds without rehearsal. Short-term memory also acts as our mental workspace while we carry out any mental activity.

What is long-term memory, and what are its subsystems?

Long-term memory is the permanent or relatively permanent memory system with a virtually unlimited capacity. Its subsystems are (1) declarative memory, which holds facts and information (semantic memory) and personal life experiences (episodic memory), and (2) non-declarative memory, which consists of motor skills acquired through repetitive practice, habits, and simple classically conditioned responses.

What are three methods of measuring retention?

Three methods of measuring retention are (1) recall, whereby information must be supplied with few or no retrieval cues; (2) recognition, whereby information must simply be recognized as having been encountered before; and (3) the relearning method, which measures retention in terms of time saved in relearning material compared with the time required to learn it originally.

 THE NATURE OF REMEMBERING

What is meant by the statement "Memory is reconstructive in nature"?

Our memory does not work like a video recorder. We reconstruct memories, piecing them together from a few highlights and using information that may or may not be accurate.

What is Bartlett's contribution to our understanding of memory?

Sir Frederic Bartlett found that people do not recall facts and experiences detail by detail. Rather, they systematically reconstruct and distort them to fit information already stored in memory.

What are schemas, and how do they affect memory?

Schemas are the integrated frameworks of knowledge and assumptions we have about people, objects, and events; schemas affect how we encode and recall information.

What conditions reduce the reliability of eyewitness testimony?

The reliability of eyewitness testimony is reduced when members of a lineup are viewed at the same time rather than one by one, when the perpetrator is of a different race from that of the eyewitness, and when leading questions are asked to elicit information.

Does hypnosis improve the memory of eyewitnesses?

Hypnotized subjects supply more information and are more confident of their recollections, but they supply more inaccurate information as well.

 FACTORS INFLUENCING RETRIEVAL

What is the serial position effect?

The serial position effect is the tendency of a person, when recalling a sequence of items, to remember the items at the beginning of the sequence (primacy effect) and the items at the end of the sequence (recency effect) better than items in the middle.

How does environmental context affect memory?

People tend to recall material more easily if they are in the same physical location during recall as during the original learning.

What is the state-dependent memory effect?

The state-dependent memory effect is our tendency to recall information better if we are in the same pharmacological or psychological state as when the information was learned.

 BIOLOGY AND MEMORY

What has the study of H. M. revealed about the role of the hippocampus in memory?

The case of H. M. reveals that the hippocampus is essential in forming declarative memories but not in forming non-declarative memories.

What is long-term potentiation, and why is it important?

Long-term potentiation is a long-lasting increase in the efficiency of neural transmission at the synapses. Long-term potentiation is important because it may be the basis for learning and memory at the level of the neurons.

How do memories of threatening situations compare with ordinary memories?

Memories of threatening situations tend to be more powerful and enduring than ordinary memories.

6E FORGETTING

What was Ebbinghaus's major contribution to psychology?

Hermann Ebbinghaus conducted the first experimental studies on learning and memory. He invented the nonsense syllable, conceived the relearning method as a test of memory, and plotted the curve of forgetting.

What are seven causes of forgetting?

Seven causes of forgetting are encoding failure, consolidation failure, decay, interference (proactive and retroactive), motivated forgetting, retrieval failure, and prospective forgetting.

What is interference, and how can it be minimized?

Interference occurs when information or associations stored either before (proactive) or after (retroactive) a given memory hinder our ability to remember it. To minimize interference, follow a learning activity with sleep, and arrange learning so that similar subjects are not studied back to back.

6F IMPROVING MEMORY

What are four study habits that can aid memory?

Four study habits that can aid memory are organization, overlearning, the use of spaced rather than massed practice, and the use of a higher percentage of time reciting than rereading material.

What is overlearning, and why is it important?

Overlearning occurs when we practise or study information beyond the minimum needed to barely learn it. Many studies suggest that we remember material better and longer if we overlearn it.

MEMORY

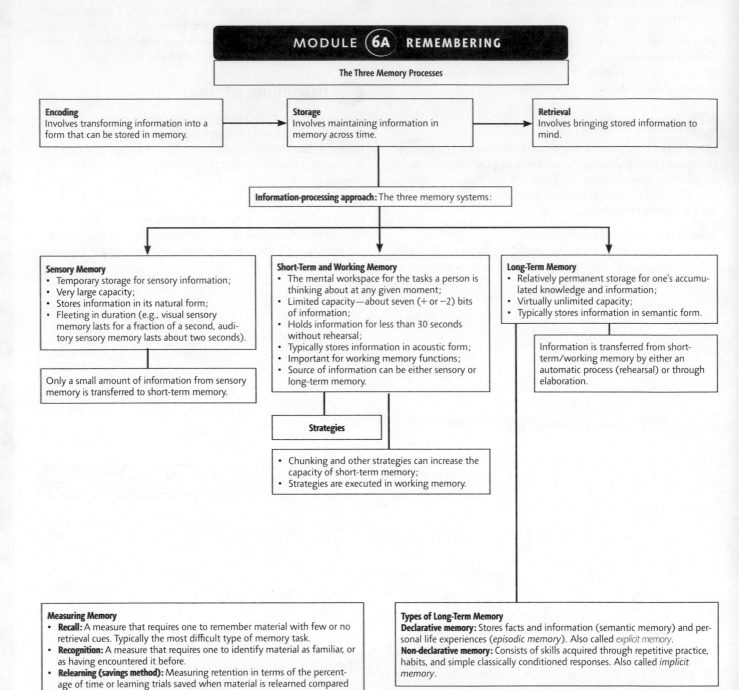

MODULE 6A REMEMBERING

The Three Memory Processes

Encoding
Involves transforming information into a form that can be stored in memory.

Storage
Involves maintaining information in memory across time.

Retrieval
Involves bringing stored information to mind.

Information-processing approach: The three memory systems:

Sensory Memory
- Temporary storage for sensory information;
- Very large capacity;
- Stores information in its natural form;
- Fleeting in duration (e.g., visual sensory memory lasts for a fraction of a second, auditory sensory memory lasts about two seconds).

Only a small amount of information from sensory memory is transferred to short-term memory.

Short-Term and Working Memory
- The mental workspace for the tasks a person is thinking about at any given moment;
- Limited capacity—about seven (+ or −2) bits of information;
- Holds information for less than 30 seconds without rehearsal;
- Typically stores information in acoustic form;
- Important for working memory functions;
- Source of information can be either sensory or long-term memory.

Strategies
- Chunking and other strategies can increase the capacity of short-term memory;
- Strategies are executed in working memory.

Long-Term Memory
- Relatively permanent storage for one's accumulated knowledge and information;
- Virtually unlimited capacity;
- Typically stores information in semantic form.

Information is transferred from short-term/working memory by either an automatic process (rehearsal) or through elaboration.

Measuring Memory
- **Recall:** A measure that requires one to remember material with few or no retrieval cues. Typically the most difficult type of memory task.
- **Recognition:** A measure that requires one to identify material as familiar, or as having encountered it before.
- **Relearning (savings method):** Measuring retention in terms of the percentage of time or learning trials saved when material is relearned compared with the time required to learn it originally.

Types of Long-Term Memory
Declarative memory: Stores facts and information (semantic memory) and personal life experiences (*episodic memory*). Also called *explicit memory*.
Non-declarative memory: Consists of skills acquired through repetitive practice, habits, and simple classically conditioned responses. Also called *implicit memory*.

Levels-of-Processing Model

Level of processing affects how long we remember the information.
- **Shallow processing:** When we are merely aware of the incoming sensory information.
- **Deeper processing:** When we form a relationship with the information, make an association, or attach meaning to information.

MODULE **6B** THE NATURE OF REMEMBERING

- Memory is a **reconstructive** process.
- The information or the construction may not be totally accurate.
- Inaccuracies may reflect the use of **schemas**—integrated frameworks of knowledge and assumptions about people, objects, and events that affect how information is both encoded and recalled.
- Distortions tend to be positive and fit a person's existing system of beliefs and expectations.

Eyewitness Testimony
- Eyewitness testimony is subject to error.
- The **misinformation effect** occurs when providing misleading information after an event causes erroneous recollections.
- Hypnosis increases confidence in memories but does not improve the accuracy of the memory.

Unusual Memory Phenomena
- **Flashbulb memory:** An extremely vivid memory of the conditions surrounding one's first hearing the news of a surprising, shocking, or highly emotional event. Although the memory is vivid, it may not be entirely accurate.
- **Eidetic memory:** The ability to retain a visual image several minutes after it has been removed. About 5 percent of children have this ability but virtually all lose it before reaching adulthood.

MODULE **6C** FACTORS INFLUENCING RETRIEVAL

Serial Position Effect
The tendency to better recall items at the beginning (primacy effect) and end (recency effect) than items in the middle of a sequence.

Environmental Context
The tendency to better recall information in the same physical location where the information was encoded.

State-Dependent Memory
The tendency to better recall information if one is in the same pharmacological or psychological state as when the information was encoded.

MODULE **6D** BIOLOGY AND MEMORY

- The **hippocampus** is essential for the formation of declarative memories.
- The **prefrontal lobe** has been shown to be involved in the encoding and retrieval of episodic memories.
- **Long-term potentiation** refers to a long-lasting increase in the efficiency of neural transmission at the synapses and is the basis for learning and memory at the level of the neuron.
- Hormones such as epinephrine and norepinephrine are involved in emotionally charged memories, while estrogen has been found to help build and maintain synapses between neurons.

MODULE **6E** FORGETTING

Encoding failure: Results from material never having been put into long-term memory.
Consolidation failure: Any disruption in the consolidation process that prevents a permanent memory from forming (e.g., loss of consciousness, grand mal seizure).
Decay theory: Suggests that the memory trace, if not used, disappears over time (a proposed cause of forgetting from sensory and short-term memory, but not long-term memory).

MODULE **6F** IMPROVING MEMORY

Four Study Habits That Aid Memory
- **Organization:** Use of conceptual hierarchies, categories, historical sequencing, and other techniques for organizing items in a meaningful way makes retrieval easier.
- **Overlearning:** Studying the material beyond the point at which it can be repeated once without error makes material harder to forget and more resistant to the effects of interference.
- **Spaced practice:** Studying for shorter time periods across many sessions reduces the effects of fatigue and interference as compared with the use of one long study period.
- **Active learning:** Use of techniques such as reciting from memory and asking questions about the material one reads is more effective than simply reading and rereading the material.

Interference: Occurs because information or associations stored either before (proactive) or after (retroactive) a given memory hinder a person's ability to remember it.
Motivated forgetting: Forgetting through suppression or repression in order to protect oneself from material that is unpleasant (e.g., too painful, anxiety- or guilt-producing).
Retrieval failure: Occurs when the information is in one's long-term memory, but cannot be retrieved.
Prospective forgetting: One fails to remember to perform some action at a certain time.

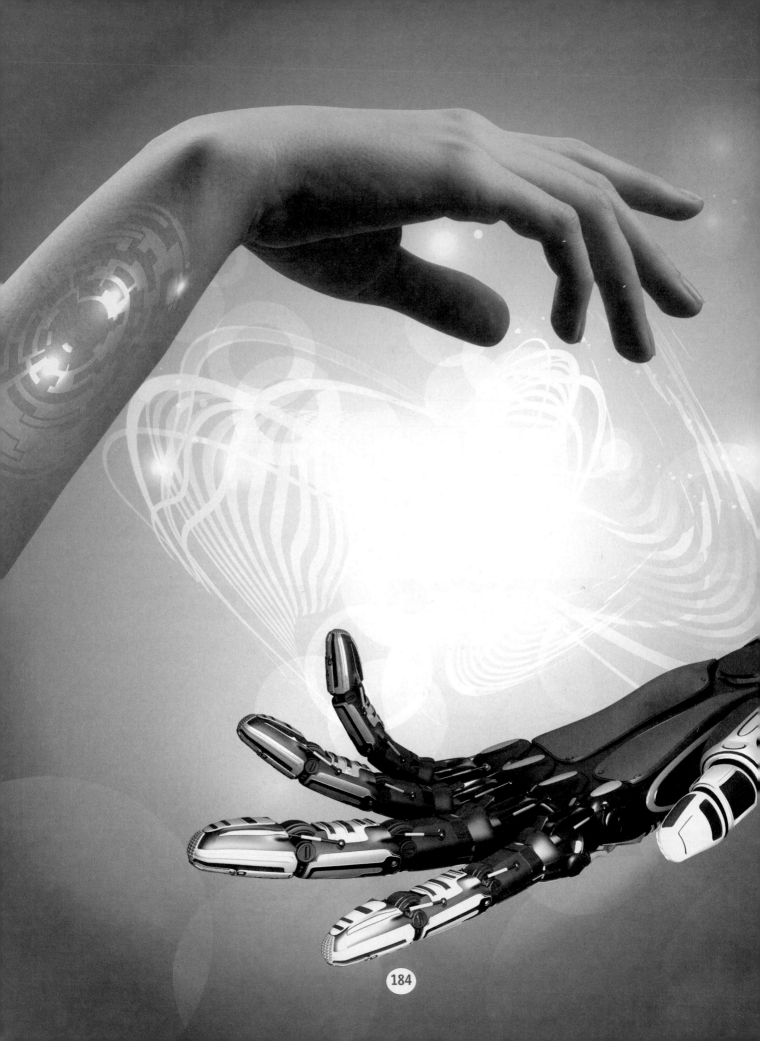

7

On a scale of 1 to 100, with 1 = not very important and 100 = very important, how vital is each of the following to your long-term happiness?

- Being involved in a stable romantic relationship
- Having enough money to live comfortably
- Achieving professional goals

Now look at these three issues from a different perspective. Imagine your life 10 years from now and assume that you are 100 percent happy, or perfectly, totally happy, at that point. How much would each of these three factors contribute to your sense that you were totally happy? Make a proportional estimate of the contribution of each factor such that they add up to 100 percent:

_____% Romance +

_____% Money +

_____% Professional goals

= 100% Happiness

Did you notice that the emphasis you placed on each factor changed when you thought about balancing them rather than when you thought about them individually? That's because our thinking is distorted by a process called *anchoring*, or the *focusing effect*, when we think about one factor in isolation from others that affect a decision (Tversky & Kahneman, 1974). As a result, we often overestimate the importance of the factor we happen to be thinking about at the moment. In fact, focusing on a single factor, such as a desire for money, can actually make us quite miserable because it causes us to emphasize what we lack rather than what we have (Kahneman, Krueger, Schkade, Schwarz, & Stone, 2006).

We address distortions such as anchoring, and how the information-processing system manages and compensates for them, in this chapter.

We will also introduce you to the universal intellectual tools that we use to make sense of the world—reasoning, imagery, and concepts—and discuss how we put these tools to work to make decisions, solve problems, and develop technological devices that mirror our own thought processes. Next, we turn to creativity and another vital cognitive tool: language. Finally, we end with a discussion of intelligence and other aspects of cognitive functioning that vary from one person to another.

©Willyam Bradberry/Shutterstock

COGNITION, LANGUAGE, AND INTELLIGENCE

MODULE **7A** COGNITION

LO 7.1 Define *cognition, imagery, concept, prototype, exemplars*, and *heuristics*.

LO 7.2 What are the roles of systematic processes, heuristics, framing, intuition, and anchoring in decision making?

LO 7.3 Compare trial and error with algorithm methods for problem solving.

LO 7.4 Explain means–end analysis and working backward.

LO 7.5 Describe two barriers to problem solving.

Cognition refers, collectively, to the mental processes involved in acquiring, storing, retrieving, and using information (Matlin, 1989). **[LO 7.1]** In addition to the cognitive processes of sensation, perception, and memory, cognition also includes our ability to contemplate abstract issues such as truth and justice, as well as the strategies we use to make decisions and solve problems. In this chapter we consider some other cognitive processes: imagery, concept formation, and problem solving.

IMAGERY AND CONCEPTS: TOOLS OF THINKING

What *are* the tools of thinking? All of us have an intuitive notion of what thinking is. We say, "I think it's going to rain" (a prediction); "I think this is the right answer" (a choice); "I think I will resign" (a decision). But our everyday use of the word *think* does not suggest the processes we use to perform the act itself. Sometimes our thinking is free-flowing rather than goal oriented. At other times, it is directed at a goal such as solving a problem or making a decision.

Just how is the act of thinking accomplished? There is general agreement that at least two tools are commonly used when we think—images and concepts.

IMAGERY: PICTURE THIS—ELEPHANTS WITH PURPLE POLKA DOTS

What is imagery?

Can you imagine hearing a recording of your favourite song, or someone calling your name? Can you picture yourself jogging or walking, pouring ice water over your hands, or kissing someone you love? In doing these things, you take advantage of your ability to use **imagery**—that is, to represent or picture a sensory experience in our mind. **[LO 7.1]**

According to psychologist Stephen Kosslyn (1988), we mentally construct the objects we image one part at a time. Studies with split-brain patients and normal people suggest that two types of processes are used in the formation of visual images. First, we retrieve stored memories of how parts of an object look; then we use mental processes to arrange or assemble those parts into the proper whole. Both hemispheres participate in the processes of forming visual images. Try forming visual images as you do the *Try It*.

TRY IT

Forming Visual Images

A. Picture an ant crawling on a newspaper about one metre away. How many legs does the ant have?

B. Picture an ant perched on the end of a toothpick right in front of your eyes. Does the ant have eyelashes?

In which mental picture is the ant larger, A or B? Which mental picture provided more detail of the ant?
Source: (Based on Finke, 1985.) Finke, R.A. (1985). Theories relating mental imagery to perception. Psychological Bulletin, 98, 236–259.

Kosslyn (1975, 1983) asked research participants many questions like those in the *Try It* and found that they answered questions about larger images about 0.2 seconds faster than questions about small images. It takes us slightly longer to zoom in on smaller images than on larger ones, just as it does when we actually look at real objects (Kosslyn & Ochsner, 1994).

But what if we are forming new images rather than answering questions about large and small images already formed? Picture an elephant standing about a metre away. Now picture a rabbit standing at the same distance. Which image took longer to form? Kosslyn (1975) discovered that it takes people longer to form large mental images—an elephant as opposed to a rabbit. It takes longer to view the elephant because there is more of it to view, and likewise more of it to image.

Not only do we form a mental image of an object, but we manipulate and move it around in our mind much as we would if we were actually holding and looking at the object (L. A. Cooper & Shepard, 1984). Shepard and Metzler (1971) asked eight participants to judge some 1600 pairs of drawings like the ones in Figure 7.1. They had to rotate the objects in their

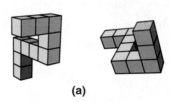

(a)

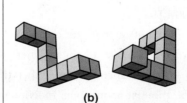

(b)

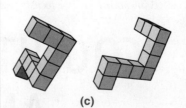

(c)

FIGURE 7.1

Samples of Geometric Patterns in Shepard and Metzler's Mental Rotation Study

Mentally rotate one of the patterns in each pair—**(a), (b),** and **(c)**—and decide whether the two patterns match. Do you find that the more you have to rotate the objects mentally, the longer it takes to decide if they match?

Republished with permission of American Association for the Advancement of Science (AAAS) from Mental rotation of three dimensional objects. Science, Shepard, R. N., & Metzler, J. (1971). 171, no 3972, 701–703 (Figure 1, p. 702). permission conveyed through Copyright Clearance Center, Inc.).

imagination to see if they matched. In Figure 7.1, the objects in (a) and (b) are a match; those in (c) are not. But the important finding is that the more the objects had to be rotated mentally, the longer it took participants to decide whether they matched. This is precisely what happens if the participants rotate real objects; the more they need to be rotated, the longer it takes to make the decision. As this study demonstrates, we manipulate objects using mental imagery in the same way as we manipulate real physical objects.

Neuroimaging studies show that, in general, the same areas of the brain and spinal cord are activated whether a person is actually performing a given task or mentally rehearsing the same task using imagery (Fourkas, Bonavolotá, Avenanti, & Aglioti, 2008; Fourkas, Ionta, & Aglioti, 2006; Lotze et al., 1999; Richter et al., 2000; Stephan et al., 1995). Thus, it isn't surprising that professionals whose work involves repetitive physical actions, such as musicians and athletes, use imaging effectively.

CONCEPTS: OUR MENTAL CLASSIFICATION SYSTEM (IS IT A PENGUIN A BIRD?)

What are concepts, and how are they formed?

Thinking is not limited to conjuring up a series of pictures, sounds, touches, tastes, and smells. We humans are capable of conceptualizing as well. A **concept** is a label that represents a class or group of objects, people, or events that share common characteristics or attributes. Concepts are useful tools that help us order our world and think and communicate with speed and efficiency. **[LO 7.1]**

Imagine that you are walking down the street with a friend, and you see approaching in the distance a hairy, brown-and-white, four-legged animal with two eyes and two ears, its mouth open, its tongue hanging out, and a long, wagging tail. You say to your friend simply, "Here comes a dog." Thanks to our ability to use concepts, we are not forced to consider and describe everything in great detail before we make an identification. We do not need a different name to identify and describe every single rock, tree, animal, or situation we meet. *Dog* is a concept that stands for a family of animals that share similar characteristics or attributes, even though they may differ in significant ways (in this case, according to breed).

We have concepts for abstractions as well as for tangible objects and organisms. Love, beauty, and justice are abstract concepts, yet we can identify and consider aspects of beauty and justice because we have formed concepts of them. We also use relational concepts in our thinking—larger than, smaller than, older than, younger than, and so on—to compare individuals, objects, and ideas.

Concept Formation: Learning What Fits a Concept

How do we acquire concepts, and how do we know what fits or does not fit a given concept? We can form concepts (1) from a formal definition of the concept, (2) by systematically memorizing a concept's common features, (3) through our experiences with positive and negative instances of the concept,

(4) through the use of prototypes, or (5) through the use of exemplars.

SYSTEMATIC OR FORMAL APPROACHES Studies have been conducted and theories proposed to explain how we form concepts. Some theorists maintain that we approach concept formation in an active, orderly, and systematic way, rather than in a random, informal, and haphazard way (Bruner, Goodnow, & Austin, 1956). Sometimes we learn a concept from a formal definition or from a formal classification system. You surely have memorized several such systems while studying biology, chemistry, English, or similar subjects.

POSITIVE AND NEGATIVE INSTANCES We acquire many simple concepts through experiences with examples or positive instances of the concept. When children are young, parents may point out examples of a car—the family car, the neighbour's car, cars on the street, and pictures of cars in a book. But if a child points to some other type of moving vehicle and says "car," the parent will say, "No, that is a truck," or "This is a bus." "Truck" and "bus" are negative instances, or *non-examples*, of the concept *car*. After experience with positive and negative instances of the concept, a child begins to grasp some of the properties of a car that distinguish it from other wheeled vehicles.

PROTOTYPES Eleanor Rosch (1973, 1978) argues that formal theories of concept formation, and the experiments on which they are based, tend to be rather artificial, contrived, and unrelated to our actual experience. She and her colleagues studied concept formation in its natural setting and concluded that in real life, our thinking and concept formation are somewhat fuzzy, not clear-cut and systematic. Sometimes we identify objects based on a memorized list of features or attributes that are common to instances of a concept. But in addition, we are likely to picture a **prototype** of the concept— an example that embodies the most common and typical features of the concept. **[LO 7.1]**

What is your prototype for the concept *bird*? Chances are it is not a penguin, an ostrich, or a kiwi. All three are birds that cannot fly. A more likely bird prototype is a robin, or perhaps a sparrow. Most birds can fly, but not all; most mammals cannot fly, but bats are mammals, have wings, and can fly. So not all examples within a concept fit equally well. Nevertheless, the prototype most closely fits a given concept, and items and

---

cognition: The mental processes involved in acquiring, storing, retrieving, and using information.

imagery: The representation in the mind of a sensory experience—visual, auditory, gustatory, motor, olfactory, or tactile.

concept: A label that represents a class or group of objects, people, or events sharing common characteristics or attributes.

prototype: An example that embodies the most common and typical features of a particular concept.

©Art Wolfe/The Image Bank/Getty Images

©Igor Kovalenko/Fotolia

A prototype is an example that embodies the most typical features of a concept. Which of the animals shown here best fits your prototype for the concept *bird*?

organisms belonging to the concept share more attributes with their prototype than with the prototype of any other concept.

EXEMPLARS Another theory of concept formation suggests that concepts are represented by their **exemplars**—individual instances, or examples, of a concept that we have stored in memory from our own experience (Estes, 1994). **[LO 7.1]** So, if you work with penguins or turkeys every day, your exemplar of *bird* might indeed be a penguin or a turkey. To decide whether an unfamiliar item belongs to a concept, we compare it with exemplars (other examples) of that concept.

Once concepts are formed, they do not exist in isolation; instead, we organize them in hierarchies. For example, the canary and the cardinal are subsets of the concept *bird*; at a higher level, birds are subsets of the concept *animal*; and at a still higher level, animals are a subset of the concept *living things*.

DECISION MAKING: GETTING AN ANSWER

What are the roles of systematic processes, heuristics, framing, intuition, and anchoring in decision making?

Do you recall the last time you made an important decision? Would you describe the process you used to make the decision as a logical one? Psychologists define **decision making** as the process of considering alternatives and choosing among them.

Systematic Decision Making

Some psychologists and other scientists maintain that humans use **systematic decision-making** processes (Loewenstein, Rick, & Cohen, 2008). This approach involves examining all possible alternatives and then choosing the one that is most beneficial **[LO 7.2]** However, in everyday life, we rarely engage in this sort of formal, systematic approach to decision making. Many limitations around the decision-making process prevent it from being entirely systematic.

Elimination by Aspects

Amos Tversky (1972) suggested that we deal with the limitations on decision making by using a strategy called **elimination by aspects**. **[LO 7.2]** Using this approach, we first have to know what are the important factors to consider. For example, cost would be one important factor in choosing a new apartment, followed by, perhaps, availability of parking. After we order these factors from most to least important, we can then eliminate the alternatives that do not match each factor. So in the search for an apartment, you might automatically eliminate all the apartments that were too expensive first, then those that didn't have parking. The process of elimination continues as each factor is considered in order, and the alternative that is left is the one chosen.

Heuristics

Decisions are often based on **heuristics**—rules of thumb that are derived from experience. **[LO 7.2]** Several kinds of heuristics exist. One that has been studied a great deal is the **availability heuristic**, a rule stating that the probability of an event corresponds to the ease with which the event comes to mind **[LO 7.2]**. For instance, if you were planning on going to a hockey game but remembered that the last time you went you were late because you were stuck in a traffic jam, you might decide to take a different route than you took last time—even if you have not checked the traffic reports to see if you should expect a problem.

Another type of heuristic is the **representativeness heuristic**, a decision strategy based on how closely a new situation resembles a familiar one. **[LO 7.2]** For instance, suppose you decide to get a puppy and have to determine which breed of dog to buy. You remember that you had such great fun with the

Is it possible that our understanding of the concept "fast-food" may follow from individual instances or examples (exemplars) of one fast-food type that we have stored in memory from our own experience?

cocker spaniel your family had when you were a child. The representative heuristic might lead you to believe that you would enjoy another cocker spaniel just as much.

The **recognition heuristic** is a strategy in which the decision-making process terminates as soon as a factor that moves one toward a decision has been recognized. **[LO 7.2]** Suppose you are voting and the only information you have is the list of candidates for a particular office on the ballot. If you recognize one of the candidates' names as being that of a woman, and you have a predisposition toward seeing more women elected to public office, the recognition heuristic may cause you to decide to vote for the female candidate.

There is little doubt that heuristics help us make rapid decisions with little mental effort, but they can also lead to errors. The challenge we face in everyday decision making is to accurately assess the degree to which a heuristic strategy is appropriate for a given decision.

Framing

Whether we use heuristics or more time-consuming strategies, we should be aware that the manner in which information is presented can affect the decision-making process. For example, **framing** refers to the way information is presented to emphasize either a potential gain or a potential loss as the outcome. **[LO 7.2]** To study the effects of framing on decision making, Kahneman and Tversky (1984) presented participants with a story about a potential outbreak of a disease. The first version of the problem was framed to focus attention on the number of lives that could be saved. And when people are primarily motivated to achieve gains (save lives), they are more likely to choose a safe option over a risky one, as 72 percent of the participants did. The second version was framed to focus attention on the 400 lives that would be lost. When trying to avoid losses, people appear much more willing to choose a risky option, as 78 percent of the participants were.

Intuition

How often have you heard someone advise another to "go with your gut feelings"? Psychologists use the term **intuition** to refer to rapidly formed judgments based on "gut feeling" or "instincts." **[LO 7.2]** Despite our faith in intuition, it's important to understand that it is strongly influenced by emotion. Thus, at times, intuition can interfere with logical reasoning (Topolinski & Strack, 2009).

Anchoring

At the beginning of the chapter, we introduced you to the concept of **anchoring**, the notion that focusing on a single factor magnifies the importance of that factor relative to others that are relevant to a decision. **[LO 7.2]** In one series of studies, British psychologist Neil Stewart examined how anchoring on the minimum payment required on a credit card bill influences decisions about repayment (Stewart, 2009). First, researchers conducted a survey in which participants answered questions about their most recent credit card bill. Respondents reported their balances, minimum payments required on their accounts, and actual payments. The researchers found that the smaller the required minimum payments were, the smaller participants' actual payments were. Moreover, there was no correlation between account balances and actual payments. In other words, survey participants anchored their payment decisions on the size of the minimum payment rather than on the size of the balance.

Review & Reflect 7.1, on the next page, summarizes the various approaches to decision making.

exemplars: The individual instances of a concept that we have stored in memory from our own experience.

decision making: The process of considering alternatives and choosing among them.

systematic decision making: Making a decision after carefully considering all possible alternatives.

elimination by aspects: A decision-making approach in which alternatives are evaluated against criteria that have been ranked according to importance.

heuristics (yur-RIS-tiks): Rules of thumb that are derived from experience and used in decision making and problem solving, even though there is no guarantee of their accuracy or usefulness.

availability heuristic: A cognitive rule of thumb that says that the probability of an event or the importance assigned to it is based on its availability in memory.

representativeness heuristic: A thinking strategy based on how closely a new object or situation is judged to resemble or match an existing prototype of that object or situation.

recognition heuristic: A strategy in which decision making stops as soon as a factor that moves one toward a decision has been recognized.

framing: The way information is presented so as to emphasize either a potential gain or a potential loss as the outcome.

intuition: Rapidly formed judgments based on "gut feelings" or "instincts."

anchoring: Overestimation of the importance of a factor by focusing on it to the exclusion of other relevant factors.

REVIEW & REFLECT 7.1 APPROACHES TO DECISION MAKING

Approach	Description
Systematic decision making	Consideration of all possible alternatives prior to making a decision.
Elimination by aspects	Factors on which alternatives are to be evaluated are ordered from most to least important; any alternatives that do not satisfy the most important factor are eliminated; elimination of alternatives then continues factor by factor until one choice remains.
Availability heuristic	Information that comes easily to mind determines the decision that is made, often because of a recent experience.
Representativeness heuristic	The decision is based on how closely an object or situation resembles or matches an existing prototype.
Recognition heuristic	A rapid decision based on recognition of one of the alternatives.
Framing	Potential gains and losses associated with alternatives are emphasized and influence the decision.
Intuition	Decisions are motivated by "gut feelings" that may be influenced by perceptions of gains.
Anchoring	Decisions are influenced by focusing on a single factor, thereby overestimating its importance.

PROBLEM SOLVING: HOW DO WE BEGIN?

What are three problem-solving techniques, and how are they used?

All of us are faced every day with a variety of problems needing to be solved. Most of our problems are simple and mundane, like what to have for dinner or what clothes to put on in the morning. But some of our problems are more far-reaching, such as what career to pursue, how to sustain or improve a relationship, or how to stretch our income from one paycheque to the next. Then there are the problems we meet in our school work, which we must think through using problem-solving techniques. How do you usually try to solve a problem? The process of decision making you have just been reading about shares many features with problem solving—the thoughts and actions required to achieve a desired goal. Among these techniques are trial and error, algorithms, and heuristics. How would you solve the problem in the *Try It*?

Trial and Error

How did you choose to solve the *Try It* problem? Many people simply start placing the numbers in the boxes and then change them around when a combination doesn't work. This is called **trial and error**. It occurs when we try one solution after another, in no particular order, until by chance we hit upon the answer. **[LO 7.3]**

Heuristics and Algorithms

Most of us find heuristics to be just as useful for solving problems as they are for making decisions. Although heuristics do not guarantee success, they offer a promising way to attack a problem and arrive at a solution. **[LO 7.1]** For instance, the **analogy heuristic** involves comparing a problem to others you have encountered in the past. The idea is that if a strategy worked with similar problems in the past, it will be effective for solving a new one.

Another heuristic that is effective for solving some problems is **working backward**, sometimes called the *backward search*. In this approach we start with the solution—a known condition—and work our way backward through the problem. **[LO 7.4]** Once our backward search has revealed the steps to be taken and their order, we can solve the problem. Try working backward to solve the water lily problem in *Try It*.

TRY IT

Testing Problem Solving

Insert the numbers 1 through 7 in the seven boxes, one digit to a box, in such a way that no consecutive numbers are next to each other horizontally, vertically, or diagonally. Several solutions are possible.

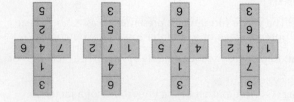

TRY IT

Working Backward to Solve a Problem

Water lilies double the area they cover every 24 hours. At the beginning of the summer there is one water lily on a pond. It takes 60 days for the pond to become covered with water lilies. On what day is the pond half covered?

Answer: The most important fact is that the lilies double in number every 24 hours. If the lake is to be completely covered on the 60th day, it has to be half covered on the 59th day.

MEANS–END ANALYSIS One popular heuristic strategy is **means–end analysis**, in which the current position is compared with a desired goal, and a series of steps are formulated and then taken to close the gap between the two (Sweller & Levine, 1982). **[LO 7.4]** Many problems are large and complex, and must be broken down into smaller steps or subproblems. If your professor assigns a term paper, for example, you probably do not simply sit down and write it. You must first determine how you will deal with your topic, research the topic, make an outline, and then probably write the subtopics over a period of time. At last you are ready to assemble the complete term paper, write several drafts, and put the finished product in final form before handing it in.

When you adopt a heuristic strategy, it may or may not lead to a correct solution. By contrast, an algorithm is a problem-solving strategy that always leads to a correct solution if it is applied appropriately.

ALGORITHMS An **algorithm** is a systematic, step-by-step procedure that guarantees a solution to a problem of a certain type if the algorithm is appropriate and executed properly. **[LO 7.3]** Formulas used in mathematics and other sciences are algorithms. Another type of algorithm is a systematic strategy for exploring every possible solution to a problem until the correct one is reached. In some cases there may be millions or even billions or more possibilities that one would have to try before reaching a solution. Often computers are programmed to solve such problems, because with a computer, an accurate

solution is guaranteed and millions of possible solutions can be tried in a few seconds.

Many problems do not lend themselves to solution by algorithms, however. Suppose you were a contestant on a game show, trying to solve this missing-letter puzzle: p_y_ _ol_ _ _. An exhaustive search algorithm would be out of the question, as nearly nine billion possibilities could be considered. The easier way to solve such problems is by using a heuristic.

IMPEDIMENTS TO PROBLEM SOLVING: MENTAL STUMBLING BLOCKS

What are the two major impediments to problem solving?

Sometimes the difficulty in problem solving lies not with the problem but with ourselves. The two major impediments to problem solving are functional fixedness and mental set. **[LO 7.5]**

Functional Fixedness

Many of us are hampered in our efforts to solve problems in daily living because of **functional fixedness**—the failure to use familiar objects in novel ways to solve problems. **[LO 7.5]** We tend to see objects only in terms of their customary functions. Just think of all the items we use daily—tools, utensils, and other equipment—that help us perform certain functions. Often the normal functions of objects become fixed in our thinking so that we do not consider using them in new and creative ways (German & Barrett, 2005).

What if you wanted a cup of coffee, but the decanter to your coffeemaker was broken? If you suffered from functional

trial and error: An approach to problem solving in which one solution after another is tried in no particular order until a workable solution is found.

analogy heuristic: A rule of thumb that applies a solution that solved a problem in the past to a current problem that shares many features with the past problem.

working backward: A heuristic strategy in which a person discovers the steps needed to solve a problem by defining the desired goal and working backward to the current condition; also called *backward search*.

means–end analysis: A heuristic problem-solving strategy in which the current position is compared with the desired goal, and a series of steps is formulated and taken to close the gap between them.

algorithm: A systematic, step-by-step procedure, such as a mathematical formula, that guarantees a solution to a problem of a certain type if the algorithm is appropriate and executed properly.

functional fixedness: The failure to use familiar objects in novel ways to solve problems because of a tendency to view objects only in terms of their customary functions.

REMEMBER IT

Cognition

1. Our images are generally as vivid as the real thing. (true/false)
2. A label that represents a class or group of objects, people, or events that share common characteristics or attributes is called a(n)
   a. image.
   b. concept.
   c. positive instance.
   d. prototype.
3. Which of the following is guaranteed, if properly applied, to result in the correct answer to a problem?
   a. an algorithm
   b. a heuristic

   c. trial and error
   d. applying prior knowledge
4. John uses a wastebasket to keep a door from closing. In solving his problem, he was not hindered by
   a. a heuristic.
   b. an algorithm.
   c. functional fixedness.
   d. mental set.

fixedness, you might come to the conclusion that there was nothing you could do to solve your problem at that moment. The solution? Rather than thinking about the object or utensil that you don't have, think about the function you need served in order to solve your problem. What you need is something to catch the coffee, rather than the specific glass decanter that came with the coffeemaker. Could you catch the coffee in some other type of bowl or cooking utensil, or even in a coffee mug? Recent research also suggests that training problem solvers to identify obscure features may help to overcome functional fixedness (McCaffrey, 2012).

Mental Set

Another impediment to problem solving, similar to functional fixedness but much broader, is mental set. **Mental set** means that we get into a mental rut in our approach to solving problems, continuing to use the same old methods even though other approaches might be better. **[LO 7.5]** Perhaps we hit on a way to solve a problem once in the past and continue to use the same technique in similar situations, even though it is not highly effective or efficient. We are much more susceptible to mental set when we fail to consider the special requirements of a problem.

MODULE 7B CREATIVITY: UNIQUE AND USEFUL PRODUCTIONS

LO 7.6 Define *creativity*.
LO 7.7 Explain the role of divergent thinking in creativity.

What is creativity, and what tests have been designed to measure it?

Creativity can be thought of as the ability to produce original, appropriate, and valuable ideas and/or solutions to problems. **[LO 7.6]** But can creativity be measured, and does it differ from conventional thought? According to psychologist J. P. Guilford (1967), who studied creativity for several decades, creative thinkers are proficient in **divergent thinking**. Divergent thinking is the ability to produce multiple ideas, answers, or solutions to a problem rather than a single, correct response. Divergent thinkers can conceive of novel or original ideas that involve the combination and synthesis of unusual associations that lead to an abundant quantity of ideas (Benedek & Neubauer, 2013; Csikszentmihalyi, 1996).

Obviously, creative thinking is divergent. **[LO 7.7]** But is divergent thinking necessarily creative thinking? No! All creative thought is divergent, but not all divergent thought is creative. Novelty is not synonymous with creativity. We are not surprised, then, to find that high scores on tests of divergent thinking do not have a very high correlation with creative thinking in real life. Guilford (1967) himself admitted that in studies of students from elementary through high school, the correlations of his divergent-thinking tests with actual creative thinking were not spectacular.

Genuine creativity rarely appears in the form of sudden flashes (Haberlandt, 1997). For the most part, creative ideas that come into conscious awareness have been incubating for some time. Creative endeavour requires hard work and persistence in the face of failure. For instance, Einstein published 248 papers on his theory of relativity before it was finished, and Mozart had created 609 musical compositions when he died at age 35 (Haberlandt, 1997).

Researchers have tried to design tests to measure creative ability. Mednick and Mednick (1967) reasoned that the essence of creativity is the thinker's ability to fit ideas together that might, to the less creative thinker, appear remote or unrelated. They created the Remote Associates Test (RAT) as a means of measuring creative ability. Try your creative skills in the *Try It*.

TRY IT

Testing Creative Ability

One indication of creativity may be the ability to make associations among several elements that seem only remotely related or unrelated. Test your ability to find associations for these 10 sets of words, which are similar to those on the Remote Associates Test. Think of a fourth word that is related in some way to all three of the words in each row. For example, the words *keeper*, *text*, and *worm* are related to the word *book* and become *bookkeeper*, *textbook*, and *bookworm*.

1. sales, collector, income
2. flower, room, water
3. red, shot, dog
4. ball, hot, stool
5. rock, man, classical
6. story, true, sick
7. news, plate, waste
8. stuffed, sleeve, sweat
9. class, temperature, bath
10. wrist, man, stop

Answers: 1. tax 2. bed 3. hot 4. foot 5. music 6. love 7. paper 8. shirt 9. room 10. watch

REMEMBER IT

Creativity: Unique and Useful Productions

1. Divergent-thinking tests and the Remote Associates Test are used to measure
   a. imaging ability.
   b. concept formation.
   c. problem-solving ability.
   d. creativity.

2. Creativity and IQ scores are _____ related.

Answers: 1. d 2. weakly to moderately

MODULE 7C LANGUAGE

LO 7.8 Define *language* and *psycholinguistics*.
LO 7.9 Identify the elements of language, and generate an English-language example for each element.
LO 7.10 Identify the progression of the development of language.
LO 7.11 Explain how learning theory and the nativist position account for the acquisition of language.
LO 7.12 Understand the similarities and differences between human and primate language.

Without language we would each live in a largely solitary and isolated world, unable to communicate or receive any information, from simple requests to our most intimate thoughts and feelings. Our knowledge would be restricted to the direct and immediate, our own experience locked within us. Scientists define **language** as a means of communicating thoughts and feelings using a system of socially shared but arbitrary symbols (sounds, signs, or written symbols) arranged according to rules of grammar. **[LO 7.8]**

Thanks to language, we can profit from the experience, the knowledge, and the wisdom of others and can benefit others with our own. Language is not confined to time and space. The wisdom of the ages from every corner of the world and spanning the centuries of recorded history is available to us through language. Truly, language is one of the most important capabilities of the human species. Civilization could not exist without it. Whether spoken, written, or signed, language is vital to us.

THE STRUCTURE OF LANGUAGE

What are the five important components of language?

Psycholinguistics is the study of how language is acquired, produced, and used and how the sounds and symbols of language are translated into meaning. **[LO 7.8]** Psycholinguists devote much of their time to the study of the structure of language and the rules governing its use. The structure and rules governing language involve five different components—phonemes, morphemes, syntax, semantics, and pragmatics. **[LO 7.9]**

Phonemes

The smallest units of sound in a spoken language are known as **phonemes**. **[LO 7.9]** Phonemes form the basic building blocks of

mental set: The tendency to apply a familiar strategy to the solution of a problem without carefully considering the special requirements of the problem.

creativity: The ability to produce original, appropriate, and valuable ideas and/or solutions to problems.

divergent thinking: Producing one or more possible ideas, answers, or solutions to a problem rather than a single, correct response.

language: A means of communicating thoughts and feelings, using a system of socially shared but arbitrary symbols (sounds, signs, or written symbols) arranged according to rules of grammar.

psycholinguistics: The study of how language is acquired, produced, and used and how the sounds and symbols of language are translated into meaning.

phonemes: The smallest units of sound in a spoken language.

a spoken language. Three phonemes together form the sound of the word *cat*—the *c* (which sounds like *k*), *a*, and *t*. Phonemes sound not like the single letters of the alphabet as we recite them, *a-b-c-d-e-f-g*, but like the sounds of the letters as they are used in words, like the *b* in *boy*, the *p* in *pan*, and so on. The sound of the phoneme *c* in the word *cat* is different from the sound of the phoneme *c* in the word *city*.

Letters combined to form sounds are also phonemes, such as the *th* in *the* and the *ch* in *child*. The same sound (phoneme) may be represented by different letters in different words, as in the *a* in *stay* and the *ei* in *sleigh*. And, as we saw with *c*, the same letter can serve as different phonemes. The letter *a*, for example, represents three different phonemes in *day*, *cap*, and *law*.

How many phonemes are there? There are perhaps 100 or so different sounds that could serve as phonemes, but most languages have far fewer. English uses about 45 phonemes; some languages may have as few as 15 or so and other languages as many as 85 (Solso, 1991). Although phonemes are the basic building blocks of language, they alone do not provide language with meaning. For meaning, we must move to the next component of language, the morphemes.

Morphemes

Morphemes are the smallest units of meaning in a language. **[LO 7.9]** In almost all cases in the English language, a morpheme is made of two or more phonemes. But a few phonemes also serve as morphemes, such as the article *a* and the personal pronoun *I*. Many words in English are single morphemes— *book*, *word*, *learn*, *reason*, and so on. In addition to root words, morphemes may also be prefixes (such as *re* in *relearn*) or suffixes (such as *–ed* to show past tense—*learned*). The single morpheme *book* becomes the two-morpheme *books*. The letter *s* gives a plural meaning to a word and is thus a morpheme. Using your knowledge of morphemes is one way to increase your vocabulary, as described in the *Apply It* at the end of this chapter.

Although morphemes, singly and in combination, form the words in a language and provide meaning, these sounds and single words alone are not enough. A language also requires rules for structuring or putting together words in an orderly and meaningful fashion. This is where syntax enters the picture.

Syntax

Syntax is the aspect of grammar that specifies the rules for arranging and combining words to form phrases and sentences. **[LO 7.9]** An important rule of syntax in English is that adjectives usually come before nouns. So we refer to the caution lights at intersections as "yellow lights" or "amber lights." But in French the noun usually comes before the adjective, and speakers would say *le feu jaune*, or "the light yellow." So the rules of word order, or syntax, differ from one language to another.

It is important to note that *grammar* includes both the rules for combining morphemes and those that govern syntax. For example, the rules for combining morphemes determine the difference between *sock* and *socks*. The difference between "Is it here?" and "Here it is" involves syntax. Both kinds of rules contribute to the grammar of a language.

Semantics

Semantics refers to the meaning we derive from morphemes, words, and sentences. **[LO 7.9]** The same word can have different meanings depending upon how it is used in sentences: "I don't mind." "Mind your manners." "He has lost his mind."

The noted linguist and theorist Noam Chomsky (1986, 1990) maintained that the ability to glean a meaningful message from a sentence is stored in a different area of the brain than are the words used to compose the sentence. Moreover, he distinguished between the surface structure and the deep structure of the sentence. **Surface structure** refers to the literal words that are written or spoken or signed. The **deep structure** is the underlying meaning of the sentence. In some sentences the surface and deep structures are the same, but in other sentences there may be one or more deep structures. For example, "John enjoys charming people" could mean two different things—John could like being with people who are charming *or* John could be the charmer.

Pragmatics is defined as the characteristics of spoken language that help you decipher the social meaning of utterances. **[LO 7.9]** For example, one component of pragmatics is prosody, or intonation. Every language has rules governing the kind of intonation you should use in different contexts. For example, when an English speaker raises the pitch at the end of an utterance it indicates a question. So if an English speaker sitting next to you at an airport says to you "Newspaper?" with a rising intonation at the end of the word, you know that she is saying, "Would you like this newspaper?"

LANGUAGE DEVELOPMENT

At birth, an infant's only means of communication is crying, but at age 17, the average high school graduate has a vocabulary of 80 000 words (G. A. Miller & Gildea, 1987).

Children do much more than simply add new words to their vocabulary. They acquire an understanding of the way words are put together to form sentences (syntax) and the way language is used in social situations. Children acquire most of their language without any formal teaching and discover the rules of language on their own. During their first few months, infants communicate distress or displeasure through crying. **[LO 7.10]** The cry is their innate reaction to an unpleasant internal state, such as hunger, thirst, discomfort, or pain.

Cooing and Babbling

During the second or third month, infants begin cooing— repeatedly uttering vowel sounds such as "ah" and "oo." **[LO 7.10]** At about six months, infants begin **babbling**. They utter phonemes. Consonant-vowel combinations are repeated in a string, like "ma-ma-ma" or "ba-ba-ba." During the first part of the babbling stage, infants babble all the basic speech sounds that occur in all the languages of the world. Language up to this point seems to be biologically determined, because all babies throughout the world, even hearing-impaired infants, vocalize this same range of speech sounds.

At about eight months, babies begin to focus attention on those phonemes common to their native tongue and on the rhythm and intonation of the language. Gradually, they cease making the sounds not found in their native language. At about one year, a French-speaking child's babbling sounds like French, and an English-speaking child's babbling sounds like English (Levitt & Wang, 1991). Hearing-impaired infants who are exposed to sign language from birth babble manually. That is, they make the hand movements that represent the basic units of language, similar to a syllable, in sign language (Petitto & Marentette, 1991).

The One-Word Stage

Sometime during the second year, infants begin to use words to communicate. Single words function as whole sentences. These are called *holophrases*. **[LO 7.10]** Depending on the context, an infant who says "milk" might mean "Where is the milk?" "I want milk," or "This is milk."

Initially, children's understanding of words differs from that of an adult. On the basis of some shared feature and because they lack the correct word, children may apply a word to a broader range of objects than is appropriate. This is known as **overextension**. For example, any man may be called "dada," any four-legged animal "doggie." **Underextension** occurs, too, when children fail to apply a word to other members of the class. Their poodle is a "doggie," but the German shepherd next door is not.

The Two-Word Stage and Telegraphic Speech

Between 18 and 20 months, when the vocabulary is about 50 words, children begin to put nouns, verbs, and adjectives together in two-word phrases and sentences. **[LO 7.10]** At this stage children depend to a great extent on gesture, tone, and context to convey their meaning (Slobin, 1972). Depending on intonation, their sentences may indicate questions, statements, or possession. Children adhere to a rigid word order. You might hear "mama drink," "drink milk," or "mama milk," but not "drink mama," "milk drink," or "milk mama."

By two years, their vocabulary has increased to about 272 words (R. Brown, 1973). At about two and a half years, short sentences are used, which may contain three or more words. Labelled **telegraphic speech** by Roger Brown (1973), these short sentences follow a rigid word order and contain only essential content words, leaving out plurals, possessives, conjunctions, articles, and prepositions. Telegraphic speech reflects the child's understanding of syntax—the rules governing how words are ordered in a sentence. When a third word is added to a sentence, it usually fills in the word missing from the two-word sentence (for example, "Mama drink milk").

Suffixes, Function Words, and Grammatical Rules

After using telegraphic speech for a time, children gradually begin to add modifiers to make words more precise. Suffixes and function words—pronouns, articles, conjunctions, and prepositions—are acquired in a fixed sequence, although the rate of acquisition varies (R. Brown, 1973; Maratsos, 1983).

Overregularization is the kind of error that results when a grammatical rule is misapplied to a word that has an irregular plural or past tense (Kuczaj, 1978). **[LO 7.10]** Thus children who have learned and correctly used words such as "went," "came," and "did" incorrectly apply the rule for past tenses and begin to say "goed," "comed," and "doed." What the parent sees as a regression in speech actually means that the child has acquired a grammatical rule (Marcus et al., 1992). **[LO 7.10]**

THEORIES OF LANGUAGE DEVELOPMENT: HOW DO WE ACQUIRE IT?

How do learning theory and the nativist position explain the acquisition of language?

The ability to acquire language has fascinated researchers and philosophers alike. Two explanations that explain how language is acquired are learning theory and the nativist approach.

Learning Theory

Learning theorists have long maintained that language is acquired in the same way that other behaviours are acquired—as a result of learning through reinforcement and imitation. **[LO 7.11]** B. F. Skinner (1957) asserted that language is shaped through reinforcement. He said that parents selectively criticize incorrect speech and reinforce correct speech through praise, approval, and attention. Thus the child's utterances are progressively shaped in the direction of grammatically correct speech. Others believe that children acquire vocabulary and sentence construction mainly through imitation (Bandura, 1977).

On the surface, what the learning theorists propose appears logical, but there are some problems with learning theory as

---

morphemes: The smallest units of meaning in a language.

syntax: The aspect of grammar that specifies the rules for arranging and combining words to form phrases and sentences.

semantics: The meaning or the study of meaning derived from morphemes, words, and sentences.

surface structure: The literal words of a sentence that we speak, write, or sign.

deep structure: The underlying meaning of a sentence.

babbling: Vocalization of the basic speech sounds (phonemes), which begins between the ages of four and six months.

overextension: The act of using a word, on the basis of some shared feature, to apply to a broader range of objects than is appropriate.

underextension: Restricting the use of a word to only a few, rather than to all, members of a class of objects.

telegraphic speech: Short sentences that follow a strict word order and contain only essential content words.

overregularization: The act of inappropriately applying the grammatical rules for forming plurals and past tenses to irregular nouns and verbs.

the sole explanation for language acquisition. Imitation cannot account for patterns of speech such as telegraphic speech or for systematic errors such as overregularization. **[LO 7.11]** Children do not hear telegraphic speech in everyday life, and "I comed" and "He goed" are not forms commonly used by parents.

There are also problems with reinforcement as an explanation for language acquisition. **[LO 7.11]** First, parents seem to reward children more for the content of the utterance than for the correctness of the grammar (R. Brown, Cazden, & Bellugi, 1968). And parents are much more likely to correct children for saying something untrue than for making a grammatical error. Regardless, correction does not seem to have much impact on a child's grammar.

Nevertheless, reinforcement plays an important part in language learning. Responsiveness to infants' vocalizations increases the amount of vocalization, and reinforcement can help children with language deficits improve (Lovaas, 1967; Whitehurst, Rischel, Caulfield, DeBaryshe, & Valdez-Menchaca, 1989). **[LO 7.11]**

The Nativist Position

A very different theory, the nativist position, was proposed by Noam Chomsky (1957), who believes that language ability is largely innate. Chomsky (1968) maintains that the brain contains a language acquisition device (LAD), which enables children to acquire language and discover the rules of grammar. **[LO 7.11]** This mechanism predisposes children to acquire language easily and naturally. Language develops in stages that occur in a fixed order and appear at about the same time in most normal children—babbling at about six months, the one-word stage at about one year, and the two-word stage at 18 to 20 months. Hearing-impaired children exposed to sign language from birth proceed along the same schedule (Meier, 1991; Petitto & Marentette, 1991). Lenneberg (1967) believes that biological maturation underlies language development in much the same way that it underlies physical and motor development.

The nativist position accounts more convincingly than does the learning theory for the fact that children throughout the world go through the same basic stages in language development. **[LO 7.11]** It can account, too, for the similarity in errors that they make when they are first learning to form plurals, past tenses, and negatives—errors not acquired through imitation or reinforcement. There remain, however, aspects of language development that the nativist position cannot explain.

The Interactionist Perspective

The interactionist perspective acknowledges the importance of both learning and inborn capacity for acquiring language (Chapman, 2000). Research reveals that language learning proceeds in a piecemeal fashion, which calls into question the assumptions of Chomsky's nativist approach (Tomasello, 2000). Children learn the concrete language expressions they hear around them, and then they imitate and build on those. One way parents support the language-learning process is by adjusting their speech to their infant's level of development. Parents often use highly simplified speech, with shorter phrases and sentences and simpler vocabulary that is uttered slowly, at a high pitch, and with exaggerated intonation and much

repetition (Fernald, 1993). This simplified presentation is often called child-directed speech, or *motherese*.

Reading to children and with them also supports language development. Parents can do many things to help their children develop their language skills. For example, parents should comment and expand on what a child says and encourage the child to say more by asking questions of the child. Supporting children's reading development is critical both at home and at school. Canadian researchers have been developing and testing a reading software program for children called ABRACADABRA, that can support educators and parents in their efforts to teach children. Read the *Canadian Connections* box to find about abiout this innovative program.

HAVING MORE THAN ONE LANGUAGE

Many countries in the world, including Canada, have more than one official language. Even within countries that formally acknowledge only one official language, considerable variation exists in the languages that are spoken by the inhabitants. This diversity in language can be attributed to many variables, such as immigration, restoration of traditional or Native languages, and the introduction of technological advances that have made communication outside one's own land commonplace. In some cases, these changes have made the acquisition of a second language necessary, and in other cases, they have made it desirable or at least noteworthy.

Psychological interests in second-language acquisition range from psycholinguistic concerns (that is, structures of language) to social issues. One important concern that affects the study of language acquisition is the age of onset. Learners can acquire a second language at any time in their lifetime (Birdsong, 2005; Humes-Bartlo, 1989). A second language can be learned either simultaneously with the first language or at a later time. A learner who is fluent in two languages is considered *bilingual*; a learner who is fluent in many languages is called *multilingual*. Many bilingual or multilingual individuals, however, are more skilled in one language than in others. Children raised in multilingual homes who have consistent and equivalent access to each language tend to follow the same steps in language development as monolingual children. It is important to note that the data do not support the myth that fluency in a second language is possible only if learners are introduced to that second language at a very early age (Genesee, 1994), although early exposure may enhance the chances of sounding like a native speaker (Abrhamsson & Hyltenstam, 2009). Learning a second language later in life requires motivation, a positive attitude, and effort and opportunity to practise the language (R. C. Gardner & Lysynchuk, 1990; Hakuta, 1987; Schulz, 1991). Research shows that the more you know about your first language—its spelling rules, grammatical structure, and vocabulary—the easier it will be for you to learn another language (Meschyan & Hernandez, 2002).

To maximize second-language learning, we have to be sensitive to the prevalence of the languages that are to be learned. In some cases when a minority language is presented in tandem with a majority language, the minority language is poorly acquired. This phenomenon is called *subtractive bilingualism* because one language detracts from the acquisition of the other

CANADIAN CONNECTIONS

Dr. Philip C. Abrami

A team of researchers and developers at the Centre for the Study of Learning and Performance (CSLP), guided by Dr. Philip Abrami at Concordia University in Montreal, designs, develops, validates, and disseminates without charge multimedia educational software for use in classrooms across Canada and around the world. These tools take advantage of the best available research in their design (i.e., are evidence-based) and are validated in methodologically rigorous field experiments (i.e., are evidence-proven).

Used with Permission from Dr. Abrami

In deciding on the software to develop, they consider both need and potential impact. Not surprisingly, their first efforts went into creating an early literacy tool, ABRACADABRA, or ABRA for short, because the evidence so clearly shows the link between reading and writing and success at school and work.

The instructional module of ABRA consists of 32 instructional activities with 17 stories and various difficulty levels, altogether creating hundreds of learning possibilities for emerging readers. The look and feel of ABRA is game-like, and young students find it a fun and effective way to learn. But there is also a serious side to ABRA, as each of the 32 activities has its basis in the summary of evidence prepared by the National Reading Panel (2000) and validated since by others (Savage et al., 2013).

Knowing that students, especially young children, learn best when given guidance and scaffolding from teachers, ABRA was designed to be used by teachers with students. A teacher module assists teachers to use the tool well, and provides a variety of teacher supports such as printable teaching materials, job aids, and just-in-time videos. ABRA also contains an assessment module, so individual students as well as a class of students can be followed to see where they are making progress and where more work is necessary. Finally, ABRA contains a parent module to help guide parents and caregivers who use the tool at home with their children.

Does ABRA work? Yes. Studies ranging from small, local interventions to pan-Canadian and even international research support the program's effectiveness (e.g., Abrami, Savage, Wade, Hipps, & Lopez, 2008; Savage et al., 2012; Savage et al., 2013).

Furthermore, the effects of ABRA are not trivial; it produces noticeable gains in learning compared to traditional means of reading instruction.

To learn more, visit http://doe.concordia.ca/cslp/. ■

---

and, overall, less is learned. Researchers suggest that one way to circumvent this problem is to provide early instruction in the minority language (S. C. Wright, Taylor, & Macarthur, 2000). For example, when Inuit children were provided early instruction in their heritage language (Inuktitut) and maintained that instruction over three years, their heritage-language and second-language skills were stronger than those of other Inuit children trained in both their heritage language and second language (English or French). In this case, early instruction in the minority heritage language alleviated the problem of subtractive bilingualism.

ANIMAL LANGUAGE

How does language in trained chimpanzees differ from human language?

Humans value their ability to communicate with one another. Non-human species also have complex ways of communicating. Our earliest attempt to share communication with non-humans dates back more than 70 years. As early as 1933, researchers attempted to teach chimpanzees to speak by raising the chimps in their homes. These experiments failed because the vocal tract in chimpanzees and the other apes is not adapted to human speech. **[LO 7.12]**

Researchers next turned to the American Sign Language (ASL) system used by hearing-impaired people in North America. R. Gardner and Beatrix Gardner (1969) took in a one-year-old chimp they named Washoe and taught her sign language. Washoe learned signs for objects, as well as certain commands and concepts such as "flower," "give me," "come," "open," and "more." Though it took Washoe an entire year to learn only 12 signs, by the end of her fifth year she had mastered about 160 (Fleming, 1974). **[LO 7.12]**

Another chimp, Sarah, was taught to use signs by David Premack (1971). Premack developed an artificial language consisting of magnetized, metal-backed plastic chips of various shapes, sizes, and colours, as shown in Figure 7.2. Premack used operant conditioning techniques. Sarah learned to select the plastic chip representing a fruit (apple, banana, etc.) and place it on a magnetized language board. The trainer would then reward Sarah with the fruit she had requested. Later, to receive the reward, Sarah had to add the name of her trainer, Mary, and select chips that symbolized "Mary apple." Still later, rewards would come only when Sarah identified herself as well and signalled, "Mary give apple Sarah."

Sarah mastered the concepts of similarities and differences, and eventually her performance in signalling whether two objects were the same or different was close to perfect (Premack & Premack, 1983). She even performed well on part–whole relationships and could match such things as half an apple and a glass half-filled with water. **[LO 7.12]** Even more remarkable was that Sarah could view a whole apple and a cut apple and, even

Give   Take   Apple

Banana   Sarah   Mary

FIGURE 7.2

Sarah's Symbols

A chimpanzee named Sarah learned to communicate using plastic chips of various shapes, sizes, and colours to represent words in an artificial language developed by her trainer, David Premack.

(Republished with permission of American Association for the Advancement of Science, from Sarah's Symbols" from "Language in Chimpanzee?, D. Premack, Science, 172, 1971; permission conveyed through Copyright Clearance Center, Inc.).

©Laurentiu Garofeanu/Barcroft USA/Barcroft Media/Getty Images

From their studies of communication among chimps and other animals, researchers have gained useful insights into the nature of language. The pygmy chimp Kanzi is skilled in using a special symbol board to communicate.

though she had not seen the apple being cut, match the apple with the utensil needed to cut it—a knife.

Another chimp, Lana, participated in a computer–controlled language training program. She learned to press keys imprinted with geometric symbols that represented words in an artificial language. Sue Savage-Rumbaugh (1986, 1990) varied the location, colour, and brightness of the keys so that Lana had to learn which symbols to use no matter where they were located. One day her trainer, Tim, had an orange that she wanted. Lana had available symbols for many fruits—apple, banana, and so on—but none for an orange. But there was a coloured symbol for the colour orange, so Lana improvised and signalled, "Tim give apple which is orange." Impressive!

But the most impressive performance to date is that of a rare species of ape known as the pygmy chimpanzee. One pygmy chimp, Kanzi, developed an amazing ability to communicate with his trainers without having formally been taught by them. Researchers worked with Kanzi's mother, Matata, during the mid-1980s, teaching her to press symbols representing words. Her progress was not remarkable, but her infant son, Kanzi, who stood by and observed her during training, learned rapidly (thanks to observational learning). When researchers gave Kanzi a chance at the symbol board, his performance quickly surpassed that of his mother and of every other chimp the researchers had tested.

Kanzi demonstrated an advanced understanding (for chimps) of spoken English and could respond correctly even to new commands, such as "Throw your ball to the river" or "Go to the refrigerator and get out a tomato" (Savage-Rumbaugh, 1990; Savage-Rumbaugh, Sevcik, Brakke, & Rumbaugh, 1992). By the time Kanzi was six years old, a team of researchers who worked with him had recorded more than 13 000 "utterances" and were reporting that he could communicate using some 200 different geometric symbols (Gibbons, 1991). Kanzi could press symbols to ask someone to play chase with him and even to ask two others to play chase while he watched. Furthermore, if Kanzi signalled someone to "chase and hide," it mattered greatly to him that his first command, "chase," be done first (Gibbons, 1991).

On the basis of research with chimps and other animals (especially dolphins), some investigators believe that language is not necessarily unique to humans (Herman, Kuczaj, & Holder, 1993). Others argue that social and cognitive underpinnings may not be present in apes that encourage or cause language to develop in humans (Kuhl & Rivera- Gaxiola, 2008; Premack, 1996). **[LO 7.12]**

LANGUAGE AND THINKING

Does the fact that you speak English or French mean that you reason, think, and perceive your world differently from someone who speaks Spanish, Chinese, or Swahili? According to one hypothesis presented some 45 years ago, it does.

The Linguistic Relativity Hypothesis

What is the linguistic relativity hypothesis, and is it supported by research?

Benjamin Whorf (1956), in his **linguistic relativity hypothesis**, suggests that the language a person speaks largely determines the nature of that person's thoughts. According to this

REMEMBER IT

Language

1. Which aspect of language acquisition is learning theory not able to explain?
   a. how reinforcement is used to encourage language
   b. why children are able to generate sentences they have not heard or used before
   c. why children imitate adults and other children in their speech
   d. why children have overregularization errors in their speech

2. The nativist position suggests that language ability is largely _____.

3. Match each utterance with the linguistic term that describes it
   _____ 1) "ba-ba-ba"
   _____ 2) "He eated the cookies"
   _____ 3) "Mama see ball"
   _____ 4) "oo," "ah"
   _____ 5) "kitty" (when seeing a lion)

   a. telegraphic speech
   b. holophrase
   c. overregularization
   d. babbling
   e. overextension
   f. cooing

4. Match the component (language) with its description.
   _____ 1) the smallest units of meaning
   _____ 2) the meaning derived from morphemes, words, and sentences
   _____ 3) grammatical rules for arranging and combining words to form phrases and sentences
   _____ 4) the smallest units of sound in a spoken language
   a. syntax
   b. morphemes
   c. semantics
   d. phonemes

Answers: 1. d 2. innate 3. (1) d (2) c (3) a (4) f (5) e 4. (1) b (2) c (3) a (4) d

hypothesis, our world view is constructed primarily by the words in our language. As proof, Whorf offered his classic example. The languages used by the Inuit have a number of different words for snow—"*apikak,* first snow falling; *aniv,* snow spread out; *pukak,* snow for drinking water"—whereas the English-speaking world has but one word, *snow* (Restak, 1988, p. 222). Whorf contended that this rich and varied selection of words for snow provides the Inuit with a different thinking process about snow relative to people whose languages lack specific words for various snow conditions.

Eleanor Rosch (1973) tested the linguistic relativity hypothesis. If language determines thinking, she reasoned, then people whose language contains many names for colours will be better at thinking about and discriminating among colours than people whose language has only a few colour names. Her participants for the comparative study were English-speaking Americans and the Dani, a remote New Guinea people whose language has only two names for colours—*mili* for dark, cool colours and *mola* for bright, warm colours. How well would these two groups perform in perceiving, discriminating, and remembering coloured chips of many different hues?

Rosch showed both groups single-colour chips of 11 colours—black, white, red, yellow, green, blue, brown, purple, pink, orange, and grey—for five seconds each. After 30 seconds, she had the participants select the 11 colours they had viewed from a larger group of 40 colour chips. If Whorf's hypothesis was accurate, she reasoned, the English speakers would perform with far greater accuracy than the Dani, for whom brown, black, purple, and blue are all *mili,* or dark. But this was not the case. Between the two groups, Rosch found no significant differences in discriminating, remembering, or thinking about the 11 basic colours used in the experiment.

Whorf appeared to go too far in suggesting that language determines how we think. But let us not go too far in the opposite direction and assume that language has little influence on how we think. Language and thought have a mutually supportive relationship.

MODULE 7D THE NATURE OF INTELLIGENCE

LO 7.13 Identify the factors underlying intelligence as defined by Spearman, Thurstone, and Guilford.
LO 7.14 Contrast the differences among factors underlying intelligence.
LO 7.15 Identify Gardner's and Sternberg's types of intelligences.

Is intelligence a single trait or capability? Is it many capabilities unrelated to each other? Or is it something in between? Is intelligence influenced more by heredity or by environment? As you might expect, there are many different points of view about the nature of intelligence, and it continues to be a hotly debated issue today.

linguistic relativity hypothesis: The notion that the language a person speaks largely determines the nature of that person's thoughts.

First, let us ask the most obvious question: What is intelligence? A task force of experts from the American Psychological Association defined intelligence as an individual's "ability to understand complex ideas, to adapt effectively to the environment, to learn from experience, to engage in various forms of reasoning, and to overcome obstacles by taking thought" (Neisser et al., 1996, p. 77).

THE SEARCH FOR FACTORS UNDERLYING INTELLIGENCE

What factors underlie intelligence, according to Spearman, Thurstone, and Guilford?

Are there certain common factors that underlie intelligence? If so, what might they be?

Spearman and General Intelligence: The *g* Factor

English psychologist Charles Spearman (1863–1945) observed that people who are bright in one area are usually bright in other areas as well. In other words, they tend to be generally intelligent. Spearman (1927) came to believe that intelligence involves a general ability, or *g* **factor**, that underlies all intellectual functions. **[LO 7.13]**

Spearman theorized that this positive relationship between the scores on intelligence subtests meant that the tests were measuring something in common—that general ability was being expressed to some degree in all of them. This, according to Spearman, was evidence of the *g* factor—general intelligence. But some of the correlations between subtests are higher than others. If the *g* factor alone defined the whole of what intelligence tests measure, then all the correlations would be nearly perfect. Because they are not, some other abilities in addition to the *g* factor must be present. These other abilities Spearman named *s factors* for specific abilities. Spearman concluded that intelligence tests tap both an individual's *g* factor, or general intelligence, and a number of *s* factors, or specific intellectual abilities. Spearman's influence can be seen in those intelligence tests, such as the Stanford–Binet, that yield one IQ score to indicate the level of general intelligence.

Thurstone's Primary Mental Abilities: Primarily Seven

Louis L. Thurstone (1938), another early researcher in the field of ability testing, rejected Spearman's notion of general ability, or the *g* factor. **[LO 7.13]** After analyzing the scores of a large number of people on some 56 separate ability tests, Thurstone identified seven **primary mental abilities**: verbal comprehension, numerical ability, spatial relations, perceptual speed, word fluency, memory, and reasoning. **[LO 7.13]** He maintained that all intellectual activities involve one or more of these primary mental abilities. Thurstone and his wife, Thelma G. Thurstone, developed their Primary Mental Abilities Tests to measure these seven abilities.

The Thurstones believed that a single IQ score obscured more than it revealed. **[LO 7.13]** They suggested that a profile showing relative strengths and weaknesses on the seven primary abilities would provide a more accurate picture of a person's mental ability.

Guilford's Structure of Intellect: A Mental House with 180 Rooms

Still another effort to shed light on the nature of intelligence was J. P. Guilford's **structure of intellect**. In 1967, Guilford proposed that the structure of intelligence has three dimensions: mental operations, contents, and products. **[LO 7.13]**

When we think, we perform a mental operation or activity. According to Guilford's theory, the mental operation can be cognition, memory, evaluation, divergent production, or convergent production. **[LO 7.13]** But we can't think in a vacuum; we must think *about* something. The something we think about, which Guilford called *contents*, can be visual, auditory, figural, symbolic, semantic, or behavioural. The result of bringing some mental activity to bear on some contents is a *product*.

Guilford (1967) hypothesized that there are 120 different intellectual abilities, depending on how the different operations, contents, and products are combined in a task. **[LO 7.13]** Shortly before his death, Guilford (1988) expanded his theory so that there were 180 abilities, and he divided the operation of memory into two categories: memory recording and memory retention.

INTELLIGENCE: MORE THAN ONE TYPE?

What types of intelligence did Gardner and Sternberg identify?

Some theorists, instead of searching for the factors that underlie intelligence, propose that there are different types of intelligence. For example, some researchers distinguish between two types of intelligence (Horn, 1982b). *Crystallized intelligence* refers to verbal ability and accumulated knowledge, whereas *fluid intelligence* refers to abstract reasoning and mental flexibility. **[LO 7.14]** Some theorists have made very refined distinctions in the types of intelligence we have. Two such modern theorists are Howard Gardner and Robert Sternberg.

Gardner's Theory of Multiple Intelligences: Eight Frames of Mind

Howard Gardner (1983) denies the existence of a *g* factor—a general intellectual ability. Instead, he proposes eight independent forms of intelligence, or *frames of mind*, as illustrated in Figure 7.3. **[LO 7.15]** The eight frames of mind are linguistic, logical-mathematical, spatial, bodily-kinesthetic, musical, interpersonal, intrapersonal, and naturalistic.

Perhaps the most controversial aspect of Gardner's theory is his view that all forms of intelligence are of equal importance. In fact, different cultures assign varying degrees of importance to the types of intelligence. For example, linguistic and logical-mathematical intelligences are valued most in Western cultures; bodily-kinesthetic intelligence is more highly prized in cultures that depend on hunting for survival.

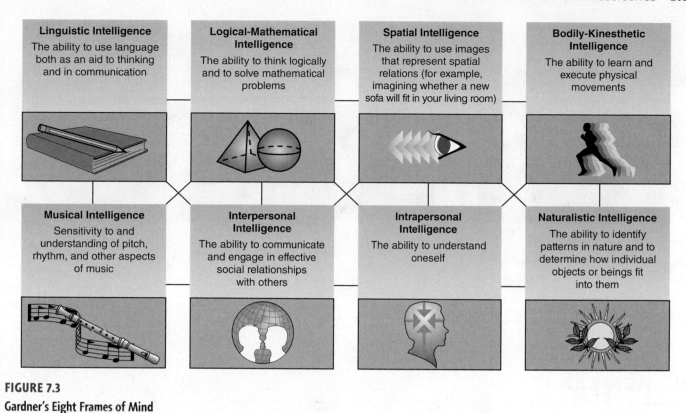

FIGURE 7.3
Gardner's Eight Frames of Mind

Gardner (1983) developed his theory of multiple intelligences after studying patients with different types of brain damage that affected some forms of intelligence but left others intact. He also studied reports of people with savant syndrome—individuals who possess a strange combination of mental disability and unusual talent or ability. Finally, he considered how various abilities and skills have been valued differently in other cultures and periods of history. Furthermore, Gardner continues to refine his model. He has proposed that a ninth type of intelligence, one that he calls *existential intelligence*, deals with the spiritual realm and enables us to contemplate the meaning of life (Halama & Strízenec, 2004).

Sternberg's Triarchic Theory of Intelligence: The Big Three

Robert Sternberg uses the information-processing approach to understanding intelligence. **[LO 7.15]** This approach involves a step-by-step analysis of the cognitive processes people employ as they acquire knowledge and use it to solve problems.

Sternberg (1985, 1986b) formulated a **triarchic theory of intelligence**, which, as the term *triarchic* implies, proposes that intelligence consists of three main parts: the componential, the experiential, and the contextual (see Figure 7.4). The first part, the *componential*, refers to the mental abilities that are most closely related to success on conventional IQ and achievement tests. He maintains that traditional intelligence tests tap only the componential, or analytical, aspect of intelligence. **[LO 7.15]**

The second part, the *experiential*, encompasses creativity and insight, although creativity has not yielded easily to conventional measurement efforts. **[LO 7.15]** The third leg of the triarchic model is *contextual*, or practical, intelligence, which some might equate with common sense or "street smarts." People with high contextual intelligence are survivors who capitalize on their strengths and compensate for their weaknesses. They adapt well to their environment, or change the environment to improve their success, or find a new environment. People who have succeeded in spite of hardships and adverse circumstances probably have a great deal of contextual intelligence. Sternberg's theory has had an impact in

***g* factor:** Spearman's term for a general intellectual ability that underlies all mental operations to some degree.

primary mental abilities: According to Thurstone, seven relatively distinct abilities that singularly or in combination are involved in all intellectual activities.

structure of intellect: The model proposed by J. P. Guilford consisting of 180 different intellectual abilities, which involve all the possible combinations of the three dimensions of intellect—mental operations, contents, and products.

triarchic theory of intelligence: Sternberg's theory that intelligence consists of three parts—the componential, the experiential, and the contextual.

Componental Intelligence

Mental abilities most closely related to success on traditional IQ and achievement tests

©Pressmaster/Shutterstock

Experiential Intelligence

Creative thinking and problem solving

©Diego Cervo/Fotolia

Contextual Intelligence

Practical intelligence or "street smarts"

©Peter Johnson/Corbis

FIGURE 7.4

Sternberg's Triarchic Theory of Intelligence

According to Sternberg, there are three types of intelligence: componental, experiential, and contextual.

REMEMBER IT

The Nature of Intelligence

1. Match the theorist with the theory of intelligence.
   - _____ 1) triarchic theory of intelligence
   - _____ 2) seven primary mental abilities
   - _____ 3) structure of intellect
   - _____ 4) the *g* factor
     - a. Spearman
     - b. Thurstone
   - c. Guilford
   - d. Sternberg
   - e. Gardner

2. The theory proposing seven distinct types of intellectual abilities was developed by _____.

3. According to Spearman, different kinds of cognitive tasks may appear to use different abilities, but they are all tied to a single type of intelligence called the _____.

Answers: 1. (1). d (2). b (3). c (4). a   2. Gardner   3. *g* factor

schools, especially for low achievers (Grigorenko, Jarvin, & Sternberg, 2002). For example, instructional interventions that focus on applying the content of lessons to practical real-world contexts and that emphasize the relevance of material can be effective.

MODULE **7E** MEASURING INTELLIGENCE

LO 7.16 List the different kinds of IQ tests.
LO 7.17 Describe how intelligence is assessed by each test.
LO 7.18 Explain what is required for a test to be a good measure of intelligence.

You have now read several competing explanations of how intelligence is structured and how intellectual processes work. But even before a workable definition of intelligence was formulated, attempts were made to measure intelligence.

ALFRED BINET AND THE FIRST SUCCESSFUL INTELLIGENCE TEST

What was Binet's major contribution to psychology?

The first successful effort to measure intelligence resulted not from a theoretical approach, but as a practical means of solving a problem. The Ministry of Public Instruction in Paris was trying to find some objective means of identifying children's

National Library of Medicine

Alfred Binet began testing Parisian students in 1904.

intelligence. The ministry wanted to ensure that average or brighter children would not be wrongly assigned to special classes and that children of limited ability would not be subjected to the regular program of instruction. In 1903, a commission was formed to study the problem. One of its members was French psychologist Alfred Binet (1857–1911).

With the help of a colleague, psychiatrist Théodore Simon, Binet published his intelligence scale in 1905; Binet and Simon revised it in 1908 and again in 1911. The Binet–Simon Intelligence Scale was an immediate success in most Western countries. **[LO 7.16]**

Test items on the scale were structured according to increasing difficulty, with the easiest item first and each succeeding item more difficult than the last. **[LO 7.17]** Children went as far as they could, and then their progress was compared with that of others of the same age. A child with the mental ability of a normal five-year-old was said to have a mental level of five. (Binet and Simon used the term *mental level*, but since then the term *mental age* has been used instead.) Binet established the concept that mental disability and mental superiority are based on the difference between chronological age (one's actual age) and mental age. An eight-year-old with a mental age of eight is normal or average. An eight-year-old with a mental age of five is mentally deficient, whereas an eight-year-old with a mental age of 11 is mentally superior.

THE INTELLIGENCE QUOTIENT, OR IQ

What does IQ mean, and how was it originally calculated?

Binet believed that children with a mental age two years below chronological age were disabled and should be placed in special education classes. But there was a flaw in his thinking: a four-year-old with a mental age of two is far more retarded than a 12-year-old with a mental age of 10. How could a similar degree of retardation at different ages be expressed?

German psychologist William Stern (1914) came up with the answer. In 1912 he devised a simple formula for calculating intelligence—the **intelligence quotient**, or IQ. He divided a child's mental age by his or her chronological age. This formula was revised later by Lewis Terman, who eliminated the decimal and multiplied by 100.

Here's how IQ is calculated:

$$\frac{\text{Mental age}}{\text{Chronological age}} \times 100 = \text{IQ}$$

Here is how some 10-year-olds' IQs would be calculated:

$$\frac{14}{10} \times 100 = 1.40 \times 100 = \text{IQ } 140 \text{ (superior IQ)}$$

$$\frac{10}{10} \times 100 = 1.00 \times 100 = \text{IQ } 100 \text{ (normal IQ)}$$

$$\frac{6}{10} \times 100 = 0.60 \times 100 = \text{IQ } 60 \text{ (below normal IQ)}$$

It is interesting to note that Binet and his partner Simon were totally against the use of IQ scores. They believed that trying to represent human intelligence with a single number was impossible, and that doing so was not only misleading but also dangerous (Hothersall, 1984).

INTELLIGENCE TESTING IN NORTH AMERICA

The Stanford–Binet Intelligence Scale

What is the Stanford–Binet Intelligence Scale?

Henry H. Goddard translated the Binet–Simon scales of 1908 and 1911 into English. Terman, of Stanford University in California, published a thorough revision of the Binet–Simon scale in 1916. Terman established new **norms**—standards based on the scores of a large number of people and used as bases for comparison. Terman's revision, known as the **Stanford–Binet Intelligence Scale**, was the first test to make use of Stern's IQ score (von Mayrhauser, 1992). **[LO 7.16]** Within two and a half years, four million children had taken the test.

The Stanford–Binet Intelligence Test is an individually administered IQ test developed for persons aged 2 to 23. It measures verbal and non-verbal IQ, knowledge, fluid and quantitative reasoning, working memory, and visual-spatial processing (Roid, 2003). **[LO 7.17]** An overall IQ score is derived from scores on the seven subscales. The Stanford–Binet is highly regarded.

intelligence quotient (IQ): An index of intelligence originally derived by dividing mental age by chronological age and then multiplying by 100.

norms: Standards based on the range of test scores of a large group of people who are selected to provide the bases of comparison for those who will take the test later.

Stanford–Binet Intelligence Scale: An individually administered IQ test for those aged 2 to 23; Lewis Terman's adaptation of the Binet–Simon Intelligence Scale.

Intelligence Testing for Adults

It quickly became obvious that the Stanford–Binet Intelligence Scale was not useful for testing adults. The original IQ formula could not be applied to adults because at a certain age, maturity in intelligence is reached, as it is for height and for other physical characteristics. According to the original IQ formula, a 40-year-old who scored the same on an IQ test as the average 20-year-old would be mentally disabled, with an IQ of only 50. Obviously, something went wrong when the formula was applied to adults. Today we still use the term *IQ*; however, for adults, IQ is a **deviation score** calculated by comparing an individual's score with the scores of others of the *same age* on whom the test's norms were formed. The deviation score is one of the contributions of David Wechsler, another pioneer in mental testing.

The Wechsler Intelligence Tests

What did Wechsler's tests provide that the Stanford–Binet did not?

In 1939, David Wechsler developed the first successful individual intelligence test for people aged 16 and older. **[LO 7.16]** The original test has been revised, restandardized, and renamed the **Wechsler Adult Intelligence Scale (WAIS-IV)** and is now one of the most common psychological tests. The test contains both verbal and performance (non-verbal) subtests, which yield separate verbal and performance IQ scores as well as an overall IQ score. **[LO 7.17]** This test is a departure from the Stanford–Binet, which yields just one IQ score.

Wechsler also published the Wechsler Intelligence Scale for Children (WISC-IV), as well as the Wechsler Preschool and Primary Scale of Intelligence (WPPSI-IV), which has established norms for children aged two and a half to seven and a half.

Group Intelligence Tests

Administering individual intelligence tests such as the Stanford–Binet and the Wechsler is expensive and time-consuming. The tests must be administered to one individual at a time by a psychologist or other qualified testing professional. When large numbers of people must be tested in a short period of time on a limited budget, individual IQ testing is out of the question. A number of widely used group intelligence tests now exist, such as the California Test of Mental Maturity, the Canadian Cognitive Abilities Test, and the Otis–Lennon Mental Ability Test. **[LO 7.16]** You may have taken one or more of these tests, all of which are good. But not all tests are created equal, as we will see in the following discussion.

REQUIREMENTS OF GOOD TESTS: RELIABILITY, VALIDITY, AND STANDARDIZATION

What is meant by the terms *reliability*, *validity*, and *standardization*?

If your watch gains six minutes one day and loses three or four minutes the next day, it is not reliable. You want a watch that you can rely on to give the correct time day after day. Like a watch, an intelligence test must have **reliability**; the test must consistently yield nearly the same scores when the same people are retested on the same test or an alternative form of the test. **[LO 7.18]** The higher the correlation between the two scores, the more reliable the test.

Even highly reliable tests are worthless if they are not valid. A test has **validity** if it measures what it is intended to measure. **[LO 7.18]** For example, a thermometer is a valid instrument for measuring temperature; a bathroom scale is valid for measuring weight. But no matter how reliable your bathroom scale is, it will not take your temperature. It is valid only for weighing.

REMEMBER IT

Measuring Intelligence

1. The first valid intelligence test was the _____ .
   a. Stanford–Binet.
   b. Binet–Simon.
   c. Wechsler.
   d. WAIS.

2. According to Stern's revised formula, what is the IQ of a child with a mental age of 12 and a chronological age of 8?
   a. 75
   b. 150
   c. 125
   d. 100

3. The Stanford–Binet and Wechsler intelligence tests must be administered individually rather than in groups. (true/false)

4. A test that measures what it claims to measure has _____; a test that gives consistent results has _____.
   a. reliability; validity
   b. equivalence; reliability
   c. validity; reliability
   d. objectivity; validity

Answers: 1. a 2. b 3. true 4. c

Once a test is proven to be valid and reliable, the next requirement is for **standardization**. [LO 7.18] There must be standard procedures for administering and scoring the test. Exactly the same directions must be given, whether written or oral, and the same amount of time must be allowed for every test taker. But even more important, standardization involves establishing norms by which all scores are interpreted. The creators of a test standardize it by administering it to a large sample of people representative of those who will be taking the test in the future. The group's scores are analyzed, and then the average score, standard deviation, percentile rankings, and other measures are computed. These comparative scores become the norms, which are used as the standard against which all other test takers will be measured. [LO 7.18]

MODULE **7F** **THE RANGE OF INTELLIGENCE**

LO 7.19 Define and describe what is meant by *norms* and *deviation scores*.

LO 7.20 Describe the outcomes of Terman's longitudinal study of intelligence.

LO 7.21 Define *giftedness*.

LO 7.22 Define intellectual disability and explain the implications for individuals at each level of ability.

What are the ranges of IQ scores that are considered average, superior, and in the range of mental disability?

When large populations are measured on mental characteristics such as intelligence or on physical characteristics such as height or weight, the test scores or results usually conform to the bell-shaped distribution known as the *normal curve*. [LO 7.19] Most of the scores cluster around the mean (average). The farther the scores deviate, or move away, from the mean, above *or* below, the fewer people there are (see Figure 7.5). [LO 7.19]

The average IQ test score for all people in the same age group is arbitrarily assigned a value of 100. On the Wechsler intelligence tests, about 50 percent of all scores fall in the average range, between 90 and 110. About 68 percent fall between 85 and 115, and about 95 percent fall between 70 and 130. About 2 percent of the scores are above 130, which is considered superior, and about 2 percent fall below 70, in the range of mental disability.

Terman's Study of Gifted People: 1528 Geniuses and How They Grew

According to the Terman study, how do gifted people differ from the general population?

In 1921, Lewis Terman began a **longitudinal study**, now a classic, in which 1528 gifted students were measured at different ages throughout their lives. The 857 males and 671 females

had IQs on the Stanford–Binet ranging from 135 to 200, with a mean (or average) of 151. Terman assumed the Stanford–Binet was "a measure of innate intelligence" and that IQ was fixed at birth (Cravens, 1992).

Terman's early findings ended the myth that mentally superior people are more likely to be physically inferior. Terman's participants excelled in almost all of the abilities he studied—intellectual, physical, emotional, moral, and social. Terman also exploded many other myths (L. M. Terman & Oden, 1947). [LO 7.20] For example, you may have heard the saying that there is a fine line between genius and madness. Actually, Terman's gifted group enjoyed better mental health than the general population and were more likely to be successful in the real, practical world.

Who Is Gifted?

In the early 1920s, the term *giftedness* was used to describe those with IQs in the upper 2 or 3 percent of the population. [LO 7.21] Since that time, the term has been expanded to include both the exceptionally creative and those excelling in the visual or performing arts.

Traditionally, special programs for gifted people have involved either acceleration or enrichment. Acceleration programs enable students to skip grades, progress through subject matter more quickly, or enter university early. Enrichment programs broaden or extend students' knowledge in foreign languages, music appreciation, and the like, or develop more advanced thinking skills.

Understanding Intellectual Disabilities/ Developmental Intellectual Disorders

What two criteria must a person meet to be classified as having an intellectual disability?

The term *intellectual disability* (previously referred to as mental retardation) has been used in conjunction with IQ scores.

---

deviation score: A test score calculated by comparing an individual's score with the scores of others of the same age on whom the test's norms were formed.

Wechsler Adult Intelligence Scale (WAIS-IV): An individual intelligence test for adults that yields separate verbal and performance (non-verbal) IQ scores as well as an overall IQ score.

reliability: The ability of a test to yield nearly the same score each time a person takes the test or an alternative form of the test.

validity: The ability of a test to measure what it is intended to measure.

standardization: The establishment of norms for comparing the scores of people who will take the test in the future; administering tests using a prescribed procedure.

longitudinal study: A type of developmental study in which the same group of individuals is followed and measured at different ages.

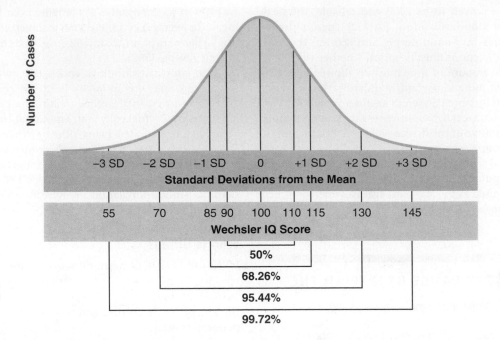

FIGURE 7.5

The Normal Curve

When a large number of test scores are compiled, they are typically distributed in a normal (bell-shaped) curve. On the Wechsler scales, the average or mean IQ score is set at 100. As the figure shows, about 68 percent of the scores fall between 15 IQ points (1 standard deviation) above and below 100 (from 85 to 115), and about 95 percent of the scores fall between 30 points (2 standard deviations) above and below 100 (from 70 to 130).

At the opposite end of the continuum from the intellectually gifted are the 2–3 percent of Canadians whose IQ scores place them in the range of an **intellectual disability**. People are not classified as having an intellectual disability unless they show deficits in intellectual functioning (scores on IQ test) and deficits in adaptive functioning that make it very hard to care for themselves and relate to others. **[LO 7.22]** Individuals with IQs two standard deviations below average or lower may qualify as having an intellectual disability.

Before the late 1960s, children with intellectual disabilities were educated almost exclusively in special schools. Since then, there has been a movement toward **mainstreaming**, which involves educating students with intellectual disabilities in regular schools and classrooms.

REMEMBER IT

The Range of Intelligence

1. The largest percentage of people taking an IQ test will score in the range from
   a. 80 to 100.
   b. 90 to 110.
   c. 100 to 130.
   a. 65 to 90.

2. In his study of gifted people, Terman found that mentally superior individuals tend to be physically smaller and weaker. (true/false)

3. People are considered as having an intellectual disability if they are clearly deficient in adaptive functioning and their IQ is at least _____ standard deviations below the norm.
   a. 1   **b.** 2   **c.** 3

Answers: 1. b 2. false 3. b

MODULE 7G THE IQ CONTROVERSY: BRAINY DISPUTE

LO 7.23 Understand the relative contributions of nature and nurture for IQ.
LO 7.24 Define *heritability*.
LO 7.25 Describe and explain the Flynn effect on IQ.

THE USES AND ABUSES OF INTELLIGENCE TESTS

Since Binet's time, intelligence testing has become a major growth industry. Virtually every college and university student in Canada has taken one or more intelligence or aptitude tests. And many people have come to believe that an IQ score gives a precise indication of a person's intellectual capacity, ability, or potential.

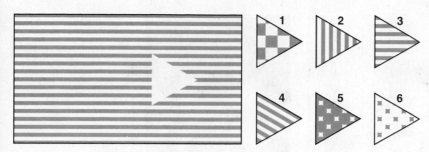

FIGURE 7.6

An Example of a Test Item on a Culture-Fair Test

This culture-fair test item does not penalize test takers whose language or cultural experiences differ from those of the urban middle or upper classes. Participants are to select, from the six samples on the right, the patch that would complete the pattern. Patch number 3 is the correct answer.

Source: Based on the Raven Standard Progressive Matrices Test.

Intelligence Test Scores: Can They Predict Success and Failure?

What do intelligence tests predict well?

What can intelligence tests really tell us? IQ scores are fairly good predictors of academic achievement and success in school. Both the Stanford–Binet Intelligence Scale and the Canadian Cognitive Abilities Test correlate highly with school grades. This is not surprising, since these scales test the same things as school work—verbal and test-taking ability. But IQ tests and aptitude tests are far from infallible.

Another important question is whether there is a high correlation between IQ and success in real life. While it is true that people in the professions (doctors, dentists, lawyers) tend to have higher IQs than people in lower-status occupations, the exact relationship between IQ score and occupational status is not clearly understood. Nevertheless, intelligence scores are related to a wide range of outcomes, including job performance, income, social status, and years of education completed (Neisser et al., 1996; Nisbett et al., 2012).

The Abuses of Intelligence Tests: Making Too Much of a Single Number

What are some of the abuses of intelligence tests?

Abuses occur when people are judged solely on their scores on intelligence tests. Intelligence tests do not measure attitude and motivation, which are critical ingredients of success.

Some people maintain that IQ tests are designed for the white middle class and that other groups are at a disadvantage when they are assessed with these tests. Attempts have been made to develop **culture-fair intelligence tests**. Such tests are designed to minimize cultural bias; the questions do not penalize individuals whose cultural experience or language differs from that of the urban middle or upper classes (e.g., Naglieri & Ronning, 2000). See Figure 7.6, for an example of the type of test item found on a culture-fair test.

THE NATURE–NURTURE CONTROVERSY: BATTLE OF THE CENTURIES

How does the nature–nurture controversy apply to intelligence?

The most vocal area of disagreement concerning intelligence has been the **nature–nurture controversy**, the debate over whether intelligence is primarily the result of heredity or environment. Most psychologists today agree that both nature and nurture contribute to intelligence (Nisbett et al., 2012; Petrill, 2003). **[LO 7.23]**

Behavioural Genetics: Investigating Nature and Nurture

What is behavioural genetics, and what are the primary methods used in the field today?

Behavioural genetics is a field of research that investigates the relative effects of heredity and environment on behaviour and ability (nature versus nurture; Plominet et al., 1997). **[LO 7.23]** Two of the primary methods used by behavioural geneticists are the twin study method—first used by Galton (1875) in his studies of heredity—and the adoption method.

In the **twin study method**, researchers study **identical (monozygotic) twins** and **fraternal (dizygotic) twins** to determine how much they resemble each other on a variety of characteristics. *Identical* twins have exactly the same genes: a single sperm cell of the father fertilizes a single egg of the mother, forming a cell that then splits to form two human beings—"carbon copies." *Fraternal* twins are no more alike genetically than other siblings born to the same parents: two separate sperm cells fertilize two separate eggs that happen to be released at the same time during ovulation.

Twins who are raised together, whether identical or fraternal, have similar environments. If identical twins raised together are found to be more alike than fraternal twins on a certain

---

intellectual disability: Evidenced by IQ scores at least two standard deviations below the norm and by adaptive functioning severely deficient for one's age.

mainstreaming: Educating students with intellectual disabilities in regular rather than special schools by placing them in regular classes for part or all of the day or having special classrooms in regular schools.

culture-fair intelligence test: An intelligence test designed to minimize cultural bias by using questions that will not penalize individuals whose culture or language differs from that of the urban middle or upper class.

nature–nurture controversy: The debate concerning the relative influences of heredity and environment on development.

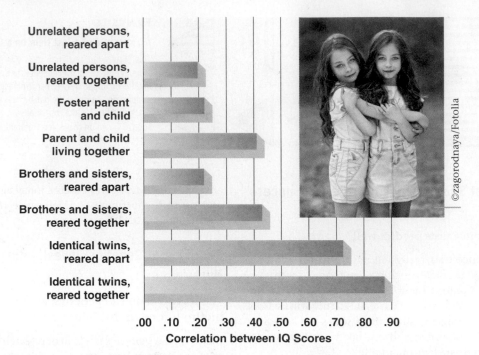

FIGURE 7.7

Correlations between the IQ Scores of Persons with Various Relationships

The more closely related two individuals are, the more similar their IQ scores tend to be. Thus, there is a strong genetic contribution to intelligence.
Source: (Based on data from T. J. Bouchard & McGue, 1981; Erlenmeyer-Kimling & Jarvik, 1963.) Based on data from Bouchard, T.J, Jr; & McGue, M. (1981). Familiar studies of intelligence: A review. *Science, 212,* 1055–1058; Erlenmeyer-Kimling, L; & Jarvik, L.F. (1963). Genetics and intelligence: A review. *Science, 142,* 1477–1479.

trait, that trait is assumed to be more influenced by heredity. If identical and fraternal twins from similar environments do not differ on a trait, that trait is assumed to be influenced more by environment. The term **heritability** refers to the index of the degree to which a characteristic is estimated to be influenced by heredity. **[LO 7.24]** Figure 7.7 shows estimates of the contribution of genetic and environmental factors to intelligence.

Behavioural geneticists also use the **adoption study method** and conduct longitudinal studies of children adopted shortly after birth. By comparing their abilities and personality traits with those of the adoptive family members with whom they live and with those of their biological parents (whom they may never have met), researchers can disentangle the effects of heredity and environment (Plomin, DeFries, & Fulker, 1988).

A Natural Experiment: Identical Twins Reared Apart

How do twin studies support the view that intelligence is inherited?

Probably the best way to assess the relative contributions of heredity and environment is to study identical twins who have been separated at birth and raised apart. **[LO 7.23]** When separated twins are found to have strikingly similar traits, it is assumed that heredity has been a major contributor. When separated twins differ on a given trait, the influence of the environment is thought to be greater.

Since 1979, researchers headed by Thomas Bouchard have studied some 60 pairs of fraternal twins and 80 pairs of identical twins who were reared apart. They conclude that "general intelligence or IQ is strongly affected by genetic factors" (T. Bouchard, Lykken, McGue, Segal, & Tellegen, 1990, p. 227). Bouchard (1997) reports that various types of twin studies have consistently revealed heritability estimates to be 0.60 to 0.70 for intelligence, indicating that 60 to 70 percent of the variation in IQ can be attributed to genetic factors. Not all researchers agree with Bouchard's estimate. Having combined data from a number of twin studies, Plomin, Owen, and McGuffin (1994) estimate heritability for general intelligence to be 0.52, and other, larger studies seem to concur with Plomin's estimates (McClearn et al., 1997).

Psychologists who consider environmental factors to be the chief contributors to differences in intelligence take issue with Bouchard's findings. They maintain that most separated identical twins are raised by adoptive parents who have been matched as closely as possible to the biological parents. This fact, the critics say, could account for the similarities in IQ. In response to their critics, Bouchard (1997) points out that studies comparing non-biologically related siblings reared in the same home reveal that IQ correlations are close to zero by the time the participants reach adolescence.

Adoption studies reveal that children adopted shortly after birth have IQs closer to their biological than to their adoptive parents' IQs. The family environment influences IQ early in life, but that influence seems to diminish; as participants reach adulthood, it is the genes that are most closely correlated with IQ (Loehlin, Horn, & Willerman, 1989; Loehlin, Willerman, & Horn, 1988; McCartney, Harris, & Bernieri, 1990; Plomin & Rende, 1991). Bouchard and colleagues (1990) assert that "although parents may be able to affect their children's rate of cognitive skill acquisition, they may have relatively little influence on the ultimate level attained" (p. 225). But does this mean that the degree to which intelligence is inherited is the degree to which it is absolutely fixed and immune to environmental intervention?

INTELLIGENCE: IS IT FIXED OR CHANGEABLE?

What kinds of evidence suggest that IQ is changeable rather than fixed?

Probably the most important issue in intelligence is whether IQ is fixed or changeable. There is little doubt that the great similarity in intelligence scores between identical twins reared apart makes a strong case that genetics is a powerful influence. But even Bouchard (Bouchard, 1997; Bouchard et al., 1990) admits that only a few of the identical twins studied were raised in impoverished environments or by illiterate parents. Consequently, they caution against trying to generalize their findings to people raised in disadvantaged environments. Moreover, they point out that their findings do not argue that IQ cannot be enhanced in a more optimal environment.

Several studies indicate that IQ test scores are not fixed, but can be modified with an enriched environment. About four decades ago, Sandra Scarr and Richard Weinberg (1976) studied 130 black and interracial children who had been adopted by highly educated, upper-middle-class white families; 99 of the children had been adopted in the first year of life. The adoptees were fully exposed to middle-class cultural experiences and vocabulary, the "culture of the tests and the school" (p. 737).

How did the children perform on IQ and achievement tests? For these children, the average 15-point black–white IQ gap was bridged by an enriched environment. Instead of an average IQ score of 90 (which would have been expected had they been reared by their biological parents), these adoptees had an average IQ of 106.3. And their achievement test scores were slightly *above* the national average. Studies in France also show that IQ scores and achievement are substantially higher when children from lower-class environments are adopted by middle- and upper-middle-class families (Duyme, 1988; Schiff & Lewontin, 1986).

Other evidence also suggests that environmental factors have a strong influence on IQ scores. In industrialized countries all over the world there have been huge IQ gains over the past 50 years. These IQ gains are known as the *Flynn effect*, after James Flynn, who analyzed 73 studies involving some 7500 participants ranging in age from 12 to 48. **[LO 7.25]** He found that "every Binet and Wechsler sample from 1932 to 1978 has performed better than its predecessor" (Flynn, 1987, p. 225). The gain, about one third of an IQ point per year (three points per decade), has been continuing for 50 years (Dickens & Flynn, 2001). That is, average IQ in industrial nations is currently about 15 IQ points, or one standard deviation, higher than 50 years ago.

Race and IQ: The Controversial Views

What are Jensen's and Herrnstein and Murray's controversial views on race and IQ?

Some studies over the past several decades have reported that, on average, blacks score about 15 points lower than whites on standardized IQ tests (Herrnstein & Murray, 1994; Jensen, 1985; Loehlin, Lindzey, & Spuhler, 1975; Rushton & Jensen, 2005). In 1969, Arthur Jensen published an article in which he attributed the IQ gap to genetic factors. He also maintained that because heredity is such a strong influence on intelligence, environment cannot make a significant difference. Jensen's views on race and intelligence sent a shock wave through the scientific community.

In a similar vein, a Canadian researcher, J. Philippe Rushton, argued that races could be ranked in order of intelligence, with Asians being the highest, followed by whites, and then blacks. His conclusions are based on differences in head circumference, brain size, and estimated cranial space (Rushton, 1991, 1992). This argument has been challenged by other researchers who question the methodology of the research, the accuracy of the measurements, and whether the studies actually test intelligence (Peters, 1995a, 1995b; Winston, 1996).

A book called *The Bell Curve* (1994) fuelled the controversy. The authors, Richard Herrnstein and Charles Murray, argued that more than any other factor, IQ explains how those at the top rungs of society got there and why those on the lower rungs remain there. According to the authors, IQ is primarily genetic and cannot be changed by environmental interventions.

Jensen's views and those of Rushton and Herrnstein and Murray run counter to the beliefs of those who argue that an enriched, stimulating environment can overcome the deficits of poverty and cultural disadvantage and thus reduce or wipe out the IQ deficit.

IS THE GAP DUE TO RACE ALONE? If average IQ differences were genetically determined by race, then the mean IQ scores of mixed-race individuals should fall somewhere between the mean scores for blacks and whites. But studies over the decades have not found such a relationship between

---

behavioural genetics: The field of research that investigates the relative effects of heredity and environment on behaviour and ability.

twin study method: Studying identical and fraternal twins to determine the relative effects of heredity and environment on a variety of characteristics.

identical (monozygotic) twins: Twins with exactly the same genes, who develop after one egg is fertilized by one sperm and the zygote splits into two parts.

fraternal (dizygotic) twins: Twins, no more alike genetically than ordinary siblings, who develop after two eggs are released during ovulation and are fertilized by two different sperm.

heritability: An index of the degree to which a characteristic is estimated to be influenced by heredity.

adoption study method: A method researchers use to study the relative effects of heredity and environment on behaviour and ability in children who are adopted shortly after birth, by comparing them with their biological and adoptive parents.

REMEMBER IT

The IQ Controversy

1. IQ tests are good predictors of success in school. (true/false)

2. What field of research investigates the relative effects of heredity and environment on behaviour and ability?
   a. genetics
   b. behavioural genetics
   c. biology
   d. physiology

3. Twin studies suggest that environment is a stronger factor than heredity in shaping IQ differences. (true/false)

4. Jensen and Herrnstein and Murray maintain that the black–white IQ gap is due primarily to _____ .
   a. genetics.
   b. environment.
   c. discrimination.
   d. racism.

Answers: 1. true 2. b 3. false 4. a

IQ and mixed ancestry. Among the earliest such research was a study by Witty and Jenkins (1936), who reported no relationship between test scores and white ancestry as reported by blacks. Other studies showed that blacks whose blood types were identical to those most commonly found in whites did not score higher than blacks with other blood types (Loehlin, Vandenberg, & Osborne, 1973; Scarr, Pakstis, Katz, & Barker, 1977).

At the end of World War II, American soldiers stationed in Germany, both black and white, fathered thousands of children with German women. Fifteen years later, Eyeferth (1961) randomly selected samples of these children (183 with black fathers and 83 with white fathers). The mean IQs of the two groups were virtually identical. Having a white father conferred no measurable IQ advantage at all.

MODULE 7H EMOTIONAL INTELLIGENCE

LO 7.26 Define and explain *emotional intelligence.*

Daniel Goleman (1995) claims that success in life is more markedly influenced by emotional intelligence than by IQ. **Emotional intelligence** is the ability to apply knowledge about emotions to everyday life (Salovey & Pizarro, 2003). **[LO 7.26]** Two leading researchers in the field, Peter Salovey and David Pizarro, argue that emotional intelligence is just as important to many important outcome variables, including how we fare in our chosen careers, as the kind of intelligence that is measured by IQ tests. Research supports this view, showing that emotional intelligence is unrelated to IQ scores (Lam & Kirby, 2002; Van der Zee, Thijs, & Schakel, 2002). At the same time, emotional intelligence is correlated with both academic and social success (Rozell, Pettijohn, & Parker, 2002; Mayer, Roberts, & Barsdale, 2008).

PERSONAL COMPONENTS OF EMOTIONAL INTELLIGENCE

What are the personal components of emotional intelligence?

The foundation of emotional intelligence is self-knowledge. **[LO 7.26]** It involves an awareness of emotions, an ability to manage those emotions, and self-motivation.

©Ghislain & Marie David de Lossy/Cultura/Getty Images

A person with high emotional intelligence shows empathy—recognizing non-verbal signals from others and making appropriate responses. Those who are high in emotional intelligence often emerge as leaders. Successful leaders can empathize with their followers, understand their needs and wants.

TRY IT

Find Your EQ

Emotional intelligence may be just as important to success in your chosen career as your actual job skills. Take this short test to assess your EQ. Check one response for each statement.

1. I am always aware of even subtle feelings as I have them.

   ____ Always ____ Usually ____ Sometimes ____ Rarely ____ Never

2. I can delay gratification in pursuit of my goals instead of getting carried away by impulse.

   ____ Always ____ Usually ____ Sometimes ____ Rarely ____ Never

3. Instead of giving up in the face of setbacks or disappointments, I stay hopeful and optimistic.

   ____ Always ____ Usually ____ Sometimes ____ Rarely ____ Never

4. My keen sense of others' feelings makes me compassionate about their plight.

   ____ Always ____ Usually ____ Sometimes ____ Rarely ____ Never

5. I can sense the pulse of a group or relationship and state unspoken feelings.

   ____ Always ____ Usually ____ Sometimes ____ Rarely ____ Never

6. I can soothe or contain distressing feelings so that they don't keep me from doing the things I need to do.

   ____ Always ____ Usually ____ Sometimes ____ Rarely ____ Never

Score your responses as follows: Always = 4 points, Usually = 3 points, Sometimes = 2 points, Rarely = 1 point, Never = 0 points. The closer your total number of points is to 24, the higher your EQ probably is.

REMEMBER IT

Emotional Intelligence

1. Identify the category in which each component of emotional intelligence belongs.

   _____ 1) empathy

   _____ 2) awareness of one's own emotions

   _____ 3) self-motivation

   _____ 4) ability to handle relationships
   a. personal
   b. interpersonal

Answers: 1(1). b (2). a (3). a (4). b

Awareness of our own emotions—recognizing and acknowledging feelings as they happen—is at the very heart of emotional intelligence. It means being aware not only of our moods, but of thoughts about those moods as well. Those who are able to monitor their feelings as they arise are more likely to be able to manage them rather than be ruled by them.

Managing emotions does not mean suppressing them, any more than it means giving free rein to every feeling and impulse. To manage emotions is to express them in an appropriate manner and not let them run out of control. You manage your emotions when you do something to cheer yourself up, soothe your own hurts, reassure yourself, or otherwise temper an inappropriate or out-of-control emotion.

Self-motivation refers to a strength of emotional self-control that enables a person to get moving and pursue worthy goals, persist at tasks even when frustrated, and resist the temptation to act on impulse.

The ability to postpone immediate gratification and to persist in working toward some greater future gain is most closely related to success—whether one is trying to build a business, get a college degree, or even stay on a diet.

INTERPERSONAL COMPONENTS OF EMOTIONAL INTELLIGENCE

What are the interpersonal components of emotional intelligence?

The interpersonal aspects of emotional intelligence are empathy and the ability to handle relationships. **[LO 7.26]** The ability to empathize—to recognize and understand the motives and emotions of others—is the cornerstone of successful interpersonal relations. Empathy appears to be a higher level of development that springs from self-awareness. If we have no insight into our own emotions, it is unlikely that we will develop sensitivity and understanding of the emotions of others.

emotional intelligence: A type of intelligence that includes an awareness of—and an ability to manage—one's own emotions, as well as the ability to motivate oneself, to empathize, and to handle relationships successfully.

Another of the interpersonal components is the capacity to manage relationships. For most people, hardly anything in life is more important than their relationships—intimate love relationships; family, professional, and work relationships; and relationships with friends. Without rewarding relationships, life would be lonely indeed. Some people are inept at forming and handling mutually satisfying relationships; others seem to be masters of the art. To effectively manage the emotional give and take involved in social relationships, we have to be able to manage our own feelings and be sensitive to those of others.

Optimism also appears to be a component of emotional intelligence. [LO 7.26] People who are optimistic have a "strong expectation in general [that] things will turn out all right in life" (p. 88). The most significant aspect of optimism in the context of emotional intelligence is the way in which optimists explain their successes and failures. When optimists fail, they attribute their failure to something in the situation that can be changed. Thus, they believe that by trying harder, they can succeed the next time. But when pessimists fail, they blame themselves and attribute their failure to some personal characteristic or flaw that cannot be changed.

To find out what your emotional intelligence score (emotional quotient, or EQ) might be, complete the *Try It*.

APPLY IT

Building a Powerful Vocabulary

Vocabulary is a powerful tool. Among children, those with high vocabularies early in life develop stronger literacy skills than those with poor vocabularies, and this advantage persists well into development (Lee, 2011). Researchers often find that vocabulary tests are strongly correlated with IQ scores (Sattler & Dumont, 2004). Of all the cognitive skills humans possess, none is more important for clarity of thinking and academic success than vocabulary. How, then, can you build a more powerful vocabulary? The best way is to realize that almost all words belong to larger networks of meaning, and to understand that your mind is already geared toward organizing information in terms of meaning. Thus, with a little effort, you can greatly increase your vocabulary by supporting the kind of learning your brain is trying to do. Here are a few techniques you can apply.

- *Learn to think analytically about words you already know and relate new words to them.* What do the words *antiseptic* and *septic tank* have in common? You use *antiseptic* to prevent bacterial infection of a wound; a *septic tank* is used for removing harmful bacteria from water containing human waste. A logical conclusion would be that *septic* has something to do with bacteria. Knowing this, what do you think a

doctor means when she says that a patient is suffering from *sepsis*? By linking *sepsis* to *septic tank* and *antiseptic*, you can guess she is referring to some kind of bacterial infection.

- *Be aware of word connections that may be hidden by spelling differences.* You may know that both *Caesar* and *czar* refer to some kind of ruler or leader. But you may not know that they are the same word, spoken or spelled somewhat differently in ancient Rome (*Caesar*) and in Russia (*czar*). Now, if you are taking a history class in which you learn about Kaiser Wilhelm, who led Germany during World War I, thinking analytically about his title might help you realize that it is exactly the same word as *Caesar* and *czar*, with a German spelling. Here's another example: Can you guess something about the location and climate of the nation of *Ecuador* by relating its name to a word that sounds very similar but differs slightly in spelling? (Answer: Equator)

- *Use your knowledge of word parts to actively seek out new words.* Don't learn new words one at a time. Instead be on the lookout for "word families"—root words and prefixes and suffixes. Here is one important root word: *spect*, which means "look," "look at," "watch,"

and "see." And spect appears in dozens of different words, such as *inspect*. What do you do when you *inspect* something? You look closely at it. Equipped with this knowledge, other *spect* words may come to mind, along with an entirely new way of thinking about their meanings: *spectacular*, *spectator*, *spectacle*, *perspective*, *prospect*, *respect*, *retrospect*, *suspect*, and so on. The word *circumspect* may be new to you. Look it up in a dictionary, and think about how the literal meaning of the word ("look around") relates to the way this word is frequently used.

And when you hear about the famous psychologist Wilhelm Wundt, who used a method of investigation called *introspection*, do you think it would now be easier to understand and remember that research method if you first thought about the *spect* part of the word? Probably so. (And if you want to check your answer go online to look up this word, or check Chapter 1).

A strong vocabulary based on root words and prefixes and suffixes will yield the word power that will "literally" profit you in many ways. If you put this *Apply It* into practice, you will be able to build a powerful vocabulary.

THINKING CRITICALLY

Evaluation

Which of the theories of intelligence best fits your notion of intelligence? Why?

Point/Counterpoint

Prepare an argument supporting each of the following positions:

a. Intelligence tests should be used in schools.

b. Intelligence tests should not be used in schools.

Psychology in Your Life

Give several examples of how tools of thinking (imagery and concepts) and problem-solving strategies (algorithms and heuristics) can be applied in your educational and personal life.

MyPsychLab go to mypsychlab (access code required) to find web resources for your text that supplement the material in chapter 7.

SUMMARY & REVIEW

 COGNITION

What is imagery?
Imagery is the ability to represent or picture a sensory experience in our mind.

What are concepts, and how are they formed?
Concepts are categories that allow us to quickly comprehend information. Rules and definitions determine formal concepts, whereas natural concepts arise out of everyday experiences. We also match information with prototypes, or examples, that include most or all of the features associated with the concepts they represent. Exemplars are examples of concepts with which we have the most familiarity.

What are the roles of systematic processes, heuristics, framing, intuition, and anchoring in decision making?
Systematic processes involve considering all possible options prior to making a decision. Sometimes we use priorities to eliminate some of these options to speed up the decision-making process. By contrast, heuristics, or "rules of thumb," allow us to make decisions quickly, with little effort. Framing causes us to weigh a decision's gains and losses, and intuition relies on "gut feelings." Anchoring on one piece of information rather than considering all of the factors that are relevant to a decision may cause distortions in thinking.

What are three problem-solving techniques, and how are they used?
We use trial and error, heuristics, and algorithms to achieve a desired goal.

What are the two major impediments to problem solving?
Two major impediments to problem solving are functional fixedness, which is the failure to use familiar objects in novel ways to solve problems, and mental set, which is the tendency to apply familiar problem-solving strategies before carefully considering the special requirements of the problem.

 CREATIVITY: UNIQUE AND USEFUL PRODUCTIONS

What is creativity, and what tests have been designed to measure it?
Creativity is the ability to produce original, appropriate, and valuable ideas and/or solutions to problems. Two tests used to measure creativity are divergent-thinking tests and the Remote Associates Test.

7C LANGUAGE

What are the five important components of language?
The five important components of language are (1) phonemes, the smallest units of sound in a spoken language; (2) morphemes, the smallest units of meaning; (3) syntax, grammatical rules for arranging and combining words to form phrases and sentences; (4) semantics, the meaning derived from phonemes, morphemes, words, and sentences; and (5) pragmatics, the characteristics of spoken language that help to convey the social meaning.

How do learning theory and the nativist position explain the acquisition of language?
Learning theory focuses on external information that is provided by parents, friends, media, and so on, as sources of information from which we develop our knowledge of language. Nativists believe that the mechanisms for acquiring language are innate.

How does language in trained chimpanzees differ from human language?
Chimpanzees do not have a vocal tract adapted to human speech, and their communication using sign language or symbols consists of constructions strung together rather than sentences.

What is the linguistic relativity hypothesis, and is it supported by research?
The linguistic relativity hypothesis suggests that language plays a significant role in determining the nature of a person's thoughts. Research does not support the idea that language determines what we think, but rather that language and thought are related.

7D THE NATURE OF INTELLIGENCE

What factors underlie intelligence, according to Spearman, Thurstone, and Guilford?
Spearman believed that intelligence is composed of a general ability (*g* factor), which underlies all intellectual functions, and a number of specific abilities (*s* factors). Thurstone points to seven primary mental abilities, which, singly or in combination, are involved in all intellectual activities. Guilford's model of the structure of intellect consists of 180 different intellectual abilities that involve all the possible combinations of the three dimensions of intellect—mental operations, contents, and products.

What types of intelligence did Gardner and Sternberg identify?
Gardner proposed eight independent forms of intelligence, which he called frames of mind. Sternberg introduced the triarchic theory of intelligence.

 MEASURING INTELLIGENCE

What was Binet's major contribution to psychology?
Binet produced an assessment tool to measure intelligence.

What does IQ mean, and how was it originally calculated?
IQ stands for *intelligence quotient*, an index of intelligence originally derived by dividing a person's mental age by his or her chronological age and then multiplying by 100.

What is the Stanford–Binet Intelligence Scale?
The Stanford–Binet Intelligence Scale is a highly regarded individual intelligence test for those aged 2 to 23. It has been revised several times since Lewis Terman's original, extensive adaptation of the Binet–Simon Intelligence Scale.

What did Wechsler's tests provide that the Stanford—Binet did not?
David Wechsler developed the first successful individual intelligence test for adults, the Wechsler Adult Intelligence Scale (WAIS-IV). His tests for adults, children, and preschoolers yield separate verbal and performance (non-verbal) IQ scores as well as an overall IQ score.

What is meant by the terms reliability, validity, and standardization?
Reliability is the ability of a test to yield nearly the same score each time a person takes the test or an alternative form of the test. *Validity* is the power of a test to measure what it is intended to measure. *Standardization* refers to prescribed procedures for administering a test and to established norms that provide a means of evaluating test scores.

 THE RANGE OF INTELLIGENCE

What are the ranges of IQ scores that are considered average, superior, and in the range of mental disability?
About 50 percent of all IQ scores fall into the average range from 90 to 110; 2 percent of the scores are above 130, which is considered superior; and 2 percent are below 70, in the range of mental disability.

According to the Terman study, how do gifted people differ from the general population?
Terman's longitudinal study revealed that, in general, gifted people enjoy better physical and mental health and are more successful than their less gifted counterparts.

What two criteria must a person meet to be classified as having an intellectual disability?
Intellectual disabilities are present when individuals show deficits in intellectual functioning (scores on IQ test) and in adaptive functioning.

 THE IQ CONTROVERSY: BRAINY DISPUTE

What do intelligence tests predict well?
IQ tests are good predictors of success in school and often predict success in other domains such as occupational success, but they are less likely to predict as well when social class and level of education are controlled.

What are some of the abuses of intelligence tests?
Abuses occur when IQ tests are the only criterion for judging people rather than considering motivation or other related variables. Many people maintain that IQ tests are biased in favour of the urban middle or upper class.

How does the nature—nurture controversy apply to intelligence?
The nature—nurture controversy in intelligence refers to the debate over whether intelligence is primarily the result of heredity or environment.

What is behavioural genetics, and what are the primary methods used in the field today?
Behavioural genetics is the field that investigates the relative effects of heredity and environment on behaviour and ability. The twin study method and the adoption method are the primary methods used.

How do twin studies support the view that intelligence is inherited?
When identical twins have been separated at birth and raised apart and are found to have strikingly similar traits, it is assumed that heredity has been a major contributor. When these same twins differ on a given trait, the influence of the environment is thought to be greater.

What kinds of evidence suggest that IQ is changeable rather than fixed?
Several adoption studies have revealed that when infants from disadvantaged environments are adopted by middle- and upper-middle-class parents, their IQ scores are about 15 points higher on average than they would otherwise be expected to be. Furthermore, IQ scores have been rising steadily over the past 50 years in many countries, including Canada and the United States, presumably because of increases in the standard of living and educational opportunities.

What are Jensen's and Herrnstein and Murray's controversial views on race and IQ?
These researchers assert that the black–white IQ gap is due to genetic differences between the races that are too strong to be changed significantly through environmental intervention.

7H EMOTIONAL INTELLIGENCE

What are the personal components of emotional intelligence?
The personal components are an awareness of and ability to control one's own emotions and the ability to motivate oneself.

What are the interpersonal components of emotional intelligence?
The interpersonal components are empathy and the ability to handle relationships.

COGNITION, LANGUAGE, AND INTELLIGENCE

MODULE **7A** COGNITION

Cognition: Mental processes involved in acquiring knowledge.

Tools of Thinking

Imagery: Mental representation of a sensory experience; perceiving and imaging may use some of the same mental processes.

Concept: A group of objects, people, or events that share common attributes.

Prototype: An example that embodies the most typical features of a particular concept.

Exemplars: Individual instances of a concept that a person has stored in memory from his or her experience.

Decision making: The process of considering alternatives and choosing among them

Approaches to Decision Making

Systematic decision making: Making a decision after carefully considering all possible alternatives.

Elimination by aspects: Factors on which alternatives are to be evaluated are identified and ordered from most to least important; alternatives are eliminated in order from the one that satisfies most factors to the one satisfying least.

Heuristics: Rules of thumb that are derived from experience;. there is no guarantee of their accuracy or usefulness.

Availability heuristic: Information that comes easily to mind determines the decision that is made.

Representativeness heuristic: The decision is based on how closely an object or situation resembles or matches an existing prototype.

Recognition heuristic: A rapid decision based on recognition of one of the alternatives.

Framing: Potential gains and losses associated with alternatives are emphasized and influence the decision.

Intuition: Decisions are motivated by "gut feelings".

Anchoring: Decisions are influenced by focusing on a single factor, thereby overestimating its importance.

Problem-Solving Methods

Trial and error: One solution after another is tried until a workable solution is found.

Algorithm: A systematic, step-by-step procedure that guarantees a solution to a problem if the algorithm is appropriate and executed properly.

Means–end analysis: A heuristic whereby the current position is compared with the desired goal, and a series of steps are formulated to reach the goal.

Working backward: A heuristic whereby the steps needed to solve a problem are discovered by defining the goal and working backward to the current position.

Barriers to Problem Solving

Functional fixedness: Viewing objects only in terms of their usual functions.

Mental set: Applying familiar strategies without considering other approaches.

MODULE **7B** CREATIVITY

Creativity: The ability to produce original, appropriate, and valuable ideas. There is a modest correlation between creativity and intelligence.

Divergent thinking: Producing multiple ideas, answers, or solutions to a problem as opposed to a single response.

MODULE **7C** LANGUAGE

Language: A form of communication using a system of symbols.

Psycholinguistics

Psycholinguistics is the study of how language is acquired, produced, and used, and how the sounds and symbols of language are translated into meaning.

Components of Language

Phonemes: Smallest units of sound

Morphemes: Smallest units of meaning

Syntax: Grammatical rules for arranging words to form phrases and sentences

Semantics: Grammatical rules and pragmatics.

Pragmatics: Characteristics of spoken language that help you decipher the social meaning of utterances

Language Development

Cooing (making vowel sounds, e.g., "oo"): 2–4 months of age

Babbling (vocalization of phonemes, e.g., "mama"): Before 6 months

Holophrases: Single words, where one word has lots of meaning

Overextension: Applying a word to a broader range of objects than is appropriate; around 12 months

Underextension: Applying a word to a restricted range of subjects; around 12 months

Two-word phrases: 18–20 months

Telegraphic speech: Short sentences containing only essential words; by 3 years

Overregularization: Inappropriately applying rules for forming plurals and past tenses to irregular nouns and verbs

Perspectives on Language Learning

Learning theories: Language is learned through reinforcement (Skinner, 1957) and imitation (Bandura, 1977b)

Nativist theories: Language ability is largely innate (Chomsky, 1957)

Interactionist theories: Both learning and inborn capacity are important for acquiring language (Chapman, 2000)

MODULE 7D — THE NATURE OF INTELLIGENCE

Intelligence: The ability to acquire knowledge, to think effectively, and to deal adequately with one's environment.

Theories of Intelligence

Spearman: A general intellectual ability, *g* factor, underlies mental abilities.

Thurstone: Seven primary mental abilities are involved in all intellectual activities—verbal comprehension, word fluency, number facility, spatial visualization, associative memory, perceptual speed, and reasoning.

Guilford: The structure of intellect consists of 180 intellectual abilities with 3 dimensions of intellect—mental operations, contents, products.

Gardner's theory of multiple intelligences: Includes 8 frames of mind—linguistic, logical-naturalistic, mathematical, musical, bodily-kinesthetic, spatial, interpersonal, intrapersonal.

Sternberg's triarchic theory of intelligence: Comprises **componential, experiential,** and **contextual ability.**

MODULE 7E — MEASURING INTELLIGENCE

Binet–Simon Intelligence Scale (1905): First test of intelligence; **mental age** is determined by the ability to solve problems at the level of a normal child at that chronological age.

Stanford–Binet Intelligence Scale (1916): Revision of the Binet–Simon Scale, which used Stern's (1914) formula to calculate the intelligence quotient (IQ) [(mental age/chronological age) × 100].

Wechsler (1939): Developed the first intelligence test for adults, now called Wechsler Adult Intelligence Scale.

A good test must be
1. **reliable** (yielding nearly the same score each time a person takes it);
2. **valid** (measuring what it is supposed to measure); and
3. **standardized** (having a set procedure for administering and scoring).

MODULE 7F — THE RANGE OF INTELLIGENCE

Norms: Test scores of a large number of people.

IQ: A deviation score calculated by comparing a person's score with scores of others of the same age; IQ scores are distributed in a normal curve with a mean of 100; about 68 percent of IQ scores are between 85 and 115, and 95 percent are between 70 and 130.

Intellectual disability: An IQ below the norm and severely deficient functioning for one's age; 2 or more standard deviations.

Giftedness: IQ above 130; exceptionally creative, or excelling in the visual or performing arts.

Terman's longitudinal study: Terman found that most gifted people (IQs above 130) had above-average physical ability, mental health, and occupational success.

MODULE 7G — THE IQ CONTROVERSY

Culture-fair intelligence tests (e.g., the Raven Standard Progressive Matrices Test): Designed to measure intelligence while minimizing cultural biases.

Nature–nurture controversy: The debate over whether intelligence and other traits are primarily the result of heredity or environment.

Behavioural genetics: Investigates the relative effects of heredity (nature) and environment (nurture) on behaviour and ability.

Heritability is an index of the degree to which a trait is due to heredity. Studies of twins suggest that heritability of IQ is between .52 and .70. Adopted children have IQs closer to their biological than to their adoptive parents' IQs.

Effects of environment are supported by the finding that IQs have been increasing in industrialized countries for the past 50 years (called the *Flynn effect*) and that enriched environments increase IQ.

MODULE 7H — EMOTIONAL INTELLIGENCE

Emotional intelligence is the ability to apply knowledge about emotions to everyday life.

8

The dense, dark jungle in Uganda, Africa, is lush with a rich variety of exotic plant life and an abundance of animal species. But civil war disturbed the peace and beauty of Uganda for many years, and brutal massacres claimed the lives of many men, women, and children.

In 1991, a woman from a nearby village spotted a rare sight among a tribe of monkeys at the edge of the jungle. She saw a larger creature unlike the other monkeys, yet acting very much like them. Intrigued, she studied the creature more closely and was amazed to discover that the strange creature was a human child.

The woman called upon other villagers to help her rescue this child. When the villagers tried to capture the child, he was terrified and threw sticks at his would-be captors. Not only did the child resist capture, but the Vervet monkeys also tried to thwart the villagers. Eventually, the child was captured and taken to an orphanage. There, he was identified as John Ssabunnya, a child whose mother was murdered and whose father had died during the civil unrest in Uganda. Left alone at three years of age, John had wandered into the jungle where he was accepted by a tribe of Vervet monkeys who "adopted" and cared for him for about three years. When he was captured, he was small for his age and unable to talk. The caretakers and other children at the orphanage found him odd because he displayed unusual mannerisms that were more like those of monkeys than humans. With extensive assistance, John eventually acquired language and appropriate human behaviours. He became a member of a youth choir and travelled beyond that part of the world.

Developmental psychologists are intrigued by cases like John's because they show the profound effect that extreme environmental conditions can have on the course of human development.

©Zurijeta/Shutterstock

DEVELOPMENT

MODULE 8A DEVELOPMENTAL PSYCHOLOGY: BASIC ISSUES AND METHODOLOGY

LO 8.1   Identify three key controversial issues in developmental psychology.

LO 8.2   Understand how each of the two opposing views in each of the controversial issues explain development.

LO 8.3   Compare and contrast the strengths and weaknesses of longitudinal and cross-sectional research designs.

Developmental psychology is the study of how we grow, develop, and change throughout the lifespan. Some developmental psychologists specialize in a particular age group on the continuum from infancy, childhood, and adolescence through early, middle, and late adulthood to the end of the lifespan. Others concentrate on a specific area of interest such as physical development, language, social or cognitive development, or moral development. Developmental psychology, therefore, is a large field of study.

CONTROVERSIAL ISSUES IN DEVELOPMENTAL PSYCHOLOGY

Developmental psychologists must consider several controversial issues as they pursue their work.

1. *To what degree do heredity and environment influence development?* This is the **nature–nurture controversy** (see also Chapter 7). **[LO 8.1]** Some take the view that our abilities are determined almost exclusively by our heredity and are transmitted to us through our genes. Others maintain that our environment—the circumstances in which we are raised—determines what we become. Today the question is not whether nature or nurture affects development, but how much each affects various aspects of development. **[LO 8.2]**

2. *Is development continuous or does it occur in stages?* This is an important question in developmental psychology.

developmental psychology: The study of how humans grow, develop, and change throughout the lifespan.

nature–nurture controversy: The debate concerning the relative influences of heredity and environment on development.

longitudinal study: A type of developmental study in which the same group of individuals is followed and measured at different ages.

cross-sectional study: A type of developmental study in which researchers compare groups of individuals of different ages with respect to certain characteristics to determine age-related differences.

genes: Within the chromosomes, the segments of DNA that are the basic units for the transmission of hereditary traits.

chromosomes: Rod-shaped structures, found in the nuclei of body cells, that contain all the genes and carry all the hereditary information.

[LO 8.1] To understand how developmentalists think about this question, consider what happens as children become taller. Children change *quantitatively* as they grow taller. In other words, the characteristic of height is the same at all ages. Older children simply have more of it than those who are younger. However, changes in other developmental variables—logical thinking, for example—occur in stages. Such changes are *qualitative* in nature. In other words, the logic of a 10-year-old is completely different from that of a three-year-old. The older child doesn't just have more logic; he thinks in an entirely different way. Developmentalists ask whether other aspects of development are best understood in terms of gradual, continuous, cumulative change or in spurts in the form of stages, with one stage *qualitatively* different from the next. **[LO 8.2]**

3. *To what extent are personal characteristics stable over time?* Developmentalists also ask whether certain personal traits, such as intelligence, aggression, and aspects of temperament, tend to be stable or changeable over time. **[LOs 8.1 & 8.2]**

APPROACHES TO STUDYING DEVELOPMENTAL CHANGE

What are two types of studies that developmental psychologists use to investigate age-related changes?

Developmental psychologists use longitudinal and cross-sectional studies to investigate age-related changes. In a **longitudinal study**, the same group of participants is followed and measured at different ages, over a period of years, sometimes over their lifespan. The benefits of this design include being able to map the stability or variability of all kinds of characteristics through all the developmental phases. There are some drawbacks to the longitudinal study. It is time-consuming and expensive, and people may drop out of the study, possibly leaving the researcher with a biased sample. **[LO 8.3]**

A **cross-sectional study** is a less expensive and less time-consuming method in which researchers compare groups of different ages, at one point in time, with respect to various characteristics to determine age-related differences. For example, a researcher may compare two-year-olds, four-year-olds, and six-year-olds in one study. But in a cross-sectional study, differences found in age groups are based on group averages, and so this approach cannot provide answers to some questions. **[LO 8.3]** For example, it cannot be used to determine whether the temperament of individuals is stable over time—an answer that could be found using a longitudinal design. Moreover, there may be certain relevant differences among groups that have less to do with ages than with the eras in which the participants grew up. Consider, for example, the experiences of your great-grandparents when they were 16 versus you, when you were 16. Many of your great-grandparents would not have had exposure to any of the technologies you use every day, and they would have experienced different world events, all of which could influence variables that developmental researchers might study. These kinds of differences, called *cohort differences*, are important variables for developmentalists to consider when designing or interpreting cross-sectional research. Figure 8.1 compares the longitudinal and cross-sectional studies.

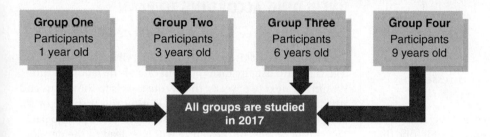

Longitudinal Study
The same group of participants is studied on several occasions over an extended period of time to determine age changes on particular characteristics.

First Study 2009	Second Study 2011	Third Study 2014	Fourth Study 2017
Participants 1 year old	Same participants at 3 years	Same participants at 6 years	Same participants at 9 years

The same group is studied over a period of 8 years.

Cross-Sectional Study
Group of participants of different ages are studied at one point in time and compared on particular characteristics.

Group One	Group Two	Group Three	Group Four
Participants 1 year old	Participants 3 years old	Participants 6 years old	Participants 9 years old

All groups are studied in 2017

FIGURE 8.1

A Comparison of Longitudinal and Cross-Sectional Studies

To study age-related changes using a longitudinal study, researchers examine the same group of individuals over an extended period of time. When using a cross-sectional study, researchers examine and compare groups of different ages at one point in time.

REMEMBER IT

Developmental Psychology

1. Developmental psychologists study changes that happen during
   a. childhood.
   c. old age.
   b. adulthood.
   d. the entire lifespan.

2. Identify the characteristics of cross-sectional studies, with the letter *c*, and the characteristics of longitudinal studies, with the letter *l*.

   _____ 1) Groups of different ages are tested at the same time.

   _____ 2) A single group is studied at different times.

   _____ 3) The method that typically costs less.

   _____ 4) The method that can reveal individual change over time.

   _____ 5) Differences may be due to factors other than development, such as the era in which participants grew up.

Answers: 1. d 2 (1). c (2). l (3). c (4). l (5). c

MODULE 8B HEREDITY AND PRENATAL DEVELOPMENT

LO 8.4 Explain how hereditary traits are transmitted.

LO 8.5 Define *dominant* and *recessive genes* and describe how they function.

LO 8.6 List the three stages of prenatal development and identify critical developments at each stage.

LO 8.7 Identify teratogens and explain their impact on development.

Development begins before birth. We will trace its course from the beginning.

THE MECHANISM OF HEREDITY: GENES AND CHROMOSOMES

How are hereditary traits transmitted?

Genes, the biological blueprints that determine and direct the transmission of all our hereditary traits, are segments of DNA located on each of the rod-shaped structures called **chromosomes** found in the nuclei of the body cells. **[LO 8.4]** Normal body cells, with two exceptions, have 23 pairs of chromosomes (so that there are 46 chromosomes in total). The two exceptions are the sperm cells and the mature egg cells, each of which has 23 single chromosomes. At conception, the sperm adds its 23 single chromosomes to the 23 of the egg. This union forms a single cell called a **zygote**, which has the full 46 chromosomes (23 pairs), which in turn contain about 30 000 genes—the genetic material needed to make a human being.

Twenty-two of the 23 pairs of chromosomes are matching pairs, called *autosomes*. Each member of these pairs carries genes for particular physical and mental traits. The chromosomes in the 23rd pair are called **sex chromosomes** because they carry the genes that determine a person's sex, primary and secondary sex characteristics, and other sex-linked traits such as red-green colour blindness, male pattern baldness, and hemophilia.

The sex chromosomes of females consist of two X chromosomes (XX); males have an X chromosome and a Y chromosome (XY). Because the egg cell always contains an X chromosome, the sex of a child depends on whether the egg is fertilized by a sperm carrying an X chromosome, which produces a female, or a sperm carrying a Y chromosome, which produces a male. Half of a male's sperm cells carry an X chromosome, and half carry a Y. Consequently, the chances of conceiving a male or a female are about equal.

Dominant and Recessive Genes: Dominants Call the Shots

When are dominant or recessive genes expressed in a person?

When two different genes are transmitted for the same trait, one of the genes is usually a **dominant gene**—that is, one that causes the dominant trait to be expressed in the individual. **[LO 8.5]** The gene for brown hair, for instance, is dominant over the gene for blond hair. An individual having one gene for brown hair and one gene for blond hair will have brown hair. And of course, two dominant genes will produce brown hair

(see Figure 8.2). The gene for blond hair is *recessive*. A **recessive gene** will be expressed if it is paired with another recessive gene. **[LO 8.5]** Blond-haired people have two recessive genes for blond hair. A recessive gene will not be expressed if it is paired with a dominant gene. Yet a person with such a pair can pass either the recessive gene or the dominant gene along to his or her offspring.

Many traits, such as height, involve several genes and are referred to as *polygenic*. Most polygenic traits do not involve dominant and recessive genes. Instead, several genes work together to produce such a trait. Many polygenic traits are also *multifactorial*; that is, they are influenced by both heredity and environment. For example, an individual's adult height is influenced by several genes, but environmental factors present during childhood (such as nutrition) also influence it.

THE STAGES OF PRENATAL DEVELOPMENT: UNFOLDING ACCORDING TO PLAN

What are the three stages of prenatal development?

Conception occurs the moment a sperm cell fertilizes the ovum (egg cell), and usually takes place in one of the fallopian tubes. Within the next two weeks, the zygote travels to the uterus and attaches itself to the uterine wall. During the first five or six days, the zygote engages in cell division and produces two parts. The cluster of cells in the centre will later lead to the development of the fetus, while the complex outside cell mass becomes the placenta and supporting structures. At the end of this first stage of **prenatal** development, called the *period of the zygote*, two weeks have passed and the zygote is only the size of the period at the end of this sentence. **[LO 8.6]**

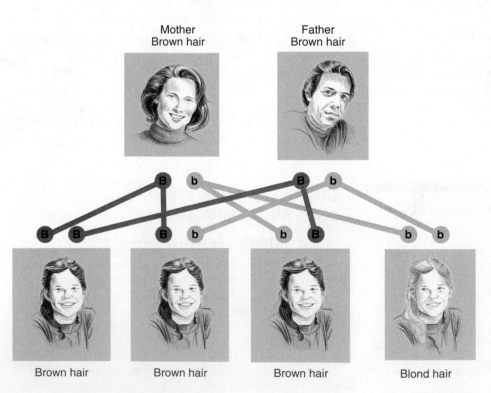

Mother
Brown hair

Father
Brown hair

Brown hair   Brown hair   Brown hair   Blond hair

FIGURE 8.2

Gene Transmission for Hair Colour

This figure shows all the possible combinations in children when both parents carry a gene for brown hair (B) and a gene for blond hair (b). The chance of their having a blond-haired child (bb) or a brown-haired child (BB) is 25 percent in each case. There is a 50 percent chance of having a brown-haired child who carries both the dominant gene (B) and the recessive gene (b).

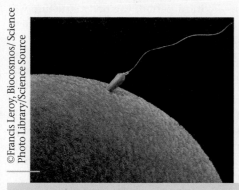
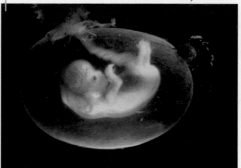
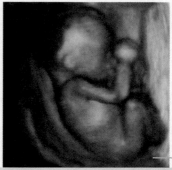

© Dr. G. Moscoso/Science Photo Library/Science Source

©Francis Leroy, Biocosmos/Science Photo Library/Science Source

©Science Photo Library/Science Source

This sequence of photos shows the fertilization of an egg by a sperm (left), an embryo at 7 weeks (middle), and a fetus at 22 weeks (right).

TABLE 8.1   Stages of Prenatal Development

Stage	Time after Conception	Major Activities of the Stage
Period of the zygote	1 to 2 weeks	Zygote attaches to the uterine lining. At 2 weeks, zygote is the size of the period at the end of this sentence.
Period of the embryo	3 to 8 weeks	Major systems, organs, and structures of the body develop. Period ends when first bone cells appear. At 8 weeks, embryo is about 2.5 cm long and weighs about 4 g.
Period of the fetus	9 weeks to birth (38 weeks)	Rapid growth and further development of the body structures, organs, and systems.

The second stage, the *embryonic stage*, is when the major systems, organs, and structures of the body develop. **[LO 8.6]** In general, the pattern of development progresses from head to toe, known as *cephalocaudal development*, and from the trunk of the body to the extremities, known as *proximodistal development*. Lasting from week 3 through week 8, this period ends when the first bone cells form. Though about 2.5 centimetres long and weighing about 4 grams, the **embryo** already has enough rudimentary features that it can be recognized as a human embryo.

The final stage, the stage of the **fetus** (the *fetal stage*), lasts from the end of the second month until birth. **[LO 8.6]** It is a time of rapid growth and further development of the structures, organs, and systems of the body. Table 8.1 describes the characteristics of each stage of prenatal development.

Multiple Births: More Than One at a Time

Most multiple births are those of twins. In the case of **identical (monozygotic) twins**, one egg is fertilized by one sperm but the zygote splits and develops into two embryos with identical genetic codes. Thus, identical twins are always of the same sex. This splitting of the zygote seems to be a chance occurrence, accounting for about 4 in 1000 births. One of the most famous cases of multiple births occurred in 1934 with the birth of the Dionne quintuplets in Corbeil, a few kilometres outside North Bay, Ontario. Although multiple births are now more common, the Dionne quints were unique even by modern standards. Their parents hadn't used fertility drugs, and the five sisters were identical, having developed from a single fertilized egg.

Fraternal (dizygotic) twins develop when two eggs are released during ovulation and are fertilized by two different sperm. The two zygotes develop into two siblings who are no

zygote: The first two weeks of development.

sex chromosomes: The 23rd pair of chromosomes, which carries the genes that determine one's sex and primary and secondary sex characteristics.

dominant gene: The gene that is expressed in the individual.

recessive gene: A gene that will not be expressed if paired with a dominant gene, but will be expressed if paired with another recessive gene.

prenatal: The stage of development between conception and birth.

embryo: The developing organism during the period (week 3 through week 8) when the major systems, organs, and structures of the body develop.

fetus: The developing organism during the period (week 9 until birth) when rapid growth and further development of the structures, organs, and systems of the body take place.

identical (monozygotic) twins: Twins with exactly the same genes, who develop after one egg is fertilized by one sperm and the zygote splits into two parts.

fraternal (dizygotic) twins: Twins, no more alike genetically than ordinary siblings, who develop after two eggs are released during ovulation and are fertilized by two different sperm.

more alike genetically than ordinary brothers and sisters. The likelihood of fraternal twins is greater if there is a family history of multiple births, if the woman is between 35 and 40, and if she has recently stopped taking birth control pills.

Fertility drugs also often cause the release of more than one egg, and some fertility procedures involve the implantation of multiple fertilized eggs. When multiple eggs are released during ovulation, when one or more eggs split before or after fertilization, when multiple eggs are implanted, or when these events occur in combination, multiple births ranging from twins to even octuplets can result.

NEGATIVE INFLUENCES ON PRENATAL DEVELOPMENT: SABOTAGING NATURE'S PLAN

What are some negative influences on prenatal development, and when is their impact greatest?

Teratogens are agents in the prenatal environment that can cause birth defects and other problems. **[LO 8.7]** The damage done by a teratogen depends on its intensity and on when it is present during prenatal development. Maternal illness, for one, can interfere with the process. A chronic condition such as diabetes, for example, can cause problems that may include intellectual deficits or acceleration of fetal growth (D. Murray, 2009). When the mother suffers from a viral disease such as rubella, chicken pox, or HIV, she may deliver an infant with physical and behavioural abnormalities (D. Murray, 2009). Some of these effects, such as the heart problems that are associated with rubella, can be lifelong.

Most teratogens (e.g., drugs, diseases, or environmental hazards such as X-rays or toxic waste) do the most harm during the first three months of development (the first trimester). During this time there are **critical periods** when certain body structures develop. If drugs, viruses, or infections interfere with

development during a critical period, the body structure will not form properly, nor will it develop later. Other viruses have an impact throughout the pregnancy and delivery stages.

Alcohol is a drug that if consumed by a pregnant woman, especially early in prenatal development, can lead to facial deformities as well as intellectual deficits and behaviour problems, a condition known as **fetal alcohol spectrum disorder (FASD)** (Mattson & Riley, 2000). **[LO 8.7]**

Although physical abnormalities are always possible, exposure to risks during the second trimester of pregnancy—the fourth, fifth, and sixth months—is more likely to result in intellectual and social impairment. **[LO 8.7]**

Prenatal malnutrition can negatively affect development of the embryo and the fetus; it can have particularly harmful effects on brain development during the final trimester. **[LO 8.7]** To maximize the chances of having a healthy baby, a woman needs proper nutrition and possibly multivitamin supplements (especially folic acid, to minimize the chances of neural tube defects) before as well as during pregnancy (Bhutte, Das, Rizvi, Gaffer, Walker, Horton, Webb, Lartey, & Black, 2013).

Newborns at High Risk

Low-birth-weight babies (babies weighing less than 2.5 kilograms) and **preterm infants** (born at or before the 37th week) are at risk. The smaller and more premature the baby, the greater the risk (Hoy, Bill, & Sykes, 1988; Page, Snowden, Cheng, Doss, Rosenstein, & Caughey, 2013). According to Apgar and Beck (1982), the handicaps of prematurity can range from subtle learning and behaviour problems (in babies closer to normal birth weight) to severe intellectual deficits, "blindness, hearing loss, and even death" in the smallest newborns (p. 69).

Poor nutrition, poor prenatal care, smoking, drug use, maternal infection, and too short an interval between pregnancies all increase the likelihood of the birth of a low-birth-weight baby with complications.

REMEMBER IT

Heredity and Prenatal Development

1. In humans, genes are located on how many pairs of chromosomes?
   a. 22
   b. 23
   c. 44
   d. 46
2. A polygenic trait is dependent upon
   a. dominant genes for one trait.
   b. recessive genes for one trait.
   c. multiple genes for one trait.
   d. either one or two dominant genes for the trait.

3. Fraternal twins are no more genetically alike than ordinary brothers and sisters. (true/false)
4. Match the stage of prenatal development with its description:
   _____ 1) first two weeks of life
   _____ 2) rapid growth and further development of body structures and systems
   _____ 3) development of major systems, organs, and structures

   a. period of the fetus
   b. period of the embryo
   c. period of the zygote

Answers: 1. b 2. c 3. true 4 (1). c (2). a (3). b

MODULE 8C PHYSICAL DEVELOPMENT AND LEARNING

LO 8.8 Map out the key physical changes in development from infancy to middle age.

LO 8.9 Describe the sensory perceptual abilities of infants.

LO 8.10 Explain how neonates learn.

THE NEONATE

Neonates (newborn babies up to one month old) come equipped with an impressive range of **reflexes**—built-in responses to certain stimuli needed to ensure survival in their new world.

Sucking, swallowing, coughing, and blinking are some important behaviours that newborns can perform right away. **[LO 8.8]** Newborns will move an arm, leg, or other body part away from a painful stimulus, and they will try to remove a blanket or a cloth placed over their face, which might hamper breathing. Stroke a baby on the cheek and you will trigger the rooting reflex—the baby's mouth opens and actively searches for a nipple. Neonates also have some reflexes that serve no apparent function; these reflexes are believed to be remnants of our evolutionary past. As the brain develops, behaviours that were initially reflexive—controlled by the lower brain centres—gradually come under the voluntary control of the higher brain centres. The presence of these reflexes at birth (as well as their disappearance between the second and fourth months) provides a means of assessing development of the nervous system. **[LO 8.8]**

PERCEPTUAL DEVELOPMENT IN INFANCY

What are the perceptual abilities of the newborn?

The five senses, although not fully developed, are functional at birth. **[LO 8.9]** The newborn already has preferences for certain odours, tastes, sounds, and visual configurations. Hearing is much better developed than vision in the neonate and is functional even before birth (Busnel, Granier-Deferre, & Lecanuet, 1992; Kisilevsky, Muir, & Low, 1992). Newborns are able to turn their head in the direction of a sound and show a general preference for female voices—especially their mother's voice (DeCasper & Fifer, 1980). A preference for the father's voice over a strange male voice does not develop until later. Newborns are able to discriminate among and show preferences for certain odours and tastes (Bartoshuk & Beauchamp, 1994). They favour sweet tastes and are able to differentiate between salty, bitter, and sour solutions. Newborns are also sensitive to pain (Porter, Porges, & Marshall, 1988) and are particularly responsive to touch, reacting positively to stroking and fondling.

Vision: What Newborns Can See

The infant's vision at birth is about 20/600 and does not reach an adult level until about age two (Held, 1993; Keech, 2002). **[LO 8.9]** Newborns focus best on objects about 20 centimetres away, and they can follow a moving object (MacFarlane, 1978). Infants 22 to 93 hours old already indicate a preference for their own mother's face over that of an unfamiliar female (T. M. Field,

When placed on the visual cliff, most infants six months and older will not crawl out over the deep side, indicating that they can perceive depth.

Cohen, Garcia, & Greenberg, 1984). At two months, infants can see all or almost all of the colours adults see (A. Brown, 1990; Franklin, Pilling, & Davies, 2005). However, they prefer red, blue, green, and yellow (M. H. Bornstein & Marks, 1982).

Eleanor Gibson and Richard Walk (1960) measured depth perception by having infants crawl across a glass table top that had a checkered pattern below it to simulate depth (see the accompanying photograph). This made it appear that there was a large drop-off, a "visual cliff," on one side. Babies from 6 to 14 months could be coaxed by their mothers to crawl to the shallow side, but few would crawl onto the deep side. Gibson and Walk concluded that "most human infants can discriminate depth as soon as they can crawl" (p. 64).

Later, Campos, Langer, and Krowitz (1970) found that six-week-old infants had distinct changes in heart rate when they faced the deep side of the cliff, but no change when they

teratogens: Harmful agents in the prenatal environment that can have a negative impact on prenatal development and even cause birth defects.

critical periods: Periods that are so important to development that a harmful environmental influence can keep a bodily structure or behaviour from developing normally.

fetal alcohol spectrum disorder (FASD): A condition, caused by maternal alcohol intake during pregnancy, in which the baby is born mentally disabled, abnormally small, and with facial, organ, and limb abnormalities.

low-birth-weight babies: Babies weighing less than 2.5 kilograms.

preterm infants: Infants born at or before the 37th week.

neonates: Newborn infants up to one month old.

reflexes: Inborn, unlearned, automatic responses to certain environmental stimuli (e.g., swallowing, coughing, blinking, sucking, grasping).

faced the shallow side. Researchers suggested that the change in heart rate indicated fear and showed that the infants could perceive depth.

LEARNING IN INFANCY

What types of learning occur in the first few days of life?

When are babies first capable of learning? We know that learning begins even before birth, because infants' experiences in the womb can affect their preferences shortly after birth. **[LO 8.10]** DeCasper and Spence (1986) had pregnant women read *The Cat in the Hat* to their developing fetuses twice a day during the final six and a half weeks of pregnancy. A few days after birth, the infants could adjust their sucking on specially designed, pressure-sensitive nipples wired to electronic equipment to hear recordings of their mothers reading either *The Cat in the Hat* or *The King, the Mice, and the Cheese*, a story they had never heard before. Which story did the infants prefer? You guessed it—their sucking behaviour signalled a clear preference for the familiar sound of *The Cat in the Hat*.

The simplest evidence of learning in infants is the phenomenon of **habituation**. When presented with a new or interesting stimulus, infants respond by generally becoming quieter. Their heart rate slows, and they fixate on the stimulus. But when they become accustomed to the stimulus, they stop responding—that is, they habituate to it. Later, if the familiar stimulus is presented along with a new stimulus, infants will usually pay more attention to the new stimulus, indicating that they remember the original stimulus but prefer the new one. Memory can be measured by (1) the speed with which habituation occurs and (2) the relative amounts of time infants spend looking at or listening to a new and an old stimulus. Amazing as it may seem, babies only 42 minutes old can imitate gestures such as sticking out the tongue (Anisfeld, 1996).

PHYSICAL AND MOTOR DEVELOPMENT: GROWING, GROWING, GROWN

Although physical and motor development persists throughout childhood, the most obvious periods of change are during infancy and adolescence. Some of the changes are due to learning and others are due to maturation. Maturation occurs naturally according to the individual's own genetically determined biological timetable. In some cases some maturational processes may be slowed down or speeded up, but in appropriate environments, these will be only temporary differences.

Infancy

In infancy, many motor milestones, such as sitting, standing, and walking (shown in Figure 8.3), are primarily a result of maturation and ultimately depend on the growth

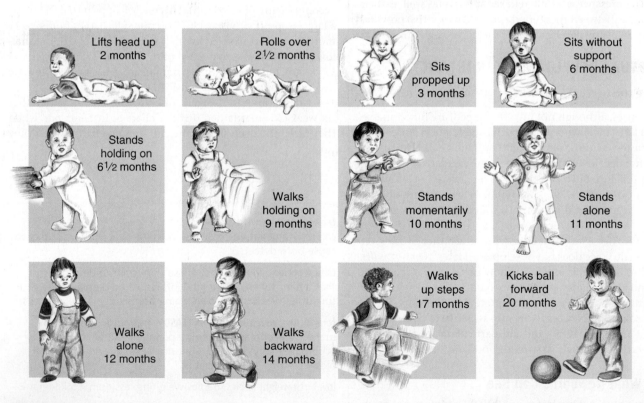

FIGURE 8.3

The Progression of Motor Development

Most infants develop motor skills in the sequence shown in the figure. The ages indicated are only averages, so normal, healthy infants may develop any of these milestones a few months earlier or later than the average.

Source: Pediatrics, Volume 89, Pages 91–97, Copyright 1992 by the American Academy of Pediatrics.

and development of the central nervous system. **[LO 8.8]** The rate at which these milestones are achieved is slowed when the infant is subjected to extremely unfavourable environmental conditions, such as severe malnutrition or maternal or sensory deprivation. In some cultures the milestones are achieved earlier because infants are exposed to special motor-training techniques (Kilbride & Kilbride, 1975). However, the faster learning of motor skills has no lasting impact on development.

Although infants follow their own individual timetables, there is a sequence in which the basic motor skills usually appear. Physical and motor development proceeds from the head downward to the trunk and legs, so babies lift their heads before they sit, and sit before they walk. Development also proceeds from the centre of the body outward—trunk to shoulders to arms to fingers. Thus, control of the arms develops before control of fingers.

Adolescence and Puberty

What physical changes occur during puberty?

Adolescence begins with the onset of **puberty**—biological changes characterized by a period of rapid physical growth and change that culminates in sexual maturity (F. P. Rice, 1992). **[LO 8.8]** The average age for onset of puberty is 10 for girls and 12 for boys; the normal *range* is 7 to 14 for girls and 9 to 16 for boys (Adelman & Ellen, 2002; Chumlea, 1982). Every individual's timetable for puberty is influenced mainly by heredity, although environmental factors also exert some influence.

Puberty begins with a surge in hormone production, which in turn causes a number of physical changes. The most startling change during puberty is the marked acceleration in growth known as the **adolescent growth spurt**. The growth spurt occurs from age 10½ to 13 in girls and about two years later in boys (Tanner, 1990). Because various parts of the body grow at different rates, the adolescent often has a lanky, awkward appearance. Girls attain their full height at 16 or 17, boys between 18 and 20 (Roche & Davila, 1972).

During puberty the reproductive organs develop and **secondary sex characteristics** appear—those physical characteristics not directly involved in reproduction that distinguish mature males from mature females. In girls the breasts develop and the hips round; in boys the voice deepens and facial and chest hair appears. In both sexes there is growth in pubic and underarm (axillary) hair.

For males, the first major landmark of puberty is the first ejaculation, which occurs on average at age 13 (Adelman & Ellen, 2002). **[LO 8.8]** For females, it is **menarche**—the onset of menstruation—which typically occurs between 12 and 13, although the range spans from 10 to 16 (Tanner, 1990). The age of menarche is influenced by heredity, but a girl's diet and lifestyle contribute as well. For example, a girl must have a certain proportion of body fat to attain menarche. Consequently, girls who eat high-fat diets and who are not physically active begin menstruating earlier than girls whose diets contain less fat and whose activities involve fat-reducing exercise (e.g., ballet, gymnastics).

Adolescent physical development clearly marks the point at which sexual maturity is reached. A question for many adolescents is when, or if, they should engage in sexual intercourse. Much Canadian research indicates that adolescents require access to relevant and accurate information about sex and sexual health as well as training in the behavioural skills that can support their healthy choices and avoid sexual health-related issues (McKay, 2004; E. Wood, Senn, Park, Verberg, & Desmarais, 2002). Open discussions and support from parents, schools, and medical practitioners can serve as a valuable support to healthy decision making regarding sexual health choices (Maticka-Tyndale, 2008; McKay, 2004; Whitaker & Miller, 2000).

Middle Age

What are the physical changes associated with middle age?

The major biological event for women during middle age is **menopause**—the cessation of menstruation—which occurs between ages 45 and 55 and signifies the end of reproductive capacity. **[LO 8.8]** Probably the most common symptom associated with menopause and the associated sharp decrease in the level of estrogen is hot flashes—sudden feelings of being uncomfortably hot. Some women also experience anxiety, irritability, mood swings, or depression, but most do not experience psychological problems (Busch, Zonderman, & Costa, 1994).

Men experience a gradual decline in their testosterone levels from about age 20 (their peak) until age 60. During late middle age, many men experience a reduction in semen production and in the sex drive. Also, the DNA carried by their sperm shows increasing amounts of fragmentation (Wyrobek et al., 2006), although the impact of this on fertility or pregnancy outcomes is not yet known. Sexual activity, sexual fantasies, and physical intimacy, for men and women, however, continue to be an important part of life even among 80- to 100-year-olds (Kamel, 2001).

Other changes among the elderly include becoming more farsighted, having increasingly impaired night vision, and experiencing hearing loss in the higher frequencies (Slawinski, Hartel, & Kline, 1993).

---

habituation: A decrease in response or attention to a stimulus as an infant becomes accustomed to it.

puberty: A period of rapid physical growth and change that culminates in sexual maturity.

adolescent growth spurt: A period of rapid physical growth that peaks in girls at about age 12 and in boys at about age 14.

secondary sex characteristics: Those physical characteristics not directly involved in reproduction but distinguishing the mature male from the mature female.

menarche (men-AR-kee): The onset of menstruation.

menopause: The cessation of menstruation, occurring between ages 45 and 55 and signifying the end of reproductive capacity.

REMEMBER IT

Physical Development and Learning

1. Compared with a neonate, the number of reflexes you possess is
   a. much larger.
   b. slightly larger.
   c. the same.
   d. smaller.

2. Which of the following statements about infant sensory development is *not* true?
   a. Vision, hearing, taste, and smell are all fully developed at birth.
   b. Vision, hearing, taste, and smell are all functional at birth.
   c. Infants can show preferences in what they want to look at, hear, taste, and smell shortly after birth.
   d. Hearing at birth is better developed than vision.

3. Two-month-old Michael likes to look at the soft, multi-coloured ball in his crib, but the new black-and-white ball has recently gained his attention. Habituation has occurred, meaning that
   a. Michael has gotten used to a stimulus (the multicoloured ball).
   b. Michael no longer remembers the stimulus he has seen previously.
   c. Michael has a short attention span.
   d. a complex form of learning has taken place.

4. The main factor influencing the attainment of the major motor milestones is
   a. experience.
   b. maturation.
   c. learning.
   d. habituation.

5. The secondary sex characteristics
   a. are directly involved in reproduction.
   b. appear at the same time in all adolescents.
   c. distinguish mature males from mature females.
   d. include the testes and ovaries.

Answers: 1. d 2. a 3. a 4. b 5. c

MODULE **8D** THE COGNITIVE STAGES OF DEVELOPMENT: CLIMBING THE STEPS TO COGNITIVE MATURITY

LO 8.11 Identify each of Piaget's stages.
LO 8.12 Explain the key cognitive achievements for each of Piaget's stages.
LO 8.13 Identify key changes in intellectual performance over the adult years.

Similar to the charting of physical development, developmental psychologists have mapped out the important cognitive advancements that children and adults progress through as they mature. One of the first and most influential researchers of cognitive development was Jean Piaget.

PIAGET'S STAGES OF COGNITIVE DEVELOPMENT

What were Piaget's beliefs regarding stages of cognitive development?

Jean Piaget formulated a comprehensive theory that systematically describes and explains how intellect develops (Piaget, 1963b, 1964; Piaget & Inhelder, 1969). He believed that cognitive development occurs in four stages, which differ not according to the amount of knowledge accumulated, but in the way individuals at different ages reason. Each stage reflects a qualitatively different way of reasoning and understanding the world. The stages occur in a fixed sequence; the accomplishments of one stage provide the foundation for the next. Although everyone is thought to progress through the stages in the same order, there are individual differences in the rates at which they pass through them, and these rates are influenced by maturation and experience.

According to Piaget, cognitive development begins with a few basic **schemas**—cognitive structures or concepts that are used to identify and interpret objects, events, and other information in the environment. When confronted with new objects, events, experiences, and information, learners attempt to fit these into their existing schemas, a process known as **assimilation**. But not everything can be assimilated into the existing schemas. If children call a stranger "daddy" or the neighbour's cat "doggie," assimilation is not appropriate. When parents correct them, or when they discover for themselves that something cannot be assimilated into an existing schema,

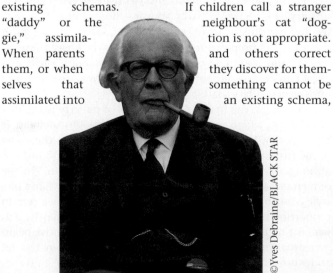

©Yves Debraine/BLACK STAR

Jean Piaget

children will use a process known as **accommodation**. In accommodation, existing schemas are modified or new schemas are created to process new information. It is through the processes of assimilation and accommodation, that schemas are formed, differentiated, and broadened.

The Sensorimotor Stage (Birth to Age Two)

What is Piaget's sensorimotor stage?

In the first stage, the **sensorimotor stage**, infants gain an understanding of the world through their senses and their motor activities (actions or body movements). **[LO 8.11]** An infant's behaviour, which is mostly reflexive at birth, becomes increasingly complex and gradually evolves into "mental actions." **[LO 8.12]** The child learns to respond to and manipulate objects and to use them in goal-directed activity.

The major achievement of the sensorimotor stage is the development of **object permanence**, which is the realization that objects (including people) continue to exist even when they are out of sight. **[LO 8.12]** This concept develops gradually and is complete when the child is able to represent objects mentally in their absence. This marks the end of the sensori-motor stage.

The Preoperational Stage (Ages Two to Seven)

What cognitive limitations characterize a child's thinking during the preoperational stage?

The **preoperational stage** is a period of rapid development in language. **[LO 8.11]** Children become increasingly able to represent objects and events mentally with words and images. **[LO 8.12]** Now their thinking is no longer restricted to objects and events that are directly perceived and present in the environment. Evidence of representational thought is the child's ability to imitate the behaviour of a person who is no longer present (*deferred imitation*). Other evidence is the child's ability to engage in imaginary play using one object to stand for another, such as using a broom to represent a horse.

Thinking is dominated by perception, and the children at this stage exhibit egocentrism in thought. They believe that everyone sees what they see, thinks as they think, and feels as they feel.

At this stage children also show animistic thinking, believing that inanimate objects such as a tree, the sun, and a doll are alive and have feelings and intentions (Piaget, 1960, 1963a). Children also believe that all things, even the sun, the moon, and the clouds, are made for people and usually even by people.

The preoperational stage is so named because children are not yet able to perform mental operations (manipulations) that follow logical rules. Children at this stage are not aware that a given quantity of matter (a given number, mass, area, weight, or volume of matter) remains the same if it is rearranged or changed in its appearance, as long as nothing has been added or taken away. This concept is known as **conservation** and is illustrated in *Try It*, on the next page.

Centration and irreversibility are two restrictions on thinking that lead children to wrong conclusions. **Centration** is the tendency to focus on only one dimension of a stimulus and ignore the other dimensions. For example, in the case described in the *Try It*, the child focused on the tallness of the glass and

failed to notice that it was also narrower. At this stage, taller means more.

Preoperational children have also not developed **reversibility** in thinking—the realization that after any change in shape, position, or order, matter can be returned mentally to its original state.

The preoperational child in *Try It* cannot mentally return the juice to the original glass and realize that once again the two glasses of juice are equal.

The Concrete Operations Stage (Ages 7 to 11 or 12)

What cognitive abilities do children acquire during the concrete operations stage?

In the third stage, the **concrete operations stage**, children gradually demonstrate less egocentric thinking, and they come to realize that other people have thoughts and feelings that may be different from their own. **[LO 8.11]** Children acquire the ability to mentally carry out the operations essential for logical thought. **[LO 8.12]** They can now decentre their thinking—that is, attend to two or more dimensions of a stimulus at the same time. They can also understand the concept of reversibility,

---

schemas: Piaget's term for cognitive structures or concepts used to identify and interpret information.

assimilation: The process by which new objects, events, experiences, or pieces of information are incorporated into existing schemas.

accommodation: The process by which existing schemas are modified and new schemas are created to incorporate new objects, events, experiences, or information.

sensorimotor stage: Piaget's first stage of cognitive development (birth to age two), culminating in the development of object permanence and the beginning of representational thought.

object permanence: The realization that objects continue to exist even when they are no longer perceived.

preoperational stage: Piaget's second stage of cognitive development (ages two to seven), characterized by rapid development of language and by thinking that is governed by perception rather than logic.

conservation: The concept that a given quantity of matter remains the same despite rearrangement or a change in its appearance, as long as nothing has been added or taken away.

centration: The child's tendency during the preoperational stage to focus on only one dimension of a stimulus and ignore the other dimensions.

reversibility: The realization, during the concrete operations stage, that any change occurring in shape, position, or order of matter can be returned mentally to its original state.

concrete operations stage: Piaget's third stage of cognitive development (ages 7 to 11 or 12), during which a child acquires the concepts of reversibility and conservation and is able to apply logical thinking to concrete objects.

TRY IT

Understanding the Conservation Concept

If you know a child of preschool age, try this conservation experiment. Show the child two glasses of the same size, and then fill them with the same amount of juice. After the child agrees they are the same, pour the juice from one glass into a tall, narrow glass. Now ask the child if the two glasses have the same amount of juice or if one glass has more than the other. Children at this stage will insist that the taller, narrower glass has more juice, although they will quickly agree that you neither added juice nor took it away.

which is crucial in problem solving. Finally, during this stage children acquire the concept of conservation. But children are able to apply logical operations only to concrete problems that they can perceive directly. They cannot apply these mental operations to verbal, abstract, or hypothetical problems. Surprisingly, the concepts of conservation of number, substance (liquid, mass), length, area, weight, and volume are not all acquired at once. They come in a certain sequence and usually at the ages shown in Figure 8.4.

The Formal Operations Stage (Age 11 or 12 and Beyond)

What new capability characterizes the formal operations stage?

In the **formal operations stage**, adolescents and adults can apply reversibility and conservation to abstract, verbal, and hypothetical situations and to problems in the past, present, and future. [LOs 8.11 &12]

Not all people attain full formal operational thinking (Kuhn, 1984; Neimark, 1981; Papalia & Bielby, 1974), and those who do attain it usually apply it only in those areas where they are most proficient (Ault, 1983; Martorano, 1977). Some suggest that some adults do not attain full operational thinking because this level of thinking requires training (Siegler, 1991).

Piaget's four stages of development are summarized in *Review & Reflect 8.1.*

AN EVALUATION OF PIAGET'S CONTRIBUTION

Although Piaget's genius and his monumental contribution to our knowledge of mental development are rarely disputed, his methods and some of his findings and conclusions have been criticized (Halford, 1989).

Piaget was limited in the information he could gather about infants because he relied on observation and on the interview technique, which depended on verbal responses. Newer techniques requiring non-verbal responses—sucking, looking, heart-rate changes, reaching, and head turning—have shown that infants and young children are more competent than Piaget proposed (Flavell, 1992).

Few developmental psychologists believe that cognitive development takes place in the general stagelike fashion proposed by Piaget. If it did, children's cognitive functioning would be similar across all cognitive tasks and content areas (Flavell, 1992). Neo-Piagetians believe that while there are important general properties in cognitive development, there is also more variability in how children perform on certain tasks than Piaget described (Case, 1987, 1992). This variability results from the expertise children acquire in different content areas through extensive practice and experience (Flavell, 1992). This also applies to adults: the expertise they have in a particular content area will influence whether they use formal operational reasoning or fall back on concrete operational reasoning when they approach a given task.

It is fair to say that Piaget has stimulated a great deal of research in developmental psychology. Piaget's work has had a profound impact on the fields of psychology and education.

COGNITIVE GAINS IN ADOLESCENCE

During adolescence, information-processing skills (such as those introduced in Chapter 6) continue to adavance. Specifically, metacognitive and metamemory skills improve dramatically (Winsler & Naglieri, 2003). Metacognition is the ability to think about and control cognitive processes, while metamemory reflects control of memory processes. You are far better equipped to handle the intellectual demands of college or university than you would have been in high school. And it isn't just because you have more knowledge. You manage the knowledge you have, as well as new information you encounter, in a more effective way.

EMERGING ADULTHOOD

What are the psychological criteria that distinguish an adolescent from an adult? Developmental psychologist Jeffrey Arnett has proposed that the educational, social, and economic demands of modern culture have given rise to a new developmental period he calls *emerging adulthood*, the period from the late teens to the early twenties when individuals experiment with options prior to taking on adult roles (Arnett, 2000, 2007).

Arnett's studies and those of other researchers indicate that young people do not tend to think of themselves as having fully attained adulthood until the age of 25 or so (Galambos,

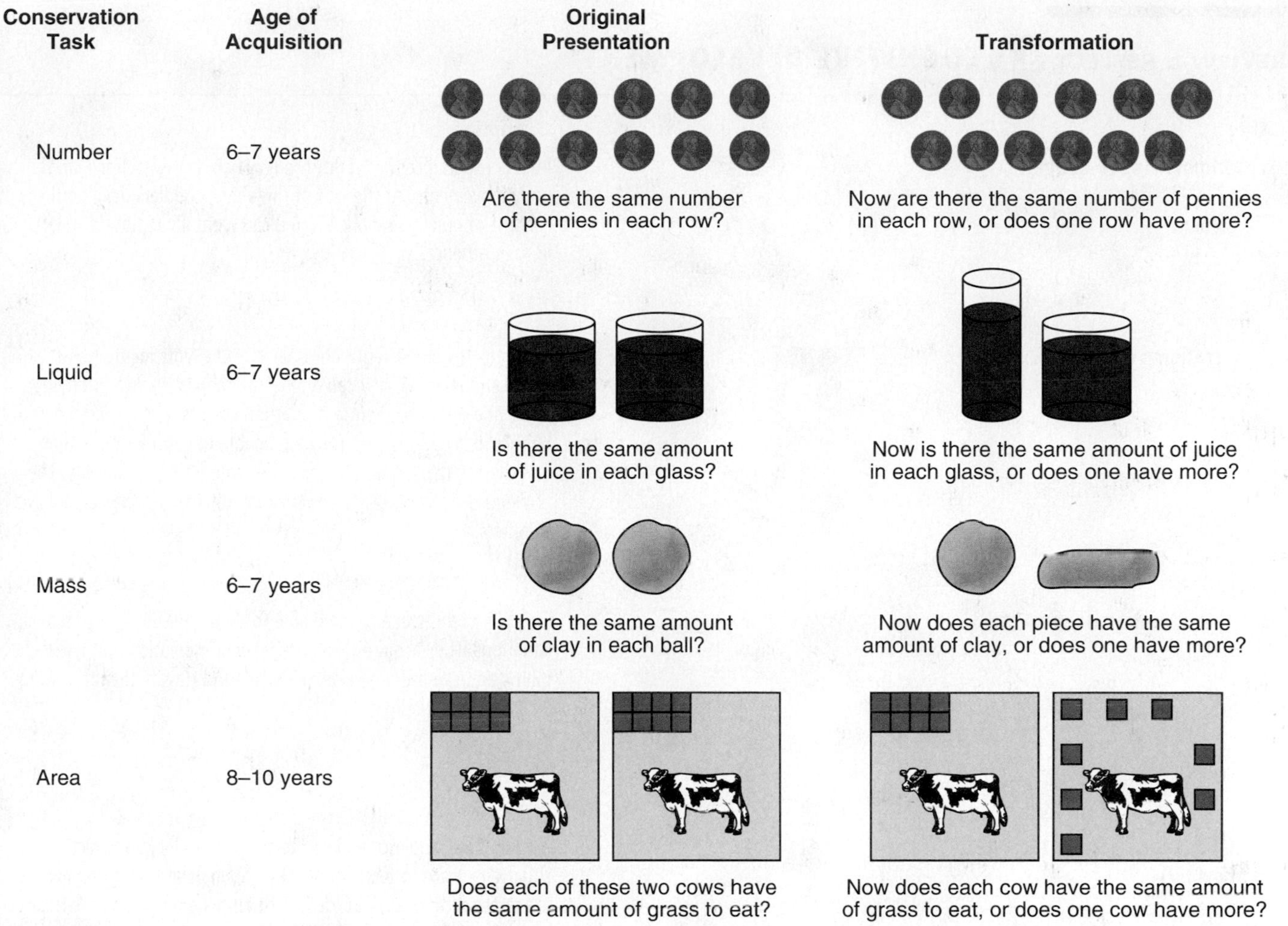

Conservation Task	Age of Acquisition	Original Presentation	Transformation
Number	6–7 years	Are there the same number of pennies in each row?	Now are there the same number of pennies in each row, or does one row have more?
Liquid	6–7 years	Is there the same amount of juice in each glass?	Now is there the same amount of juice in each glass, or does one have more?
Mass	6–7 years	Is there the same amount of clay in each ball?	Now does each piece have the same amount of clay, or does one have more?
Area	8–10 years	Does each of these two cows have the same amount of grass to eat?	Now does each cow have the same amount of grass to eat, or does one cow have more?

FIGURE 8.4

Piaget's Conservation Tasks

Pictured here are several of Piaget's conservation tasks. The ability to answer correctly develops over time according to the ages indicated for each task. (Bee, Helen; Boyd, Denise, The Developing Child, 11th Ed., ©2007, p. 158. Reprinted and Electronically reproduced by permission of Pearson Education, Inc., New York, NY.).

Turner, & Tilton-Weaver, 2005). Neuroimaging studies have provided some support for the notion that emerging adulthood is a unique period of life. These studies suggest that the parts of the brain that underlie rational decision making, impulse control, and self-regulation mature during these years (Crone, Wendelken, Donohue, van Leijenhorst, & Bunge 2006; Gogtay et al., 2004). As a result, early on in this phase of life, individuals make poorer decisions about matters such as risky behaviours (e.g., unprotected sex) than they do when these brain areas may reach full maturity in the early to mid-20s.

INTELLECTUAL CAPACITY DURING EARLY, MIDDLE, AND LATE ADULTHOOD

In general, can adolescents and adults look forward to an increase or a decrease in intellectual performance?

Conventional wisdom has held that intellectual ability reaches its peak in the late teens or early 20s, and that it's all downhill after that. Fortunately, conventional wisdom is wrong. Although adolescents and younger adults tend to do better on tests requiring speed or rote memory, intellectual performance in adults continues to increase in other areas. In tests measuring general information, vocabulary, reasoning ability, and social judgment, older individuals usually do better than younger ones because of their greater experience and education. **[LO 8.13]**

formal operations stage: Piaget's fourth and final stage, characterized by the ability to apply logical thinking to abstract, verbal, and hypothetical situations and to problems in the past, present, and future.

REVIEW & REFLECT 8.1 COGNITIVE DEVELOPMENT

Stage		Description
Sensorimotor (birth to age 2)		Infants experience the world through their senses, actions, and body movements. At the end of this stage, toddlers develop the concept of object permanence and can mentally represent objects in their absence.
Preoperational (ages 2 to 7)		Children are able to represent objects and events mentally with words and images. They can engage in imaginary play (pretend), using one object to represent another. Their thinking is dominated by their perceptions, and they are unable to consider more than one characteristic of an object at the same time (centration). Their thinking is egocentric—that is, they fail to consider the perspective of others.
Concrete operational (ages 7 to 11 or 12)		Children at this stage become able to think logically in concrete situations. They acquire the concepts of conservation and reversibility, and can order objects in a series and classify them according to multiple dimensions.
Formal operational (age 11 or 12 and beyond)		At this stage, adolescents learn to think logically in abstract situations, learn to test hypotheses systematically, and become interested in the world of ideas. Not all people attain full formal operational thinking.

Adults continue to be able to acquire complex cognitive skills into their 70s and beyond (Boron, Turiano, Willis, & Schaie, 2007). Moreover, regardless of age, people who select appropriate strategies for processing new information are more likely to remember it than those who use inappropriate strategies (Lange & Verhaegen, 2009). And individual differences in background knowledge contribute to differences in memory performance at all ages (Soederberg Miller, 2009). For example, a person who knows a lot about baseball will find it easier to remember the events of a particular game than someone who is unfamiliar with the sport will. Nevertheless, there is no doubt that some intellectual functions deteriorate with age (Salthouse, 2009). Declines are particularly pronounced for cognitive tasks that depend on working-memory capacity and processing speed, both of which decline as we get older (Kim, Bayles, & Beeson, 2008; Meijer, de Groot, van Gerven, van Boxtel, & Jolles, 2009).

Canadian data from the Victoria Longitudinal Study were used to determine whether actively participating in the activities of everyday life could buffer individuals against cognitive decline as they aged. Findings from this research and other studies suggest that living an "engaged" life protects against cognitive decline (Hultsch, Hertzog, Small, & Dixon, 1999; Pushkar et al., 1999; Shimamura, Brerry, Mangela, Rusting, & Jurica, 1995). Several factors are positively correlated with good cognitive functioning in the elderly. They are education level (Lyketsos, Chen, & Anthony, 1999; Van der Elst, Van Boxtel, Van Breukelen, & Jolles, 2006), a complex work environment, a long marriage to an intelligent spouse, and a higher income (Schaie, 2005). Gender is a factor as well: women not only outlive men, but generally show less cognitive decline during old age. Moreover, there is some evidence that physical exercise positively affects cognitive functioning in old age (Lindwall, Rennemark, & Berggren, 2008; Taaffe et al., 2008).

REMEMBER IT

The Cognitive Stages of Development

1. Which statement reflects Piaget's thinking about the cognitive stages?
   a. All people pass through the same stages but not necessarily in the same order.
   b. All people progress through the stages in the same order but not at the same rate.
   c. All people progress through the stages in the same order and at the same rate.
   d. Very bright children sometimes skip stages.

2. Three-year-old Danielle says "Airplane!" when she sees a helicopter for the first time. She is using the process Piaget called _____ .
   a. assimilation.
   b. accommodation.
   c. centration.
   d. conservation.

3. Four-year-old Kendra rolls her ball of clay into the shape of a wiener to make "more" clay. Her actions demonstrate that she has not acquired the concept of _____ .

   a. reversibility.
   b. animism.
   c. centration.
   d. conservation.

4. Match the stage with the relevant concept.
   _____ 1) abstract thought
   _____ 2) conservation, reversibility
   _____ 3) object permanence
   _____ 4) egocentrism, centration
   a. concrete operations stage
   b. sensorimotor stage
   c. formal operations stage
   d. preoperational stage

Answers: 1.b 2.a 3.d 4(1).c (2).a (3).b (4).d

LO 8.14 Identify and describe each of Erikson's psychosocial stages.
LO 8.15 Explain what Harlow's studies revealed about maternal deprivation and attachment in infant monkeys.
LO 8.16 Describe the four types of attachment.
LO 8.17 Understand how each of the three styles of parenting impacts on child development.
LO 8.18 Define and describe *adolescent egocentrism*.
LO 8.19 Identify and explain each of Kohlberg's three levels of moral reasoning.

Every one of us is born into a society. To function effectively and comfortably within that society, we must come to know the patterns of behaviour that it considers desirable and appropriate. The process of learning socially acceptable behaviours, attitudes, and values is called **socialization**. Many people play a role in our socialization, including parents and peers. School, the media, and religion are also important influences.

ERIKSON'S THEORY OF PSYCHOSOCIAL DEVELOPMENT

What is Erikson's theory of psychosocial development?

Erik Erikson proposed a theory that emphasizes the role of social forces on human development throughout the lifespan. He was the first to stress that society plays an important role in personality development as well as individuals themselves. He did not focus exclusively on the influence of parents. Erikson's is the only major theory of development to include the entire lifespan.

According to Erikson, individuals progress through eight **psychosocial stages** during the lifespan. Each stage is defined by a conflict involving the individual's relationship with the social environment that must be resolved satisfactorily in order for healthy development to occur. Although failure to resolve a conflict impedes later development, resolution may occur at a later stage and reverse any damage done earlier.

Stage 1: Basic Trust versus Basic Mistrust (Birth to 12 Months)

During the first stage, **basic trust versus basic mistrust**, infants develop a sense of trust or mistrust depending on the degree and regularity of care, love, and affection they receive from the mother or primary caregiver. **[LO 8.14]** Erikson (1980) considered "basic trust as the cornerstone of a healthy personality" (p. 58).

socialization: The process of learning socially acceptable behaviours, attitudes, and values.

psychosocial stages: Erikson's eight developmental stages, which are each defined by a conflict that must be resolved in order for healthy personality development to occur.

basic trust versus basic mistrust: Erikson's first psychosocial stage (birth to 12 months), when infants develop trust or mistrust depending on the quality of care, love, and affection provided.

Stage 2: Autonomy versus Shame and Doubt (Ages One to Three)

The second stage, **autonomy versus shame and doubt** (ages one to three), is one in which infants are developing their physical and mental abilities and want to do things for themselves. **[LO 8.14]** They begin to express their will or independence and develop a "sudden violent wish to have a choice" (Erikson, 1963, p. 252). "No!" becomes one of their favourite words. Erikson believed that parents must set appropriate limits but at the same time facilitate children's desires for autonomy by encouraging their appropriate attempts at independence. If parents are impatient or overprotective, they may make children feel shame and doubt about their efforts to express their will and explore their environment.

Stage 3: Initiative versus Guilt (Ages Three to Six)

In the third stage, **initiative versus guilt**, children go beyond merely expressing their autonomy and begin to develop initiative. **[LO 8.14]** Enjoying their new locomotor and mental powers, they begin to plan and undertake tasks. They initiate play and motor activities and ask questions.

If children's appropriate attempts at initiative are encouraged and their inappropriate attempts are handled firmly but sensitively, they will leave this stage with a sense of initiative that will form "a basis for a high and yet realistic sense of ambition and independence" (Erikson, 1980, p. 78).

Stage 4: Industry versus Inferiority (Age Six to Puberty)

During the fourth stage, **industry versus inferiority**, children develop enjoyment and pride in making things and doing things. **[LO 8.14]** The encouragement of teachers as well as parents is important for a positive resolution of this stage. "But parents who see their children's efforts at making and doing as 'mischief' and as simply 'making a mess,' help to encourage in children a sense of inferiority" (Elkind, 1970, pp. 89–90).

Stage 5: Identity versus Role Confusion (Adolescence)

Erikson's fifth stage of psychosocial development, **identity versus role confusion**, is the developmental struggle of adolescence. **[LO 8.14]** "Who am I?" becomes the critical question at this stage, as adolescents seek to establish their identity and find values to guide their lives (Erikson, 1963). They must develop a sense of who they are, where they have been, and where they are going. Adolescents are seriously looking to the future for the first time and considering an occupational identity—what they will choose as their life's work. Erikson (1968) believed that "in general it is the inability to settle on an occupational identity that most disturbs young people" (p. 132). The danger at this stage, he said, is that of role confusion—not knowing who one is or where one belongs.

Stage 6: Intimacy versus Isolation (Young Adulthood)

Erikson contended that if healthy development is to continue, young adults must establish intimacy in a relationship. He

According to Erikson, in middle adulthood people develop generativity—an interest in guiding the next generation.

©Monkey Business/Fotolia

called this sixth stage of psychosocial development **intimacy versus isolation**. **[LO 8.14]**

What kind of intimacy was Erikson referring to? He meant more than sexual intimacy alone. Intimacy means the ability to share with, care for, make sacrifices for, and commit to another person. Erikson believed that avoiding intimacy results in a sense of isolation and loneliness. Erikson and others argue that young adults must first establish their own identity before true intimacy is possible.

Stage 7: Generativity versus Stagnation (Middle Adulthood)

Erikson's seventh psychosocial stage is called **generativity versus stagnation**. **[LO 8.14]** Erikson (1980) maintained that in order for mental health to continue into middle adulthood, individuals must develop generativity—an "interest in establishing and guiding the next generation" (p. 103). This interest should extend beyond the immediate family to include making the world a better place for all young people.

People who do not develop generativity become self-absorbed and "begin to indulge themselves as if they were their own one and only child" (p. 103). Personal impoverishment and a sense of stagnation often accompany such self-absorption. We enlarge ourselves when we have concern for others.

Stage 8: Ego Integrity versus Despair (Late Adulthood)

In Erikson's eighth stage, **ego integrity versus despair**, the outcome depends primarily on whether a person has resolved the conflicts at the previous stages (Erikson, Erikson, & Kivnick, 1986). **[LO 8.14]** Those who have a sense of ego integrity believe their life has had meaning. They can look back on their life with satisfaction and a sense of accomplishment, and they are not burdened with major regrets:

> At the other extreme is the individual who looks back upon [his or her] life as a series of missed opportunities and missed directions; now in the twilight years [she or he] realizes that it is too late to start again. For such a person the inevitable result is a sense of despair at what might have been. (Elkind, 1970, p. 112)

Review & Reflect 8.2 describes Erikson's stages.

REVIEW & REFLECT 8.2 PSYCHOSOCIAL STAGES OF DEVELOPMENT

Stage	Ages	Description
Trust vs. mistrust	Birth to 12 months	Infants learn to trust or mistrust depending on the degree and regularity of care, love, and affection from their mother or primary caregiver.
Autonomy vs. shame and doubt	Ages 1 to 3	Children learn to express their will and independence, to exercise some control, and to make choices. If not, they experience shame and doubt.
Initiative vs. guilt	Ages 3 to 6	Children begin to initiate activities, to plan and undertake tasks, and to enjoy developing motor and other abilities. If not allowed to initiate or if made to feel stupid and a nuisance, they may develop a sense of guilt.
Industry vs. inferiority	Age 6 to puberty	Children develop industriousness and feel pride in accomplishing tasks, making things, and doing things. If not encouraged, or if rebuffed by parents and teachers, they may develop a sense of inferiority.
Identity vs. role confusion	Adolescence	Adolescents must make the transition from childhood to adulthood, establish an identity, develop a sense of self, and consider a future occupational identity. Otherwise, role confusion can result.
Intimacy vs. isolation	Young adulthood	Young adults must develop intimacy—the ability to share with, care for, and commit themselves to another person. Avoiding intimacy brings a sense of isolation.
Generativity vs. stagnation	Middle adulthood	Middle-aged people must find some way of contributing to the development of the next generation. Failing this, they may become self-absorbed, personally impoverished, and reach a point of stagnation.
Ego integrity vs. despair	Late adulthood	Individuals review their lives. If they are satisfied and feel a sense of accomplishment, ego integrity will result. If dissatisfied, they will sink into despair.

THE PARENTS' ROLE IN THE SOCIALIZATION PROCESS

For children, the parents' role in the socialization process consists of the examples they set, their teachings, and their approach to discipline. Parents are usually more successful if they are loving, warm, nurturant, and supportive (Maccoby & Martin, 1983). In fact, a longitudinal study (Franz, McClelland, & Weinberger, 1991) that followed individuals from ages 5 to 41 revealed that "children of warm, affectionate parents were more likely to be socially accomplished adults who, at age 41, were mentally healthy, coping adequately, and psychosocially mature in work, relationships, and generativity" (p. 593).

The first social relationship in our lives is the one we forge with our caretakers. Human newborns are among the most helpless and dependent of all animal species and cannot survive alone. Fortunately, infants form a strong attachment to their primary caregivers. Because their attachment is a two-way affair, the term *bonding* has been used to describe this mutual attachment (Brazelton, Tronick, Adamson, Als, & Wise, 1975).

What precisely is the glue that binds caregiver and infant? For decades people believed that an infant's attachment to its caregiver was formed primarily because the caregiver provided the nourishment that sustains life. However, a series of classic studies by Harry Harlow on attachment in rhesus monkeys suggests that life-sustaining physical nourishment is not enough to bind infants to their primary caregivers.

autonomy versus shame and doubt: Erikson's second psychosocial stage (ages one to three), when infants develop autonomy or shame depending on how parents react to their expression of will and their wish to do things for themselves.

initiative versus guilt: Erikson's third psychosocial stage (ages three to six), when children develop a sense of initiative or guilt depending on how parents react to their initiation of play, their motor activities, and their questions.

industry versus inferiority: Erikson's fourth psychosocial stage (age six to puberty), when children develop a sense of industry or inferiority depending on how parents and teachers react to their efforts to undertake projects.

identity versus role confusion: Erikson's fifth psychosocial stage, when adolescents need to establish their own identity and to form values to live by; failure can lead to an identity crisis.

intimacy versus isolation: Erikson's sixth psychosocial stage, when the young adult must establish intimacy in a relationship in order to avoid feeling isolated and lonely.

generativity versus stagnation: Erikson's seventh psychosocial stage, occurring during middle age, when the individual becomes increasingly concerned with guiding and assisting the next generation rather than becoming self-absorbed and stagnating.

ego integrity versus despair: Erikson's eighth and final psychosocial stage, occurring during old age, when individuals look back on their lives with satisfaction and a sense of accomplishment or have major regrets about missed opportunities and mistakes.

Harlow found that infant monkeys developed a strong attachment to a cloth-covered surrogate mother and little or no attachment to a wire surrogate mother—even when the wire mother provided nourishment.

©Science Source

Attachment in Infant Monkeys: Like Humans in So Many Ways

What did Harlow's studies reveal about maternal deprivation and attachment in infant monkeys?

To investigate systematically the nature of attachment and the effects of maternal deprivation on infant monkeys, Harlow constructed two artificial monkey "mothers." One was a plain wire-mesh cylinder with a wooden head; the other was a wire-mesh cylinder that was padded, covered with soft terry cloth, and fitted with a somewhat more monkey-like head (see the accompanying photograph). A baby bottle could be attached to one or the other "mother" for feeding.

Newborn monkeys were placed in individual cages with equal access to the cloth surrogate and the wire surrogate. For the monkeys, the source of their nourishment (cloth or wire surrogate) was unimportant; they preferred to be with the cloth monkey: "The infants developed a strong attachment to the cloth mothers and little or none to the wire mothers" (Harlow & Harlow, 1962, p. 141). Harlow found that it was contact comfort—the comfort supplied by bodily contact—rather than nourishment that formed the basis of the infant monkey's attachment to its mother. **[LO 8.15]**

The Need for Love

Harlow's research reveals the disastrous effects that maternal deprivation can have on infant monkeys. Human infants, too, need love in order to grow physically and psychologically. **[LO 8.15]** Between 1900 and 1920, many infants under a year old who were placed in orphanages did not survive, even though they were given adequate food and medical care (Montagu, 1962). Usually kept in cribs, the sides draped with sheets, these unfortunate infants were left to stare at the ceiling. Lacking a warm, close, personal caregiver and the all-important ingredient of love, the infants who survived their first year failed to gain weight and grow normally—a condition known as *deprivation dwarfism* (L. I. Gardner, 1972). And they were far behind other children in their mental and motor development (Spitz, 1946). To survive, infants need to become attached to someone. That someone can be nearly anyone.

The Development of Attachment in Humans

When does the infant have a strong attachment to the mother?

No strong emotional attachment between caregiver and infant is present at birth; nor does it develop suddenly. Rather, as a result of the caregiver and the infant responding to each other with behaviours that provide mutual satisfaction, the attachment develops gradually. Virtually all infants will develop an attachment to a caregiver by age two, with early signs of attachment formation beginning around six to eight months. John Bowlby (1951), one of the foremost theorists on attachment, maintains that to grow up mentally healthy, infants and young children "should experience a warm, intimate, and continuous relationship" with their attachment figure that is mutually satisfying and enjoyable (p. 13).

Once the attachment has formed, infants show **separation anxiety**—fear and distress when the parent leaves them with another caretaker.

Ainsworth's Study of Attachment: The Importance of Being Securely Attached

What are the four attachment patterns identified in infants?

Vast differences exist in the quality of the attachment to a caregiver. In a classic study of mother–child attachment, Mary Ainsworth (1973, 1979) observed mother–child interactions in a laboratory procedure called the "Strange Situation." On the basis of infants' reactions to their mothers after two brief separations, Ainsworth and others identified four patterns of attachment: secure, avoidant, resistant, and disorganized/disoriented (M. D. S. Ainsworth, Blehar, Walters, & Wall, 1978; Main & Solomon, 1990).

SECURE ATTACHMENT Securely attached infants (about 65 percent of North American infants) are usually distressed when separated from their mothers. **[LO 8.16]** They eagerly seek to re-establish contact after separation and then show an interest in play. Moreover, securely attached infants use their mothers as a "safe base" from which to explore, much as Harlow's monkeys did when unfamiliar objects were placed in their cages. Securely attached infants are the most responsive, obedient, and content. The mothers of securely attached infants tend to be the most sensitive, accepting, and affectionate, as well as the most responsive to their infants' cries and needs (Isabella, Belsky, & von Eye, 1989; D. R. Pederson et al., 1990). This finding contradicts the notion that mothers who respond promptly to an infant's cries end up with spoiled babies who cry more.

Securely attached infants are likely to grow up to be more sociable, more effective with peers, more interested in exploring the environment, and generally more competent than less securely attached infants (Masters, 1981; K. A. Park & Waters, 1989).

Secure attachment is the most common type across cultures. However, there are exceptions. Cross-cultural research has revealed a higher incidence of insecure attachment patterns in Israel, Japan, and Germany than in the United States (Collins & Gunnar, 1990), suggesting cultural variation in attachment preferences or in the validity of the Strange Situation as an assessment for attachment.

AVOIDANT ATTACHMENT About 20 percent of North American infants are considered to have an avoidant attachment to their mothers. **[LO 8.16]** Infants with this attachment pattern are usually unresponsive to the mother when she is present and are not troubled when she leaves. When the mother returns, the infant may actively avoid contact with her or, at least, not readily greet her. The mother of an avoidant infant tends to show little affection and to be generally unresponsive to her infant's needs and cries.

RESISTANT ATTACHMENT Between 10 and 15 percent of North American infants show a resistant attachment pattern toward their mothers. **[LO 8.16]** Prior to a period of separation, resistant infants seek and prefer close contact with their mothers. Yet they do not tend to branch out and explore like securely attached infants. And when the infant's mother returns to the room after a period of separation, the resistant infant displays anger, and many push the mother away or hit her. When picked up, the infant is hard to comfort and may continue crying.

DISORGANIZED/DISORIENTED ATTACHMENT Between 5 and 10 percent of North American infants show a disorganized/disoriented attachment pattern, which is the most puzzling and apparently least secure pattern. **[LO 8.16]** When reunited with their mothers, these infants exhibit contradictory and disoriented responses. Rather than looking at the parent while being held, the infant may purposely look away or approach the parent with an expressionless or depressed demeanour.

FATHER–CHILD ATTACHMENT RELATIONSHIPS Although mother–child rather than father–child attachment relationships have been the traditional focus of research, fathers can be as responsive and competent as mothers (P. Roberts & Moseley, 1996). On the negative side, children whose fathers exhibit antisocial behavior, such as deceitfulness and aggression, are more likely to demonstrate such behaviour themselves (Jaffee, Moffitt, Caspi, & Talor, 2003). More often, though, fathers exert a positive influence on their children's development. For instance, children who experience regular interaction with their fathers tend to have higher IQs and to do better in social situations and at coping with frustration than children lacking such interaction. They also persist longer in solving problems, are less impulsive, and are less likely to become violent (J. Adler, 1997; Bishop & Lane, 2000; P. Roberts & Moseley, 1996). In addition, positive father–son relationships are associated with higher-quality parenting behaviour of sons when they have children of their own (Shears, Robinson, & Emde, 2002).

What aspect of authoritative parenting might this mother be demonstrating?

Parenting Styles: What Works and What Doesn't

What are the three parenting styles discussed by Baumrind, and which did she find most effective?

Diana Baumrind (1971, 1980, 1991) has identified three parenting styles—the authoritarian, the authoritative, and the permissive. She related these styles first to different patterns of behaviour in preschool children and later to those in older children and adolescents. The outcomes found for each parenting style are based on research with predominantly white, middle-class children.

AUTHORITARIAN PARENTS Authoritarian parents make the rules, expect unquestioned obedience from their children, punish misbehaviour (often physically), and value obedience to authority. **[LO 8.17]** Rather than giving a rationale for a rule, authoritarian parents consider "because I said so" a sufficient reason for obedience. Parents using this parenting style tend to be uncommunicative, unresponsive, and somewhat distant. Baumrind (1967) found preschool children disciplined in this manner to be withdrawn, anxious, and unhappy.

If the goal of discipline is eventually to have children internalize parental standards, the authoritarian approach leaves much to be desired. When parents fail to provide a rationale for rules, children find it hard to see any reason for following them. When a parent says, "Do it because I said so" or "Do it or you'll be punished," the child may do what is expected when the parent is present, but not when the parent is not around.

AUTHORITATIVE PARENTS Authoritative parents set high but realistic and reasonable standards, enforce limits,

separation anxiety: The fear and distress an infant feels when left with another caretaker.

authoritarian parents: Parents who make arbitrary rules, expect unquestioned obedience from their children, punish transgressions, and value obedience to authority.

authoritative parents: Parents who set high but realistic standards, reason with their children, enforce limits, and encourage open communication and independence.

and at the same time encourage open communication and independence. **[LO 8.17]** They are willing to discuss rules and supply rationales for them. When children know why the rules are necessary and important, they find it easier to internalize and follow them, whether or not their parents are present. Authoritative parents are generally warm, nurturant, supportive, and responsive; they also show respect for their children and their opinions. Children raised in this way are the most mature, happy, self-reliant, self-controlled, assertive, socially competent, and responsible. Furthermore, this parenting style is associated with higher academic performance, independence, higher self-esteem, and internalized moral standards in middle childhood and adolescence (Dornbusch, Ritter, Leiderman, Roberts, & Fraleigh, 1987; Lamborn, Mounts, Steinberg, & Dronbusch, 1991; Steinberg, Elman, & Mounts, 1989).

PERMISSIVE PARENTS **Permissive parents**, although rather warm and supportive, make few rules or demands and usually do not enforce those that are made. **[LO 8.17]** They allow children to make their own decisions and control their own behaviour. Children raised in this manner are the most immature, impulsive, and dependent; they also seem to be the least self-controlled and the least self-reliant.

Permissive parents also come in the indifferent, unconcerned, and uninvolved variety (Maccoby & Martin, 1983). In adolescents, this parenting style is associated with drinking problems, promiscuous sex, delinquent behaviour, and poor academic performance.

SOCIALIZATION IN ADOLESCENCE

How do peers contribute to the socialization process?

Infants begin to show an interest in each other at a very young age. At only six months, they already demonstrate an interest in other infants by looking, reaching, touching, smiling, and vocalizing (Vandell & Mueller, 1980). Friendships begin to develop by age three or four. Relationships with peers become increasingly important, and by middle childhood, membership in a peer group is central to a child's happiness. At a time when adolescents feel the need to become more independent from their family, friends become a vital source of emotional support and approval. Adolescents usually choose friends who have similar values, interests, and backgrounds (Altermatt & Pomerantz, 2003; Duck, 1983; J. Epstein, 1983).

The peer group serves a socializing function by providing models of appropriate behaviour, dress, and language. It is a continuing source of both reinforcement for appropriate behaviour and punishment for deviant behaviour. The peer group also provides an objective measure against which individuals can evaluate their own traits and abilities (e.g., how smart or how good at sports they are).

©Samott/Fotolia

Adolescents frequently engage in high-risk behaviours even though they understand the risks involved. What underlying factors might explain this behaviour?

Adolescent Egocentrism: On Centre Stage, Unique, and Indestructible

David Elkind (1967, 1974) believes that the early teenage years are marked by adolescent egocentrism, which takes two forms—the imaginary audience and the personal fable. **[LO 8.18]**

Do you remember, as a young teenager, picturing how your friends would react to the way you looked when you made your grand entrance at a big party? At this stage of life, it never occurred to us that most of the other people at the party were preoccupied not with us, but with the way *they* looked and the impression *they* were making. This **imaginary audience** of admirers (or critics) that an adolescent conjures up exists only in the imagination, "but in the young person's mind, he/she is always on stage" (Buis & Thompson, 1989, p. 774). **[LO 8.18]**

Adolescents also have an exaggerated sense of personal uniqueness and indestructibility that Elkind calls the **personal fable**. **[LO 8.18]** They cannot fathom that anyone has ever felt as deeply as they feel or loved as they love. Elkind suggests that this compelling sense of personal uniqueness may be why many adolescents believe they are somehow protected from the misfortunes that befall others, such as unwanted pregnancies, car accidents, or drug overdoses. Belief in the personal fable may account for many of the risks teens take during adolescence.

Quadrel, Fischhoff, and Davis (1993) dispute Elkind's explanation for adolescent risk taking. They found that both high-risk adolescents (from group homes or juvenile centres) and middle-class, low-risk adolescents were more likely than adults (the parents of the group of middle-class adolescents) to anticipate experiencing certain negative events—injury in a car accident, alcohol dependency, mugging, and so forth. Apparently some adolescents are willing to engage in high-risk

CANADIAN CONNECTIONS

Risk Taking in Adolescence

Despite the fact that adolescence is noted for rapid increases in mental and physical capabilities, overall morbidity and mortality rates increase 200 percent from early childhood to late adolescence and early adulthood (Dahl, 2004). Much of this rise in morbidity and mortality rates is due to adolescent participation in behaviours that are risky, such as substance abuse, unprotected sexual activity, aggression, and delinquency. As a result, a great deal of research and attention has been given to how adolescent brain development might be implicated in risk behaviours. A popular theory is that adolescents do not have the cognitive maturity to effectively regulate the heightened emotions and arousal that occur as a result of puberty; that is, adolescents are thought to be vulnerable to risk taking because of a gap between an early maturing affective/approach brain system and a slower maturing cognitive control brain system.

Teena Willoughby and colleagues from Brock University recently provided a critical analysis of the adolescent brain development literature (see Willoughby et al., 2013). They point out that although mortality and morbidity rates increase significantly from childhood to adolescence, very few children or adolescents die or are injured (Public Health Agency of Canada, 2005a, b). In fact, the survival rate of high school students in North America is an impressive 99.96 percent. Furthermore, although there is a widely held perception by researchers, parents, media, and policy makers that risk taking behaviours are more common during adolescence than at any other age period (e.g., Dahl, 2004; Galvan, 2013; Steinberg, 2005), high school students on average report low levels of involvement in risk behaviours, with the exception of alcohol use in senior grades. Instead, the highest levels of risk taking occur among young adults, particularly university/college students (Willoughby et al., 2013), highlighting the role of the social context on engagement in risk behaviours. One does not have to look far to see that impulsivity and lapses in self-control are evident also among adults, and can incur significant costs to individuals and society. For example, millions of adults engage in impulse buying (Vohs & Faber, 2007) and overeating (Hedley et al., 2004). Approximately 11 percent of new HIV infection diagnoses in the United States occur in adults aged 50 or older (Brooks, Buchacz, Gebo, & Mermin, 2012).

Teena Willoughby

Used by permission of Teena Willoughby

One assumption of adolescent brain development models is that risk taking in adolescence is generally impulsive and due to a lack of self-control. Willoughby and colleagues contend, however, that risk taking is not necessarily unregulated or impulsive, but instead might be planned (Willoughby et al., 2013). Specifically, adolescents may deliberately engage in risk taking behaviour in order to gain social rewards, such as interpersonal acceptance (Rawn & Vohs, 2011). Planned risk taking may even require the *exertion* of self-control to overcome aversions to risky behaviour, such as the distaste for alcohol or cigarettes, or the fear of negative consequences from having unprotected sex or using illicit drugs.

According to Willoughby and colleagues, adopting a lifespan perspective, with a focus on how associations between neural systems and behaviours are moderated by both the social context and trait-level characteristics (e.g., impulsivity, working memory) *from childhood to old age*, will help to address these limitations in the adolescent brain development and risk taking literature. ∎

behaviours *in spite of* the risks involved, perhaps because of peer pressure, or because the pleasure outweighs the risk.

Some forms of risk taking may have positive consequences (Bjorklund and Green, 1992; Willoughby et al., 2007). It may enable adolescents to "experiment with new ideas and new tasks and generally behave more independently. Many of these experiences will be adaptive for adult life and for making the transition to adulthood" (Bjorklund & Green, 1992, p. 49). For more information about adolescent risk taking, see the *Canadian Connections* box.

The Development of Physical Aggression

Stabbings, shootings, fights, and other acts of violence by teenagers are a prevalent feature in news stories across the country. What makes these teens become so physically

aggressive? According to Richard Tremblay at the University of Montreal, that may be the wrong question to ask. Instead,

permissive parents: Parents who make few rules or demands and allow children to make their own decisions and control their own behaviour.

imaginary audience: A belief of adolescents that they are or will be the focus of attention in social situations and that others will be as critical or approving as they are of themselves.

personal fable: An exaggerated sense of personal uniqueness and indestructibility, which may be the basis of the risk taking that is common during adolescence.

Tremblay (2002) suggests that we ask when children start to become physically aggressive and what is the developmental pattern of aggression.

In a longitudinal study of children in Quebec, Tremblay asked mothers to rate the frequency and age of onset of their children's aggression (pushing others to get what they want, threatening to hit, physically attacking another) when children were 17 months old and again when they were 30 months old. Physical aggression such as pushing appears early, with 50 percent of children engaging in this activity by 17 months old. Threatening to hit and physically attacking another also appears early, but boys with siblings are the most likely to engage in this early in their development. All three types of aggression were evident by the 30-month mark. Interestingly, studies showed that the frequency of physical aggression decreased from 48 months of age onward (R. E. Tremblay, 2002, 2003).

Tremblay's work suggests that genetic, physical, cognitive, and social changes account for these developmental patterns in aggression, and that it is the children who fail to learn alternatives to physical aggression during these critical preschool years who are most at risk for later delinquent behaviour (R. E. Tremblay, 2002, 2003).

KOHLBERG'S THEORY OF MORAL DEVELOPMENT

What are Kohlberg's three levels of moral reasoning?

How do we develop our ideas of right and wrong? Lawrence Kohlberg (1981, 1984, 1985) believed that moral reasoning is closely related to cognitive development and that it, too, evolves in stages. Kohlberg (1969) studied moral development by presenting a series of moral dilemmas to male participants from a number of countries.

Read one of his best-known dilemmas in the next *Try It*.

Levels of Moral Reasoning

Kohlberg was less interested in how people judged Heinz's behaviour (described in the *Try It*) than in the *reasons* for their responses. He found that moral reasoning had three levels, with each level having two stages.

THE PRECONVENTIONAL LEVEL At the **preconventional level**, moral reasoning is governed by the standards of others rather than by an individual's own internalized standards of right and wrong. **[LO 8.19]** An act is judged good or bad on the basis of its physical consequences. In Stage 1, "right" is whatever avoids punishment; in Stage 2, "right" is whatever is rewarded, benefits the individual, or results in a favour being returned. "You scratch my back and I'll scratch yours" is the thinking common at this stage. Children through age 10 usually function at the preconventional level.

THE CONVENTIONAL LEVEL At the **conventional level**, the individual has internalized the standards of others and judges right and wrong in terms of those standards. **[LO 8.19]** Stage 3 is sometimes called the "good boy–nice girl orientation." "Good behaviour is that which pleases or helps others and is approved by them" (Kohlberg, 1968, p. 26). At Stage 4, the orientation is toward "authority, fixed rules, and

TRY IT

Test Your Moral Judgment

In Europe, a woman was near death from a special kind of cancer. There was one drug that the doctors thought might save her. It was a form of radium that a druggist in the same town had recently discovered. The drug was expensive to make, and the druggist was charging 10 times what the drug cost him to make. He paid $200 for the radium and charged $2000 for a small dose of the drug. The sick woman's husband, Heinz, went to everyone he knew to borrow the money, but he could get together only $1000, which was half of what it cost. He told the druggist that his wife was dying and asked him to sell it cheaper or let him pay later. But the druggist said, "No, I discovered the drug, and I am going to make money from it." So Heinz got desperate and broke into the man's store to steal the drug for his wife (Colby, Kohlberg, Gibbs, & Lieberman, 1983, p. 77).

What moral judgment would you make about the dilemma? Should Heinz have stolen the drug? Explain.

the maintenance of the social order. Right behaviour consists of doing one's duty, showing respect for authority, and maintaining the given social order for its own sake" (p. 26). Kohlberg believed that a person must have reached Piaget's concrete operations stage in order to reason morally at the conventional level.

Couldn't this kind of moral reasoning provide a convenient justification for any act at any time? Not according to Kohlberg, who insisted that an action must be judged in terms of whether it is right and fair from the perspective of *all* the people involved. In other words, the person must be convinced that the action would be proper even if he or she had to change positions with any individual, from the most favoured to the least favoured, in the society.

THE POSTCONVENTIONAL LEVEL Kohlberg's highest level of moral reasoning is the **postconventional level**, which requires the ability to think at Piaget's level of formal operations. **[LO 8.19]** According to Kohlberg, most often this level is found among middle-class, well-educated people. At this level, people do not simply internalize the standards of others. Instead, they weigh moral alternatives, realizing that at times the law may conflict with basic human rights. At Stage 5, the person believes that laws are formulated to protect both society and the individual and that they should be changed if they fail to do so. At Stage 6, ethical decisions are based on universal ethical principles, which emphasize respect for human life, justice, equality, and dignity for all people. People who reason morally at Stage 6 believe that they must follow their conscience even if it results in a violation of the law.

We should point out that Kohlberg had second thoughts about this sixth stage and was unsure whether it exists except as a matter of theoretical and philosophical speculation (Levine, Kohlberg, & Hewer, 1985).

Review & Reflect 8.3 describes Kohlberg's stages of moral development.

REVIEW & REFLECT 8.3 KOHLBERG'S STAGES OF MORAL DEVELOPMENT

Level	Stage
Level I: Preconventional Level (ages birth to 10 years) Moral reasoning is governed by the standards of others; an act is good or bad depending on its physical consequences—whether it is punished or rewarded.	**Stage 1** The stage where whatever avoids punishment is right. Children obey out of fear of punishment. **Stage 2** The stage of self-interest. Whatever benefits the individual or gains a favour in return is right. "You scratch my back and I'll scratch yours."
Level II: Conventional Level (ages 10 to 13) The person internalizes the standards of others and judges right and wrong according to those standards.	**Stage 3** The morality of mutual relationships. The "good boy–nice girl" orientation. Child acts to please and help others. **Stage 4** The morality of the social system and conscience. Orientation toward authority. Morality is doing one's duty, respecting authority, and maintaining the social order.
Level III: Postconventional Level (after age 13, at young adulthood, or never) Moral conduct is under internal control; this is the highest level and the mark of true morality.	**Stage 5** The morality of contract; respect for individual rights and laws that are democratically agreed on. Rational valuing of the wishes of the majority and welfare of the people. Belief that society is best served if citizens obey the law. **Stage 6** The highest stage of the highest social level. The morality of universal ethical principles. The person acts according to internal standards independent of legal restrictions or opinions of others.

The Development of Moral Reasoning

According to Kohlberg, we progress through moral stages one stage at a time in a fixed order. We do not skip stages, and if movement occurs, it is to the next higher stage. Postconventional reasoning is not possible, Kohlberg said, until people fully attain Piaget's level of formal operations. They must be able to think in terms of abstract principles and be able to think through and apply ethical principles in hypothetical situations (Kohlberg & Gilligan, 1971; Kuhn, Kohlberg, Langer, & Haan, 1977). Attaining a high level of cognitive development, however, does not guarantee advanced moral reasoning.

Research on Kohlberg's Theory

What do cross-cultural studies reveal about the universality of Kohlberg's theory?

In a review of 45 studies of Kohlberg's theory conducted in 27 countries, Snarey (1985) found support for the virtual universality of Stages 1 through 4 and for the invariant sequence of these stages in all groups studied. Stage 5 was evident in almost all samples from urban or middle-class populations and was absent in all of the tribal or village societies studied. A subsequent study by Snarey (1995) a decade later supported these conclusions.

Kohlberg indicated gender differences, with most women remaining at Stage 3, while most men attained Stage 4. Carol Gilligan (1982) believed that Kohlberg's theory was sex-biased.

Not only did Kohlberg fail to include any females in his original research and limited morality to abstract reasoning about moral dilemmas, but at his highest level, Stage 6, Kohlberg emphasized justice and equality but not mercy, compassion, love, or concern for others. Gilligan and others (Wark & Krebs, 1996) suggest that females tend more than males to view moral behaviour in terms of compassion, caring, and concern for others. Thus Gilligan agrees that the content of moral reasoning differs between the sexes, but she contends that males and females do not differ in the complexity of their moral reasoning. Kohlberg's theory does emphasize rights and justice over concern for others; even so, other researchers have found that females score as highly as males in their moral reasoning (L. Walker, 1989; L. Walker, de Vries, & Trevethan, 1987).

preconventional level: Kohlberg's lowest level of moral reasoning, based on the physical consequences of an act; "right" is whatever avoids punishment or gains a reward.

conventional level: Kohlberg's second level of moral reasoning, in which right and wrong are based on the internalized standards of others; "right" is whatever helps or is approved of by others, or whatever is consistent with the laws of society.

postconventional level: Kohlberg's highest level of moral reasoning, in which moral reasoning involves weighing moral alternatives; "right" is whatever furthers basic human rights.

REMEMBER IT

Socialization and Social Relationships

1. Match the psychosocial stage with the appropriate phrase.
   - _____ 1) needs regular care and love
   - _____ 2) initiates play and motor activities, asks questions
   - _____ 3) strives for sense of independence
   - _____ 4) undertakes projects, makes things
      - a. basic trust versus basic mistrust
      - b. industry versus inferiority
      - c. initiative versus guilt
      - d. autonomy versus shame and doubt

2. Infants raised with adequate physical care but without the attention of a close, personal caregiver often become mentally and/or physically disabled. (true/false)

3. Match the parenting style with the approach to discipline.
   - _____ 1) expect unquestioned obedience
   - _____ 2) set high standards, give rationale for rules
   - _____ 3) set few rules or limits
      - a. permissive parents
      - b. authoritative parents
      - c. authoritarian parents

4. Match Kohlberg's level of moral reasoning with the rationale for engaging in a behaviour.
   - _____ 1) to avoid punishment or gain a reward
   - _____ 2) to ensure that human rights are protected
   - _____ 3) to gain approval or to follow the law
      - a. conventional
      - b. preconventional
      - c. postconventional

MODULE 8F SPECIAL CONCERNS IN LATER ADULTHOOD

LO 8.20 Identify and describe the five stages Kübler-Ross proposed to explain the process of coming to terms with death and dying.
LO 8.21 Understand the process of bereavement.

Age 65 or 70 is generally considered the beginning of old age. What are your perceptions of life after 65? Complete the *Try It* by answering *true* or *false* to the statements about older adults.

Life satisfaction in older adults appears to be most strongly related to good health, as well as to a feeling of control over one's life (Berg, Hoffman, Hassing, McClearn, & Johansson 2009). Elders who have an optimistic outlook report higher levels of satisfaction (Hagberg, Hagberg, & Saveman, 2002; Litwin, 2005; Mehlsen, 2005). Adequate income, participation in social activities, and a satisfactory marital relationship also are associated with high levels of life satisfaction (Litwin, 2006). Many older adults experience a rich, rewarding old age; however, they also experience losses (cognitive, health, social, and love), which can negatively impact on their lives.

TERMINAL ILLNESS AND DEATH

One of the developmental tasks for the elderly is to accept the inevitability of death and to prepare themselves for it. At no time does this become more critical than when people face a terminal illness.

Kübler-Ross on Death and Dying

According to Kübler-Ross, what stages do terminally ill patients experience as they come to terms with death?

TRY IT

Testing Perceptions of Older Adults

Are the following statements true or false?

1. Older adults tend to express less satisfaction with life in general than younger adults do.
2. A lack of money is a serious problem for most people over 65.
3. Marital satisfaction declines in old age.
4. Mandatory retirement forces most workers out of jobs before they are ready to leave.
5. The majority of retirees do not adjust well to retirement.
6. A large percentage of individuals over 85 end up in nursing homes or institutions.

Psychiatrist Elisabeth Kübler-Ross (1969) interviewed some 200 terminally ill people and found commonalities in their reactions to dying. She identified five stages that most of those she interviewed experienced in coming to terms with death.

In the first stage, *denial and isolation*, most patients feel shock and disbelief. **[LO 8.20]** The second stage, *anger*, is marked by envy of those who are young and healthy, and by resentment. **[LO 8.20]** "Why me?" is the question that rages inside. In the third stage, *bargaining*, the person attempts to postpone death for a specific period of time in return for "good behaviour." **[LO 8.20]**

Eventually the bargaining gives way to the fourth stage, *depression*. **[LO 8.20]** This stage brings a great sense of loss—physical loss, loss of ability to work, loss of the role of mother, father, spouse. This depression takes two forms—depression over past losses and depression over impending losses.

If enough time remains, patients usually reach the final stage, *acceptance*, in which they are neither depressed nor angry. **[LO 8.20]** They stop struggling against death and are able to contemplate its coming without fear or despair. Kübler-Ross found that the family also goes through stages similar to those experienced by the patient.

Kübler-Ross was one of the first researchers to make the public aware of the needs and feelings of the dying. Although other researchers acknowledge that her proposed stages often do occur, they deny their universality and their invariant sequence (R. Butler & Lewis, 1982; Kastenbaum, 1992). We should not expect the reactions of all the terminally ill to conform to some rigid sequence of stages; nor should we dismiss their anguish as merely a stage they are going through.

Older adults who stay active and socialize have a better chance of remaining healthy.

Bereavement

Many of us have experienced the grieving process—the period of bereavement that follows the death of a loved one and sometimes lingers long after. **[LO 8.21]** Contrary to what many believe, those who suffer the most intense grief initially, who weep inconsolably and feel the deepest pain, do not get through their bereavement more quickly than others (Bonanno, Keltner, Holen, & Horowitz, 1995). According to one proposed model for how married people cope with bereavement, the grieving spouse at times actively confronts and at other times avoids giving full vent to grief. This dual-process coping, with periods of grieving and periods of relief, seems effective in dealing with the stress of losing a spouse (Hansson & Stroebe, 2007; Stroebe & Schut, 1999).

Death and dying are not pleasant subjects, but remember that life itself is a terminal condition, and each day of life should certainly be treasured like a precious gift.

REMEMBER IT

Special Concerns in Later Adulthood

1. Greater life satisfaction is related to all but which of the following?
   a. good education
   b. good health
   c. optimism
   d. adequate finances

2. According to Kübler-Ross, the first stage experienced by terminally ill patients in coming to terms with death is _____; the last stage is _____.
   a. anger; depression
   b. denial; depression
   c. bargaining; acceptance
   d. denial; acceptance

Answers: 1. a 2. d

APPLY IT

Choosing a Non-parental Care Arrangement

Although you, as a parent, are a vital support for your child, any other care setting you arrange for your child is also important. Thus, even though your child is not in direct contact with you when she is receiving care from someone else, you will still be influencing her through the criteria that you use to select the non-parental care arrangement. One of the most daunting and stress-inducing tasks that a parent faces is that of choosing a non-parental care arrangement for an infant or young child. Here is a systematic approach that may help reduce the stress associated with making this important decision.

Step 1: Define Your Parenting Goals

Child psychologist Sandra Scarr (1997) suggests that non-parental care is best thought of as an extension of your own parenting priorities. Thus, it's worthwhile to spend some time thinking about your parenting goals before you start your search. Think about the kind of home environment you plan to provide for your child's early years and look for the non-parental care arrangement that best matches it.

Step 2: Know Your Child's Temperament and Preferences

Research suggests that temperament interacts with care arrangements (Crockenberg & Leerkes, 2005; Wachs, Gurkas, & Kontos, 2004). For example, slow-to-warm-up children may be overwhelmed by the sheer number of children in a daycare centre (Watamura, Donzella, Alwin, & Gunnar, 2003). Thus, it helps to know what kind of temperament your child has and the kinds of situations in which she is most comfortable.

A child's likes and dislikes are important as well. For a picky eater, a care arrangement in which the child can have her beloved peanut butter and banana sandwich at every meal may be more practical than a centre where she will only be offered food that she will refuse to eat. Similarly, an active child may be happiest in a situation in which children can go outdoors whenever their caregivers sense that they need to burn off some energy.

Step 3: Consider the Research

The importance of child care to families and to society in general has motivated psychologists to conduct thousands of studies aimed at identifying the differences between high- and low-quality non-parental care (see Feine, 2002 for a summary). Here are a few criteria that most experts recommend taking into account:

- *Health practices.* Take note of handwashing rules (for both children and caregivers), food-handling practices, and the nutritional quality of meals.

- *Caregiver–child ratio, sensitivity, stability, and training.* Look for a low ratio of adults to children, sensitive responses to children's behaviour, low turnover, and formal training requirements for all caregivers.

- *Group size.* Smaller is generally better, especially for infants.

- *Appropriate learning environment.* Look for toys, games, books, activities, and a daily routine that are appropriate for your child's age group.

Step 5: Evaluate Your Choice

The evaluation process shouldn't stop once you have made your choice. Drop in unexpectedly from time to time to see how things are going, and keep track of personnel changes. Above all, do not hesitate to withdraw your child if you become dissatisfied or uncomfortable in any way with the arrangement you have chosen.

THINKING CRITICALLY

Evaluation

In your opinion, do Erikson's psychosocial stages for adolescence and early adulthood accurately represent the major conflicts of these periods of life? Explain.

Point/Counterpoint

Prepare an argument supporting each of these positions:

a. Physical development peaks in the early adult years and declines thereafter.

b. Physical development can be maintained throughout life.

Psychology in Your Life

Using Erikson's theory, try to relate the first four stages of psychosocial development to your life.

Using Baumrind's scheme, classify the parenting style your mother and/or father used in rearing you.

a. Cite examples of techniques they used that support your classification.

b. Do you agree with Baumrind's conclusions about the effects of that parenting style on children? Explain.

MyPsychLab — go to mypsychlab (access code required) to find web resources for your text that supplement the material in chapter 8.

SUMMARY & REVIEW

 8A DEVELOPMENTAL PSYCHOLOGY: BASIC ISSUES AND METHODOLOGY

What are two types of studies that developmental psychologists use to investigate age-related changes?
To investigate age-related changes, developmental psychologists use (1) the longitudinal study, in which the same group of participants is followed and measured at different ages; and (2) the cross-sectional study, in which researchers compare groups of participants of different ages with respect to various characteristics to determine age-related differences.

 8B HEREDITY AND PRENATAL DEVELOPMENT

How are hereditary traits transmitted?
Hereditary traits are transmitted through genes.

When are dominant or recessive genes expressed in a person?
When there are alternative forms of a gene for a specific trait, the dominant gene will be expressed. A recessive gene is expressed when it is paired with another recessive gene.

What are the three stages of prenatal development?
The three stages of prenatal development are the period of the zygote, the period of the embryo, and the period of the fetus.

What are some negative influences on prenatal development, and when is their impact greatest?
Some common hazards in the prenatal environment include drugs, environmental agents, poor maternal nutrition, and maternal infections and illnesses. Their impact is greatest during the first trimester.

8C PHYSICAL DEVELOPMENT AND LEARNING

What are the perceptual abilities of the newborn?
All of the newborn's senses are functional at birth, and the neonate already has preferences for certain odours, tastes, sounds, and visual configurations.

What types of learning occur in the first few days of life?
Newborns are capable of habituation.

What physical changes occur during puberty?
Puberty is a period marked by rapid physical growth (the adolescent growth spurt), further development of the reproductive organs, and the appearance of the secondary sex characteristics. The major event for girls is menarche (first menstruation); for boys it is the first ejaculation.

What are the physical changes associated with middle age?
Physical changes associated with middle age are a need for reading glasses, menopause (for women), and a declining reproductive capacity (for men).

8D THE COGNITIVE STAGES OF DEVELOPMENT

What were Piaget's beliefs regarding stages of cognitive development?
Piaget believed that intellect develops in four stages, each representing a qualitatively different form of reasoning and understanding. He also believed the stages to be universal and to occur in an invariant sequence, although the rate at which children progress through them might differ.

What is Piaget's sensorimotor stage?
In the sensorimotor stage (birth to age two), infants learn about the world through their senses and motor activities. The major accomplishment of this stage is the development of object permanence.

What cognitive limitations characterize a child's thinking during the preoperational stage?
In the preoperational stage (ages two to seven), children are increasingly able to represent objects and events mentally, but they exhibit egocentrism and centration; they have not developed the concepts of reversibility and conservation.

What cognitive abilities do children acquire during the concrete operations stage?
In the concrete operations stage (ages 7 to 11 or 12 years), children become able to decentre their thinking and to understand the concepts of reversibility and conservation.

What new capability characterizes the formal operations stage?
In the formal operations stage (age 11 or 12 and beyond), adolescents and adults are able to apply logical thinking to abstract, verbal, and hypothetical situations and to problems in the past, present, and future.

In general, can adolescents and adults look forward to an increase or a decrease in intellectual performance?
Although younger people tend to do better on tests requiring speed or rote memory, intellectual performance shows modest gains until the mid-40s. A modest decline occurs from the 60s to the 80s.

8E SOCIALIZATION AND SOCIAL RELATIONSHIPS

What is Erikson's theory of psychosocial development?
Erikson believed that individuals progress through eight psychosocial stages during the lifespan, each defined by a conflict with the social environment that must be resolved. The four stages in childhood are basic trust versus basic mistrust (birth to age two), autonomy versus shame and doubt (ages one to three), initiative versus guilt (ages three to six), and industry versus inferiority (age six to puberty). Adolescents experience the fifth stage, identity versus role confusion. The three stages of adulthood are intimacy versus isolation (young adulthood), generativity versus stagnation (middle adulthood), and ego integrity versus despair (late adulthood).

What did Harlow's studies reveal about maternal deprivation and attachment in infant monkeys?
Harlow found that the basis of attachment in infant monkeys is contact comfort, and that monkeys raised with surrogates showed abnormal social and emotional behaviour.

When does the infant have a strong attachment to the mother?
The infant usually starts to show signs of a strong attachment to the mother at six to eight months, and virtually all children show attachment by the age of two.

What are the four attachment patterns identified in infants?
Ainsworth identified four attachment patterns: secure, avoidant, resistant, and disorganized/disoriented.

What are the three parenting styles discussed by Baumrind, and which did she find most effective?
The three parenting styles discussed by Baumrind are the authoritarian, the permissive, and the authoritative; she found the authoritative to be best.

How do peers contribute to the socialization process?
The peer group serves a socializing function by modelling and reinforcing behaviours it considers appropriate, by punishing inappropriate behaviour, and by providing an objective measurement against which children can evaluate their own traits and abilities.

What are Kohlberg's three levels of moral reasoning?
At Kohlberg's preconventional level, moral reasoning is based on the consequences of an act—"right" is whatever averts punishment or brings a reward. At the conventional level, right and wrong are based on the internalized standards of others—"right" is whatever helps or is approved of by others or is consistent with the laws of society. Postconventional moral reasoning involves weighing moral alternatives—"right" is whatever furthers basic human rights.

What do cross-cultural studies reveal about the universality of Kohlberg's theory?
Cross-cultural studies support the universality of Kohlberg's Stages 1 through 4 and their invariant sequence. Stage 5 was found in most urban or middle-class samples but not in the tribal and village societies studied.

8F SPECIAL CONCERNS IN LATER ADULTHOOD

According to Kübler-Ross, what stages do terminally ill patients experience as they come to terms with death?
Kübler-Ross maintains that terminally ill patients go through five stages in coming to terms with death: denial and isolation, anger, bargaining, depression, and acceptance.

DEVELOPMENT

MODULE (8A) DEVELOPMENTAL PSYCHOLOGY

Developmental psychology studies how humans grow, develop, and change throughout their lifespan.

Developmental Issues
Nature–nurture controversy: To what degree do heredity and environment influence development?
Is development **continuous** or does it occur in **stages**?
Are personal traits **stable** or **changeable**?

Developmental Research Designs
Longitudinal designs test the same group of individuals at different ages.
Cross-sectional designs test different groups of people who differ in age at one time.

MODULE (8B) HEREDITY AND PRENATAL DEVELOPMENT

Genes are segments of DNA that determine transmission of hereditary traits and bodily functions. Genes can be dominant (expressed whenever they occur) or recessive (expressed only if paired with another recessive gene).
Chromosomes contain genes. In humans the 23rd pair of chromosomes are called **sex chromosomes** because they determine one's primary and secondary sex characteristics.
Identical (monozygotic) twins form when one egg is fertilized by one sperm and the zygote splits into two parts, whereas **fraternal (dizygotic) twins** form when two eggs are fertilized by two different sperm.

Prenatal Development

Period of the zygote (conception to 2 weeks) lasts from when a sperm cell fertilizes an ovum to implantation in uterus.

Embryonic stage (3 to 8 weeks) ends when the first bone cells form. Major systems, organs, and structures of the body begin to develop.

Fetal stage (9 to 38 weeks) ends at birth. Period of growth for organs and body systems.

Effects of Teratogens
Teratogens are harmful agents that can have a negative effect on prenatal development and are usually most harmful during the first three months of development.
They can result in low birth weight (less than 2.5 kilograms), preterm deliveries (before the 37th week with low birth weight), cognitive or physical delays, or death.
A **critical period** is a specific time in development where teratogens can prevent a bodily structure or behaviour from developing normally.

MODULE (8C) PHYSICAL DEVELOPMENT AND LEARNING

Neonates
A **neonate** is a newborn infant up to one month old.
Newborns have many survival-based **reflexes** (unlearned automatic responses to certain stimuli) and fairly well-developed senses.
One measure of learning is **habituation** (decreased response to a stimulus that is repeated).

Adolescence and Puberty
Puberty begins with an increase in hormone production, which in turn causes a number of physical changes that culminates in sexual maturity.
The adolescent growth spurt peaks around age 12 in girls and around age 14 in boys. Major landmarks of puberty are first ejaculation for males and menarche for females.

Middle Age and the Elderly
Major landmarks are menopause for females and gradual decline in testosterone production in males.
The elderly may experience decrements in vision and hearing.

MODULE 8D THE COGNITIVE STAGES OF DEVELOPMENT

Piaget's Cognitive Stages

Sensorimotor (birth to 2 years)
Infants think about events that are directly perceived and by moving their body. They gradually learn that objects continue to exist even when they are no longer perceived (object permanence).

Preoperational (2 to 7 years)
Children can think using words and images but cannot follow logical rules. Preoperational children focus on only one dimension (centration), believe that everyone sees what they see and thinks as they think (egocentrism), and believe that inanimate objects are alive and have feelings (animistic thinking).

Concrete Operational (7 to 11 or 12 years)
Children can follow logical rules only for problems that they can directly perceive. Children come to understand that changes in shape, position, or order can be undone (reversibility) and that changes in appearance do not alter the amount of matter (conservation).

Formal Operational (11 or 12 years and beyond)
Adolescents and adults can perform mental operations that follow logical rules for abstract, verbal, and hypothetical problems.

Cognitive Capacity in Adolescence and Adulthood
During adolescence information-processing skills such as metamemory continue to advance.
Adults continue to be able to acquire complex cognitive skills into their 70s and beyond.

Attachment in Infants
Without a warm, close, personal caregiver, many human infants fail to grow normally and may not survive.
Harlow observed that contact comfort, rather than nourishment, forms the basis for infant monkeys' attachment to their mothers.
Types of Attachments in Infants and Responses to Parent in the Stranger Situation
Secure attachment (65%): Distressed when separated from mother, eagerly re-establishes contact after separation, and then plays.
Avoidant attachment (20%): Unresponsive to mother when she is present, and not troubled when she leaves.
Resistant attachment (10%): Preferring close contact with mother, but displaying anger toward mother after a separation.
Disorganized/disoriented attachment (5%): Either looking away from mother when being held or looking expressionless or depressed and sometimes changing response on different occasions.

Adolescent **egocentrism** has two forms. **Imaginary audience** occurs when adolescents believe that they are the centre of attention in social situations. **Personal fable** is evidenced through an exaggerated sense of personal uniqueness and indestructibility.

Kohlberg's Moral Stages

Preconventional level (up to 10 years): Behaviour is judged good or bad based on its consequences. Good is whatever avoids punishment (Stage 1) or benefits oneself (Stage 2).

Conventional level (10 to 13 years): A person has internalized the standards of others. Good is whatever is approved by others close to oneself (Stage 3) or by society (Stage 4).

Postconventional level (after 13 years or never):
Moral reasoning is based on weighing moral alternatives and determining what best furthers basic human rights. Good is whatever protects both society and individuals (Stage 5) or is consistent with universal ethical principles (Stage 6).

MODULE 8E SOCIALIZATION AND SOCIAL RELATIONSHIPS

Erikson's Psychosocial Stages
Each stage is defined by a conflict with the social environment.
1. **Basic trust vs. mistrust** (birth to 12 months): Is my world caring and predictable?
2. **Autonomy vs. shame and doubt** (1 to 3 years): Can I do things myself?
3. **Initiative vs. guilt** (3 to 6 years): Am I responsible?
4. **Industry vs. inferiority** (6 years to puberty): Am I proud of my accomplishments?
5. **Identity vs. role confusion** (adolescence): Who am I and where am I going?
6. **Intimacy vs. isolation** (early adulthood): Can I commit to another person?
7. **Generativity vs. stagnation** (middle adulthood): Can I contribute to society?
8. **Ego integrity vs. despair** (late adulthood): Am I satisfied with my life?

Parenting Styles

Authoritarian parents make arbitrary rules, expect unquestioned obedience, and punish transgression.

Authoritative parents set high but realistic standards, reason with children, enforce limits, and encourage open communication and independence.

Permissive parents make few rules and allow children to make their own decisions and control their own behaviour.

MODULE 8F SPECIAL CONCERNS IN LATER ADULTHOOD

Kübler-Ross's Stages of Dying
Denial and isolation: A person feels shock and disbelief.
Anger: A person is envious of healthy people and resents his or her fate.
Bargaining: A person tries to postpone death in return for good behaviour.
Depression: A person is depressed over past and impending losses.
Acceptance: A person accepts death without fear or despair.

9

Much has been written about the cognitive nature of humans. The fact that people can think is a central tenet of Western philosophy as defined in René Descartes's famous statement "I think, therefore I am." By contrast, all of us can also appreciate the fact that emotions often govern our understanding of the world and that the decisions we make are frequently based on the way we feel about certain things.

The emotional nature of people was demonstrated at a recent Game Developers Conference in San Francisco. David Mark, an artificial intelligence expert, wanted to demonstrate to an audience of games developers that the only way to create successful games is to appeal to the gamers' emotions (see Crecente, 2012). He argued that, even in the absence of defining information, people project what they believe should be there—they make emotional connections with even a minimum of information.

To prove his point, Mark showed the Heider–Simmel demonstration, an animated video created by psychologists Fritz Heider and Marianne Simmel in the 1940s. The short video shows two animated triangles, an animated circle, and a box.

There was no audio, just the crude line drawings moving around. After David Mark showed the video, most viewers interpreted what they saw as a story filled with emotional connections. For example, some viewers described the story as a conflict between a couple and a bully; others perceived it as a mother, a child, and a bad guy. Each viewer created his or her own story, and many invented an elaborate backstory for the simple drawings shown in the video. "It's really just two triangles, a circle, and some lines," Mark pointed out. But even in the absence of information, its viewers created their own fiction and their own emotional attachments.

This illustration suggests that while deliberate and thoughtful decision making matters, so do emotions. We are emotional beings, and we cannot, or should not, discount this important aspect of being human. Later in the chapter, you will learn more about human emotions, how they occur and why. But before we discuss this fascinating topic, we will first examine the topic of motivation—why we do what we do.

©Mike Ehrmann/Getty Images Sport/Getty Images

MOTIVATION AND EMOTION

MODULE 9A THEORIES OF MOTIVATION

LO 9.1 Compare and contrast internal and external motivation.

LO 9.2 Identify and contrast the four main theories of motivation described in the chapter: instinct theories, drive-reduction theory, arousal theory, and Maslow's hierarchy of needs.

LO 9.3 Explain how stimulus motives and arousal affect behaviour and performance.

LO 9.4 Describe the effects of sensory deprivation.

LO 9.5 Describe Maslow's hierarchy of needs and explain how it connects to motivation.

What is the difference between intrinsic and extrinsic motivation?

When you say "I need to study for an exam, but I'm just not motivated to do it right now," what do you really mean? You probably mean that there is nothing pushing you toward that goal. In this chapter on **motivation**, we look at the underlying processes that initiate, direct, and sustain behaviour in order to satisfy physiological and psychological needs. At any given time, our behaviour may be explained by one or a combination of **motives**—needs or desires that energize and direct behaviour toward a goal. Motives can arise from an internal need, such as when we are hungry and look for something to eat. In such cases we are pushed into action from within. Other motives come from outside: Some external stimulus, or **incentive**, pulls or entices us to act. After finishing a huge meal, some people yield to the temptation of a delicious dessert. At times like this, it is the external tempter, not the internal need for food, that moves us.

The intensity of our motivation, which depends on the number and strength of the motives involved, has a bearing on the effort and the persistence with which we pursue our goals. Sometimes we pursue an activity as an end in itself simply because it is enjoyable, not because any external reward is attached to it. This type of motivation is known as **intrinsic motivation**. **[LO 9.1]** On the other hand, when we engage in activities not because they are enjoyable but to gain some external reward or to avoid some undesirable consequence, we are pulled by **extrinsic motivation**. **[LO 9.1]** If you are working hard in this course solely because you find the subject interesting, your motivation is intrinsic. But if you are studying only to meet a requirement or to satisfy some other, external need, your motivation is extrinsic. In real life, the motives for many activities are both intrinsic and extrinsic. You may love your job, but you would probably be motivated to leave if your salary—an important extrinsic motivator—were taken away. Table 9.1 gives examples of intrinsic and extrinsic motivation.

What do the experts say about the motives behind our behaviour? Consider some theories of motivation and find out.

INSTINCT THEORIES OF MOTIVATION

How do instinct theories explain motivation?

Scientists have learned much about instincts by observing animal behaviour. Spiders instinctively spin their intricate webs

TABLE 9.1 Intrinsic and Extrinsic Motivation

	Description	Examples
Intrinsic motivation	An activity is pursued as an end in itself because it is enjoyable and rewarding.	A person anonymously donates a large sum of money to a university to fund scholarships for hundreds of deserving students. A child reads several books each week because reading is fun.
Extrinsic motivation	An activity is pursued to gain an external reward or to avoid an undesirable consequence.	A person agrees to donate a large sum of money to a university for the construction of a building, provided it will bear the family name. A child reads two books each week to avoid losing television privileges.

without having *learned* the technique from other spiders. It is neither a choice they make nor a task they learn, but an instinct. An **instinct** is an inborn, unlearned, fixed pattern of behaviour that is characteristic of an entire species. An instinct does not improve with practice, and an animal will perform it the same way even if it has never seen another member of its species. Even when their web-spinning glands are removed, spiders still perform the complex spinning movements and then lay their eggs in the imaginary web they have spun. So instincts tell us a great deal about animal behaviour.

But can human motivation be explained by **instinct theory**—the notion that we are motivated by certain innate, unlearned tendencies that are part of the genetic makeup of all individuals? **[LO 9.2]** Instinct theory was widely accepted by psychologists and others for the first 20 or 30 years of the twentieth century. Over the course of those decades, the list of instincts expanded until thousands of instincts were being proposed to explain human behaviour. Common experience alone suggests that human behaviour is too richly diverse, and often too unpredictable, to be considered fixed and invariant across our species. Today, most psychologists reject the instinct theory as an explanation of human motivation.

DRIVE-REDUCTION THEORY: STRIVING TO KEEP A BALANCED INTERNAL STATE

What is the drive-reduction theory of motivation?

Another major attempt to explain motivation, human and otherwise, is the **drive-reduction theory**, or drive theory, popularized by Clark Hull (1943). **[LO 9.2]** According to Hull, all living organisms have certain biological needs that must be met if they are to survive. A need gives rise to an internal state of tension or arousal called a **drive**, and we are motivated to reduce it. For example, when we are deprived of food or go too long without water, our biological need causes a state of tension, in this case the hunger or thirst drive. We become motivated to seek food or water to reduce the drive and satisfy our biological need.

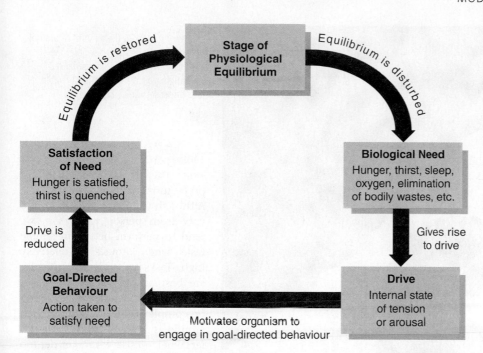

FIGURE 9.1

Drive-Reduction Theory

Drive-reduction theory is based on the biological concept of homeostasis—the body's natural tendency to maintain a state of internal balance, or equilibrium. When the equilibrium becomes disturbed (e.g., when we are thirsty and need water), a drive (internal state of arousal) emerges. Then the organism is motivated to take action to satisfy the need, thus reducing the drive and restoring equilibrium.

Drive-reduction theory is derived largely from the biological concept of **homeostasis**—the tendency of the body to maintain a balanced internal state to ensure physical survival. Body temperature, blood sugar, water, oxygen—in short, everything required for physical existence—must be maintained in a state of equilibrium, or balance. When this state is disturbed, a drive is created to restore the balance, as shown in Figure 9.1. But drive theory cannot fully account for the broad range of human motivation.

It is true that we are sometimes motivated to reduce tension, as the drive-reduction theory states, but often we are just as motivated to increase it. Why do people seek activities that actually create a state of tension—hang-gliding, horror movies, bungee jumping, and so on? Why do animals and humans alike engage in exploratory behaviour when it does not serve to reduce any primary drive?

AROUSAL THEORY: STRIVING FOR AN OPTIMAL LEVEL OF AROUSAL

How does arousal theory explain motivation?

Arousal theory can answer some of the puzzling questions that drive-reduction theory cannot answer. **[LO 9.2]** **Arousal** refers to a person's state of alertness and mental and physical activation. It ranges from no arousal (as in comatose) to moderate arousal (when we are pursuing normal day-to-day activities) to high arousal (when we are excited and highly stimulated).

Unlike drive-reduction theory, **arousal theory** does not suggest that we are always motivated to reduce arousal or tension. Arousal theory states that we are motivated to maintain an optimal level of arousal. If arousal is less than the optimal level, we do something to stimulate it; if arousal exceeds the optimal level, we seek to reduce it.

motivation: The process that initiates, directs, and sustains behaviour to satisfy physiological or psychological needs.

motives: Needs or desires that energize and direct behaviour toward a goal.

incentive: An external stimulus that motivates behaviour (e.g., money, fame).

intrinsic motivation: The desire to perform an act because it is satisfying or pleasurable in and of itself.

extrinsic motivation: The desire to perform an act in order to gain a reward or to avoid an undesirable consequence.

instinct: An inborn, unlearned, fixed pattern of behaviour that is characteristic of an entire species.

instinct theory: The notion that human behaviour is motivated by certain innate tendencies, or instincts, shared by all individuals.

drive-reduction theory: A theory of motivation suggesting that a need creates an unpleasant state of arousal or tension called a *drive*, which impels the organism to engage in behaviour that will satisfy the need and reduce tension.

drive: A state of tension or arousal brought about by an underlying need, which motivates one to engage in behaviour that will satisfy the need and reduce the tension.

homeostasis: The tendency of the body to maintain a balanced internal state with regard to body temperature, blood sugar, water, oxygen level, and so forth to ensure physical survival.

arousal: A state of alertness and mental and physical activation.

arousal theory: A theory suggesting that the aim of motivation is to maintain an optimal level of arousal.

Biological needs, such as the needs for food and water, increase our arousal. But we also become aroused when we encounter new stimuli or when the intensity of stimuli is increased, as with loud noises, bright lights, or foul odours. And of course, certain kinds of drugs—stimulants such as caffeine, nicotine, amphetamines, and cocaine—also increase arousal.

Psychologists once believed that people generally felt better when their arousal level was moderate (Berlyne, 1971). But current theories suggest that people differ in the level of arousal they prefer. Some people are sensation seekers who love the thrills of new experiences, while others prefer the routine of a predictable life (Zuckerman, 2014).

Review & Reflect 9.1 summarizes the three major motivation theories that we have discussed: instinct, drive reduction, and arousal.

Stimulus Motives: Increasing Stimulation

When arousal is too low, **stimulus motives**, such as curiosity and the motives to explore, to manipulate objects, and to play, cause us to increase stimulation. **[LO 9.3]** Think about sitting at a place where people are waiting. How many people do you see playing games on their cellphones or listening to music? Many? This shouldn't be surprising, since waiting is boring and provides no sources of arousal.

Arousal and Performance

There is often a close link between arousal and performance. **[LO 9.3]** According to the **Yerkes–Dodson law** (Yerkes & Dodson,

People vary greatly in the amount of arousal they can tolerate. For some people, the heightened level of arousal experienced when hanging off a precipice is enjoyable. Others prefer less arousing activities.

©Greg Epperson/ Fotolia

1908), performance on tasks is best when the arousal level is appropriate to the difficulty of the task. Although optimal levels of arousal vary from person to person, we tend to perform better on simple tasks when arousal is relatively high. Tasks of moderate difficulty are best accomplished when our arousal is moderate; we do better on complex or difficult tasks when arousal is lower. Performance suffers when arousal level is either too high or too low for the task.

The Effects of Sensory Deprivation: Sensory Nothingness

How would you like to be paid to do absolutely nothing? In an early experiment, Bexton, Herron, and Scott (1954) at McGill University gave student volunteers this opportunity when they studied the effects of **sensory deprivation**—a condition in which sensory stimulation is reduced to a minimum or eliminated.

Students had to lie motionless in a specially designed sensory-deprivation chamber in which sensory stimulation was severely restricted, as in the photograph. The participants could eat, drink, and go to the bathroom when they wanted to. Occasionally they were tested for motor and mental function. Otherwise they were confined to their sensationless prison.

Did they enjoy the experience? Hardly! Half the participants quit the experiment after the first two days. **[LO 9.4]** Those who remained eventually became irritable, confused, and unable to concentrate. They began to have visual hallucinations. Some began to hear imaginary voices and music and felt as if they were receiving electric shocks or being hit by pellets.

REVIEW & REFLECT 9.1 THEORIES OF MOTIVATION

Theory	View	Example
Instinct theory	Behaviour is the result of innate, unlearned tendencies. (This view has been rejected by most modern psychologists.)	Two people fight because of their aggressive instinct.
Drive-reduction theory	Behaviour results from the need to reduce an internal state of tension or arousal.	A person eats to reduce hunger.
Arousal theory	Behaviour results from the need to maintain an optimal level of arousal.	A person climbs a mountain for excitement; a person listens to classical music for relaxation.

Need for Self-Actualization
Need to realize one's fullest potential

Esteem Needs
Need to achieve, to gain competence, to gain respect and recognition from others

Belonging and Love Needs
Need to love and be loved; need to affiliate with others and be accepted

Safety Needs
Need for safety and security

Physiological Needs
Need to satisfy the basic biological needs for food, water, oxygen, sleep, and elimination of bodily wastes

FIGURE 9.2

Maslow's Hierarchy of Needs

(Maslow, Abraham H.; Frager, Robert D..; Fadiman, James, Motivation and Personality, 3rd Ed., ©1987. Reprinted and Electronically reproduced by permission of Pearson Education, Inc., New York, NY.).

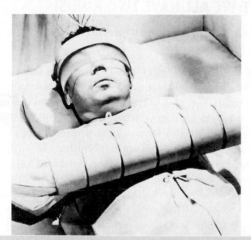

Sensory stimulation is reduced to a minimum for participants in sensory-deprivation experiments.

Their performance on motor and cognitive tasks deteriorated. None said they liked the experiment.

MASLOW'S HIERARCHY OF NEEDS: PUTTING OUR NEEDS IN ORDER

How does Maslow's hierarchy of needs account for human motivation?

Humans have a variety of needs, or motives. Clearly, some needs are more critical to sustaining life than others. We could live without self-esteem, but obviously we could not live long without air to breathe, water to drink, or food to eat.

Abraham Maslow (1908–1970) proposed a **hierarchy of needs** (see Figure 9.2) to account for the range of human motivation (1970). **[LOs 9.2 & 9.5]** He placed physiological needs such as food and water at the base of the hierarchy, stating that these needs must be adequately satisfied before higher ones can be considered.

Once our physiological needs (for water, food, sleep, sex, and shelter) are met, the motives at the next higher level—the safety and the security needs—come into play. Once these needs are satisfied, we climb to the next level to satisfy our needs to belong, and to love and be loved. Maslow believed that failure to meet the belonging and love needs deprives individuals of acceptance, affection, and intimacy and is the most prominent factor in human adjustment problems. Still higher in the hierarchy are the needs for self-esteem and the esteem of others. These needs involve our sense of worth and competence,

stimulus motives: Motives that cause us to increase stimulation and that appear to be unlearned (e.g., curiosity and the need to explore, manipulate objects, and play).

Yerkes–Dodson law: The principle that performance on tasks is best when arousal level is appropriate to the difficulty of the task—higher arousal for simple tasks, moderate arousal for tasks of moderate difficulty, and lower arousal for complex tasks.

sensory deprivation: A condition in which sensory stimulation is reduced to a minimum or eliminated.

hierarchy of needs: Maslow's theory of motivation, in which needs are arranged in order of urgency ranging from physiological needs to safety needs, belonging and love needs, esteem needs, and finally the need for self-actualization.

REMEMBER IT

Theories of Motivation

1. In its original form, drive-reduction theory focused primarily on which of the following needs and the drives they produce?
   a. cognitive
   b. psychological
   c. biological
   a. emotional

2. Which theory suggests that human behaviour is motivated by certain innate, unlearned tendencies that are shared by all individuals?
   a. arousal theory
   b. instinct theory
   c. Maslow's theory
   d. drive-reduction theory

3. According to arousal theory, people seek _____ arousal.
   a. minimized
   b. increased
   c. decreased
   d. optimal

4. According to Maslow's hierarchy of needs, which needs must be satisfied before a person will try to satisfy the belonging and love needs?
   a. safety and self-actualization needs
   b. self-actualization and esteem needs
   c. physiological and safety needs
   d. physiological and esteem needs

Answers: 1. c 2. b 3. d 4. c

our need to achieve and be recognized for it, and our need to be respected. At the top of Maslow's hierarchy is the need for **self-actualization**, the need to realize our full potential. People may reach self-actualization through achievement in virtually any area of life's work.

Maslow's hierarchy of needs has been a popular notion, appealing to many, but much of it has not been verified by empirical research. The steps on the hierarchy may not be the same for all people (Wahba & Bridwell, 1976). It is well known that in some people the desire for success and recognition is so strong that they are prepared to sacrifice safety, security, and personal relationships to achieve it. A few people are willing to sacrifice their very lives for others or for a cause to which they are committed.

MODULE 9B THE PRIMARY DRIVES: HUNGER AND THIRST

LO 9.6 Describe and compare the two kinds of thirst.
LO 9.7 Explain the role of the lateral and ventromedial hypothalamus in moderating hunger.
LO 9.8 Describe the biologically driven internal hunger cues.
LO 9.9 Describe the various types of external cues that influence hunger and explain how they function.
LO 9.10 Describe how social and genetic factors contribute to weight.
LO 9.11 Describe and contrast the fat-cell and set-point theories and contrast their main arguments.

Drive-reduction theory, as we have seen, suggests that motivation is based largely on the **primary drives**, those that are unlearned and that seek to satisfy biological needs. Two of the most important primary drives are thirst and hunger.

THIRST: WE ALL HAVE TWO KINDS

Under what kinds of conditions do the two types of thirst occur?

Thirst is a basic biological drive. Adequate fluid is critical because the body itself is about 75 percent water. Without any intake of fluids, we can survive only about four or five days.

But how do we know when we are thirsty? When we have a dry mouth and throat, or a powerful urge to drink? Yes, of course. But thirst is more complex than that. There are two types of thirst signalling us to drink. **[LO 9.6]** One type,

A rat whose satiety centre has been destroyed can weigh up to six times as much as a normal rat.

©Kay Chernush/Photolibrary/Getty Images

extracellular thirst, occurs when fluid is lost from the body tissues. When you are exercising heavily or doing almost anything in hot weather, you perspire and lose bodily fluid. Bleeding, vomiting, and diarrhea also rob your body of fluid. Perhaps you have heard that it is not a good idea to drink a cold beer or any other type of alcohol to quench your thirst on a very hot day. Alcohol increases extracellular fluid loss. This is why most people awaken with a powerful thirst after drinking heavily the night before.

Another type of thirst, intracellular thirst, involves the loss of water from inside the body cells. When we eat a lot of salty food, the water–sodium balance in the blood and in the tissues outside the cells is disturbed. The salt cannot readily enter the cells, so the cells release some of their own water to restore the balance. As the body cells become dehydrated, thirst is stimulated so that we drink to increase the water volume (G. L. Robertson, 1983).

THE BIOLOGICAL BASIS OF HUNGER: INTERNAL HUNGER CUES

The Role of the Hypothalamus: Our Feeding and Satiety Centre

What are the roles of the lateral hypothalamus and the ventromedial hypothalamus in the regulation of eating behaviour?

Like thirst, hunger is influenced by physiological processes. Researchers have found two areas of the hypothalamus that are of central importance in regulating eating behaviour and thus affect the hunger drive (Steffens, Scheurink, & Luiten, 1988). **[LO 9.7]** As researchers discovered long ago, the **lateral hypothalamus (LH)** acts in part as a feeding centre to excite eating. Stimulating the feeding centre causes animals to eat even when they are full (Delgado & Anand, 1953). When the feeding centre is destroyed, animals initially refuse to eat until they adapt to this condition (Anand & Brobeck, 1951).

The **ventromedial hypothalamus (VMH)** presumably acts as a satiety centre. When active, it inhibits eating (Hernandez & Hoebel, 1989). Electrically stimulating the satiety centre causes animals to stop eating (Duggan & Booth, 1986). If the VMH is surgically removed, experimental animals soon eat their way to gross obesity (Hetherington & Ranson, 1940; Parkinson & Weingarten, 1990).

Hunger regulation, however, is not as simple as an off/on switch regulated by the LH and VMH. This view fails to convey the subtle ways in which the neurons in these organs influence eating and body weight (King, 2013). Therefore, although it is clear that the hypothalamus plays a role in eating behaviour, researchers have yet to determine precisely how it interacts with biochemical signals from other components of the body's hunger management system.

The Role of the Stomach: Hunger Pangs

What are some of the body's hunger and satiety signals?

The fullness of the stomach affects our feeling of hunger. The stomach has a capacity of about 0.5 litres when empty and stretches to hold 1.2 litres when full (Yamada, 2009). Generally, the fuller or more distended the stomach, the less hunger we feel.

How do you know when you are hungry? **[LO 9.8]** Do you have stomach contractions, or "hunger pangs"? In a classic experiment, Cannon and Washburn (1912) demonstrated a close correlation between stomach contractions and the perception of hunger. But their discovery does not necessarily mean that the sensation of hunger is caused by stomach contractions. Additional research has confirmed that humans and other animals continue to experience hunger even when it is impossible for them to feel stomach contractions.

Other Hunger and Satiety Signals

So what causes us to feel hungry? **[LO 9.8]** Many body structures and processes contribute to feelings of hunger and satiety. For example, the brain's pleasure system influences eating behaviour even when we aren't really hungry (Berthoud & Morrison, 2008). Changes in blood sugar level and the hormone that regulates it also contribute to sensations of hunger. Blood levels of the sugar called *glucose* are monitored by nutrient detectors in the liver, which send this information to the brain (M. I. Friedman, Tordoff, & Ramirez, 1986). Hunger is stimulated when the brain receives the message that blood glucose

Just the sight of mouth-watering foods can make us want to eat, even when we aren't actually hungry.

self-actualization: The development of one's full potential; the highest need on Maslow's hierarchy.

primary drives: States of tension or arousal arising from a biological need; states not based on learning.

lateral hypothalamus (LH): The part of the hypothalamus that apparently acts as a feeding centre and, when activated, signals an animal to eat; when the LH is destroyed, the animal initially refuses to eat.

ventromedial hypothalamus (VMH): The part of the hypothalamus that presumably acts as a satiety centre and, when activated, signals an animal to stop eating; when the area is destroyed, the animal overeats, becoming obese.

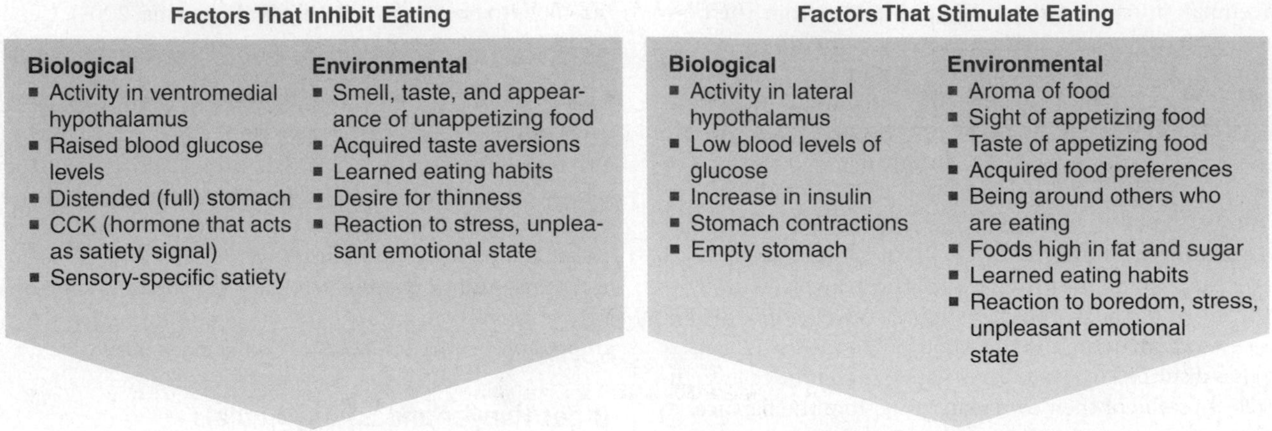

Factors That Inhibit Eating	
Biological	**Environmental**
▪ Activity in ventromedial hypothalamus	▪ Smell, taste, and appearance of unappetizing food
▪ Raised blood glucose levels	▪ Acquired taste aversions
▪ Distended (full) stomach	▪ Learned eating habits
▪ CCK (hormone that acts as satiety signal)	▪ Desire for thinness
▪ Sensory-specific satiety	▪ Reaction to stress, unpleasant emotional state

Factors That Stimulate Eating	
Biological	**Environmental**
▪ Activity in lateral hypothalamus	▪ Aroma of food
▪ Low blood levels of glucose	▪ Sight of appetizing food
▪ Increase in insulin	▪ Taste of appetizing food
▪ Stomach contractions	▪ Acquired food preferences
▪ Empty stomach	▪ Being around others who are eating
	▪ Foods high in fat and sugar
	▪ Learned eating habits
	▪ Reaction to boredom, stress, unpleasant emotional state

FIGURE 9.3

Factors That Inhibit and Stimulate Eating

Both biological and environmental factors combine to inhibit or to stimulate eating.

---

levels are low. When blood glucose is high, insulin, a hormone produced by the pancreas, chemically converts glucose into energy that is usable by the cells, thus regulating glucose levels. Elevations in insulin cause an increase in hunger, in food intake, and in a desire for sweets (Rodin, Wack, Ferrannini, & DeFronzo, 1985). Chronic oversecretion of insulin often leads to obesity.

Hunger is also influenced by some of the substances secreted by the gastrointestinal tract during digestion, which are released into the blood and act as satiety signals (Feinle-Bisset, 2014). The hormone cholecystokinin (CCK) is one satiety signal that causes people to limit the amount of food they eat during a meal (Veldhorst et al., 2008).

We are pushed to eat not only by our hunger drive within. There are also external factors that stimulate hunger.

OTHER FACTORS INFLUENCING HUNGER: EXTERNAL EATING CUES

What are some non-biological factors that influence what and how much we eat?

Smell that coffee brewing. Look at that mouth-watering chocolate cake. Listen to the bacon sizzling in the morning. Apart from our internal hunger, there are external factors influencing what, where, and how much we eat. **[LO 9.9]** Sensory cues such as the taste, smell, and appearance or variety of food stimulate the appetite (Coelho, Jansen, Roefs, & Nederkoorn, 2009). For many, the hands of the clock alone, signalling mealtime, are enough to prompt a quest for food. And when we eat with other people, we tend to eat more than when we are eating alone (de Castro & de Castro, 1989).

Susceptibility to External Eating Cues: Can You Resist Them?

Are we all equally susceptible to such external eating cues? Psychologist Judith Rodin (1981) has shown that our responsiveness to internal or external cues does not strongly correlate with the degree of overweight. But external cues *can* trigger internal

processes that motivate a person to eat. The sight and smell of appetizing food can trigger the release of insulin, particularly in those who are externally responsive (Rodin, Slochower, & Fleming, 1977). For some individuals, simply seeing and thinking about food can cause an elevated level of insulin. Such people have a greater tendency to gain weight (Rodin, 1985).

The Palatability of Food: Tempting Tastes

How good a particular food tastes—that is, how palatable the food is—seems to work somewhat independently of hunger and satiety in determining how much we eat (Jager & Witkamp, 2014); otherwise, most of us would refuse the pie after eating a big dinner. **[LO 9.9]**

Foods that are sweet (Ball & Grinker, 1981) and high in fat (Samra, 2010) tend to stimulate the human appetite, even when the sweetness is provided by artificial sweeteners (Blundel, Rogers, & Hill, 1988; Tordoff, 1988). Figure 9.3 summarizes the factors that stimulate and inhibit eating.

UNDERSTANDING VARIATIONS IN BODY WEIGHT: WHY WE WEIGH WHAT WE WEIGH

What are some factors that account for variations in body weight?

Pencil-thin models seen in fashion magazines have come to represent the ideal body for many women. **[LO 9.10]** But most of these models have only 10 to 15 percent body fat, far below the 18.5 to 24.9 percent considered normal for women (Health Canada, 2003). *Fat* has become a negative term, a development clearly reflected in the finding that nearly 60 percent of North Americans are actively attempting to lose weight (Saad, 2011). But some body fat is necessary to maintain life. Men need 3 percent and women need 12 percent just for survival. And in order for a woman's reproductive system to function properly, she must maintain 20 percent body fat. Of course, there is a range of weight that is considered healthy, and this range varies according to height, as illustrated in Figure 9.4.

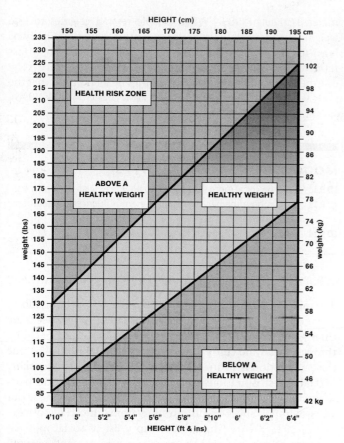

FIGURE 9.4

Healthy Weight by Height

This comparison chart shows healthy and potentially unhealthy weight.

Extremes in either fatness or thinness can pose health risks. An abnormal desire for thinness can result in eating disorders such as anorexia nervosa (self-starvation) and bulimia nervosa (a pattern of bingeing and purging). Read the *Apply It* box later in this chapter for more details on eating disorders. At the other extreme are those Canadians—slightly over 60 percent of men and nearly 44 percent of women (Statistics Canada, 2011b)— who are overweight, including the 18 percent of us who are obese, which increases the risk of high blood pressure, coronary heart disease, stroke, and cancer (Public Health Agency of Canada [PHAC], 2011). The term **obesity** means excessive fatness and is usually used in the medical profession to refer to men and women whose body mass index (BMI) exceeds 30 (Tjepkema, 2005a). BMI is a measure of body fat based on height and weight, calculated using the person's weight in kilograms divided by the square of their height in metres. While obesity rates among Canadian adults have nearly doubled between 1979 and 2004 (Statistics Canada, 2011b), perhaps the most disturbing weight-related trend in Canada is the increase in childhood obesity, which has soared by 424 percent between 1981 and 1996 (M. Tremblay, 2003)—a change that will surely affect the overall health status of Canadians in the years to come.

The Role of Genetic Factors in Body Weight

Studies of adopted children and twins reveal the strong influence of heredity on body size (T. J. Bouchard, 1997; de Castro, 1998). **[LO 9.10]** Across all weight classes, from very thin to very obese, children adopted at birth tend to resemble their biological parents more than their adoptive parents in body size. A review of studies that include more than 100 000 participants found that 74 percent of identical twins had similar body weights, whereas only 32 percent of fraternal twins had comparable body weight (Barsch, Farooqi, & O'Rahilly, 2000). But genes interact in such complex ways that obesity isn't simply a matter of inheriting particular genes from one's parents (Grigorenko, 2003). Moreover, environmental characteristics and lifestyle also make a strong contribution to overall body mass (Nelson, Gordon-Larsen, North, & Adair, 2006).

What exactly do people inherit that affects body weight? Researchers have identified the hormone leptin, which directly affects the feeding and satiety centres of the brain's hypothalamus and is now known to be one of the key elements in body-weight regulation (J. M. Friedman, 2014). Leptin is produced by the body's fat tissues, and the amount produced is a direct measure of body fat—the higher the leptin produced, the higher the level of body fat. Obese mice injected with leptin lost 30 percent of their body weight within two weeks because the injection fooled their metabolism into thinking they were even more obese than they were (Halaas et al., 1995). In humans, a mutation of the gene that controls leptin receptors can cause obesity as well as pituitary abnormalities (Farooqi & O'Rahilly, 2005).

Metabolic Rate: Burning Energy—Slow or Fast

The term *metabolism* refers to all the physical and chemical processes that are carried out in the body to sustain life. **[LO 9.10]** Food provides the energy required to carry out these processes. The rate at which the body burns calories to produce energy is called the **metabolic rate**. Physical activity uses up only about one third of our energy; the other two thirds is consumed by the maintenance processes that keep us alive (Shah & Jeffery, 1991). When there is an imbalance between energy intake (how much we eat) and output (how much energy we use), our weight changes. If our caloric intake exceeds our daily energy requirement, we gain weight. If our daily energy requirement exceeds our caloric intake, we lose weight. There are, however, significant individual differences in the efficiency with which energy is burned, which results in some people being able to consume more calories than others without gaining weight.

Fat-Cell Theory: Tiny Storage Tanks for Fat

Fat-cell theory proposes that fatness is related to the number of **fat cells** in the body. **[LO 9.11]** It is estimated that people of

obesity (o-BEE-sih-tee): Excessive fatness; a term applied to men whose body fat exceeds 20 percent of their weight and to women whose body fat exceeds 30 percent of their weight.

metabolic rate (meh-tuh-BALL-ik): The rate at which the body burns calories to produce energy.

fat cells: Numbering between 30 and 40 billion, cells that serve as storehouses for liquefied fat in the body; with weight loss, they decrease in size but not in number.

normal weight have between 25 and 35 billion fat cells (adipose cells), whereas those whose weight is twice normal may have between 100 and 125 billion fat cells (Brownell & Wadden, 1992). The number of fat cells is determined by both our genes and our eating habits (W. Bennett & Gurin, 1982; Grinker, 1982). These cells serve as storehouses for liquefied fat. When we lose weight, we do not lose the fat cells themselves. We lose the fat that is stored in them—the cells simply shrink (Dietz, 1989). Researchers once believed that all the fat cells a person would ever have were formed early in life. This is no longer the accepted view. Researchers now believe that when people overeat beyond the point at which the fat cells reach their capacity, the number of fat cells increases (Rodin & Wing, 1988).

Set-Point Theory: Thin/Fat Thermostat

How does set point affect body weight?

Set-point theory suggests that humans and other mammals are genetically programmed to carry a certain amount of body weight (Levin, 2005). **[LO 9.11]** Set point is affected by the number of fat cells in the body and by metabolic rate, both of which are influenced by the genes (de Castro, 1993; Gurin, 1989).

According to set-point theory, an internal homeostatic system functions to maintain set-point weight, much as a thermostat works to keep temperature near the point at which it is set. Whether we are lean, overweight, or average, when our weight falls below our set point, our appetite increases. When our weight climbs above our set point, our appetite decreases so as to restore the original weight.

The theory also holds that our rate of energy expenditure adjusts to maintain the body's set-point weight (Keesey & Powley, 1986). When people gain weight, their metabolic rate

REMEMBER IT

The Primary Drives: Hunger and Thirst

1. Body cells lose water and become dehydrated when an individual
   a. perspires heavily.
   b. consumes too much salt.
   c. has diarrhea or vomiting.
   d. drinks too much alcohol.

2. The lateral hypothalamus (LH) acts as a (feeding/satiety) centre; the ventromedial hypothalamus (VMH) acts as a (feeding/satiety) centre.

3. Which factor is most responsible for how fast your body burns calories to produce energy?
   a. set point
   b. fat cells
   c. eating habits
   d. metabolic rate

4. Fat cells never decrease in number. (true/false)

Answers: 1. b   2. feeding; satiety   3. d   4. true

increases (Dietz, 1989). When people restrict calories to lose weight, their metabolic rate *decreases*; this causes the body to burn fewer calories, which in turn makes further weight loss more difficult. Increasing the amount of physical activity is the one method recommended for lowering the set point so that the body will store less fat (Forey, Walker, Poston, & Goodrick, 1996).

MODULE 9C SOCIAL MOTIVES

LO 9.12 Describe social motives and explain how they relate to motivation.
LO 9.13 Explain how the need for achievement influences expectations and performance.
LO 9.14 Describe the various characteristics of achievers.

What is Murray's contribution to the study of motivation?

Do you have a strong need to be with other people (affiliation), or a need for power, or a need for achievement? These needs are three examples of **social motives**, which we learn or acquire through social and cultural experiences. **[LO 9.12]** While it is true that motivation is strongly affected by biological needs, many of our highest aspirations—the professions we choose, the partners we are drawn to, and the methods we use to achieve our sense of importance—result primarily from our social motives.

In 1935, Henry Murray drew up a list of social motives, or needs, which included the needs for achievement, recognition, affiliation, dominance, and order. Murray believed that people have social motives in varying degrees. To investigate the strength of those various needs, Murray (C. D. Morgan & Murray, 1935) developed the **Thematic Apperception Test (TAT)**, which consists of a series of pictures of ambiguous situations. People are asked to write a story about each picture—to describe what is going on in the picture, what the person or persons pictured are thinking about, what they may be feeling, and what is likely to be the outcome of the situation. The stories are presumed to reveal the individual's needs and the strength of those needs. The TAT has also been used as a more general personality test.

THE NEED FOR ACHIEVEMENT: THE DRIVE TO EXCEL

What is the need for achievement?

Both men and women are driven by social motives. Among these is the **need for achievement**, defined by Henry Murray (1938) as the need "to accomplish something difficult. . . . To overcome obstacles and attain a high standard. To excel one's self" (p. 164). This need has been researched vigorously, but the participants have been almost exclusively male (D. C. McClelland, 1958, 1961, 1985).

Atkinson's Theory of Achievement Motivation: When Do We Try?

J. R. Atkinson (1964) suggests that when we approach any situation, two conflicting factors are operating—our hope for success and our fear of failure. **[LO 9.13]** Motivation to avoid failure

CANADIAN CONNECTIONS

The Motivation to Exercise: A Matter of Willpower

We all know that exercising is good for us. Aside from helping people regulate their weight and improve their psychological well-being, regular exercise has many other health benefits, including preventing chronic diseases like cancer, Type 2 dia-betes, and heart disease (PHAC, 2011). Both Canadian and international guidelines indicate that adults should accumulate at least 150 minutes of moderate to vigorous physical activity a week to obtain significant health benefits. Yet, according to recent data from the Canadian Health Measures Survey (CHMS), only 15 percent of Canadian adults attain this level of activity (Statistics Canada, 2011a). The data are even more worrisome when it comes to the activity level of young people, including teenagers. Young people aged 5 to 17 should accumulate at least 60 minutes of moderate to vigorous physical activity daily, but only 7 percent of young people do so.

Why, then, do most of us have such difficulty starting or maintaining a fitness routine? The short answer to this important question, according to psychologist Roy Baumeister and Tierney (2011), is threefold—setting clear goals, monitoring your goals, and willpower. *Willpower* can be defined as the combination of two psychological processes: the ability to delay gratification—resisting short-term tempta-

tions in order to meet long-term goals—and the capacity to override an unwanted thought, feeling, or impulse.

Maintaining willpower is one of life's most challenging tasks. Yet individuals who are self-disciplined benefit tremendously from their ability to control themselves. Aside from getting better grades and being more physically fit, recent research has shown that individuals who have a high degree of self-control in childhood have greater physical and mental health, fewer substance-abuse problems and criminal convictions, and better savings behaviour and financial security as adults (Moffitt et al., 2011).

Keeping the benefits of willpower in mind should assist you in keeping your motivation to maintain your fitness goals, but what tips does the Public Health Agency of Canada (2011) recommend? Consider the following steps:

- Make a goal.
- Set a plan.
- Choose a variety of physical activities you enjoy.
- Get into a routine.
- Spread your sessions of moderate to vigorous aerobic activity throughout the week.
- Consider joining a team. ∎

can cause us to work harder at a task to try to ensure success, or it can cause us to avoid the task altogether.

Whether you strive for a goal depends on three factors: (1) the strength of your need to achieve, (2) your expectation of success, and (3) the incentive value of success or failure at a particular activity—that is, how much you value success in the activity and how distressed you would be if you failed at it (Wigfield & Eccles, 2000). For example, whether you try to achieve an A in psychology will depend on how important an A is to you, on whether you believe an A is possible, and on how much pride you will feel in getting an A as opposed to how upset you will be if you do not. Of course, other factors have also been shown to affect our motivation. The *Canadian Connections* box highlights how willpower influences our ability to succeed.

Complete the *Try It*, which describes a game that is said to reveal high or low achievement motivation.

Characteristics of Achievers: Successful People Have Them

What are some characteristics shared by people who are high in achievement motivation?

McClelland and colleagues (D. C. McClelland, Atkinson, Clark, & Lowell, 1953) found that high achievers differ from low achievers in several ways. **[LO 9.14]** People with a high achievement motivation tend to set goals of moderate difficulty—in other words, goals that are realistic (Conroy, Elliot, & Thrash, 2009). They pursue goals that are challenging yet attainable with hard work, ability, determination, and persistence.

Goals that are too easy offer no challenge and hold no interest, because success would not be rewarding (D. C. McClelland, 1985). Impossibly high goals and high risks are also not pursued because they offer little chance of success and are considered a waste of time.

People with a low need for achievement are not willing to take chances when it comes to testing their own skills and abilities. They are motivated more by their fear of failure than by their hope and expectation of success, which is why they set either ridiculously low goals or else impossibly high goals (Geen, 1984). After all, who can fault a person for failing to reach a goal that is impossible for almost anyone?

set point: The weight the body normally maintains when one is trying neither to gain nor to lose weight (if weight falls below the normal level, appetite increases and metabolic rate decreases; if weight is gained, appetite decreases and metabolic rate increases so that the original weight is restored).

social motives: Motives acquired through experience and interaction with others (e.g., need for achievement, need for affiliation).

Thematic Apperception Test (TAT): A projective test consisting of drawings of ambiguous human situations, which the subject describes; thought to reveal inner feelings, conflicts, and motives.

need for achievement: The need to accomplish something difficult and to perform at a high standard of excellence.

TRY IT

Test Your Need for Achievement

Imagine you are playing a ring-toss game. You have three rings to toss at any of the six pegs pictured here. You will be paid a few pennies each time you are able to ring a peg.

Which peg would you try to ring with your three tosses—peg 1 or 2 nearest you, peg 3 or 4 at a moderate distance, or peg 5 or 6 at the far end of the room?

People with a high need for achievement can overcome even serious disabilities in their efforts to succeed.

In view of this description, which peg in the ring toss game in the *Try It* would people low in achievement motivation try for? If you guessed peg 1 or 2 or peg 5 or 6, you are right. People low in achievement motivation are likely to stand right over peg 1 so they can't possibly fail. Or they may toss the rings at peg 6, hoping they might get lucky. People with a high need for achievement tend to toss their rings at peg 3 or 4, an intermediate distance that offers some challenge. Which peg did you aim for?

People with high achievement motivation see their success as a result of their own talents, abilities, persistence, and hard work (Kukla, 1972). They typically do not credit luck or the influence of other people for their successes; nor do they blame luck or other people for their failures. When individuals with low achievement motivation fail, they usually give up quickly and attribute their failure to lack of ability. They also believe that luck or fate, rather than effort, is responsible for accomplishment (B. Weiner, 1972, 1974).

Developing Achievement Motivation: Can We Learn It?

If achievement motivation, like the other social motives, is primarily learned, *how* is it learned? Some experts believe that child-rearing practices and values in the home are

REMEMBER IT

Social Motives

1. Social motives are, for the most part, unlearned. (true/false)

2. According to Atkinson's theory of achievement motivation, which of the following is not a major factor in determining whether an individual approaches a goal?
   a. the strength of the individual's need to achieve
   b. the person's expectation of success
   c. how much pride the person has in achieving the goal as opposed to how upsetting failure would be
   d. the financial reward attached to the goal

3. Which of these statements is not true of people high in achievement motivation?
   a. They set very high goals for which success will be extremely difficult to obtain.
   b. They set goals of moderate difficulty.
   c. They attribute their success to their talents, abilities, and hard work.
   d. They are likely to choose careers as entrepreneurs.

Answers: 1. false 2. d 3. a

important factors in developing achievement motivation (D. C. McClelland, 1985; D. C. McClelland & Pilon, 1983). Parents may be more likely to have children with high achievement motivation if they give their children responsibilities, stress independence when the children are young, and praise them sincerely for genuine accomplishments (Gottfried, Fleming, & Gottfried, 1994, 2001). And when it comes to motivation for school performance, recent research has shown that parental aspiration for their children's education is positively correlated to the children's own educational motivation (W. Fan, Williams, & Wolters, 2012).

MODULE **9D** THE WHAT AND WHY OF EMOTIONS

LO 9.15 Explain the connection between motivation and emotion.

LO 9.16 Describe and contrast the physical, cognitive, and behavioural components of emotions and contrast how these components affect emotions.

LO 9.17 Compare and contrast the four theories of emotion described in the chapter: the James–Lange theory, the Cannon–Bard theory, the Schachter–Singer theory, and the Lazarus theory.

MOTIVATION AND EMOTION: WHAT IS THE CONNECTION?

Motivation does not occur in a vacuum. **[LO 9.15]** Much of our motivation to act is fuelled by our emotional state. In fact, the root of the word **emotion** means "to move," indicating the close relationship between motivation and emotion. When we observe the emotion of sadness in another, we often feel empathy, and this may motivate us to acts of altruism (helping behaviour). Fear motivates us either to flee (to escape danger) or to perform protective behaviours that provide security and safety (Izard, 1992). Emotions prepare and motivate us to respond adaptively to a variety of situations in life. They enable us to communicate our feelings and intentions more effectively than we could with words alone; thus, they make it more likely that others will respond to us. But what, precisely, are emotions?

THE COMPONENTS OF EMOTIONS: THE PHYSICAL, THE COGNITIVE, AND THE BEHAVIOURAL

What are the three components of emotions?

Are emotions more than just feelings? We say that we feel lonely or sad, happy or content, or angry, embarrassed, or afraid. Most people describe emotions in terms of feeling states; psychologists, however, study emotions according to their three components—physical, cognitive, and behavioural (Moors & Scherer, 2013). **[LO 9.16]**

The physical component is the physiological arousal (the internal body state) that accompanies the emotion. **[LO 9.16]** Without the physiological arousal, we would not feel

TABLE 9.2 **The Components of Emotions**

Physical Component	Cognitive Component	Behavioural Component
Physiological arousal (internal bodily state accompanying the emotion)	The way we interpret a stimulus or situation	Outward expression of the emotion (facial expressions, gestures, body posture, tone of voice)

the emotion in all its intensity. The surge of powerful feeling we know as emotion is due largely to the physiological arousal we experience.

The cognitive component—the way we perceive or interpret a stimulus or situation—determines the specific emotion we feel. **[LO 9.16]** If you are home alone and the wind is banging a tree limb on your roof, you may become fearful if you perceive the knocking and the banging as a burglar trying to break into your house. An emotional response to an imaginary threat is every bit as powerful as a response to a real threat. Perceptions make it so. Have you ever worked yourself into a frenzy before a first date, a job interview, or an oral presentation for one of your classes? Then your thinking was contributing to your emotional state.

The behavioural component of emotions is the outward expression of the emotions. **[LO 9.16]** Our facial expressions, gestures, body posture, and tone of voice stem from and convey the emotions we are feeling within. Some of the facial expressions that accompany emotion are innate and are the same across cultures. But some of our emotional expressions are more influenced by our culture and its rules for displaying emotion. Table 9.2 summarizes the components of emotions.

THEORIES OF EMOTION: WHICH COMES FIRST, THE THOUGHT OR THE FEELING?

There is no doubt that we react to certain experiences with emotion. For example, if you think you are making a fool of yourself in front of your friends, the emotion you feel is embarrassment, which triggers a physiological response that may cause you to blush. This type of reaction seems logical—it seems to fit our everyday experience. But is this sequence of events the course that an emotional experience really follows?

The James–Lange Theory

According to the James–Lange theory, what sequence of events occurs when we experience an emotion?

William James (1884) argued that the sequence of events in an emotional experience is exactly the reverse of what our

---

emotion: A feeling state involving physiological arousal, a cognitive appraisal of the situation arousing the state, and an outward expression of the state.

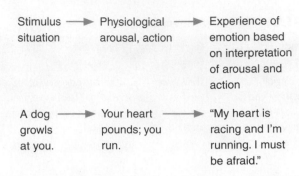

FIGURE 9.5

The James–Lange Theory of Emotion

The James–Lange theory of emotion is the exact opposite of what our subjective experience tells us. If an angry dog growls at you, the James–Lange interpretation is this: The dog growls, your heart begins to pound, and only by observing that your heart is pounding do you conclude that you must be afraid.

subjective experience tells us. James believed that first an event causes physiological arousal and a physical response. Only then do we perceive or interpret the physical response as an emotion. In other words, saying something stupid causes us to blush, and we interpret our physical response, the blush, as an emotion, embarrassment. James (1890) went on to suggest that "we feel sorry *because* we cry, angry *because* we strike, afraid *because* we tremble" (p. 1066).

At about the same time that James proposed his theory, a Danish physiologist and psychologist, Carl Lange, independently formulated nearly the same theory. Hence, we have the **James–Lange theory** of emotion (C. G. Lange & James, 1922; see Figure 9.5). **[LO 9.17]** The theory suggests that different patterns of arousal in the autonomic nervous system produce the different emotions we feel, and that the physiological arousal appears before the emotion is perceived.

If the physical arousal itself were the sole cause of what we know as emotion, however, there would have to be a distinctly different set of physical changes associated with each emotion.

Otherwise we wouldn't know whether we were sad, embarrassed, frightened, or happy.

The Cannon–Bard Theory

What is the Cannon–Bard theory of emotion?

An early theory of emotion that challenged the James–Lange theory was proposed by Walter Cannon (1927), who claimed that the bodily changes caused by the various emotions are not sufficiently distinct to allow people to distinguish one emotion from another.

Physiologist Philip Bard (1934) later expanded Cannon's original theory. **[LO 9.17]** The **Cannon–Bard theory** suggests that the following chain of events occurs when we feel an emotion: Emotion-provoking stimuli are received by the senses and are then relayed simultaneously to the thalamus; to the cerebral cortex, which provides the conscious mental experience of the emotion; and to the sympathetic nervous system, which produces the physiological state of arousal. In other words, your feeling of emotion (e.g., fear) occurs at about the same time that you experience physiological arousal (e.g., pounding heart). One does not cause the other.

The Schachter–Singer Theory

According to the Schachter–Singer theory, what two things must occur in order for us to experience an emotion?

Stanley Schachter looked at these early theories of emotion and concluded that they left out a critical component—our own cognitive interpretation of why we become aroused. Schachter and Jerome Singer (1962) proposed a two-factor theory. According to the **Schachter–Singer theory**, two things must happen for a person to feel an emotion: (1) The person must first experience physiological arousal; (2) then there must be a cognitive interpretation or explanation of the physiological

---

REVIEW & REFLECT 9.2 THEORIES OF EMOTION

Theory	View	Example
James–Lange theory	An event causes physiological arousal. We experience an emotion only after we interpret the physical response.	You are walking home late at night and hear footsteps behind you. Your heart pounds and you begin to tremble. You interpret these physical responses as fear.
Cannon–Bard theory	An event causes a physiological and an emotional response simultaneously. One does not cause the other.	You are walking home late at night and hear footsteps behind you. Your heart pounds, you begin to tremble, and you feel afraid.
Schachter–Singer theory	An event causes physiological arousal. We must then be able to identify a reason for the arousal in order to label the emotion.	You are walking home late at night and hear footsteps behind you. Your heart pounds, and you begin to tremble. You know that walking alone at night can be dangerous, and so you feel afraid.
Lazarus theory	An event occurs, a cognitive appraisal is made, and then the emotion and physiological arousal follow.	You are walking home late at night and hear footsteps behind you. You think it could be a mugger. So you feel afraid, and your heart starts to pound and you begin to tremble.

REMEMBER IT

The What and Why of Emotions

1. According to the text, emotions have all of the following except a _____ component.
   a. physical
   b. cognitive
   c. sensory
   d. behavioural

2. Which theory of emotion holds that we feel a true emotion only when we become physically aroused and can identify some cause for the arousal?
   a. Schachter–Singer theory
   b. James–Lange theory
   c. Cannon–Bard theory
   d. Lazarus theory

3. Which theory of emotion suggests that we would feel fearful because we were trembling?
   a. Schachter–Singer theory
   b. James–Lange theory
   c. Cannon–Bard theory
   d. Lazarus theory

4. Which theory suggests that our feeling of an emotion and our physiological response to an emotional situation occur at about the same time?
   a. Schachter–Singer theory
   b. James–Lange theory
   c. Cannon–Bard theory
   d. Lazarus theory

Answers: 1. c   2. a   3. b   4. c

arousal so that the person can label it as a specific emotion. **[LO 9.17]** Thus, according to this theory, a true emotion can occur only if we are both physically aroused and can find some reason for it. However, attempts to replicate the findings of Schachter and Singer have been largely unsuccessful (G. D. Marshall & Zimbardo, 1979; Friedman, 2010).

The Lazarus Cognitive-Appraisal Theory

According to Lazarus, what sequence of events occurs when an individual feels an emotion?

Richard Lazarus (1991a, 1991b, 1995) has proposed a theory of emotion that most heavily emphasizes cognition (Ekman & Campos, 2003). According to the **Lazarus theory** of emotion, a cognitive appraisal is the first step in an emotional response, and all other aspects of an emotion, including physiological arousal, depend on the cognitive appraisal. **[LO 9.17]** Contrary to what Schachter and Singer proposed, Lazarus believes that when faced with a stimulus or event, a person first appraises it. This cognitive appraisal determines whether the person will have an emotional response and, if so, what type of response it should be. The physiological arousal and all other aspects of the emotion flow from the appraisal. In short, Lazarus contends that emotions are provoked when cognitive appraisals of events are positive or negative—but not neutral.

Critics of the Lazarus theory point out that some emotional reactions are instantaneous—occurring too rapidly to pass through cognitive appraisal (Zajonc, 1980, 1984, 1998). Lazarus (1991b) responds that some mental processing occurs without conscious awareness, and that there must be some form of cognitive realization, however brief, or else a person would not know what he or she is supposed to feel. This issue is still hotly debated among experts. What do you think? Do emotions or cognitions come first?

Review & Reflect 9.2 summarizes the four major theories of emotion: James–Lange, Cannon–Bard, Schachter–Singer, and Lazarus.

MODULE 9E THE EXPRESSION OF EMOTIONS

LO 9.18 Identify the basic emotions.
LO 9.19 Describe the developmental process associated with emotional expression.
LO 9.20 Describe display rules and explain how context and culture affect them.
LO 9.21 Explain how emotions can serve as a form of communication.

James–Lange theory: The theory that emotional feelings result when we become aware of our physiological response to an emotion-provoking stimulus (in other words, we are afraid because we tremble).

Cannon–Bard theory: The theory that physiological arousal and the feeling of emotion occur simultaneously after an emotion-provoking stimulus is relayed to the thalamus and the cerebral cortex.

Schachter–Singer theory: A two-stage theory stating that for an emotion to occur, there must be (1) physiological arousal and (2) an interpretation or explanation of the arousal.

Lazarus theory: The theory that an emotion-provoking stimulus triggers a cognitive appraisal, which is followed by the emotion and the physiological arousal.

Expressing emotions comes as naturally to humans as breathing. No one has to be taught how to smile or frown, or how to express fear, sadness, surprise, or disgust. Only actors practise making the facial expressions to convey various emotions. And the facial expressions of the basic emotions are much the same across human cultures all over the world.

THE RANGE OF EMOTION: HOW WIDE IS IT?

What are basic emotions?

How many emotions are there? The number of emotions people list depends on their culture, the language they speak, and other factors. Two leading researchers in the field, Paul Ekman (1993) and Carroll Izard (1992), insist that there are a limited number of basic emotions. **Basic emotions** are unlearned and universal—that is, they are found in all cultures, are reflected in the same facial expressions, and emerge in children according to their own biological timetable of development. Fear, anger, disgust, surprise, joy or happiness, and sadness or distress are usually considered basic emotions. **[LO 9.18]** Izard (1992, 1993) suggests that there are distinct neural circuits that underlie each of the basic emotions; and Levenson, Ekman, and Friesen (1990) point to specific autonomic nervous system activity associated with the basic emotions.

Ekman (1993, 1999) suggests that we consider studying emotions as "families." Clearly there are gradients, or degrees, of intensity within a single emotion. For example, people experience fear in various degrees, from mild uneasiness to outright terror. Anger as a "family" could range from annoyance to irritation to rage.

Obviously, the facial expression for annoyance is quite different from the facial expression for rage. But can you imagine 60 different facial expressions for the different types and intensities of anger? Ekman and Friesen (1975) identified 60 anger expressions; each was different from the others, but all shared the basic properties of the face of anger (Ekman, 1993). Just as there are many words in our vocabulary to describe the variations in any emotion, there are subtle distinctions in the facial expression of a single emotion that convey its intensity.

How do we learn to express our emotions? **[LO 9.19]** Or *do* we learn? There is considerable evidence that the basic emotions (fear, anger, sadness, happiness, disgust, and surprise), or the facial expressions we make when we feel them, are biologically rather than culturally determined (Santos, Pezawas, & Meyer-Lindenberg, 2014).

THE DEVELOPMENT OF FACIAL EXPRESSIONS IN INFANTS: SMILES AND FROWNS COME NATURALLY

How does the development of facial expressions of different emotions in infants suggest a biological basis for emotional expression?

Emotional expressions are natural, but what patterns are associated with their development? Newborn babies don't even smile, but one-year-olds exhibit almost as many facial expressions as older children and adults. Facial expressions of emotions

develop naturally, just as do the motor skills of crawling and walking. **[LO 9.19]** By 12 weeks, babies can express happiness and sadness (Lewis, 2008), and laughter appears somewhere around 14 to 16 weeks (Provine, 1996). Between the ages of 16 weeks and 6 months, the emotions of anger and surprise appear, and by about seven months, infants show fear. The self-conscious emotions do not emerge until later. Between 18 months and 3 years, children begin to show empathy, envy, and embarrassment, followed by shame, guilt, and pride (Lewis, 2008).

Another strong indication that the facial expressions of emotion are biologically determined, rather than learned, comes from studies done on children who were visually or hearing impaired from birth. Their smiles and frowns, their laughter and crying, and their facial expressions of anger, surprise, and pouting were the same as those of children who could hear and see (Eibl-Eibesfeldt, 1973).

Although recent studies have contributed much to our understanding of facial expressions, the biological connection between emotions and facial expressions was proposed many years ago, as described in the *World of Psychology* box on the next page.

CULTURAL RULES FOR DISPLAYING EMOTION

While the facial expressions of the basic emotions are much the same in cultures around the world, cultures can have very different **display rules**—cultural rules that dictate how emotions should generally be expressed and where and when their expression is appropriate (Ekman, 1993; Hwang & Matsumoto, 2015; Safdar et al., 2009; Scherer & Wallbott, 1994). **[LO 9.20]** Society often expects us to give evidence of certain emotions that we may not actually feel. We are expected to be sad at funerals, to hide our disappointment when we lose, and to refrain from showing disgust if the food we are served tastes bad to us. Gender differences in display rules have also been reported with some consistency in a variety of contexts (Brody, 2010).

The stern faces of these young Masai warriors from Kenya reflect their culture's display rules banning the public expression of emotion.

WORLD OF PSYCHOLOGY

Facial Expressions for the Basic Emotions: A Universal Language

The relationship between emotions and facial expressions was first studied by Charles Darwin (1872/1965). He believed that the facial expression of emotion was an aid to survival in that it enabled people, before they developed language, to communicate their internal states and react to emergencies. Darwin maintained that most of the emotions we feel and the facial expressions that convey them are genetically inherited and characteristic of the entire human species. To test his belief, he asked missionaries and people of different cultures around the world to record the facial expressions that accompany the basic emotions. On the basis of those data, he concluded that facial expressions were similar across cultures.

In some cases, modern research supports Darwin's view that facial expressions are universal. Ekman and Friesen (1971) showed photographs portraying facial expressions of the primary emotions—sadness, surprise, happiness, anger, fear, and disgust—to members of the Fore tribe in a remote area in New Guinea. The Fore people were able to identify the emotional expressions of happiness, sadness, anger, and disgust; however, they had difficulty distinguishing fear and surprise.

Ekman then had the tribespeople make faces to reflect the same emotional expressions, and he videotaped them. The tapes were shown to students in the United States, who could readily identify the emotions portrayed except for the same two expressions that had posed a problem for the Fore—surprise and fear.

While it appears that there is a certain degree of universality in emotion recognition, more recent studies indicate clear cultural variation (Jack, Blais, Scheepers, Schyns, & Caldara, 2009). For instance, a study by Saba Safdar (Safdar et al., 2009) at the University of Guelph compared the emotional expressions of Canadian, American, and Japanese students and found that Japanese display rules permit the expression of anger, contempt, and disgust significantly less than those of the two Western sample groups. Japanese students also believed that they should express positive emotions (happiness, surprise) significantly less than the Canadian sample.

Research indicates as well that each culture appears to have an "accent" for facial expressions (Elfenbein, 2013; Marsh, Elfenbein, & Ambady, 2003). This accent is a pattern of minute muscle movements that are used by most members of a culture when they exhibit a particular facial expression. In other words, there appear to be slight differences in the way a Japanese, a German, or a Canadian person would make a happy or sad face, and these differences are enough to influence perceptions of emotion.

Do Ekman's test in *Try It*, on the next page, and see if you can identify the faces of emotion. ∎

Different cultures, neighbourhoods, and even families may have very different display rules. [LO 9.20] Display rules in Japanese culture dictate that negative emotions must be disguised when others are present (Ekman, 1972; Matsumoto, Yoo, Hirayama, & Petrova, 2005; Safdar et al., 2009). In many Western societies, women are expected to smile often, whether they feel happy or not. It appears that much of our communication of emotion is not authentic, and instead is influenced by our cultural context.

One clear illustration of the disconnection between felt emotions and emotional expression has been shown in studies of North American teens (Salisch, 2001). Teens conform to unspoken display rules, acquired from peers, that discourage the public display of emotion. The resulting subdued emotional expressions can cause them to appear aloof, uncaring, and even rude to parents and other adults, which is often the basis of much miscommunication between teens and their parents and teachers.

Most of us learn display rules very early and abide by them most of the time. Yet we may not be fully aware that the rules we have learned dictate where, when, how, and even for how long certain emotions should be expressed.

EMOTION AS A FORM OF COMMUNICATION

Why are emotions considered a form of communication?

Emotions enable us to communicate our feelings, intentions, and needs more effectively than just words alone; thus, they make it more likely that others will respond to us. And researchers maintain that not only are we biologically wired to convey certain emotion signals, but we are biologically predisposed to read and interpret them as well (Dimberg, Thunberg, & Elmehed, 2000).

By communicating emotions, we motivate others to act. [LO 9.21] When we communicate sadness or distress, people close to us are likely to be sympathetic and to try to help us. By expressing emotions, infants communicate their feelings and needs before they can speak. And research shows that adults are quite skilled at interpreting infants' non-verbal emotional signals—for instance, they can determine whether a baby is looking at a new or familiar object by simply observing the change in the baby's facial expression and body language (Camras et al., 2002; Mesman et al., 2012).

basic emotions: Emotions that are found in all cultures (e.g., fear, anger, disgust, surprise, joy, happiness, sadness, distress) that are reflected in the same facial expressions across cultures and that emerge in children according to their biological timetable.

display rules: Cultural rules that dictate how emotions should be expressed, and when and where their expression is appropriate.

TRY IT

Identifying Facial Expressions of Emotion

Look carefully at the six photographs. Which basic emotion is portrayed in each?
Match the number of the photograph with the basic emotion it portrays:

a. happiness   **c.** fear   **e.** surprise
b. sadness   **d.** anger   **f.** disgust

  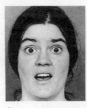  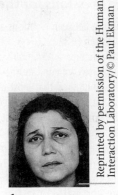

1. _____ 2. _____ 3. _____ 4. _____ 5. _____ 6. _____

Reprinted by permission of the Human Interaction Laboratory/© Paul Ekman

Answers: 1. d   2. c   3. f   4. e   5. a   6. b

Source: Based on Strack, Martin, & Stepper, 1988.

Do you feel happier when you are around others who are happy? Emotions are contagious. Infants will usually begin to cry when they hear another infant cry. Your own emotional expressions can infect others with the same emotion. Parents seem to know this intuitively when they display happy expressions to infect their babies with happy moods (Sauter et al., 2014). Mothers in many cultures—Trobriand Island, Yanomamo, Greek, German, Japanese, and American—attempt to regulate the moods of their babies through facial communication of emotions (Keller, Schlomerich, & Eibl-Eibesfeldt, 1988; Sauter et al., 2014).

Humans begin to perceive the emotions of others early in the first year of life and use this information to guide behaviour (Pollak, Messner, Kistler, & Cohn, 2009). Infants pay close attention to the facial expressions of others, especially their mothers. And when they are confronted with an ambiguous situation, they use the mother's emotion as a guide to whether they should approach or avoid the situation. This phenomenon is known as *social referencing* (Klinnert, Campos, Sorce, Emde, & Svejda, 1983). Researchers argue that there is survival value in the ability to interpret various states instantly and reliably, which may be why such emotional recognition is fast and efficient (Horstmann, 2003; Niedenthal & Brauer, 2012).

REMEMBER IT

The Expression of Emotions

1. Which of the following is not one of the emotions represented by a distinctive facial expression?
   a. happiness
   b. hostility
   c. surprise
   d. sadness

2. Facial expressions associated with the basic emotions develop naturally according to a child's own biological timetable of maturation. (true/false)

3. All of the following are true of display rules except that
   a. they are the same in all cultures.
   b. they dictate when and where emotions should be expressed.
   c. they dictate what emotions should not be expressed.
   d. they often cause people to display emotions they do not feel.

4. Which of the following statements is not true about emotion as a form of communication?
   a. Emotions communicate our feelings better than just words alone.
   b. Emotions communicate our intentions.
   c. Emotions are often contagious.
   d. Infants under one year of age are unable to use the emotions of others to guide their behaviour.

Answers: 1. b   2. true   3. a   4. d

MODULE **9F** EXPERIENCING EMOTIONS

LO 9.22 Explain the facial-feedback hypothesis.

LO 9.23 Describe how facial expressions can affect emotions.

LO 9.24 Compare and contrast passionate and companionate love.

LO 9.25 Describe the six styles of love identified by John Alan Lee.

LO 9.26 Describe Sternberg's triangular theory of love and explain the various kinds of love that can emerge as a result of these components.

THE FACIAL-FEEDBACK HYPOTHESIS: DOES THE FACE CAUSE THE FEELING?

What is the facial-feedback hypothesis?

Silvan Tomkins (1962, 1963) suggested that facial expressions of the basic emotions are genetically programmed. But he went a step further: He asserted that the facial expression itself—that is, the movement of the facial muscles producing the expression—triggers both the physiological arousal and the conscious feeling associated with the emotion. The notion that the muscular movements involved in certain facial expressions produce the corresponding emotion is called the **facial-feedback hypothesis** (Izard, 1971, 1977, 1990; Strack et al., 1988). **[LO 9.22]**

In an extensive review of research on the facial-feedback hypothesis, Adelmann and Zajonc (1989) found impressive evidence to support an association between facial expression and the subjective experience of the emotion. In addition, they found considerable support for the notion that simply the act of making the facial expression can initiate the subjective feeling of the emotion.

The Simulation of Facial Expressions: Put On a Happy Face

Over 125 years ago, Darwin (1872/1965) wrote, "Even the simulation of an emotion tends to arouse it in our minds" (p. 365). Ekman and colleagues (1983) put this notion to the test using 16 participants (12 professional actors and 4 scientists). Participants were guided to contract specific muscles in the face so that they could assume the facial expressions of six basic emotions—surprise, disgust, sadness, anger, fear, and happiness. However, they were never actually told to smile, frown, or put on an angry face.

They were hooked up to electronic instruments, which monitored changes in heart rate, skin response (to measure perspiring), muscle tension, and hand temperature. While hooked up to the devices, the participants were also asked to imagine or relive six actual experiences in which they had felt each of the six emotions.

Ekman reported that a distinctive physiological response pattern emerged for the emotions of fear, sadness, anger, and disgust, whether the participants relived one of their emotional experiences or simply made the corresponding facial expression. **[LO 9.23]** In fact, in some cases the physiological measures of emotion were greater when the actors and scientists made the facial expression than when they imagined an actual

TRY IT

Do Facial Expressions Affect Emotions?

Hold a pencil between your lips with your mouth closed, as shown in the left-hand drawing, for about 15 seconds. Pay attention to your feelings. Now hold the pencil between your teeth, letting your teeth show, as shown in the right-hand drawing, for about 15 seconds.

Did you have more pleasant feelings with the pencil between your lips or your teeth? Why?

Source: Adapted from Strack et al., 1988.

emotional experience (Ekman, Levenson, & Friesen, 1983). The researchers found that both anger and fear accelerate heart rate and that fear produces colder fingers than does anger.

Do you think that making particular facial expressions will affect your emotions? A simple experiment you can try alone or with friends or classmates is described in the *Try It*. When you hold a pencil between your teeth, you activate the facial muscles used to express happiness. When you hold it between your lips, you activate the muscles involved in the expression of anger.

Controlling Our Facial Expressions to Regulate Our Feelings

If facial expressions can activate emotions, is it possible that intensifying or weakening a facial expression can intensify or weaken the corresponding state of feeling?

Izard (1990) believes that by learning to regulate our own emotional expressions, we may be able to gain control over our emotions. We may learn to change the intensity of an emotion by inhibiting or amplifying its expression, or change the emotion by simulating another emotion. Izard proposes that this might be a useful adjunct to psychotherapy.

Regulating or modifying an emotion by simulating an expression of its opposite may be effective if the emotion is not unusually intense. What is it about intense emotional states that make them so difficult to control or regulate?

facial-feedback hypothesis: The idea that the muscular movements involved in certain facial expressions trigger the corresponding emotions (for example, smiling makes us happy).

©Gary Blakeley/Fotolia

There are many situations in which people must disguise their emotions to comply with the display rules of their culture, which dictate when and how feelings should be expressed. For example, these Buckingham Palace guards are expected to remain expressionless, even if it means hiding their true feelings.

EMOTION AND RATIONAL THINKING

Have you ever been so "swept away" by emotion that you did something you later regretted? Could there be a negative correlation between emotional intensity and rational thinking?

TRY IT

Events That Cause Extreme Emotion

List as many news events as you can that seem to support the notion that when people are consumed by emotion, rational thinking can decrease or disappear, with disastrous consequences.

Event   Extreme Emotion

_____   _____

_____   _____

_____   _____

This idea is contrary to the belief that venting emotions, a process known as *catharsis*, is good for mental health. In reality, the opposite is true. Venting anger makes a person angrier and may even make him or her more likely to express the anger aggressively (Bushman, 2002).

Intense emotional states are frequently described in phrases that suggest these states are devoid of rational thinking—"insanely jealous," "blinded by love," "frozen with fright," "consumed by passion." Can you think of examples that would suggest that rational thinking lessens as emotional states intensify?

WORLD OF PSYCHOLOGY

The Art and Science of Lie Detection

Do you recall the TV show called *Lie to Me* that was popular a few years ago? The show followed the work of Dr. Cal Lightman (played by Tim Roth) and his colleagues, who had devised ways to detect when someone was lying or telling the truth by analyzing facial expressions, body movements, and changes in voice and speech. In other words, the show was based on the premise that people, even very good liars, display some small and uncontrollable expressions of emotions that can be detected by someone who is trained to identify them.

Was this show based on science or was it a total work of fiction? The correct answer to this question is that it is a bit of both. Psychological research is currently being done to determine whether it is possible to train individuals to increase their accuracy in perceiving lies. While there appears to be some people who are fairly accurate, efforts to train people to become lie–perceiving experts have not been very encouraging.

While many people think that they can perceive deceit, the strategies most people use to assess truthfulness are no more effective than flipping a coin—roughly a 50–50 chance. Research about professionals whose work often depends on assessing another person's truthfulness has produced mixed results. Some studies have shown that individuals who are experienced in the detection of lies, such as law enforcement officers, do slightly better than the rest of us (Ekman & O'Sullivan, 1991; Ekman, O'Sullivan,

& Frank, 1999). However, more recent studies have tended to show that experts perform just as poorly as inexperienced people do (Akehurst, Bill, Vrij, & Kohnken, 2004; Leach, Talwar, Lee, Bala, & Lindsay, 2004). More studies will need to be conducted in real-world lie detection situations before researchers can make a final judgment on the matter.

Our inability to identify deception may be caused by the inconsistencies in liars' behaviour. Many people believe that there are common signs of lying, such as looking away or fidgeting, but there are actually very few consistencies across deceivers (Lock, 2004). This is one of the reasons why it has even been difficult to design a machine that can do a better job than we do of distinguishing between liars and truth-tellers.

Some gifted people appear to be extraordinarily good at catching liars. Psychologist Paul Ekman, whose work on emotions is described earlier in this chapter, suggests that these people are better able than the rest of us to detect *microemotions*—facial expressions that last no longer than one twenty-fifth of a second. Individuals who are good at detecting microemotions are also good at detecting deception (Ekman & O'Sullivan, 1991), but training people to detect these microemotions has been a real challenge. Undoubtedly, those who developed the TV show *Lie to Me* were aware of these findings and simply extended them beyond current research reality. ∎

Some dramatic examples of how extreme emotional states can diminish rational thinking and result in tragedy are major depression resulting in suicide, and rage resulting in spousal abuse, child abuse, or murder. Do the *Try It* to find other emotion-causing events that could affect rational thinking.

Emotional experience is a central part of human existence. But we all realize that, at times, the emotions we show are not consistent with those we feel. This is especially true when someone lies. Can we accurately detect when someone lies to us? Are some people better than others in their ability to detect a lie? The *World of Psychology* box addresses these questions.

LOVE: THE STRONGEST EMOTIONAL BOND

The emotion of love comes in many varieties. And although we often use the term rather loosely or casually—"I love ice cream," "I love to dance"—love is usually experienced as a deep and abiding affection. We feel love for our parents, for our sisters and brothers, for our children, and ideally for our friends and neighbours and other humans. There is also love of country and love of learning. There seems to be a virtually endless list of people, things, and situations that may produce in humans the emotion of love.

The variety of love most written about by poets, most set to music by composers, and most longed for by virtually all of us is—romantic love.

But the first question to ask is, How many components are there to this thing we call love?

Romantic Love: Lost in Each Other

When we say we have "fallen" in love, it is probably romantic love we have fallen into. Romantic love (sometimes called *passionate love*) is an intense emotional response characterized by a turmoil of emotion, coupled with sexual arousal and a tremendous longing for that person (Hatfield, 1988). **[LO 9.24]** Does it mean that love is over when passion fades? Probably not. Love often changes into what has been termed *companionate love* (Hatfield, 1988). **[LO 9.24]** This is characterized by a less sexualized sense of affection. As love grows, couples often focus on the stability of the relationship, and on the commitment and sense of liking for the other person.

The Six Styles of Love

Canadian psychologist John Alan Lee (1973, 1988) proposed that love is characterized by six different "styles of loving," all of which may be present in differing degrees for each individual. **[LO 9.25]** These dimensions of love are (a) romantic and passionate, (b) friendly, (c) game-playing, (d) possessive, (e) pragmatic, and (f) unselfish.

Sternberg's Theory of Love: Three Components, Seven Types

How does Sternberg's triangular theory of love account for the different kinds of love?

Robert Sternberg (1986, 1987, 2006), whose triarchic theory of intelligence was discussed earlier, has also proposed a three-component **triangular theory of love. [LO 9.26]** The three

components are intimacy, passion, and commitment. Sternberg (1987) explains intimacy as "those feelings in a relationship that promote closeness, bondedness, and connectedness" (p. 339). *Passion* refers to those drives in a loving relationship "that lead to romance, physical attraction, [and] sexual consummation" (Sternberg, 1986, p. 119). The commitment component consists of a short-term aspect (i.e., the decision that one person loves another) and a long-term aspect (i.e., the commitment the person makes to maintaining that love over time).

Sternberg proposes that these three components combine in various ways to form different kinds of love. **[LO 9.26]** Each component can vary in intensity, from very strong to very weak, and the kind of love that is experienced depends on the strengths of each of the three components relative to one another. Liking, for example, has only one of the love components—intimacy. People who experience empty love feel a strong commitment to their relationship, but the intimacy and passion components are no longer present. Infatuated love consists of strong passion combined with little intimacy and weak commitment, while romantic love is a combination of strong passion and great intimacy with weak commitment. Fatuous love has the passion and commitment required for a strong relationship, but lacks the intimacy. This type of love can be exemplified by a whirlwind courtship and marriage in which a commitment is motivated largely by passion without the stabilizing influence of intimacy. By contrast, companionate love consists of high intimacy and commitment with little passion. This type of love is often found in marriages in which the passion has gone out of the relationship but a deep affection and commitment remains. Finally, **consummate love** is the only type that has all three components in great intensity and is certainly perceived to be the ideal type of love relationship, for which many people strive. However, Sternberg cautions that maintaining consummate love may be even harder than achieving it!

Sternberg stresses the importance of translating the components of love into action. "Without expression," he warns, "even the greatest of loves can die" (1987, p. 341).

Love in all its fullness, its richness, and its power is such an intense and consuming human experience that researchers find it hard to capture. It is almost too personal to be viewed and studied with passionless objectivity.

---

triangular theory of love: Sternberg's theory that three components—intimacy, passion, and commitment—singly or in various combinations produce seven different kinds of love.

consummate love: According to Sternberg's theory, the most complete form of love, consisting of three components—intimacy, passion, and commitment.

REMEMBER IT

Experiencing Emotions

1. The idea that making a happy, sad, or angry face can actually trigger the physiological response and feeling associated with the emotion is called the
   a. emotion production theory.
   b. emotion control theory.
   c. facial-feedback hypothesis.
   d. facial expression theory.

2. Heightened emotion tends to facilitate rational thinking. (true/false)

3. Which of the following is not one of the central components of love, according to Sternberg's triangular theory?
   a. compatibility
   b. passion
   c. commitment
   d. intimacy

4. What is the complete form of love, according to Sternberg?
   a. romantic love
   b. fatuous love
   c. companionate love
   d. consummate love

Answers: 1. c 2. false 3. a 4. d

APPLY IT

Eating Disorders: The Tyranny of the Scale

Imagine this: The thought of even the slightest layer of fat on your body repels you. You have been dieting and exercising strenuously for months, but you still feel fat, even though your friends comment that you're nothing but skin and bones. And you're unbelievably hungry: Your dreams and daydreams are all about food—delicious food, lots of it. You leaf through cookbooks, go grocery shopping, and prepare meals whenever you get a chance, but when you sit down to eat you merely play with your food, because if you ate it you might get fat.

Now imagine this: Driven by an uncontrollable urge, you buy a dozen packages of cookies, perhaps a box of doughnuts. You take them home, lock the door, and start eating them. Once you've started, you can't stop—you gorge yourself on cookies and doughnuts until you feel as if you're about to explode. At that point you are overcome with disgust and anger at yourself; you take a double dose of laxatives in an effort to get rid of the excess volume of food you have consumed.

These two scenarios are not as unusual as you might think. They represent two surprisingly common eating disorders: anorexia nervosa and bulimia nervosa. What causes these disorders, and how can they be treated?

Although there are some similarities between them, anorexia and bulimia are very different disorders. Anorexia nervosa is characterized by an overwhelming, irrational fear of gaining weight or becoming fat, compulsive dieting to the point of self-starvation, and excessive weight loss. Some anorexics lose as much as 20 to 25 percent of their original body weight. Anorexia typically begins in adolescence, and 90 percent of those afflicted are females (Bekker & Spoor, 2008). Unfortunately, 4 percent of people who are diagnosed with anorexia nervosa die within 30 years of having been diagnosed in adolescence or early adulthood (Papadopoulos, Ekbom, Brandt, & Ekselius, 2009). Their average age at death is just 34. Anorexia is diagnosed when an individual weighs less than 85 percent of her or his expected weight but still expresses an intense fear of becoming fat (American Psychiatric Association [APA], 2000). Anorexia often begins with dieting, perhaps in reaction to a gain in weight after the onset of menstruation. Gradually the dieting develops into an obsession. Anorexic individuals continue to feel hunger and are strangely preoccupied with food.

Anorexic individuals also have a gross distortion in the perception of their body size. No matter how thin they become, they continue to perceive themselves as fat. They are so obsessed with their weight that frequently they not only starve themselves, but they also exercise relentlessly and excessively in an effort to accelerate their weight loss. Research suggests that this tendency to obsess about their weight is associated with a more general tendency toward distorted thinking (Tchanturia et al., 2007). Moreover, an unusually high rate of obsessive-compulsive disorder—a psychiatric disorder characterized by an obsessive need for control—has been found among anorexics (Milos, Spindler, Ruggiero, Klaghofer, & Schnyder, 2002). The tendency toward eating disorders may be genetically transmitted (Kortegaard, Hoerder, Joergensen, Gillberg, & Kyvik, 2001), but it is difficult to pinpoint the actual cause of this disorder. Some investigators believe that young women who refuse to eat are attempting to control a portion of their lives, which they may feel unable to control in other respects.

Up to 50 percent of anorexics also develop symptoms of bulimia nervosa, a chronic disorder characterized by repeated and uncontrolled episodes of binge eating, often in secret (APA, 2000). An episode of binge eating has two main features: (1) much larger amounts of food than most people would eat during the same period of time and (2) a feeling of inability to stop the eating or control the amount eaten. Binges are frequently followed by purging: self-induced vomiting and/or the use of large quantities of laxatives and diuretics. Bulimics may also engage in excessive dieting and exercise. Athletes are especially susceptible to this disorder. Many bulimics are average in size, and they purge after an eating binge simply to maintain their weight (APA, 2000).

Bulimia nervosa can cause a number of health problems. The stomach acid in vomit eats away at the teeth and may cause them to rot, and the delicate balance of body chemistry is destroyed by excessive use of laxatives and diuretics. The disorder also has a strong emotional component: the bulimic individual is aware that the eating pattern is abnormal and feels unable to control it. Depression, guilt, and shame often accompany the binges and subsequent purging.

Bulimia nervosa tends to appear in the late teens and affects about 1 in 25 women during their lifetime (Kendler et al., 1991). An even larger number of young women regularly binge and purge, but not frequently enough to warrant the diagnosis of

bulimia nervosa (Drewnowski, Yee, Kurth, & Krahn, 1994). Like those with anorexia, individuals with bulimia have high rates of obsessive-compulsive disorder and exhibit poor decision-making skills (Liao et al., 2009). Further, perhaps as many as a third of them have engaged in other kinds of self-injurious behaviour, such as cutting themselves intentionally (Favaro et al., 2008).

Bulimia, like anorexia, is difficult to treat. Sometimes treatment is complicated by the fact that a person with an eating disorder is also likely to have a personality disorder, or may interact ineffectively with therapists (R. D. Goodwin & Fitzgibbon, 2002; Rosenvinge, Matinuseen, & Ostensen 2000). Cognitive-behavioural therapy has been

used successfully to help modify eating habits and abnormal attitudes about body shape and weight (G. Wilson & Sysko, 2006). Antidepressant drugs have been found to reduce the frequency of binge eating and purging in some individuals with bulimia (Monteleone et al., 2005).

If you or someone you know is showing signs of suffering from either of these disorders, you can get help by contacting the National Eating Disorder Information Centre, ES 7-421, 200 Elizabeth St., Toronto ON, M5G 2C4, or call toll free (1-866-633-4220) or email nedic@uhn.ca. You can also contact a local agency through the public health department or your local hospital.

THINKING CRITICALLY

Evaluation

In your view, which theory or combination of theories best explains motivation: drive-reduction theory, arousal theory, or Maslow's hierarchy of needs? Which theory do you find least convincing? Support your answers.

Using what you have learned about body weight and dieting, select any well-known weight-loss plan (for example, Weight Watchers®, Jenny Craig®, Slim-Fast®) and evaluate it, explaining why it is or is not an effective way to lose weight and keep it off.

Point/Counterpoint

Recent research suggests that individuals who work in the prevention of crime, such as police officers, airport security, and border officials, should be trained to read people's emotions, since it is difficult to fake a true emotion. Prepare a convincing argument supporting each of the following positions:

a. Training security personnel to read facial expressions accurately should not be allowed.

b. Training security personnel to read facial expressions accurately should be allowed.

Psychology in Your Life

Which level of Maslow's hierarchy (shown in Figure 9.2) provides the strongest motivation for your behaviour in general? Give specific examples to support your answer.

MyPsychLab   go to mypsychlab (access code required) to find web resources for your text that supplement the material in chapter 9.

SUMMARY & REVIEW

THEORIES OF MOTIVATION

What is the difference between intrinsic and extrinsic motivation?

With intrinsic motivation, an act is performed because it is satisfying or pleasurable in and of itself; with extrinsic motivation, an act is performed to bring a reward or to avert an undesirable consequence.

How do instinct theories explain motivation?

An instinct is an inborn, unlearned, fixed pattern of behaviour that is characteristic of an entire species. Instinct theory was widely accepted by psychologists for the first 30 years of the twentieth century. Today, most researchers reject instinct theory as an explanation of human motivation. Our behaviours are too complex and unpredictable to be considered fixed and invariant across our species.

What is the drive-reduction theory of motivation?

Drive-reduction theory suggests that a biological need creates an unpleasant state of arousal or tension called a *drive*, which impels the organism to engage in behaviour that will satisfy the need and reduce tension.

How does arousal theory explain motivation?

Arousal theory suggests that the aim of motivation is to maintain an optimal level of arousal. If arousal is less than optimal, we engage in activities that stimulate arousal; if arousal exceeds the optimal level, we seek to reduce stimulation.

How does Maslow's hierarchy of needs account for human motivation?

Maslow's hierarchy of needs arranges needs in order of urgency—from physical needs (food, water, air, shelter) to security needs, belonging needs, esteem needs, and finally the need for self-actualization (developing to one's full potential), at the top of the hierarchy. Theoretically, the needs at the lower levels must be satisfied adequately before a person will be motivated to fulfill the higher needs.

THE PRIMARY DRIVES: HUNGER AND THIRST

Under what kinds of conditions do the two types of thirst occur?

One type of thirst, extracellular thirst, results from a loss of bodily fluid that can be caused by perspiration, vomiting, bleeding, diarrhea, or excessive intake of alcohol. Another type of thirst, intracellular thirst, results from excessive intake of salt, which disturbs the water–sodium balance.

What are the roles of the lateral hypothalamus and the ventromedial hypothalamus in the regulation of eating behaviour?

The lateral hypothalamus (LH) apparently acts in part as a feeding centre to excite eating: when activated, it signals the animal to start eating; when it is destroyed, the animal initially refuses to eat.

The ventromedial hypothalamus (VMH) presumably acts as a satiety centre: when activated, it signals the animal to stop eating; when it is destroyed, the animal overeats, becoming obese.

What are some of the body's hunger and satiety signals?

Some biological hunger signals are stomach contractions, low blood glucose levels, and high insulin levels. Some satiety signals are a full or distended stomach, high blood glucose levels, and the presence in the blood of other satiety substances (such as CCK) that are secreted by the gastrointestinal tract during digestion.

What are some non-biological factors that influence what and how much we eat?

External eating cues, such as the taste, smell, and appearance of food, the variety of food offered, and the time of day, can cause people to eat more food than they actually need.

What are some factors that account for variations in body weight?

Body weight is affected mainly by genetics and metabolic rates—which are influenced by patterns of food consumption and levels of activity.

How does set point affect body weight?

Set-point theory suggests that an internal homeostatic system functions to maintain a certain body weight by adjusting appetite and metabolic rate.

SOCIAL MOTIVES

What is Murray's contribution to the study of motivation?

Murray defined a list of social motives, or needs, and developed the Thematic Apperception Test (TAT) to assess the strength of a person's needs.

What is the need for achievement?

The need for achievement is the need to accomplish something difficult and to perform at a high standard of excellence.

What are some characteristics shared by people who are high in achievement motivation?

People high in achievement motivation enjoy challenges and like to compete. They tend to set goals of moderate difficulty, are more motivated by hope of success than by fear of failure, and attribute their success to their abilities and hard work.

THE WHAT AND WHY OF EMOTIONS

What are the three components of emotions?

An emotion is a feeling state that involves a physical component (physiological arousal), a cognitive component (appraisal of the situation arousing the emotion), and a behavioural component (outward expression of the emotion).

According to the James–Lange theory, what sequence of events occurs when we experience an emotion?

According to the James–Lange theory of emotion, environmental stimuli produce a physiological response, and then our awareness of this response causes the emotion.

What is the Cannon–Bard theory of emotion?
The Cannon–Bard theory suggests that emotion-provoking stimuli received by the senses are relayed to the thalamus, which simultaneously passes the information to the cerebral cortex, giving us the conscious mental experience of the emotion, and to the sympathetic nervous system, producing physiological arousal.

According to the Schachter—Singer theory, what two things must occur in order for us to experience an emotion?
This theory states that for an emotion to occur, (1) the person must experience physiological arousal and (2) the person must interpret or explain the arousal in order to label it as an emotion.

According to Lazarus, what sequence of events occurs when an individual feels an emotion?
Lazarus's theory of emotions suggests that, first, an emotion-provoking stimulus triggers a person's cognitive appraisal of that stimulus. This first step is then followed by the emotion and the physiological arousal.

THE EXPRESSION OF EMOTIONS

What are basic emotions?
The basic emotions (happiness, sadness, disgust, etc.) are those that are unlearned and that are reflected in the same facial expressions in all cultures.

How does the development of facial expressions of different emotions in infants suggest a biological basis for emotional expression?
The facial expressions of different emotions develop in a particular sequence in infants and seem to be the result of maturation rather than learning. The same sequence occurs even in children who have been visually or hearing impaired since birth.

Why are emotions considered a form of communication?
Emotions enable us to communicate our feelings, intentions, and needs more effectively than words alone can. Research suggests that we are both biologically wired to convey certain emotion signals, and also biologically predisposed to read and interpret them.

EXPERIENCING EMOTIONS

What is the facial-feedback hypothesis?
The facial-feedback hypothesis suggests that the muscular movements involved in certain facial expressions trigger the corresponding emotion (for example, smiling makes us happy).

How does Sternberg's triangular theory of love account for the different kinds of love?
In his triangular theory of love, Sternberg proposes that three components—intimacy, passion, and commitment—singly or in various combinations, produce seven different kinds of love—infatuated love, empty love, romantic love, fatuous love, companionate love, and consummate love, as well as liking.

MOTIVATION AND EMOTION

MODULE (9A) THEORIES OF MOTIVATION

Motivation is the process that initiates, directs, and sustains behaviour to satisfy physiological or psychological needs.

Types of Motivation
Intrinsic motivation: The desire to perform an act because it is satisfying or pleasurable in and of itself.
Extrinsic motivation: The desire to perform an act in order to gain a reward or to avoid an undesirable consequence.

Motives, Drives, and Incentives
Motive: A need or desire that energizes and directs behaviour toward a goal.
Drive: A state of tension brought about by an underlying need, which motivates one to engage in behaviour that will satisfy the need and reduce tension.
Incentive: An external stimulus that motivates behaviour.

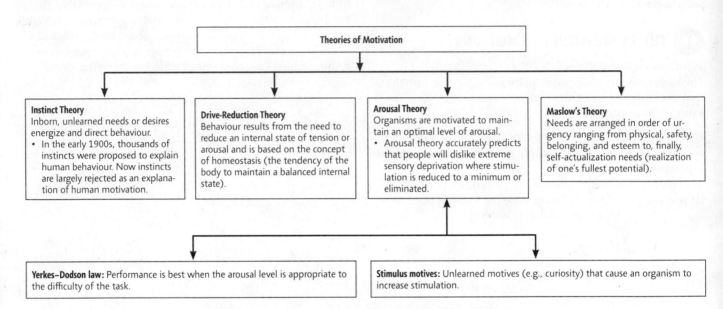

Theories of Motivation

Instinct Theory
Inborn, unlearned needs or desires energize and direct behaviour.
• In the early 1900s, thousands of instincts were proposed to explain human behaviour. Now instincts are largely rejected as an explanation of human motivation.

Drive-Reduction Theory
Behaviour results from the need to reduce an internal state of tension or arousal and is based on the concept of homeostasis (the tendency of the body to maintain a balanced internal state).

Arousal Theory
Organisms are motivated to maintain an optimal level of arousal.
• Arousal theory accurately predicts that people will dislike extreme sensory deprivation where stimulation is reduced to a minimum or eliminated.

Maslow's Theory
Needs are arranged in order of urgency ranging from physical, safety, belonging, and esteem to, finally, self-actualization needs (realization of one's fullest potential).

Yerkes–Dodson law: Performance is best when the arousal level is appropriate to the difficulty of the task.

Stimulus motives: Unlearned motives (e.g., curiosity) that cause an organism to increase stimulation.

MODULE (9B) THE PRIMARY DRIVES

A **primary drive** is an unlearned state of tension or arousal arising from a biological need.
• Two of the most important primary drives are hunger and thirst.

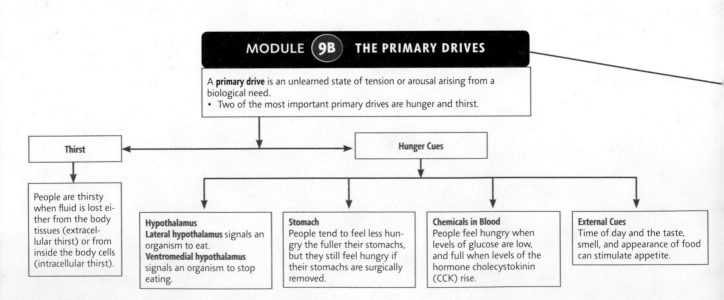

Thirst

Hunger Cues

People are thirsty when fluid is lost either from the body tissues (extracellular thirst) or from inside the body cells (intracellular thirst).

Hypothalamus
Lateral hypothalamus signals an organism to eat.
Ventromedial hypothalamus signals an organism to stop eating.

Stomach
People tend to feel less hungry the fuller their stomachs, but they still feel hungry if their stomachs are surgically removed.

Chemicals in Blood
People feel hungry when levels of glucose are low, and full when levels of the hormone cholecystokinin (CCK) rise.

External Cues
Time of day and the taste, smell, and appearance of food can stimulate appetite.

MODULE 9C SOCIAL MOTIVES

Social motives are acquired through experience and interaction with others.
- Need for achievement is a social motive to accomplish something difficult and to perform at a high standard. J. W. Atkinson (1964) suggests that when we approach any situation, two conflicting factors are operating—our hope for success and our fear of failure.

MODULE 9D THE WHAT AND WHY OF EMOTIONS

Emotion is a feeling state involving **physiological** arousal, **cognitive** appraisal of the situation arousing the state, and an outward (**behavioural**) expression of the state.

Theories of Emotions

James–Lange Theory
Emotion is the awareness of our physiological response to an emotion-provoking stimulus.

Cannon–Bard Theory
The feeling of emotion and physiological arousal occur simultaneously after an emotion-provoking stimulus is relayed to the thalamus.

Schachter–Singer Theory
For emotion to occur, there must be physiological arousal and cognitive appraisal.

Lazarus Theory
An emotion-provoking stimulus triggers a cognitive appraisal, which is followed by the emotion and physiological arousal.

MODULE 9E THE EXPRESSION OF EMOTIONS

Basic Emotions
Basic emotions are emotions that are unlearned and universal. Humans are biologically predisposed to show specific facial expressions for some emotions and to correctly interpret those emotions in other people.
Fear, anger, disgust, surprise, happiness, and sadness or distress are usually considered basic emotions.

Display Rules
Display rules are cultural rules that dictate how emotions should be expressed, and when and where their expression is appropriate.
Most people learn display rules early and abide by them most of the time.

MODULE 9F EXPERIENCING EMOTIONS

Facial-feedback hypothesis states that muscular movements involved in certain facial expressions trigger the corresponding emotion.

Research indicates that having people simulate an emotional expression produces physiological changes typical for that emotion.

Types of Love
Hatfield classifies love in two categories:
1) **Passionate love:** An intense emotional response coupled with sexual arousal and longing.
2) **Companionate love:** A less sexualized, more stable, and committed form of love.
John Alan Lee proposed that love is characterized by six different "styles of loving": romantic and passionate, friendly, game-playing, possessive, pragmatic, and unselfish.
Sternberg's triangular theory of love asserts that various combinations of three components of love—**passion, intimacy,** and **commitment**—give rise to **seven** different **types of love.**

Body Weight

Genetic factors alter body size and the number of fat cells in a body.
- Mutation of a gene can cause obesity.

Metabolic rate: The rate at which the body burns calories to produce energy.
- Body weight varies depending on calorie intake and metabolic rate.

Fat-cell theory: Body weight depends on the number and size of fat cells in the body.
- The number of fat cells depends on heredity and eating habits.

Set-point theory: An internal homeostatic system functions to maintain a certain body weight.

Body Fat
Women need 12 percent body fat to survive and 20 percent body fat for their reproductive system to function properly. Men need 3 percent body fat to survive.
Obesity is excessive fatness, defined as a body mass index of 30 for men and women.

10

Imagine that you have just been in an auto accident with the man in this photo. He hit your car from behind, so there is no doubt that he was legally at fault. However, you don't know exactly what it was that caused him to crash into your car. Based strictly on the photo, estimate on a scale from 1 to 10 the likelihood that each of the following factors contributed to the accident, with 1 being "not likely" and 10 being "very likely."

1. He was intoxicated.
2. His sunglasses were fogged up.
3. He was talking on a cellphone.
4. He is an angry person who takes out his frustrations on other drivers.
5. He was distracted by the erratic behaviour of another driver.
6. He is an irresponsible person who has little concern for the rights of others.

Did the man's appearance influence your responses? All of us tend to be influenced by the first information we receive about a person. In face-to-face interactions, the first thing we learn about anyone is what they look like. Thus, we often use a person's appearance to form hypotheses about characteristics such as their personalities and moral values.

The nature of the statements in the list may have influenced your responses as well. Notice that items 1, 4, and 6 refer to characteristics of the man, whereas items 2, 3, and 5 refer to the situation. If you tended to see the accident as the product of the man's characteristics rather than those of the situation, then you may have committed a common error in thinking that causes us to see another person's mistakes as a function of personality and our own as caused by situational factors that are beyond our control.

© Kirk Weddle/Photodisc/Getty Images

SOCIAL PSYCHOLOGY

First impression and the ways in which we think about the causes of our own and others' behaviours are just two of the topics of interest in **social psychology**, the area of study that attempts to explain how the actual, imagined, or implied presence of others influences the thoughts, feelings, and behaviour of individuals. No human being lives in a vacuum. How we think about, respond to, and interact with other people provides the scientific territory that social psychology explores. Research in social psychology yields some surprising and provocative explanations about human behaviour, from the atrocious to the altruistic.

In this chapter, we will explore some of the main topics of social psychology, including how we form impressions of other people, how we develop friendships and romantic relationships, and how social factors and the presence of others influence conformity and obedience, performance, and decision making. We will also discuss how attitudes are formed and how they can be changed, and we will explore prejudice and discrimination. Finally, we will look at the conditions under which people are likely to help each other (prosocial behaviour) and hurt each other (aggression).

MODULE 10A SOCIAL PERCEPTION

LO 10.1 Describe the primacy effect.

LO 10.2 Explain how our expectations of people can become self-fulfilling prophecies.

LO 10.3 Describe and contrast situational and dispositional attributions.

LO 10.4 Identify three attribution biases when we explain our own vs. other people's behaviour.

---

social psychology: The study of the way in which the actual, imagined, or implied presence of others influences the thoughts, feelings, and behaviour of individuals.

primacy effect: The likelihood that an overall impression or judgment of another will be influenced more by the first information received about that person than by information that comes later.

attributions: Inferences about the cause of our own or another's behaviour.

situational attribution: Attribution of a behaviour to some external cause or factor operating in the situation; an external attribution.

dispositional attribution: Attribution of one's own or another's behaviour to some internal cause such as a personal trait, motive, or attitude; an internal attribution.

actor–observer bias: The tendency of observers to make dispositional attributions for the behaviours of others but situational attributions for their own behaviours.

fundamental attribution error: The tendency to overemphasize internal factors and underemphasize situational ones when explaining other people's behaviour.

self-serving bias: Our tendency to attribute our successes to dispositional causes, and our failures to situational causes.

We spend a significant portion of our lives in contact with other people. Not only do we form impressions of others, but we also attempt to understand why they behave as they do.

IMPRESSION FORMATION: SIZING UP THE OTHER PERSON

Why are first impressions so important and enduring?

When we meet people for the first time, we start forming impressions of them right away. And, of course, they are busy forming impressions of us. Naturally we notice the obvious attributes first—gender, ethnicity, age, dress, and physical attractiveness (Maner, Miller, Moss, Leo, & Plant, 2012). The latter, as shallow as it may seem, has a definite impact on our first impressions. Beyond noticing physical appearance, we may wonder, What is her occupation? Is he married? Answers to our questions, combined with a conscious or unconscious assessment of the person's verbal and nonverbal behaviour, all play a part in forming a first impression. Our own moods also play a part—when we are happy, our impressions of others are usually more positive than when we are unhappy (Forgas & Bower, 1987). First impressions are powerful and can colour many of the later impressions we form about people.

A number of studies reveal that our overall impression or judgment of another person is influenced more by the first information we receive than by later information (Asch, 1946; Luchins, 1957). For example, psychologist Stephanie Buchert and her colleagues found that professors' scores on students' end-of-semester evaluations did not differ from those they were given by students just two weeks into the term (Buchert, Laws, Apperson, & Bregman, 2008). This phenomenon is called the **primacy effect**. **[LO 10.1]** It seems that we attend to initial information more carefully, and once an impression is formed, it provides the framework through which we interpret later information (Forgas, 2011). Any information that is consistent with the first impression is likely to be accepted, thus strengthening the impression. Information that does not fit with the earlier information is more likely to be disregarded.

Remember that any time you list your personal traits or qualities, always list your most positive ones first. It pays to put your best foot forward—first.

Expectations: Seeing What We Expect to See

Sometimes our expectations become a self-fulfilling prophecy and actually influence the way other people act. **[LO 10.2]** Expectations may be based on a person's gender, age, racial or ethnic group, social class, role or occupation, personality traits, past behaviour, relationship with us, and so on. Once formed, our expectations affect how we perceive the behaviour of others—what we pay attention to and what we ignore. Rarely do we consider that our own expectations may colour our attitude and manner toward other people—that we ourselves partly bring about the very behaviour we expect (E. E. Jones, 1986; D. T. Miller & Turnbull, 1986).

ATTRIBUTION: OUR EXPLANATION OF BEHAVIOUR

What is the difference between a situational attribution and a dispositional attribution for a specific behaviour?

How often do you ask yourself why people (yourself included) do the things they do? When trying to explain behaviour, we make **attributions**—that is, we assign or attribute causes to explain the behaviour of others and to explain our own behaviour as well. We are particularly interested in the causes when behaviours are unexpected, when goals are not attained (B. Weiner, 1985), and when actions are not socially desirable (E. E. Jones & Davis, 1965).

Although we can actually observe behaviour, we usually can only infer its cause or causes. Whenever we try to determine why we or someone else behaved in a certain way, we can make two types of attributions. **[LO 10.3]** In some instances we make a **situational attribution** (an external attribution) and attribute the behaviour to some external cause or factor operating within the situation. After failing an exam, we might say, "The test was unfair" or "The professor didn't teach the material well." Or we might make a **dispositional attribution** (an internal attribution) and attribute the behaviour to some internal cause such as a personal trait, motive, or attitude. Thus, we might attribute a poor grade to our own lack of ability or to a poor memory.

Attributional Biases: Different Attributions for Ourselves and Others

How do the kinds of attributions we tend to make about ourselves differ from those we make about other people?

A basic difference exists in how we make attributions for our own behaviour and that of others—a phenomenon called the **actor–observer bias** (E. E. Jones, 1976, 1990; E. E. Jones & Nisbett, 1971). **[LO 10.4]** We tend to use situational attributions to explain our own behaviour, because we are aware of factors in the situation that influenced us to act the way we did. In addition, being aware of our past behaviour, we know whether our present actions are typical or atypical.

In explaining the behaviour of others, we focus more on personal factors than on factors within the situation (Stewart, Latu, Kawakami, & Myers, 2010). Not knowing how a person has behaved in different situations in the past, we assume a consistency in his or her behaviour. Thus, we are likely to attribute the behaviour of the individual to some personal quality. The tendency to overemphasize internal factors and underemphasize situational factors when we explain other people's behaviour is so fundamental, so commonplace, that it has been named the **fundamental attribution error** (L. Ross, 1977). **[LO 10.4]**

There is one striking inconsistency in the way we view our own behaviour—the self-serving bias. **[LO 10.4]** We use the **self-serving bias** when we attribute our successes to internal or dispositional causes and blame our failures on external or situational causes (Park, Bauer, & Arbuckle, 2009). If we interview for a job and get it, it is probably because we have the right qualifications. If someone else gets the job, it is probably because he or she knew the right people. The self-serving bias allows us to take credit for our successes and to shift the blame for our failures to the situation. Doing so helps protect our self-esteem and positive self-identity (Alicke & Sedikides, 2009; Sharma & Sharma, 2010), both of which are associated with well-being (S. E. Taylor & Brown, 1988).

REMEMBER IT

Social Perception

1. Which of the following statements about first impressions is false?
   a. We usually pay closer attention to early information than to later information we receive about a person.
   b. Early information forms a framework through which other information is interpreted.
   c. First impressions often serve as self-fulfilling prophecies.
   d. The importance of first impressions is greatly overrated.

2. We tend to make _____ attributions to explain our own behaviour and _____ attributions to explain the behaviour of others.
   a. situational; situational
   b. situational; dispositional
   c. dispositional; situational
   d. dispositional; dispositional

3. The tendency of people to overemphasize dispositional causes and underemphasize situational causes when they explain the behaviour of others is called the
   a. fundamental attribution error.
   b. false consensus error.
   c. self-serving bias.
   d. actor–observer bias.

4. The tendency of people to emphasize situational explanations for their own behaviours but dispositional attributions for the behaviours of others is called the
   a. fundamental attribution error.
   b. false consensus error.
   c. self-serving bias.
   d. actor–observer bias.

Answers: 1. d 2. b 3. a 4. d

MODULE 10B ATTRACTION

LO 10.5 Describe the influence of proximity, reciprocal liking, and similarity on attraction.

LO 10.6 Explain the halo effect.

LO 10.7 Explain the matching hypothesis.

LO 10.8 Identify four qualities both men and women across cultures look for in a mate.

Think for a moment about the people you consider to be your closest friends. What causes you to like or even love one person yet ignore or react negatively to someone else? What factors influence interpersonal attraction—the degree to which we are drawn to or like one another?

FACTORS INFLUENCING ATTRACTION

Proximity: Close to You

Why is proximity an important factor in attraction?

One major factor influencing our choice of friends is physical **proximity**, or geographic closeness. **[LO 10.5]** If you live in an apartment complex, you are probably friendlier with people who live next door or only a few doors away (Festinger, Schachter, & Back, 1950). What about the people you like best in your classes? Do they sit next to you or not more than a seat or two away?

It is much easier to make friends or even fall in love with people who are close at hand. One possible explanation for this is that mere exposure to people, objects, and circumstances probably increases our liking for them (Zajonc, 1968). The **mere-exposure effect** refers to our tendency to feel more positive toward stimuli with repeated exposure. People, food, songs, and styles become more acceptable the more we are exposed to them. Advertisers rely on the positive effects of repeated exposure to increase our liking for products, trends, and even political candidates.

Reciprocal Liking: Liking Those Who Like Us

We tend to like people who like us—or who we believe like us (Curtis & Miller, 1986). **[LO 10.5]** This effect was the source of a recent Canadian study by Stinson and her colleagues (2009), who examined how our impression of people's feelings toward us become self-fulfilling. Their results showed that if people expect acceptance from a person they just meet, "they will behave warmly, which in turn will lead other people to accept them; if they expect rejection, they will behave coldly, which will lead to less acceptance" (p. 1165). People's positive expectations affected their behaviours, which consequently affected other people to also view them positively.

©Kurhan/Fotolia

Attractiveness: Good Looks Attract

How important is physical attractiveness in attraction?

Although people are quick to deny that mere physical appearance is the main factor that attracts them to someone initially, a substantial body of evidence indicates that it is. People of all ages have a strong tendency to prefer physically attractive people (Dion, 1973, 1979; Feingold, 1992; Langlois et al., 2000). Children as young as two months old, when shown photographs of attractive and unattractive people, will spend more time looking at attractive faces. Attractive male and female professors also receive significantly higher student evaluations (Lewandowski, Higgins, & Nardone, 2012)!

What constitutes physical beauty? Researchers Langlois and Roggman (1990) found that physical beauty consists not of rare physical qualities but of facial features that are more or less the average of the features in a given general population. Studies show, for instance, that symmetrical faces and bodies are seen as more attractive and sexually appealing (R. D. Green, MacDorman, Ho, & Vasudevan, 2008). Judgments of physical attractiveness seem to have some definite consistency across cultures for both women and men (Singh & Singh, 2011). Whether this level of agreement is associated with similar views of beauty across cultures or the influence of the media on our perceptions of beauty is still debated. Evolutionary psychologists suggest that this cross-cultural similarity is the result of a tendency, shaped by natural selection, to look for indicators of health in potential mates, especially waist-to-hip ratio (Weeden & Sabini, 2005).

Why is physical attractiveness so important? When people have one trait or quality that we either admire or dislike very much, we often assume that they also have other admirable or negative traits—a phenomenon known as the **halo effect** (Nisbett & Wilson, 1977; Thorndike, 1920). **[LO 10.6]** Attractive people are seen as more exciting, personable, interesting, and socially desirable than unattractive people. Perhaps as a result, candidates who are being considered for a job are more likely to be selected if they are attractive (López Bóo, Rossi, & Urzua, 2012).

Feingold's (1992) studies have confirmed that positive characteristics are indeed attributed to physically attractive people. Being attractive is an

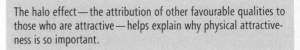
The halo effect—the attribution of other favourable qualities to those who are attractive—helps explain why physical attractiveness is so important.

advantage to children and adults, and to males and females. According to some studies, women's looks contribute more to how they are judged on other personal qualities than is the case with men (Bar-Tal & Saxe, 1976; Feingold, 1990). Not surprisingly, physical attractiveness seems to have its greatest impact in the context of romantic attraction, particularly in initial encounters (Feingold, 1988; Hatfield & Sprecher, 1986).

Does this mean that unattractive people don't have a chance? Fortunately not. Eagly and her colleagues (1991) suggest that the impact of physical attractiveness is strongest in the perception of strangers. But once we get to know people, other qualities assume more importance. In fact, as we come to like people, they begin to look more attractive to us.

Similarity: A Strong Basis of Attraction

Are people, as a rule, more attracted to those who are opposite or to those who are similar to them?

To sum up research on attraction, the saying that "birds of a feather flock together" is more accurate than "opposites attract." **[LO 10.5]** Beginning in elementary school, people are more likely to pick friends of the same age, gender, ethnic background, and socioeconomic class. These variables continue to influence the choice of friends through college or university and later in life. Of course, choosing friends who are similar to us could be related to proximity—that is, to the fact that we tend to come into contact with people who are more similar to us in a variety of ways.

For both sexes, liking people who have similar attitudes begins early in childhood and continues throughout life (Griffitt, Nelson, & Littlepage, 1972). We are likely to choose friends and lovers who have similar views on most things that are important to us. Similar interests and attitudes make it more likely that time spent together is rewarding. It is similarities, then, not differences, that usually stimulate liking and loving (Morry, Kito, & Ortiz, 2011).

ROMANTIC ATTRACTION

> Moderately attractive, unskilled, unemployed, 50-year-old divorced man with 7 children seeks beautiful, wealthy, exciting woman between ages 20 and 30 for companionship, romance, and possible marriage. No smokers or drinkers.

Can you imagine reading this ad in the personals column of your newspaper? Somehow, we all recognize that this "match" is not reasonable. Even though most of us may be attracted to beautiful people, the **matching hypothesis** suggests that we are more likely to end up with someone similar to ourselves in attractiveness and other assets (Taylor, Fiore, Mendelsohn, & Cheshire, 2011). **[LO 10.7]** It has been suggested that most people estimate their social assets and realistically expect to attract someone with more or less equal assets. Fear of rejection keeps many people from pursuing those who are much more attractive than they are. Nevertheless, once a relationship is formed, both men and women develop the ability to screen out the attractiveness of alternative partners (Maner, Gailliot,

& Miller, 2009). Thus, although continuing to be attentive to a partner's attractiveness is important to maintaining a romantic relationship, ignoring the attractiveness of other potential partners may be just as important to relationship stability and longevity.

MATE SELECTION: THE MATING GAME

In 1958, Robert Winch proposed that men and women tend to choose mates whose needs and personalities complement their own. A talkative person might seek a quiet mate who prefers to listen. Although there is some research to support this view (Dryer & Horowitz, 1997), the weight of research suggests that similarity in needs leads to attraction (Buss, 1984; Gebauer, Leary, & Neberich, 2012). Similarities in personality, as well as in "physical characteristics, cognitive abilities, age, education, religion, ethnic background, attitudes and opinions, and socioeconomic status," play a role in marital choice (O'Leary & Smith, 1991, p. 196; see also Watson, Beer, & McDade-Montez, 2014) and seem to be related to marital success.

If you were to select a marital partner, what qualities would attract you? Do the *Try It* to evaluate your own preferences.

How do your selections in the *Try It* compare with those of men and women from more than 30 countries and cultures? Generally, men and women across cultures agree on the first four values in mate selection: (1) mutual attraction/love, (2) dependable character, (3) emotional stability and maturity, and (4) pleasing disposition (Buss et al., 1990). **[LO 10.8]** Beyond these first four, however, men and women differ somewhat in the attributes they prefer. According to Buss (1994), "Men prefer to mate with beautiful young women, whereas women prefer to mate with men who have resources and social status" (p. 239). These preferences, Buss believes, have been adaptive in human evolutionary history: To a male, beauty and youth suggest health and fertility—the best opportunity to send his genes into the next generation; to a female, resources and social status provide security for her and her children (Buss & Shackelford, 2008). Others, however, see this pattern as a simple reflection of men's greater economic power in our society along with other social norms that foster different choices by women and men (Eagly & Wood, 1999).

---

proximity: Geographic closeness; a major factor in attraction.

mere-exposure effect: The tendency of people to develop a more positive evaluation of some person, object, or other stimulus with repeated exposure to it.

halo effect: The tendency to attribute generally positive or negative traits to a person as a result of observing one major positive or negative trait.

matching hypothesis: The notion that people tend to have spouses, lovers, or friends who are similar to themselves in social assets such as physical attractiveness.

TRY IT

What Qualities Are You Looking for in a Mate?

In your choice of a mate, which qualities are most and least important to you? Rank these 18 qualities of a potential mate from most important (1) to least important (18) to you.

_____ Ambition and industriousness
_____ Chastity (no previous sexual intercourse)
_____ Desire for home and children
_____ Good cooking and housekeeping skills
_____ Education and intelligence
_____ Emotional stability and maturity
_____ Favourable social status or rating
_____ Similar political background
_____ Similar religious background
_____ Good health
_____ Good looks
_____ Similar education
_____ Pleasing disposition
_____ Refinement/neatness
_____ Sociability
_____ Good financial prospects
_____ Dependable character
_____ Mutual attraction/love

©Andrey Yurlov/Shutterstock

REMEMBER IT

Attraction

1. Physical attractiveness is a very important factor in initial attraction. (true/false)
2. People are usually drawn to those who are more opposite than similar to themselves. (true/false)
3. Match the example with the term.
   _____ 1) Brian sees Susan at the library often and begins to like her.
   _____ 2) Liane assumes that because Boyd is handsome, he must be popular and sociable.
   _____ 3) Alan and Carol are dating each other and are both very attractive.
   a. matching hypothesis
   b. halo effect
   c. mere-exposure effect

Answers: 1. true 2. false 3. (1) c (2) b (3) a

MODULE 10C CONFORMITY, OBEDIENCE, AND COMPLIANCE

LO 10.9 Describe and compare conformity and compliance.
LO 10.10 Explain the findings of Asch's experiment on conformity.
LO 10.11 Explain the findings of Milgram's experiment on obedience.
LO 10.12 Describe three techniques used to gain compliance.

CONFORMITY: GOING ALONG WITH THE GROUP

Whether we like it or not, we all conform to some norms. The real question is, to *what* do we conform? **Conformity** involves changing or adopting a behaviour or an attitude in order to be consistent with the norms of a group or the expectations of other people. **[LO 10.9]** Norms are the standards of behaviour and the attitudes that are expected of members of the group. Some conformity is necessary if we are to have a society at all. We cannot drive on either side of the street as we please, or park anywhere we want, or drive as fast as we choose. Norms are in place to create a predictable and stable environment.

We need other people, so we must conform to their expectations to some extent in order to have their esteem or approval, their friendship or love, or even their company (P. N. Christensen, Rothberger, Wood, & Matz, 2004). For instance, teens who attend schools where the majority of students are opposed to smoking, drinking, and drug use are less likely to use these substances than are peers who attend schools where the majority approve of these behaviours (Eisenberg, Toumbourou, Catalano, & Hemphill, 2014). It is easy to see why people conform to norms and standards of groups that are important to them, such as family, peer groups, social groups, and sports teams. But what is even more amazing is that people also conform to the majority opinion even when they are among strangers.

Asch's Experiment: The Classic on Conformity

What did Asch find in his famous experiment on conformity?

The best-known experiment on conformity was conducted by Solomon Asch (1951, 1955), who designed the simple test shown in Figure 10.1. Look at the standard line at the top. Then pick the line—1, 2, or 3—that is the same length. Did you pick line 2? Can you imagine any circumstances in which you might

Standard Line

FIGURE 10.1
Asch's Classic Study of Conformity
If you were one of eight participants in the Asch experiment who were asked to pick the line (1, 2, or 3) that matched the standard line, which line would you choose? If the other participants all chose line 3, would you conform and answer line 3?
Source: (Based on Asch, 1955) Based on Asch, S.E. (1955). Opinions and social pressure. Scientific American, 193, 31–35.

1   2   3

In this scene from Asch's experiment on conformity, all but one of the "participants" were really confederates of the experimenter. They deliberately chose the wrong line to try to influence the naive subject (second from right) to go along with the majority.

tell the experimenter that either line 1 or line 3 matched the standard line? You could be surprised by the influence of others on your own behaviour if people around you insisted that the wrong line—say, line 3—was of the same length as the standard line. And many participants were so influenced in Asch's classic experiment, even when the tests were so simple that they otherwise picked the correct line more than 99 percent of the time.

Eight males were seated around a large table and were asked, one by one, to tell the experimenter which of the three lines matched the standard line, as in Figure 10.1. Only one of the eight was an actual participant; the others were confederates assisting the experimenter. There were 18 trials—18 different lines to be matched. During 12 of these trials, the confederates all gave the same wrong answer, which of course puzzled the naive participant. Would the participant continue to believe his eyes and select the correct line, or would he feel pressure to conform to the group's selection and give the wrong answer himself?

Asch found that 5 percent of the participants conformed to the incorrect, unanimous majority *all* of the time; 70 percent conformed *some* of the time; and 25 percent remained completely independent and were *never* swayed by the group. **[LO 10.10]**

Asch wondered how group size would influence conformity. Varying the experiment with groups of 2, 3, 4, 8, and 10 to 15, he found that the tendency to "go along" with the majority opinion was in full force even when the unanimous majority consisted of only 3 confederates. **[LO 10.10]** Surprisingly, unanimous majorities of 15 produced no higher conformity rates than did those of 3. Asch also found that if just one other person voiced a dissenting opinion, the tendency to conform was not as strong. When just one confederate in the group disagreed with the incorrect majority, the naive participants' errors dropped drastically, from 32 percent to 10.4 percent. **[LO 10.10]**

OBEDIENCE: FOLLOWING ORDERS

Some obedience is necessary if society is to function; however, unquestioned obedience can bring people to commit unbelievably horrible acts. In one of the darkest chapters in human history, officials in Nazi Germany obeyed Hitler's orders to exterminate six million Jews and other "undesirables." The civilized world was stunned and sickened by their actions, and nearly everyone wondered how human beings could be capable of committing such atrocities. Stanley Milgram, a young researcher at Yale University in the 1960s, designed a study to investigate how far ordinary citizens would go to obey orders.

The Milgram Study: The Classic on Obedience

What did Milgram find in his classic study of obedience?

In the 1960s this advertisement appeared in newspapers in New Haven, Connecticut, and in other communities near Yale:

> **Wanted:** Volunteers to serve as subjects in a study of memory and learning at Yale University.

Many people responded to the ad, and 40 males between the ages of 20 and 50 were selected, among them "postal clerks, high school teachers, salesmen, engineers, and laborers" (Milgram, 1963, p. 372). But no experiment on memory and learning was to take place. Instead, Milgram planned a staged drama. Imagine that you are one of the naive participants selected for the experiment.

The researcher actually wants to know how far you will go in obeying orders to administer what you believe are increasingly painful electric shocks to a "learner" who misses questions on a test. The cast of characters is as follows:

> **The experimenter:** A 31-year-old high school biology teacher dressed in a grey laboratory coat who assumes a stern and serious manner.

> **The learner:** A pleasant, heavy-set accountant about 50 years of age (an accomplice of the experimenter).

> **The teacher:** You—the only naive member of the cast.

The experimenter leads you and the learner into one room. The learner is then strapped into an electric-chair apparatus. You, the teacher, are given a sample shock of 45 volts, which stings you and is supposedly for the purpose of testing the equipment and showing you what the learner will feel. The learner complains of a heart condition and says that he hopes the electric shocks will not be too painful. The experimenter admits that the stronger shocks will hurt but hastens to add, "Although the shocks can be extremely painful, they cause no permanent tissue damage" (Milgram, 1963, p. 373).

Then the experimenter takes you to an adjoining room, out of sight of the learner. The experimenter seats you in front of an instrument panel (shown in the left-hand photograph on this page), on which 30 lever switches are set horizontally. The first switch on the left, you are told, delivers only 15 volts, but each successive switch is 15 volts stronger than the last—30 volts, 45 volts, and so on, up to the last switch, which carries 450 volts. The instrument panel has labels ranging from "Slight Shock" to "Danger: Severe Shock."

conformity: Changing or adopting a behaviour or an attitude to be consistent with the norms of a group or the expectations of others.

norms: The attitudes and standards of behaviour expected of members of a particular group.

On the left is the shock generator used by Milgram in his famous experiment. On the right is the learner (actually an accomplice) being strapped into his chair by the experimenter and the unsuspecting participant.

From the film Obedience, copyright © 1968 by Stanley Milgram, copyright © renewed 1993 by Alexandra Milgram.

The experimenter explains that you are to read a list of word pairs to the learner and then test his memory. When the learner makes the right choice, you go on to the next pair. If he misses a question, you are to flip a switch and shock him, moving one switch to the right—delivering 15 additional volts—for each miss. The learner does well at first but then begins missing about three out of every four questions. You begin pulling the switches, which you believe are delivering stronger and stronger shocks for each incorrect answer. When you hesitate, the experimenter urges you, "Please continue" or "Please go on." If you still hesitate, the experimenter orders you, "The experiment requires that you continue," or, more strongly, "You have no other choice, you *must* go on" (Milgram, 1963, p. 374).

At the twentieth switch, 300 volts, the learner begins to pound on the wall and screams, "Let me out of here, let me out, my heart's bothering me, let me out!" (P. Meyer, 1972, p. 461). From this point on, the learner answers no more questions. Alarmed, you protest to the experimenter that the learner, who is pounding the wall frantically, does not want to continue. The experimenter answers, "Whether the learner likes it or not, you must go on" (Milgram, 1963, p. 374). When the learner fails to respond, you are told to count that as an incorrect response and shock him again.

Do you continue? If you do, you flip the next switch—315 volts—and only groans are heard from the learner. You look at the experimenter, obviously distressed, your palms sweating, your heart pounding. The experimenter states firmly, "You have no other choice, you *must* go on." If you refuse at this point, the experiment is ended. Would you refuse, or would you continue to shock a silent learner nine more times until you delivered the maximum of 450 volts?

How many of the 40 participants do you think obeyed the experimenter to the end—to 450 volts? The answer is quite disturbing: Almost everyone in the study (87.5 percent) continued to administer the shock to the 20th switch, supposedly 300 volts, when the learner began pounding the wall. Amazingly, 26 people—65 percent of the sample—obeyed the experimenter to the bitter end, as shown in Figure 10.2. But this experiment took

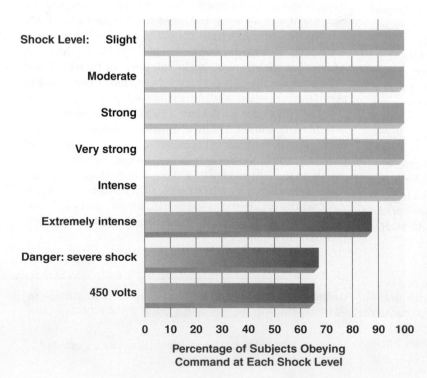

Percentage of Subjects Obeying Command at Each Shock Level

FIGURE 10.2

The Results of Milgram's Classic Experiment on Obedience

In his classic study, Stanley Milgram showed that a large majority of his participants would obey authority even if obedience caused great pain or was life-threatening to another person. **[LO 10.11]** Milgram reported that 87.5 percent of the participants continued to administer what they thought were painful electric shocks of 300 volts to a victim who complained of a heart condition. Amazingly, 65 percent of the participants obeyed authority to the bitter end and continued to deliver what they thought were dangerous, severe shocks to the maximum of 450 volts.

Source: (Data from Milgram, S. (1963). Behavioral study of obedience, *Journal of Abnormal and Social Psychology*, 67, 371–378).

a terrible toll on the participants. "Subjects were observed to sweat, tremble, stutter, bite their lips, groan, and dig their fingernails into their flesh. These were characteristic rather than exceptional responses to the experiment" (Milgram, 1963, p. 375).

Variations of the Milgram Study

Would the same results have occurred if the experiment had not been conducted at a famous university like Yale? The same experiment was carried out in a three-room office suite in a run-down building identified by a sign, "Research Associates of Bridgeport." Even there, 48 percent of participants administered the maximum shock, compared with the 65 percent in the Yale setting (P. Meyer, 1972).

Milgram (1965) conducted a variation of the original experiment in which each trial included three teachers: two were confederates and the third a naive participant. One confederate was instructed to refuse to continue after 150 volts, the other after 210 volts. In this situation 36 out of 40 naive participants (90 percent) defied the experimenter before the maximum shock could be given, compared with only 14 in the original experiment (Milgram, 1965). In Milgram's experiment, as in Asch's conformity study, the presence of another person who *refused to go along* gave many of the participants the courage to defy authority.

It is important to note that a study like the one conducted by Milgram could not be performed today because it would violate both the Canadian Psychological Association's and the American Psychological Association's codes of ethics for researchers. The use of deception as well as the potentially serious impact of the study would make the study inappropriate and unethical.

COMPLIANCE: GIVING IN TO REQUESTS

What are three techniques used to gain compliance?

Often, people act not out of conformity or obedience but in accordance with the wishes, suggestions, or direct requests of another person. **[LO 10.9]** This type of action is called **compliance**. Almost daily we are confronted by people who make requests of one sort or another. Do we comply with these requests? Quite often we do. People use several techniques to gain the compliance of others. **[LO 10.12]**

The Foot-in-the-Door Technique: Upping the Ante

One strategy, the **foot-in-the-door technique**, is designed to secure a favourable response to a small request first. **[LO 10.12]** The intent is to make a person more likely to agree later to a larger request (the request that was desired from the beginning). In one study, a researcher pretending to represent a consumers' group called a number of homes and asked whether the people answering the phone would mind answering a few questions about the soap products they used. Then, a few days later, the same person called those who had agreed to the first request and asked if he could send five or six of his assistants to conduct a two-hour inventory of the products in their home. Would you agree to such an imposition?

In fact, nearly 53 percent of the foot-in-the-door group agreed to this large request, compared with 22 percent of a control group who were contacted only once, with the large request (Freedman & Fraser, 1966). A review of many studies on the foot-in-the-door approach suggests that it is highly effective (Beaman, Cole, Preston, Klentz, & Steblay, 1983; DeJong, 1979), and even works when used online (Grassini, Pascual, & Guéguen, 2013). But strangely enough, exactly the opposite approach will work just as well, as shown in the next section.

The Door-in-the-Face Technique: An Unreasonable Request First

With the **door-in-the-face technique**, a large, unreasonable request is made first. **[LO 10.12]** The expectation is that the person will refuse but will then be more likely to respond favourably to a smaller request later (the request that was desired from the beginning). In one of the best-known studies of the door-in-the-face technique, university students were approached on campus. They were asked to agree to serve without pay as counsellors to young offenders for two hours each week for a minimum of two years. As you would imagine, not a single person agreed (Cialdini, Cacioppo, Basset, & Miller, 1978). Then the experimenters countered with a much smaller request, asking the students if they would agree to take a group of young offenders on a two-hour trip to the zoo. Half the students agreed—a fairly high compliance rate. The researchers used another group of university students as controls, asking them to respond only to the smaller request, the zoo trip. Only 17 percent agreed when the smaller request was presented alone. Studies now suggest that the foot-in-the-door and door-in-the-face techniques are equally effective (Pascual & Guéguen, 2005).

The Low-Ball Technique: Not Telling the Whole Truth Up Front

Another method used to gain compliance is the **low-ball technique**. **[LO 10.12]** A very attractive initial offer is made to get people to commit themselves to an action, and then the terms are made less favourable. In one study, university students were asked to enrol in an experimental course for which they would receive credit. But they were low-balled: Only after the students had agreed to participate were they informed that the class would meet at 7:00 a.m. But 55 percent of the low-balled group agreed to participate anyway. When another group of students were told up front that the class would meet at 7:00 a.m., only about 25 percent agreed to take the class (Cialdini et al., 1978).

---

compliance: Acting in accordance with the wishes, suggestions, or direct requests of another person.

foot-in-the-door technique: A strategy designed to secure a favourable response to a small request first, with the aim of making the subject more likely to agree later to a larger request.

door-in-the-face technique: A strategy in which someone makes a large, unreasonable request with the expectation that the person will refuse but will then be more likely to respond favourably to a smaller request later.

low-ball technique: A strategy to gain compliance by making a very attractive initial offer to get a person to agree to an action and then making the terms less favourable.

REMEMBER IT

Conformity, Obedience, and Compliance

1. What percentage of the participants in the original Asch study never conformed to the majority's unanimous incorrect response?
   a. 70 percent
   b. 33 percent
   c. 25 percent
   d. 5 percent

2. What percentage of the participants in Milgram's original obedience experiment administered what they thought was the maximum 450-volt shock?
   a. 85 percent
   b. 65 percent
   c. 45 percent
   d. 25 percent

3. Match the compliance technique with the appropriate example.
   _____ 1) Julie agrees to sign a letter supporting an increase in taxes for road construction. Later she agrees to make 100 phone calls urging people to vote for the measure.
   _____ 2) Rick refuses a phone request for a $24 donation to send four needy children to the circus but does agree to give $6.
   _____ 3) Linda finds her dream car for a bargain price and then finds out that she'll have to pay extra to get all the options she assumed were standard equipment.
   a. door-in-the-face technique
   b. low-ball technique
   c. foot-in-the-door technique

Answers: 1. c   2. b   3 (1). c   (2). a   (3). b

MODULE 10D GROUP INFLUENCE

LO 10.13 Describe social facilitation.
LO 10.14 Explain the influence of audience effects and co-action effects on individual performance.
LO 10.15 Identify factors that can lessen social loafing.
LO 10.16 Explain group polarization and why it does not affect all group decisions.
LO 10.17 Describe social roles.

THE EFFECTS OF THE GROUP ON INDIVIDUAL PERFORMANCE

Our performance of tasks can be enhanced or impaired by the mere presence of others, and the decisions we reach as part of a group can be quite different from those we would make when acting alone.

Social Facilitation: Performing in the Presence of Others

Under what conditions does social facilitation have either a positive or a negative effect on performance?

The term **social facilitation** refers to any effect on performance, positive or negative, that can be attributed to the presence of others. **[LO 10.13]** Research on this phenomenon has focused on two types of effects: (1) **audience effects**, the impact of passive spectators on performance, and (2) **co-action effects**, the impact on performance caused by the presence of other people engaged in the same task. **[LO 10.14]**

One of the first studies in social psychology was conducted by Norman Triplett (1898), who looked at co-action effects. **[LO 10.14]** Triplett had observed in official bicycle records that bicycle racers pedalled faster when they were pedalling against other racers than when they were racing against the clock. Was this pattern of performance peculiar to competitive bicycling? Or was it part of a more general phenomenon in which individuals worked faster and harder in the presence of others than when performing alone? Triplett set up a study in which he told 40 children to wind fishing reels as quickly as possible under two conditions: (1) alone and (2) in the presence of other children performing the same task. He found that the children worked faster when other reel turners were present.

Later studies on social facilitation found just the opposite effect—the presence of others, whether co-acting or just watching, could impede individual performance. **[LO 10.14]** Robert Zajonc (1965; Zajonc & Sales, 1966) reasoned that we become aroused by the presence of others and that arousal facilitates the dominant response—that is, the one most natural to us. This would account for the repeated findings that in the presence of others, performance improves on tasks that people do easily, but suffers on difficult tasks (Michaels, Bloomel, Brocato, Linkous, & Rowe, 1982; see Figure 10.3).

Social Loafing: Not Pulling Our Weight in a Group Effort

What is social loafing, and what factors can lessen or eliminate it?

Have you ever been assigned by a teacher or professor to work in a group and, at the end of the project, felt that you had carried more than your fair share of the workload? Such feelings are not uncommon. Researcher Bibb Latané used the term **social loafing** for the tendency of people to exert less effort when they are working with others on a common task than when they are working alone on the same task (Latané, Williams, & Harkins, 1979). Social loafing takes place in situations in which no one person's contribution to the group can be identified and in which individuals are neither praised for a good performance nor blamed for a poor one (K. Williams, Harkins, & Latané, 1981). Social loafing is a problem in many workplaces, especially where employees have unlimited access to the internet (Andreasen, Torsheim, & Pallesen, 2014).

Several studies have found that social loafing disappears when participants in a group are led to believe that each person's output can be monitored and his or her performance evaluated (Lount Jr. & Wilk, 2014). **[LO 10.15]** When group size is relatively small and group evaluation is important, some members will even expend extra effort if they know that some of their co-workers are unwilling, unreliable, or incompetent (Karau & Williams, 1995; K. D. Williams & Karau, 1991). Social loafing is not likely to take place when participants can evaluate their own individual contributions (Szymanski & Harkins, 1987), when they are personally involved in the outcome or feel that the task is challenging (Meyer, Schermuly, &

Studying in a group could lead to social loafing through a diffusion-of-responsibility effect.

Kauffeld, 2015), and when they are working with close friends or teammates (Hertel, 2011). **[LO 10.15]**

THE EFFECTS OF THE GROUP ON DECISION MAKING

The group can have profound and predictable effects on decision making, depending on the attitudes of group members before discussion begins.

Group Polarization: When Group Decisions Become More Extreme

How are the initial attitudes of group members likely to affect group decision making?

It is commonly believed that groups tend to make more moderate, conservative decisions than individuals make, but some research in social psychology tells us otherwise.

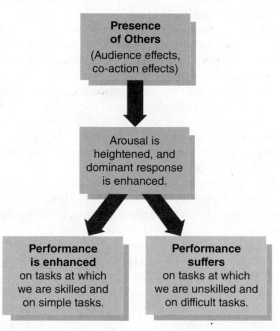

FIGURE 10.3

Social Facilitation: Performing in the Presence of Others

The presence of others (either as an audience or as co-actors engaged in the same task) may have opposite effects, either helping or hindering our performance. Why? Robert Zajonc explained that (1) the presence of others heightens our arousal and (2) heightened arousal leads to better performance on tasks we are good at and worse performance on tasks that are difficult for us. **[LO 10.14]**

Source: Based on Zajonc, R.B; & Sales, S.M (1966). Social facilitation of dominant and subordinate responses. Journal of Experimental Social Psychology, 2, 160–168.

social facilitation: Any positive or negative effect on performance due to the presence of others; either an audience effect or a co-action effect.

audience effects: The impact of passive spectators on performance.

co-action effects: The impact on performance caused by the presence of others engaged in the same task.

social loafing: The tendency to put forth less effort when working with others on a common task than when working alone.

Group discussion often causes members of the group to shift to a more extreme position in whatever direction the group was leaning initially—a phenomenon known as **group polarization** (Isenberg, 1986; Lamm, 1988). Group members, it seems, will decide to take a greater risk if they were leaning in a risky direction to begin with, but they will shift toward a more cautious position if they were somewhat cautious at the beginning of the discussion (Moscovici & Zavalloni, 1969; D. G. Myers & Lamm, 1975). **[LO 10.16]**

Why, then, aren't all group decisions either very risky or very cautious? The reason is that the members of a group do not always all lean in the same direction at the beginning of a discussion. **[LO 10.16]** When subgroups within a larger group hold opposing views, compromise rather than polarization is the likely outcome (Vinokur & Burnstein, 1978).

Groupthink: When Group Cohesiveness Leads to Bad Decisions

Group cohesiveness refers to the degree to which group members are attracted to the group and experience a feeling of oneness. **Groupthink** is the term that social psychologist Irving Janis (1982) applies to the decisions that are often reached by overly cohesive groups. When a tightly knit group is more concerned with preserving group solidarity and uniformity than with objectively evaluating all possible alternatives in decision making, individual members hesitate to voice any dissent. The group may also discredit opposing views from outsiders. Even plans bordering on madness can be hatched and adopted when groupthink prevails.

To guard against groupthink, Janis suggests that the group encourage an open discussion of alternative views and encourage the expression of any objections and doubts. He further recommends that outside experts sit in and challenge the views of the group. At least one group member should take the role of devil's advocate whenever a policy alternative is evaluated. Finally, to avoid groupthink in the workplace, managers should withhold their own opinions during problem solving and decision making (Bazan, 1998).

Groups exert an even more powerful influence on individuals by prescribing social roles.

SOCIAL ROLES

The group is indispensable to human life. We are born into a family group, a culture, a racial and ethnic group, and usually a religious group. And as we grow and mature, we may choose to join many other groups, such as social groups and professional groups.

The groups to which we belong define certain roles. **Roles** are the behaviours considered to be appropriate for individuals occupying certain positions within a group. **[LO 10.17]**

Roles are useful because they tell us beforehand how people—even people we have never met before—are likely to act toward us in many situations. **[LO 10.17]** If you have ever been stopped for speeding by a police officer, you were at that moment unwillingly cast in the role of speeder, and you had few doubts about the role the officer would play. But both you and the police officer assume many different roles

in life—family roles, social roles, work roles, and so on—and your behaviour can differ dramatically as you shift from role to role.

Roles can shape human behaviour to an alarming degree. This is best illustrated in a classic study by Philip Zimbardo.

Zimbardo's Prison Study: Our Roles Dictate Our Actions

Picture the following scene: On a quiet Sunday morning in a peaceful university town, the scream of sirens splits the air as the local police conduct a surprise mass arrest, rounding up nine male university students. The students are searched, handcuffed, read their rights, and hauled off to jail. Here they are booked and fingerprinted, then transported to "Stanford County Prison." At the prison, each student is stripped naked, searched, deloused, given a uniform and a number, and placed in a cell with two other prisoners. All of this is more than sufficiently traumatic, but then there are the guards in their khaki uniforms, wearing reflector sunglasses that make eye-to-eye contact impossible and carrying clubs that resemble small baseball bats.

The prisoners have to get permission from the guards for the most simple, routine matters, such as using the toilet. And the guards are severe in the punishments they impose. Prisoners are made to do pushups while the guards sometimes step on them or force another prisoner to sit on them. Some prisoners are placed in solitary confinement. (This anecdote is adapted from Zimbardo, 1972.)

But wait a minute! People are not arrested, charged, and thrown into prison without a trial. What happened? In truth the guards were not guards and the prisoners were not prisoners. All were university students who had been selected to participate in a two-week experiment on prison life (Zimbardo, Haney, & Banks, 1973). Guards and prisoners were selected randomly from a pool of volunteers who had been judged to be mature, healthy, psychologically stable, law-abiding citizens. Those who were to be prisoners were not aware of their selection until they were "arrested" on that quiet Sunday morning.

This was only an experiment, but it became all too real—for the guards and especially for the prisoners. How could some of the guards, though mild-mannered pacifists, so quickly become sadistic, heartless tormentors in their new role?

The prisoners fell into their roles quickly as well. How could autonomous, self-respecting students allow themselves to become debased, to suffer physical and mental abuse, and to behave as if they were real prisoners? The experiment was to be run for two weeks but had to be called off after only six days.

What could have caused the "prisoners" and the "guards" to behave in the way they did? Zimbardo has argued that deindividuation explains the study's outcome (Zimbardo, 1969). Deindividuation occurs when individuals lose their sense of personal identity as a result of identification with a group. This interpretation has recently been challenged by British psychologists Haslam and Reicher (2008), who believe that the nature of the instructions given to the "guards" may have caused them to act harshly and may have rendered the "prisoners" powerless.

REMEMBER IT

Group Influence

1. Which of the following statements regarding the effects of social facilitation is true?
   a. Performance improves on all tasks.
   b. Performance worsens on all tasks.
   c. Performance improves on easy tasks and worsens on difficult tasks.
   d. Performance improves on difficult tasks and worsens on easy tasks.

2. Social loafing is most likely to occur when
   a. individual output is monitored.
   b. individual output is evaluated.
   c. a task is challenging.
   d. individual output cannot be identified.

3. When group polarization occurs following group discussion, the group will decide to take a greater risk
   a. if members were leaning in a cautious direction to begin with.
   b. if members were leaning in a risky direction to begin with.
   c. if members were leaning in different directions to begin with.
   d. regardless of the initial position of the members.

4. What occurs when members of a very cohesive group are more concerned with preserving group solidarity than with evaluating all possible alternatives in making a decision?
   a. groupthink
   b. group polarization
   c. social facilitation
   d. social loafing

Answers: 1. c   2. d   3. b   4. a

MODULE 10E ATTITUDES AND ATTITUDE CHANGE

LO 10.18 Identify the three components of an attitude.

LO 10.19 Describe ways that individuals try to reduce cognitive dissonance.

LO 10.20 Identify four elements of persuasion.

LO 10.21 Describe the influence of credibility, attractiveness, and likeability on persuasion.

LO 10.22 Describe when fear-based appeals are most effective in persuading an audience.

ATTITUDES: COGNITIVE, EMOTIONAL, AND BEHAVIOURAL POSITIONS

What are the three components of an attitude?

What is your attitude toward abortion? Or gun control? Or same-sex marriage? An **attitude** is a relatively stable evaluation of a person, object, situation, or issue that varies along a continuum from negative to positive (Ajzen, 2001). Most of our attitudes have three components: (1) a cognitive component—our thoughts and beliefs about the attitudinal object; (2) an emotional component—our feelings toward the attitudinal object; and (3) a behavioural component—how we are predisposed to act toward the object (Petty & Wegener, 1998; Zanna & Rempel, 1988). **[LO 10.18]** Figure 10.4, on the next page, shows the three components of an attitude.

Attitudes enable us to appraise people, objects, and situations; in this way they provide structure and consistency to our social environment (Fazio, 1989). Attitudes help us process social information (Pratkanis, 1989); they also guide our

behaviour (Sanbonmatsu & Fazio, 1990) and influence our social judgments and decisions (Devine, 1989a; Jamieson & Zanna, 1989).

How do we form our attitudes? Some of our attitudes are acquired through first-hand experience with people, objects, situations, and issues. Others are acquired vicariously. When we hear parents, family, friends, and teachers express positive or negative attitudes toward certain issues or people, we may adopt the same attitudes. The media, including advertisers, greatly influence our attitudes and reap billions of dollars annually for their efforts. As you might expect, however, the attitudes we form through direct experience are stronger than those we acquire vicariously and are more resistant to change (Nieto-Hernandez, Rubin, Cleare, Weinman, & Wessely, 2008). Once formed, however, attitudes tend to strengthen when we associate with others who share them (Visser & Mirabile, 2004).

---

group polarization: The tendency of members of a group, after group discussion, to shift toward a more extreme position in whatever direction they were leaning initially.

groupthink: The tendency for members of a very cohesive group to feel such pressure to maintain group solidarity and to reach agreement on an issue that they fail to adequately weigh available evidence or to consider objections and alternatives.

roles: The behaviours considered to be appropriate for individuals occupying certain positions within a group.

attitude: A relatively stable evaluation of a person, object, situation, or issue.

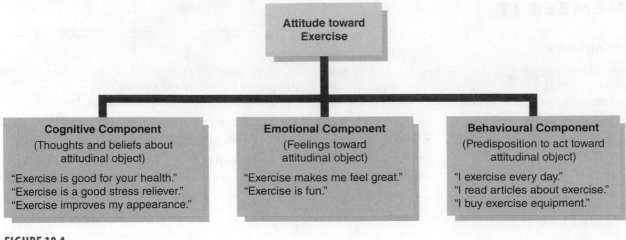

FIGURE 10.4

The Three Components of an Attitude

An attitude is a relatively stable evaluation of a person, object, situation, or issue. Most of our attitudes have (1) a cognitive component, (2) an emotional component, and (3) a behavioural component.

The Relationship between Attitudes and Behaviour

We often hear that attitude change is the key to behaviour change. However, research indicates that attitudes are rather low predictors of actual behaviours (Webb & Sheeran, 2006; Wicker, 1969). Why, then, aren't attitude measurements better predictors of behaviour? Attitude measurements may often be too general for this. For example, people may express strong attitudes in favour of protecting the environment, but this doesn't mean they recycle or own a car that has low gas consumption. However, many studies have also shown that attitudes are better predictors of behaviour if they are strongly held and are easily accessible in memory (Bassili, 1995; Fazio & Williams, 1986), and vitally affect our interests (Miller, 1999).

Cognitive Dissonance: The Mental Pain of Inconsistency

What is cognitive dissonance, and how can it be resolved?

If we discover that some of our attitudes are in conflict with others or are not consistent with our own behaviour, we are likely to experience an unpleasant state. Leon Festinger (1957) called this **cognitive dissonance**. We usually try to reduce the dissonance by changing our behaviour or our attitude, or by somehow explaining away the inconsistency or reducing its importance (Festinger, 1957; Matz & Wood, 2005). **[LO 10.19]**

Smoking provides a perfect example of cognitive dissonance. What are smokers to do? The healthiest, but perhaps not the easiest, way for them to reduce cognitive dissonance is to change their behaviour—to quit smoking. Another way is to change their attitude—to convince themselves that smoking is not as dangerous as research suggests. Smokers can also tell themselves that they will stop smoking long before any permanent damage is done, or that medical science is advancing so rapidly that a cure for cancer is just around the corner. Figure 10.5 illustrates the methods that smokers can use to reduce cognitive dissonance.

If people voluntarily make a statement or take a position that is counter to what they believe, they will experience cognitive dissonance because of the inconsistency. To resolve this dissonance, they are likely to change their beliefs to make them more consistent with their behaviour (Festinger & Carlsmith, 1959). **[LO 10.19]** Cognitive dissonance can also be reduced by trivializing or minimizing the dissonant cognitions instead of changing one's attitudes (Simon, Greenberg, & Brehm, 1995).

PERSUASION: TRYING TO CHANGE ATTITUDES

What are the four elements in persuasion?

Persuasion is a deliberate attempt to influence the attitudes and/or the behaviour of another person. Persuasion is a pervasive part of our work experience, social experience, and family life.

Researchers have identified four elements in persuasion: (1) the source of the communication (who is doing the persuading), (2) the audience (who is being persuaded), (3) the message (what is being said), and (4) the medium (the means by which the message is transmitted). **[LO 10.20]**

The Source: Look Who's Talking

What qualities make a source persuasive?

Some factors that make the source (communicator) persuasive are credibility, attractiveness, and likeability. Credibility refers to how believable a source is. **[LO 10.21]** A credible communicator is one who has expertise (knowledge of the topic at hand) and trustworthiness (truthfulness and integrity), and this credibility has been shown to strongly influence the persuasiveness of the message (Smith, De Houwer, & Nosek, 2013). The influence of a credible source is even greater if the audience knows the communicator's credentials beforehand. Moreover, we attach greater credibility to sources who have nothing to gain from persuading us or, better yet, who seem to be arguing against their own best interests.

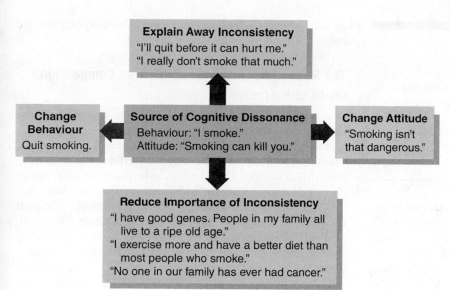

FIGURE 10.5

FIGURE 10.5

Methods of Reducing Cognitive Dissonance

Cognitive dissonance can occur when people become aware of inconsistencies in their attitudes or between their attitudes and their behaviour. People try to reduce dissonance by (1) changing their behaviour, (2) changing their attitude, (3) explaining away the inconsistency, or (4) reducing its importance. Here are examples of how a smoker might use these methods to reduce the cognitive dissonance created by his or her habit.

In matters that involve our own personal tastes and preferences rather than issues, attractive people and celebrities can be very persuasive (Chaiken, 1979). **[LO 10.21]** Movie and TV stars, athletes, and even unknown attractive models have long been used to persuade us to buy certain products. Likeable, down-to-earth, ordinary people who are perceived to be similar to the audience are sometimes even more effective persuaders. **[LO 10.21]** Political candidates try to appear more likeable, and more like voters, by visiting construction sites and coal mines, by kissing babies, and by posing with farmers.

The Audience and the Message

Audience characteristics also influence responses to persuasion. In general, people are more easily persuaded by a message that they deem personally relevant than by one that seems to be only remotely connected to their everyday lives (Hirsh, Kang, & Bodenhausen, 2012). Research suggests that a one-sided message (in which only one side of an issue is given) is usually most persuasive if the audience is not well informed on the issue, is not overly intelligent, or is already in agreement with the point of view. A two-sided approach (in which both sides of an issue are mentioned) works best when the audience is well informed, fairly intelligent, or initially opposed to the point of view. The two-sided approach usually sways more people than a one-sided appeal (Hovland, Lumsdaine, & Sheffield, 1949; McGuire, 1969, 1985). People tend to scrutinize arguments that are contrary to their existing beliefs more carefully and exert more effort refuting them; they are also more likely to judge such arguments as weaker than those that support their beliefs (K. Edwards & Smith, 1996).

A message can be well reasoned, logical, and unemotional ("just the facts"); or it can be strictly emotional ("scare the hell out of them"); or it can be a combination of the two. Which type of message works best? Arousing fear seems to be an effective method for persuading people to quit smoking, get regular chest X-rays, and wear seat belts (Dillard & Anderson, 2004). **[LO 10.22]** However, appeals based on fear have only minimal short-term effects and are not that effective in the long run (Ruiter, Kessels, Peters, & Kok, 2014).

Another important factor in persuasion is repetition (Claypool et al., 2004). However, the effects of repetition are strongest when the audience perceives the subject of the message to be personally relevant (Claypool et al., 2004). Consequently, in order to be certain that a repetitive message will be persuasive, the persuader must send it to the appropriate audience.

REMEMBER IT

Attitudes and Attitude Change

1. The three components of an attitude are _____, _____, and _____.
2. All of the options listed below are ways to reduce cognitive dissonance except
   a. changing an attitude.
   b. changing a behaviour.
   c. explaining away the inconsistency.
   d. strengthening the attitude and behaviour.
3. With a well-informed audience, two-sided messages are more persuasive than one-sided messages. (true/false)
4. High-fear appeals are more effective than low-fear appeals if they provide definite actions that people can take to avoid dreaded outcomes. (true/false)

Answers: 1. cognitive, emotional, behavioura 2. d 3. true 4. true

cognitive dissonance: The unpleasant state that can occur when people become aware of inconsistencies between their attitudes or between their attitudes and their behaviour.

persuasion: A deliberate attempt to influence the attitudes and/or behaviour of another.

MODULE **10F** PREJUDICE AND DISCRIMINATION

LO 10.23 Describe the difference between prejudice and discrimination.

LO 10.24 Describe the effects of in-group and out-group categorizations and their role in discrimination.

LO 10.25 Explain prejudice according to social learning theory.

LO 10.26 Explain when the contact hypothesis will work to reduce prejudice.

Canada is among the most culturally diverse nations in the world. Can we all learn to live and work peacefully no matter what racial, ethnic, cultural, or other differences exist among us? The answer is a conditional yes—we can do it *if* we can learn how to combat prejudice and discrimination. Dealing with these issues is complex, as illustrated in the *Canadian Connections* box, which provides some insights into factors that predict homophobia.

THE ROOTS OF PREJUDICE AND DISCRIMINATION

What is the difference between prejudice and discrimination?

Prejudice consists of attitudes (usually negative) toward others based on their gender, religion, race, or membership in a particular group. Prejudice involves beliefs and emotions (not actions) that can escalate into hatred. **Discrimination** consists of behaviour—that is, actions (usually negative) toward members of a group. **[LO 10.23]** Many Canadians have experienced prejudice and discrimination—minority racial groups (racism), women (sexism), the elderly (ageism), people with disabilities,

gays and lesbians, religious groups, and others. What, then, are the roots of prejudice and discrimination?

The Realistic Conflict Theory: When Competition Leads to Prejudice

One of the oldest explanations offered for prejudice is competition among various social groups for scarce economic resources—good jobs, land, political power, and so on. Commonly called the **realistic conflict theory**, this view suggests that as competition increases, so do prejudice, discrimination, and hatred among the competing groups. Some historical evidence supports this theory. Prejudice and hatred were high between the Europeans and the Native Canadians who struggled over land during Canada's westward expansion. Many of the millions of immigrants to Canada have felt the sting of prejudice and hatred from native-born Canadians. This has been especially true in times of economic scarcity. As nations around the world experience hard economic times in the twenty-first century, will we see an increase in prejudice and discrimination? The realistic conflict theory predicts that we will. But prejudice and discrimination are too complex to be explained simply by economic conflict. What are some other causes?

Us versus Them: Dividing the World into In-Groups and Out-Groups

What is meant by the terms *in-group* and *out-group*?

Prejudice can also spring from the distinct social categories into which we divide our world—*us versus them* (J. C. Turner, Hogg, Oakes, Reicher, & Wetherell, 1987). **[LO 10.24]** An **in-group** is a social group with a strong feeling of togetherness and from which others are excluded. An **out-group** consists of individuals or groups specifically identified by the in-group as not

CANADIAN CONNECTIONS

What Factors Affect Homophobic Attitudes?

For the most part, Canadians have relatively liberal attitudes when it comes to social issues. Canadians have been shown to have more positive attitudes toward immigrants, gender equality, and gays and lesbians than citizens of many European countries or the United States. To illustrate this fact, consider a study by Melanie Morrison, Todd Morrison, and Randall Franklin (2009) that examined Canadian and American students' attitudes toward gays and lesbians. The researchers found that, on average, Canadian students had significantly fewer negative attitudes than did their American counterparts.

Given our generally positive views about diversity, many Canadians were shocked to learn of the news that a prominent Halifax gay activist, Raymond Taavel, had been killed in the early morning of April 17, 2012, after attempting to break up a fight between two men. Witnesses told police that the attacker used homophobic slurs while repeatedly slamming Taavel's head into the street, where the victim was found by police and later pronounced dead by paramedics

("Gay Activist's Death," 2012). While reports suggest that the assailant had a history of mental illness and criminality, the use of homophobic slurs as Taavel was assaulted show us that negative views of gays and lesbians persist within our society.

Recent Canadian research indicates that while hate crimes appear to be on the decline, the rate of reported homophobic attacks remained the same during recent years (Statistics Canada, 2012a). The roots of homophobia are complex, and years of study have shown that people with homophobic attitudes, on average, tend to have had little personal contact with lesbians or gays; are more likely to have resided in areas where negative attitudes are the norm; tend to be older and less well educated; and are more likely to be religious, to attend church frequently, and to subscribe to a conservative religious ideology.

As psychology students, how would you devise a strategy to reduce negative attitudes toward gays and lesbians? What information found in this chapter would guide your approach? ■

belonging. Us-versus-them thinking can lead to excessive competition, hostility, prejudice, discrimination, and even war.

Prejudiced individuals who most strongly identify with their racial in-group are most reluctant to admit others to the group if there is the slightest doubt about their racial purity (Blascovich, Wyer, Swart, & Kibler, 1997). Note, however, that groups need not be composed of particular races, religions, nations, or any other particular category for in-group/out-group hostility to develop (Tajfel, 1982). Sometimes even the slightest form of affiliation can lead to in-group/out-group differences.

THE ROBBERS CAVE EXPERIMENT A famous study by Sherif and Sherif (1967) shows how in-group/out-group conflict can escalate into prejudice and hostility rather quickly, even between groups that are very much alike. The researchers set up their experiment at the Robbers Cave summer camp. Their subjects were 22 bright, well-adjusted 11- and 12-year-old white, middle-class boys. Divided into two groups and housed in separate cabins, the boys were kept apart for all their daily activities and games. During the first week, in-group solidarity, friendship, and cooperation developed within each of the groups. One group called itself the Rattlers; the other group took the name Eagles.

During the second week of the study, competitive events were purposely scheduled so that the goals of one group could be achieved "only at the expense of the other group" (Sherif, 1958, p. 353). The groups were happy to battle each other, and intergroup conflict quickly emerged. Name-calling began, fights broke out, and accusations were hurled back and forth. During the third week of the experiment, the researchers tried to put an end to the hostility and to turn rivalry into cooperation. They simply brought the groups together for pleasant activities such as eating meals and watching movies. "But far from reducing conflict, these situations only served as opportunities for the rival groups to berate and attack each other. . . . They threw paper, food, and vile names at each other at the tables" (Sherif, 1956, pp. 57–58).

Finally, the last stage of the experiment was set in motion. The experimenters manufactured a series of crises that could be solved only if all the boys combined their efforts and resources, and cooperated. The water supply, sabotaged by the experimenters, could be restored only if all the boys worked together. After a week of several activities requiring cooperation, cutthroat competition gave way to cooperative exchanges. Friendships developed between groups, and before the end of the experiment, peace was declared. Working together toward shared goals had turned hostility into friendship.

The Social Learning Theory: Acquiring Prejudice through Modelling and Reinforcement

How does prejudice develop, according to the social learning theory?

According to the social learning theory, people learn attitudes of prejudice and hatred the same way they learn other attitudes. [LO 10.25] If children hear their parents, teachers, peers, and others openly express prejudices toward different racial, ethnic, or cultural groups, they may be quick to learn such

attitudes. And if parents, peers, and others reward children with smiles and approval for mimicking their own prejudices (operant conditioning), children may learn these prejudices even more quickly.

It is good to note that people can also learn to be non-prejudiced. For example, imagining positive contact with members of a different group (Al Ramiah & Hewstone, 2013) and reducing power differences between groups (Birtel & Crisp, 2012) have been shown to reduce prejudice.

Social Cognition: Natural Thinking Processes Can Lead to Prejudice

What are stereotypes?

Social cognition also plays a role in giving birth to prejudice. **Social cognition** refers to the ways in which we typically process social information, or to the natural thinking processes whereby we notice, interpret, remember, and apply information about our social world. The processes we use to simplify, categorize, and order our world are the very same processes we use to distort it. Thus, prejudice may arise not only from heated negative emotions and hatred toward other social groups, but also from cooler cognitive processes that govern how we think and process social information (Kunda & Oleson, 1995).

One way people simplify, categorize, and order their world is through stereotypes. **Stereotypes** are widely shared beliefs about the characteristics of members of various social groups (racial, ethnic, religious); among these beliefs is the assumption that *they* are usually all alike. Once a stereotype is in place, people tend to pay more attention to information that confirms their beliefs rather than challenges them (Wigboldus, Dijksterhuis, & van Knippenberg, 2003). But even though stereotypes help us process information more quickly, they may also carry *symbolic beliefs* about a specific group—that is,

prejudice: Attitudes, usually negative, toward others based on their gender, religion, race, or membership in a particular group.

discrimination: Behaviour, usually negative, directed toward others based on their gender, religion, race, or membership in a particular group.

realistic conflict theory: The notion that prejudices arise when social groups must compete for scarce economic resources.

in-group: A social group with a strong sense of togetherness and from which others are excluded.

out-group: A social group specifically identified by the in-group as not belonging.

social cognition: Mental processes that people use to notice, interpret, remember, and apply information about the social world and that enable them to simplify, categorize, and order their world.

stereotypes: Widely shared beliefs about the characteristic traits, attitudes, and behaviours of members of various social groups (racial, ethnic, religious); these include the assumption that group members are usually all alike.

stereotypes may imply that a specific group threatens our values and norms (Esses, Haddock, & Zanna, 1993).

Macrae, Milne, and Bodenhausen (1994) suggest that people apply stereotypes in their interactions with others because doing so requires less mental energy than trying to understand others as individuals. Stereotyping allows people to make quick, automatic (thoughtless) judgments about others and apply their mental resources to other activities (Sherman et al., 2009). However, individuals who are prejudiced do not necessarily apply stereotypes equally to all members of a given group. For one thing, people are less likely to apply stereotypes to others with whom they have personal relationships than they are to strangers (R. Turner, Hewstone, Voci, & Vonofakou, 2008).

Do you use stereotypes in your thinking? To find out, complete the *Try It*.

Are women nurturant and non-competitive, and men strong, dominant, and the best leaders? Are beautiful people more vain? All these beliefs are stereotypes. Once developed, stereotypes strongly influence our evaluations of incoming information about specific groups. The stereotypes we hold can powerfully affect our reactions to and judgments of people in various groups.

When you did the *Try It*, how many group characteristics could you list? We know that not *all* members of a group possess the same traits or characteristics, but we tend to use stereotypic thinking nonetheless.

Social stereotypes can involve more than overgeneralization about the traits or characteristics of members of certain groups (Judd, Ryan, & Park, 1991; B. Park & Judd, 1990). People tend to perceive more variability within the groups to which they belong (in-groups) and less variability among members of other groups (out-groups) (Brauer & Er-Rafiy, 2011). Thus, whites see more diversity among themselves but more sameness within groups of blacks and Asians. This tendency in thinking can extend from race to gender to any other category of people (Hewstone, Crisp, & Turner, 2011). Age stereotypes can often be

more pronounced and negative than gender stereotypes (Kite, Deaux, & Miele, 1991).

Stereotypes can be positive or negative, but all are distortions of reality. One of the most insidious things about stereotypes is that we often are not even aware that we are using them. The *World of Psychology* box illustrates the way gender stereotyping affects women's income.

COMBATTING PREJUDICE AND DISCRIMINATION

What are several strategies for reducing prejudice and discrimination?

Prejudice and discrimination have been pervasive in human societies throughout recorded history. We have seen that both may take many forms, ranging from bigotry and hatred to kindness and compassion (though misplaced). Given that prejudice and discrimination may grow from many roots, are there effective ways to reduce them? Many experts believe so. One way is through education: To the extent that prejudice is learned, it can also be unlearned. Sustained educational programs designed to increase teachers' and parents' awareness of the damage caused by prejudice and discrimination can be very effective (Aronson, 1990).

Direct Contact: Bringing Diverse Groups Together

Prejudice separates us, keeping us apart from other racial, ethnic, religious, and social groups. Can we reduce our prejudices and stereotypic thinking by increasing our contact and interaction with people in other social groups? Yes, according to the **contact hypothesis. [LO 10.26]**

Increased contact with members of groups about which we hold stereotypes can teach us that *they* are not all alike. But the contact hypothesis works to reduce prejudice only under certain conditions. In fact, if people from diverse groups are simply thrown together, prejudice and even hostility are likely to increase rather than decrease, as we learned from Sherif and Sherif's Robbers Cave experiment. We also learned from that experiment the conditions under which intergroup contact reduces prejudice. These findings have been confirmed and extended by others (Aronson, 1990; Finchilescu, 1988).

The contact hypothesis will work to reduce prejudice most effectively under the following conditions: **[LO 10.26]**

- Interacting groups should be about equal in social and economic status and in their ability to perform the contact-situation tasks.

- The intergroup contact must be cooperative (not competitive) in nature, and work should be confined to shared goals.

- The contact should be informal, so that friendly interactions can develop more easily and group members can get to know each other individually.

- The conditions of the contact situation should favour group equality.

- The individuals involved should perceive each other as typical members of the groups to which they belong.

TRY IT

Do You Use Stereotypes?

Can you list characteristics for each of the following groups?

Jamaican Canadians

White, male top-level executives

Native Canadians

Gays

Feminists

Members of fundamentalist religious groups

Jews

Arabs

Italians

Germans

WORLD OF PSYCHOLOGY

Gender Stereotyping: Who Wins? Who Loses?

Most of the people on our planet are women, yet around the world women are vastly underrepresented in positions of power. Gender stereotypes define men as decisive, aggressive, unemotional, logical, and ambitious. These qualities are perceived by many men and women alike as precisely the "right stuff" for leaders, decision makers, and powerful people at all levels of society. But women, too, can be strong, bold, and decisive, and yet, according to the most recent reports (Swanson, 2015), only 5 percent of women lead North America's top 500 corporations despite making up over 45 percent of these companies' workforces.

In addition, although most women and men agree that they should receive equal pay for equal work, the most recent findings from Statistics Canada indicate that the average female worker in Canada is still paid just over 83 cents for every dollar paid to a male worker (83.5 percent; Statistics Canada, 2009a). And women are more likely to hold low-paying, low-status jobs. Table 10.1 shows the male–female wage gap in 10 different industrialized countries.

As you can see, the gender wage gap occurs in all parts of the world. Of the 10 industrialized nations shown in Table 10.1, Italy has the smallest wage gap between men and women, at only 5.5 percent (in other words, women earn 94.5 cents for every dollar paid to male workers). Germany has the highest wage gap of all industrialized countries, with the United States, the United Kingdom, and Canada not far behind. The data (Tijdens & Van Klaveren, 2012) show that Zambia has the highest wage gap of all, with women, on average, earning 54 cents for every dollar earned by a man in that country.

TABLE 10.1 Wage Gap between Full-Time Working Women and Men in 10 Industrialized Countries, 1985 and 2008–2010

Country	Wage Gap (1985)	Wage Gap (2008–2010)
Australia	12.8	16.9*
Denmark	17.0**	16.0**
France	18.6	16.0*
Italy	32.6	5.5*
Netherlands	23.6	18.5*
Belgium	25.4	8.8*
Germany	27.2	23.1*
United Kingdom	30.5	19.5*
United States	35.4	19.8*
Japan	40.5	13.5*

*2012, **2011

Source: For 1985 data: Roos & Gatta, 1999, p. 105; all 2008–2010 data from Tijdens & Van Klaveren (2012); 2011 data from OECD, 2011. ∎

Us versus Them: Extending the Boundaries of Narrowly Defined Social Groups

Our tendency to separate ourselves into social categories (in-groups and out-groups) creates an us-versus-them mentality. This mentality heightens prejudice, stereotypic thinking, and discrimination—for example, "Our group (or school, or country, or race, or religion) is better than theirs." But the boundary lines between us and them are not eternally fixed. If such boundaries can be extended, prejudice and in-group/out-group conflict can be reduced. We saw in the Sherif and Sherif study that the Rattlers and Eagles became a larger "us" group when they were brought together to work cooperatively on shared goals.

If your college or university wins the regional championship in a competitive event, then local rival colleges and universities will often join your group because you represent the region in national competition. Many researchers have shown that this recategorization reduces us-versus-them bias and prejudice (Gaertner, Mann, Dovidio, & Murrell, 1990; S. C. Wright, Taylor, & Moghaddam, 1990).

PREJUDICE: IS IT INCREASING OR DECREASING?

Few people would readily admit to being prejudiced. Gordon Allport (1954), a pioneer in research on prejudice, noted that while "defeated intellectually, prejudice lingers emotionally"

(p. 328). However, most people feel guilty when they catch themselves having prejudiced thoughts or engaging in discriminatory behaviour (Amodio, Devine, & Harmon-Jones, 2007). Is there any evidence that prejudice is decreasing in our society? According to some researchers, we are not making much progress toward reducing either prejudice *or* discrimination (Gaertner & Dovidio, 2005). But national polls reveal that Canadians of all backgrounds are becoming more racially tolerant than they were in decades past, and that our ethnic tolerance appears to be greater than that found in some other industrialized countries (Parkin & Mendelsohn, 2003). In a nationally representative study, fewer than 10 percent of Canadians opposed interracial marriages, a rate that compares favourably with that found by a similar poll conducted in the United States, wherein 30 percent of Americans opposed interracial marriages. And fewer than 12 percent of Canadians indicated that relations between different racial and ethnic groups were a very big problem, compared with 30 to 50 percent who hold the same opinion in the United States, United Kingdom, France, and Italy. A more recent survey conducted by the

contact hypothesis: The notion that prejudice can be reduced through increased contact with members of different social groups.

Organisation for Economic Co-operation and Development (2011) supports this trend. The study indicates that Canadians report the highest community tolerance of minority groups—ethnic minorities, migrants, and gays and lesbians—in the OECD.

We can make things better for all by examining our own attitudes and actions, and then by using what we have learned here and elsewhere to combat prejudice and discrimination in ourselves. Prejudice has no virtues. It immediately harms those who feel its sting and ultimately harms those who practise it.

REMEMBER IT

Prejudice and Discrimination

1. Match the example with the appropriate term.
   _____ 1) Darlene thinks all whites are racists.
   _____ 2) Betty's salary is $5000 less than that of her male counterpart.
   _____ 3) Bill can't stand Jews.
       a. stereotypic thinking
       b. discrimination
       c. prejudice
2. From the in-group perspective, out-group members are often liked as individuals. (true/false)
3. Researchers have found that bringing diverse social groups together almost always decreases hostility and prejudice. (true/false)

Answers: 1(1). a (2). b (3). c 2. false 3. false

MODULE 10G PROSOCIAL BEHAVIOUR: BEHAVIOUR THAT BENEFITS OTHERS

LO 10.27 Describe when the bystander effect is most likely to occur.
LO 10.28 Provide two possible explanations for the bystander effect.
LO 10.29 Describe altruism.
LO 10.30 Identify people who are more likely to receive help in an emergency.

Kitty Genovese was returning home alone late one night. But this was no ordinary night. Nearly 40 of her neighbours who lived in the apartment complex nearby watched as she was attacked and stabbed, but they did nothing. The attacker left. Kitty was still screaming, begging for help, and then . . . he returned. He dragged her around, stabbing her again while her neighbours watched. Some of them turned off their bedroom lights to see more clearly, pulled up chairs to the window, and watched. Someone yelled, "Leave the girl alone," and the attacker fled again. But even then, no one came to her aid. A third time the attacker returned. Again there was more

stabbing and screaming, and still they only watched. Finally, Kitty Genovese stopped screaming. When he had killed her, the attacker fled for the last time. (This anecdote is adapted from Rosenthal, 1964.)

This actual event might not seem so unusual today, but it was a rare occurrence in the early 1960s—so rare, in fact, that people wondered how Genovese's neighbours could have been so callous and cold-hearted that they did nothing but watch as she begged for help that never came. Social psychologists Bibb Latané and John Darley looked deeper for an explanation. Perhaps there were factors in the situation itself that would help explain why so many people only watched and listened.

THE BYSTANDER EFFECT: THE GREATER THE NUMBER OF BYSTANDERS, THE LESS LIKELY THEY ARE TO HELP

What is the bystander effect, and what factors have been suggested to explain why it occurs?

If you were injured or ill and needed help, would you feel safer if one or two other people were near or if a large crowd of onlookers was present? You may be surprised to learn of the **bystander effect**: as the number of bystanders at an emergency increases, the probability that the victim will be helped by them decreases, and the help, if given, is likely to be delayed. **[LO 10.27]**

Why should this be? Darley and Latané (1968a) set up a number of experiments to study helping behaviour. In one study, participants were placed one at a time in a small room and told they would be participating in a discussion group by means of an intercom system. It was explained that because personal problems were being discussed, a face-to-face group discussion might be inhibiting. Some participants were told they would be communicating with only one other person, some believed that two other participants would be involved, and some were told that five other people would be participating. In fact, there were no other participants in the study—only the prerecorded voices of confederates assisting the experimenter.

Shortly after the discussion began, the voice of one confederate was heard over the intercom calling for help, indicating that he was having an epileptic seizure. Of the participants who believed that they alone were hearing the victim, 85 percent went for help before the end of the seizure. When they believed that one other person was hearing the seizure, 62 percent sought help. When they believed there were four other people, only 31 percent sought help. Figure 10.6 shows how the number of bystanders affects both the number of people who try to help and the speed of response.

Darley and Latané suggest two possible explanations for the bystander effect: diffusion of responsibility and the influence of apparently calm bystanders.

Diffusion of Responsibility: An Explanation for the Bystander Effect

When bystanders are present in an emergency, they generally feel that the responsibility for helping is shared by the group, a phenomenon known as **diffusion of responsibility**. **[LO 10.27]** Consequently, each person feels less compelled to act than if she

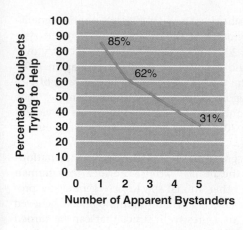

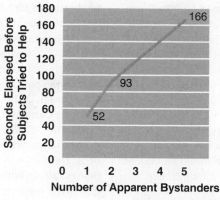

FIGURE 10.6

The Bystander Effect

In their intercom experiment, Darley and Latané showed that the more people a participant believed were present during an emergency, the longer it took that participant to respond and help a person in distress.

Source: (Data from Darley & Latané, 1968a.) Darley, J. M., & Latané, B. (1968a). Bystander intervention in emergencies: Diffusion of responsibility. Journal of Personality and Social Psychology, 8, 377–383. American Psychological Association.

or he were alone and thus totally responsible. Kitty Genovese's neighbours were aware that other people were watching because they saw lights go off in the other apartments. They did not feel that the total responsibility for action rested only on their shoulders. Or they may have thought, "Somebody else must be doing something" (Darley & Latané, 1968a, p. 378).

The Influence of Apparently Calm Bystanders: When Faces Deceive

Sometimes it may not be clear that an actual emergency exists. Bystanders often hesitate to act until they are sure that intervention is appropriate (R. D. Clark & Word, 1972). They may stand there watching other apparently calm bystanders and conclude that nothing is really wrong and that no intervention is necessary (Darley & Latané, 1968b). **[LO 10.28]**

More than a few people have died while many potential helpers stood and watched passively because of the bystander effect. Picture an orthopedic surgeon's large waiting room in which eight patients are waiting to see the doctor. In one chair a middle-aged man sits slumped over, yet he does not appear to be sleeping. His position resembles that of a person who is unconscious. If you were a patient in such a setting, would you check on the man's condition or just continue sitting?

This was the actual scene one of the authors of this text entered a few years ago as a patient. She sat down and immediately noticed the man slumped in his chair. She scanned the faces of the other waiting patients but saw no sign of alarm or even concern. Was there really no emergency, or was this a case of the bystander effect? Knowing that the reaction of onlookers is a poor indicator of the seriousness of a situation, she quickly summoned the doctor, who found that the man had suffered a heart attack. Fortunately, the doctor's office was attached to a large hospital complex, and almost immediately a hospital team appeared and rushed the victim to the emergency room.

PEOPLE WHO HELP IN EMERGENCIES

There are many kinds of **prosocial behaviour**—behaviour that benefits others, such as helping, cooperation, and sympathy. Prosocial impulses arise early in life. Researchers agree that children respond sympathetically to companions in distress by at least their second birthday (Roth-Hanania, Davidov, & Zahn-Waxler, 2011). The term **altruism** is usually reserved for behaviour aimed at helping others that requires some self-sacrifice,

Why do people often ignore someone who is unconscious on the sidewalk? Diffusion of responsibility is one possible explanation.

is not performed for personal gain, and carries no expectation of external reward (Bar-Tal, 1976). **[LO 10.29]** What motivates us to help or not to help in an emergency? Batson (2006) believes that we help out of empathy—the ability to feel what another feels.

People are more likely to receive help if they are physically attractive (P. L. Benson, Karabenick, & Lerner, 1976), if they are perceived by potential helpers as similar to them (Dovidio, 1984), and if they are in a positive mood (Carlson, Charlin, & Miller, 1988). **[LO 10.30]** Cultures vary in their norms for helping others—that is, in their social responsibility norms. According

bystander effect: As the number of bystanders at an emergency increases, the probability that the victim will receive help decreases, and help, if given, is likely to be delayed.

diffusion of responsibility: The feeling among bystanders at an emergency that the responsibility for helping is shared by the group, so that each individual feels less compelled to act than if he or she alone bore the total responsibility.

prosocial behaviour: Behaviour that benefits others, such as helping, cooperation, and sympathy.

altruism: Behaviour aimed at helping another, requiring some self-sacrifice and not designed for personal gain.

to J. G. Miller, D. M. Bersoff, and R. L. Harwood (1990), North Americans tend to feel an obligation to help family, friends, and even strangers in life-threatening circumstances, but only family in moderately serious situations. In contrast, in India social responsibility extends to strangers whose needs are only moderately serious or even minor. But whatever the motive for altruism, people who regularly engage in behaviour that helps others also reap significant benefits (Poulin & Cohen Silver, 2008). One interesting benefit is that the more people help, the more altruistic they become. Along with this attitude comes an increased appreciation of life. Perhaps we would all benefit from considering this the next time people ask for our help.

REMEMBER IT

Prosocial Behaviour

1. The bystander effect is influenced by all of the following except
   a. the number of bystanders.
   b. the personalities of bystanders.
   c. whether the situation is ambiguous.

2. As the number of bystanders to an emergency increases, the probability that the victim will receive help decreases. (true/false)

3. In an ambiguous situation, a good way to determine whether an emergency exists is to look at the reactions of other bystanders. (true/false)

4. Altruism is one form of prosocial behaviour. (true/false)

Answers: 1. b 2. true 3. false 4. true

MODULE **10H** AGGRESSION: INTENTIONALLY HARMING OTHERS

LO 10.31 Identify biological and social factors that can contribute to aggression.

LO 10.32 Explain the frustration–aggression hypothesis.

LO 10.33 Describe the practice of scapegoating.

LO 10.34 Identify aversive events that have been related to aggression.

LO 10.35 Explain aggression according to social learning theory.

We humans have a long history of **aggression**—intentionally inflicting physical or psychological harm on others. Consider the tens of millions of people killed by other humans in wars and even in times of peace. The rate of violent crime in Canada has followed a surprising pattern over the past 30 years or so. Violent crimes increased steadily between 1981 and 1991 and then began a steady decline; the most recent statistics indicate that 2012 saw the lowest rates of violent crimes in Canada since 1989 (Perreault, 2013). Over two thirds of all violent crimes were minor assaults, while robbery made up the second most

frequent category (Statistics Canada, 2013). Note that the rate of sexual assault, which was the second most frequent type of violent crime in 2004, has also declined significantly over the past 10 years and is now 23 percent lower than in 1998. However, despite the positive signs in Canadian rates of violent crime, police reported close to 1.95 million Criminal Code incidents in 2012, and just over 415 000 incidents of violent crime in Canada in 2012, which remains a disturbing number (Perreault, 2013).

What causes aggression? One of the earliest explanations of aggression was the *instinct theory*—the idea that human beings, along with other animal species, are genetically programmed for aggressive behaviour. Sigmund Freud believed that humans have an aggressive instinct that can be turned inward (as self-destruction) or outward (as aggression or violence toward others). Konrad Lorenz (1966), who won a Nobel Prize for his research in animal behaviour, maintained that aggression springs from an inborn fighting instinct common in many animal species. Most social psychologists, however, consider human behaviour too complex to attribute to instincts.

BIOLOGICAL VERSUS SOCIAL FACTORS IN AGGRESSION

What biological factors are thought to be related to aggression?

While rejecting the instinct theory of aggression, many psychologists believe that biological factors are involved. **[LO 10.31]** Twin and adoption studies suggest a genetic link for both aggression (Yancey, Venables, Hicks, & Patrick, 2013) and criminal behaviour (DiLalla & Gottesman, 1991). Twin and adoption studies have also revealed a genetic link for aggressive behaviour in children (L. A. Baker, Jacobson, Raine, Lozano, & Bezdjian, 2007). Moreover, many researchers now believe that genes that predispose individuals to aggressive behaviour may also cause them to be more sensitive to models of aggressiveness in the environment (Rowe, 2003).

One biological factor that seems very closely related to aggression is a low arousal level of the autonomic nervous system (Caramaschi, de Boer, & Koolhaas, 2008). Low arousal level (low heart rate and lower reactivity) has been linked to antisocial behaviour, and the tendency to display low levels of arousal appears to be genetic (Herpetz et al., 2007). People with a low arousal level tend to seek stimulation and excitement and often exhibit fearlessness, even in the face of danger. Much research suggests there is a substantial gender difference in aggressiveness, especially physical aggressiveness. Men are more physically aggressive than women (Hyde, 2005); a correlation between high testosterone levels and aggressive behaviour has been found in males (Denson, Ronay, von Hippel, & Schira, 2013); and gender differences in aggression are heritable (Soler, Vinayak, & Quadagno, 2000). **[LO 10.31]** Moreover, the connection between testosterone and aggression has a social component. Adolescent males with both high testosterone levels and a tendency to take risks that can lead to aggression, such as insulting someone without provocation, prefer to associate with peers who have similar hormonal and behavioural profiles (Vermeersch, T'Sjoen, Kaufman, & Vincke, 2008). Researchers speculate that a cycle of risky behaviour and aggression maintains high levels of testosterone secretion among such males.

Alcohol and aggression are also frequently linked. [LO 10.31] A meta-analysis of dozens of experimental studies indicated that use of alcohol is related to aggression (Foran & O'Leary, 2008). The use of alcohol and other drugs that affect the brain's frontal lobes may lead to aggressive behaviour in humans and other animals by disrupting normal executive functions (Lyvers, 2000).

AGGRESSION IN RESPONSE TO FRUSTRATION: SOMETIMES, BUT NOT ALWAYS

What is the frustration–aggression hypothesis?

Does **frustration**—the blocking of an impulse, or interference with the attainment of a goal—lead to aggression? The **frustration–aggression hypothesis** suggests that frustration produces aggression (Dollard, Doob, Miller, Mowrer, & Sears, 1939; N. E. Miller, 1941). [LO 10.32] If a traffic jam kept you from arriving at your destination on time and you were frustrated, what would you do—lean on your horn, shout obscenities out of your window, or just sit patiently and wait? Berkowitz (1988) points out that even when a feeling of frustration is justified, it can cause aggression if it arouses negative emotions.

Aggression in response to frustration is not always aimed at the people causing it. If the preferred target is too threatening or not available, the aggression may be displaced. For example, children who are angry with their parents may take out their frustrations on a younger sibling. Sometimes minorities and others who have not been responsible for a frustrating situation become targets of displaced aggression—a practice known as **scapegoating** (Koltz, 1983). [LO 10.33]

AGGRESSION IN RESPONSE TO AVERSIVE EVENTS: PAIN, HEAT, NOISE, AND MORE

What kinds of aversive events and unpleasant emotions have been related to aggression?

According to a leading researcher on aggression, Leonard Berkowitz (1988, 1989), aggression in response to frustration is only one special case of a broader phenomenon—aggression resulting from unpleasant or aversive events in general. People often become aggressive when they are in pain (Berkowitz, 1983), when they are exposed to loud noise or foul odours (Rotton, Frey, Barry, Milligan, & Fitzpatrick, 1979), and even when they are exposed to irritating cigarette smoke. [LO 10.34] Extreme heat has also been linked to aggression (C. A. Anderson, 1989; C. A. Anderson & Anderson, 1996; Rotton & Cohn, 2000).

THE SOCIAL LEARNING THEORY OF AGGRESSION: LEARNING TO BE AGGRESSIVE

According to social learning theory, what causes aggressive behaviour?

The social learning theory of aggression holds that people learn to behave aggressively by observing aggressive models

Children learn to behave aggressively by observing aggressive models, often their parents.

and by having their aggressive responses reinforced (Bandura, 1973). [LO 10.35] It is well known that aggression is higher in groups and subcultures that condone violent behaviour and accord high status to aggressive members. A leading advocate of the social learning theory of aggression, Albert Bandura (1976), believes that aggressive models in the subculture, the family, and the media all play a part in the increasing levels of aggression in North American society.

aggression: The intentional infliction of physical or psychological harm on another.

frustration: Interference with the attainment of a goal or the blocking of an impulse.

frustration–aggression hypothesis: The hypothesis that frustration produces aggression.

scapegoating: Displacing aggression onto minority groups or other innocent targets who were not responsible for the frustration causing the aggression.

Abused children certainly experience aggression and see it modelled day after day. Moreover, individuals who were sexually abused as children are more likely than others to become child sexual abusers as adults (Jespersen, Lalumière, & Seto, 2009). On the basis of original research and an analysis of 60 other studies, Oliver (1993) concluded that one third of people who are abused go on to become abusers and one third do not, while the final one third may become abusers if the social stress in their lives is sufficiently high.

Most abusive parents, however, were not abused as children (Widom, 1989). Although abused and neglected children run a higher risk of becoming delinquent, criminal, or violent, the majority do not become abusive themselves (DuMont, Widom, & Czaja, 2007).

The Media and Aggression: Is There a Connection?

Several years ago, a study by Huston and colleagues (1992) noted that by the time the average North American child completes elementary school, he or she will have watched on TV over 8000 murders and more than 100 000 violent acts. But is there a causal link between viewing aggressive acts and committing them? Current research evidence overwhelmingly supports a relationship between TV violence and viewer aggression (Coyne & Nelson, 2011; Huesmann, Moise-Titus, Podolski, & Eron, 2003). And the negative effects of TV violence are even worse for individuals who are highly aggressive by nature (Bushman, 1995). Researchers have also found a correlation between playing violent video games and aggression (Anderson et al., 2010), with aggressiveness increasing as more time is spent playing such games. However, boys who chose aggressive video games tend to be more aggressive, less intelligent, and less prosocial in their behaviour (Weigman & van Schie, 1998). So the link between aggression and video games may reflect the tendency of individuals who are more aggressive to prefer entertainment media that feature aggression.

REMEMBER IT

Aggression

1. Pain, extreme heat, loud noise, and foul odours have all been associated with an increase in aggressive responses. (true/false)
2. The social learning theory of aggression emphasizes all of the following except that
   a. aggressive responses are learned from the family, the subculture, and the media.
   b. aggressive responses are learned through modelling.
   c. most aggression results from frustration.
   d. when aggressive responses are reinforced, they are more likely to continue.

3. According to the frustration–aggression hypothesis, frustration _____ leads to aggression.
   a. always
   b. frequently
   c. rarely
   d. never
4. The weight of research suggests that media violence is probably related to increased aggression. (true/false)

Answers: 1. true   2. c   3. b   4. true

APPLY IT

"Unlearning" Prejudice

Today's college and university population is more diverse than ever before. In addition to the broad diversity of students who are Canadian citizens, people from many other countries come to Canada to further their education. Consequently, for many young people, campus life represents a unique opportunity to interact with others of different racial, ethnic, or cultural groups. How can students make the most of this opportunity to "unlearn" the prejudices they may bring with them to college or university?

Intergroup Contact

As you learned from the Robbers Cave experiment (Sherif & Sherif, 1967), intergroup contact can sometimes lead to increased stereotyping. Under the right conditions, though, intergroup contact can reduce prejudice. Colleges and universities can provide a context in which students from diverse backgrounds study together, endure the same trials (midterms and finals), develop a shared sense of school spirit, join clubs in which members from different backgrounds share common goals, and so on. Thus, under the right conditions,

intergroup contact can reduce prejudice (Page-Gould, Mendoza-Denton, & Tropp, 2008).

The Jigsaw Technique

Methods such as the *jigsaw technique*, a strategy that works well in college and university classrooms and as a game in less formal interactions, represent a more direct approach. Each participant in a jigsaw group is given a small amount of information and asked to teach it to other participants. The group must use all the individual pieces of information to solve a problem. This approach increases interaction among participants and helps them develop empathy for members of other ethnic and racial groups (Aronson, Stephan, Sikes, Blaney, & Snapp, 1978; Singh, 1991). A side benefit is that it is an effective way of learning a new solution to a problem.

Diversity Education

Many colleges and universities offer students and faculty opportunities to participate in seminars and workshops designed to combat racism. In such settings, participants learn about racial and cultural perspectives that may differ from their own. They also learn to identify behaviours that may be construed as racist by others, even when the behaviour is not motivated by racism. Researchers have found that such programs help to reduce automatic stereotyping among participants (Hill & Augoustinos, 2001; Rudman, Ashmore, & Gary, 2001).

Open Discussions of Prejudice and Discrimination

Perhaps the greatest potential of the college or university campus for reducing prejudice and discrimination lies in the nature of its intellectual climate. Traditionally, classes, as well as club meetings, gatherings at restaurants, all-night study sessions in coffee shops, and late-night debates in dorm rooms, often feature lively discussions of a variety of topics. And when we hear others speak passionately about racism, sexism, and other types of injustice, we are likely to adopt more tolerant attitudes ourselves.

So the next time you hear someone make a statement you feel is racist or sexist or prejudiced in any way, speak up! You never know how influential your voice might be.

THINKING CRITICALLY

Evaluation

Many Canadians and Americans were surprised to note that many people in China are quickly adapting to a society with more economic choice and, at least to some extent, moving away from the communist system. Using what you have learned about attribution bias and conformity, try to explain why many Canadians mistakenly believed that the Chinese population preferred to operate under a communist system.

Point/Counterpoint

Prepare a convincing argument supporting each of the following positions:

a. Aggression results largely from biological factors (nature).

b. Aggression is primarily learned (nurture).

Psychology in Your Life

Review the factors influencing impression formation and attraction as discussed in this chapter. Prepare a dual list of behaviours indicating what you should and should not do if you wish to make a better impression on other people and increase their liking for you.

MyPsychLab go to mypsychlab (access code required) to find web resources for your text that supplement the material in chapter 10.

SUMMARY & REVIEW

10A SOCIAL PERCEPTION

Why are first impressions so important and enduring?
First impressions are important because we attend more carefully to the first information we receive about a person and because, once formed, this impression acts as a framework through which later information is interpreted.

What is the difference between a situational attribution and a dispositional attribution for a specific behaviour?
An attribution is our inference about the cause of our own or another's behaviour. When we use situational attributions, we attribute the behaviour to some external cause or factor. When we use dispositional attributions, we attribute the behaviour to some internal cause—a personal trait, motive, or attitude.

How do the kinds of attributions we tend to make about ourselves differ from those we make about other people?
We tend to overemphasize dispositional factors when making attributions about the behaviour of other people, and to overemphasize situational factors in explaining our own behaviour.

10B ATTRACTION

Why is proximity an important factor in attraction?
Proximity allows us to have repeated exposure to certain people, and research has shown that we tend to feel more positive toward any stimuli when we encounter them frequently. This phenomenon is called the mere-exposure effect.

How important is physical attractiveness in attraction?
Proximity influences attraction because relationships are easier to develop with people close at hand. Proximity also increases the likelihood of repeated contacts, and mere exposure tends to increase attraction (the *mere-exposure effect*). Physical attractiveness is a major factor in attraction for people of all ages. People attribute other positive qualities to those who are physically attractive—a phenomenon called the *halo effect*.

Are people, as a rule, more attracted to those who are opposite or those who are similar to them?
People are generally attracted to those who have similar attitudes and interests and who are similar in economic status, ethnicity, and age.

10C CONFORMITY, OBEDIENCE, AND COMPLIANCE

What did Asch find in his famous experiment on conformity?
In Asch's classic study on conformity, 5 percent of the subjects went along with the incorrect, unanimous majority all the time; 70 percent went along some of the time; and 25 percent remained completely independent and were never swayed by the group.

What did Milgram find in his classic study of obedience?
In Milgram's classic study of obedience, 65 percent of the subjects obeyed the experimenter's orders to the end of the experiment and administered what they believed were increasingly painful shocks to the learner up to the maximum of 450 volts.

What are three techniques used to gain compliance?
Three techniques used to gain compliance are the foot-in-the-door technique, the door-in-the-face technique, and the lowball technique.

10D GROUP INFLUENCE

Under what conditions does social facilitation have either a positive or a negative effect on performance?
When others are present, either as an audience or as co-actors, one's performance on easy tasks is usually improved but performance on difficult tasks is usually impaired.

What is social loafing, and what factors can lessen or eliminate it?
Social loafing is the tendency of people to put forth less effort when they are working with others on a common task than when they are working alone. This is less likely to take place when individual output can be monitored or when people are highly involved with the outcome.

How are the initial attitudes of group members likely to affect group decision making?
The initial attitudes of group members tend to shift decisions to a more extreme position in whatever direction the group was leaning initially—a phenomenon known as group polarization.

10E ATTITUDES AND ATTITUDE CHANGE

What are the three components of an attitude?
Attitudes usually have a cognitive, an emotional, and a behavioural component.

What is cognitive dissonance, and how can it be resolved?
Cognitive dissonance is an unpleasant state that can occur when we become aware of inconsistencies between our attitudes or between our attitudes and our behaviour. We can resolve cognitive dissonance by changing the attitude or the behaviour or by rationalizing away the inconsistency.

What are the four elements in persuasion?
Researchers have identified four elements in persuasion: (1) the source of the communication (who is doing the persuading); (2) the audience (who is being persuaded); (3) the message (what is being said); and (4) the medium (the means by which the message is transmitted).

What qualities make a source persuasive?
Persuasive attempts are most successful when the source is credible (expert and trustworthy), attractive, and likeable.

10F PREJUDICE AND DISCRIMINATION

What is the difference between prejudice and discrimination?
Prejudice consists of attitudes (usually negative) toward others based on their gender, religion, race, or membership in a particular group. Discrimination consists of actions against others based on the same factors.

What is meant by the terms in-group and out-group?
An *in-group* is a social group with a strong sense of togetherness and from which others are excluded; an *out-group* consists of individuals or groups specifically identified by the in-group as not belonging.

How does prejudice develop, according to the social learning theory?
According to the social learning theory, people learn attitudes of prejudice and hatred the same way they learn other attitudes. If children hear their parents, teachers, peers, or others openly express prejudices toward different racial, ethnic, or cultural groups, they may be quick to learn such attitudes.

What are stereotypes?
Stereotypes are widely shared beliefs about the characteristics of members of various social groups (racial, ethnic, religious); they usually include the assumption that group members are all alike.

What are several strategies for reducing prejudice and discrimination?
Strategies for reducing prejudice include (1) arranging appropriate educational experiences for children, (2) providing

situations where diverse social groups can interact under certain favourable conditions, and (3) extending the boundaries of narrowly defined social groups.

 PROSOCIAL BEHAVIOUR: BEHAVIOUR THAT BENEFITS OTHERS

What is the bystander effect, and what factors have been suggested to explain why it occurs?

The *bystander effect* means that as the number of bystanders at an emergency increases, the probability that the victim will receive help decreases, and help, if given, is likely to be delayed. The bystander effect may be due in part to diffusion of responsibility or, in ambiguous situations, to the assumption that no emergency exists.

10H AGGRESSION: INTENTIONALLY HARMING OTHERS

What biological factors are thought to be related to aggression?

Biological factors thought to be related to aggression are a genetic link, in both aggression and criminal behaviour, and high testosterone levels. By contrast, social learning theory suggests that people acquire aggressive responses by observing aggressive models in the family, the subculture, and the media, and by having aggressive responses reinforced. Research suggests that both of these views are partially correct.

What is the frustration–aggression hypothesis?

The frustration–aggression hypothesis holds that frustration produces aggression and that this aggression may be directed at the frustrater or displaced onto another target, as in scapegoating.

What kinds of aversive events and unpleasant emotions have been related to aggression?

Aggression may result from unpleasant or aversive events in general. People often respond aggressively when they feel pain; when they are exposed to loud noise, foul odours, or irritating cigarette smoke; and when they feel extreme heat.

According to social learning theory, what causes aggressive behaviour?

The social learning theory of aggression holds that people learn to behave aggressively by observing aggressive models and by having their aggressive responses reinforced.

SOCIAL PSYCHOLOGY

Social psychology studies how the actual, imagined, or implied presence of others influences individuals.

MODULE (10A) SOCIAL PERCEPTION

Impression formation: The process of integrating information to form a coherent impression of a person. Impressions of others are influenced by their physical appearance.

Attribution: An inference about the cause of behaviour. Biases occur when people overemphasize external (situational) or internal (dispositional) causes of behaviour.

Primacy Effect: First information has a greater effect than later information on overall impression formation.

Self-fulfilling Prophecies: Expectations about others cause others to act as expected.

Actor–Observer Bias: Tendency to attribute the behaviour of others to internal causes, and own behaviour to external causes.

Fundamental Attribution Error: Observers over-emphasize internal factors and under-emphasize external ones when explaining behaviour of others.

Self-serving Bias: Tendency to attri-bute our own suc-cesses to internal causes, and failures to external causes.

MODULE (10B) ATTRACTION

Factors Influencing Attraction
Proximity refers to geographic closeness.
Mere-exposure effect is the tendency to feel more positive toward stimuli with repeated exposure.
Reciprocal liking is liking those who like us.
People prefer **physically attractive** people.
People prefer others who are **similar** to them.
Halo effect occurs when, after observing one major positive or negative trait in a person, people infer that the person has other generally positive or negative traits.

Romantic Attraction
Matching hypothesis predicts that we have friends, lovers, or spouses who are similar to us in social assets.

Mate Selection
Across cultures, people prefer others who have mutual attraction, dependable char-acter, emotional stability, and pleasing disposition.

MODULE (10C) CONFORMITY, OBEDIENCE, AND COMPLIANCE

Conformity involves changing one's behaviour or attitude in order to be consistent with the norms of a group or the expectations of others.

Norms are attitudes and standards of behaviour expected of members of a group.

Asch found that most people conformed some of the time when confederates selected the same wrong answer on a visual task.

Obedience refers to following orders.

Milgram found that most people obeyed author-ity even if obedience caused great pain and was life-threatening to another person.

Compliance involves acting in accordance with the wishes, suggestions, or direct requests of another person.

Foot-in-the-door technique increases the likeli-hood that a person will agree to a larger request after getting the person to agree to a small request.

Door-in-the-face technique increases the likeli-hood that a person will agree to a smaller request by first getting the person to reject an unreasonable large request.

Low-ball technique involves changing the terms of a request after a person has agreed to it.

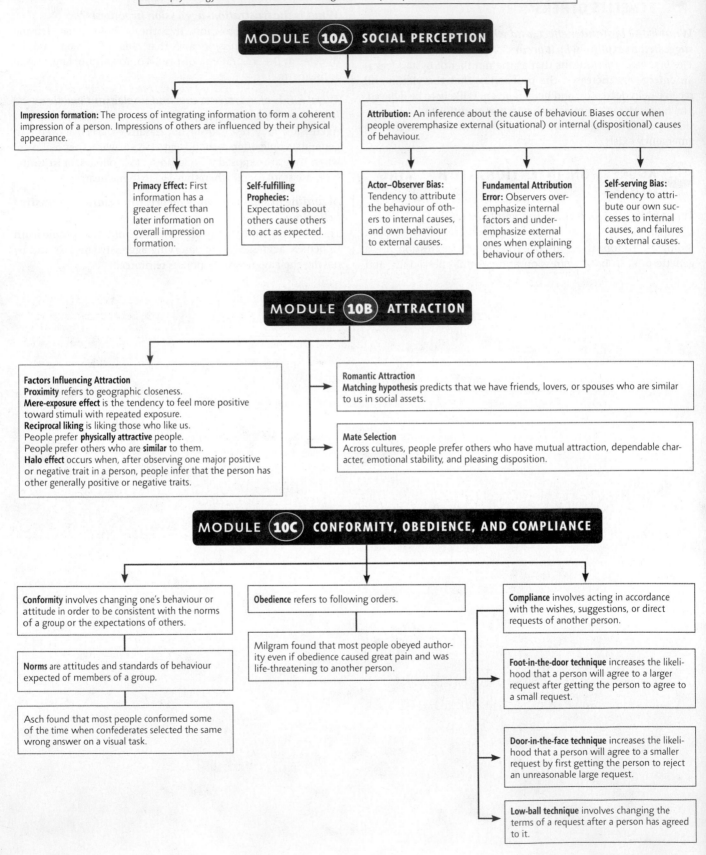

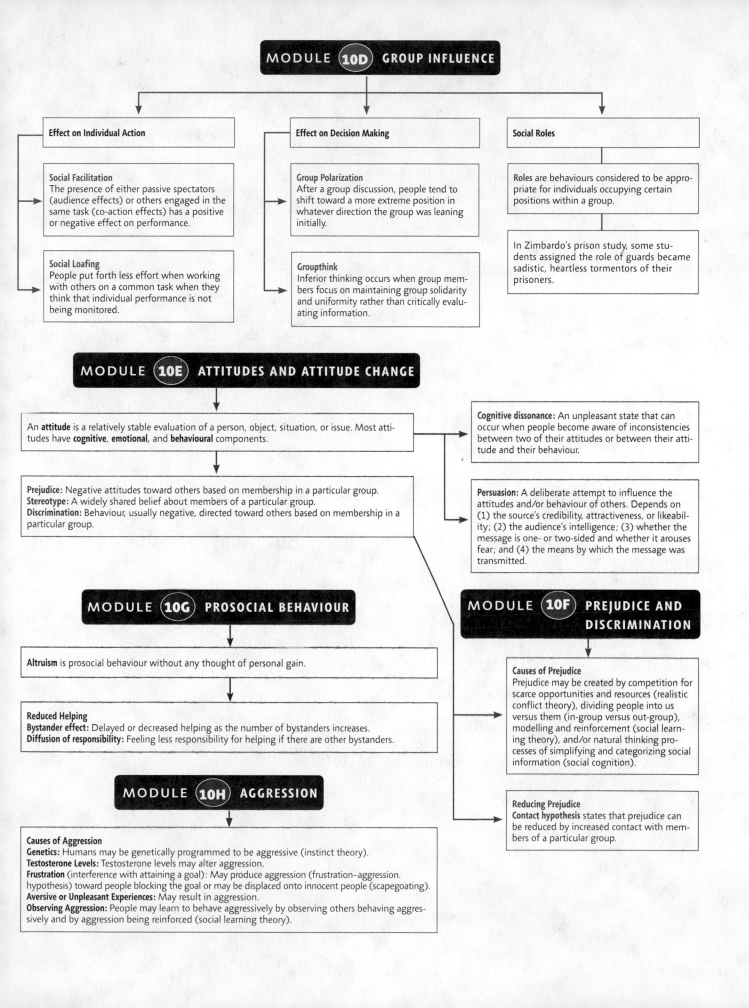

MODULE 10D GROUP INFLUENCE

Effect on Individual Action

Social Facilitation
The presence of either passive spectators (audience effects) or others engaged in the same task (co-action effects) has a positive or negative effect on performance.

Social Loafing
People put forth less effort when working with others on a common task when they think that individual performance is not being monitored.

Effect on Decision Making

Group Polarization
After a group discussion, people tend to shift toward a more extreme position in whatever direction the group was leaning initially.

Groupthink
Inferior thinking occurs when group members focus on maintaining group solidarity and uniformity rather than critically evaluating information.

Social Roles

Roles are behaviours considered to be appropriate for individuals occupying certain positions within a group.

In Zimbardo's prison study, some students assigned the role of guards became sadistic, heartless tormentors of their prisoners.

MODULE 10E ATTITUDES AND ATTITUDE CHANGE

An **attitude** is a relatively stable evaluation of a person, object, situation, or issue. Most attitudes have **cognitive**, **emotional**, and **behavioural** components.

Prejudice: Negative attitudes toward others based on membership in a particular group.
Stereotype: A widely shared belief about members of a particular group.
Discrimination: Behaviour, usually negative, directed toward others based on membership in a particular group.

Cognitive dissonance: An unpleasant state that can occur when people become aware of inconsistencies between two of their attitudes or between their attitude and their behaviour.

Persuasion: A deliberate attempt to influence the attitudes and/or behaviour of others. Depends on (1) the source's credibility, attractiveness, or likeability; (2) the audience's intelligence; (3) whether the message is one- or two-sided and whether it arouses fear; and (4) the means by which the message was transmitted.

MODULE 10G PROSOCIAL BEHAVIOUR

Altruism is prosocial behaviour without any thought of personal gain.

Reduced Helping
Bystander effect: Delayed or decreased helping as the number of bystanders increases.
Diffusion of responsibility: Feeling less responsibility for helping if there are other bystanders.

MODULE 10F PREJUDICE AND DISCRIMINATION

Causes of Prejudice
Prejudice may be created by competition for scarce opportunities and resources (realistic conflict theory), dividing people into us versus them (in-group versus out-group), modelling and reinforcement (social learning theory), and/or natural thinking processes of simplifying and categorizing social information (social cognition).

Reducing Prejudice
Contact hypothesis states that prejudice can be reduced by increased contact with members of a particular group.

MODULE 10H AGGRESSION

Causes of Aggression
Genetics: Humans may be genetically programmed to be aggressive (instinct theory).
Testosterone Levels: Testosterone levels may alter aggression.
Frustration (interference with attaining a goal): May produce aggression (frustration–aggression. hypothesis) toward people blocking the goal or may be displaced onto innocent people (scapegoating).
Aversive or Unpleasant Experiences: May result in aggression.
Observing Aggression: People may learn to behave aggressively by observing others behaving aggressively and by aggression being reinforced (social learning theory).

11

Who or what is in control of your life? We all know that we don't have total control over our lives or what happens to us, but what do you believe about your ability to at least influence what happens to you? Let's check to see what your beliefs are about how much control you have. For each statement below, indicate whether you agree or disagree.

1. Heredity determines most of a person's personality.
2. Chance has a lot to do with being successful.
3. Whatever plans you make, something will always interfere.
4. Being at the right place at the right time is essential for getting what you want in life.
5. Intelligence is a given, and it cannot be improved.
6. If I successfully accomplish a task, it's because it was an easy one.
7. You cannot change your destiny.
8. School success is mostly a result of one's socioeconomic background.
9. People are lonely because they are not given the chance to meet new people.
10. Setting goals for yourself is of little use because nobody knows what might happen in the future to interfere with them.

PERSONALITY THEORY AND ASSESSMENT

Give yourself 1 point for each "agree" and 0 points for each "disagree." Is your score closer to 0 or closer to 10? Scores ranging from 0 to 4 suggest that you believe that you have some degree of control over what happens to you, and scores from 7 to 10 indicate just the opposite. Psychologists are interested in people's answers to such questions because we know that believing you have at least some degree of control over some things, such as stressors, can help you to cope with challenges, including stress, more effectively. Psychologists also wonder whether the beliefs, feeling and behaviours we see in people are stable or temporary. Understanding whether beliefs, feelings, or behaviours are flexible or relatively stable has become a central theme in psychological research that examines aspects of our personality. But what do psychologists mean when they speak of personality? **Personality** is defined as an individual's unique characteristic patterns of behaving, thinking, and feeling (Carver & Scheier, 1996). For years psychologists assumed that our personality stabilizes early in life and did not change much over time—that it became a stable and fixed aspect of ourselves. Others now endorse the idea that a person can change his or her personality (Moskowitz & Fournier, 2015). A sense of personal control is an important feature of personality.

In this chapter, we will explore some of the theories that have been proposed to explain personality as well as a variety of tests and inventories used to assess personality. We will begin with the theory that established the study of personality as a central issue in the field of psychology: the psychoanalytic theory of Sigmund Freud.

MODULE 11A SIGMUND FREUD AND PSYCHOANALYSIS

LO 11.1 Describe the three levels of awareness in Freud's theory of consciousness.

LO 11.2 Explain the roles of the id, ego, and superego.

LO 11.3 Describe the role of defence mechanisms.

LO 11.4 Explain fixation and how it can develop during the early stages of psychosexual development.

LO 11.5 Describe how fixations and the relative balance of the id, ego, and superego influence personality.

To what two aspects of Freud's work does the term *psychoanalysis* apply?

Most textbooks begin their exploration of personality theory with Sigmund Freud, and for good reason. Freud created one of the first and most controversial personality theories. Using information gained from the treatment of his patients and from his own life experiences, Freud developed the theory of psychoanalysis.

When you hear the term **psychoanalysis**, you may picture a psychiatrist treating a troubled patient on a couch. But psychoanalysis is much more than that. The term refers not only to a therapy for treating psychological disorders, but also to a personality theory.

Freud's theory of psychoanalysis is largely original, and it was revolutionary and shocking to the nineteenth- and early twentieth-century European audience to which it was introduced. The major components of Freud's theory, and perhaps the most controversial, are (1) the central role of the sexual instinct, (2) the concept of infantile sexuality, and (3) the dominant part played by the unconscious in moving and shaping our thoughts and behaviour. Freud's theory assumes a psychic determinism: the view that there is a cause for our every thought, idea, feeling, action, or behaviour. Nothing happens by chance or accident; everything we do and even everything we forget to do has an underlying cause.

THE CONSCIOUS, THE PRECONSCIOUS, AND THE UNCONSCIOUS: LEVELS OF AWARENESS

What are the three levels of awareness in consciousness?

Freud believed that there are three levels of awareness in consciousness: the conscious, the preconscious, and the unconscious. **[LO 11.1]** The **conscious** consists of whatever we are aware of at any given moment—a thought, a feeling, a sensation, or a memory. When we shift our attention or our thoughts, a change occurs in the content of the conscious.

Freud's **preconscious** is very much like the present-day concept of long-term memory. It contains all the memories, feelings, experiences, and perceptions that we are not consciously thinking about at the moment but that may be brought to consciousness—which high school you went to or the year in which you were born, for example. This information resides in your preconscious but can easily be brought to consciousness.

The most important of the three levels is the **unconscious**, which Freud believed to be the primary motivating force of our behaviour. The unconscious holds memories that once were conscious but that were so unpleasant or anxiety-provoking that they were repressed (involuntarily removed from consciousness). The unconscious also contains all of the instincts (sexual and aggressive), wishes, and desires that have never been allowed into consciousness. Freud traced the roots of psychological disorders to these impulses and repressed memories.

THE ID, THE EGO, AND THE SUPEREGO: WARRING COMPONENTS OF THE PERSONALITY

What are the roles of the id, the ego, and the superego?

Sigmund Freud (1923/1961) proposed a new conception of personality that contained three systems: the id, the ego, and the superego. **[LO 11.2]** Figure 11.1 shows these three systems and how they relate to his conscious, preconscious, and unconscious levels of awareness. These systems do not exist physically; they are only concepts, or ways of looking at personality.

The **id** is the only part of the personality that is present at birth. It is inherited, primitive, inaccessible, and completely unconscious. The id contains (1) the life instincts, which are the sexual instincts and the biological urges such as hunger and thirst, and (2) the death instinct, which accounts for our aggressive and destructive impulses (S. Freud, 1933/1965). The id operates according to the **pleasure principle**—that is, the drive to seek pleasure, avoid pain, and gain immediate gratification of its wishes. The id is the source of the **libido**—the psychic, often sexual, energy that fuels the entire personality—yet the id cannot act on its own. It can only wish, image, fantasize, and demand.

FIGURE 11.1

Freud's Conception of Personality

According to Freud, personality is composed of three structures, or systems: the id, the ego, and the superego. Conceptualized here as parts of an iceberg, the id, completely unconscious, is wholly submerged. The ego is largely conscious and visible but partly unconscious. The superego also operates at both the conscious and the unconscious levels.

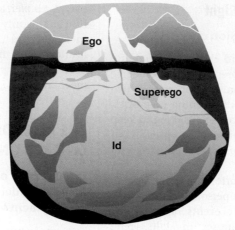

Conscious mind

Preconscious (outside awareness but accessible)

Unconscious mind

The **ego** is the logical, rational, realistic part of the personality. The ego evolves from the id and draws its energy from the id. One of the ego's functions is to satisfy the id's urges. But the ego, which is mostly conscious, acts according to the reality principle; it must consider the constraints of the real world in determining appropriate times, places, and objects to gratify the id's wishes. It allows compromises to be made—for example, settling for a burger instead of having the lobster or steak you had wanted.

When a child is five or six years old, the **superego**—the moral component of the personality—is formed. The superego has two parts: (1) the *conscience*, which consists of all the behaviours for which we have been punished and about which we feel guilty, and (2) the *ego ideal*, which contains the behaviours for which we have been praised and rewarded and about which we feel pride and satisfaction. At first the superego reflects only the parents' expectations of what is good and right, but it expands over time to incorporate teachings from the broader social world. In its quest for moral perfection, the superego sets moral guidelines that define and limit the flexibility of the ego.

DEFENCE MECHANISMS: PROTECTING THE EGO

What is a defence mechanism?

All would be well if the id, the ego, and the superego had compatible aims. But the id's demands for sensual pleasure are often in direct conflict with the superego's desire for moral perfection. At times the ego needs some way to defend itself against the anxiety created by the excessive demands of the id, by the harsh judgments of the superego, or by the sometimes threatening conditions in the environment. Often the ego can relieve anxiety by solving its problems rationally and directly. When it cannot do so, it must resort to irrational defences against anxiety called *defence mechanisms*.

A **defence mechanism** is a technique used to defend against anxiety and to maintain self-esteem, but it involves self-deception and the distortion of internal and external reality (Vaillant, 2012). **[LO 11.3]** All people use defence mechanisms to some degree (Vaillant, 2000), but research supports Freud's view that the overuse of defence mechanisms can adversely affect mental health (Cramer, 2006; Diehl, Chui, Hay, Lumley, Grühn, & Labouvie-Vief, 2014).

personality: A person's characteristic patterns of behaving, thinking, and feeling.

psychoanalysis (SY-co-ah-NAL-ih-sis): Freud's term for both his theory of personality and his therapy for the treatment of psychological disorders.

conscious (KON-shus): Those thoughts, feelings, sensations, and memories of which we are aware at any given moment.

preconscious: The thoughts, feelings, and memories that we are not consciously aware of at the moment but that may be brought to consciousness.

unconscious (un-KON-shus): Considered by Freud to be the primary motivating force of behaviour, containing repressed memories as well as instincts and wishes that have never been allowed into consciousness.

id: The unconscious system of the personality, which contains the life and death instincts and operates on the pleasure principle.

pleasure principle: The principle by which the id operates to seek pleasure, avoid pain, and obtain immediate gratification.

libido (lih-BEE-doe): Freud's name for the psychic, often sexual, energy that comes from the id and provides the energy for the entire personality.

ego (EE-go): In Freudian theory, the rational and largely conscious system of one's personality; operates according to the reality principle and tries to satisfy the demands of the id without violating moral values.

superego (sue-per-EE-go): The moral system of the personality, which consists of the conscience and the ego ideal.

defence mechanism: An unconscious, irrational means used by the ego to defend against anxiety; involves self-deception and the distortion of reality.

repression: The act of removing unpleasant memories from one's consciousness so that one is no longer aware of the painful event.

Repression: Out of Mind, Out of Sight

What are two ways in which repression operates?

Repression is the most important and the most frequently used defence mechanism, and it is present to some degree in all other defence mechanisms. Repression operates in two ways: (1) it can remove painful or threatening memories, thoughts, ideas, or perceptions from consciousness and keep them in the unconscious or (2) it can prevent unconscious but disturbing sexual and aggressive impulses from breaking into consciousness.

Even though repressed, the memories lurk in the unconscious and exert an active influence on personality and behaviour. This is why repressed traumatic events of childhood can cause psychological disorders (neuroses) in adults. Freud believed that the way to cure such disorders is to bring the repressed material back to consciousness. This was what he tried to accomplish through his therapy, psychoanalysis.

Other Defence Mechanisms: Excuses, Substitutions, and Denials

What are some other defence mechanisms?

There are several other defence mechanisms that we may use from time to time. We use **projection** when we attribute our own undesirable thoughts, impulses, personality traits, or behaviour to others, or when we minimize the undesirable in ourselves and exaggerate it in others.

Denial is a refusal to consciously acknowledge or to believe that a danger or a threatening condition exists. For instance, smokers use denial when they refuse to admit that cigarettes are a danger to their health.

Rationalization occurs when we unconsciously supply a logical, rational, or socially acceptable reason rather than the real reason for an action or event. When we rationalize, we make excuses for, or justify, our failures and mistakes. A teacher may blame students for their low grades, arguing that they are unmotivated and lazy, rather than evaluating the impact of his or her teaching techniques.

Sometimes, when frustrated or anxious, we may use **regression**—that is, we revert to behaviour that might have reduced anxiety at an earlier stage of development. A five-year-old child with a new baby sibling may regress and suck her thumb.

Reaction formation is at work when people express exaggerated ideas and emotions that are the opposite of their disturbing, unconscious impulses and desires, usually of ones that are sexual or aggressive. In reaction formation, the conscious thought or feeling masks the unconscious one. Unconscious hatred may be expressed as love and devotion, cruelty as kindness.

Displacement occurs when we substitute a less threatening object or person for the original object of a sexual or aggressive impulse. If your boss makes you angry, you may take out your hostility on your boyfriend or girlfriend.

With **sublimation**, we rechannel sexual or aggressive energy into pursuits or accomplishments that society considers acceptable or even praiseworthy. An aggressive person may rechannel that aggression and become a football or hockey player, a boxer, a surgeon, or a butcher. Freud viewed sublimation as the only completely healthy ego defence mechanism. In fact, Freud (1930/1962) considered all advances in civilization to be the result of sublimation. *Review & Reflect 11.1* describes and provides additional examples of the defence mechanisms.

THE PSYCHOSEXUAL STAGES OF DEVELOPMENT: CENTRED ON THE EROGENOUS ZONES

What are the psychosexual stages, and why did Freud consider them so important in personality development?

The sex instinct, Freud said, is the most important factor influencing personality; but it does not just suddenly appear full-blown at puberty. It is present at birth and then develops through a series of **psychosexual stages** (see Table 11.1). Each stage centres on a particular erogenous zone—a part of the body that provides pleasurable sensations and around which a conflict arises (S. Freud, 1905/1953b, 1920/1963b). If the conflict is not resolved without undue difficulty, the child may develop a **fixation**. **[LO 11.4]** This means that a portion of the libido (psychic energy) remains invested at that stage, leaving less energy to meet the challenges of future stages. Overindulgence at a stage may leave a person unwilling psychologically to move on to the next stage. But too little gratification may leave the person trying to make up for unmet needs. Freud believed that certain personality characteristics develop as a result of difficulty at one or another of the psychosexual stages.

The Oral Stage (Birth to 12 or 18 Months)

During the **oral stage**, the mouth is the primary source of sensual pleasure (Freud, 1920/1963b). The conflict at this stage centres on weaning. Too much or too little gratification may result in an oral fixation—an excessive preoccupation with oral activities such as eating, drinking, smoking, gum chewing, nail biting, and even kissing. **[LO 11.4]** Freud believed that difficulties at the oral stage can result in personality traits such as excessive dependence, optimism, and gullibility or extreme pessimism, sarcasm, hostility, and aggression.

The Anal Stage (12 or 18 Months to Age 3)

During the **anal stage**, children derive sensual pleasure from expelling and withholding feces. A conflict arises when toilet training begins, because this is one of the parents' first attempts to have children withhold or postpone gratification. When parents are harsh in their approach, children may rebel openly, defecating whenever and wherever they please. This may lead to an anal expulsive personality—someone who is sloppy, irresponsible, rebellious, hostile, and destructive. Other children may defy their parents and gain attention by withholding feces. They may develop anal retentive personalities, gaining security through what they possess and becoming stingy, stubborn, rigid, and excessively neat and clean, orderly, and precise (Freud, 1933/1965).

REVIEW & REFLECT 11.1 DEFENCE MECHANISMS

Defence Mechanism	Description	Example
Repression	Involuntarily removing an unpleasant memory from consciousness or barring disturbing sexual and aggressive impulses from consciousness.	Jill forgets a traumatic incident from childhood.
Projection	Attributing one's own undesirable traits or impulses to another.	A very lonely divorced woman accuses all men of having only one thing on their minds.
Denial	Refusing to consciously acknowledge the existence of danger or a threatening situation.	Amy is severely injured when she fails to take a storm warning seriously.
Rationalization	Supplying a logical, rational reason rather than the real reason for an action or event.	Fred tells his friend that he didn't get the job because he didn't have connections.
Regression	Reverting to a behaviour characteristic of an earlier stage of development.	Susan bursts into tears whenever she is criticized.
Reaction formation	Expressing exaggerated ideas and emotions that are the opposite of disturbing, unconscious impulses and desires.	A former purchaser of pornography, Bob is now a tireless crusader against it.
Displacement	Substituting a less threatening object for the original object of an impulse.	After being spanked by his father, Bill hits his baby brother.
Sublimation	Rechannelling sexual and aggressive energy into pursuits that society considers acceptable or even admirable.	Tim goes to a gym to work out when he feels hostile and frustrated.

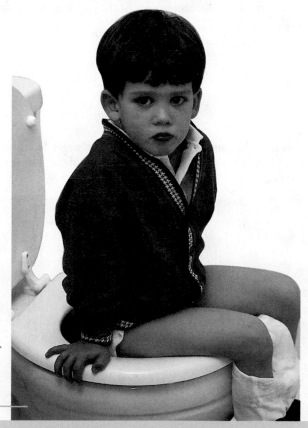

Freud believed that a fixation at the anal stage, resulting from harsh parental pressure, could lead to an anal retentive personality—characterized by excessive stubbornness, rigidity, and neatness.

projection: The act of attributing our own undesirable thoughts, impulses, personality traits, or behaviours to others, or of minimizing the undesirable in ourselves and exaggerating it in others.

denial: The act of refusing to consciously acknowledge the existence of a danger or a threatening condition.

rationalization: The act of supplying a logical, rational, socially acceptable reason rather than the real reason for an unacceptable thought or action.

regression: The act of reverting to a behaviour that might have reduced anxiety at an earlier stage of development.

reaction formation: The process of denying an unacceptable impulse, usually sexual or aggressive, by giving strong conscious expression to its opposite.

displacement: The substitution of a less threatening object for the original object of an impulse; taking out frustrations on objects or people who are less threatening than those who provoked us.

sublimation: The rechannelling of sexual or aggressive energy into pursuits or accomplishments that society considers acceptable or even praiseworthy.

psychosexual stages: A series of stages through which the sexual instinct develops; each stage is defined by an erogenous zone that becomes the centre of new pleasures and conflicts.

fixation: Arrested development at a psychosexual stage occurring because of excessive gratification or frustration at that stage.

oral stage: The first of Freud's psychosexual stages (birth to 12 or 18 months), in which sensual pleasure is derived mainly through stimulation of the mouth (e.g., sucking, biting, chewing).

anal stage: Freud's second psychosexual stage (12 or 18 months to 3 years), in which the child derives sensual pleasure mainly from expelling and withholding feces.

©Tom Prettyman/PhotoEdit Inc.

The Phallic Stage (Ages Three to Five or Six)

What is the Oedipus complex?

During the **phallic stage**, children learn that they can get pleasure by touching their genitals, and masturbation is common. They become aware of the anatomical differences between males and females.

The conflict that develops at this stage is a sexual desire for the parent of the opposite sex and a hostility toward the same-sex parent. **[LO 11.4]** For boys, Freud (1925/1963a) called this the **Oedipus complex** (after the central character in the Greek tragedy *Oedipus Rex*, by Sophocles). "Boys concentrate their sexual wishes upon their mother and develop hostile impulses against their father as being a rival," he wrote (Freud, 1925/1963a, p. 61). But the young boy eventually develops castration anxiety—an intense fear that his father might retaliate and harm him by cutting off his penis (Freud, 1933/1965). This fear becomes so intense, Freud believed, that the boy usually resolves the Oedipus complex by identifying with his father and repressing his sexual feelings for his mother. With identification, the child takes on his father's behaviours, mannerisms, and superego standards. In this way the superego develops (Freud, 1930/1962).

Girls experience a similar conflict, often referred to as the *Electra complex*, although Freud did not use that term. Freud (1933/1965) contended that when young girls discover that they have no penis, they develop "penis envy" and turn to their father because he has the desired organ. They feel sexual desires for him and develop a jealous rivalry with their mother. But eventually girls, too, experience anxiety as a result of their hostile feelings. They repress their sexual feelings toward the father and identify with the mother, and this leads to the formation of their superego (Freud, 1930/1962).

According to Freud, failure to resolve these conflicts can have serious consequences for both boys and girls. Freud thought that tremendous guilt and anxiety could be carried over into adulthood and cause many negative outcomes, especially sexual problems such as high promiscuity or, by contrast, extreme concerns about sexuality resulting in chastity or in great difficulty relating to members of the opposite sex. Freud also believed that an unresolved phallic stage could lead to homosexuality.

The Latency Period (Age Five or Six to Puberty)

The **latency period** is one of relative calm. The sex instinct is repressed and temporarily sublimated in school and play activities, hobbies, and sports.

The Genital Stage (from Puberty On)

In the **genital stage**, for the vast majority of people, the focus of sexual energy gradually shifts to the opposite sex. This culminates in heterosexual love and the attainment of full adult sexuality. Freud believed that the few who reach the genital stage without having fixations at earlier stages can achieve the state of psychological health that he equated with the ability to love and work.

Table 11.1 provides a summary of the psychosexual stages of development.

TABLE 11.1 Freud's Psychosexual Stages of Development

In Freud's view, the most important factor influencing personality is the sex instinct, which develops through a series of psychosexual stages. Each stage is centred on a particular erogenous zone. Certain adult personality traits can result from a failure to resolve problems or conflicts at one of the psychosexual stages.

Stage	Oral	Anal	Phallic	Latency	Genital
	Birth to 12–18 months	12–18 months to 3 years	3 to 5–6 years	5–6 years to puberty	Puberty onward
Erogenous zone	Mouth	Anus	Genitals	None	Genitals
Conflicts/experiences	Weaning; oral gratification from sucking, eating, biting	Toilet training; gratification from expelling and withholding feces	Oedipal conflict; sexual curiosity; masturbation	Period of sexual calm; interest in school, hobbies, play, sports, and same-sex friends	Revival of sexual interests; establishment of mature sexual relationships
Adult traits associated with problems at this stage	Excessive optimism, gullibility, dependency; or pessimism, passivity, hostility, sarcasm, aggression	Excessive cleanliness, orderliness, stinginess; or messiness, rebelliousness, destructiveness	Flirtatiousness, vanity, promiscuity; or pride, chastity		

FREUD'S EXPLANATION OF PERSONALITY

According to Freud, what are the two primary sources of influence on the personality?

Freud suggested that personality is almost completely formed by age five or six, when the Oedipal conflict is resolved and the superego is formed. He believed that there are two primary influences on personality: (1) the traits that develop because of fixations at any of the psychosexual stages and (2) the relative strengths of the id, the ego, and the superego. **[LO 11.5]** In psychologically healthy people, there is a balance among the three components.

EVALUATING FREUD'S CONTRIBUTION

Freud's contribution has influenced an enormous body of research across many areas of psychology, and he remains one of the most influential figures of the twentieth century (Westen, 1998). Freud's theory is so comprehensive (he wrote more than 24 volumes) that its elements must be evaluated separately. His belief that women are inferior to men sexually, morally, and intellectually and that they suffer penis envy seems ridiculous today. Moreover, research contradicts Freud's notion that personality is almost completely formed by age five or six. However, we are indebted to him for introducing the idea that unconscious forces may motivate behaviour, for making people more aware of the importance of sexuality in their lives, and for emphasizing the influence of early childhood experiences on later development. But when we consider Freud's vision of the unconscious, it is now clear that the reality is not exactly what Freud had envisioned. Rather, unconscious mental activity is now viewed as information processing that often precedes conscious thought and takes place below the level of awareness (Bargh & Morsella, 2008).

Other aspects of Freud's theory have also been valuable. Freud's concept of defence mechanisms has been shown to provide a useful way of categorizing the cognitive strategies people use to manage stress (Diehl, Chui, Hay, Lumley, Grühn, & Labouvie-Vief, 2014). Psychoanalytic theory continues to be used in explanations of psychological disorders (Lingiardi, McWilliams, Bornstein, Gazzillo, & Gordon, 2015). Moreover, today's psychodynamic therapies are direct descendants of Freud's techniques (Borden, 2009).

When tests of Freud's hypotheses are available, the results show a mixed pattern. For instance, his suggestion that catharsis, the release of pent-up emotions, is good for one's psychological health has been refuted by studies showing that expressing negative emotions such as anger actually intensifies such feelings (Farber, Khurgin-Bott, & Feldman, 2009). In contrast, his claim that childhood trauma leads to the development of psychological disorders in adulthood has received partial support. While much research has shown that childhood sexual victimization is likely to result in the development of psychological disorders, other studies suggest that victims of sexual abuse display a greater degree of resilience.

Critics of Freud's theory argue that it interprets behaviour after the fact (Grünbaum, 2006), although some even go as far as to say that the entire theory can neither be supported scientifically nor justified therapeutically (Crews, 1996; Erwin, 1996). How, for instance, can we ever test the idea that little

Sigmund Freud (1856–1939) with his daughter Anna.

boys are in love with their mothers and want to get rid of their fathers? How can we verify or falsify the idea that one component of personality is motivated entirely by the pursuit of pleasure? Chiefly because of the difficulty involved in finding scientific answers to such questions, there are very few strict Freudians among today's psychologists.

phallic stage: The third of Freud's psychosexual stages (ages three to five or six), during which sensual pleasure is derived mainly through touching the genitals; the stage when the Oedipus complex arises.

Oedipus complex (EE-duh-pus): Occurring in the phallic stage, a conflict in which the child is sexually attracted to the opposite-sex parent and feels hostility toward the same-sex parent.

latency period: The period following Freud's phallic stage (age five or six to puberty), in which the sex instinct is largely repressed and temporarily sublimated in school, sports, and play activities.

genital stage: The last of Freud's psychosexual stages (from puberty on), in which for most people the focus of sexual energy gradually shifts to the opposite sex, culminating in the attainment of full adult sexuality.

REMEMBER IT

Sigmund Freud and Psychoanalysis

1. The part of the personality that would make you want to eat, drink, and be merry is your
   a. id.
   b. ego.
   c. superego.
   d. unconscious.

2. Match the example with the corresponding defence mechanism.
   _____ 1) sublimation
   _____ 2) repression
   _____ 3) displacement
   _____ 4) rationalization
        a. forgetting a traumatic childhood experience
        b. supplying a logical reason for arriving late
        c. creating a work of art
        d. venting anger on a friend or spouse after getting a speeding ticket from a police officer

3. Excessive concern with cleanliness and order could indicate a fixation at the _____ stage.
   a. oral
   b. anal
   c. phallic
   d. genital

4. According to Freud, which of the following represents a primary source of influence on our personality?
   a. our heredity
   b. life experiences after we begin school
   c. the relative strengths of our id, ego, and superego
   d. the problems we experience during adolescence

Answers: 1. a   2. (1) c (2) a (3) d (4) b   3. b   4. c

MODULE 11B THE NEO-FREUDIANS

LO 11.6 Describe the three components of personality according to Jung.

LO 11.7 Explain archetypes in relation to the collective unconscious.

LO 11.8 Compare and contrast Adler's theory of personality with Freud's.

LO 11.9 Describe an inferiority complex.

LO 11.10 Identify factors that Horney believed help us to be psychologically healthy.

Is it possible to construct a theory of personality that builds on the strengths of Freud's approach and avoids its weaknesses? Several personality theorists, referred to as *neo-Freudians*, have attempted to do so. They modified some aspects of the theory and presented their own original ideas about personality. We will discuss Carl Jung (analytical psychology), Alfred Adler (individual psychology), and Karen Horney (feminine psychology).

CARL GUSTAV JUNG: DELVING INTO THE COLLECTIVE UNCONSCIOUS

Carl Gustav Jung (1875–1961), unlike Freud, did not consider the sexual instinct to be the main factor in personality, nor did he believe that the personality is almost completely formed in early childhood. He maintained that middle age is an important period for personality development (Jung, 1933).

Jung's View of the Personality: A Different View of the Unconscious

According to Jung, what are the three components of personality?

Jung conceived of the personality as consisting of three parts, as shown in Figure 11.2: the ego, the personal unconscious, and the collective unconscious. **[LO 11.6]** He saw the ego as the conscious component of personality, which carries out our

Carl Jung

©Bettmann/Corbis

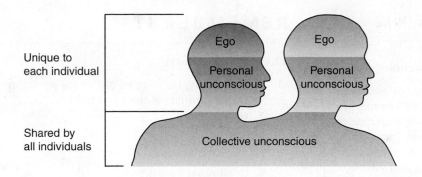

FIGURE 11.2
Jung's Conception of Personality
Like Freud, Carl Jung saw three components in personality. The ego and the personal unconscious are unique to each individual. The collective unconscious is shared by all people and accounts for the similarity of myths and beliefs in diverse cultures.

Structure	Characteristics
Ego	The conscious component of personality; carries out normal daily activities.
Personal unconscious	The component containing all the individual's memories, thoughts, and feelings that are accessible to consciousness, and all repressed memories, wishes, and impulses; similar to a combination of Freud's preconscious and unconscious.
Collective unconscious	The most inaccessible layer of the unconscious, shared by all people; contains the universal experiences of humankind throughout evolution, as well as the archetypes.

normal daily activities. Like Freud, he believed the ego to be secondary in importance to the unconscious.

The **personal unconscious** develops as a result of our own individual experience and is therefore unique to each individual. It contains all the experiences, thoughts, and perceptions accessible to the conscious, as well as repressed memories, wishes, and impulses. The personal unconscious resembles a combination of Freud's preconscious and unconscious.

The **collective unconscious** is the deepest and most inaccessible layer of the unconscious. Jung thought that the universal experiences of humankind throughout evolution are transmitted to each individual through the collective unconscious. This is how he accounted for the similarity of certain myths, dreams, symbols, and religious beliefs in cultures widely separated by distance and time.

The collective unconscious contains what Jung called *archetypes*. **[LO 11.7]** An **archetype** is an inherited tendency to respond to universal human situations in particular ways. Jung would say that the tendencies of people to believe in a god, a devil, evil spirits, and heroes and to have a fear of the dark all result from inherited archetypes that reflect the shared experience of humankind.

ALFRED ADLER: OVERCOMING INFERIORITY

What did Adler consider to be the driving force of the personality?

Alfred Adler (1870–1937) disagreed with most of Freud's basic beliefs; on many points his views were the exact opposite. **[LO 11.8]** Adler emphasized the unity of the personality rather than the separate warring components of id, ego, and superego. He believed that our behaviour is motivated more by the conscious than by the unconscious and that we are influenced more by future goals than by early childhood experiences.

Unlike Freud, who believed that sex and pleasure-seeking are our primary motives, Adler (1927, 1956) maintained that we are driven by the need to compensate for inferiority and to strive for superiority or significance. **[LO 11.8]** He believed that feelings of weakness and inferiority are an inevitable experience in every child's early life. Adler himself had felt a particularly keen sense of inferiority as a child because he was small, sickly, and unable to walk until he was four.

According to Adler (1956), at an early age people develop a "style of life"—a unique way in which the child and later the adult will go about the struggle to achieve superiority. Sometimes inferiority feelings are so strong that they prevent personal development. Adler originated a term to describe this condition—the *inferiority complex* (Dreikurs, 1953). **[LO 11.9]** Adler (1964) also maintained that birth order influences personality, making first-born children more likely than their siblings to be high achievers.

personal unconscious: In Jung's theory, the layer of the unconscious containing all of the experiences, thoughts, and perceptions that are accessible to the conscious, as well as repressed memories, wishes, and impulses.

collective unconscious: In Jung's theory, the most inaccessible layer of the unconscious, which contains the universal experiences of humankind transmitted to each individual.

archetype (AR-keh-type): Existing in the collective unconscious, an inherited tendency to respond in particular ways to universal human situations.

KAREN HORNEY: CHAMPION OF FEMININE PSYCHOLOGY

Why is Horney considered a pioneer in psychology?

The work of Karen Horney (1885–1952) centred on two main themes—the neurotic personality (1937, 1945, 1950) and feminine psychology (1967). She considered herself a disciple of Freud, accepting his emphasis on unconscious motivation and the basic tools of psychoanalysis. However, she did not accept his division of personality into id, ego, and superego, and she flatly rejected his psychosexual stages and the concepts of the Oedipus complex and penis envy. Furthermore, she thought Freud overemphasized the role of the sexual instinct and neglected cultural and environmental influences on personality. While she did stress the importance of early childhood experiences (Horney, 1939), she believed that personality could continue to develop and change throughout life. She argued forcefully against Freud's notion that women had penis envy. Instead, Horney insisted that what women really want are the same opportunities, rights, and privileges that society grants to men.

Horney believed that to be psychologically healthy, we all need safety and satisfaction. **[LO 11.10]** But these needs can be frustrated in early childhood by parents who are indifferent, unaffectionate, rejecting, or hostile. Such early experiences may cause a child to develop *basic anxiety* (Horney, 1945). To minimize this basic anxiety and to satisfy the need for safety, children develop coping strategies that form their basic attitude toward life—including moving *toward* people, moving *against* people, or moving *away from* people. If we are normal, we move in all three ways as different situations demand. But if we are neurotic, we are restricted to only one way to reduce anxiety, and we use it excessively and inappropriately.

Horney (1950) believed that the idealized self brings with it the "tyranny of the should"—unrealistic demands for personal

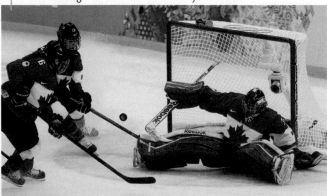

©U T San Diego/ZUMAPRESS.com/Alamy Live News

Karen Horney insisted that, rather than envying the penis, as Freud believed, women really want the same opportunities and privileges as men—to play sports at the Olympic and professional levels, for example.

REMEMBER IT

The Neo-Freudians

1. In Jung's theory, the inherited part of the personality that stores the experiences of humankind is the _____
   a. ego.
   b. collective conscious.
   c. personal unconscious.
   d. collective unconscious.

2. Which personality theorist believed that our basic drive is to overcome and compensate for inferiority feelings and strive for superiority and significance?
   a. Sigmund Freud
   b. Carl Jung
   c. Alfred Adler
   d. Karen Horney

3. Horney traced the origin of psychological maladjustment to
   a. the inferiority feelings of childhood.
   b. basic anxiety resulting from the parents' failure to satisfy the child's needs for safety and satisfaction.
   c. excessive frustration or overindulgence of the child at early stages of development.
   d. the failure to balance opposing forces in the personality.

Answers: 1. d 2. c 3. b

perfection that "no human being could fulfill" (p. 66). Her influence may be seen in modern cognitive-behavioural therapies, especially the rational-emotive therapy of Albert Ellis, which we explore in Chapter 14.

MODULE 11C TRAIT THEORIES

LO 11.11 Describe traits and trait theories of personality.
LO 11.12 Identify the three types of individual traits according to Allport.
LO 11.13 Describe surface and source traits, according to Cattell.
LO 11.14 Identify the three most important dimensions of personality according to Eysenck.
LO 11.15 Identify the five factors of the five-factor theory of personality.

What are trait theories of personality?

How would you describe yourself—cheerful, moody, talkative, quiet, shy, friendly, outgoing? When you describe your own personality or that of someone else, you probably list several relatively stable and consistent personal characteristics called **traits**. **Trait theories** are attempts to explain personality and differences between people in terms of personal characteristics that are stable across situations. **[LO 11.11]**

GORDON ALLPORT: PERSONALITY TRAITS IN THE BRAIN

How did Allport differentiate between cardinal and central traits?

Gordon Allport (1897–1967) asserted that personality traits are real entities, physically located somewhere in the brain (Allport & Odbert, 1936). Each of us inherits a unique set of raw materials for given traits, which are then shaped by our experiences. Traits describe how we respond to the environment and the consistency of that response. If we are shy, we respond to strangers differently than if we are friendly; if we are self-confident, we approach tasks differently than if we feel inferior.

Allport (1961) identified two main categories of traits: common and individual. *Common traits* are those traits we share or hold in common with most others in our own culture. Far more important to Allport were three types of individual traits: cardinal, central, and secondary traits.

A **cardinal trait** is "so pervasive and so outstanding in a life that . . . almost every act seems traceable to its influence" (Allport, 1961, p. 365). [LO 11.12] It is so strong a part of a person's personality that he or she may become identified with or known for that trait. **Central traits** are those we would "mention in writing a careful letter of recommendation" (Allport, 1961). [LO 11.12] Do the *Try It* exercise to learn more about central traits.

We also possess numerous *secondary traits*, but these are less obvious, less consistent, and not as critical as the cardinal and central traits in defining our personality. [LO 11.12] Secondary traits are such things as food preferences, favourite music, and specific attitudes. We have many more secondary traits than cardinal or central traits.

RAYMOND CATTELL'S 16 PERSONALITY FACTORS

How did Cattell differentiate between surface and source traits?

Raymond Cattell (1905–1998) considered personality to be a pattern of traits providing the key to understanding and predicting a person's behaviour (Cattell, 1950). He identified two types: surface traits and source traits.

If you were asked to describe your best friend, you might list such traits as kind, honest, helpful, generous, and so on. These observable qualities of personality Cattell called **surface traits**. [LO 11.13] (Allport called these qualities *central traits*.) Using observations and questionnaires, Cattell studied thousands of people; he found certain clusters of surface traits that appeared together time after time. He thought these were evidence of deeper, more general personality factors. Using a statistical technique called *factor analysis*, Cattell tried to identify these factors, which he called *source traits*.

Source traits make up the most basic personality structure and, according to Cattell, cause behaviour. [LO 11.13] We all possess the same source traits; however, we do not all possess them in the same degree. Intelligence is a source trait, and every person has a certain amount of it, but obviously not exactly the same amount or the same kind.

TRY IT

Identifying Central Traits

Which adjectives in this list best describe you? Which characterize your mother or your father? In Allport's terms, you are describing her or his *central traits*.

decisive	funny	intelligent
disorganized	shy	fearful
jealous	controlled	responsible
rigid	outgoing	inhibited
religious	arrogant	loyal
competitive	liberal	friendly
compulsive	quiet	generous
sloppy	laid-back	rebellious
calm	good-natured	nervous
serious	humble	lazy
industrious	deceptive	cooperative
reckless	sad	honest
happy	selfish	organized

Cattell found 23 source traits in normal individuals, 16 of which he studied in great detail. Cattell's 16 Personality Factor Questionnaire, commonly called the *16 PF*, yields a personality profile (Cattell, Eber, & Tatsuoka, 1977). This test continues to be used in research, personality assessment, and career counselling.

You can chart your own source traits in the *Try It*.

traits: Stable and consistent personal characteristics that are used to describe or explain personality.

trait theories: Theories that attempt to explain personality and differences between people in terms of personal characteristics.

cardinal trait: Allport's name for a personal quality that is so strong a part of a person's personality that he or she may become identified with that trait.

central traits: Allport's name for the type of trait you would mention in writing a letter of recommendation.

surface traits: Cattell's name for observable qualities of personality, such as those used to describe a friend.

source traits: Cattell's name for the traits that underlie the surface traits, make up the most basic personality structure, and cause behaviour.

TRY IT

Charting a Personality Profile

This hypothetical personality profile is based on Cattell's 16 Personality Factor Questionnaire. Using it as a model, circle the point along each of the 16 dimensions of bipolar traits that best describes your personality.

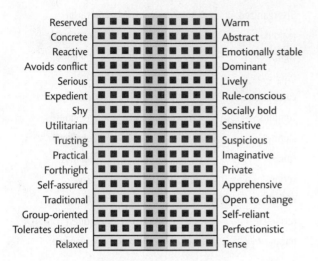

Reserved	Warm
Concrete	Abstract
Reactive	Emotionally stable
Avoids conflict	Dominant
Serious	Lively
Expedient	Rule-conscious
Shy	Socially bold
Utilitarian	Sensitive
Trusting	Suspicious
Practical	Imaginative
Forthright	Private
Self-assured	Apprehensive
Traditional	Open to change
Group-oriented	Self-reliant
Tolerates disorder	Perfectionistic
Relaxed	Tense

HANS EYSENCK: STRESSING THREE FACTORS

What did Eysenck consider to be the two most important dimensions of personality?

British psychologist Hans Eysenck (1916–1997) believed that personality is largely determined by genes, and that environmental influences are slight at best (Eysenck, 1990). Eysenck proposed that three higher-order factors or dimensions are needed to capture the essence of personality: psychotisicm, **extraversion** (versus **introversion**), and neuroticism (versus emotional stability). **[LO 11.14]** Eysenck depicted each of these as continuums. Psychoticism represents an individual's link to reality. At one extreme are "psychotics," those who live in a world of hallucinations and delusions, and at the other are people whose thought processes are so rigidly tied to the material world that they lack creativity. Extraverts are sociable, outgoing, and active, whereas introverts are withdrawn, quiet, and introspective. Emotionally stable people are calm, even-tempered, and often easygoing, whereas emotionally unstable (neurotic) people are anxious, excitable, and easily distressed.

Eysenck proposed that all three of the PEN dimensions are rooted in neurological functioning. As a result, his theory has served as a useful framework for neurological studies of personality. In addition, Eysenck developed a series of personality tests that is still widely used by researchers and clinicians today (Littlefield, Sher, & Wood, 2009).

THE FIVE-FACTOR MODEL OF PERSONALITY: THE BIG FIVE

What are the five personality dimensions in the five-factor model as described by McCrae and Costa?

The most talked-about trait theory today is the **five-factor model**, the view that personality can be explained in terms of five broad dimensions, each of which is composed of a cluster of personality traits (R. McCrae & Costa, 2008). The assertion that five factors are needed to account for personality dates back to the early 1960s (e.g., W. Norman, 1963). However, the model has become most closely associated with the research of Robert McCrae and Paul Costa (Costa & McCrae, 1985). Another important five-factor model, known as the *Big Five*, proposed by psychologist Lewis Goldberg (1993), varies somewhat from that of McCrae and Costa in its approach to measuring the factors. However, research based on both models supports the hypothesis that personality can be usefully described in terms of five factors and that the factors predict important outcomes such as academic and occupational success (B. W. Roberts, Kuncel, Shiner, Caspi, & Goldberg, 2007). You will notice that the names of these factors can be easily remembered by using the acronym OCEAN. **[LO 11.15]**

- *Openness to experience.* Are you eager to try new things and consider new ideas? If so, then you might get a high score on a test that measures openness. This dimension contrasts individuals who seek out varied experiences and who are imaginative, intellectually curious, and broad-minded with those whose interests are narrower. Openness may be a critical factor in learning. Research suggests that the higher a person is in openness, the more general knowledge he or she possesses (Furnham, Swami, Arteche, & Chamorro-Premuzic, 2008). Openness may also be an important factor in adapting to new situations.

- *Conscientiousness.* Do you always fold your laundry before putting it away? This factor differentiates individuals who are dependable, organized, reliable, responsible, thorough, hard-working, and persevering from those who are undependable, disorganized, impulsive, unreliable, irresponsible, careless, negligent, and lazy. Conscientiousness has been shown to predict both academic and job performance (Chamorro-Premuzic & Furnham, 2014).

- *Extraversion.* If you have a free evening, would you rather go to a party or stay home and read a book or watch a movie? Individuals who are high in extraversion prefer being around people. This dimension contrasts such traits as sociable, outgoing, talkative, assertive, persuasive, decisive, and active with more introverted traits such as withdrawn, quiet, passive, retiring, and reserved.

- *Agreeableness.* Do people describe you as easygoing? Individuals who are high in agreeableness are often characterized in this way. A person high on agreeableness would be a pleasant person, good-natured, warm, sympathetic, and cooperative; whereas one low on agreeableness would tend to be unfriendly, unpleasant, aggressive, argumentative, cold, and even hostile. People who are high in agreeableness also seem to be more likely to succumb to peer influence with regard to decisions about risky behaviour, such as binge drinking (van Schoor, Bott, & Engels, 2008).

- *Neuroticism.* If you see an 8-ounce glass that contains 4 ounces of water, is it half empty or half full? People who are high in neuroticism tend to be pessimistic and always see the negative aspects of situations—the "half-empty" interpretation of life. At the same time, people high in neuroticism are prone to emotional instability. They tend to experience negative emotions and to be moody, irritable, nervous, and prone to worry. Neuroticism differentiates people who are anxious, excitable, and easily distressed from those who are emotionally stable and thus calm, even-tempered, easygoing, and relaxed. In real life, individuals who are high in neuroticism have difficulty maintaining social relationships and are at higher risk than others for a variety of psychological disorders (Hur, 2009; Kurdek, 2009).

Researchers from many different traditions have found five factors when they have subjected self-ratings, observer ratings, and peer ratings to analysis. Most studies that examine the Big Five personality factors have used a personality measure called the NEO Personality Inventory (NEO-PI), which was originally developed by Paul Costa and Robert McCrae (1985, 1992a, 1992b, 1997) and has been recently revised (NEO-PI-R). Support for the five factors persists regardless of the language of the study, the participants' age groups or sex, or the country in which the research was conducted.

There has been a lot of recent research support for the five factors model, and the Big Five factors remain helpful in predicting general trends of behaviour in a wide variety of situations. Genetic research also indicates that heredity makes substantial contributions to individual differences in the five personality factors (Caspi, 2000; A. Johnson, Vernon, Harris, & Jang, 2004; Lonsdorf et al., 2009).

EVALUATING THE TRAIT PERSPECTIVE

Do we possess stable and enduring traits that predictably guide the way we will act across time and changing situations? Critics of trait theories say no; they maintain that the consistency of our behaviour across situations is very low and not predictable on the basis of personality traits. However, after several decades of study, the weight of evidence supports the view that there are internal traits that strongly influence behaviour across situations (B. W. Roberts & DelVechio, 2000) or even across cultures (K. Lee et al., 2005; R. R. McCrae & Terracciano, 2005). However, studies have also shown that there are subtle age-related changes in the five factors across the years of adulthood and that the patterns of change differ depending on which factor is considered (Terracciano, McCrae, & Costa, 2010). Studies that follow individuals into old age show that openness, extraversion, and neuroticism decline as adults age. Agreeableness increases, as does conscientiousness up until around age 70, when it begins to show decline. Perhaps not surprisingly, then, the recognition

REMEMBER IT

Trait Theories

1. According to Allport, the kind of trait that is used in a letter of recommendation is a _____; the kind of trait that is a defining characteristic of one's personality is a _____ .
   a. common trait; secondary trait
   d. cardinal trait; common trait
   c. cardinal trait; central trait
   d. central trait; cardinal trait

2. Which of the following statements is not true of source traits, according to Cattell?
   a. Differences in personality can be explained primarily in terms of the degree to which people possess the same source traits.
   b. Source traits can be viewed as the cause of behaviour.
   c. The differences between people are explained by the number of source traits they possess.
   d. Source traits can be used to compare one person with another.

3. We can best understand personality by assessing people on two major dimensions: extraversion and neuroticism. This view is championed by:
   a. Hans Eysenck.
   b. Gordon Allport.
   c. Raymond Cattell.
   d. Carl Jung.

4. According to a growing number of trait theorists, there are _____ major dimensions of personality.
   a. 3
   b. 5
   c. 7
   d. 16

Answers: 1. d 2. c 3. a 4. b

that personality is a complex interaction of both enduring traits and social context has recently fostered the development of a more integrated theory of personality that tries to merge both of these aspects of our lives (McAdams & Pals, 2006).

extraversion: The tendency to be outgoing, adaptable, and sociable.

introversion: The tendency to focus inward.

five-factor model: A trait theory that attempts to explain personality using five broad dimensions, each of which is composed of a constellation of personality traits.

MODULE (11D) LEARNING THEORIES AND PERSONALITY

LO 11.16 Explain the origins of abnormal behaviour from Skinner's behaviourist perspective.

LO 11.17 Compare and contrast the behaviourist and social-cognitive perspectives.

LO 11.18 Identify the components of reciprocal determinism and how they interact.

LO 11.19 Describe self-efficacy.

LO 11.20 Describe and contrast internal locus of control and external locus of control.

According to the learning perspective, personality consists of the learned tendencies that have been acquired over a lifetime.

THE BEHAVIOURIST VIEW OF B. F. SKINNER

How did Skinner account for what most people refer to as personality?

B. F. Skinner (1904–1990) and other behaviourists have an interesting view of personality: They deny that there is any such thing. What we call "personality," they believe, is nothing more or less than a collection of learned behaviours or habits that have been reinforced in the past. Skinner denied that a personality or self initiates and directs behaviour. The causes of behaviour, he stated, lie outside the person, and they are based on past and present rewards and punishments. Thus, Skinner did not use the term *personality*. He simply described the variables in the environment that shape an individual's observable behaviour. Healthy experiences in a healthy environment make a healthy person.

But what about the psychologically unhealthy individual? Where does abnormal behaviour originate? Skinner (1953) believed that psychologically unhealthy people have been reinforced by the environment for behaving abnormally. **[LO 11.16]** For example, an overly dependent person may have been punished by his parents for asserting his independence and reinforced for dependency. To change an individual's behaviour, then, we must restructure the environment so that it will reinforce normal rather than abnormal behaviour.

THE SOCIAL-COGNITIVE THEORISTS: EXPANDING THE BEHAVIOURIST VIEW

There is no doubt that some of our behaviours can be traced to classical and operant conditioning; but can all of personality, or even all of learning, be explained in this way? Not according to social-cognitive theorists, who consider both the environment *and* personal/cognitive factors in their attempts to understand human personality and behaviour. **[LO 11.17]** Personal/cognitive factors include personal dispositions, feelings, expectancies, perceptions, and cognitions, such as thoughts, beliefs, and attitudes.

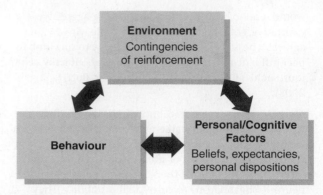

FIGURE 11.3

Albert Bandura's Reciprocal Determinism

Albert Bandura takes a social-cognitive view of personality. He suggests that three components—our environment, our behaviour, and personal/cognitive factors such as our beliefs, expectancies, and personal dispositions—play reciprocal roles in determining personality and behaviour.

Albert Bandura's Views on Personality

What are the components that make up Bandura's concept of reciprocal determinism, and how do they interact?

The chief advocate of the social-cognitive theory is Albert Bandura (1925–), who maintains that personal/cognitive factors, our behaviour, and the external environment all influence each other and are influenced by each other (Bandura, 1999). This mutual relationship he calls **reciprocal determinism**. **[LO 11.18]** Figure 11.3 provides a diagram of Bandura's model of reciprocal determinism.

Consider how Bandura's concept of reciprocal determinism might work in the following situation: A waiter who normally works in a section of a restaurant where good tippers habitually sit is reassigned to tables in an area where tips are normally poor. This new environment influences the waiter's beliefs and expectancies (personal/cognitive factors). Now, because he believes that good service will not be appropriately rewarded, his behaviour changes. He is inattentive, is not very pleasant, and provides poor service. In this way, the new environment alters the waiter's beliefs, which then affect his behaviour; subsequently, this affects the customers—their thinking, feelings, and attitudes. And these, in turn, influence their behaviour. Not surprisingly, these customers *do* tip poorly. As this example illustrates, reciprocal determinism does a good job of explaining the mutual influences that occur among personal, environmental, and behavioural variables. Each of the three influences the other two. Consequently, the three domains are inseparable components of a dynamic system of personality that adapts to whatever situational demands an individual faces.

One of the cognitive factors Bandura (1999, 2001) considers especially important is self-efficacy. **Self-efficacy** is the perception people hold of their ability to perform competently and successfully in whatever they attempt. **[LO 11.19]** People high in self-efficacy will approach new situations confidently and will persist in their efforts because they believe success is likely. People low in self-efficacy, on the other hand, will expect failure and avoid challenges.

Locus of Control

What is meant by the terms *internal* and *external locus of control*?

Julian Rotter (1916–2014) proposes another concept, **locus of control**, which provides additional insight into why people behave as they do (Rotter, 1966, 1971, 1990). Some people see themselves as primarily in control of their behaviour and its consequences. That is, they exhibit an *internal* locus of control. **[LO 11.20]** Others perceive that whatever happens to them is in the hands of fate, luck, or chance; they exhibit an *external* locus of control and may contend that it does not matter what they do because "whatever will be, will be." **[LO 11.20]** Rotter contends that people with an external locus of control are less likely to change their behaviour as a result of reinforcement, because they do not see reinforcers as being tied to their own actions. Students who have an external locus of control are more likely to procrastinate and, thus, are less likely to be academically successful (Janssen & Carton, 1999). Further, external locus of control is associated with lower levels of life satisfaction (Denny & Steiner, 2009).

Evaluating the Social-Cognitive Perspective

Studies indicate that self-efficacy and locus of control contribute to important outcomes independently from the five personality factors. For example, both locus of control and self-efficacy are correlated with the number of job offers a person receives after a round of interviews (Tay et al., 2006). Similarly, the five factors and locus of control make separate contributions to academic achievement (Hattrup, O'Connell, & Labrador, 2005). That is, a person who is high in conscientiousness is most likely to be a high achiever if she also has an internal locus of control.

As you can see, a model of personality that includes the five factors, self-efficacy, and locus of control provides us with a more comprehensive understanding of individual differences in personality than any of these variables does when considered alone. Moreover, Bandura's reciprocal determinism provides us with a useful explanation of how these variables and many others work together to produce the kind of behaviour and mental processes that we typically think of as being a function of personality.

The social-cognitive perspective cannot be criticized for lacking a strong research base. Yet some argue that it emphasizes the *situation* too strongly. They ask: What about *unconscious* motives or *internal* dispositions (traits) that we exhibit fairly consistently across many different situations? Other critics highlight the contribution of behavioural genetics in their criticisms of the social-cognitive perspective and point to the

accumulating evidence that heredity may explain 40 to 50 percent or more of the variation in personality characteristics (T. J. Bouchard, 1994).

REMEMBER IT

Learning Theories and Personality

1. Which of the following concepts does Skinner find useful in explaining behaviour?
   a. Behaviour is initiated by inner forces called *personality*.
   b. Behaviour is caused by forces outside the person and based upon past rewards and punishments.
   c. Behaviour is an interaction of inner forces and situational forces.
   d. Behaviour and personality are for the most part determined by our heredity.
2. Bandura's concept of reciprocal determinism refers to the mutual effects of
   a. our behaviour, personality, and thinking.
   b. our feelings, attitudes, and thoughts.
   c. our behaviour, personal/cognitive factors, and the environment.
   d. classical and operant conditioning and observational learning.
3. Which statement is not true of people low in self-efficacy?
   a. They persist in their efforts.
   b. They lack confidence.
   c. They expect failure.
   d. They avoid challenge.
4. Who proposed the concept of locus of control?
   a. B. F. Skinner
   b. Albert Bandura
   c. Hans Eysenck
   d. Julian Rotter

Answers: 1. b 2. c 3. a 4. d

reciprocal determinism: Bandura's concept that personal/cognitive factors, our behaviour, and the external environment all influence and are influenced by each other.

self-efficacy: A person's belief in his or her ability to perform competently in whatever is attempted.

locus of control: A concept used to explain how people account for what happens in their lives—people with an internal locus of control see themselves as primarily in control of their behaviour and its consequences; those with an external locus of control perceive what happens to be in the hands of fate, luck, or chance.

MODULE 11E HUMANISTIC PERSONALITY THEORIES

LO 11.21   Describe humanistic psychology.
LO 11.22   Identify the characteristics that self-actualizing people share.
LO 11.23   Explain the emergence of the self-concept according to Rogers.
LO 11.24   Describe conditions of worth and its role in our experience of stress and anxiety.

Abraham Maslow

©Bettmann/Corbis

Who were the two pioneers in humanistic psychology, and how did they view human nature?

In **humanistic psychology**, people are assumed to have a natural tendency toward growth and the realization of their fullest potential. Humanistic psychology seeks to give a more complete and positive picture of the human personality. **[LO 11.21]** Humanistic psychologists largely deny that there is a dark or evil side of human nature. They do not believe that people are shaped strictly by the environment or ruled by mysterious, unconscious forces. Rather, they see people as creative beings with an active, conscious free will who can chart their own course in life.

The pioneering humanistic psychologists were Abraham Maslow and Carl Rogers.

ABRAHAM MASLOW: THE SELF-ACTUALIZING PERSON

What is self-actualization, and how did Maslow study it?

For Abraham Maslow (1908–1970), motivational factors were at the root of personality (Maslow, 1970). As we saw in Chapter 9, Maslow constructed a hierarchy of needs, with physiological needs at the bottom and the need for self-actualization at the top. **Self-actualization** means developing to one's fullest potential. A healthy person is one who is always growing and becoming all that he or she can be.

humanistic psychology: The school of psychology that focuses on the uniqueness of human beings and their capacity for choice, growth, and psychological health.

self-actualization: Developing to one's fullest potential; the highest need on Maslow's hierarchy.

conditions of worth: Conditions upon which others' positive regard rests.

unconditional positive regard: A condition required of person-centred therapists, involving a caring for and acceptance of clients regardless of the client's feelings, thoughts, or behaviour.

behavioural genetics: The field of research that investigates the relative effects of heredity and environment on behaviour and ability.

Maslow maintained that if you want to know what makes a healthy personality, you must study people who are healthy. So he studied individuals he believed were using their talents and abilities to their fullest—in other words, individuals who exemplified self-actualization. Maslow studied historical figures and figures who made significant contributions during their lifetime to identify characteristics that self-actualizing people seem to share.

Maslow found self-actualizers to be accurate in perceiving reality—able to judge honestly and to spot quickly the fake and the dishonest. **[LO 11.22]** Self-actualizers are comfortable with life; they accept themselves and others, and nature as well, with good humour and tolerance. Most of them believe they have a mission to accomplish or the need to devote their life to some larger good. Self-actualizers tend not to depend on external authority or on other people; they are autonomous and independent. They feel a strong fellowship with humanity, and their relationships with others are characterized by deep and loving bonds. They have a good sense of humour, can laugh at themselves, and are not critical of others. Finally, self-actualizers often have *peak experiences*—experiences of harmony within and with the universe. Current researchers have modified Maslow's definition of self-actualization to include effective personal relationships, religious transformations, and spirituality as well as peak experiences (Dy-Liacco, Piedmont, Murray-Swank, Rodgerson, & Sherman, 2009; Hanley & Abell, 2002).

CARL ROGERS: THE FULLY FUNCTIONING PERSON

According to Rogers, why don't all people become fully functioning persons?

Carl Rogers (1902–1987) developed his theory of personality through insights gained from his patients in therapy sessions (C. R. Rogers, 1951, 1961). Rogers viewed human nature as basically good. If left to develop naturally, he thought, people would be happy and psychologically healthy.

According to Rogers, each of us lives in a private subjective reality, the *phenomenological field*. It is in this personal, subjective field, rather than in the objective, real, physical environment, that we act, think, and feel. In other words, the way we see it is the way it is—for us. Gradually, a part of the phenomenological field becomes differentiated as the self. The self-concept emerges as a result of repeated experiences involving such terms as *I*, *me*, and *mine*. **[LO 11.23]** With the emerging self comes the need for positive regard. We need such things as warmth, love, acceptance, sympathy, and respect from the people who are significant in our lives.

Usually our parents do not view us positively regardless of our behaviour. They set up **conditions of worth**—conditions on which their positive regard hinges. **[LO 11.24]** Conditions of worth force us to live and act according to someone else's values rather than our own. In our efforts to gain positive regard, we deny our true self by inhibiting some of our behaviour, denying and distorting some of our perceptions, and closing ourselves to parts of our experience. In so doing, we experience stress and anxiety, and our whole self-structure may be threatened.

For Rogers, a major goal of psychotherapy is to enable individuals to open themselves up to experiences and begin to live according to their own values rather than the values of others. He called his therapy *person-centred therapy*, preferring not to use the term *patient*. Rogers believed that the therapist must give the client **unconditional positive regard**—that is, the therapist must give positive regard no matter what the client says, does, has done, or is thinking of doing. Unconditional positive regard is designed to reduce threats, eliminate conditions of worth, and bring the person back in tune with his or her true self.

EVALUATING THE HUMANISTIC PERSPECTIVE

Humanism has become much more than a personality theory and an approach to therapy. Its influence has spread significantly as a social movement in the schools and in society in general. Some of its severest critics charge that an all-consuming personal quest for self-fulfillment can lead to a self-centred, self-serving, self-indulgent personality that lacks moral restraint or genuine concern for others (D. T. Campbell & Sprecht, 1985; M. A. Wallach & Wallach, 1983). And a review of research evidence regarding Maslow's hierarchy suggests that, while the initial concept was useful, there now seems to be little agreement about the identification of basic human needs and how they are ordered (Huitt, 2007).

Humanistic psychologists do not accept such criticisms as valid. By and large, they trust in the inherent goodness of human nature, and their perspective on personality is consistent with that trust. But how do humanists explain the evil we see around us—assaults, murder, rape? Where does this originate? Rogers replied, "I do not find that this evil is inherent in human nature. . . . So my experience leads me to believe that it is cultural influences which are the major factor in our evil behaviors" (C. R. Rogers, 1981, p. 16).

Though the humanists have been criticized for being unscientific and having an overly positive view of the human psyche, they have inspired the study of the positive qualities—altruism, cooperation, love, and acceptance of self and others.

MODULE 11F PERSONALITY: IS IT IN THE GENES?

LO 11.25 Describe behavioural genetics.
LO 11.26 Describe the findings of twin studies related to the heritability of personality traits.
LO 11.27 Describe and contrast the influence of the shared environment and the non-shared environment on personality traits.

What has research in behavioural genetics revealed about the influence of the genes and the environment on personality?

Behavioural genetics is a field of research that investigates the relative effects of heredity and environment on behaviour and ability (Plomin, DeFries, Knopik, & Neiderhiser, 2013). **[LO 11.25]**

THE TWIN STUDY METHOD: STUDYING IDENTICAL AND FRATERNAL TWINS

One approach used in behavioural genetics is the twin study method, in which identical (monozygotic, or MZ) and fraternal (dizygotic, or DZ) twins are studied to determine similarities and differences. Ideal subjects are identical twins separated at birth and reared apart. When these twins have strikingly similar traits, it is assumed that heredity has been a major contributor. When twins differ on a given trait, the influence of the environment is thought to be greater.

Tellegen and colleagues (1988) found that identical twins raised together or apart were quite similar on several personality factors. The term **heritability** refers to the degree to which a characteristic is estimated to be influenced by heredity. Altruism and aggressiveness—traits one would expect to be strongly influenced by parental upbringing—also appear to be more strongly influenced by heredity (Brandt & Wetherell, 2012). **[LO 11.26]** When considered as a whole, hundreds of twin studies and research examining the impact of genetics on personality reveal a strong genetic influence on most aspects of personality, from social attitudes to moral perspectives to one's view of one's environment, to relationships and sense of well-being (T. J. Bouchard & McGue, 2003). The genetic influences we have been discussing involve many genes, each with small effects (Plomin, DeFries, Knopk, & Neiderhiser, 2013). Research evidence suggests that heredity may explain 40 to 50 percent or more of the variation in personality characteristics (T. J. Bouchard, 1994, 1997; Lonsdorf et al., 2009). However, new studies point to variations across the lifespan such that environmental effects increase from childhood to adulthood, whereas the influence of heredity stabilizes over time (Briley & Tucker-Drob, 2014). At this point, genetic research clearly demonstrates that both nature and nurture contribute to human development, including individual differences in personality. Behavioural geneticists further differentiate between two types of environmental influences. First, some personality traits may result from the *shared environment*: all those influences that tend to make family members similar. **[LO 11.27]** The effects of shared environment tend to be modest, however (T. J. Bouchard, 1994). By far the most important environmental influences involve the *non-shared environment* among children in the same family (Turkheimer & Waldron, 2000). **[LO 11.27]** Non-shared influences occur because individual children tend to elicit different responses from their parents, owing to their temperament, gender, or birth order, to give a few examples (Plomin, 1989).

REMEMBER IT

Research Methods

1. Many behavioural geneticists believe that personality may be as much as _____ inherited.
   a. 10 to 20 percent
   b. 25 to 35 percent
   c. 40 to 50 percent
   d. 65 to 75 percent

2. Behavioural geneticists have found that the _____ environment has a greater effect on personality than the _____ environment.

Answers: 1. c 2. non-shared, shared

Although heredity influences most psychological traits, this influence does not lessen the value or reduce the importance of environmental factors such as social influences, parenting, and education.

MODULE **11G** PERSONALITY ASSESSMENT

LO 11.28 Identify the three major methods used in personality assessment.

LO 11.29 Describe the use of observation, interviews, and rating scales in personality assessment.

LO 11.30 Describe the MMPI–2 and the use of inventories to assess personality.

LO 11.31 Explain how projective tests are used to gain insight into personality.

What are the three major methods used in personality assessment?

Just as there are many different personality theories, there are many different methods for measuring personality. Various personality tests are used by clinical and counselling psychologists and psychiatrists to diagnose patients and assess progress in therapy. Personality assessment is also used by businesses and industries to aid in hiring decisions, and by counsellors for vocational and educational counselling. Personality assessment methods can be grouped in a few broad categories: (1) observation, interviews, and rating scales; (2) inventories; and (3) projective tests. **[LO 11.28]**

OBSERVATION, INTERVIEWS, AND RATING SCALES

Observation

All of us use observation, though informally, to form opinions about other people. Psychologists use observation in personality assessment and evaluation in a variety of settings, including hospitals, clinics, schools, and workplaces.

Using an observational technique known as *behavioural assessment*, psychologists can count and record the frequency of particular behaviours they are studying. **[LO 11.29]** This method is often used in behaviour modification programs in settings such as psychiatric hospitals, where psychologists may chart the progress of patients in reducing aggressive acts or other undesirable or abnormal behaviours. Although much can be learned from observation, it has its shortcomings: it is time-consuming; what is observed may be misinterpreted; and the very presence of the observer can alter the behaviour that is observed.

Interviews

Clinical psychologists and psychiatrists use interviews to help diagnose and treat patients. **[LO 11.29]** Counsellors use interviews to screen applicants for admission to colleges, universities, and special programs. Employers use them to evaluate job applicants and candidates for job promotions. You can use the *Apply It* for tips on how to use the interview process to your advantage.

Interviewers consider not only a person's answers, but also tone of voice, speech, mannerisms, gestures, and general appearance. Psychologists and other professionals use both structured and unstructured interviews in making their assessments. In unstructured situations, the direction the interview will take and the questions to be asked are not all planned beforehand; thus, the interview can be highly personalized. In structured situations, the content of the questions and the manner in which questions are asked are carefully planned ahead of time. The interviewer tries not to deviate in any way from the structured format so that more reliable comparisons can be made between different participants.

Rating Scales

Sometimes examiners use rating scales to record data from interviews or observations. **[LO 11.29]** Rating scales are useful because they provide a standardized format, including a list of traits or behaviours on which to evaluate. The rating scale helps to focus the rater's attention on all relevant traits so that some are not overlooked or weighed too heavily. The major limitation of these scales is that the ratings are often subjective. A related problem is the *halo effect*—the tendency of raters to be excessively influenced in their overall evaluation of a person by one or a few favourable or unfavourable traits. Often, traits or attributes that are not even on the rating scale, such as physical attractiveness or similarity to the rater, heavily influence a rater's perception of an individual. To overcome these limitations, it is often necessary to have individuals rated by more than one interviewer.

PERSONALITY INVENTORIES: TAKING STOCK

What is an inventory, and what is the MMPI–2 designed to reveal?

There is an objective method for measuring personality, a method in which the personal opinions and ratings of observers or interviewers do not unduly influence the results. This method is the **inventory**, a paper-and-pencil test with questions about an individual's thoughts, feelings, and behaviours, which measures several dimensions of personality and can be scored according to a standard procedure. Psychologists favouring the trait approach to personality prefer the inventory because it can assess where people fall on various dimensions of personality and it yields a personality profile.

The MMPI and MMPI–2

The **Minnesota Multiphasic Personality Inventory–2 (MMPI–2)** is a revision of the most popular, the most heavily researched, and the most widely used personality test for screening and diagnosing psychiatric problems and disorders, and for use in psychological research (Butcher, 2006). **[LO 11.30]**

There have been more than 115 recognized translations of the MMPI, which is used in more than 65 countries. Published in 1943 by J. C. McKinley and Starke R. Hathaway, the MMPI was originally intended to identify tendencies toward various psychiatric disorders.

Because it was published in 1943, some aspects of the MMPI had become outdated by the 1980s. It was revised, and

the MMPI–2 was published in 1989 (Butcher, Dahlstrom, Graham, Tellegen, & Kaemmer, 1989). Most of the original test items were retained, some were deleted because they were obsolete, and new items were added to provide more adequate coverage of areas such as alcoholism, drug abuse, and suicidal tendencies. Although the MMPI–2 now has 567 items, updating has made it more user-friendly and easier for the person being tested (Butcher & Hostetler, 1990).

The MMPI–2 provides scores on 4 validity scales and 10 clinical scales. Here are examples of items on the test:

> I wish I were not bothered by thoughts about sex.
>
> When I get bored I like to stir up some excitement.
>
> In walking I am very careful to step over sidewalk cracks.
>
> If people had not had it in for me, I would have been much more successful.

Evaluating the MMPI–2

The MMPI–2 is reliable, easy to administer and score, and inexpensive to use. It is useful in the screening, diagnosis, and clinical description of abnormal behaviour; however, it is not very good at revealing differences among normal personalities (Hiller, Rosenthal, & Bornstein, 1999; T. L. Morrison, Edwards, & Weissman, 1994). Some researchers have cautioned against making diagnoses based exclusively on the MMPI and MMPI–2 (Libb, Murray, Thurstin, & Alarcon, 1992) and suggest that clinicians should integrate MMPI results with other sources of clinical information before making a diagnosis (G. J. Meyer et al., 2001).

The *Canadian Connections* box describes Canadian researchers' efforts to translate popular personality tests into French, Chinese, and Japanese.

PROJECTIVE TESTS: PROJECTIONS FROM THE UNCONSCIOUS

How do projective tests provide insight into personality, and what are some of the most commonly used projective tests?

Responses on interviews and questionnaires are conscious responses; for this reason, they are less useful to therapists who wish to probe the unconscious. Such therapists may choose a completely different technique called a *projective test*. A **projective test**

---

heritability: An index of the degree to which a characteristic is estimated to be influenced by heredity.

inventory: A paper-and-pencil test with questions about a person's thoughts, feelings, and behaviours, which measures several dimensions of personality and can be scored according to a standard procedure.

Minnesota Multiphasic Personality Inventory–2 (MMPI–2): A revision of the most extensively researched and widely used personality test; used to screen and diagnose psychiatric problems and disorders.

projective test: A personality test in which people respond to inkblots, drawings of ambiguous human situations, incomplete sentences, and the like by projecting their own inner thoughts, feelings, fears, or conflicts onto the test materials.

CANADIAN CONNECTIONS

Personality Scales for Canadians from Different Cultural Groups

So far in this chapter, we have discussed how personality inventories are used to assess people's personalities on particular dimensions, such as self-esteem, motivation, or self-control. But do these personality constructs hold across cultures? Research suggests that this is the case, but careful test development is needed to ensure the reliability and validity of these instruments when they are used in different cultures. How then do psychologists make sure that they are measuring the same dimensions when people are from different linguistic groups? This is a question that has been at the forefront of much research by Québec psychologists.

For well over two decades, psychologists at many Québec universities have worked to develop new French personality inventories and have translated existing English inventories to be used in Québec and other francophone communities in Canada and elsewhere. Since 2010, more than 10 personality scales have been translated and validated on French-speaking samples to ensure the suitability of the translated format of the original English scale.

Creating a new inventory is not a simple task. Scale development requires that data be collected on hundreds and often thousands of participants. Recent work by Québec researchers has led to the development of scales that assess such diverse individual difference variables as goal orientation (Lauzier & Haccoun, 2010) and marital satisfaction (Brodard et al., 2015).

In a similar line of research, Canadian researchers have also begun to work with members of other linguistic communities to translate well-established psychological scales originally developed in English into various languages. Two recent examples are the translation of the depressive symptoms scale into Chinese (Yao, Fang, Zhu, & Zuroff, 2009) and the translation of two emotional intelligence scales into Japanese (Fukuda et al., 2011). Such research efforts have provided French-speaking, and now Chinese- and Japanese-speaking, researchers and practitioners with more valid methods of assessments that take into consideration both cultural and linguistic factors that would otherwise limit the usefulness of the scales. ■

is a personality test consisting of inkblots, drawings of ambiguous human situations, or incomplete sentences for which there are no obvious correct or incorrect responses. People respond by projecting their own inner thoughts, feelings, fears, or conflicts onto the test materials, just as a movie projector projects film images onto a screen. **[LO 11.31]**

The Rorschach Inkblot Test: What Do You See?

One of the oldest and most popular projective tests is the **Rorschach Inkblot Test**, developed by Swiss psychiatrist Hermann Rorschach (1884–1922) in 1921. It consists of 10 inkblots, which people are asked to describe (see Figure 11.4).

To develop his test, Rorschach put ink on paper and then folded the paper so that symmetrical patterns resulted. Earlier, psychologists had used standardized series of inkblots to study imagination and other personal attributes; Rorschach was the first to use inkblots to investigate personality. He experimented with thousands of inkblots on different groups of people and found that 10 of the inkblots could be used to discriminate between different diagnostic groups: manic depressives, paranoid schizophrenics, and so on. These 10 inkblots—5 black and white, and 5 in colour—were standardized and are still widely used.

ADMINISTRATION AND SCORING OF THE RORSCHACH The 10 inkblots are shown to a person, who is asked to tell everything that each inkblot looks like or resembles. The examiner writes down the person's responses and then goes through the cards again, asking questions to clarify what the person has reported.

The interpretation of the Rorschach has always been a problem, mainly due to its low reliability and validity (J. M Wood, Lilienfeld, & Garb, 2000). Some recent research has demonstrated some improvement in the reliability of the Rorschach (Bornstein, 2012), but others continue to question it (Wood et al., 2010).

The Thematic Apperception Test: Seeing Ourselves in Scenes of Others

Another projective test is the **Thematic Apperception Test (TAT)** developed by Henry Murray and his colleagues in 1935 (C. D. Morgan & Murray, 1935; H. Murray, 1938). The TAT consists of 1 blank card and 19 other cards showing vague or ambiguous black-and-white drawings of human figures in various situations. The test taker is asked to make up a story about each scene in the test.

The test "is based upon the well-recognized fact that when a person interprets an ambiguous social situation he is apt to expose his own personality as much as the phenomenon to

Rorschach Inkblot Test (ROR-shok): A projective test composed of 10 inkblots to which a participant responds; used to reveal unconscious functioning and the presence of psychiatric disorders.

Thematic Apperception Test (TAT): A projective test consisting of drawings of ambiguous human situations, which the subject describes; thought to reveal inner feelings, conflicts, and motives, which are projected onto the test materials.

FIGURE 11.4
An Inkblot Similar to One on the Rorschach Inkblot Test

which he is attending" (C. D. Morgan & Murray, 1962, p. 531). If many of a person's story themes are about illness (or sex, or fear of failure, or aggression, or power, or interpersonal conflicts, and so on), it is thought to reveal a problem in the person's life. Murray also maintains that TAT "can reveal things that the patient is unwilling to tell or is unable to tell because he is unconscious of them" (H. A. Murray, 1965, p. 427).

The TAT is time-consuming and difficult to administer and score. Although it has been used extensively in personality research, it suffers from the same weaknesses as other projective tests: (1) it relies heavily on the interpretation skills of the examiner and (2) it may reflect too strongly a person's temporary motivational and emotional state and not get at the more permanent aspects of personality.

The Value of Projective Tests

How effective are projective tests? Although the Rorschach has recently received some better evaluations (R. F. Bornstein, 2012; G. J. Meyer et al., 2005), research evidence on the validity of projective techniques as a whole is disappointing. Projective tests suffer from a lack of objectivity in scoring and an absence of adequate norms. Nevertheless, in clinical practice, projective tests continue to be a popular and valued diagnostic tool (R. F. Bornstein, 2012; G. J. Meyer et al., 2001, 2005; I. B. Weiner, 1997).

Review & Reflect 11.2 summarizes the three methods of personality assessment. We also summarize the major theories of personality, their assumptions, and their assessment techniques in *Review & Reflect 11.3*.

REMEMBER IT

Personality Assessment

1. Match the personality test with its description.
   _____ 1) MMPI–2
   _____ 2) Rorschach
   _____ 3) TAT
   a. inventory used to diagnose psychopathology
   b. projective test using inkblots
   c. projective test using drawings of ambiguous human situations

2. Dr. X and Dr. Y are both experts in personality assessment. They would be most likely to agree on their interpretation of results from the _____

   a. Rorschach.
   b. MMPI–2.
   c. TAT.
   d. sentence-completion method.

3. George has an unconscious resentment toward his father. Which test might best detect this?
   a. MMPI–2
   b. Rating scales
   c. Rorschach
   d. TAT

Answers: 1. (1). a (2). b (3). c 2. b 3. d

REVIEW & REFLECT **11.2** THREE METHODS OF PERSONALITY ASSESSMENT

Method	Examples	Description
Observation and rating	Observation	Performance (behaviour) is observed in a specific situation, and personality is assessed on the basis of observation.
	Interviews	In interviews, the responses to questions are taken to reveal personality characteristics.
	Rating scales	Rating scales are used to score or rate subjects on the basis of traits, behaviours, or results of interviews.
		Assessment is subjective, and accuracy depends largely on the ability and experience of the evaluator.
Inventories	Minnesota Multiphasic Personality Inventory–2 (MMPI–2)	Subjects reveal their beliefs, feelings, behaviour, and/or opinions on paper-and-pencil tests.
		Subjects respond to ambiguous test materials and presumably reveal elements of their own personality.
Projective tests	Rorschach Inkblot Test Thematic Apperception Test (TAT)	This is done through an analysis of the themes each person describes, either orally or in writing.
		Scoring is subjective, and accuracy depends largely on the ability and experience of the evaluator.

REVIEW & REFLECT 11.3 SUMMARY OF MAJOR THEORIES OF PERSONALITY

Theory	Associated Theorists	Assumptions about Behaviour	Assessment Techniques	Research Methods
Psychoanalytic	Freud	Behaviour arises mostly from unconscious conflicts between pleasure-seeking id and moral-perfectionist superego, with reality-oriented ego as mediator.	Projective tests to tap unconscious motives; interviews for purposes of analysis	Case studies
Trait	Allport Cattell Eysenck McCrae and Costa	Behaviour springs from personality traits that may be influenced by both heredity and environment.	Self-report inventories; adjective checklists; inventories	Analysis of test results for identifying strength of various traits
Learning: Behaviourist	Skinner	Behaviour is determined strictly by environmental influences.	Direct observation of behaviour; objective tests; interviews; rating scales	Analysis of observations of behaviour; quantifying behaviours; analysis of person–situation interactions
Learning: Social-cognitive	Bandura Rotter	Behaviour results from an interaction between internal cognitive factors and environmental influences.	Direct observation of behaviour; objective tests; interviews	Analysis of interactions between internal cognitive factors and environmental influences
Humanistic	Maslow Rogers	Behaviour springs from the person's own unique perception of reality and conscious choices. Humans are innately good.	Interviews and tests designed to assess the person's self	Analysis of the relationship between the person's feelings or perceptions and behaviour

APPLY IT

Put Your Best Foot Forward

Did you ever think of a job interview as a personality assessment? You should, because that's precisely what it is. The interviewer isn't measuring your personality as a psychologist would. Instead, he or she is assessing whether you fit the organization's needs and whether you can fit in with the others who work there. Here are a few tips for successful interviewing.

Impression Management

Think of the interview as an opportunity to make a particular impression on a potential employer. However, you should refrain from exaggerating your qualifications or experience. Experienced interviewers are skilled at recognizing such exaggerations and tend to look unfavourably upon interviewees who use them (Paulhus, Harms, Bruce, & Lysy, 2003).

Educate Yourself

Learn as much as you can about the business or industry you want to work in and about the particular firm to which you are applying. Study the qualifications for the job you are seeking, both required and preferred, if they're available, and get a good idea of how your qualifications match up.

Prepare an Effective Resumé

Even if the job you're applying for doesn't require a resumé, it's a good idea to prepare one and take it—along with some extra copies—with you to the interview. A good resumé is a quick source of information for the interviewer, who needs to know about your entire work history to create questions based on it. Most colleges and universities have career centres that provide advice on resumé preparation, as well as related services.

Practise

Practise answering interview questions with a friend. Many university and college career centres have lists of frequently asked interview questions, and you should always create your own list of questions that you think the interviewer might ask. Try to avoid saying negative things about yourself. Remember, too, that consistent eye contact will show the interviewer that you have confidence.

Dress Professionally

When you are interviewing for a job, your clothing, visible adornments on your body (e.g., tattoos, jewellery), how well groomed you are, and even the way you smell can be forms of communication. Your appearance should communicate to the interviewer that you understand the environment in which you hope to be working. Keep in mind, too, that your appearance influences your own self-confidence. Researchers have found that the more formal interviewees' clothing is, the more positive are the remarks they make about themselves during the interview (Kwantes, 2011).

Be Punctual

Do you feel frustrated when others keep you waiting? Interviewers respond emotionally to tardiness, just as you do. Consequently, it's best to arrive early. And if you are unavoidably delayed, call and reschedule.

Greet the Interviewer Appropriately

Your greeting plays an important role in the interview process as well. In Canada, it's best to look your interviewer directly in the eyes, shake hands firmly, pronounce her or his name correctly, and have good posture.

Follow Up

After the interview, it's a good idea to send a thank-you note—an email will be fine. If you met with more than one interviewer, send a note to each of them, mentioning some specific aspect of the discussion that you found interesting. This will indicate that you were fully engaged in the conversation, listening intently, and interested in the interviewer's knowledge about the open position and the organization. The note should also express your appreciation for the interviewer's time and your interest in the position.

THINKING CRITICALLY

Evaluation

In your opinion, which personality theory is the most accurate, reasonable, and realistic? Which is the least accurate, reasonable, and realistic? Support your answers.

Point/Counterpoint

Are personality characteristics mostly learned? Or are they mostly transmitted through the genes? Using what you have learned in this chapter and other evidence you can gather, make a case for each position. Support your answers with research and expert opinion.

Psychology in Your Life

Consider your own behaviour and personality attributes from the standpoint of each of the theories: psychoanalysis, trait theory, and the learning, humanistic, and genetic perspectives. Which theory or theories best explain your personality? Why?

MyPsychLab Go to mypsychlab (access code required) to find web resources for your text that supplement the material in chapter 11.

SUMMARY & REVIEW

SIGMUND FREUD AND PSYCHOANALYSIS

To what two aspects of Freud's work does the term psycho-analysis *apply?*
Psychoanalysis is the term Freud used for both his theory of personality and his therapy for the treatment of psychological disorders.

What are the three levels of awareness in consciousness?
The three levels of awareness in consciousness are the conscious, the preconscious, and the unconscious.

What are the roles of the id, the ego, and the superego?
The id is the primitive, unconscious part of the personality, which contains the instincts and operates on the pleasure principle. The ego is the rational, largely conscious system, which operates according to the reality principle. The superego is the moral system of the personality, consisting of the conscience and the ego ideal. Freud believed that differences in personality result from the relative strengths of the id, the ego, and the superego, and from the personality traits that develop as a result of problems during the psychosexual stages.

What is a defence mechanism?
A defence mechanism is an unconscious, irrational means that the ego uses to defend against anxiety and to maintain self-esteem; it involves self-deception and the distortion of reality.

What are two ways in which repression operates?
Repression can remove painful or threatening memories, thoughts, ideas, or perceptions from consciousness and keep them in the unconscious; or it can prevent unconscious but disturbing sexual and aggressive impulses from breaking into consciousness.

What are some other defence mechanisms?
Aside from repression, the most common defence mechanisms are projection, denial, rationalization, regression, reaction formation, displacement, and sublimation.

What are the psychosexual stages, and why did Freud consider them so important in personality development?
Freud believed that the sexual instinct is present at birth, develops through a series of psychosexual stages, and provides the driving force for thought and activity. The psychosexual stages are the oral stage, anal stage, phallic stage (followed by the latency period), and genital stage.

What is the Oedipus complex?
The Oedipus complex, occurring in the phallic stage, is a conflict in which the child is sexually attracted to the opposite-sex parent and feels hostility toward the same-sex parent.

According to Freud, what are the two primary sources of influence on personality?
Freud believed that there are two primary influences on personality: (1) the traits that develop because of fixations at any of the psychosexual stages; and (2) the relative strengths of the id, the ego, and the superego. In psychologically healthy people, there is a balance among the three components.

11B THE NEO-FREUDIANS

According to Jung, what are the three components of personality?
Jung conceived of the personality as having three parts: the ego, the personal unconscious, and the collective unconscious.

What did Adler consider to be the driving force of the personality?
Adler maintained that the predominant force of the personality is the drive to overcome and compensate for feelings of weakness and inferiority and to strive for superiority or significance.

Why is Horney considered a pioneer in psychology?
Horney took issue with Freud's sexist view of women and added the feminine dimension to the world of psychology.

11C TRAIT THEORIES

What are trait theories of personality?
Trait theories of personality are attempts to explain personality and differences between people in terms of their personal characteristics.

How did Allport differentiate between cardinal and central traits?
Allport defined a cardinal trait as a personal quality that is so strong a part of a person's personality that he or she may become identified with that trait or known for it. A central trait is the type you would mention in writing a letter of recommendation.

How did Cattell differentiate between surface and source traits?
Cattell used the term *surface traits* to refer to observable qualities of personality, those you might use in describing a friend. *Source traits* underlie the surface traits, exist in all of us in varying degrees, make up the most basic personality structure, and cause behaviour.

What did Eysenck consider to be the two most important dimensions of personality?
Eysenck considered extraversion (versus introversion) and neuroticism (versus emotional stability) to be the most important dimensions of personality.

What are the five personality dimensions in the five-factor model as described by McCrae and Costa?
According to McCrae and Costa, the five personality dimensions are extraversion, neuroticism, conscientiousness, agreeableness, and openness to experience.

11D LEARNING THEORIES AND PERSONALITY

How did Skinner account for what most people refer to as personality?
B. F. Skinner viewed personality as simply a collection of behaviours and habits that have been reinforced in the past.

What are the components that make up Bandura's concept of reciprocal determinism, and how do they interact?
Personal/cognitive factors, our behaviour, and the external environment are the three components of reciprocal determinism, each influencing and influenced by the others.

What is meant by the terms internal *and* external locus of control*?*
According to Rotter, people with an internal locus of control see themselves as primarily in control of their behaviour and its consequences; those with an external locus of control believe their destiny is in the hands of fate, luck, or chance.

11E HUMANISTIC PERSONALITY THEORIES

Who were the two pioneers in humanistic psychology, and how did they view human nature?
Abraham Maslow and Carl Rogers, the two pioneers in humanistic psychology, believed that human nature is innately good and that people have free will and a tendency toward growth and realization of their potential. Maslow emphasized people's motivation to become self-actualized and develop their fullest potential, whereas Rogers emphasized the importance of unconditional positive regard in human development.

What is self-actualization, and how did Maslow study it?
Self-actualization is developing ourselves to our fullest potential. To explore this concept, Maslow studied individuals he believed were using their talents and abilities—in other words, individuals, such as historical figures, who exemplified self-actualization.

According to Rogers, why don't all people become fully functioning persons?
Rogers theorized that we as people need unconditional love, acceptance, and respect from the people who are significant in our lives. However, in reality, we do not receive such unconditional support, and instead, we must live and act according to someone else's values rather than our own. To gain the positive regard of others, we deny our true selves and close ourselves to parts of our experience. In doing so, we experience stress and anxiety, and our whole self-structure may be threatened.

11F PERSONALITY: IS IT IN THE GENES?

What has research in behavioural genetics revealed about the influence of the genes and the environment on personality?

Research in behavioural genetics has revealed that about 40 to 50 percent of personality can be attributed to the genes, and that the environmental influences on personality are mainly from the non-shared environment.

11G PERSONALITY ASSESSMENT

What are the three major methods used in personality assessment?

The major methods used in personality assessment are (1) observation, interviews, and rating scales; (2) inventories; and (3) projective tests.

What is an inventory, and what is the MMPI–2 designed to reveal?

An inventory is a paper-and-pencil test with questions about a person's thoughts, feelings, and behaviours, which measures several dimensions of personality and can be scored according to a standard procedure. The MMPI–2 is the most widely used personality inventory, and it is designed to screen and diagnose psychiatric problems and disorders.

How do projective tests provide insight into personality, and what are some of the most commonly used projective tests?

In a projective test, people respond to inkblots, drawings of ambiguous human situations, incomplete sentences, and the like by projecting their own inner thoughts, feelings, fears, or conflicts onto the test materials. Examples are the Rorschach Inkblot Test and the Thematic Apperception Test (TAT).

PERSONALITY THEORY AND ASSESSMENT

Personality is an individual's unique and stable pattern of characteristics and behaviours.
Personality theories have provided diverse explanations for why people have different personalities.

MODULE 11A SIGMUND FREUD AND PSYCHOANALYSIS

People are primarily motivated by unconscious instincts. Personality is almost completely formed by age five or six years. The two primary influences on personality are traits that develop due to fixation at any psychosexual stage and the relative strengths of id, ego, and superego.

Personality contains three components.

Id is present at birth, inherited, and totally unconscious; it operates on the **pleasure principle** (seeks immediate pleasure, avoids pain, and seeks immediate gratification).

Ego is rational, largely conscious, and operates on the **reality principle** (tries to satisfy the id without violating moral values). The ego may use **defence mechanisms** (ways to reduce anxiety by unconsciously distorting reality).

Superego contains mainly unconscious memories of behaviours that have been either punished (the **conscience**) or rewarded (the **ego ideal**).

Defence mechanisms
Repression: blocking or removing unpleasant thoughts.
Denial: refusing to consciously acknowledge the existence of a threatening condition.
Rationalization: supplying a logical, rational, or socially acceptable reason in place of the real reason.
Regression: reverting to behaviour that might have reduced anxiety at an earlier age.
Reaction formation: expressing the opposite of one's true feelings.
Displacement: substituting a less threatening object for the original object.
Projection: attributing one's own undesirable thoughts to others.
Sublimation: redirecting sexual or aggressive energy to pursuits or accomplishments that society considers acceptable or praiseworthy.

The Psychosexual Stages of Development: Centred on the Erogenous Zones.

Psychosexual stages are defined by the erogenous zone, which becomes the centre of new pleasures and conflicts.

Oral stage (birth to 1 year or 18 months): Pleasure is derived mainly through stimulation of the mouth.

Anal stage (12 or 18 months to 3 years): Pleasure is derived mainly through expelling and withholding feces.

Phallic stage (3 to 5 or 6 years): Pleasure is derived mainly from the genitals. The **Oedipus complex** refers to a child's sexual attraction to the opposite-sex parent and hostility toward the same-sex parent.

Latency period (5 or 6 years to puberty): Sexual instinct is largely repressed and temporarily sublimated in school and play activities.

Genital stage (puberty onward): The focus of sexual energy gradually shifts to the opposite-sex peers with whom a person establishes mature sexual relationships.

MODULE 11B THE NEO-FREUDIANS

Carl Jung (1875–1961)
Middle age is an important period for personality development. Personality consists of the ego, the personal unconscious, and the collective unconscious. The **collective unconscious** contains **archetypes**, which are inherited tendencies to respond in particular ways to universal human experiences.

Alfred Adler (1870–1937)
People are motivated by the conscious, are influenced by future goals, need to compensate for inferiority, and strive for superiority or significance. People develop a **style of life**; however, inferiority feelings may prevent personal development causing an **inferiority complex**.

Karen Horney (1885–1952)
Culture and environment have a large effect on females' traits and can create a neurotic personality.
- **Basic anxiety** is the feeling of being isolated and helpless in a potentially hostile world.
- The **tyranny of the should** is an unrealistic demand for personal perfection that is unattainable.

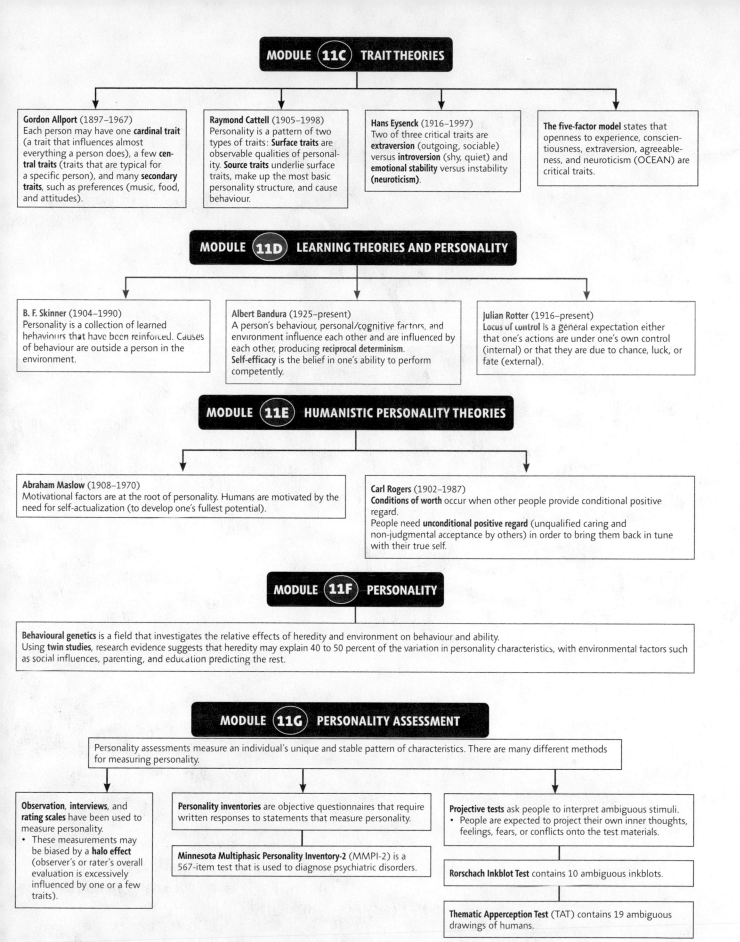

MODULE 11C TRAIT THEORIES

Gordon Allport (1897–1967)
Each person may have one **cardinal trait** (a trait that influences almost everything a person does), a few **central traits** (traits that are typical for a specific person), and many **secondary traits**, such as preferences (music, food, and attitudes).

Raymond Cattell (1905–1998)
Personality is a pattern of two types of traits: **Surface traits** are observable qualities of personality. **Source traits** underlie surface traits, make up the most basic personality structure, and cause behaviour.

Hans Eysenck (1916–1997)
Two of three critical traits are **extraversion** (outgoing, sociable) versus **introversion** (shy, quiet) and **emotional stability** versus instability (**neuroticism**).

The five-factor model states that openness to experience, conscientiousness, extraversion, agreeableness, and neuroticism (OCEAN) are critical traits.

MODULE 11D LEARNING THEORIES AND PERSONALITY

B. F. Skinner (1904–1990)
Personality is a collection of learned behaviours that have been reinforced. Causes of behaviour are outside a person in the environment.

Albert Bandura (1925–present)
A person's behaviour, personal/cognitive factors, and environment influence each other and are influenced by each other, producing **reciprocal determinism**.
Self-efficacy is the belief in one's ability to perform competently.

Julian Rotter (1916–present)
Locus of control is a general expectation either that one's actions are under one's own control (internal) or that they are due to chance, luck, or fate (external).

MODULE 11E HUMANISTIC PERSONALITY THEORIES

Abraham Maslow (1908–1970)
Motivational factors are at the root of personality. Humans are motivated by the need for self-actualization (to develop one's fullest potential).

Carl Rogers (1902–1987)
Conditions of worth occur when other people provide conditional positive regard.
People need **unconditional positive regard** (unqualified caring and non-judgmental acceptance by others) in order to bring them back in tune with their true self.

MODULE 11F PERSONALITY

Behavioural genetics is a field that investigates the relative effects of heredity and environment on behaviour and ability.
Using **twin studies**, research evidence suggests that heredity may explain 40 to 50 percent of the variation in personality characteristics, with environmental factors such as social influences, parenting, and education predicting the rest.

MODULE 11G PERSONALITY ASSESSMENT

Personality assessments measure an individual's unique and stable pattern of characteristics. There are many different methods for measuring personality.

Observation, **interviews**, and **rating scales** have been used to measure personality.
• These measurements may be biased by a **halo effect** (observer's or rater's overall evaluation is excessively influenced by one or a few traits).

Personality inventories are objective questionnaires that require written responses to statements that measure personality.

Minnesota Multiphasic Personality Inventory-2 (MMPI-2) is a 567-item test that is used to diagnose psychiatric disorders.

Projective tests ask people to interpret ambiguous stimuli.
• People are expected to project their own inner thoughts, feelings, fears, or conflicts onto the test materials.

Rorschach Inkblot Test contains 10 ambiguous inkblots.

Thematic Apperception Test (TAT) contains 19 ambiguous drawings of humans.

12

Are you a victim of "technostress"?

In his classic book on the subject, Craig Brod (1984) defined *technostress* as "a modern disease of adaptation caused by an inability to cope with the new computer technologies in a healthy manner. It manifests itself in two distinct ways: in the struggle to accept computer technology, and in the more specialized form of over-identification with computer technology" (p. 16). When some of the technologies we now take for granted were first introduced, these potentially time- and labour-saving devices implied the possibility of a better future, with more time for leisure and social relationships. Instead, our world has simply adapted to the new technology by requiring that all aspects of our lives, and especially our work or school life, operate at an increasingly fast pace.

In the past few years it has become apparent that some people—especially the young—are not only undisturbed by the speed of communication, but in fact prefer rapid and short bursts of communication such as texting or Twitter. However, others often feel overwhelmed by the rapid pace of change in technological gadgetry and the need for the constant contact it represents. In the last few years, Larry Rosen, past chair and professor of psychology at California State University, has provided much research evidence to support the view that our dependence on technology is affecting us negatively. In his most recent book (Rosen, Cheever, & Carrier, 2012), Rosen argues that our overreliance on technology fosters "obsessions, dependence and stress reactions" that can cause significant psychological problems or, as he calls it, an "idisorder." Today the Information Age is increasingly being blamed for making simple things more complicated—and stressing us out in the process.

As you will learn in this chapter, stress—any type of stress—affects our ability to function and tends to have a negative impact on our health. That we should never take our health for granted is good advice indeed, but it's advice that most of us easily forget. In this chapter we discuss many issues related to health and stress.

©Silvano Rebai/Fotolia

HEALTH AND STRESS

There are two main approaches to health and illness. The **biomedical model**, the predominant view in medicine, focuses on illness rather than health. It explains illness in terms of biological factors without considering psychological and social factors that might contribute to the condition.

Another approach that is gaining serious attention is the **biopsychosocial model** of health and wellness (see Figure 12.1). This approach focuses on health as well as illness, and holds that both are determined by a combination of biological, psychological, and social factors (Engel, 1977, 1980; G. E. Schwartz, 1982). Growing acceptance of this model gave rise to the subfield of **health psychology**, "the field within psychology devoted to understanding psychological influences on how people stay healthy, why they become ill, and how they respond when they do get ill" (S. E. Taylor, 1991, p. 6). Health psychology is particularly important today because several prevalent diseases, including heart disease and cancer, are related to unhealthy lifestyles and stress (S. E. Taylor, 2008).

Why do people become ill in the modern age? At the beginning of the twentieth century, the primary causes of death in Canada were pneumonia and infectious diseases such as diphtheria and tuberculosis. The health menaces of modern times are diseases related to unhealthy lifestyle and stress—heart attack, stroke, hardening of the arteries, cancer, and cirrhosis of the liver. In this chapter we will discuss stress, disease, and behaviours that promote and compromise health.

MODULE **12A** THEORIES OF STRESS

LO 12.1 Describe Selye's concept of general adaptation syndrome.

LO 12.2 Describe the physiological responses during the alarm, resistance, and exhaustion stages of general adaptation.

LO 12.3 Explain the four phases of response to a potentially stressful event according to Lazarus's cognitive theory of stress and coping.

LO 12.4 Describe the primary and secondary appraisal processes that occur in response to a potentially stressful event.

How would you define *stress*? Is stress something in the environment? Is it a physiological or psychological reaction that occurs within a person? Most psychologists define **stress** as the physiological and psychological response to a condition that threatens or challenges the individual and requires some form of adaptation or adjustment.

HANS SELYE AND THE GENERAL ADAPTATION SYNDROME

An early, classic contribution to stress research was made by Walter Cannon (1932), who described the fight-or-flight response. Cannon discovered that when any threat is perceived by an organism (animal or human), the sympathetic nervous system and the endocrine glands prepare the body to fight the

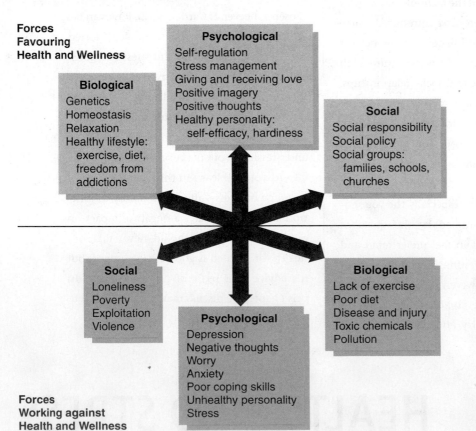

FIGURE 12.1

The Biopsychosocial Model of Health and Wellness

The biopsychosocial model focuses on health as well as illness, and holds that both are determined by a combination of biological, psychological, and social factors. Most health psychologists endorse the biopsychosocial model.

Source: (Based on J. A. Green & Shellenberger, 1990.) Green, J.A; & Shellenberger, R. (1990). The dynamics of health and wellness: A biopsychosocial approach. Fort Worth, TX: Holt, Rinehart & Winston. Houghton Mifflin Harcourt.

AP Images

Hans Selye

threat or flee from it. Cannon considered the fight-or-flight response wonderfully adaptive, because it helps the organism respond rapidly to threats. He also considered it potentially harmful in the long run if an organism is not able to fight or flee and experiences prolonged stress and continuing physical arousal (Sapolsky, Romero, & Munck, 2000).

Canadian scientist Hans Selye (1907–1982) is the researcher most prominently associated with the study of stress and health. Selye spent most of his pioneering career at McGill University (1932–1945) and the Université de Montréal (1945–1977). At McGill, he conducted research on the effects of sex hormones. In one experiment he injected rats with hormone-rich extracts of cow ovaries. What happened to the rats? To Selye's amazement, (1) their adrenal glands became swollen, (2) their immune systems were weakened, and (3) they developed bleeding ulcers in the stomach and intestines. Never before had a hormone been shown to cause such clear physical symptoms. Selye thought he might be on the verge of discovering a new hormone. But after further experiments he found that he could produce the same symptoms by trying almost anything on the rats—for example, exposing them to toxic chemicals or freezing temperatures. Even extreme muscle fatigue caused the same symptoms. It seemed that Selye had not discovered anything at all. He was crushed. Then brooding gave way to reflection.

He realized that the body responds in much the same way to all harmful agents (toxic substances, injuries, electric shock) and a host of other stressors. The physical response was so predictable, so general, that Selye named it the **general adaptation syndrome (GAS)**. As a medical student in the 1920s, Selye had been struck by the fact that patients admitted to the hospital with an amazingly wide variety of illnesses all had many of the same physical symptoms. Now he was seeing general symptoms in rats exposed to a variety of stressors.

Selye was elated by his discovery, but the medical world was skeptical. The notion that organisms react in the same way to a wide range of dangers was completely contrary to the orthodox medical thinking of the day. Within five years, however, Selye had proved that the general stress reaction was indeed the body's way of responding to stress.

The General Adaptation Syndrome: A General Physical Response to Many Stressors

What is the general adaptation syndrome?

Selye knew that all living organisms are constantly confronted with **stressors**—stimuli or events that place a demand on the organism for adaptation or readjustment. Each stressor causes both specific and non-specific responses. Extreme cold, for example, causes the *specific* response of shivering. Apart from this, the body makes a *non-specific* response to a wide variety of stressors. The heart of Selye's concept of stress is the *general adaptation syndrome*, his term for the non-specific response to stress (see Figure 12.2). The GAS consists of three stages: alarm, resistance, and exhaustion (Selye, 1956). **[LO 12.1]**

The body's first response to a stressor is the **alarm stage**, when emotional arousal occurs and the body prepares its defensive forces to meet the threat. **[LO 12.2]** In the alarm stage the sympathetic nervous system, through the release of hormones, mobilizes the body to fight or flee. If the stressor cannot be quickly conquered or avoided, the organism enters the **resistance stage**, which is characterized by intense physiological efforts to either resist or adapt to the stressor. **[LO 12.2]** During the resistance stage, the adrenal glands pour out powerful hormones (glucocorticoids) to help the body resist stressors.

biomedical model: A perspective that focuses on illness rather than health, explaining illness in terms of biological factors without regard to psychological and social factors.

biopsychosocial model: A perspective that focuses on health as well as illness, and holds that both are determined by a combination of biological, psychological, and social factors.

health psychology: The field concerned with the psychological factors that contribute to health, illness, and response to illness.

stress: The physiological and psychological response to a condition that threatens or challenges a person and requires some form of adaptation or adjustment.

general adaptation syndrome (GAS): The predictable sequence of reactions (the alarm, resistance, and exhaustion stages) that organisms show in response to stressors.

stressors: Any events capable of producing physical or emotional stress.

alarm stage: The first stage of the general adaptation syndrome, when there is emotional arousal and the defensive forces of the body are prepared for fight or flight.

resistance stage: The second stage of the general adaptation syndrome, during which there are intense physiological efforts to resist or adapt to the stressor.

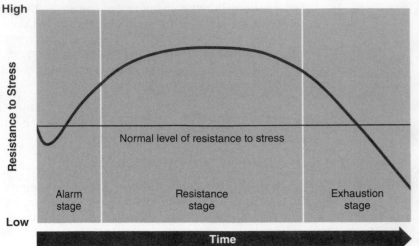

FIGURE 12.2
The General Adaptation Syndrome
The three stages in Hans Selye's general adaptation syndrome are (1) the alarm stage, during which there is emotional arousal and the defensive forces of the body are mobilized for fight or flight; (2) the resistance stage, in which intense physiological efforts are exerted to resist or adapt to the stressor; and (3) the exhaustion stage, when the organism fails in its efforts to resist the stressor. *Source:* (Based on Selye, 1956.) The stress of life. New York: McGraw-Hill.

Resistance may last a long time. According to Selye (1956), the length of the resistance stage depends both on the strength or intensity of the stressor and on the body's power to adapt.

If the organism fails in its efforts to resist, it reaches the **exhaustion stage**: "The stage of exhaustion after a temporary demand upon the body is reversible, but the complete exhaustion of all stores of deep adaptation energy is not" (Selye, 1974, p. 29). **[LO 12.2]** If exposure to the stressor continues, all the stores of deep energy are depleted, and disintegration, disease, or death may follow.

Selye claimed that any event requiring a readjustment, positive or negative, will produce stress in an organism. He did, however, differentiate between the positive and negative aspects of stress. *Eustress* is positive or good stress, including exhilaration, excitement, and the thrill of accomplishment. *Distress* is damaging or unpleasant stress, such as frustration, inadequacy, loss, disappointment, insecurity, helplessness, or desperation.

Criticisms of Selye's Theory: A Missing Cognitive Factor

The connection between extreme, prolonged stress and certain diseases is now widely accepted by medical experts, but some criticism of Selye's work seems justified. The major criticism is directed at Selye's contention that the intensity of the stressor determines one's physical reaction to it. His theory does not provide for a psychological component—that is, it does not consider how a person perceives and evaluates the stressor. This criticism led to the development of the cognitive theory of stress.

exhaustion stage: The final stage of the general adaptation syndrome, occurring if the organism fails in its efforts to resist the stressor.

primary appraisal: Evaluating the significance of a potentially stressful event according to how it will affect one's well-being—whether it is perceived as irrelevant or as involving harm or loss, threat, or challenge.

secondary appraisal: Evaluating one's coping resources and deciding how to deal with a stressful event.

RICHARD LAZARUS'S COGNITIVE THEORY OF STRESS

Richard Lazarus (1922–2002) argued that it is not the stressor itself that causes stress, but a person's perception of the stressor (Lazarus, 1966; Lazarus & Folkman, 1984). Because Lazarus emphasized the importance of perceptions and the appraisal of stressors, his is a *cognitive* theory of stress and coping. To Lazarus, the stress process can be understood in terms of four phases. **[LO 12.3]** First, there is a causal agent, either external or internal, commonly referred to as *stress* or *the stressor*. Second, the mind or the body evaluates the stressor as either threatening or benign. Third, the mind or the body uses coping processes to deal with the stressor. Finally, there is the stress reaction—the "complex pattern of effects on mind and body" (Lazarus, 1993, p. 4). Lazarus believed that physiological and psychological stress must be analyzed differently. He argued that whereas Selye's general adaptation syndrome describes how the body copes with physiological stress, his model focuses on how we cope with psychological stressors.

The Cognitive Appraisal of Stressors: Evaluating the Stressor and Considering Your Options

What are the roles of primary and secondary appraisal when people are confronted with a potentially stressful event?

According to Lazarus, when people are confronted with a potentially stressful event, they engage in a cognitive process that involves a primary and a secondary appraisal. A **primary appraisal** is an evaluation of the meaning and significance of a situation—whether its effect on our well-being is positive, irrelevant, or negative. **[LO 12.4]** An event appraised as negative or stressful could involve (1) harm or loss—damage that has already occurred; (2) threat—the potential for harm or loss; or (3) challenge—the opportunity to grow or gain. An appraisal of threat, harm, or loss can be made in relation to anything important to us—a friendship, a part of our body, our property, our finances, or our self-esteem.

The same event can be appraised differently by different people. Some students may welcome the opportunity to give an oral presentation in class, seeing it as a challenge and a chance to impress their professor and raise their grade. Other students may feel threatened, fearing that they may embarrass themselves in front of their classmates and lower their grade in the process. Still others may view the assignment as both a challenge and a threat. When we appraise a situation as one involving harm, loss, or threat, we have negative emotions such as anxiety, fear, anger, and resentment (Folkman, 1984). A challenge appraisal, on the other hand, is usually accompanied by positive emotions such as excitement, hopefulness, and eagerness. When we assess an event as stressful, we engage in a **secondary appraisal**. During secondary appraisal, if we judge the situation to be within our control, we make an evaluation of our available coping resources: physical (health, energy, stamina), social (support network), psychological (skills, morale, self-esteem), material (money, tools, equipment), and time. **[LO 12.4]** Then we consider our options and decide how we will deal with the stressor. The level of stress we feel depends largely on whether our resources are adequate to cope with the threat, and how severely our resources will be taxed in the process. Figure 12.3 summarizes Lazarus and Folkman's psychological model f stress.

Research generally supports Lazarus and Folkman's contention that the physiological, emotional, and behavioural reactions to stressors depend partly on whether the stressors are appraised as challenging or threatening. Recent Canadian research also suggests that some stressful situations can even be anticipated in advance, allowing people to use a strategy called *proactive coping*, which consists of efforts or actions taken in advance of a potentially stressful situation to prevent its occurrence or to minimize its consequences (Greenglass & Fiksenbaum, 2009). Proactive copers anticipate and then prepare for upcoming stressful events and situations.

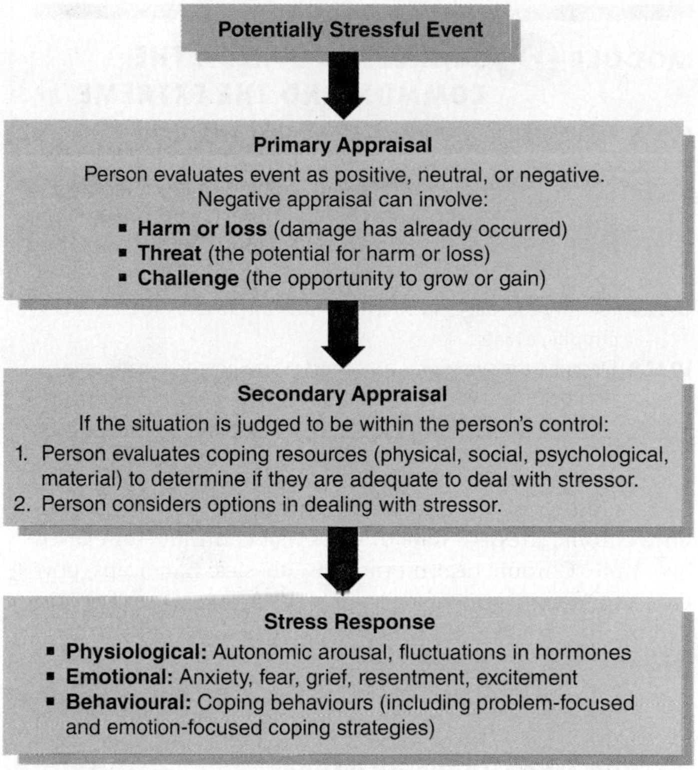

Potentially Stressful Event

Primary Appraisal
Person evaluates event as positive, neutral, or negative. Negative appraisal can involve:
- **Harm or loss** (damage has already occurred)
- **Threat** (the potential for harm or loss)
- **Challenge** (the opportunity to grow or gain)

Secondary Appraisal
If the situation is judged to be within the person's control:
1. Person evaluates coping resources (physical, social, psychological, material) to determine if they are adequate to deal with stressor.
2. Person considers options in dealing with stressor.

Stress Response
- **Physiological:** Autonomic arousal, fluctuations in hormones
- **Emotional:** Anxiety, fear, grief, resentment, excitement
- **Behavioural:** Coping behaviours (including problem-focused and emotion-focused coping strategies)

FIGURE 12.3
Lazarus and Folkman's Psychological Model of Stress

Lazarus and Folkman emphasize the importance of a person's perceptions and appraisal of stressors. The stress response depends on the outcome of the primary and secondary appraisals, whether the person's coping resources are adequate to cope with the threat, and how severely the resources are taxed in the process.
Source: (Based on Folkman, 1984.) Folkman, S. (1984). Personal control and stress and coping processes: A theoretical analysis. Journal of Personality and Social Psychology, 46, 839–852. American Psychological Association.

REMEMBER IT

Theories of Stress

1. Selye focused on the _____ aspects of stress; Lazarus focused on the _____ aspects of stress.
   a. physiological; physiological
   b. physiological; psychological
   c. psychological; physiological
   d. psychological; psychological

2. Which stage of the general adaptation syndrome is marked by intense physiological efforts to adapt to the stressor?
   a. The readjustment stage
   b. The resistance stage
   c. The alarm stage
   d. The exhaustion stage

3. Susceptibility to illness increases during what stage of the general adaptation syndrome?
   a. The readjustment stage
   b. The resistance stage
   c. The alarm stage
   d. The exhaustion stage

4. During secondary appraisal, we _____
   a. evaluate our coping resources and consider options in dealing with the stressor.
   b. determine whether an event is positive, neutral, or negative.
   c. determine whether an event involves loss, threat, or challenge.
   d. determine whether an event causes physiological or psychological stress.

MODULE **12B** SOURCES OF STRESS: THE COMMON AND THE EXTREME

LO 12.5 Describe approach–approach, approach–avoidance, and avoidance–avoidance conflicts in motivation.

LO 12.6 Explain how the unpredictability of and lack of control over a stressor affect its impact.

LO 12.7 Explain the relationship between racism and the experience of stress.

LO 12.8 Identify the stages in which victims tend to react to catastrophic events.

LO 12.9 Describe the symptoms that characterize post-traumatic stress disorder.

Some stressors produce temporary stress, whereas others produce chronic stress—a state of stress that continues unrelieved over time. Chronic health problems, physical handicaps, poverty, and unemployment are sources of chronic stress. The burden of chronic stress is disproportionately heavy for the poor, for minorities, and for the elderly.

EVERYDAY SOURCES OF STRESS

How do approach–approach, avoidance–avoidance, and approach–avoidance conflicts differ?

Sometimes conflicting motives can be sources of stress. When we must make a choice between desirable alternatives, we are facing an **approach–approach conflict**, and stress may be the result. **[LO 12.5]** Some approach–approach conflicts are minor, such as deciding which movie to see. Others can have major consequences, such as whether to continue building a promising career or to interrupt the career to raise a child.

In an **avoidance–avoidance conflict**, we must choose between two undesirable alternatives. **[LO 12.5]** You may want to avoid studying for an exam but at the same time you want to avoid failing the test. In an **approach–avoidance conflict**, we are simultaneously drawn to and repelled by a choice; for example, you may want to take a wonderful vacation but you would have to empty your savings account to do so. **[LO 12.5]**

Unpredictability and Lack of Control: Factors That Increase Stress

How do the unpredictability of, and lack of control over a stressor affect its impact?

Our physical and psychological well-being is profoundly influenced by the degree to which we feel a sense of control over our lives (Rodin & Salovey, 1989). **[LO 12.6]** Ellen J. Langer and Judith Rodin (1976) studied the effects of control on nursing-home residents. One group of residents was given some measure of control over their lives, such as choices in arranging their rooms and in the times they could see movies. They showed improved health and well-being and had a lower death rate than another group that was not given control. Within

18 months, 30 percent of the residents given no choices had died, compared with only 15 percent of those who had been given some control over their lives.

Several studies suggest that we are less subject to stress when we believe we have control over the source of stress, whether we exercise that power or not. It is likely that our expectations about unpredictable stressors may influence the manner in which we respond to them. For instance, in one study, experimenters exposed participants to an annoying noise (a randomly sounded buzzer) but offered them the opportunity to control the intensity of the noise (Bollini, Walker, Hamann, & Kestler, 2004). Even though all participants had an equal opportunity to exert some control over the stressor, only those who had a general belief in their own ability to moderate the effects of the stressor appeared to benefit. These participants were found to have lower levels of the stress hormone cortisol than participants who believed they lacked the ability to control stressors.

Racism and Stress

A significant source of chronic stress is being a member of a minority group in a majority culture (Ong, Fuller-Rowell, & Burrow, 2009). A study of white and black participants' responses to a survey about ways of coping suggests that a person may experience racial stress from simply being one of the few members of a particular race in any of a variety of settings (such as a classroom, workplace, or social setting). **[LO 12.7]** The feeling of stress can be intense, even in the absence of racist attitudes, discrimination, or any other overt evidence of racism (Plummer & Slane, 1996).

Some theorists have proposed that *historical racism*—the history of repression of members of particular groups—can also be a source of stress. Historical racism has been studied most extensively with African Americans in the United States, and many of these researchers who focus on this line of research claim that the higher incidence of high blood pressure and other chronic medical conditions among African Americans is attributable to stress associated with historical racism (D. R. Williams & Mohammed, 2009). Researchers now argue that this phenomenon must be studied more thoroughly with other historically repressed groups, such as Aboriginal peoples (Belcourt-Dittloff & Stewart, 2000).

CATASTROPHIC EVENTS AND CHRONIC INTENSE STRESS

How do people typically react to catastrophic events?

Do you remember how you felt when you found out about the terrorist attacks at the *Charlie Hebdo* headquarters in Paris where 11 people were killed in January 2015, or when you saw the image of a dead child whose family tried to escape war torn Syria? Like many people, you were probably a bit stunned and emotionally numb. Although the reactions of those who are directly affected are usually more extreme, catastrophes are stressful not only for people who experience them directly but also for those who learn of the events via news media.

CANADIAN CONNECTIONS

War and Post-traumatic Stress Disorder

In the spring of 2003, as Canadian soldiers were preparing to increase their participation in the peacekeeping efforts in Afghanistan, former Canadian Forces ombud André Marin warned the military that "Post Traumatic Stress Disorder is an operational hazard that is a fact of modern peacekeeping missions." In his report, Marin noted that nearly 20 percent of those in uniform and 50 percent of reservists experience PTSD (Dineen, 2003). He also noted that soldiers suffering from PTSD-related illnesses were often stigmatized by their peers and superiors, and that many were considered "fakers." Regrettably, recent evidence suggests that the situation may only have worsened since the ombud's original report (Statistics Canada, 2014).

Since the beginning of Canada's military involvement in Afghanistan, roughly 25 percent of Canadian soldiers have returned from this mission with mental health problems. The most recent assessment suggests that 12 percent of soldiers had one or more mental-health problems, including post-traumatic stress disorder (PTSD) and depression. Another 13 percent of them reported "harmful" or "hazardous" drinking. Canadian Forces ombud Pierre Daigle has called PTSD and related stress illnesses "a real hardship for Canada's soldiers, sailors, airmen and airwomen for many years to come" (Sher, 2011). ■

Victims tend to react to catastrophic events in a series of stages. **[LO 12.8]** First, they seem disoriented and may wander about aimlessly, often unaware of their own injuries and without attempting to help themselves or others. Following this stage, victims show a concern for others; although unable to act efficiently on their own, they are willing to follow the directions of rescue workers. As victims begin to recover, this shock is replaced by generalized anxiety.

Recovering victims typically have recurring nightmares and feel a compulsive need to retell the event over and over. Perhaps re-experiencing the event through dreaming and retelling helps desensitize them to the horror of the experience. Crisis intervention therapy can provide victims with both coping strategies and realistic expectations about the problems they may face in connection with the trauma. Although most people eventually manage the stress associated with such catastrophes quite well, some people experience an extreme form of stress reaction known as *post-traumatic stress disorder.*

When writer Pico Iyer's home was destroyed by arson, he saved only his cat and his manuscript. A fairly common reaction to such catastrophic events is post-traumatic stress disorder.

©Mark Richard/PhotoEdit Inc.

POST-TRAUMATIC STRESS DISORDER

What is post-traumatic stress disorder?

Post-traumatic stress disorder (PTSD) is a prolonged and severe stress reaction to a catastrophic event (such as a plane crash, an earthquake, or rape) or to chronic intense stress, such as that which occurs in combat or during imprisonment as a hostage. PTSD can also be the result of living in a neighbourhood in which violent crime is a daily occurrence (Kilpatrick et al., 2003) or even in an environment wherein one is exposed to domestic violence (Griffin et al., 2006). The disorder may show up immediately, or it may not appear until six months or more after the traumatic experience, in which case it is called *delayed* post-traumatic stress disorder. The most serious cases of PTSD are found among those who have witnessed brutal atrocities: victims of sexual violence and child abuse (Filipas & Ullman, 2006; Hedtke et al., 2008) and soldiers who have experienced combat (M. Price, Gros, Strachan, Ruggiero, & Acierno, 2012). The *Canadian Connections* box looks at the PTSD suffered by soldiers returning from combat.

approach–approach conflict: A conflict arising from having to choose between desirable alternatives.

avoidance–avoidance conflict: A conflict arising from having to choose between equally undesirable alternatives.

approach–avoidance conflict: A conflict arising when a choice has both desirable and undesirable features, so that you are both drawn to and repelled by the same choice.

post-traumatic stress disorder (PTSD): A prolonged and severe stress reaction to a catastrophic or otherwise traumatic event; characterized by anxiety, psychic numbing, withdrawal from others, and the feeling that one is reliving the traumatic experience.

REMEMBER IT

Sources of Stress

1. Rick cannot decide whether to go out or stay home and study for his test. What kind of conflict does he have?
   a. approach–approach conflict
   b. avoidance–avoidance conflict
   c. approach–avoidance conflict
   d. ambivalence–ambivalence conflict

2. Victims of catastrophic events typically want to talk about their experience. (true/false)

3. What has research shown to increase stress?
   a. predictability of the stressor
   b. unpredictability of the stressor
   c. predictability of and control over the stressor
   d. unpredictability of and lack of control over the stressor

4. Post-traumatic stress disorder is a prolonged and severe stress reaction that results when a number of common sources of stress occur simultaneously. (true/false)

Answers: 1. c 2. true 3. d 4. false

People with post-traumatic stress disorder often have flashbacks, nightmares, or intrusive memories in which they feel as if they are actually re-experiencing the traumatic event. [LO 12.9] They suffer increased anxiety and startle easily, particularly in response to anything that reminds them of the trauma (APA, 2013). Many survivors of war or catastrophic events experience *survivor guilt* because they lived while others died; some feel that perhaps they could have done more to save others (Southwick, Gilmartin, Mcdonough, & Morrissey, 2006). People who develop PTSD are also quite likely to experience depression (Bleich, Koslowsky, Dolev, & Lerer, 1997) and cognitive difficulties such as poor concentration (Vasterling et al., 2002).

MODULE 12C COPING WITH STRESS

LO 12.10 Describe coping.
LO 12.11 Explain and compare problem-focused and emotion-focused coping.
LO 12.12 Describe an effective stress management strategy.

When we encounter stressful situations, we try either to alter them or to reinterpret them to make them seem more favourable. **Coping** refers to our efforts to deal with demands that we perceive as taxing or overwhelming (Lazarus, 1993). [LO 12.10]

PROBLEM-FOCUSED AND EMOTION-FOCUSED COPING

What is the difference between problem-focused and emotion-focused coping?

Coping strategies fall into two categories: problem focused and emotion focused (Lazarus & Folkman, 1984). **Problem-focused coping** is direct; it involves reducing, modifying, or eliminating the source of stress. [LO 12.11] If you are getting a poor grade in history and appraise this as a threat, you may study harder, talk over your problem with your professor, form a study group with other class members, get a tutor, or drop the course.

But what can we do when we face stress that we cannot fight, escape from, avoid, or modify in any way? We can use

REVIEW & REFLECT 12.1 PROBLEM-FOCUSED AND EMOTION-FOCUSED COPING STRATEGIES

Coping Strategy	Definition	Examples
Problem focused	A response aimed at reducing, modifying, or eliminating the source of stress.	Acting to remove or lessen the threat.
		Removing oneself from the stressful situation.
		Enlisting the help of others in dealing with the threat.
		Seeking professional help or advice.
		Acting to prevent recurrence of similar stressful situations.
Emotion focused	A response aimed at reducing the emotional distress caused by the stressor.	Viewing the stressor as a challenge rather than a threat.
		Using one of these responses: prayer, denial, wishful thinking, fantasizing, humour, relaxation, biofeedback, alcohol, drugs, overeating, promiscuous sex.

REMEMBER IT

Coping with Stress

1. Lazarus's research focused on the _____ aspects of coping.
   a. complex
   b. psychological
   c. physiological
   d. emotion-focused

2. Experts who have studied how to cope with traumatic events suggest that it is often best to isolate yourself from others in order to cope successfully. (true/false)

3. Coping aimed at reducing, modifying, or eliminating a source of stress is called _____ coping; coping aimed at reducing an emotional reaction to stress is called _____ coping.
   a. emotion-focused; problem-focused
   b. problem-focused; emotion-focused
   c. primary; secondary
   d. secondary; primary

4. Researchers recommend that people use a combination of problem-focused and emotion-focused coping when dealing with a stressful situation. (true/false)

Answers: 1. b 2. false 3. b 4. true

---

emotion-focused coping to change the way we respond emotionally. **[LO 12.11]** Emotion-focused coping may involve reappraising a stressor by using many possible strategies. Some people may use prayer, denial, or wishful thinking. They may also fantasize about various options or use humour. Others may prefer to use relaxation, biofeedback, or even alcohol, drugs, overeating, or promiscuous sex in order to reduce the emotional impact of a serious problem. A person who loses his job, for example, may decide that it isn't a major tragedy and instead view it as a challenge—an opportunity to find a better job with a higher salary. And despite what you may have heard, ignoring a stressor, one form of emotion-focused coping, can be an effective way of managing stress. Other emotion-focused strategies, such as keeping a journal in which you write about your worries and track how they change over time, may be even more effective (Alford, Malouff, & Osland, 2005). But a combination of problem-focused and emotion-focused coping is probably the most effective stress management strategy (Folkman & Lazarus, 1980). **[LO 12.12]** *Review & Reflect 12.1* summarizes the problem-focused and emotion-focused coping strategies.

MODULE 12D EVALUATING LIFE STRESS: MAJOR LIFE CHANGES, HASSLES, AND UPLIFTS

LO 12.13 Describe what the Social Readjustment Rating Scale is designed to measure.
LO 12.14 Explain the connection between life stress and health problems.
LO 12.15 Explain the balance between daily hassles and uplifts in the experience of stress.

There are two major approaches to evaluating life stress and its relation to illness. One approach focuses on major life events, which cause life changes that require adaptation. A second approach focuses on life's daily hassles.

HOLMES AND RAHE'S SOCIAL READJUSTMENT RATING SCALE: ADDING UP THE STRESS SCORES

What is the Social Readjustment Rating Scale designed to reveal?

Interested in the relationship between life changes and illness, Thomas Holmes and Richard Rahe (1967) developed the **Social Readjustment Rating Scale (SRRS)**. The SRRS is designed to measure stress by ranking different life events from most to least stressful. **[LO 12.13]** Each life event is assigned a point value. Life events that produce the greatest life changes and require the greatest adaptation are considered the most stressful, regardless of whether the events are positive or negative. The original scale assesses whether a person has experienced one of 43 life events that include the death of a spouse (100 stress points), divorce (73 points), death of a close family member (63 points), marriage (50 points), pregnancy (40 points), and trouble with the boss (23 points), and minor law violations such as getting

coping: Efforts through action and thought to deal with demands that are perceived as taxing or overwhelming.

problem-focused coping: A response aimed at reducing, modifying, or eliminating a source of stress.

emotion-focused coping: A response aimed at reducing the emotional impact of the stressor.

Social Readjustment Rating Scale (SRRS): A stress scale, developed by Holmes and Rahe, which ranks 43 life events from most to least stressful and assigns a point value to each.

Even positive life events, such as getting married, can cause stress.

©Roman Pyshchyk/Fotolia

a traffic ticket (11 points). More recent research has shown that scores on the scale developed by Holmes and Rahe in 1967 are still correlated with a variety of health indicators (Dohrenwend, 2006; Thorsteinsson & Brown, 2009).

Holmes and Rahe maintain that there is a connection between the degree of life stress and major health problems. **[LO 12.14]** After analyzing more than 5000 medical case histories, they concluded that major life changes often precede serious illness (Rahe, Meyer, Smith, Kjaer, & Holmes, 1964). However, one of the main shortcomings of the SRRS is that it assigns a point value to each life change without taking into account whether the change is for the better or the worse. For example, life changes such as divorce, separation, pregnancy, retirement from work, and changing jobs or residences may be either welcome or unwelcome.

Paul Insel and Walter Roth (1985) developed a similar scale to assess the degree of stress experienced by students. Would you like to learn the number of stress points in your life? Complete the *Try It.*

THE HASSLES OF LIFE: LITTLE THINGS STRESS A LOT

What roles do hassles and uplifts play in the stress of life, according to Lazarus?

Which do you think is more stressful—major life events or those little problems and frustrations that seem to crop up every day? Richard Lazarus believes that the little stressors, which he calls **hassles**, add up to more stress than major life events.

Daily hassles are the "irritating, frustrating, distressing demands and troubled relationships that plague us day in and day out" (Lazarus & DeLongis, 1983, p. 247). **[LO 12.15]** Lazarus and colleagues (Kanner, Coyne, Schaefer, & Lazarus, 1981) developed the Hassles Scale to assess various categories of hassles that include irritating, frustrating experiences such as standing in line, being stuck in traffic, waiting for an appliance repair technician to come to your home, and so on. People completing the scale indicate which items have been a hassle for

TRY IT

Student Stress Scale

The Student Stress Scale is scored by adding the points listed for the checked life events. Insel and Roth suggest the following interpretations: Scores of 300 and higher indicate a relatively high health risk; scores of 150 to 299 indicate a 50–50 chance of serious health problems within two years. What stress management skills that you have studied could you apply to the results of this scale?

Instructions: Check those events you have experienced in the past six months or are likely to experience in the next six months. Add up the points to derive your total stress score.

Rank	Life Event	Past	Future	Stress Value	Your Scores	Rank	Life Event	Past	Future	Stress Value	Your Scores
1	Death of a close family member			100		18	Outstanding personal achievement			36	
2	Death of a close friend			73		19	First quarter/semester in college/university			35	
3	Divorce between parents			65		20	Change in living conditions			31	
4	Jail term			63		21	Serious argument with instructor			30	
5	Major personal injury or illness			63		22	Lower grades than expected			29	
6	Marriage			58		23	Change in sleeping habits			29	
7	Fired from job			50		24	Change in social activities			29	
8	Failed important course			47		25	Change in eating habits			28	
9	Change in health of a family member			45		26	Chronic car trouble			26	
10	Pregnancy			45		27	Change in number of family get-togethers			26	
11	Sex problems			44		28	Too many missed classes			25	
12	Serious argument with a close friend			40		29	Change of college/university			24	
13	Change in financial status			39		30	Dropped more than one class			23	
14	Change of major			39		31	Minor traffic violations			20	
15	Trouble with parents			39							
16	New girl or boy friend			38						**Total:**	
17	Increased workload			37							

Source: Insel & Roth, 1985. Insel, P., & Roth, W. (1985). Core Concepts in Health (4th ed.). Palo Alto, CA: Mayfield Publishing Co. Reprinted by permission from McGraw-Hill Companies.

them and rate them for severity on a three-point scale. Research indicates that minor hassles that accompany stressful major life events are better predictors of the level of psychological distress than are the major life events themselves (Pillow, Zautra, & Sandler, 1996). **[LO 12.15]**

According to Lazarus, "A person's morale, social functioning, and health don't hinge on hassles alone, but on a balance between the good things that happen to people—that make them feel good—and the bad" (quoted in Goleman, 1979, p. 52). Hassles are part of everyone's life, but what are the specific

hassles that affect students? In a 2005 study, researchers examined this question and found that balancing the time needed for class assignments, studying, and social relationships was identified as the most challenging hassle for students. Other

hassles: Little stressors that include the irritating demands and troubled relationships that are encountered daily and that, according to Lazarus, cause more stress than do major life changes.

REMEMBER IT

Evaluating Life Stress

1. On the Social Readjustment Rating Scale, only negative life changes are considered stressful. (true/false)

2. The Social Readjustment Rating Scale takes account of the individual's perceptions of the stressfulness of the life change in assigning stress points. (true/false)

3. According to Lazarus, hassles typically account for more life stress than do major life changes. (true/false)

4. Lazarus's approach in measuring hassles and uplifts considers individual perceptions of stressful events. (true/false)

Answers: 1. false 2. false 3. true 4. true

---

important sources of hassles were: not having enough money; feeling that they were treated differently because of race, cultural stereotypes, or gender; and concerns about being lonely, not having enough friends, or having difficulty making friends (Pett & Johnson, 2005) .

Fortunately, life's **uplifts**—that is, the positive experiences—may neutralize or cancel out many of the hassles. **[LO 12.15]** But events viewed as uplifts by some people may actually be stressors for other people. For example, for middle-aged people, uplifts are often health or family related, whereas for college or university students uplifts often take the form of having a good time.

MODULE **12E** HEALTH AND DISEASE

LO 12.16 Identify positive strategies for coping with cancer and cancer treatment.

LO 12.17 Describe the psychological impact of HIV infection and AIDS and strategies for coping psychologically.

LO 12.18 Describe psychoneuroimmunology and the effects of stress and depression on the immune system.

LO 12.19 Explain the role of optimism in physical health.

LO 12.20 Discuss social support as a factor that contributes to better health.

Health psychologists study the myriad ways in which we respond to illness risk factors, and the factors that affect whether we seek treatment. Let's look at two examples: cancer and AIDS.

CANCER: A DREADED DISEASE

Cancer. The word alone is frightening. Cancer is second only to heart disease as the leading cause of death. The Canadian Cancer Society estimated in 2014 that in that year, 191 300 Canadians would be diagnosed with cancer and 76 600 would die of it (Canadian Cancer Society, 2014). Young people are not spared the scourge of cancer, which takes the lives of more children between the ages of 3 and 14 than any other disease.

We speak of cancer as a single disease, but actually it is a complicated collection of diseases. Cancer can invade the cells in any part of a living organism—humans, other animals, and even plants. Cancer always starts small, because it is a disease of the body's cells. Normal cells in all parts of the body reproduce (divide), and they have built-in instructions about when to stop doing so. If they did not, every part of the body would continue to grow as long as it lived. Unlike normal cells, cancerous cells do not stop dividing. Unless they can be caught in time and destroyed, they continue to grow and spread, eventually killing the organism.

Risk Factors for Cancer

Health psychologists warn that an unhealthy diet, smoking, excessive alcohol consumption, promiscuous sexual behaviour, and becoming sexually active in the early teens (especially for females) are all behaviours that increase the risk of cancer. Compared with those who do not get cancer, many cancer patients report that they faced more high-stress situations in their lives before their cancer was diagnosed.

Coping with Cancer

What can cancer patients do to help themselves cope with having cancer?

People who are diagnosed with cancer must adjust to the chronic stressors associated with it. They must cope with difficult medical therapies along with "continued emotional distress, disrupted life tasks, social and interpersonal turmoil and fatigue and low energy" (B. L. Anderson, Kiecolt-Glaser, & Glaser, 1994, p. 390). The chronic stress associated with cancer can damage the autonomic, endocrine, and immune systems. Researchers suggest that patients need more than medical treatment: their therapy should also involve helping them maintain their quality of life. Patients should be able to discuss their fears and anxieties, be given information about their disease and treatment, and be taught how to lower their arousal. **[LO 12.16]**

What have health psychologists found that can help cancer patients? Carver and colleagues (1993, 2005) found that breast-cancer patients who maintained an optimistic outlook, accepted the reality of their situation, and maintained a sense of humour experienced less distress three months and six months after surgery. Patients who refused to accept the reality of the situation and who had thoughts of giving up experienced much higher levels of distress. Social support and focusing on the positive have also been identified as effective coping strategies (Dunkel-Schetter, Feinstein, Taylor, & Falke, 1992). **[LO 12.16]** Avoidant coping strategies such as fantasizing, denial, and social withdrawal were associated with more emotional distress.

AIDS

What happens to a person from the time of infection with HIV to the development of full-blown AIDS?

The most feared disease related to the immune system is AIDS (acquired immune deficiency syndrome), which is caused by the human immunodeficiency virus (HIV). The virus attacks the helper cells, gradually but relentlessly weakening the immune system. The first case of AIDS was diagnosed in Canada in the early 1980s; there is still no cure for it and no vaccine to protect against it. Finding a cure is urgent—worldwide statistics for 2010 estimate that 34 million people around the world live with HIV or AIDS (Avert.org, 2011).

When a person is first infected, HIV enters the bloodstream. This initial infection usually causes no symptoms, and the immune system begins to produce HIV antibodies. It is these antibodies that are detected in the AIDS test. Individuals then progress to the asymptomatic carrier state, during which they experience no symptoms at all and thus can unknowingly infect others.

HIV attacks the immune system until it becomes essentially non-functional. The diagnosis of AIDS is made when the immune system is so damaged that victims develop rare forms of cancer or pneumonia or other "opportunistic" infections. Such infections would not usually affect people with a normal immune response; in people who have a very impaired immune system, these infections can be life-threatening. At this point, patients typically experience progressive weight loss, weakness, fever, swollen lymph nodes, and diarrhea; 25 percent develop a rare cancer that produces red-purple spots on the skin. Other infections develop as the immune system weakens further.

The Transmission of AIDS

HIV is transmitted primarily through the exchange of blood, semen, or vaginal secretions during sexual contact or when IV (intravenous) drug users share contaminated needles or syringes (Des Jarlais & Friedman, 1994). Infected mothers can also infect the fetus prenatally, during childbirth, and when breastfeeding. There currently is no cure or vaccine available to treat AIDS. The most effective treatment to date consists of a combination of at least three medications, referred to as "highly active antiretroviral therapy" (HAART) (World Health Organization, 2010).

The Psychological Impact of HIV Infection and AIDS

Most people are psychologically devastated when they are diagnosed with the AIDS virus. **[LO 12.17]** Not only are they being sentenced to an early death, but there is a social stigma associated with AIDS that few other diseases have.

To cope psychologically, AIDS patients and those infected with HIV need education and information about the disease. **[LO 12.17]** They can be helped by psychotherapy, self-help groups, and medications such as antidepressants and anti-anxiety drugs. Self-help groups and group therapy may serve as substitute family for some patients. An ever-present concern voiced by patients in psychotherapy is whether to tell others and, if so, what to tell them and how. Patients may feel a compelling need to confide in others and, at the same time, to conceal their condition.

Protection against Sexually Transmitted Diseases: Minimizing Risk

Although everyone has seen or heard the messages about "safer" behaviours, many people still ignore the message. Even when people indicate that they are concerned about contracting AIDS, many do not use any form of protection when engaged in new sexual encounters (Lewis, Miguez-Burbano, & Malow, 2009). People who choose to practise promiscuous sex are never entirely safe, but they can reduce the risks by using a condom.

STRESS AND THE IMMUNE SYSTEM

What are the effects of stress and depression on the immune system?

In a field of study known as **psychoneuroimmunology**, psychologists, biologists, and medical researchers combine their expertise to learn how psychological factors (emotions, thinking, and behaviour) affect the immune system. **[LO 12.18]**

Several studies show that emotions, psychological factors, and stress are related to immune system functioning (Glaser & Kiecolt-Glaser, 2014). **[LO 12.18]** These relationships are incredibly complex, given that our immune system is an interconnected defence system working with the brain to keep the body healthy. For example, social factors, such as close social ties to family, friends, and others, have been shown to have positive effects on the immune system, whereas poor marital relationships, sleep deprivation, exams, and academic pressures have been linked to lowered immune response (Glaser & Kiecolt-Glaser, 2014). This pattern of protection holds across age and racial groups, for both sexes, at all educational levels, and at every season of the year. Severe, incapacitating depression is

---

uplifts: The positive experiences in life, which can neutralize the effects of many of the hassles.

psychoneuroimmunology (sye-ko-NEW-ro-IM-you-NOLL-oh-gee): A field in which psychologists, biologists, and medical researchers study the effects of psychological factors on the immune system.

related to lowered immune activity (Robles, Shaffer, Malarkey, & Kiecolt-Glaser, 2006). After the death of a spouse, the widow or widower suffers weakened immune system function and is at a higher risk of mortality; this risk may last for up to two years following a partner's death (Prigerson et al., 1997).

Periods of high stress have been correlated with increased symptoms of many infectious diseases, including oral and genital herpes, mononucleosis, colds, and flu. Stress can cause decreased levels of the immune system's B and T cells. People who experience stress may indeed be more susceptible to coronary heart disease, stroke, and poorer pregnancy outcomes (Steptoe & Kivimäki, 2012; Hobel, Goldstein, & Barrett, 2008). But even more ominous is the growing evidence that stress can impair the functioning of the immune system itself. **[LO 12.18]** For instance, people exposed to cold viruses are more likely to develop colds if they have experienced a greater number of life changes in the previous year (S. Cohen, Miller, & Rabin, 2001). In fact, physicians have long observed that stress and anxiety can worsen autoimmune diseases (Chrousos, 2009).

PERSONAL FACTORS REDUCING THE IMPACT OF STRESS AND ILLNESS

What three personal factors are associated with health and resistance to stress?

Researchers have identified three personal factors that may contribute to better health: optimism, psychological hardiness, and social support.

Optimism and Pessimism

Researchers have shown a strong relationship between positive attitudes and physical health (Pressman & Cohen, 2005). Recent longitudinal research has even shown that an optimistic outlook can reduce the risk of a first heart attack by 50 percent when compared to the least optimistic (Boehm, Peterson, Kivimaki, & Kubzandky, 2011). It should not be surprising, then, that people who are generally optimistic tend to cope more effectively with stress, and this in turn may reduce their risk of illness (Scheier, Carver, & Bridge, 2001; Seligman, 1990). **[LO 12.19]** Optimists generally expect good outcomes, and this helps make them more stress resistant than pessimists, who tend to expect bad outcomes. Researchers suspect that associations between optimism and resistance to stress are explained by the finding that, in response to similar stressors, optimists secrete lower levels of stress hormones than pessimists do (Lai et al., 2005). Optimism seems to be especially important in the prevention of stress-induced symptom flare-ups among patients with chronic disorders such as multiple sclerosis (Mitsonis, Potagas, Zervas, Sfagos, 2009).

Optimism is at the heart of a movement called *positive psychology*. The main proponent of the movement, Martin Seligman, argues that psychologists should focus more attention on using research to improve people's lives than they do on treating psychological disorders (Seligman & Csikszentmihalyi, 2000). Perhaps you too should consider taking a more positive outlook on life . . . doing so could have many social and health-related benefits.

A strong social support network can help a person recover faster from an illness.

Psychological Hardiness: Commitment, Challenge, and Control

Suzanne Kobasa (1979; Kobasa, Maddi, & Kahn, 1982) wondered why some people under great stress succumb to illness while others do not. She studied 670 male executives, who identified stressful life events and symptoms of illness that they had experienced in the preceding three years. She then administered personality questionnaires to 200 executives who ranked high for both stress and illness and to 126 who had faced equally stressful life events but had few symptoms of illness. She found three qualities that distinguished those who remained healthy from those who had a high incidence of illness: *commitment*, *control*, and *challenge*. Kobasa collectively called these psychological qualities **hardiness**.

Hardy individuals feel a strong sense of commitment to their work and personal life. They see themselves as having control over consequences and outcomes, and they welcome challenges. Being hardy also has some positive impact for students. Research has shown that hardiness can also reduce your academic stress and, consequently, reduce students' reported health complaints (Hystad, Eid, Laberg, Johnsen, & Bartone, 2009).

Social Support: Help in Time of Need

Another factor that seems to contribute to better health is **social support** (Thoits, 2011). **[LO 12.20]** This includes support provided by a spouse or other family members, friends, neighbours, colleagues, support groups, and members of the larger community. Social support can direct help, information, and advice to the individual, as well as emotional support. Social support provides the feeling that we are loved, valued, esteemed, and cared for by those to whom we feel a mutual obligation (S. Cohen, 1988, 2004).

Social support appears to have positive effects on the body's immune system as well as on the cardiovascular and endocrine systems (Uchino & Birmingham, 2011). Social

REMEMBER IT

Health and Disease

1. Lowered immune response has been associated with_____
   a. stress.
   b. depression.
   c. stress and depression.
   d. neither stress nor depression.

2. Some research suggests that optimists are more stress resistant than pessimists. (true/false)

3. Social support tends to reduce stress but is unrelated to health outcomes. (true/false)

4. Which of the following is not a dimension of psychological hardiness?
   a. A feeling that adverse circumstances can be controlled and changed.
   b. A sense of commitment and deep involvement in personal goals.
   c. A tendency to look upon change as a challenge rather than a threat.
   d. Close, supportive relationships with family and friends.

Answers: 1. c 2. true 3. false 4. d

---

support may encourage health-promoting behaviours and reduce the impact of stress so that people are less likely to resort to unhealthy methods of coping, such as smoking and drinking. Further, social support has been shown to reduce depression and enhance self-esteem in individuals who suffer from chronic illnesses (Symister & Friend, 2003). People with strong social support recover more quickly from illnesses and have a significantly lower risk of death from specific diseases (Holt-Lunstad, Smith, & Layton, 2010).

MODULE 12F YOUR LIFESTYLE AND YOUR HEALTH

LO 12.21 Explain factors that constitute an unhealthy lifestyle.

LO 12.22 Identify factors apart from the physical addiction that can diminish a smoker's ability to quit smoking.

LO 12.23 Describe the disease model of alcoholism and the limitations of this model.

LO 12.24 Identify the benefits of regular exercise to promoting better health.

What constitutes an unhealthy lifestyle, and how serious a factor is lifestyle in illness and disease?

If you are not healthy or physically hardy, who or what is to blame? There are a number of enemies of good health: environmental pollutants; job, family, and personal stressors; genetic and congenital defects; accidents and injury; and others. But the number one concern with most people is lifestyle habits. The specific culprits are all well known: an unhealthy diet, overeating, lack of exercise, alcohol and drug abuse, too much coffee, too little sleep, and so on. **[LO 12.21]** The most dangerous unhealthy behaviour of all is smoking.

SMOKING: HAZARDOUS TO YOUR HEALTH

Why is smoking considered the single most preventable cause of death?

According to the most recent Canadian statistics, 16 percent of Canadians aged 15 or older smoke (Health Canada, 2013). According to the most recent Canadian statistics, in 2011 alone, smoking was directly related to more than 37 000 deaths in Canada; "of those," Health Canada predicted at the time, "more than 300 non-smokers will die of lung cancer and at least 700 non-smokers will die of coronary heart disease caused by exposure to second-hand smoke" (Health Canada, 2011a). Add to these statistics the suffering from chronic bronchitis, emphysema, and other respiratory diseases; death and injury from fires caused by smoking; and low birth weight and impaired fetal development in babies born to mothers who smoke.

Why do adult smokers continue the habit even though most admit they would prefer to be non-smokers? There seems little doubt that smoking is an addiction. Nicotine is a powerful substance that increases the release of acetylcholine, norepinephrine, dopamine, and other neurotransmitters, which improve mental alertness, sharpen memory, and reduce tension and anxiety (Pomerleau & Pomerleau, 1989). Withdrawal

---

hardiness: A combination of three psychological qualities shared by people who can undergo high levels of stress yet remain healthy: commitment to one's personal goals, a sense of control over one's life, and a tendency to view change as a challenge rather than as a threat.

social support: Tangible support, information, advice, and/or emotional support provided in time of need by family, friends, and others; the feeling that we are loved, valued, and cared for.

symptoms from smoking typically last two to four weeks and the average smoker makes five or six attempts to quit before succeeding. But quitting smoking is more complex than overcoming the physical addiction. Rates of success vary substantially depending on the strategy used and the commitment made to quitting. **[LO 12.22]** For instance, research has shown that only 20 percent of smokers using nicotine replacement, such as patches or gum, succeed (Rose, 2006). Unfortunately, research to date suggests that the effectiveness of nicotine replacement strategies do not seem to improve as a result of the social support provided to the individual who is trying to quit (Stead, Perera, Bullen, Mant, & Lancaster, 2008).

ALCOHOL: A PROBLEM FOR MILLIONS

What are some health risks of alcohol consumption?

The health and social costs of alcohol—in fatalities, lost work, family problems, and so on—are staggering. According to the most recent comprehensive study conducted in Canada, direct alcohol-related health care costs alone totalled $3.3 billion in 2002 (Rehm, Patra, & Popova, 2006). Alcohol abuse and dependence are significantly more prevalent among men than among women. People who begin drinking before age 15 are more likely to become dependent on alcohol than those who begin later (Grant & Dawson, 1998; Prescott & Kendler, 1999). Research suggests that alcohol is related to 6 percent of all deaths in Canada for people below the age of 70, with a much higher rate for men (7.6 percent) than women (3.5 percent) (Rehm, Patra, & Popova, 2006)

Alcohol can damage virtually every organ in the body, but it is especially harmful to the liver and is the major cause of cirrhosis. Alcoholics are about three times as likely to die in automobile accidents or of heart disease as non-alcoholics, and they have twice the rate of death from cancer. Pregnant women should avoid all alcohol because of its potentially disastrous effects on the developing fetus. Alcohol also affects the brain. For instance, research using MRI scans has shown damage to the brains of long-term alcoholics (Zahr, Kaufman, & Harper, 2011). Even shorter-term heavy drinking can cause cognitive damage and dysfunction that continues for several months after the drinking has stopped (Harper, 2009; Maurage, Joassin, Speth, Modvae, Philippot, & Campenella, 2012). The only good news in recent studies is that some of alcohol's effects on the brain seem to be partially reversible with prolonged abstinence.

Alcoholism's toll goes beyond physical damage to the alcoholic. Drunk drivers kill and injure. Alcohol has also been implicated in drownings, suicides, sexual assaults, burglaries, and assaults.

Alcoholism: Causes and Treatment

The Canadian Medical Association maintains that alcoholism is a disease, and "once an alcoholic, always an alcoholic."

According to this view, even a small amount of alcohol causes an irresistible craving for more, leading alcoholics to lose control of their drinking. Total abstinence is seen as the only acceptable recourse. The medical establishment and Alcoholics Anonymous endorse both the disease concept and the total abstinence approach to treatment.

Recent studies suggest that there is a genetic factor in alcoholism and lend support to the disease model. **[LO 12.23]** For example, neuroscience research suggests that the brains of alcoholics respond differently to visual and auditory stimuli than do those of non-alcoholics, and that these differences act as a genetic marker associated with a predisposition to alcoholism (Hada, Porjesz, Chorlian, Begleiter, & Polich, 2001; Porjesz et al., 2005). Relatives of alcoholics have been found to be more likely to become alcoholics themselves or to suffer from other types of addictions (Kamarajan et al., 2006; Zhang, Cohen, Projesz, & Begleiter, 2001).

The hypothesis that there is a greater genetic risk of alcoholism for men is also supported by years of research on identical and fraternal twins. **[LO 12.23]** Studies have revealed a substantial genetic influence (Kendler, Gardner, & Prescott, 2011; Tyndale, 2003). A study of 1000 pairs of female identical and fraternal twins found that alcoholism in women is 50 to 60 percent heritable, which is a rate similar to that for male alcoholics (Kendler, Gruenberg, & Kinney, 1994; Prescott & Kendler, 1999).

Is alcoholism a disease? Some experts reject the disease concept and contend that alcoholism can take various forms and have various causes. Both genetic and environmental factors, such as one's culture and family, have been shown to influence the development of alcoholism (Enoch, 2006). **[LO 12.23]**

EXERCISE: KEEPING FIT IS HEALTHY

What are some benefits of regular aerobic exercise?

For years medical experts, especially health psychologists, have promoted regular exercise. Yet only a small proportion of the population is highly active, and slightly more than 50 percent of the Canadian population aged 12 and older are physically inactive (Gilmour, 2007). Many studies show that regular **aerobic exercise** pays rich dividends in the form of physical and mental fitness. **[LO 12.24]** Aerobic exercise, such as running, swimming, brisk walking, bicycling, rowing, and jumping rope, is exercise that uses the large muscle groups in continuous, repetitive action and requires increased oxygen intake and increased breathing and heart rates. According to the Public Health Agency of Canada (2012), adults should perform aerobic exercise for a minimum of 2.5 hours per week to achieve health benefits. The importance of regular, systematic aerobic exercise in keeping the cardiovascular system healthy cannot be overemphasized. This is true for people of all ages. Even preschoolers receive cardiovascular benefits from as little as an additional 60 minutes per week of exercise. And regular, planned exercise yields dramatic increases in muscle and bone strength in older people. Strength training, for example, has been found to reduce sarcopenia, the age-related process in which muscles deteriorate. Such training also appears to prevent the loss of bone mass, called *osteoporosis* (CDC, 2011).

We do not need to become marathon runners to enjoy the maximum benefits of exercise, but individuals who engage in

---

aerobic exercise (eh-RO-bik): Exercise involving the use of large muscle groups in continuous, repetitive action and requiring increased oxygen intake and increased breathing and heart rates.

Strength training moderates the effects of aging on older adults' muscles and bones.

more than three hours of aerobic activity each week are more successful at losing excess weight and keeping it off than are those who exercise less (Votruba, Horvitz, & Schoeller, 2000).

And a daily brisk walk of 30 minutes or more helps to reduce stress and yields the fitness standard associated with a much lower death rate.

In case you are not yet convinced, consider the following benefits of exercise and other small lifestyle changes that may improve your health:

- Engage in moderate physical activity every day (e.g., walk up and down stairs for 15 minutes; spend 30 minutes washing a car). Such small amounts of activity will reduce your feelings of anxiety and sadness, will increase your bone density, and will reduce your risk of diabetes, heart disease, high blood pressure, and many other life-shortening diseases (Health Canada, 2011b). And it will also likely help you lose weight.

- While we are on the topic of weight loss, if you are overweight, try to lose just 5 kilograms. Doing so will result in a 34 percent reduction in triglyceride levels, a 16 percent decrease in total cholesterol, and an 18 percent increase in HDL ("good" cholesterol); will significantly reduce your blood pressure; and will decrease your risk for diabetes, sleep apnea, and osteoarthritis (CDC, 2011).

- Add just 20 to 30 grams of fibre to your diet each day. Doing so will improve your bowel function, reduce your risk of colon cancer and other digestive-system diseases, decrease your total blood cholesterol, reduce your blood pressure, and improve your insulin function (FiberFoods.net, 2012).

- Of course, stop smoking! Doing so will result in immediate health improvement. It will improve your circulation, reduce your blood level of carbon monoxide, stabilize your pulse rate and blood pressure, improve your sense of smell and taste, improve your lung function and endurance, and reduce your risk of lung infections such as pneumonia and bronchitis. In the long term, stopping smoking will reduce your risk of lung cancer and decrease your likelihood of developing other smoking-related illnesses such as emphysema and heart disease (Health Canada, 2011).

REMEMBER IT

Your Lifestyle and Your Health

1. Which is the most important factor leading to disease and death?
   a. unhealthy lifestyle
   b. a poor health care system
   c. environmental hazards
   d. genetic disorders

2. Which health-compromising behaviour is responsible for the most deaths?
   a. overeating
   b. smoking

   c. lack of exercise
   d. excessive alcohol use

3. (Alcohol/Smoking) damages virtually every organ in the body.

4. To improve cardiovascular fitness, aerobic exercise should be done:
   a. 15 minutes daily.
   b. 1 hour daily.
   c. 20 to 30 minutes daily.
   d. 20 to 30 minutes 3 or 4 times a week.

APPLY IT

Interpreting Health Information on the Internet

All of us now use the internet to access information. From reviews of new music, to booking hotels for an upcoming trip, to answering any of our small queries, the Web has become a most valued tool. But how reliable is health information available on the internet? In an American Medical Association–sponsored large-scale study of health-related websites, researchers found that the quality of information varied widely from one site to another (Eysenbach, Powell, Kuss, & Sa, 2002).

Despite these difficulties, physicians' organizations acknowledge the potential value of the internet in helping patients learn about and manage their own health. And because we all tend to rely extensively on the Web to gather information, here are some suggestions from the U.S. Food and Drug Administration website (2013) about how to become wise consumers of online health information:

- Remember that there are no rules governing what is published on the internet. Unlike scientific journal articles, which are usually written and reviewed by experts in the field, internet articles can be posted by anyone, without review of any kind. Without expert knowledge, it is extremely difficult to tell whether the information and advice these articles contain are valid. Any good health website should make it easy to learn who is responsible for the site and its information.
- Consider the source. Generally, websites sponsored by medical schools, government agencies, and public health organizations are reliable. Others, especially those promoting a health-related product, should be considered suspect.
- Examine references. Reliable sites refer to credible sources and give information about the medical credentials of the people who prepare or review the material on the website. Also, reliable sites are reviewed and updated on a regular basis.
- Is it too good to be true? As in all areas of life, if something sounds too good to be true (e.g., a vitamin that cures cancer), it probably is. Try to find experimental, placebo-controlled studies that support any claims.

Using these guidelines, you can become a better consumer of internet-based health information.

THINKING CRITICALLY

Evaluation

Can people always cure themselves of illnesses? What are the limits to what people can do to help themselves?

Point/Counterpoint

Prepare two arguments, one supporting the position that alcoholism is a genetically inherited disease, and the other supporting the position that alcoholism is not a medical disease but results from learning.

Psychology in Your Life

Choose several stress-producing incidents from your own life and explain what problem-focused and emotion-focused coping strategies you used. From the knowledge you have gained in this chapter, list other coping strategies that might have been more effective.

MyPsychLab

Go to mypsychlab (access code required) to find web resources for your text that supplement the material in chapter 12.

SUMMARY & REVIEW

12A THEORIES OF STRESS

What is the general adaptation syndrome?
The general adaptation syndrome is the predictable sequence of reactions that organisms show in response to stressors. It consists of the alarm stage, the resistance stage, and the exhaustion stage.

What are the roles of primary and secondary appraisal when people are confronted with a potentially stressful event?
Lazarus maintains that when we are confronted with a potentially stressful event, we engage in a cognitive appraisal process consisting of (1) a primary appraisal, to evaluate the relevance

of the event to our well-being (whether it will be positive, will be irrelevant, or will involve harm or loss, threat, or challenge), and (2) a secondary appraisal to determine how we will cope with the stressor.

12B SOURCES OF STRESS: THE COMMON AND THE EXTREME

How do approach–approach, avoidance–avoidance, and approach–avoidance conflicts differ?
In an approach–approach conflict, we must decide between equally desirable alternatives; in an avoidance–avoidance conflict, between two undesirable alternatives. In an approach–avoidance conflict, we are both drawn to and repelled by a choice.

How do the unpredictability of, and lack of control over a stressor affect its impact?
Stressors that are unpredictable and uncontrollable are more stressful than those that are predictable and controllable.

How do people typically react to catastrophic events?
Victims of catastrophic events are initially dazed and stunned. When they begin to recover from the shock, they typically experience anxiety, nightmares, and a compulsive need to retell the event over and over.

What is post-traumatic stress disorder?
Post-traumatic stress disorder (PTSD) is a prolonged, severe stress reaction to a catastrophic event. The victim relives the trauma in flashbacks, nightmares, or intrusive memories.

12C COPING WITH STRESS

What is the difference between problem-focused and emotion-focused coping?
Problem-focused coping is a response aimed at reducing, modifying, or eliminating the source of stress; emotion-focused coping is aimed at reducing the emotional impact of the stressor.

12D EVALUATING LIFE STRESS: MAJOR LIFE CHANGES, HASSLES, AND UPLIFTS

What is the Social Readjustment Rating Scale designed to reveal?
The SRRS assesses stress in terms of life events that necessitate life change. Holmes and Rahe found a relationship between degree of life stress (as measured on the scale) and major health problems.

What roles do hassles and uplifts play in the stress of life, according to Lazarus?
According to Lazarus, daily hassles typically cause more stress than do major life changes. The positive experiences in life—the uplifts—can neutralize the effects of many of the hassles.

12E HEALTH AND DISEASE

What can cancer patients do to help themselves cope with having cancer?
Cancer patients need medical treatment and social support that will help them maintain their quality of life. They need to have opportunities to discuss their treatment and emotions openly. In addition, if patients maintain an optimistic outlook and are able to accept their condition, they may experience less distress.

What happens to a person from the time of infection with HIV to the development of full-blown AIDS?
When a person is initially infected with HIV, the body begins to produce HIV antibodies, eventually detectable in a blood test. For a period of time, the victim has no symptoms, but HIV gradually renders the immune system non-functional. The diagnosis of AIDS is made when the person succumbs to various opportunistic infections.

What are the effects of stress and depression on the immune system?
Both stress and depression have been associated with lowered immune response, and stress has been linked to increased symptoms of various infectious diseases.

What three personal factors are associated with health and resistance to stress?
Personal factors related to health and resistance to stress are optimism, psychological hardiness, and social support.

12F YOUR LIFESTYLE AND YOUR HEALTH

What constitutes an unhealthy lifestyle, and how serious a factor is lifestyle in illness and disease?
The number one health concern with most people is unhealthy lifestyle factors, which include smoking, overeating, an unhealthy diet, too much coffee or alcohol, drug abuse, and/or too little exercise and rest.

Why is smoking considered the single most preventable cause of death?
Smoking is considered the single most preventable cause of death because each year in Canada it is directly related to tens of thousands of deaths from heart disease, cancer, lung disease, and stroke.

What are some health risks of alcohol consumption?
Alcohol damages virtually every organ in the body, including the liver, stomach, skeletal muscles, heart, and brain.

What are some benefits of regular aerobic exercise?
Regular aerobic exercise reduces the risk of cardiovascular disease, increases muscle strength, moderates the effects of stress, makes bones denser and stronger, and helps maintain a desirable weight.

HEALTH AND STRESS

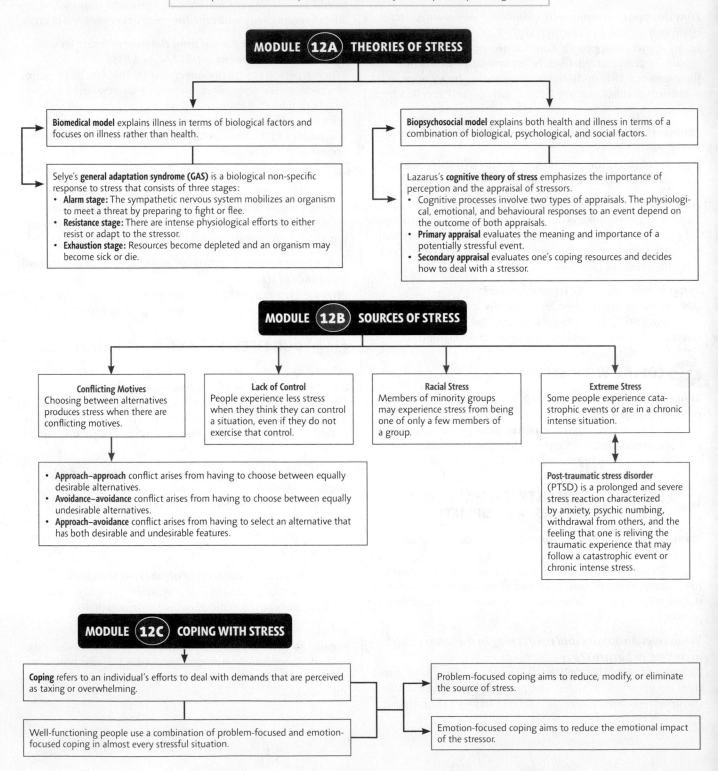

Health psychology examines psychological factors that contribute to health, illness, and recovery. **Stress** is the physiological and psychological response to a condition that threatens an individual and requires some form of adjustment. A **stressor** is any event capable of producing stress.

MODULE 12A THEORIES OF STRESS

Biomedical model explains illness in terms of biological factors and focuses on illness rather than health.

Selye's **general adaptation syndrome (GAS)** is a biological non-specific response to stress that consists of three stages:
- **Alarm stage:** The sympathetic nervous system mobilizes an organism to meet a threat by preparing to fight or flee.
- **Resistance stage:** There are intense physiological efforts to either resist or adapt to the stressor.
- **Exhaustion stage:** Resources become depleted and an organism may become sick or die.

Biopsychosocial model explains both health and illness in terms of a combination of biological, psychological, and social factors.

Lazarus's **cognitive theory of stress** emphasizes the importance of perception and the appraisal of stressors.
- Cognitive processes involve two types of appraisals. The physiological, emotional, and behavioural responses to an event depend on the outcome of both appraisals.
- **Primary appraisal** evaluates the meaning and importance of a potentially stressful event.
- **Secondary appraisal** evaluates one's coping resources and decides how to deal with a stressor.

MODULE 12B SOURCES OF STRESS

Conflicting Motives
Choosing between alternatives produces stress when there are conflicting motives.

Lack of Control
People experience less stress when they think they can control a situation, even if they do not exercise that control.

Racial Stress
Members of minority groups may experience stress from being one of only a few members of a group.

Extreme Stress
Some people experience catastrophic events or are in a chronic intense situation.

- **Approach–approach** conflict arises from having to choose between equally desirable alternatives.
- **Avoidance–avoidance** conflict arises from having to choose between equally undesirable alternatives.
- **Approach–avoidance** conflict arises from having to select an alternative that has both desirable and undesirable features.

Post-traumatic stress disorder (PTSD) is a prolonged and severe stress reaction characterized by anxiety, psychic numbing, withdrawal from others, and the feeling that one is reliving the traumatic experience that may follow a catastrophic event or chronic intense stress.

MODULE 12C COPING WITH STRESS

Coping refers to an individual's efforts to deal with demands that are perceived as taxing or overwhelming.

Well-functioning people use a combination of problem-focused and emotion-focused coping in almost every stressful situation.

Problem-focused coping aims to reduce, modify, or eliminate the source of stress.

Emotion-focused coping aims to reduce the emotional impact of the stressor.

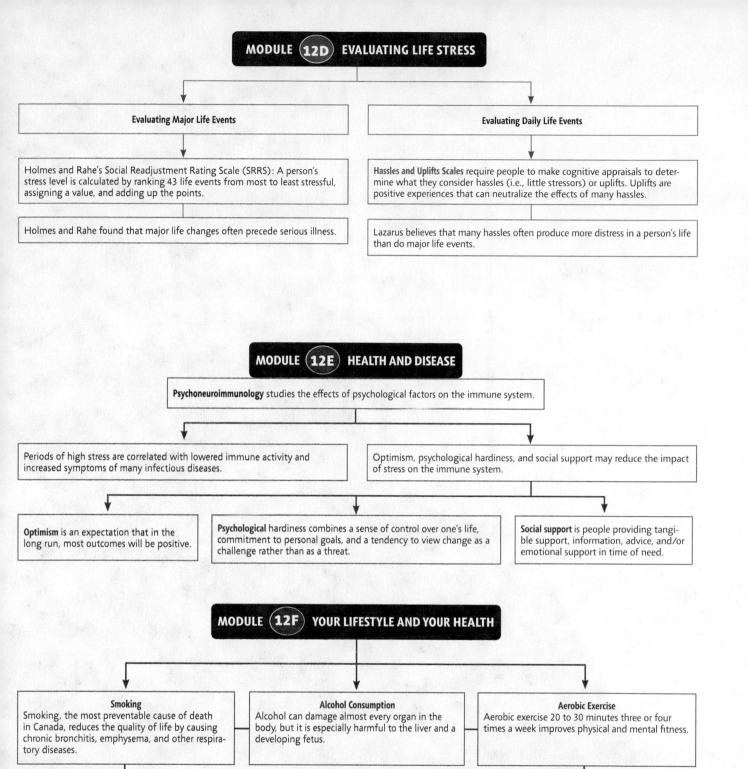

MODULE (12D) EVALUATING LIFE STRESS

Evaluating Major Life Events

Holmes and Rahe's Social Readjustment Rating Scale (SRRS): A person's stress level is calculated by ranking 43 life events from most to least stressful, assigning a value, and adding up the points.

Holmes and Rahe found that major life changes often precede serious illness.

Evaluating Daily Life Events

Hassles and Uplifts Scales require people to make cognitive appraisals to determine what they consider hassles (i.e., little stressors) or uplifts. Uplifts are positive experiences that can neutralize the effects of many hassles.

Lazarus believes that many hassles often produce more distress in a person's life than do major life events.

MODULE (12E) HEALTH AND DISEASE

Psychoneuroimmunology studies the effects of psychological factors on the immune system.

Periods of high stress are correlated with lowered immune activity and increased symptoms of many infectious diseases.

Optimism, psychological hardiness, and social support may reduce the impact of stress on the immune system.

Optimism is an expectation that in the long run, most outcomes will be positive.

Psychological hardiness combines a sense of control over one's life, commitment to personal goals, and a tendency to view change as a challenge rather than as a threat.

Social support is people providing tangible support, information, advice, and/or emotional support in time of need.

MODULE (12F) YOUR LIFESTYLE AND YOUR HEALTH

Smoking
Smoking, the most preventable cause of death in Canada, reduces the quality of life by causing chronic bronchitis, emphysema, and other respiratory diseases.

Most smokers use cigarettes to either increase their arousal or to reduce stress and anxiety.

Alcohol Consumption
Alcohol can damage almost every organ in the body, but it is especially harmful to the liver and a developing fetus.

Many people use alcohol to reduce stress and anxiety.

Aerobic Exercise
Aerobic exercise 20 to 30 minutes three or four times a week improves physical and mental fitness.

Exercise moderates the effects of stress.

13

In the early days of September 2006, Jeff Ingram, a 39-year-old Canadian man living in Olympia, Washington, said goodbye to his fiancée and left to visit his parents in northern Alberta. He never made it to his parents' home that day—in fact, he completely disappeared, without calling or contacting anyone including his fiancée, Penny Hansen, who feared the worst. What she did not know, and only uncovered more than one month later, was that Jeff had been found four days after he left on his trip in front of the Denver World Trade Center without any recollection of who he was. Many people he met on that day thought he was drunk or homeless. However, Jeff was none of these things—he simply didn't know who he was or how he got there.

What no one he met on that day realized was that Jeff was suffering from a rare form of amnesia called dissociative fugue—a condition that affects only 0.2 percent of the general population in their lifetime. People who have this condition are unable to recall any personal information from either recent memories or the distant past. The condition can last from days to years. Some sufferers never reclaim their memories.

But what happened to Jeff? He checked himself into a Denver hospital on the day he was found, and the police department was contacted to assist him in finding any clues that would allow him to return to his life. It would be more than a month and a half before he learned his true identity. The Denver police held a press conference for the media during which Jeff asked the public for help. The national news in the United States and Canada quickly jumped on the story and an old friend recognized him on television and telephoned Jeff's mother. Friends and family quickly contacted Denver police, and within 24 hours Jeff was on a flight bound for Washington to reunite with his fiancée.

When Jeff met his fiancée at the airport, he could not remember her but sensed that she was a familiar presence. Since then, Jeff has struggled to piece together the elements of his former life. But on a positive note, within weeks of reuniting, Jeff and Penny wed. (Story adapted from Derrick, 2007; Köhler, 2007.)

©katalinks/123RF

PSYCHOLOGICAL DISORDERS

What happened to Jeff Ingram is difficult to understand. What would cause an otherwise stable individual, with good family connections and a solid relationship, to forget his identity?

How can we know whether *our* behaviour is normal or abnormal? At what point do our fears, thoughts, mood changes, and actions move from normal to mentally disturbed? This chapter explores many psychological disorders, their symptoms, and their possible causes. But first let us ask the obvious question: What is abnormal?

MODULE **13A** WHAT IS ABNORMAL?

LO 13.1 Identify criteria for differentiating normal from abnormal behaviour.

LO 13.2 Identify five current perspectives that attempt to explain the causes of psychological disorders.

LO 13.1 Describe what the *DSM-5* is used for and how it assists mental health professionals.

LO 13.2 Describe and contrast neurosis and psychosis.

What criteria might be used to differentiate normal from abnormal behaviour?

Some psychological disorders are so extreme that virtually everyone would agree that the behaviours associated with them are abnormal. But most abnormal behaviours are not so extreme and clear-cut. There are not two clearly separate and distinct kinds of human beings, with one kind always mentally healthy and well adjusted and another kind always abnormal and mentally disturbed. Behaviour lies along a continuum, with most of us fairly well adjusted and experiencing only occasional maladaptive thoughts or behaviour. At one extreme of the continuum are the unusually mentally healthy; at the other extreme are the seriously disturbed. What criteria might be used to differentiate normal from abnormal behaviour?

And where along the continuum does behaviour become abnormal? Several questions can help determine what behaviour is abnormal: **[LO 13.1]**

- *Is the behaviour considered strange within the person's own culture?* What is considered normal and abnormal in one culture will not necessarily always be considered so in another. Even within the same culture, conceptions about what is normal can change from time to time.

- *Does the behaviour cause personal distress?* When people experience considerable emotional distress without any life experience that warrants it, they may be diagnosed as having a psychological or mental disorder. But not all people with psychological disorders feel distress. Some feel perfectly comfortable, even happy, with the way they are and the way they feel.

- *Is the behaviour maladaptive?* Some experts believe that the best way to differentiate between normal and abnormal behaviour is to consider whether the behaviour is adaptive or maladaptive—that is, whether it leads to healthy or impaired functioning. Maladaptive behaviour interferes with the quality of people's lives and can cause a great deal of distress to family members, friends, and co-workers.

- *Is the person a danger to self or others?* Another consideration is whether people are a threat or danger to themselves or others. In order to be committed to a mental institution, a person has to be judged both mentally ill and a danger to himself or herself or to others.

- *Is the person legally responsible for his or her acts?* Traditionally, the term *insanity* was used to label those who behaved abnormally. "Not guilty due to mental disorder" is a legal phrase used by the Canadian courts to declare people not legally responsible for their acts; the term, however, is not used by mental health professionals.

PERSPECTIVES ON THE CAUSES AND TREATMENT OF PSYCHOLOGICAL DISORDERS

What are five current perspectives that attempt to explain the causes of psychological disorders?

The earliest explanation of psychological disorders was that disturbed people were possessed by evil spirits or demons. At present, there are five main perspectives that attempt to explain the causes of psychological disorders and to recommend the best methods of treatment: biological, psychodynamic, learning,

Abnormal behaviour is defined by each culture. For example, homelessness is considered abnormal in some cultures and completely normal in others. Thus, the lack of a permanent dwelling place, in and of itself, is not necessarily indicative of a psychological disorder.

REVIEW & REFLECT 13.1 PERSPECTIVES ON PSYCHOLOGICAL DISORDERS: SUMMARY

Perspective	Cause of Psychological Disorders	Treatment
Biological perspective	A psychological disorder is a symptom of an underlying physical disorder caused by a structural or biochemical abnormality in the brain, by genetic inheritance, or by infection.	Diagnose and treat like any other physical disorder Drugs, electroconvulsive therapy, or psychosurgery
Psychodynamic perspective	Psychological disorders stem from early childhood experiences; unresolved unconscious sexual or aggressive conflicts; and/or imbalance among the id, ego, and superego.	Bring disturbing repressed material to consciousness and help patient work through unconscious conflicts Psychoanalysis
Learning perspective	Abnormal thoughts, feelings, and behaviours are learned and sustained like any other behaviours, or there is a failure to learn appropriate behaviours.	Use classical and operant conditioning and modelling to extinguish abnormal behaviours and to increase adaptive behaviour Behaviour therapy, behaviour modification
Cognitive perspective	Faulty and negative thinking can cause psychological disorders.	Change faulty, irrational, and/or negative thinking Beck's cognitive therapy, rational-emotive therapy
Humanistic perspective	Psychological disorders result from blocking of the normal tendency toward self-actualization.	Increase self-acceptance and self-understanding; help patient become more inner-directed Client-centred therapy, Gestalt therapy

cognitive, and humanistic. **[LO 13.2]** They are summarized in *Review & Reflect 13.1*.

Mental health professionals often disagree about the causes of abnormal behaviour and the best treatments; there is less disagreement about diagnosis. Standard criteria have been established and are used by most mental health professionals to diagnose psychological disorders.

DEFINING AND CLASSIFYING PSYCHOLOGICAL DISORDERS

What is the *DSM-5*?

In 1952, the American Psychiatric Association (APA) published a diagnostic system for describing and classifying psychological disorders: the *Diagnostic and Statistical Manual of Mental Disorders* (*DSM*). Over the years, this system has been revised several times. The fifth edition of the DSM was published in 2013. This latest revision is a substantial change from past versions of the *DSM* and has resulted in significant differences in the way disorders are described and classified. However, like previous versions, the *DSM-5* describes about 300 specific psychological disorders and lists the criteria for diagnosing them. **[LO 13.3]**

The DSM system is the most widely accepted diagnostic system in Canada and the United States and is used by researchers, therapists, and mental health workers. It enables a diverse group of professionals to speak the same language when diagnosing, treating, researching, and conversing about a variety of psychological disorders. **[LO 13.3]** *Review & Reflect 13.2*, on the next page, summarizes the major categories of disorders in the *DSM-5*.

You may have heard the terms *neurotic* and *psychotic* used in relation to mental disturbances. **[LO 13.4]** The term **neurosis** (now obsolete) used to be applied to disorders that cause people considerable personal distress and some impairment in functioning but do not cause them to lose contact with reality or to violate important social norms. A **psychosis** is a more serious disturbance that greatly impairs everyday functioning. It can cause people to lose touch with reality and to suffer from delusions or hallucinations, or both; it sometimes requires hospitalization. The term *psychosis* is still used by mental health professionals.

The most recent report on mental health in Canada conducted by the federal ministry of health highlighted the prevalence of various forms of mental illness in Canada (Public Health Agency of Canada [PHAC], 2012). This report was completed prior to the release of the *DSM-5*, which means that some of the categories are slightly different than would be reported today. Table 13.1, however, captures the prevalence estimates for mood disorders, schizophrenia, anxiety disorders, eating disorders, and deaths from suicide by age cohorts. (Note the high incidence of anxiety disorders—the subject of the next module.)

DSM-5 The *Diagnostic and Statistical Manual of Mental Disorders* (fifth edition) describes about 300 mental disorders and the symptoms that must be present for diagnosing each disorder.

neurosis (new-RO-sis): An obsolete term for a disorder causing personal distress and some impairment in functioning, but not causing one to lose contact with reality or to violate important social norms.

psychosis (sy-CO-sis): A severe psychological disorder, sometimes requiring hospitalization, in which one typically loses contact with reality, suffers delusions and/or hallucinations, and has a seriously impaired ability to function in everyday life.

REVIEW & REFLECT 13.2 MAJOR *DSM-5* CATEGORIES OF MENTAL DISORDERS

Category	Description	Examples of Disorders
Anxiety disorders	Disorders characterized by anxiety and avoidance behaviour	Generalized anxiety disorder Panic disorder Panic attack (specifier) Agoraphobia Specific phobia Social anxiety disorder
Obsessive-compulsive and related disorders[1]	Disorders characterized by the presence of obsessive preoccupation and repetitive behaviours	Obsessive-compulsive disorder Hoarding disorder Trichotillomania (hair-pulling disorder) Excoriation (skin picking) disorder
Trauma- and stress-related disorders[1]	Disorders which are preceded by specific stressful and potentially traumatic events	Acute stress disorder Adjustment disorder Post-traumatic stress disorder Reactive attachment disorder
Somatic symptom and related disorders	Disorders in which physical symptoms are present that are psychological in origin rather than due to a medical condition	Somatic symptom disorder Illness anxiety disorder Conversion disorder
Dissociative disorders	Disorders in which one handles stress or conflict by forgetting important personal information or one's whole identity	Dissociative identity disorder Dissociative amnesia Depersonalization/derealization disorder
Schizophrenia spectrum and other psychotic disorders	Disorders characterized by the presence of psychotic symptoms, including hallucinations	Schizophrenia Schizoaffective disorder Delusional disorder Brief psychotic disorder Catatonia
Depressive disorders[2]	Disorders characterized by periods of extreme or prolonged depression	Major depressive disorder Disruptive mood dysregulation disorder Persistent depressive disorder (dysthymia) Premenstrual dysphoric disorder
Bipolar and related disorders[2]	Disorders characterized by periods of extreme or prolonged depression and mania	Bipolar I disorder Bipolar II disorder Cyclothymic disorder
Personality disorders	Disorders characterized by long-standing, inflexible, maladaptive patterns of behaviour beginning early in life and causing personal distress or problems in social and occupational functioning	Paranoid personality disorder Schizoid personality disorder Antisocial personality disorder Histrionic personality disorder Narcissistic personality disorder Borderline personality disorder
Paraphilic disorders	Disorders where paraphilia(s) cause distress or impairment or risk of harm to self or others	Fetishistic disorder Transvestic disorder Pedophilic disorder Sexual masochism Voyeuristic disorder
Substance-related and addictive disorders	Disorders in which undesirable behavioural changes result from substance abuse, dependence, or intoxication	Substance-related disorders • Alcohol-related disorders • Opioid-related disorders • Cannabis-related disorders • Hallucinogen-related disorders Gambling disorder

Category	Description	Examples of Disorders
Neurodevelopmental disorders	Disorders with onset in the developmental period, characterized by deficits in learning, intelligence, control of executive functions or social skills	Intellectual disabilities Communication disorders Autism spectrum disorder Attention-deficit hyperactivity disorder Tic disorders
Disruptive, impulse-control, and conduct disorders[3]	Conditions involving the self-control of emotions and behaviours	Conduct disorder Oppositional defiant disorder Intermittent explosive disorder
Sleep-wake disorders	Disorders including dyssomnias (disturbance in the amount, quality, or timing of sleep) and parasomnias (abnormal occurrences during sleep)	Insomnia disorder Narcolepsy Hypersomnolence disorder Parasomnias
Feeding and eating disorders	Disorders characterized by severe disturbances in eating behaviour	Anorexia nervosa Bulimia nervosa Pica Rumination disorder

The following notes identify areas where changes occurred between the *DSM-IV-TR* and the *DSM-5*:

[1]These disorders were captured under the category of Anxiety Disorders in the *DSM-IV-TR* system, but are separate categories in the *DSM-5*.

[2]These disorders were categorized together under Mood Disorders in the *DSM-IV-TR* system, but are separate categories in the *DSM-5*.

[3]This category brings together disorders that were previously included in Disorders Usually First Diagnosed in Infancy, Childhood, or Adolescent and in Impulse-Control Disorders Not Otherwise Specified.

Source: Based on DSM-IV-TR, American Psychiatric Association. (2000). Diagnostic and Statistical manual of mental disorders (4th ed; text revision). Arlington, VA: Author. American Psychiatric Association.

TABLE 13.1 Estimated One-Year Prevalence of Mental Illnesses among Adults in Canada

Mental Illness	Estimates of One-Year Prevalence*	
Mood disorders		
Major (Unipolar) depression	4.1–4.6%	
Bipolar disorder	0.2–0.6%	
Dysthymia	0.8–3.1%	
Schizophrenia	0.3%	
Anxiety disorders	12.2%	
Personality disorders	<0.1%	
Eating disorders		
Anorexia	0.7% women	0.2% men
Bulimia	1.5% women	0.1% men
Deaths from suicide (2014)	10.8 per 100 000 1.5% of all deaths 24.5% of all deaths among those aged 15–24 years 20.4% of all deaths among those aged 25–34 years	

*Estimated percentage of the population diagnosed with the disorder during any one-year period.

Sources: (© All rights reserved. A report on Mental Illness in Canada. Public Health Agency of Canada, 2015. Reproduced with permission from the Minister of Health, 2015).

Note: Because these data measure occurrence within a given year, rates will generally be lower than lifetime prevalence rates. Even chronic disorders such as schizophrenia and bipolar disorder will probably be underestimated by this method. For example, lifetime prevalence rates of schizophrenia are estimated to be 1% of the Canadian adult population, whereas yearly estimates are much lower (0.3%). Similarly, the rates of personality disorders in the general population are between 6 and 9%, whereas they are extremely low when considering yearly estimates (,0.1%) (PHAC, 2012, Chapters 1 and 2).

REMEMBER IT

What Is Abnormal?

1. It is relatively easy to differentiate normal behaviour from abnormal behaviour. (true/false)

2. Match the perspective with its suggested cause of abnormal behaviour.

   _____ 1) faulty learning

   _____ 2) unconscious, unresolved conflicts

   _____ 3) blocking of the natural tendency toward self-actualization

   _____ 4) genetic inheritance or biochemical or structural abnormalities in the brain

   _____ 5) faulty thinking

   a. psychodynamic

   b. biological

   c. learning

   d. humanistic

   e. cognitive

3. The *DSM-5* is a manual published by the American Psychiatric Association that is used to_____

   a. diagnose psychological disorders.

   b. explain the causes of psychological disorders.

   c. outline treatments for various psychological disorders.

   d. assess the effectiveness of treatment programs.

Answers: 1. false   2.(1).c (2).a (3).d (4).b (5).e   3. a

MODULE **13B** **ANXIETY AND OBSESSIVE-COMPULSIVE DISORDERS: WHEN ANXIETY IS EXTREME**

LO 13.5 Describe and contrast normal and abnormal anxiety.

LO 13.6 Describe generalized anxiety disorder.

LO 13.7 Identify the social and health consequences of panic disorder.

LO 13.8 Identify and describe the characteristics of three categories of phobias.

LO 13.9 Describe the obsessions and compulsions that characterize obsessive-compulsive disorder.

When is anxiety healthy, and when is it unhealthy?

Anxiety is a vague, general uneasiness or feeling that something bad is about to happen. Anxiety may be associated with a particular situation or object, or it may be free-floating—not associated with anything specific. None of us is a stranger to anxiety. We have all felt it.

Some anxiety is normal and appropriate. Imagine that you are driving on a highway late at night when you notice that your gas tank indicator is on empty. A wave of anxiety sweeps over you, and you immediately begin to look for a service station. You are feeling normal anxiety—a response to a real danger or threat. Normal anxiety prompts us to take useful action and is therefore healthy. **[LO 13.5]** Anxiety is abnormal if it is out of proportion to the seriousness of the situation, if it does not fade soon after the danger has passed, or if it interferes with a person's social and work activities. In such instances, a person may be suffering from one of many types of anxiety disorders.

Anxiety disorders, combined with obsessive-compulsive and related disorders, represent the most common category of mental disorders in Canada, affecting more than 2 900 000 Canadians, or 12 percent of the population (PHAC, 2012).

Anxiety disorders, characterized by severe anxiety, can be divided into several categories, including generalized anxiety disorder, panic disorder, and phobias, as well as obsessive-compulsive disorder and related disorders.

GENERALIZED ANXIETY DISORDER

Generalized anxiety disorder is the diagnosis given to people who experience *excessive* anxiety and worry that they find difficult to control. **[LO 13.6]** They may be unduly worried about their finances or their own health or the health of family members. They may worry unnecessarily about their performance at work or their ability to function socially. Their excessive anxiety may cause them to feel tense, on edge, tired, and irritable, and to have difficulty concentrating and sleeping. Their symptoms may include trembling, palpitations, sweating, dizziness, nausea, diarrhea, and frequent urination. It is estimated that about 9 percent of North Americans will suffer from generalized anxiety disorder sooner or later, with many more women being affected compared to men (Kessler, Petukhova, Sampson, Zaslavsky, & Wittchen, 2012). Bienvenu and colleagues (Bienvenu, Davydow, & Kendler, 2011) estimate the heritability of generalized anxiety disorder to be about 28 percent. Previously thought of as a mild disorder, generalized anxiety disorder is now considered to substantially reduce the quality of life for those who suffer from it (Revicki et al., 2012).

PANIC DISORDER

What are the symptoms of a panic disorder?

People who have recurring panic attacks may be diagnosed with panic disorder. During **panic attacks**—attacks of overwhelming anxiety, fear, or terror—people commonly report a pounding heart, uncontrollable trembling or shaking, and a feeling of being choked or smothered. They may report being afraid that they are going to die or that they are "going crazy." Recent studies suggest that the more catastrophic such events are, the more intense the panic attack is likely to be (Hedley, Hoffart, Dammen, Ekeberg, & Friis, 2000).

Panic disorder is characterized by recurrent, unpredictable panic attacks that cause apprehension about the occurrence and consequences of further attacks. **[LO 13.7]** This apprehension can cause people to avoid situations that have been associated with previous panic attacks.

The biological perspective sheds some light on panic disorder. PET scans reveal that even in a non-panic state, many panic-disorder patients show a greatly increased blood flow to parts of the right hemisphere of the limbic system—the part of the brain involved in emotion (Gecici et al., 2005). Family and twin studies, too, suggest that genetic factors play a role in panic disorder (Gregersen et al., 2012; Kessler et al., 2006).

Panic disorder can have significant social and health consequences (Davidoff, Christensen, Khalili, Nguyen, & IsHak, 2012). **[LO 13.7]** Panic-disorder patients tend to visit doctors' offices and emergency rooms quite frequently. However, most individuals with this disorder respond to a combination of medication and psychotherapy (Biondi & Picardi, 2003).

©Dennis Galante/Corbis

People who have social anxiety disorder limit their interactions with others because of their fear of embarrassment.

PHOBIAS: PERSISTENT, IRRATIONAL FEARS

What are the characteristics of the three categories of phobias?

People suffering from a **phobia** experience a persistent, irrational fear of some specific object, situation, or activity that poses no real danger (or whose danger they blow out of proportion). Phobics realize their fear is irrational; they nevertheless feel compelled to avoid the feared object or situation. There are three classes of phobias—agoraphobia, social anxiety disorder, and specific phobia. **[LO 13.8]**

Agoraphobia

A person who suffers from **agoraphobia** has an intense fear of being in a situation where immediate escape is not possible or help would not be readily available in case of incapacitating anxiety. **[LO 13.8]** In some cases, an individual's entire life must be planned around avoiding feared situations such as busy streets, crowded stores, restaurants, or public transportation. People with agoraphobia will rarely, if ever, leave home; if they do, they will not go out by themselves.

As is the case for many anxiety disorders, a person is at greater risk of developing agoraphobia if other family members have it. The closer the relative, the higher the risk (Hettema et al., 2001). Also, women are twice as likely as men to be diagnosed with agoraphobia (McLean, Asnaani, Litz, & Hofmann, 2011).

Social Anxiety Disorder

Those who suffer from **social anxiety disorder** have an irrational fear of social or performance situations in which they

might embarrass or humiliate themselves in front of others—where they might shake, blush, sweat, or in some other way appear clumsy, foolish, or incompetent. **[LO 13.8]** They may fear eating, talking, or writing in front of others, or doing anything else that would cause people to think poorly of them. About one third of those with social anxiety disorders fear only speaking in public (Kessler, Stein, & Berglund, 1998).

Although less so than agoraphobia, social anxiety disorder can be disabling. In its extreme form, it can seriously harm people's prospects at work and at school, and severely restrict their social life (Aderka et al., 2012). Recent research suggests

anxiety: A generalized feeling of apprehension, fear, or tension that may be associated with a particular object or situation, or may be free-floating, not associated with anything specific.

generalized anxiety disorder: An anxiety disorder in which people experience excessive anxiety or worry that they find difficult to control.

panic attack: An attack of overwhelming anxiety, fear, or terror.

panic disorder: An anxiety disorder in which a person experiences recurrent unpredictable attacks of overwhelming anxiety, fear, or terror.

phobia (FO-bee-ah): A persistent, irrational fear of an object, situation, or activity that the person feels compelled to avoid.

agoraphobia (AG-or-uh-FO-bee-uh): An intense fear of being in a situation where immediate escape is not possible or help is not immediately available in case of incapacitating anxiety.

social anxiety disorder: An irrational fear and avoidance of social situations in which people believe they might embarrass or humiliate themselves by appearing clumsy, foolish, or incompetent.

TRY IT

Identifying Some Specific Phobias

Can you match the following specific phobias with their descriptions?

_____ 1. acrophobia   a. fear of high places

_____ 2. anthropophobia   b. fear of fire

_____ 3. arachnophobia   c. fear of animals

_____ 4. monophobia   d. fear of human beings

_____ 5. pyrophobia   e. fear of spiders

_____ 6. zoophobia   f. fear of being alone

Answers: 1. a 2. d 3. e 4. f 5. b 6. c

---

that those with social anxiety disorder have higher incidence of drug use (Marmorstein, 2012).

Specific Phobia

Specific phobia is a catch-all category for any phobias other than agoraphobia and social anxiety disorder. **[LO 13.8]** The categories of specific phobias, in order of frequency of occurrence, are as follows: (1) situational phobias (fear of elevators, airplanes, enclosed places, tunnels, bridges); (2) fear of the natural environment (storms, water, heights); (3) animal phobias (fear of dogs, snakes, insects, or mice); and (4) blood-injection-injury phobia (fear of seeing blood or an injury, or of receiving an injection). Two types of situational phobia—claustrophobia (fear of closed spaces) and acrophobia (fear of heights)—are the specific phobias treated most often by therapists (Fredrikson, Annas, Fischer, & Wik, 1996).

People with specific phobias generally fear the same things others fear, but their fears are grossly exaggerated. A fear is not considered a phobia unless it causes a great deal of distress or interferes with a person's life in a major way. Those who suffer from phobias will go to great lengths to avoid the feared object or situation because they experience intense anxiety, even to the point of shaking or screaming.

Causes of Phobias

What do psychologists believe are some probable causes of phobias?

The causes of phobias vary depending on their type, but heredity is clearly an important factor, especially for agoraphobia (Smoller, Block, & Young, 2009). People are at three times the risk if a close relative suffers from a phobia (Domschke, 2013). Beyond genetics, it is likely that most specific phobias and social anxiety disorders result from learning—that is, direct conditioning, modelling, or the transmission of information (Loken, Hettema, Aggen, & Kendler, 2014). Frightening experiences, most experts agree, set the stage for phobias, although not all phobics recall the experience that produced the phobia. For instance, a person with a dog phobia may be able to trace its beginning to a painful dog bite (Coelho & Purkis, 2009). Many phobias may be acquired through observational learning that occurred in childhood (Kashdan & Herbert, 2001). For example, children who hear their parents talk about frightening experiences with the dentist or with bugs, snakes, or thunderstorms may develop similar fears themselves. Phobias are most likely acquired through a combination of genetic predisposition, conditioning, and observational learning.

OBSESSIVE-COMPULSIVE AND RELATED DISORDERS

Unlike previous versions of the *DSM,* which included obsessive-compulsive disorders in the anxiety disorder category, the *DSM-5* lists these disorders in separate categories.

What is obsessive-compulsive disorder?

What is wrong with a person who is endlessly counting, checking, or performing other time-consuming rituals over and over? Why would a person wash his or her hands 100 times a day until they are raw and bleeding? People with **obsessive-compulsive disorder (OCD)** suffer from recurrent obsessions, or compulsions, or both.

Obsessions

Have you ever had a tune or the words of a song run through your mind over and over without being able to stop it? If so, you have experienced obsessive thinking in a mild form. Imagine how miserable you would be if every time you touched something you thought you were being contaminated, or if the thought of stabbing your mother kept popping into your mind. **Obsessions** are persistent, recurring, involuntary thoughts, images, or impulses that invade consciousness and cause great distress. **[LO 13.9]**

People with obsessions might worry about contamination by germs or about whether they performed a certain act, such as turning off the stove or locking the door (W. M. Greenberg, 2011). People with obsessional doubt may have a persistent fear that they failed to turn off the stove or put out a cigarette. Other types of obsessions centre on aggression, religion, or sex.

Do people ever act on their obsessive thoughts? It is not unheard of, but it is extremely rare. Yet many people are so horrified by their obsessions that they think they are going insane.

Compulsions

A person who has a **compulsion** feels literally compelled to repeat certain acts over and over or to perform specific rituals repeatedly. **[LO 13.9]** The individual knows such acts are irrational and senseless, but resistance to performing them would result in an intolerable build-up of anxiety—anxiety that can be relieved only by yielding to the compulsion. Many of us have engaged in compulsive behaviour from time to time (e.g., stepping over cracks on the sidewalk, counting stairs).

Like this woman, many people with obsessive-compulsive disorder take great pains to avoid contamination from germs and dirt.

©Karen Foley Photo/Fotolia

The behaviour becomes a psychological problem only when the person cannot resist performing it, when it is very time-consuming, and when it interferes with the person's normal activities and relationships.

Compulsions usually involve cleanliness, counting, checking, touching objects, or excessive ordering (Stasik, Naragon-Gainey, Chmielewski, & Watson, 2012). Sometimes compulsive acts or rituals resemble "magical" thinking and must be performed faithfully in order to ward off some danger. People with OCD do not enjoy the time-consuming rituals—the endless counting, checking, handwashing, or cleaning. They realize that their behaviour is not normal, but they simply cannot help themselves, as shown in the following example:

> Mike, a 32-year-old patient, performed checking rituals that were preceded by a fear of harming other people. When driving, he had to stop the car often and return to check whether he had run over people, particularly babies. Before flushing the toilet, he had to check to be sure that a live insect had not fallen into the toilet, because he did not want to be responsible for killing a living thing. At home he repeatedly checked to see that the doors, stoves, lights, and windows were shut or turned off. . . . Mike performed these and many other checking rituals for an average of four hours a day. (Kozak, Foa, & McCarthy, 1988, p. 88)

Are there many Mikes out there, or is his case unusual? Mike's checking compulsion is quite extreme. That being said, between 1.1 and 1.8 percent of Canadians suffer from OCD (PHAC, 2012).

About 70 percent of people in treatment for OCD have both obsessions and compulsions, but in the general population only 16 percent of OCD sufferers have both obsessions and compulsions (Weissman et al., 1994). When both occur together, the compulsion most often serves to relieve the anxiety caused by the obsession.

Causes of Obsessive-Compulsive Disorder

For many years, people with obsessive-compulsive disorder were seen as extremely insecure individuals who viewed the world as threatening and unpredictable. Their ritualistic behaviour was thought to be a means for imposing some order, structure, and predictability on the world. However, more recent studies point to a biological basis for obsessive-compulsive disorder in some patients. Research has shown that early autoimmune system diseases, early strep infections, and changes in the brain caused by infection may predispose a person to develop OCD (Giedd, Rapoport, Garvey, Perlmutter, & Swedo, 2000; Swedo et al., 2004). Several twin and family studies also suggest that a genetic factor may be involved (Pauls, Abramovitch, Rauch, & Geller, 2014). Genes affecting serotonin functioning are suspected of causing OCD in some people (van Dijk, Klompmakers, & Denys, 2008), many of whom are helped by antidepressant drugs that increase serotonin levels in the brain (Ravindran, da Silva, Ravindran, Richter, & Rector, 2009).

specific phobia: A marked fear of a specific object or situation, and a catch-all category for any phobia other than agoraphobia and social anxiety disorder.

obsessive-compulsive disorder (OCD): A disorder in which a person suffers from obsessions and/or compulsions.

obsessions: Persistent, recurring, involuntary thoughts, images, or impulses that invade consciousness and cause great distress.

compulsion: A persistent, irresistible, irrational urge to perform an act or ritual repeatedly.

REMEMBER IT

Anxiety and Obsessive-Compulsive Disorders

1. Anxiety serves no useful function. (true/false)

2. Match the psychological disorder with the example.

   _____ 1) Renée refuses to eat in front of others for fear her hand will shake.

   _____ 2) Juan is excessively anxious about his health and his job, even though there is no concrete reason for it.

   _____ 3) Betty has been housebound for four years.

   _____ 4) Jackson gets hysterical when a dog approaches him.

   _____ 5) Laura has incapacitating attacks of anxiety that come over her suddenly.

   _____ 6) Max repeatedly checks his doors, windows, and appliances before he goes to bed.

a. panic disorder
b. agoraphobia
c. specific phobia
d. generalized anxiety disorder
e. social anxiety disorder
f. obsessive-compulsive disorder

3. Most phobias result from frightening experiences and observational learning. (true/false)

4. Obsessive-compulsive disorder appears to be caused primarily by psychological rather than biological factors. (true/false)

Answers: 1. false   2. (1). e (2). d (3). b (4). c (5). a (6). f   3. true   4. false

---

MODULE 13C SOMATIC SYMPTOM AND RELATED DISORDERS, AND DISSOCIATIVE DISORDERS

LO 13.10 Describe and contrast illness anxiety disorder (previously hypochondriasis) and conversion disorder.
LO 13.11 Describe dissociative disorders.
LO 13.12 Describe the main characteristics of dissociative amnesia.
LO 13.13 Identify the symptoms and causes of dissociative identity disorder.

SOMATIC SYMPTOM AND RELATED DISORDERS: PHYSICAL SYMPTOMS WITH PSYCHOLOGICAL CAUSES

What are two somatic disorders, and what symptoms do they share?

The word *soma* means "body." The **somatic symptom disorders** involve bodily symptoms that cannot be explained by known medical conditions. Although they are psychological in origin, patients are sincerely convinced that their symptoms spring from real physical disorders. People with somatic symptom disorders are not consciously faking illness to avoid work or other activities. Illness anxiety disorder and conversion disorder are two disorders related to somatic symptom disorders.

Illness Anxiety Disorder

People with **illness anxiety disorder** (previously known as hypochondriasis) are overly concerned about their health. **[LO 13.10]** They are preoccupied with the fear that their bodily symptoms are a sign of some serious disease, but their symptoms are not usually consistent with known physical disorders. Even when a medical examination reveals no physical problem,

people with illness anxiety disorders are not convinced. They may "doctor shop," going from one physician to another, seeking confirmation of their worst fears. Unfortunately, illness anxiety disorder is not easily treated, and there is usually a poor chance of recovery.

Conversion Disorder: When Thoughts and Fears Can Paralyze

A man is suddenly struck blind, or an arm, a leg, or some other part of his body becomes paralyzed. Extensive medical tests find nothing wrong—no possible physical reason for the blindness or the paralysis. How can this be?

A diagnosis of **conversion disorder** is made when there is a loss of motor or sensory functioning in some part of the body that (a) is not due to a physical cause and (b) solves a psychological problem. **[LO 13.10]** Psychologists think that conversion disorder can act as an unconscious defence against any intolerable anxiety situation that the individual cannot otherwise escape. For example, a soldier who desperately fears going into battle may escape the anxiety by developing a paralysis or some other physically disabling symptom.

You would expect normal people to show great distress if they suddenly lost their sight or hearing, or became paralyzed. Yet many patients with conversion disorder exhibit a calm and cool indifference to their symptoms, called *la belle indifférence.* Furthermore, many seem to enjoy the attention, sympathy, and concern their disability brings them.

DISSOCIATIVE DISORDERS: MENTAL ESCAPES

We are consciously aware of who we are. Our memories, our identity, our consciousness, and our perception of the environment are integrated. But some people, in response to unbearable stress, develop a **dissociative disorder** and lose this integration. **[LO 13.11]** Their consciousness becomes dissociated either from their identity or from their memories of important personal events. Dissociative disorders provide a mental escape from intolerable circumstances. Two types of dissociative disorders are dissociative amnesia and dissociative identity disorder (commonly known as "multiple personality").

Dissociative Amnesia: "Who Am I?"

What is dissociative amnesia?

Amnesia is a complete or partial loss of the ability to recall personal information or identify past experiences that cannot be attributed to ordinary forgetfulness or substance use. Popular books, movies, and TV shows have used amnesia as a central theme in which, usually after a blow to the head, characters cannot remember who they are or anything about their past. In **dissociative amnesia**, however, no physical cause such as a blow to the head is present. **[LO 13.12]** Rather, a traumatic experience—a *psychological* blow, so to speak—or an unbearable anxiety situation causes the person to escape by "forgetting." Such cases illustrate one of the strange quirks of dissociative amnesia: sufferers forget items of personal reference, such as their name, age, and address, and may even fail to recognize their parents, spouse, or friends, but they do not forget how to carry out routine tasks, read and write, and solve problems, and their basic personality structure remains intact.

In extreme cases, sufferers can forget their entire identity, with no recollection of their personality, friends, family, or habits. At the beginning of the chapter we introduced the case of Jeff Ingram, who was found in Denver without any recollection of his identity. This case gave you some insight into the most extreme and puzzling subset of dissociative amnesia, formerly known as **dissociative fugue** in previous versions of the *DSM*. In this state, people not only forget their identity, they also physically leave the scene and travel away from home. **[LO 13.12]** Some take on a new identity that is usually more outgoing and uninhibited than their former identity (Spiegel et al., 2013). The dissociative state may last for hours, days, or even months and is usually a reaction to some severe psychological stress.

Dissociative Identity Disorder: Multiple Personality

What are some of the identifying symptoms of dissociative identity disorder?

In **dissociative identity disorder**, two or more distinct, unique personalities exist in the same individual. **[LO 13.13]** In 50 percent of dissociative identity disorder cases, there are more than 10 different personalities. The change from one personality to another often occurs suddenly—usually during stress. The *host personality* is "the one who has executive control of the body the greatest percentage of time" (Kluft, 1984, p. 23). The alternate personalities, or *alter personalities*, may differ radically in intelligence, speech, accent, vocabulary, posture, body language, hairstyle, taste in clothes, manners, and even handwriting. And incredibly, within the same individual, the alter personalities may differ in gender, age, and even sexual orientation. Some alters may be right-handed, others left-handed.

Many patients with dissociative identity disorder report hearing voices and sometimes the sounds of crying, screaming, or laughter. For this reason, such patients have often been misdiagnosed as schizophrenic.

In the great majority of dissociative identity disorder cases, the host personality does not know of the alters, but "the alter personalities will possess varying levels of awareness for one another" (Putnam 1989, p. 114). The host and alter personalities commonly show amnesia for certain periods of time or for important life episodes (e.g., their wedding, the birth of a child). There is the common complaint of "lost time"—periods for which a given personality has no memory because he or she was not in control of the body.

CAUSES OF DISSOCIATIVE IDENTITY DISORDER

Various forms of early trauma, such as severe physical and/or sexual abuse, have been linked to dissociative identity disorders (Dalenberg et al., 2012). This type of disorder usually begins in early childhood (Silberg, 2014) and is significantly more common in women than in men (Ross, Norton, & Wozney, 1989). The splitting off of separate personalities is apparently a way of coping with such intolerable abuse. **[LO 13.13]** Furthermore, the link between trauma and dissociative disorders supports the view that these disorders should most likely be thought of as manifestations of post-traumatic stress disorder rather than diagnoses in their own right (Rocha-Rego et al., 2009). Regardless of cause, this disorder can be treated, often by psychotherapy, and empirical evidence suggests patients respond well to treatment (C. A. Ross, 2009).

---

somatic symptom disorders: Disorders in which physical symptoms are present that are due to psychological rather than physical causes.

illness anxiety disorder: A disorder in which persons are preoccupied with their health and convinced they have some serious disorder despite reassurance from doctors to the contrary.

conversion disorder: A somatic symptom disorder in which a loss of motor or sensory functioning in some part of the body has no physical cause but solves some psychological problem.

dissociative disorder: A disorder in which, under stress, one loses the integration of consciousness, identity, and memories of important personal events.

dissociative amnesia: A dissociative disorder in which there is a loss of memory for limited periods in one's life or for one's entire personal identity.

dissociative fugue: A disorder associated with dissociative amnesia in which one not only has a complete loss of memory for one's entire identity, but also travels away from home, and may assume a new identity.

dissociative identity disorder: A dissociative disorder in which two or more distinct personalities occur in the same individual, each taking over at different times; also called *multiple personality*.

REMEMBER IT

Somatic Symptom and Related Disorders, and Dissociative Disorders

1. Match the psychological disorder with the example.

_____ 1) Mark is convinced he has some serious disease although his doctors can find nothing physically wrong.

_____ 2) Jamal is found far away from his hometown, calling himself by another name and having no memory of his past.

_____ 3) Theresa suddenly loses her sight, but doctors can find no physical reason for the problem.

_____ 4) Larry has no memory of being in the boat with other family members on the day his older brother drowned.

_____ 5) Nadine has no memory for blocks of time in her life and often finds clothing in her closet that she cannot remember buying.
   a. dissociative identity disorder
   b. dissociative fugue
   c. dissociative amnesia
   d. illness anxiety disorder
   e. conversion disorder

2. Somatic symptom disorders have physiological rather than psychological causes. (true/false)

3. Dissociative disorders are psychological in origin. (true/false)

Answers: 1(1). d (2). b (3). e (4). c (5). a 2. false 3. true

MODULE 13D SCHIZOPHRENIA

LO 13.14 Describe the major positive symptoms of schizophrenia and contrast these with the negative symptoms.

LO 13.15 Identify brain abnormalities that have been associated with schizophrenia.

LO 13.16 Identify the four historical subtypes of schizophrenia presented in the *DSM-IV-TR*.

LO 13.17 Explain the cause of schizophrenia according to the diathesis–stress model.

To a mild degree we can identify with most people who suffer from most psychological disorders. We can imagine being anxious, fearful, depressed; we can picture ourselves having an obsession or a compulsion. But schizophrenia is so far removed from our common, everyday experience that it is all but impossible for most people to imagine what it is like to be schizophrenic.

Schizophrenia is the most serious of the psychological disorders. It affects about one person in a hundred. Schizophrenia usually begins in adolescence or early adulthood. For this reason, most researchers think that normal developmental processes in the brain that happen in late adolescence set the stage for the appearance of the disease (Uhlhaas, 2011). Schizophrenia is probably the most devastating of all the psychological disorders because of the social disruption and misery it brings to those who suffer from it and to their families.

THE SYMPTOMS OF SCHIZOPHRENIA: MANY AND VARIED

There are many symptoms associated with schizophrenia. Any given individual with the disorder may have one or more of the major symptoms, but there is no one single symptom or brain abnormality that is shared by all schizophrenics (Andreasen, 1999). The symptoms of schizophrenia fall into two categories: positive and negative.

Positive Symptoms

What are some of the major positive symptoms of schizophrenia?

Positive symptoms are so named not because they are desirable, but rather because they are present (as opposed to absent). Positive symptoms include hallucinations, delusions, disorganized thinking and speech, and grossly disorganized or bizarre behaviour or inappropriate affect **[LO 13.14]**

HALLUCINATIONS One of the clearest symptoms that suggests schizophrenia is the presence of **hallucinations**—imaginary sensations. Schizophrenic patients may see, hear, feel, taste, or smell strange things in the absence of any stimulus in the environment. Hearing voices is the most common type of hallucination. Schizophrenic patients may believe they hear the voice of God or Satan, the voices of family members or friends, and even their own voice broadcasting aloud what they are thinking. Most often the voices are unpleasant, accusing or cursing the patient or engaging in a running commentary on his or her behaviour. Sometimes the voices are menacing and order the patient to kill someone or commit suicide.

Visual hallucinations are less common than auditory ones. They are usually in black and white, and commonly take the form of friends, relatives, God, Jesus, or the devil. Patients who have schizophrenia may also experience bodily sensations that are exceedingly frightening and painful. They may feel they are being beaten, burned, or sexually violated.

DELUSIONS Imagine how upset you would be if you believed that your every thought was being broadcast aloud for everyone to hear. What if you were convinced that some strange agent or force was stealing your thoughts or inserting in your head thoughts that were not your own? These are examples of **delusions**—false beliefs that are not generally shared by others in the culture. Usually patients cannot be persuaded that their beliefs are false, even in the face of strong evidence.

Delusions may be of several different types. Schizophrenics with **delusions of grandeur** may believe they are a famous person (the Queen or Jesus Christ, for example) or a powerful or important person who possesses some great knowledge, ability, or authority. Those with **delusions of persecution** have the false notion that some person or agency is trying to harass, cheat, spy on, conspire against, injure, kill, or in some other way harm them.

DISTURBANCES IN THE FORM OF THOUGHT OR SPEECH Schizophrenia is often marked by thought disturbance. The most common type involves a loosening of associations—the individual does not follow one line of thought to completion, but shifts from one subject to another on the basis of vague connections. The speech of schizophrenics is often very difficult, if not impossible, to understand. The content of the message may be extremely vague, or the person may invent words or use them inappropriately.

> I am writing on paper. The pen I am using is from a factory called "Perry & Co." This factory is in England. . . . The city of London is in England. I know this from my school-days. Then, I always liked geography. My last teacher in that subject was . . . a man with black eyes. I also like black eyes. There are also blue and gray eyes and other sorts, too. I have heard it said that snakes have green eyes. All people have eyes. There are some, too, who are blind. (Bleuler, 1950, p. 17)

GROSSLY DISORGANIZED BEHAVIOUR Grossly disorganized behaviour can include such things as childlike silliness, inappropriate sexual behaviour (masturbating in public), dishevelled appearance, and peculiar dress. There may also be unpredictable agitation, including shouting and swearing, and unusual or inappropriate motor behaviour, including strange gestures, facial expressions, or postures.

INAPPROPRIATE AFFECT Schizophrenics may have grossly **inappropriate affect**—that is, their facial expressions, tone of voice, and gestures may not reflect the emotion that would be expected under the circumstances. A person might cry when watching a TV comedy and laugh when watching a news story showing bloody bodies being removed from a fatal automobile accident.

Negative Symptoms

What are some of the major negative symptoms of schizophrenia?

Negative symptoms of schizophrenia involve a loss of or deficiency in thoughts and behaviours that are characteristic in normal functioning. Negative symptoms may include social withdrawal, apathy, loss of motivation, lack of goal-directed activity, very limited speech, slow movements, poor hygiene and grooming, poor problem-solving abilities, and a distorted

sense of time (Bell, Corbera, Johannesen, Fiszdon, & Wexler, 2013). **[LO 13.14]** Some schizophrenic patients show *flat affect*—practically no emotional response at all. They may speak in a monotone, and their facial expressions may be blank and emotionless. Such patients may act and move more like robots than humans.

Some researchers who have followed schizophrenics over a number of years have found that those with negative symptoms seem to have the poorest outcomes (Rabinowitz et al., 2012). They tend to withdraw from others and retreat into their own world. Often their functioning is too impaired for them to hold a job or even care for themselves.

Brain Abnormalities in Some Schizophrenics

Several abnormalities in brain structure and function have been found in schizophrenic patients, including low levels of neural activity in frontal lobes (Glantz, Gilmore, Lieberman, & Jarskog, 2006). **[LO 13.15]** Many schizophrenic patients have defects in the neural circuitry of the cerebral cortex and limbic system (Benes, 2000; Mitelman, Shihabuddin, Brickman, Hazlett, & Buchsbaum, 2005). There is also evidence of reduced volume in the hippocampus, amygdala, thalamus, and front lobe grey matter (Mahon et al., 2015; Szeszko et al., 2008). Further, individuals with schizophrenia display abnormal lateralization of brain functions and slow communication between left and right hemispheres (Hulshoff Pol et al., 2004).

TYPES OF SCHIZOPHRENIA

What are the four historical subtypes of schizophrenia?

Previous versions of the *DSM* categorized schizophrenia into four subtypes based on specific sets of behavioural

---

schizophrenia (SKIT-soh-FREE-nee-ah): A severe psychological disorder characterized by loss of contact with reality, hallucinations, delusions, inappropriate or flat affect, some disturbance in thinking, social withdrawal, and/or bizarre behaviour.

hallucinations: Sensory perceptions in the absence of any external sensory stimulus; imaginary sensations.

delusions: False beliefs, not generally shared by others in the culture, that cannot be changed despite strong evidence to the contrary.

delusions of grandeur: False beliefs that one is a famous person or that one has some great knowledge, ability, or authority.

delusions of persecution: An individual's false beliefs that a person or group is trying in some way to harm him or her.

inappropriate affect: A symptom common in schizophrenia in which an individual's behaviour (including facial expression, tone of voice, and gestures) does not reflect the emotion that would be expected under the circumstances—for example, a person laughs at a tragedy, cries at a joke.

©Will Hart/PhotoEdit

A person with catatonic schizophrenia symptoms may become frozen in an unusual position, like a statue, for hours at a time.

characteristics. We will review them briefly here because these terms are still in popular use. However, it is important to note that these subtypes have been eliminated in the *DSM-5* and are no longer used in clinical diagnosis. The four subtypes of schizophrenia previously identified were: catatonic, disorganized, paranoid, and undifferentiated. **[LO 13.16]**

People with **catatonic schizophrenia** were described as displaying complete stillness and stupor, or great excitement and agitation. **[LO 13.16]** Frequently they alternate rapidly between the two. They may become frozen in a strange posture or position, as shown in the accompanying photograph, and remain for hours without moving.

Disorganized schizophrenia was described as the most serious type, marked by extreme social withdrawal, hallucinations, delusions, silliness, inappropriate laughter, grimaces, grotesque mannerisms, and bizarre behaviour. **[LO 13.16]** These people show flat or inappropriate affect and are frequently incoherent. They often exhibit obscene behaviour, masturbate openly, and swallow almost any kind of object or material. Patients with this type of schizophrenia were seen as having the poorest chance of recovery (Fenton & McGlashan, 1991; Kane, 1993).

People with **paranoid schizophrenia** were described as displaying delusions of grandeur or persecutions. **[LO 13.16]** They may be convinced that they have an identity other than their own. Their delusions may include the belief that they possess great ability or talent, or that they have some special mission. Paranoid schizophrenics often show exaggerated anger and suspiciousness. If they have delusions of persecution and feel that they are being harassed or threatened, they may become violent in an attempt to defend themselves against their imagined persecutors.

Undifferentiated schizophrenia was a general catch-all category for individuals who clearly have symptoms of schizophrenia but whose symptoms either do not conform to the criteria of any other type of schizophrenia or conform to more than one type. **[LO 13.16]**

Currently, the *DSM-5* does not make discriminations among these four categories, as data suggests that distinctions among these subtypes are not as stable or valid as previously thought.

THE CAUSES OF SCHIZOPHRENIA

What are some suggested causes of schizophrenia?

During the 1950s and 1960s, many psychiatrists and some researchers pointed to unhealthy patterns of communication and interaction in the entire family as the breeding ground for schizophrenia (Bateson, Jackson, Haley, & Weakland, 1956; Lidz, Fleck, & Cornelison, 1965). There is no convincing evidence to justify pointing the finger of blame at mothers, fathers, or other family members (D. L. Johnson, 1989; Torrey, 1983). Instead, research evidence strongly suggests that a complex interaction of both biological and experiential factors are involved in the onset of schizophrenia (Walder, Faraone, Glatt, Tsuang, & Seidman, 2014).

Genetic Inheritance

Research indicates that schizophrenia tends to run in families and that genetic factors play a major role (Plomin, DeFries, Craig, & McGuffin, 2003; Riley & Kendler, 2005). Figure 13.1 shows how the likelihood of developing schizophrenia varies with the degree of relationship to a schizophrenic person. Note that genes also play a role in how well or how poorly individuals with schizophrenia respond to treatment with antipsychotic drugs (Pouget & Müller, 2014).

catatonic schizophrenia (KAT-uh-TON-ik): A type of schizophrenia identified in the *DSM-IV-TR*, characterized by extreme stillness or stupor and/or periods of great agitation and excitement; patients may assume an unusual posture and remain in it for long periods.

disorganized schizophrenia: The most serious type of schizophrenia identified in the *DSM-IV-TR*, marked by extreme social withdrawal, hallucinations, delusions, silliness, inappropriate laughter, grotesque mannerisms, and bizarre behaviour.

paranoid schizophrenia (PAIR-uh-noid): A type of schizophrenia identified in the *DSM-IV-TR*, characterized by delusions of grandeur or persecution.

undifferentiated schizophrenia: A catch-all category in the *DSM-IV-TR*; marked by symptoms of schizophrenia that do not conform to the other types or that conform to more than one type.

diathesis–stress model: The idea that people with a constitutional predisposition (diathesis) toward a disorder, such as schizophrenia, may develop the disorder if they are subjected to sufficient environmental stress.

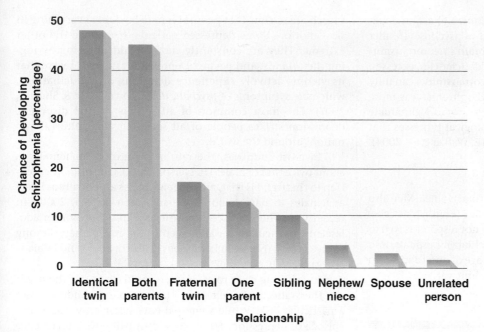

FIGURE 13.1

Genetic Similarity and Probability of Developing Schizophrenia

Research strongly indicates a genetic factor operating in many cases of schizophrenia. Identical twins have identical genes, and if one twin develops schizophrenia, the other twin has a 48 percent chance of developing it also. In fraternal twins, the chance is only 17 percent. Similarly, a person with one schizophrenic parent has a 13 percent chance of developing schizophrenia, but a 46 percent chance if both parents are schizophrenic (McNeil, Cantor-Graae, & Weinberger, 2000).

Source: From Schizophrenia Genesis: The Origins of Madness, by Irving I. Gottesman. © 1991 by Irving I Gottesman. Used with permission of Irving Gottesman.

It is important to note that genes are not destiny and that no one factor appears to be most significant in the genesis of schizophrenia (Rapoport, Giedd, & Gogtay, 2012). The most recent theorizing on the roots of schizophrenia suggests that it develops when there is both a genetic predisposition toward the disorder, along with highly stressful environmental conditions (van Os, Kenis, & Rutten, 2010). [LO 13.17] Elaine Walker and her colleagues (2008) point out that there is no evidence suggesting that individuals who develop schizophrenia experience more stress than people who do not get the disease. Instead, some individuals appear to be more vulnerable to stress than others. Thus, stress plays a role in the development of schizophrenia but only among those who have the relevant constitutional vulnerability. Other environmental factors—birth trauma, a virus such as influenza, malnutrition, a head injury, and so on—that can interfere with normal brain development bring an increased risk of schizophrenia (Khandaker, Zimbron, Lewis, & Jones, 2013; Molloy, Conroy, Cotter, & Cannon, 2011).

Excessive Dopamine Activity

Abnormal activity in the brain's dopamine systems is common in many schizophrenics (Benes, 2006). Many studies suggest that dopamine plays an important role in schizophrenia,

REMEMBER IT

Schizophrenia

1. Match the symptom of schizophrenia with the example.
   _____ 1) Joe believes he is Moses.
   _____ 2) Elena thinks her family is spreading rumours about her.
   _____ 3) Peter hears voices cursing him.
   _____ 4) Marco laughs at tragedies and cries when he hears a joke.
   a. delusions of grandeur
   b. hallucinations
   c. inappropriate affect
   d. delusions of persecution

2. Match the historical subtype of schizophrenia (from *DSM-IV-TR*) with the example:
   _____ 1) Louise stands for hours in the same strange position.
   _____ 2) Ron believes that CSIS is plotting to kill him.

   _____ 3) Harry makes silly faces, laughs a lot, and masturbates openly.
   _____ 4) Yasuko has the symptoms of schizophrenia but does not fit any one type.
   a. paranoid schizophrenia
   b. disorganized schizophrenia
   c. catatonic schizophrenia
   d. undifferentiated schizophrenia

3. There is substantial research evidence that all of the following help to cause schizophrenia except_____
   a. genetic factors.
   b. stress in people predisposed to the disorder.
   c. excessive dopamine activity.
   d. unhealthy family interaction patterns.

primarily because medications that are known to act on dopamine are usually helpful in the treatment of psychoses (Müller et al., 2006). However, the nature of the brain's neurotransmitter system is such that it is unlikely that deficiencies, excesses, or malfunctions that involve a single neurotransmitter can fully account for the complex features of schizophrenia. It is more likely that many other neurotransmitters, notably glutamate and GABA, also participate in the neurological processes that underlie the symptoms of schizophrenia (E. Walker et al., 2004).

GENDER AND SCHIZOPHRENIA

Schizophrenia is more likely to strike men than women. Men also tend to develop the disorder at an earlier age (Eranti, MacCabe, Bundy, & Murray, 2013), they typically do not respond as well to treatment, they spend more time in psychiatric hospitals, and they are more likely to relapse. The earlier age of onset appears to be independent of culture and socio-economic variables.

MODULE **13E** DEPRESSIVE AND BIPOLAR DISORDERS

LO 13.18 Identify the symptoms that characterize major depressive disorder.

LO 13.19 Contrast major depressive disorder and persistent depressive disorder (dysthymia).

LO 13.20 Describe a major manic episode and its negative effects.

LO 13.21 Explain the role of genetic inheritance and neurotransmitters in major depressive disorder.

LO 13.22 Describe the distortions in thinking that characterize depression.

Mood disorders, such as depression and bipolar disorders, involve moods or emotions that are extreme and unwarranted. In the most serious disorders, mood ranges from the depths of severe depression to the heights of extreme elation. These disorders fall into two broad categories: depressive and bipolar disorders.

DEPRESSIVE DISORDERS AND BIPOLAR DISORDERS: EMOTIONAL HIGHS AND LOWS

Major Depressive Disorder

What are the symptoms of major depressive disorder?

It is normal to feel blue, down, sad, or depressed in response to many of life's common experiences—death of a loved one, loss of a job, or an unhappy ending to a long-term relationship. Major depression, however, is not normal. People with **major depressive disorder** feel an overwhelming sadness, despair, and hopelessness, and they usually lose their ability to experience pleasure. **[LO 13.18]** They may have appetite and weight changes, sleep disturbance, loss of energy, and difficulty thinking or concentrating. Key symptoms of major depressive disorder include psychomotor disturbances (Lohr, May, & Caligiuri, 2013). For example, body movements and

speech are so slow that people seem to be doing everything in slow motion. Some depressed patients experience the other extreme: They are constantly moving and fidgeting, wringing their hands, and pacing. Depression can be so severe that its victims actually experience delusions or hallucinations, which are symptoms of *psychotic depression* (Swartz & Shorter, 2007). The most common of all serious mental disorders, depression strikes people of all social classes, cultures, and nations around the world.

In most countries, the rate of depression for females is about twice that of males (Halverson, 2011). One notable exception to this trend is that, among Jews, males are equally as likely as females to have major depression (Loewenthal, 2009). In recent years there has been an increase in depression in adolescents, particularly in adolescent girls, and perhaps among Native people (National Institutes of Health, 2005) and lesbians and gay men (Cochran, 2001).

In fulfilling their roles, women are likely to put the needs of others ahead of their own. Having young children poses a particular risk. While some patients suffer only one major episode of depression, 50 to 60 percent will have a recurrence (Halverson, 2011). People who experienced depression before age 20 (Hardeveld, Spijker, De Graaf, Nolen, & Beekman, 2013) and those with a family history of mood disorders (Pettit, Hartley, Lewinsohn, Seeley, & Klein, 2013) are also at significantly greater risk of recurrence. Risk of recurrence is twice as high for women as it is for men (Halverson, 2011), and hospitalization rates for depression are one and a half times higher among women than among men (PHAC, 2012). Recurrences may be frequent or infrequent. For 20 to 35 percent of patients, the depressive episodes are chronic, lasting two years or longer. Unfortunately, many people who suffer from depression never even receive treatment. Depression is related to more than one half of all suicide attempts, and about 15 percent of people with depression commit suicide (Halverson, 2011). To learn more about teen suicide, read the *World of Psychology* box.

Many people suffer from a milder form of depression called *persistent depressive disorder (dysthmia)*, which is nonetheless chronic (lasting two years or longer). Individuals with persistent depressive disorder suffer from depressed mood but have fewer of the symptoms associated with major depressive disorder. **[LO 13.19]**

Although depression is more common among women, it also affects men. Comedian Jim Carrey is among many adults who have this disorder.

The Canadian Press (© Warner Brothers/ Everett Collection)

WORLD OF PSYCHOLOGY

Teen Suicide in Canada

The rate of suicide among 15- to 19-year-olds has tripled over the past several decades, from 3.2 per 100 000 in 1962 to 9.2 per 100 000. While Canada ranks roughly in the middle of the world's nations in terms of suicides in the general population (World Health Organization, 2012), suicide in Canada still accounts for nearly 25 percent of all deaths of young people aged 15 to 24 years. Teenage boys are much more likely to commit suicide than teenage girls (Statistics Canada, 2014), and this is especially true for First Nations boys, for whom rates of suicide are five to seven times higher than those for non-Aboriginal youth (Health Canada, 2006). Rates of teen suicide for Inuit youth are among the highest in the world, with levels 11 times higher than the national average (Health Canada, 2006). The root causes of the high level of youth suicide in Aboriginal and Inuit communities are complex and include factors such as poverty, isolation, inadequate social support networks, lack of opportunities, and systemic issues related to colonization and the disconnection to a more traditional way of life.

Canadian researchers have been extensively involved in studying both the genetics and the social factors that affect suicide rates. Factors such as exposure to violence, along with physical and sexual abuse early in life, significantly increase the likelihood of suicide attempts by teens (Séguin, Renaud, Lesage, Robert, & Turecki, 2011). Genetic links are also associated with suicidal behaviour; for instance, early-life adversity increases risk of suicide in susceptible individuals, a pattern that seems especially true for males (Fiori, Zouk, Himmelman, & Turecki, 2011; Turecki, Ernst, Jollang, Labonté, & Mechawar, 2012).

Preventing Suicide

There are cultural differences in suicide rates, but the methods used, the reasons, and the warning signs for suicide are very similar across ethnic, gender, and age groups. Most suicidal individuals communicate their intent; in fact, about 90 percent of them leave clues (National Institute of Mental Health, 2010). They may communicate verbally: "You won't be seeing me again," "You won't have to worry about me anymore," "Life isn't worth living." They may leave behavioural clues—for example, they may give away their most valued possessions; withdraw from friends, family, and associates; take unnecessary risks; show personality changes; act and look depressed; and lose interest in favourite activities. These warning signs should always be taken seriously. Suicidal individuals need compassion, emotional support, and the opportunity to express the feelings and problems that are the source of their psychological pain.

But we should not be amateur psychologists if we are dealing with a suicidal person. Probably the best service you can render is to encourage the person to get professional help. There are 24-hour-a-day suicide hotlines all over the country. A call might save a life. One number to call is Kids Help Phone (1-800-668-6868). ■

Seasonal Depression

Many people find that their moods seem to change with the seasons. People suffering from **seasonal affective disorder (SAD)** experience a significant depression that tends to come and go with the seasons (Sohn & Lam, 2005). There is a spring/summer depression that remits in winter; but the most common type, winter depression, seems to be triggered by light deficiency (Magnusson, 2000). During the winter months, when the days are shorter, some people become very depressed and tend to sleep and eat more, gain weight, and crave carbohydrates.

Reasoning that the obvious difference between the seasons was the amount and intensity of light, researchers have shown the effectiveness of exposing patients with winter depression to bright light, which simulates the longer daylight hours of summer (M. Terman & Terman, 2005; Westrin & Lam, 2007). After several days of the light treatment, most of the participants improve.

Bipolar Disorder

What are the extremes of mood suffered in bipolar disorder?

Bipolar disorder is a disorder in which patients experience two radically different moods: extreme highs (called *manic episodes*, or *mania*) and extreme lows (major depression), usually with relatively normal periods in between. A **manic episode** is marked by excessive euphoria, inflated self-esteem, wild optimism, and hyperactivity. During a manic episode, people are wound up and full of energy. They rarely sleep, are frantically engaged in a flurry of activity, and talk loud and fast, skipping from one topic to another. **[LO 13.20]**

You may wonder what is wrong with being euphoric, energetic, and optimistic. Obviously, nothing—as long as it is warranted. But people in a manic state have temporarily lost touch with reality. **[LO 13.20]** Their high-spirited optimism is not merely irrational—it is delusional. They may go on wild spending sprees or waste large sums of money on grand get-rich-quick schemes. If family members try to stop them or talk them out of their irrational plans, they are likely to become irritable, hostile, enraged, or even dangerous. Quite often, patients must be hospitalized during manic episodes to protect them and others from the disastrous consequences of their poor judgment.

Bipolar disorder is much less common than major depressive disorder. Its lifetime prevalence rate is about the same for men and women (Kessler et al., 1994), with just under 1 percent of the Canadian population affected in any given year (PHAC, 2012). Unfortunately, about 90 percent of those with bipolar

---

major depressive disorder: A disorder characterized by feelings of great sadness, despair, guilt, worthlessness, hopelessness, and, in extreme cases, suicidal intentions.

seasonal affective disorder (SAD): A disorder in which depression comes and goes with the seasons.

bipolar disorder: A disorder in which manic episodes alternate with periods of depression, usually with relatively normal periods in between.

manic episode (MAN-ik): A period of extreme elation, euphoria, and hyperactivity, often accompanied by delusions of grandeur and by hostility if activity is blocked.

disorder have recurrences, and, in nearly 60 percent of the cases, the manic episodes directly precede or follow the depressive episodes (Tohen et al., 2003). The good news is that 70 to 80 percent of patients return to normal after an episode (APA, 2000), and many people who suffer from bipolar disorder can manage their symptoms and live a normal life with the help of drugs such as lithium and divalproex. Moreover, psychotherapy can help them cope with the stress of facing life with a potentially disabling mental illness (Gitlin & Frye, 2012).

CAUSES OF DEPRESSIVE DISORDERS AND BIPOLAR DISORDERS

What are some suggested causes of depressive disorders and bipolar disorders?

The biological and cognitive perspectives offer some insight into the causes of depressive and bipolar disorders and suggest treatments that have been helpful to many people.

The Biological Perspective

Biological factors such as genetic inheritance and abnormal brain chemistry play a major role in bipolar and depressive disorders. PET scans have revealed abnormal patterns of brain activity in both of these disorders (Drevets, Price, & Furey, 2008).

THE ROLE OF GENETIC INHERITANCE

Does depression tend to run in families? Apparently so: People who have relatives with a depressive disorder are at higher risk of developing mood disturbances, and this risk is due to shared genetic factors rather than shared environmental factors (Kendler et al., 1992). **[LO 13.21]** A comprehensive national study of 15 493 twin pairs estimated the heritability of major depression to be 38 percent, with a greater rate for women (42 percent) versus men (29 percent) (Kendler, Gatz, Gardner, & Pedersen, 2006). A person is nearly three times more likely to develop depression if a close relative has had an early onset of depression and if the depression was recurring rather than single-episode (Sullivan, Neale, & Kendler, 2000). And the genetic link is much

stronger in bipolar disorder than in depression (Kalidindi & McGuffin, 2003), with the odds of developing bipolar disorder being more than 20 times greater among persons who have first-degree relatives (parents, children, or siblings) with the disorder.

THE ROLE OF SEROTONIN AND NOREPINEPHRINE

We all know that mood can be altered by the substances people put into their bodies. Alcohol, caffeine, various other uppers and downers, and a host of additional psycho-active substances are known to alter mood. Researchers now know that our moods are also altered and regulated by our own body's biochemicals, which of course include the neurotransmitters. Norepinephrine, serotonin, and dopamine are three neurotransmitters thought to play an important role in disorders that affect mood (Nutt, 2007). **[LO 13.21]** All are localized in the limbic system and the hypothalamus, parts of the brain that help regulate emotional behaviour.

An important question remains: Do these biochemical differences in the brain cause psychological changes or result from them? Theorists who emphasize psychological causes see biochemical changes as the result, not the cause, of mood disorders.

The Cognitive Perspective

Cognitive explanations, such as that of Aaron Beck (1967, 1991), maintain that depression is characterized by distortions in thinking. **[LO 13.22]** According to Beck, depressed individuals view themselves, their world, and their future negatively. They see their interactions with the world as defeating—a series of burdens and obstacles that end mostly in failure. Depressed persons believe they are deficient, unworthy, and inadequate, and they attribute their perceived failures to their own physical, mental, or moral inadequacies. Finally, according to the cognitive perspective, depressed patients believe that their future holds no hope. They may reason "Everything always turns out wrong," "I never win," "Things will never get better," "It's no use."

For several years, clinicians have known that depression is related to distorted thinking (Garratt, Ingram, Rand, & Sawalani, 2007). The cognitive perspective has much to offer for us to apply in our daily lives. Read the *Apply It* box at the end of this chapter to learn more.

REMEMBER IT

Depressive and Bipolar Disorders

1. Sanju has periods during which he is so depressed that he becomes suicidal. At other times he is energetic and euphoric. He would probably receive the diagnosis of_____
    a. persistent depressive disorder (dysthymia).
    b. seasonal mood disorder.
    c. bipolar disorder.
    d. major depressive disorder.

2. Match the theory of depression with the proposed cause.
    _____ 1) negative thoughts about oneself, the world, and one's future
    _____ 2) a deficiency of serotonin and norepinephrine
    _____ 3) turning resentment and hostility inward
    _____ 4) a family history of depression
    a. psychodynamic theory
    b. cognitive theory
    c. genetic theory
    d. biochemical theory

Answers: 1.c   2(1).b   (2).d   (3).a   (4).c

MODULE 13F OTHER PSYCHOLOGICAL DISORDERS

LO 13.23 Describe personality disorders.

LO 13.24 Describe and compare Cluster A, Cluster B, and Cluster C personality disorders.

LO 13.25 Identify the symptoms associated with borderline personality disorder.

LO 13.26 Describe three categories of sexual disorders.

PERSONALITY DISORDERS: TROUBLESOME BEHAVIOUR PATTERNS

What are the main attributes of personality disorders?

A *personality disorder* is an enduring pattern of inner experience and behaviour that deviates markedly from the expectations of the individual's culture, is pervasive and inflexible, has an onset in adolescence or early adulthood, is stable over time, and leads to distress or impairment (APA, 2013). **[LO 13.23]**. People with this type of disorder tend to have problems in their social relationships and in their work; they may experience personal distress as well. Some realize that their behaviour is a problem, yet they seem unable to change. More commonly, they are self-centred and do not see themselves as responsible for their difficulties. Rather, they tend to blame other people or situations for their problems. In most cases, the causes of personality disorders have yet to be identified.

The *DSM-5* lists 10 categories of personality disorders, and the criteria used to classify them overlap considerably. The *DSM-5* groups personality disorders into *clusters*, as shown in Table 13.2. The disorders within each cluster have similarities. For example, all the personality disorders in Cluster A are characterized by odd behaviour, such as extreme suspiciousness (*paranoid*), isolation and lack of emotional bond (*schizoid*), or odd appearance and unusual thought patterns (*schizotypal*). **[LO 13.24]** People with other disorders, especially mood disorders, are often diagnosed with personality disorders (D. Kopp et al., 2009; Valtonen et al., 2009). In most cases, the causes of personality disorders have yet to be identified.

Cluster B disorders are characterized by erratic and overly dramatic behaviours. **[LO 13.24]** These disorders are associated with an increased risk of suicide (May, Klonsky, & Klein, 2012). A strong desire to be the centre of others' attention is characteristic of both *narcissistic* and *histrionic* personality disorders, as is a lack of concern for others.

A more serious Cluster B disorder is *borderline personality disorder*, whose sufferers are highly unstable. **[LO 13.25]** Fear of abandonment is the primary theme of their social relationships. Consequently, they tend to cling to those for whom they feel affection but, if the relationship ends, the individual with borderline disorder views the former lover as a mortal enemy. For the most part, they direct their negative emotion toward themselves. The often harm themselves, for example by pulling out their hair or making tiny cuts on their forearms.

A significant portion of patients with borderline personality disorder have histories of childhood abuse or disturbances in attachment relationships (B. Allen, 2008). Many of these patients also suffer from mood disorders (Brieger, Ehrt, & Marneros, 2003). Thus, suicidal thoughts and behaviours are often a major concern of therapists working with them (Joiner, Van Orden, Witte, & Rudd, 2009). However, research indicates that antidepressant medication, combined with psychotherapy, can be effective in treating this disorder (Soler, Pascual, Campins, Barrachina, Puigdemont, Alvarez, & Pérez, 2005).

The media are frequently captivated with people who suffer from the last category of Cluster B disorders. All too often we read or hear about people who commit horrible crimes and show no remorse whatsoever. Many of these people have **antisocial personality disorder**, which is characterized by a pattern of disregard for and violation of the rights of others (APA, 2013). This pattern of behaviours often begins in childhood or adolescence. As children, people with this disorder lie, steal, vandalize, initiate fights, skip school, and run away from home; they may be physically cruel to others and to animals (Arehart-Treichel, 2002). By early adolescence, they usually drink excessively, use drugs, and engage in promiscuous sex. In adulthood, they typically fail to keep a job, to act as a responsible parent, to honour financial commitments, and to obey the law. Con artists and many criminals could be diagnosed as having antisocial personality disorder, which may explain why experts estimate that as many as 20 percent of people who are in prisons may have this disorder. Research suggests that slightly less than 2 percent of Canadians suffer from this disorder (PHAC, 2012).

Brain-imaging studies indicate that people with antisocial personality disorder do not show the same level of arousal in response to emotionally charged words and stimuli (Seara-Cardoso & Viding, 2014). This finding suggests a neurophysiological basis for the lack of normal empathic responses in most individuals with antisocial personality disorder.

Finally, Cluster C disorders are associated with fearful or anxious behaviours. Individuals diagnosed with *obsessive compulsive personality disorder* fear being less than perfect. **[LO 13.24]** As a result, they tend to have shallow emotional relationships because of their tendency to hold others to equally unrealistic standards of behaviour. There is some degree of similarity between this disorder and the anxiety disorder called obsessive-compulsive disorder; however, patients with obsessive-compulsive personality disorders do not experience the kinds of irrational compulsions and obsessions that dominate the lives of people who have obsessive-compulsive disorders.

The two other Cluster C disorders, *avoidant personality disorder* and *dependent personality disorder*, represent opposite approaches to social relationships. A person with avoidant personality disorder avoids relationships because of excessive

---

personality disorder: An enduring pattern of inner experience and behaviour that deviates markedly from the expectations of the individual's culture, is pervasive and inflexible, has an onset in adolescence or early adulthood, is stable over time, and leads to distress or impairment.

antisocial personality disorder: A disorder marked by lack of feeling for others; selfish, aggressive, irresponsible behaviour; and willingness to break the law, lie, cheat, or exploit others for personal gain.

TABLE 13.2 Examples of *DSM-5* Categories of Personality Disorders

Personality Disorder	Symptoms
Cluster A: Odd behaviour	
Paranoid	Individual is highly suspicious, untrusting, guarded, hypersensitive, easily slighted, lacking in emotion; holds grudges.
Schizoid	Individual isolates self from others; appears unable to form emotional attachments; behaviour may resemble that of autistic children.
Schizotypal	Individual dresses in extremely unusual ways; lacks social skills; may have odd ideas resembling the delusions of schizophrenia.
Cluster B: Erratic, overly dramatic behaviour	
Narcissistic	Individual has exaggerated sense of self-importance and entitlement; is self-centred, arrogant, demanding, exploitive, envious; craves admiration and attention; lacks empathy.
Histrionic	Individual seeks attention and approval; is overly dramatic, self-centred, shallow, demanding, manipulative, easily bored, suggestible; craves excitement; is often attractive and sexually seductive.
Borderline	Individual is unstable in mood, behaviour, self-image, and social relationships; has intense fear of abandonment; exhibits impulsive and reckless behaviour and inappropriate anger; makes suicidal gestures and performs self-mutilating acts.
Antisocial	Individual disregards rights and feelings of others; is manipulative, impulsive, selfish, aggressive, irresponsible, and reckless; is willing to break the law, lie, cheat, and exploit others for personal gain, without remorse; fails to hold jobs.
Cluster C: Anxious, fearful behaviour	
Obsessive-compulsive	Individual is concerned with doing things the "right" way and is generally a perfectionist; relationships are emotionally shallow.
Avoidant	Individual fears criticism and rejection; avoids social situations in order to prevent being judged by others.
Dependent	Person is overly dependent on others for advice and approval; may cling to lovers and friends, fearing abandonment.

sensitivity to criticism and fear of rejection. By contrast, someone with dependent personality disorder relies on others to an inappropriate degree. He or she can't make an everyday decision, such as what to have for dinner, without seeking others' advice and approval. Because of fear of abandonment, people with this disorder tend to be very "clingy" in social relationships.

SEXUAL DYSFUNCTION, PARAPHILIC DISORDERS, AND GENDER DYSPHORIA DISORDERS

What are the sexual disorders?

The *DSM-5* has three categories of sexual disorders: sexual dysfunctions, paraphilic disorders, and gender dysphoria. **[LO 13.26]** Sexual dysfunctions are persistent problems that cause marked distress and interpersonal difficulty; they may involve sexual desire, sexual arousal, or the pleasure associated with sex or orgasm. The most common sexual dysfunction in men is *male erectile disorder*—the repeated inability to have or sustain an erection firm enough for coitus. For women the most common sexual dysfunction is *female orgasmic disorder*—a persistent inability to reach orgasm.

Paraphilias are recurrent sexual urges, fantasies, or behaviours involving children, other non-consenting partners, non-human objects, or suffering or humiliation. **[LO 13.26]** To be diagnosed as having a paraphilia, the person must experience considerable psychological distress or an impairment in functioning in an important area of his or her life.

Table 13.3 describes a number of paraphilic disorders listed in the *DSM-5*.

Gender dysphoria involves difficulties accepting one's identity as male or female. Recent studies suggest that genes may strongly influence the development of gender dysphoria.

sexual dysfunctions: Persistent or recurrent problems that cause marked distress and interpersonal difficulty that may involve any or some combination of the following: sexual desire, sexual arousal, or the pleasure associated with sex or orgasm.

paraphilias: Sexual disorders in which sexual urges, fantasies, and behaviour generally involve children, other non-consenting partners, non-human objects, or the suffering and humiliation of oneself or one's partner.

gender dysphoria: Disorder characterized by a problem accepting one's identity as male or female.

TABLE 13.3 *DSM-5 Categories of Paraphilic Disorders*

Disorder	Symptoms
Paraphilias	Disorders in which recurrent sexual urges, fantasies, and behaviours involve non-human objects, children, other non-consenting persons, or the suffering or humiliation of the individual or one's partner.
Fetishism	A disorder in which sexual urges, fantasies, and behaviour involve an inanimate object, such as women's undergarments or shoes.
Transvestism	A disorder in which sexual urges, fantasies, and behaviour involve cross-dressing.
Pedophilia	A disorder in which sexual urges, fantasies, and behaviour involve sexual activity with a prepubescent child or children.
Exhibitionism	A disorder in which sexual urges, fantasies, and behaviour involve exposing one's genitals to an unsuspecting stranger.
Voyeurism	A disorder in which sexual urges, fantasies, and behaviour involve watching unsuspecting people naked, undressing, or engaging in sexual activity.
Sexual masochism	A disorder in which sexual urges, fantasies, and behaviour involve being beaten, humiliated, bound, or otherwise made to suffer.
Sexual sadism	A disorder in which sexual urges, fantasies, and behaviour involve inflicting physical or psychological pain and suffering on another.
Frotteurism	A disorder in which sexual urges, fantasies, and behaviour involve touching or rubbing against a non-consenting person, usually in a crowded place.
Other paraphilias	Disorders in which sexual urges, fantasies, and behaviour involve, among other things, animals, feces, urine, corpses, filth, or enemas.

Source: Based on the DSM-5 (APA, 2013). Based on American Psychiatric Association. (2013). Diagnostic and statistical manual of mental disorders (5th ed.). Washington, DC: Author.

REMEMBER IT

Other Psychological Disorders

1. Which statement is true of personality disorders?
   a. Personality disorders usually begin in adulthood.
   b. Persons with these disorders usually realize their problem.
   c. Personality disorders typically cause problems in social relationships and at work.
   d. Persons with these disorders typically seek professional help.

2. Tim lies, cheats, and exploits others without feeling guilty. He most likely has _____ personality disorder.
   a. avoidant
   b. histrionic
   c. antisocial
   d. narcissistic

3. What is the name for disorders in which sexual urges, fantasies, and behaviours involve children, other non-consenting partners, or non-human objects?
   a. paraphilias
   b. gender identity disorders
   c. dysfunctional object disorder
   d. sexual dysfunctions

4. What is the general term used to describe disturbances in sexual desire, sexual arousal, or the ability to attain orgasm?
   a. paraphilias
   b. gender identity disorders
   c. dysfunctional object disorder
   d. sexual dysfunctions

Answers: 1. c 2. c 3. a 4. d

APPLY IT

Overcoming the Fear of Public Speaking

Do you break out in a cold sweat and start trembling when you have to speak in public? If so, cheer up; you're in good company: Fear of public speaking is one of the most common fears reported by North American adults (P. L. Witt et al., 2006)!

What Causes It?

Fear of public speaking is a form of performance anxiety, a common type of social anxiety disorder. Much of the fear of public speaking stems from fear of being embarrassed or of being judged negatively by others. Some people cope with this fear by trying to avoid situations in which they may be required to speak in public. A more practical approach is to examine the incorrect beliefs that can cause the fear of public speaking and then take specific steps to overcome it. Here are some incorrect beliefs associated with public speaking:

- To succeed, a speaker has to perform perfectly. (Not true; no audience expects perfection.)
- A good speaker presents as many facts and details about the subject as possible. (Not true; all you need is two or three main points.)
- If some members of the audience aren't paying attention, the speaker needs to do something about it. (Not true; you can't please everyone, and it's a waste of time to try to do so.)

What Can You Do?

Some of the steps you can take to manage fear of public speaking deal with how you present yourself to your audience; others focus on what's going on inside you. Here are some of the many suggestions:

- Know your material well. Practise aloud, and revise your speech, if necessary.
- Visualize your speech. Imagine yourself giving your speech in a confident, clear manner.
- Relax. Reduce your tension by doing deep breathing or relaxation exercises.
- Be familiar with the place where you will speak. Arrive early, and practise using the microphone and any other equipment you plan to use.
- Connect with the audience. Greet some members of the audience as they arrive; then, when you give your speech, speak to the audience as though they were a group of your friends.

- Project confidence through your posture. Stand or sit in a self-assured manner, smile, and make eye contact with the audience.
- Focus on your message, not on yourself. Turn your attention away from your nervousness and focus on the purpose of your speech, which is to transmit information to your audience.
- Remember that the audience doesn't expect you to be perfect. Don't apologize for any problems you think you have with your speech. Just be yourself.

By applying these few simple tips, you can overcome nervousness and speak confidently on any topic—even on the spur of the moment.

THINKING CRITICALLY

Evaluation

Some psychological disorders are more common in women (depression, agoraphobia, and specific phobia), and some are more common in men (antisocial personality disorder and substance-related disorders). Give some possible reasons why such gender differences exist in these disorders. Support your answer.

Point/Counterpoint

There is continuing controversy over whether specific psychological disorders are chiefly biological in origin (nature) or result primarily from learning and experience (nurture). Select any two disorders from this chapter and prepare arguments for both nature and nurture for both disorders.

Psychology in Your Life

Formulate a specific plan for your own life that will help you recognize and avoid the five cognitive traps that contribute to unhealthy thinking. You might enlist the help of a friend to monitor your negative statements.

MyPsychLab Go to mypsychlab (access code required) to find web resources for your text that supplement the material in chapter 13.

SUMMARY & REVIEW

WHAT IS ABNORMAL?

What criteria might be used to differentiate normal from abnormal behaviour?
Behaviour might be considered abnormal if it deviates radically from what is considered normal in one's own culture, if it leads to personal distress or impaired functioning, or if it results in one's being a danger to oneself and/or others.

What are five current perspectives that attempt to explain the causes of psychological disorders?
Five current perspectives on the causes of abnormal behaviour are (1) the biological perspective, which views it as a symptom

of an underlying physical disorder; (2) the psychodynamic perspective, which maintains that it is caused by unconscious, unresolved conflicts; (3) the learning perspective, which argues that it is learned and sustained in the same way as other behaviour; (4) the cognitive perspective, which suggests that it results from faulty thinking; and (5) the humanistic perspective, which views it as a result of the blocking of one's natural tendency toward self-actualization.

What is the DSM-5?
The *Diagnostic and Statistical Manual of Mental Disorders (Fifth Edition)*, published by the American Psychiatric Association in 2013, is used in North America to diagnose psychological disorders.

13B ANXIETY AND OBSESSIVE-COMPULSIVE DISORDERS: WHEN ANXIETY IS EXTREME

When is anxiety healthy, and when is it unhealthy?
Anxiety is healthy when it is the normal response to danger or threat. However, anxiety is maladaptive if it is out of proportion to the seriousness of the situation, if it does not fade soon after the danger has passed, or if it interferes with a person's social and work activities.

What are the symptoms of a panic disorder?
Panic disorder is marked by recurrent, unpredictable panic attacks: attacks of overwhelming anxiety, fear, or terror during which people experience palpitations, trembling or shaking, choking or smothering sensations, and the feeling that they are going to die or go crazy.

What are the characteristics of the three categories of phobias?
The three categories of phobic disorders are (1) agoraphobia, fear of being in situations in which immediate escape is impossible or help is not available in the case of incapacitating anxiety; (2) social anxiety disorder, fear of social situations in which one might be embarrassed or humiliated by appearing clumsy or incompetent; and (3) specific phobia, a marked fear of a specific object or situation and a catch-all category for all phobias other than agoraphobia or social anxiety disorder.

What do psychologists believe are some probable causes of phobias?
Phobias result primarily from frightening experiences or through observational learning. Genes may also play a role.

What is obsessive-compulsive disorder?
Obsessive-compulsive disorder is characterized by obsessions (persistent, recurring, involuntary thoughts, images, or impulses that cause great distress) and/or compulsions (persistent, irresistible, irrational urges to perform an act or ritual repeatedly).

13C SOMATIC SYMPTOM AND RELATED DISORDERS, AND DISSOCIATIVE DISORDERS

What are two somatic disorders, and what symptoms do they share?
Somatic symptom disorders involve bodily symptoms that cannot be explained by known medical conditions. Illness anxiety disorder involves a preoccupation with the fear that bodily symptoms are the sign of some serious disease. Conversion disorder involves a loss of motor or sensory functioning in some part of the body, such as paralysis or blindness.

What is dissociative amnesia?
People with dissociative amnesia have a loss of memory for limited periods of their life or for their entire personal identity.

What are some of the identifying symptoms of dissociative identity disorder?
In dissociative identity disorder (often called *multiple personality*), two or more distinct, unique personalities occur in the same person, each taking over at different times. Most patients are female and victims of early, severe physical and/or sexual abuse. They typically complain of periods of "lost time."

13D SCHIZOPHRENIA

What are some of the major positive symptoms of schizophrenia?
The positive symptoms of schizophrenia are abnormal behaviours and characteristics; they include hallucinations, delusions, disorganized thinking and speech, bizarre behaviour, and inappropriate affect.

What are some of the major negative symptoms of schizophrenia?
The negative symptoms of schizophrenia involve a loss of or deficiency in thoughts and behaviours characteristic of normal functioning; they include social withdrawal, apathy, loss of motivation, very limited speech, slow movements, flat affect, and poor hygiene and grooming.

What are the four historical subtypes of schizophrenia?
The four subtypes of schizophrenia are catatonic, disorganized, paranoid, and undifferentiated.

What are some suggested causes of schizophrenia?
Some suggested causes of schizophrenia are a genetic predisposition, sufficient stress in people who are predisposed to the disorder, and excessive dopamine activity in the brain.

13E DEPRESSIVE AND BIPOLAR DISORDERS

What are the symptoms of major depressive disorder?
Major depressive disorder is characterized by feelings of great sadness, despair, guilt, worthlessness, hopelessness, and, in extreme cases, suicidal intentions.

What are the extremes of mood suffered in bipolar disorder?
Bipolar disorder is a disorder in which a person suffers from manic episodes (periods of extreme elation, euphoria, and hyperactivity) alternating with major depression, usually with relatively normal periods in between.

What are some suggested causes of depressive and bipolar disorders?
Some of the proposed causes are (1) a genetic predisposition; (2) an imbalance in the neurotransmitters norepinephrine and serotonin; (3) a tendency to turn hostility and resentment inward rather than expressing it; (4) distorted and negative views of oneself, the world, and the future; and (5) stress.

13F OTHER PSYCHOLOGICAL DISORDERS

What are the main attributes of personality disorders?
Personality disorders are continuing, inflexible, maladaptive patterns of behaviour and inner experience that cause personal distress and/or impairment in social and occupational functioning.

What are the sexual disorders?
Three categories of sexual disorders are sexual dysfunctions (problems with sexual desire, sexual arousal, or orgasm); paraphilic disorders (needing unusual or bizarre objects, conditions, or acts for sexual gratification); and gender dysphoria (having a problem accepting one's identity as male or female).

PSYCHOLOGICAL DISORDERS

MODULE 13A WHAT IS ABNORMAL?

Psychological disorder: Any recurrent abnormal behaviour or mental state.
Abnormal behaviour: Behaviour that is strange within a culture, causes personal distress, is maladaptive, or is dangerous to self or others.

Neurosis and Psychosis

Neurosis: Obsolete term for mild mental disorder.
Psychosis: A severe psychological disorder. A person with psychosis suffers delusions (false beliefs) and/or hallucinations (false sensations) and has greatly impaired everyday functioning.
Two types of delusions:
Delusions of grandeur (falsely believing one is famous or has great knowledge, ability, or authority). Delusion of persecution (falsely believing that others are trying to harm one).

Defining and Classifying Psychological Disorders

The *Diagnostic and Statistical Manual of Mental Disorders, fifth edition (DSM-5)*, lists about 300 psychological disorders and symptoms for classification. The DSM-5 is the most widely accepted diagnostic system of abnormal behaviour in Canada and the United States.

Possible Causes of Psychological Disorders

- **Biological:** Disorders involve structural or biochemical abnormalities in the brain. The diathesis–stress model states that schizophrenia develops when there is both a genetic predisposition and more stress than a person can handle. Imbalance in neurotransmitters may cause mood disorders (norepinephrine and serotonin), obsessive-compulsive disorder (serotonin), and schizophrenia (dopamine).
- **Psychodynamic:** Disorders are caused by unconscious sexual or aggressive conflicts that are unresolved. Many pedophiles and people with dissociative identity disorder report having been sexually abused in the past.
- **Learning:** Disorders derive from inappropriate learning. Most phobias result from learning.
- **Cognitive:** Disorders originate from faulty thinking. People may be depressed because they view themselves, their world, and their future negatively.
- **Humanistic:** Disorders result from blocking one's natural tendency toward self-actualization.

MODULE 13B ANXIETY AND OBSESSIVE-COMPULSIVE DISORDERS

Anxiety disorder: Unrealistic fear and apprehension.

Generalized anxiety disorder: Experiencing excessive irrational anxiety and worry that one finds difficult to control.	**Panic disorder:** Recurring attacks of overwhelming anxiety, fear, or terror.	**Phobias:** Persistent, irrational fears of something. Three classes of phobias are agoraphobia, social anxiety disorder, and specific phobia.	**Obsessive-compulsive disorder:** Persistent, recurring, involuntary thoughts (obsessions) or behaviours (compulsions), or both.

MODULE 13C SOMATIC SYMPTOM AND RELATED DISORDERS, AND DISSOCIATIVE DISORDERS

Somatic Symptom Disorders	Dissociative Disorders
Unwarranted physical symptoms	Loss of personal identity due to a non-organic cause

Illness anxiety disorder: A preoccupation with one's health and fear that bodily symptoms are a sign of a serious disease despite reassurances from doctors to the contrary.	**Conversion disorder:** The loss of motor or sensory functioning that has no apparent physical cause but that solves some psychological problem.	**Dissociative amnesia:** Loss of memory for limited periods of one's life or for one's entire personal identity.	**Dissociative identity disorder:** Having two or more distinct, unique personalities in the same individual, with each identity in control at different times.

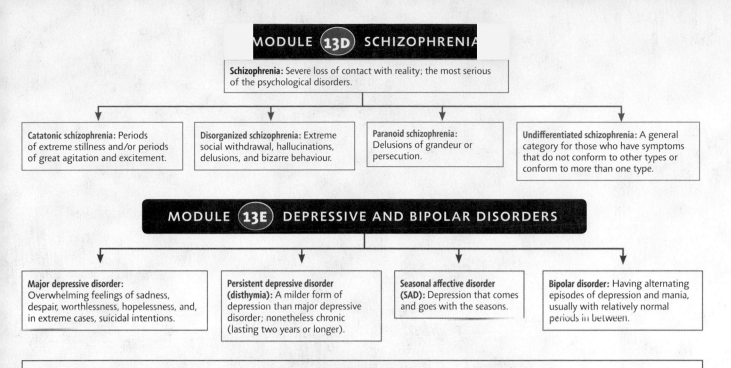

MODULE (13D) SCHIZOPHRENIA

Schizophrenia: Severe loss of contact with reality; the most serious of the psychological disorders.

Catatonic schizophrenia: Periods of extreme stillness and/or periods of great agitation and excitement.

Disorganized schizophrenia: Extreme social withdrawal, hallucinations, delusions, and bizarre behaviour.

Paranoid schizophrenia: Delusions of grandeur or persecution.

Undifferentiated schizophrenia: A general category for those who have symptoms that do not conform to other types or conform to more than one type.

MODULE (13E) DEPRESSIVE AND BIPOLAR DISORDERS

Major depressive disorder: Overwhelming feelings of sadness, despair, worthlessness, hopelessness, and, in extreme cases, suicidal intentions.

Persistent depressive disorder (disthymia): A milder form of depression than major depressive disorder; nonetheless chronic (lasting two years or longer).

Seasonal affective disorder (SAD): Depression that comes and goes with the seasons.

Bipolar disorder: Having alternating episodes of depression and mania, usually with relatively normal periods in between.

Bad Thoughts Produce Bad Feelings
Mental misery can be produced by setting unrealistic and unachievable standards, negative what-if thinking, making mountains out of molehills, regarding anything short of perfection as total failure, and setting impossible conditions for happiness.

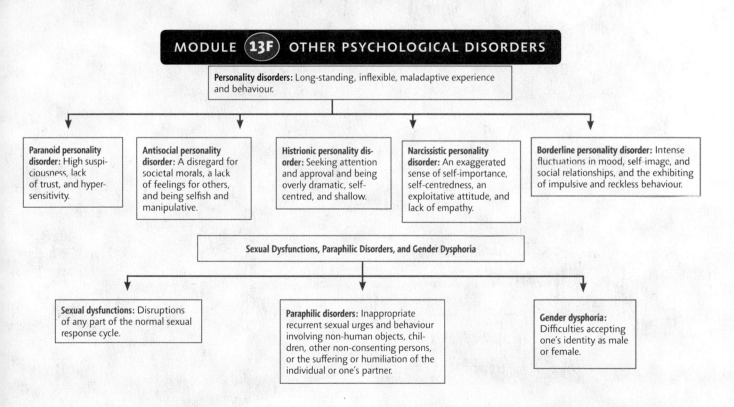

MODULE (13F) OTHER PSYCHOLOGICAL DISORDERS

Personality disorders: Long-standing, inflexible, maladaptive experience and behaviour.

Paranoid personality disorder: High suspiciousness, lack of trust, and hypersensitivity.

Antisocial personality disorder: A disregard for societal morals, a lack of feelings for others, and being selfish and manipulative.

Histrionic personality disorder: Seeking attention and approval and being overly dramatic, self-centred, and shallow.

Narcissistic personality disorder: An exaggerated sense of self-importance, self-centredness, an exploitative attitude, and lack of empathy.

Borderline personality disorder: Intense fluctuations in mood, self-image, and social relationships, and the exhibiting of impulsive and reckless behaviour.

Sexual Dysfunctions, Paraphilic Disorders, and Gender Dysphoria

Sexual dysfunctions: Disruptions of any part of the normal sexual response cycle.

Paraphilic disorders: Inappropriate recurrent sexual urges and behaviour involving non-human objects, children, other non-consenting persons, or the suffering or humiliation of the individual or one's partner.

Gender dysphoria: Difficulties accepting one's identity as male or female.

14

A simple web search for online therapy in Canada yields over 40 million hits. Clearly, online therapy is receiving a lot of attention. Is it something you should try? Research highlights both pros and cons for online therapy. On the plus side is the potential for greater portability, greater accessibility, and more anonymity (Segall, 2000).

If this is sounding good, think again! User safety is an important concern (Recupero, Harms, & Noble, 2008; Tangney, 2008). Although many services are advertised, the challenge of finding a qualified therapist is much greater online. You don't have physical access to these individuals, their diplomas, their offices, or their colleagues, which means that you do not have any tangible evidence of their qualifications. Because online services cross provincial and international boundaries, the standards that operate in your community do not necessarily affect the person you are contacting. That makes the search for a qualified practitioner quite a bit more challenging. Anyone can post a website. Anonymity works two ways on the Web—you can be whoever you want to be, and so can other people! In some cases, you might even connect with someone promoting dangerous practices under the guise of help (Recupero, Harms, & Noble 2008).

It's also good to remember that a therapist's understanding of what's happening to you is based on more than just what you say. He or she observes non-verbal communications as well. Although webcams could provide some visual contact with the person on the other end, they may not provide a full or clear picture, and communications may be disrupted, delayed, or impossible depending on the type of connection you have available. In many cases on the Web, it's only you and your words. And how comfortable are you spilling your heart out when you're not sure who else is reading your mail? Although some websites are secure, you always run the risk of undesired external parties looking in on your most personal exchanges. Technical issues (Tangney, 2008) such as limitations of servers, system crashes, and other unforeseen technical problems surface as a common difficulty.

THERAPIES

Although trained psychologists have established guidelines for ethical and caring conduct when using the internet to connect with clients (CPA, 2015), at present, online service providers are not regulated to ensure high quality service, and online therapy has yet to be proven an effective method of therapy. In this chapter we will discuss a variety of recognized therapies designed to treat psychological disorders.

MODULE **14A** INSIGHT THERAPIES

LO 14.1 Define *psychotherapy* and *insight therapy*.

LO 14.2 Identify the four basic techniques of psychoanalysis and how they are used to help patients.

LO 14.3 Explain similarities and differences between person-centred and Gestalt therapies.

What comes into your mind when you hear the word *psychotherapy*? Many people picture a patient on a couch talking to a grey-haired, bearded therapist with a heavy accent. But that picture is hopelessly out of date, as you will see. **Psychotherapy** uses psychological rather than biological means to treat emotional and behavioural disorders; it usually involves a conversation between the client and the therapist. **[LO 14.1]**. Today, the couch has generally been replaced by a comfortable chair. And psychotherapy is relatively brief, lasting from eight sessions to several months for most clients (APA, 2015), rather than years.

There are also many types of psychotherapy. Some forms of psychotherapy are collectively referred to as **insight therapies** because their assumption is that our psychological well-being depends on self-understanding—understanding of our own thoughts, emotions, motives, behaviour, and coping mechanisms. **[LO 14.1]** The major insight therapies are psychoanalysis, person-centred therapy, and Gestalt therapy.

Freud's famous couch was used by his patients during psychoanalysis.

AP Images

PSYCHODYNAMIC THERAPIES: FREUD REVISITED

Freud proposed that the cause of psychological disorders lies in early childhood experiences and in unresolved, unconscious conflicts, usually of a sexual or aggressive nature. **Psychoanalysis** was the first formal psychotherapy; it was the dominant influence on psychotherapy in the 1940s and 1950s (Garfield, 1981) and is still used by some therapists today. The goals of psychoanalysis are to uncover repressed memories and to bring to consciousness the buried, unresolved conflicts believed to lie at the root of the person's problem.

Psychoanalysis: From the Couch of Freud

What are the four basic techniques of psychoanalysis, and how are they used to help disturbed patients?

Freudian psychoanalysis uses four basic techniques: free association, analysis of resistance, dream analysis, and analysis of transference. **[LO 14.2]**

FREE ASSOCIATION The central technique of psychoanalytic therapy is **free association**, in which the patient is instructed to reveal whatever thoughts, feelings, or images come to mind, no matter how embarrassing, terrible, or trivial they might seem. Freud believed that free association allows important unconscious material to surface—for example, repressed memories, threatening impulses, and traumatic episodes of childhood. **[LO 14.2]** The analyst pieces together the free-flowing associations, explains their meaning, and helps patients gain insight into the thoughts and behaviours that are troubling them.

ANALYSIS OF RESISTANCE How do you think you would react if an analyst told you to express *everything* that came into your mind? Would you try to avoid revealing certain painful or embarrassing thoughts? Freud's patients did, and he called this **resistance**. If the patient hesitates, balks, or becomes visibly upset about any topic touched on, the analyst assumes that the topic is emotionally important to the patient. **[LO 14.2]** Freud also pointed out other forms of resistance, such as "forgetting" appointments with the analyst or arriving late.

DREAM ANALYSIS Freud believed that areas of emotional concern repressed in waking life are sometimes expressed in symbolic form in dreams. He believed that dreams convey hidden meanings and identify important repressed thoughts, memories, and emotions. **[LO 14.2]**

ANALYSIS OF TRANSFERENCE Freud said that at some point during psychoanalysis, the patient inevitably begins to react to the analyst with the same feelings and attitudes that were present in another significant relationship—usually with the mother or father. This reaction he called **transference**. Transference allows the patient to relive or re-enact troubling experiences from the past with the analyst as parent substitute. **[LO 14.2]** The unresolved childhood conflicts can then be replayed in the present, this time with a parent figure who does not reject, provoke guilt, or punish as the actual parent did.

Psychodynamic Therapy Today: The New View

Traditional psychoanalysis can be a long and costly undertaking. Patients attend four or five therapy sessions per week for two to four years. The number of people opting for classical psychoanalysis has dropped. Many psychoanalysts today practise *brief psychodynamic therapy*, in which the therapist and patient decide on the issues to explore at the outset rather than waiting for them to emerge in the course of treatment. The therapist assumes a more active role and places more emphasis on the present than is the case in traditional psychoanalysis. Brief psychodynamic therapy may require only one or two visits per week for as few as 12 to 20 weeks (Altshuler, 1989). Research indicates that brief psychodynamic therapy is as effective as other kinds of psychotherapy (Crits-Christoph et al., 2008; Hager, Leichsenring, & Schiffler, 2000). Brief psychotherapy appears to be most effective with patients who do not have multiple psychological disorders, who lack significant social relationship problems, and who believe that the therapy will be effective (Crits-Christoph et al., 2004).

HUMANISTIC THERAPY

Humanistic therapy stands in stark contrast to psychoanalysis in that it is based on a more optimistic and hopeful picture of human nature and human potential. Individuals are viewed as unique and basically self-determining, with the ability and freedom to lead rational lives and make rational choices. It encourages personal growth; it seeks to teach clients how to fulfill their potential and take responsibility for their behaviour and for what they become in life. The focus is primarily on current relationships and experiences.

Person-Centred Therapy: The Patient Becomes the Person

What is the role of the therapist in person-centred therapy?

Person-centred therapy (sometimes called *client-centred* therapy), developed by Carl Rogers (1951), is based on the humanistic view of human nature. **[LO 14.3]** According to this view, people are innately good and, if allowed to develop naturally, will grow toward self-actualization (the realization of their inner potential).

If people grow naturally toward self-actualization, then why is everyone not self-actualized? The humanistic perspective suggests that psychological disorders result when a person's natural tendency toward self-actualization is blocked. **[LO 14.3]** Rogers (1959) insisted that individuals block their natural tendency toward growth and self-actualization when they act in ways that are inconsistent with their true self in order to gain the positive regard of others.

In person-centred therapy, the focus is on conscious thoughts and feelings. **[LO 14.3]** The therapist attempts to create a warm, accepting climate in which clients are free to be themselves so that their natural tendency toward growth can be released. Person-centred therapy is a **non-directive therapy**.

Carl Rogers (at upper right) facilitates discussion in a therapy group.

The direction of the therapy sessions is controlled by the client. The therapist acts as a facilitator of growth, giving understanding, support, and encouragement rather than proposing solutions, answering questions, or actively directing the course of therapy.

According to Rogers, only three things are required of therapists. First, they must have **unconditional positive regard** for, or total acceptance of, the client, regardless of the client's feelings, thoughts, or behaviour. **[LO 14.3]** In such an atmosphere,

psychotherapy: The treatment for psychological disorders that uses psychological rather than biological means and primarily involves conversations between patient and therapist.

insight therapies: Any type of psychotherapy based on the notion that psychological well-being depends on self-understanding.

psychoanalysis (SY-ko-uh-NAL-ul-sis): The psychotherapy that uses free association, analysis of resistance, dream analysis, and transference to uncover repressed memories, impulses, and conflicts thought to cause psychological disorder.

free association: A psychoanalytic technique used to explore the unconscious; patients reveal whatever thoughts or images come to mind.

resistance: In psychoanalytic therapy, the patient's attempts to avoid expressing or revealing painful or embarrassing thoughts or feelings.

transference: An intense emotional situation occurring in psychoanalysis when one comes to behave toward the analyst as one had behaved toward a significant figure from the past.

person-centred therapy: A non-directive, humanistic therapy in which the therapist creates a warm, accepting atmosphere, thus freeing clients to be themselves and releasing their natural tendency toward positive growth; developed by Carl Rogers.

non-directive therapy: An approach in which the therapist acts to facilitate growth, giving understanding and support rather than proposing solutions, answering questions, or actively directing the course of therapy.

unconditional positive regard: A condition required of person-centred therapists, involving a caring for and acceptance of clients regardless of the client's feelings, thoughts, or behaviour.

REMEMBER IT

Insight Therapies

1. In psychoanalysis the technique whereby a patient reveals every thought, idea, or image that comes to mind is called _____; the patient's attempt to avoid revealing certain thoughts is called _____.
   a. transference; resistance
   b. free association; transference
   c. revelation; transference
   d. free association; resistance

2. What is the directive therapy that emphasizes the importance of the client's fully experiencing, in the present moment, his or her thoughts, feelings, and actions?
   a. person-centred therapy
   b. Gestalt therapy
   c. brief psychodynamic theory
   d. psychoanalytic therapy

3. What is the non-directive therapy developed by Carl Rogers in which the therapist creates a warm, accepting atmosphere so that the client's natural tendency toward positive change can be released?
   a. person-centred therapy
   b. Gestalt therapy
   c. brief psychodynamic theory
   d. psychoanalytic therapy

4. Which therapy presumes that the causes of the patient's problems are repressed memories, impulses, and conflicts?
   a. person-centred therapy
   b. Gestalt therapy
   c. brief psychodynamic theory
   d. psychoanalytic therapy

Answers: 1. d 2. b 3. a 4. d

---

clients feel free to reveal their weakest points, relax their defences, and begin to accept and value themselves. Second, therapists' feelings toward their clients must be genuine—no facade, no putting up a professional front. Third, therapists must have empathy with their clients—that is, they must be able to put themselves in the clients' place. Therapists must show that they comprehend the clients' feelings, emotions, and experiences, and that they understand and see the clients' world as the clients see it. When clients speak, the therapist follows by restating or reflecting back their ideas and feelings. In this way clients begin to see themselves more clearly; eventually, they resolve their own conflicts and make positive decisions about their lives.

Gestalt Therapy: Getting in Touch with Your Feelings

What is the major emphasis in Gestalt therapy?

Gestalt therapy, developed by Fritz Perls (1969), emphasizes the importance of clients fully experiencing, in the present moment, their feelings, thoughts, and actions, and then taking responsibility for both their feelings and their behaviour. **[LO 14.3]** Perls maintains that many of us block out aspects of our experience and are often not aware of how we really feel.

Gestalt therapy is a **directive therapy**, one in which the therapist takes an active role in determining the course of therapy sessions. **[LO 14.3]** "Getting in touch with one's feelings" is an ever-present objective for those in Gestalt therapy. The therapist helps, prods, or badgers clients to experience their feelings as deeply and genuinely as possible and then admit responsibility for them.

Perls suggests that those of us who need therapy carry around a heavy load of unfinished business, which may be in the form of resentments of or conflicts with parents, siblings, lovers, employers, or others. If not resolved, these conflicts are carried forward into our present relationships. One method of dealing with unfinished business is the "empty chair" technique, which is used to help clients express their true feelings about significant people in their lives. The client imagines, for example, that a wife, husband, father, mother, or friend sits in the empty chair. The client then proceeds to tell the "chair" what he or she truly feels about that person. Then the client trades places and sits in the empty chair and role-plays the imagined person's response to what the client has said.

The ultimate goal of Gestalt therapy is not merely to relieve symptoms. Rather, it is to help clients achieve a more integrated self and become more authentic and self-accepting. **[LO 14.3]** In addition, clients must learn to assume personal responsibility for their behaviour rather than blame society, past experiences, parents, or others.

MODULE 14B RELATIONSHIP THERAPIES: THERAPIES EMPHASIZING INTERACTION WITH OTHERS

LO 14.4 Describe the characteristics that define relationship therapies.
LO 14.5 Explain the differences between traditional and integrated behavioural couple therapies.
LO 14.6 Understand the goals of family therapy.
LO 14.7 Identify the advantages of group therapy.

Insight therapies focus on the self, which is not always the most appropriate approach to a psychological problem. **Relationship therapies** look not only at the individual's internal struggles, but also at interpersonal relationships. **[LO 14.4]**

COUPLES THERAPY: HEALING OUR RELATIONSHIPS

How do traditional and integrated behavioural couples therapies differ?

Some therapists work with couples to help them resolve problems. There are many approaches to premarital and other forms of couples therapy, but two models have become prominent in recent years—traditional and integrated behavioural couples therapy (A. Christensen, Wheeler, & Jacobson, 2008; D. K. Snyder, Castellani, & Whisman, 2006).

The older of the two, **traditional behavioural couples therapy (TBCT)**, focuses on identification and modification of behaviours that contribute to a couple's conflicts (Jacobson & Margolin, 1979). **[LO 14.5]** For example, suppose that a spouse complains that her partner is a poor listener. In response, the partner justifies the tendency to tune out as a reaction to his spouse's habit of communicating in vague generalities and her tendency to become defensive whenever asked for clarification. A TBCT therapist would observe interactions between the couple to assess the accuracy of these complaints and to identify each spouse's communication strengths. Next, the therapist would work with each of them individually to modify the behaviours that contribute to the couple's communication difficulties. At the same time, the therapist would seek to enhance whatever behaviours each spouse exhibits that are helpful to the communication process.

A variation on TBCT, **integrated behavioural couples therapy (IBCT)**, targets emotions as well as behaviours (Jacobson & Christensen, 1996). **[LO 14.5]** A central premise of IBCT is that a couple's problems arise from changeable behaviours as well as from the individual—and less changeable—personality traits of both partners (e.g., openness, conscientiousness, extroversion, agreeableness, and neuroticism). Thus, when couples complain about behaviours in their partners that reflect such traits, IBCT therapists seek to help them accept and adjust to each other's personalities rather than to try to change them.

In summary, couples therapy helps couples achieve higher levels of relationship satisfaction and can be useful in the treatment of psychological disorders. For example, sexual dysfunctions, as well as mood, anxiety, and substance use disorders, can be treated in the context of couples therapy (Gehring, 2003; McCrady, Epstein, Cook, Jensen, & Hildebrandt, 2009; D. K. Snyder et al., 2006; Walitzer & Demen, 2004).

FAMILY THERAPY: HOME IS WHERE THE HELP IS

What are the goals of family therapy?

For most of us, the most significant group to which we will ever belong is the family. But even the strongest families sometimes have problems, and there are therapists of all types who

©Izabela Habur/E+/Getty Images

Family and marital therapists pay attention to the dynamics of the family unit—how members communicate, act toward each other, and view each other.

specialize in treating troubled families. In **family therapy**, parents and children enter therapy as a group. The therapist pays attention to the dynamics of the family unit—how family members communicate, how they act toward one another, and how they view each other. The goal of the therapist is to help family members reach agreement on certain changes that will help heal the wounds of the family unit, improve communication patterns, and create more understanding and harmony within the group (Hawley & Weisz, 2003). **[LO 14.6]**

As you can imagine, there are some things a family member may want to discuss privately with the therapist. Family therapists realize this and do not conduct every session with the entire family together. Sometimes they work with only one or a few family members at a time.

Gestalt therapy: A therapy originated by Fritz Perls that emphasizes the importance of clients fully experiencing, in the present moment, their feelings, thoughts, and actions and then taking responsibility for their feelings and behaviour.

directive therapy: An approach to therapy in which the therapist takes an active role in determining the course of therapy sessions and provides answers and suggestions to the patient.

relationship therapies: Therapies that look not only at individual struggles, but also at interpersonal relationships.

traditional behavioural couples therapy (TBCT): An approach to couples therapy that focuses on behaviour change.

integrated behavioural couples therapy (IBCT): A type of couples therapy that emphasizes both behaviour change and mutual acceptance.

family therapy: Therapy involving an entire family, with the goal of helping family members reach agreement on changes that will help heal the family unit, improve communication problems, and create more understanding and harmony within the group.

REMEMBER IT

Relationship Therapies

1. All of the following are true of group therapy except that it _____
   a. allows individuals to get feedback from other members.
   b. allows individuals to receive help and support from other members.
   c. is not conducted by trained therapists.
   d. is less expensive than individual therapy.

2. _____ behavioural couples therapy focuses on behaviour change, while _____ behavioural couples therapy emphasizes mutual acceptance.

3. In family therapy, the therapist pays attention to the _____ of the family unit.

4. Match each description with the appropriate type(s) of therapy.
   _____ 1) led by professional therapists
   _____ 2) effective for supporting individuals recovering from alcoholism
   _____ 3) provides members with a sense of belonging
   _____ 4) less expensive than individual therapy but still provides contact with trained therapists
   a. group therapy
   b. self-help groups
   c. both group therapy and self-help groups

Answers: 1. c 2. Traditional, integrated 3. dynamics 4. (1) a (2) b (3) c (4) a

GROUP THERAPY: HELPING ONE AT A TIME, TOGETHER

What are some advantages of group therapy?

Group therapy is a form of therapy in which several clients (usually 7 to 10) meet regularly with one or more therapists to resolve personal problems. Besides being less expensive than individual therapy, group therapy has other advantages. It gives the individual a sense of belonging and an opportunity to express feelings, get feedback from other members, and give and receive help and emotional support. **[LO 14.7]** Discovering that others share the same problems leaves individuals feeling less alone and ashamed.

Psychodrama, originated by J. L. Moreno (1959a, 1959b), is a technique whereby one client acts out a problem situation or relationship with the assistance and participation of the other group members. Sometimes the client plays the part of the person who is a problem—a technique called *role reversal*. In doing so, he or she may gain some understanding of the other person's feelings. When group members act out their own frustrations and role-play the frustrations of others, they often gain insight into the nature of their problems and troublesome relationships.

Group Help of a Different Sort

Some people seek help for their problems from sources other than mental health professionals—through encounter groups and self-help groups.

ENCOUNTER GROUPS: WHERE ANYTHING GOES

Encounter groups claim to promote personal growth and self-knowledge and to improve personal relationships through intense emotional encounters with other group members. Groups are composed of 10 to 20 people who meet with a leader or leaders over a period of several weeks or months. Encounter group participants are urged to express their true feelings about themselves and others. Not all exchanges are oral. Relating to others physically (i.e., touching, hugging) is also encouraged.

Some studies indicate that only about one third of encounter group participants benefit from the experience, one third are unaffected, and one third are harmed (Lieberman, Yalom, & Miles, 1973).

SELF-HELP GROUPS: LET'S DO IT OURSELVES

Self-help groups are not usually led by professional therapists. They are simply groups of people who share a common problem and meet to support one another.

One of the oldest and best-known self-help groups is Alcoholics Anonymous (AA), which is believed to have more than two million members worldwide (Alcoholics Anonymous, 2005). Other self-help groups, patterned after AA, have been formed to help individuals overcome many other addictive behaviours—for example, Overeaters Anonymous, Gamblers Anonymous, and Cocaine Anonymous. There are self-help groups for people with a variety of physical and mental illnesses, and groups to help people deal with crises, from divorce and bereavement to victimization.

Self-help groups offer comfort because people can talk about their problems with others who have "been there." **[LO 14.7]** They can exchange useful information, discuss their coping strategies, and gain hope by seeing people who are coping with the same problems successfully. Research assessing the effectiveness of self-help groups is mixed (Ferri, Amato, Davoli, 2006; Finch, Lambert, & Brown, 2000; Kaskatus, 2009; Lieberman, 1986; Zilbergeld, 1986).

MODULE **14C** BEHAVIOUR THERAPIES: UNLEARNING THE OLD, LEARNING THE NEW

LO 14.8 Define *behaviour modification*.
LO 14.9 Identify two operant-based behaviour modification techniques and explain how each changes behaviour.
LO 14.10 Identify four therapies based on classical conditioning and explain how they are implemented.
LO 14.11 Understand how modelling helps people overcome fears.

What is behaviour therapy?

Behaviour therapy is a treatment approach associated with the learning perspective on psychological disorders—the perspective that holds that abnormal behaviour is learned. According to the behaviourists, unless people are suffering from some physiological disorder, such as brain pathology, those who seek therapy need it for one of two reasons: (1) they have learned inappropriate or maladaptive responses or (2) they have never had the opportunity to learn appropriate behaviour in the first place. Instead of viewing the maladaptive behaviour as a symptom of some underlying disorder, the behaviour therapist sees the behaviour itself as the disorder. Thus, if a person comes to a therapist with a fear of flying, that fear of flying is seen as the problem.

Behaviour therapy applies the principles of operant conditioning, classical conditioning, and/or observational learning to eliminate inappropriate or maladaptive behaviours and replace them with more adaptive responses. Sometimes this approach is referred to as **behaviour modification**. **[LO 14.8]** The goal is to change the troublesome behaviour, not to change the individual's personality structure or to search for the origin of the problem behaviour. The therapist's role is active and directive.

BEHAVIOUR MODIFICATION TECHNIQUES BASED ON OPERANT CONDITIONING

How do behaviour therapists modify behaviour using operant conditioning techniques?

Behaviour modification techniques based on operant conditioning seek to control the consequences of behaviour. Undesirable behaviour is eliminated by withholding or removing reinforcement for the behaviour. As you have learned, behaviour that is not reinforced will eventually stop.

Behaviour therapists also seek to reinforce desirable behaviour in order to increase its frequency, and they use reinforcement to shape entirely new behaviours. Institutional settings such as hospitals, prisons, and school classrooms lend themselves well to these techniques, because they provide a restricted environment in which the consequences (or *contingencies*) of behaviour can be more tightly controlled.

Token Economies: What Would You Do for a Token?

Some institutions use behaviour modification programs called **token economies,** which reward appropriate behaviour with poker chips, play money, gold stars, and the like. **[LO 14.9]** These tokens can later be exchanged for desired goods (candy, gum, cigarettes) and/or privileges (weekend passes, free time, participation in desirable activities). Sometimes individuals are fined a certain number of tokens for undesirable behaviour. To start these programs, patients have to know which appropriate behaviours will be rewarded. The appropriate behaviours are usually established with the patient and the institutional support staff team. Each time a patient performs the desired behaviour, he or she receives a token. Tokens are collected over time. For decades, institutions have used token economies to improve self-care skills and social interaction among patients

with chronic schizophrenia—with good results (Ayllon & Azrin, 1965, 1968). Similar interventions have been helpful in motivating clients at substance abuse clinics to remain abstinent (Petry et al., 2004).

Time Out: All Alone with No Reinforcers

Another effective method used to eliminate undesirable behaviour, especially in children and adolescents, is **time out** (Donaldson & Vollmer, 2011; Kazdin & Benjet, 2003). **[LO 14.9]** The principle is simple. Children are told in advance that if they engage in certain undesirable behaviours, they will be removed calmly from the situation and will have to pass a period of time (usually no more than 15 minutes) in a place containing no reinforcers (no television, books, toys, friends, and so on). Theoretically, the undesirable behaviour will stop if it is no longer followed by attention or any other positive reinforcers.

Other Applications of Operant Approaches: Where Do They Work?

Behaviour therapies based on operant conditioning have a history of being effective in modifying some behaviours of seriously disturbed individuals (Ayllon & Azrin, 1968; Paul & Lentz, 1977). Although these techniques do not presume to cure severe psychological disorders, they can increase the frequency of desirable behaviours and decrease the frequency of undesirable ones.

group therapy: A form of therapy in which several clients (usually between 7 and 10) meet regularly with one or two therapists to resolve personal problems.

psychodrama: A group therapy in which one group member acts out a personal problem situation or relationship, assisted by other members, to gain insight into the problem.

encounter groups: Intense emotional group experiences designed to promote personal growth and self-knowledge; participants are encouraged to let down their defences and relate honestly and openly with one another.

behaviour therapy: A treatment approach that employs the principles of operant conditioning, classical conditioning, and/or observational learning theory to eliminate inappropriate or maladaptive behaviours and replace them with more adaptive responses.

behaviour modification: The systematic application of the learning principles of operant conditioning, classical conditioning, or observational learning to individuals or groups in order to eliminate undesirable behaviour and/or encourage desirable behaviour.

token economies: Behavioural techniques used to encourage desirable behaviours by reinforcing them with tokens that can be exchanged later for desired objects, activities, and/or privileges.

time out: A behavioural technique used to decrease the frequency of undesirable behaviour; involves withdrawing an individual from all reinforcement for a period of time.

Behaviour modification techniques can also be used to break bad habits such as smoking (e.g., Tidey, O'Neill, & Higgins, 2002) and overeating, or to develop good habits such as a regular exercise regime. If you want to modify any of your behaviours, devise a reward system for desirable behaviours, and remember the principles of shaping. Reward gradual changes in the direction of your ultimate goal. If you are trying to develop better eating habits, don't try to change a lifetime of bad habits all at once. Begin with a small step such as substituting frozen yogurt for ice cream. Set realistic and achievable weekly goals.

THERAPIES BASED ON CLASSICAL CONDITIONING

What behaviour therapies are based on classical conditioning?

Some behaviour therapies are based mainly on the principles of classical conditioning, which can account for how we acquire many of our emotional reactions. In classical conditioning, a neutral stimulus—some object, person, or situation that initially does not elicit any strong positive or negative emotional reaction—is paired with either a very positive or a very negative stimulus. After conditioning, our strong feeling toward the positive or negative stimulus transfers to the original, neutral stimulus.

Therapies based on classical conditioning can be used to rid people of fears and other undesirable behaviours. Recent research also suggests that exposing individuals to such stimuli via virtual reality can be a useful addition to the standard ways in which such therapies are implemented (Mühlberger, Weik, Pauli, & Wiedemann, 2006; Parsons & Rizzo, 2008). We will discuss four types of therapy based primarily on classical conditioning: systematic desensitization, flooding, exposure and response prevention, and aversion therapy.

Systematic Desensitization: Overcoming Fears One Step at a Time

How do therapists use systematic desensitization to rid people of fears?

One of the pioneers in the application of classical conditioning techniques to therapy, psychiatrist Joseph Wolpe (1958, 1973), reasoned that if he could get people to relax and stay relaxed while they thought about a feared object, person, place, or situation, they could conquer their fear. In Wolpe's therapy, **systematic desensitization**, clients are trained in deep muscle relaxation. **[LO 14.10]** Then they confront a hierarchy of anxiety-producing situations—either in real life or in their imagination—until they can remain relaxed even in the presence of the most feared situation. The therapy can be used for everything from fear of animals to acrophobia (fear of high places), claustrophobia (fear of enclosed places), test anxiety, and social and other situational fears.

What do you fear most? Many students would say that they fear speaking in front of a group. If that were your fear and you went to a behaviour therapist who used systematic desensitization, here is what she or he would have you do. First the therapist would ask you to identify the fear causing your anxiety and everything connected with it. Then all the aspects of the fear would be arranged in a hierarchy from least to most anxiety-producing.

After the hierarchy was prepared, you would be taught deep muscle relaxation—how to progressively relax parts of your body until you achieve a completely relaxed state. During the actual desensitization procedure, you would be asked to picture, as vividly as possible, the least fear-producing item on your hierarchy—for example, reading in the syllabus that the presentation will be assigned. Once you were able to remain relaxed while visualizing this item, the therapist would have you picture the next item—your professor assigning the oral presentation. This procedure would be followed until you were able to remain calm and relaxed while you vividly imagined the most fear-producing stimulus—actually making your presentation in class. If, during the desensitization process, anxiety crept in as you imagined items on the hierarchy, you would signal the therapist, who would instruct you to stop thinking about that item. You would then clear your mind, come back to a state of complete relaxation, and begin again. Try creating your own hierarchy in the *Try It.*

How effective is systematic desensitization? Many experiments, demonstrations, and case reports confirm that it is highly successful in eliminating fears and phobias in a relatively short time (Kalish, 1981; Kolivas, Riordan, & Gross, 2008; Zinbarg & Griffith, 2008). It has proved effective for specific

TRY IT

Using Systematic Desensitization to Overcome Fear

Use what you have learned about systematic desensitization to create a step-by-step approach to help someone overcome a fear of making a class presentation. The person's hierarchy of fears begins with reading in the syllabus that an oral presentation will be assigned, and it culminates in actually making the oral presentation. Fill in the sequence of steps, according to a possible hierarchy of fears, that will lead to the final step.

Try to fill in the steps in the following example:

1. Being assigned the oral presentation and given a due date.
2.
3.
4.
5.
6.
7.
8. Giving the oral presentation.

problems such as test anxiety, stage fright, and anxiety related to sexual disorders.

Several other therapies used to treat phobias and obsessive-compulsive disorder use exposure as the key therapeutic element.

Flooding: Confronting Our Fears All at Once

What is flooding?

Flooding is a behaviour therapy used in the treatment of phobias. **[LO 14.10]** Clients are exposed to the feared object or event (or asked to vividly imagine it) for an extended period until their anxiety decreases. Flooding is almost the opposite of systematic desensitization. The person is exposed to the fear all at once, not gradually and certainly not in a state of relaxation. A person with a fear of heights, for example, might have to go onto the roof of a tall building and remain there until the fear subsided.

The key to success is keeping the person in the feared situation long enough for it to become clear that none of the dreaded consequences actually come to pass (Marks, 1978). Flooding sessions typically last from 30 minutes to two hours and should not be terminated until patients are markedly less afraid than they were at the beginning of the session. It is rare for a patient to need more than six treatment sessions (W. L. Marshall & Segal, 1988).

Confronting the real object works faster and is more effective than simply imagining it (Chambless & Goldstein, 1979; Marks, 1972). Flooding may be quite painful for the patient. But flooding often works when other therapies have failed; and it works faster than other therapies.

Exposure and Response Prevention: Cutting the Tie That Binds Fears and Rituals

How is exposure and response prevention used to treat people with obsessive-compulsive disorder?

Exposure and response prevention is a successful therapy for treating obsessive-compulsive disorder (Baer, 1996; Foa, 1995; Rhéaume & Ladouceur, 2000). **[LO 14.10]** The therapy consists of two components. The first component involves *exposure*—clients are exposed to objects or situations they have been avoiding because they trigger obsessions and compulsive rituals. The second component is *response prevention*—patients agree to resist performing their compulsive rituals for progressively longer periods of time.

The therapist begins by identifying the thoughts, objects, or situations that trigger the compulsive ritual. For example, touching a doorknob, a piece of unwashed fruit, or garbage might ordinarily send people with a fear of contamination to the nearest bathroom to wash their hands. Clients are gradually exposed to stimuli that they find more and more distasteful and anxiety-provoking. They must agree not to perform the normal ritual (handwashing, bathing, or the like) for a specified period of time after exposure. Gradually, clients learn to tolerate the anxiety evoked by the various "contaminants." A typical treatment course—about 10 sessions over a period of three to

Virtual reality phobia therapy research. Researchers testing a virtual reality therapy system to treat spider phobia (arachnophobia). The system contains eye-tracking software to study a person's response when exposed to virtual spiders in a virtual environment (on screen). Photographed at the Clinical Cyberpsychology Laboratory, University of Quebec, Outaouais, Canada.

©Thierry Berrod, Mona Lisa Production/Science Photo Library/Science Source

seven weeks—can bring about considerable improvement in 60 to 70 percent of patients (Jenike, 1990). This therapy has also proved useful in the treatment of post-traumatic stress disorder (Cloitre, Koenen, Cohen, & Han, 2002).

systematic desensitization: A behaviour therapy, used to treat phobias, that involves training clients in deep muscle relaxation and then having them confront a graduated series of anxiety-producing situations (real or imagined) until they can remain relaxed while confronting even the most feared situation.

flooding: A behavioural therapy used to treat phobias; clients are exposed to the feared object or event (or asked to imagine it vividly) for an extended period until their anxiety decreases.

exposure and response prevention: A behaviour therapy that exposes obsessive-compulsive disorder patients to objects or situations generating increasing anxiety; patients must agree not to carry out their normal rituals for a specified period of time after exposure.

Systematic desensitization, flooding, and exposure help people *stop* avoiding feared objects and situations. But what type of therapy exists to help people *start* avoiding situations? The answer: aversion therapy.

Aversion Therapy: Making Us Sick to Make Us Better

How does aversion therapy rid people of a harmful or undesirable behaviour?

Aversion therapy rids clients of a harmful or socially undesirable behaviour by pairing that behaviour with a painful, sickening, or otherwise aversive stimulus. **[LO 14.10]** Electric shock, emetics (which cause nausea and vomiting), and other unpleasant stimuli are paired with the undesirable behaviour time after time until a strong negative association is formed and the person comes to avoid that behaviour, habit, or substance. Treatment continues until the bad habit loses its appeal because it has become associated with pain or discomfort.

Alcoholics given a nausea-producing substance (e.g., disulfiram, also known as Antabuse®), which reacts violently with alcohol, retch and vomit until their stomach is empty (J. B. Grossman & Ruiz, 2004).

But for most problems, aversion therapy need not be so intense as to make a person physically ill. A controlled comparison of treatments for chronic nail biting revealed that mild aversion therapy—painting a bitter-tasting substance on the fingernails—yielded significant improvement (K. W. Allen, 1996).

THERAPIES BASED ON OBSERVATIONAL LEARNING: JUST WATCH THIS!

How does participant modelling help people overcome fears?

A great deal of what we learn in life, we learn from watching and then copying or imitating others. Therapies derived from Albert Bandura's work on observational learning are based on the belief that people can overcome fears and acquire social skills through modelling. **[LO 14.11]**

For example, therapists have effectively treated fears and phobias by having clients watch a model (on film or in real life) responding to a feared situation in appropriate ways with no dreaded consequences. **[LO 14.11]** Bandura (1967) describes how nursery-school children lost their fear of dogs after watching a film showing a child who was not afraid of dogs first approaching a dog, then playing with it, petting it, and so on.

The most effective type of therapy based on observational learning theory is called **participant modelling** (Bandura, 1977; Bandura, Adams, & Beyer, 1977; Bandura, Jeffery, & Gajdos, 1975). In this therapy, not only does the model demonstrate the appropriate response in graduated steps, but also the client attempts to imitate the model step by step while the therapist gives encouragement and support. Most specific phobias can be extinguished in only three or four hours of client participation in modelling therapy. Participant modelling is more effective than simple observation for some specific phobias (Bandura, Blanchard, & Ritter, 1969).

REMEMBER IT

Behaviour Therapy

1. Behaviour therapy techniques that try to change behaviour by reinforcing desirable behaviour and removing reinforcers for undesirable behaviour are based on_____
   a. operant conditioning.
   b. observational learning.
   c. classical conditioning.
   d. modelling.

2. Behaviour therapies based on classical conditioning are used mainly to
   a. shape new, more appropriate behaviours.
   b. rid people of fears and undesirable behaviours or habits.
   c. promote development of social skills.
   d. demonstrate appropriate behaviours.

3. Exposure and response prevention is a treatment for people with _____
   a. panic disorder.
   b. phobias.

   c. generalized anxiety disorder.
   d. obsessive-compulsive disorder.

4. Match the description with the therapy.
   _____ 1) flooding
   _____ 2) aversion therapy
   _____ 3) systematic desensitization
   _____ 4) participant modelling
   a. practising deep muscle relaxation during gradual exposure to the feared object
   b. associating painful or sickening stimuli with the undesirable behaviour
   c being exposed directly to the feared object without relaxation
   d. imitating a model responding appropriately in the feared situation

MODULE 14D COGNITIVE THERAPIES: IT'S THE THOUGHT THAT COUNTS

LO 14.12 Define *cognitive therapies*.

LO 14.13 Explain what is meant by the *ABC*s of rational-emotive therapy.

LO 14.14 Describe how Beck's cognitive therapy can be used to assist people with depression and anxiety disorders.

LO 14.15 Identify the key components of cognitive-behavioural therapy.

We have seen that behaviour therapies based on classical and operant conditioning and modelling are effective in eliminating many types of troublesome behaviour. What if the problem is not an observable, undesirable behaviour, but rather is in our thinking, attitudes, beliefs, or self-concept? There are therapies for these problems as well. **Cognitive therapies** assume that maladaptive behaviour can result from irrational thoughts, beliefs, and ideas, which the therapist tries to change. **[LO 14.12]** The emphasis in cognitive therapies is on conscious rather than unconscious processes, and on the present rather than the past. We will explore three types of cognitive therapy—rational-emotive therapy, Beck's cognitive therapy, and cognitive-behavioural therapy.

RATIONAL-EMOTIVE THERAPY: HUMAN MISERY—THE LEGACY OF FALSE BELIEFS

What is the aim of rational-emotive therapy?

Picture this scenario: Harry received two free tickets to a Saturday-night concert featuring his favourite group. Excited and looking forward to a great time on Saturday, Harry called Sally, whom he had dated a couple of times, to ask her to share the evening with him. But she turned him down with some lame excuse like "I have to do my laundry." He was stunned and humiliated. "How could she do this to me?" he wondered. As the week dragged on, he became more and more depressed.

What caused Harry's depression? Sally's turning him down, right? Not according to Albert Ellis (1961, 1977, 1993), a clinical psychologist who developed **rational-emotive therapy** in the 1950s. Rational-emotive therapy is based on Ellis's ABC theory. *A* refers to the *activating* event, *B* to the person's *belief* about the event, and *C* to the emotional *consequence*. **[LO 14.13]** Ellis argues that it is not the event that causes the emotional consequence, but rather the person's belief about the event. In other words, *A* does not cause *C*; *B* causes *C*. If the belief is irrational, the emotional consequence can be extreme distress, as illustrated in Figure 14.1.

Irrational beliefs cause people to view an undesirable event as a catastrophe rather than a disappointment or inconvenience; this leads them to say "I can't stand this" rather than "I don't like this." Irrational beliefs cause people to feel depressed, worthless, or enraged instead of simply disappointed or annoyed. To make matters worse, people go on to feel "anxious about their anxiety" and "depressed about their depression" (Ellis, 1987, p. 369).

Rational-emotive therapy (RET) is a directive, confrontational form of psychotherapy designed to challenge clients'

TRY IT

Using Rational-Emotive Therapy

Use what you have learned about Albert Ellis's rational-emotive therapy to identify—and perhaps even eliminate—an irrational belief that you hold about yourself.

First, identify an irrational belief, preferably one that causes some stress in your life. For example, perhaps you feel that you must earn all A's in order to think of yourself as a good person.

Ask yourself the following questions, and write down your answers in as much detail as possible.

- Where does this belief come from? Can you identify the time in your life when it began?
- Why do you think this belief is true? What evidence can you provide that "proves" your belief?
- Can you think of any evidence to suggest that this belief is false? What evidence contradicts your belief? What people do you know who do not cling to this belief?
- How does holding this belief affect your life, both negatively and positively?
- How would your life be different if you stopped holding this belief? What would you do differently?

irrational beliefs about themselves and others. As clients begin to replace irrational beliefs with rational ones, their emotional reactions become more appropriate, less distressing, and more likely to lead to constructive behaviour. Try challenging an irrational belief of your own in the *Try It*.

Most clients in rational-emotive therapy are seen individually, once a week, for 5 to 50 sessions. In stark contrast to person-centred therapists (and most other therapists, for that matter), "rational-emotive therapists do not believe a warm relationship between counsellee and counsellor is a necessary or a sufficient condition for effective personality change" (Ellis, 1979, p. 186).

aversion therapy: A behaviour therapy used to rid clients of a harmful or socially undesirable behaviour by pairing it with a painful, sickening, or otherwise aversive stimulus until the behaviour becomes associated with pain and discomfort.

participant modelling: A behaviour therapy in which an appropriate response is modelled in graduated steps and the client attempts each step, while encouraged and supported by the therapist.

cognitive therapies: Any therapies designed to change maladaptive thoughts and behaviour, based on the assumption that maladaptive behaviour can result from one's irrational thoughts, beliefs, and ideas.

rational-emotive therapy: A directive, confrontational psychotherapy designed to challenge and modify the client's irrational beliefs, which are thought to cause personal distress; developed by Albert Ellis.

Harry's View: Sally's refusal caused his upset. *A* caused *C*.

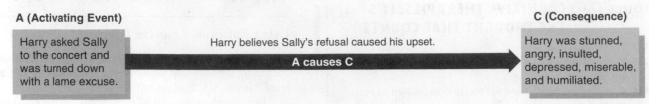

A (Activating Event)

Harry asked Sally to the concert and was turned down with a lame excuse.

Harry believes Sally's refusal caused his upset.
A causes C

C (Consequence)

Harry was stunned, angry, insulted, depressed, miserable, and humiliated.

Ellis's View: Harry's *belief* about the event caused his upset. *B* caused *C*.

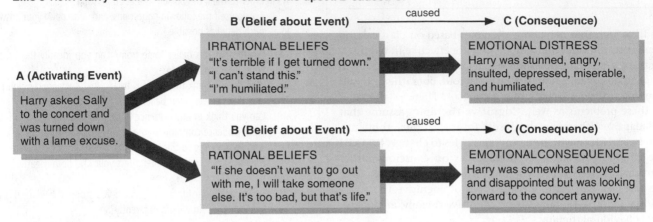

B (Belief about Event) ——— caused ———▶ **C (Consequence)**

IRRATIONAL BELIEFS
"It's terrible if I get turned down."
"I can't stand this."
"I'm humiliated."

EMOTIONAL DISTRESS
Harry was stunned, angry, insulted, depressed, miserable, and humiliated.

A (Activating Event)

Harry asked Sally to the concert and was turned down with a lame excuse.

B (Belief about Event) ——— caused ———▶ **C (Consequence)**

RATIONAL BELIEFS
"If she doesn't want to go out with me, I will take someone else. It's too bad, but that's life."

EMOTIONAL CONSEQUENCE
Harry was somewhat annoyed and disappointed but was looking forward to the concert anyway.

FIGURE 14.1

The ABCs of Albert Ellis's Rational-Emotive Therapy

Rational-emotive therapy teaches clients that it is not the activating event (A) that causes the upsetting consequences (C). Rather, it is the client's beliefs (B) about the activating event. Irrational beliefs cause emotional distress, according to Albert Ellis. Rational-emotive therapists help clients identify their irrational beliefs and replace them with rational ones.

In Ellis's view, "giving a client RET with a good deal of warmth, approval and reassurance will tend to help this client 'feel better' rather than 'get better'" (1979, p. 194).

Two meta-analyses indicated that patients receiving rational-emotive therapy did better than those receiving systematic desensitization (Engles, Garnefski, & Diekstra, 1993), and that rational emotive therapy is also effective for youth and children (Gonzalez Nelson, Gutkin, Saunders, Galaway, & Shrewy, 2004).

BECK'S COGNITIVE THERAPY: OVERCOMING THE "POWER OF NEGATIVE THINKING"

How does Beck's cognitive therapy help people overcome depression and anxiety disorders?

"To be happy, I have to be successful in whatever I undertake."
"To be happy, I must be accepted (liked, admired) by all people at all times."
"If people disagree with me, it means they don't like me."

If you agree with all of these statements, you probably spend a good part of your time upset and unhappy. Psychiatrist Aaron T. Beck (1976) maintains that much of the misery of depressed and anxious people can be traced to **automatic thoughts**—unreasonable but unquestioned ideas that rule the person's life. **[LO 14.14]** Beck believes that depressed individuals hold "a negative view of the present, past, and future experiences" (1991,

p. 369). They tend to view themselves as "deficient, defective, and/or undeserving"; their environment as "unduly demanding, depriving, and/or rejecting"; and their future as "without promise, value, or meaning" (Karasu, 1990, p. 138). These people notice only negative, unpleasant things and jump to upsetting conclusions. Anxious people expect the worst; they "catastrophize" and at the same time underestimate their ability to cope with situations.

Aaron T. Beck, an early proponent of cognitive therapy.

©Hollandse Hoogte/Redux Pictures

REMEMBER IT

Cognitive Therapies

1. Cognitive therapists believe that, for the most part, maladaptive behaviours result from _____
   a. physical causes.
   b. unconscious conflicts and motives.
   c. irrational thinking.
   d. environmental stimuli.

2. Rational-emotive therapy is a non-directive therapy that requires a warm, accepting therapist. (true/false)

3. The goal of cognitive therapy is best described as helping people _____
   a. develop effective coping strategies.
   b. replace negative thoughts with more objective thoughts.
   c. develop an external locus of control.
   d. develop realistic goals and aspirations.

4. Cognitive therapy has proved very successful in the treatment of _____
   a. depression and mania.
   b. schizophrenia.
   c. fears and phobias.
   d. anxiety disorders and depression.

Answers: 1. c 2. false 3. b 4. d

The goal of **Beck's cognitive therapy** is to help clients stop their negative thoughts as they occur and replace them with more objective thoughts. **[LO 14.14]** After challenging clients' irrational thoughts, the therapist sets up a plan and guides clients so that their own experience in the real world provides evidence to refute their false beliefs. Clients are given homework assignments, such as keeping track of automatic thoughts and the feelings evoked by them, and substituting more rational thoughts.

Beck's cognitive therapy is brief—usually only 10 to 20 sessions. This therapy has been researched extensively and is reported to be highly successful in the treatment of mildly to moderately depressed patients (Hollon, Thase, & Markowitz, 2002; Whisman, 2008). There is some evidence that depressed people who have received Beck's cognitive therapy are less likely to relapse than those who have been treated with antidepressants (Hollon, Stewart, & Strunk, 2006; J. Scott, 1996).

Cognitive therapy is also effective for generalized anxiety disorder (Beck, 1993; Wetherell, Gatz, & Craske, 2003), bulimia (Agras, Walsh, Fairburn, Wilson, & Kraemer, 2000), and panic disorder (Grey, Salkovskis, Quigley, Clark, & Ehlers, 2008; Power, Sharp, Swanson, & Simpson, 2000). An alternative to Beck's cognitive therapy was developed by University of Waterloo psychologist Donald Meichenbaum (1985). He proposed that individuals can be "inoculated" against negative events by being taught in advance to make positive and optimistic self-evaluations. In this way, the positive evaluations act as a buffer against negative experiences.

COGNITIVE-BEHAVIOURAL THERAPY: CHANGES IN THOUGHT CHANGE BEHAVIOUR

The important role that our thoughts have in how we feel and how we act is evident in a form of psychotherapy called **cognitive-behavioural therapy (CBT)** (Dobson, 2001). It is one of the most popular forms of therapy today, and rightfully so—it's effective. But since it draws upon other therapeutic approaches, the mechanisms that make this therapy successful and the range of psychological difficulties it can be used to treat are not fully understood (Dobson, 2001).

Therapists using CBT believe that changing how a person thinks about a situation can result in changes in how a person feels and behaves in that situation, even if the situation itself does not change. The three assumptions that underlie this form of therapy are that (1) what we think (our cognitions) affects behaviour, (2) our cognitions may be monitored and changed, and (3) desired changes in behaviour can be achieved by changing our cognitions (Dobson, 2001, p. 4). **[LO 14.15]** Therapists work with patients to encourage them to change negative or inappropriate cognitions to more desirable ones. Treatment using CBT is (like Beck's cognitive therapy) generally shorter than many other forms of therapy (some of which may take years). Cognitive-behavioural therapy has been shown to be effective in treating a wide variety of problems, including anxiety disorders (R. McCabe & Gifford, 2009; Wilbram, Kellett, & Beail, 2008), hypochondriasis (Martinez & Belloch, 2004), psychological drug dependence (Babor, 2004), mood disorders (Totterdell & Kellett, 2008), and pathological gambling (Petry, 2002).

automatic thoughts: Unreasonable and unquestioned ideas that rule a person's life and lead to depression and anxiety.

Beck's cognitive therapy: A brief cognitive therapy for depression and anxiety, designed to help people recognize their automatic thoughts and replace them with more objective thoughts.

cognitive-behavioural therapy (CBT): A therapy based on the belief that changing how a person thinks about a situation can result in changes in how a person feels and behaves in that situation, even if the situation itself does not change.

MODULE 14E EYE MOVEMENT DESENSITIZATION AND REPROCESSING (EMDR)

LO 14.16 Identify what the letters in EMDR represent.
LO 14.17 Explain how EMDR works.

What is EMDR?

In 1989, Francine Shapiro (1989, 2001) introduced a new treatment for traumatic memories: Eye Movement Desensitization and Reprocessing (EMDR). **[LO 14.16]** She also developed a theoretical model to describe and explain its mechanisms and principles. EMDR is a method of psychotherapy that draws upon components of other therapies (e.g., psychodynamic, cognitive-behavioural, interpersonal, experiential, and body-centred therapies), psychological theories (e.g., attachment, learning, and cognition), and biological information related to brain functioning (EMDR International Association, 2006). **[LO 14.17]** Much of this treatment is based on an information-processing approach (Shapiro, 2001; Shapiro & Maxfield, 2002).

Recall that information-processing approaches assume that our experiences, thoughts, emotions, and sensations are stored in memory in a way that allows us to access them later. However, "when a traumatic or very negative event occurs, information processing may be incomplete, perhaps because strong negative feelings or dissociation interfere with information processing" (EMDR Institute, 2006). EMDR is used as a means for "correcting" or completing the processing of information to allow for more adaptive thinking. **[LO 14.17]**

How does EMDR work? Its important feature is dual attention, whereby a client is asked to attend to two pieces of information at the same time. **[LO 14.17]** Specifically, the client is asked to think about disturbing past and present experiences while focusing on an external stimulus (EMDR Institute, 2006). In most cases this stimulus is the therapist's fingers. The therapist moves his or her fingers in a controlled way while the client attempts to both focus on the disturbing information and follow the controlled finger movements. These movements in turn produce controlled eye movements (from which the therapy gets its name). The role of eye movements in this therapeutic approach is not wholly understood, but researchers such as Louise Maxfield (see *Canadian Connections*) are attempting to understand the unique contribution of eye movements to this therapy.

Is the therapy effective? A great deal of the research on EMDR deals with the potency of this therapy for treating victims of trauma, specifically those experiencing post-traumatic stress disorder (e.g., Pearlman & Courtois, 2005; Rothbaum, Astin, & Marsteller, 2005), and success has also been reported for other anxiety disorders.

CANADIAN CONNECTIONS

The Role of Eye Movements in EMDR

Post-traumatic stress disorder (PTSD) is a debilitating condition whereby those who have experienced or witnessed highly stressful or traumatic events subsequently suffer from a variety of distressing psychological experiences, including recurring nightmares, flashbacks, anxiety, avoidance of guilt, and depression. One therapy that is proving to be particularly effective for individuals suffering from PTSD is Eye Movement Desensitization and Reprocessing (EMDR).

Both therapists and their clients typically report that EMDR decreases the distress of the traumatic memory. EMDR also increases awareness of related positive and adaptive information. For example, after EMDR a sexual assault victim no longer feels responsible for the assault, and is not troubled by the experience. Exactly how does EMDR achieve these results? One feature of EMDR, as you can tell by its name, is that the therapist directs the client's eye movement while the client thinks of the disturbing experience. Research has yet to determine whether these directed eye movements contribute to the treatment outcomes, and if so, what effect they have.

Louise Maxfield (2003, 2007), a psychologist at the London Health Sciences Centre in Ontario, and editor of the *Journal of EMDR Practice and Research* (2014), has found evidence that when people think of a memory and move their eyes, the vividness of the memory and its associated emotions are decreased. This effect is thought to be the result of cognitive overload; when people attempt to do two similar tasks at the same time, their performance is impaired. (Just try reading this textbook while listening to your professor's lecture!) It is uncertain

Louise Maxfield

Used by permission of Louise Maxfield

whether this decrease in the memory's vividness and distress allows the individual to access more positive information or whether there is something about the eye movements themselves that increases the person's cognitive flexibility; that is, the ability to think about things from more than one perspective. Alternatively, the eye movements may result in brain activation similar to that which occurs in REM sleep. The role of eye movements opens many intriguing lines of investigation. Already this new therapy has developed an increasing presence (Maxfield, 2009). ■

REMEMBER IT

Eye Movement Desensitization and Reprocessing (EMDR)

1. For which disorder has EMDR proven most effective? _____ _____

2. When clients are asked to follow the therapist's fingers while thinking about a disturbing event, they are engaging in the dual attention component of EMDR. Which other theory is this based on?

a. operant conditioning

b. information processing

c. dual processing

d. repression

Answers: 1. post-traumatic stress disorder   2. c

MODULE (14F) THE BIOMEDICAL THERAPIES

LO 14.18 Identify for which disorders the following drugs are used: neuroleptics, tricyclics, selective serotonin reuptake inhibitors, monoamine oxidase inhibitors, lithium, and tranquilizers.

LO 14.19 Explain how the following drugs function: neuroleptics, tricyclics, selective serotonin reuptake inhibitors, monoamine oxidase inhibitors, lithium, and tranquilizers.

LO 14.20 Explain how electroconvulsive therapy (ECT) is used as a therapy.

LO 14.21 Define *psychosurgery* and list the disorders it is used to treat.

What are the three main biological therapies?

Professionals who favour the biological perspective—the view that psychological disorders are symptoms of underlying physical disorders—usually favour a **biological therapy**. The three treatment categories in biological therapy are drug therapy, electroconvulsive therapy (ECT), and psychosurgery.

DRUG THERAPY: PILLS FOR PSYCHOLOGICAL ILLS

The most frequently used biological treatment is drug therapy. A major breakthrough in drug therapy came in the mid-1950s when antipsychotic drugs—sometimes called the *major tranquilizers*—began to be used to treat schizophrenia. In the late 1950s, antidepressants were discovered. Finally, in 1970, lithium, the miracle drug for bipolar disorder, was introduced into psychiatry (S. H. Snyder, 1984). Modern drug therapy is now capable of relieving the debilitating symptoms of schizophrenia, depression, bipolar disorder, and some anxiety disorders; it has had a tremendous impact on the treatment of psychological disorders.

Antipsychotic Drugs

How do antipsychotic drugs help schizophrenic patients?

Antipsychotic drugs, or *neuroleptics*, are prescribed mainly for schizophrenia to control severe psychotic symptoms, such

as hallucinations, delusions, and other disorders in thinking. **[LO 14.18]** They are also effective in reducing restlessness, agitation, and excitement. You may have heard of these drugs under some of their brand names—Thorazine®, Stelazine®, and Mellaril®. Neuroleptics work primarily by inhibiting the activity of the neurotransmitter dopamine. **[LO 14.19]** About 50 percent of patients have a good response to the standard antipsychotics (Bobes et al., 2003; Kane, 1996). However, even those patients who are helped by antipsychotics often stop taking them because of unpleasant side effects such as restless pacing and fidgeting, muscle spasms and cramps, and a shuffling gait. Long-term use of antipsychotic drugs carries a high risk of the most severe side effect, tardive dyskinesia. Tardive dyskinesia involves almost continual twitching and jerking movements of the face and tongue and squirming movements of the hands and trunk (Glazer, Morgenstern, & Doucette, 1993).

Several newer "atypical" neuroleptics, such as clozapine (Clozaril®), risperidone (Risperdal®), aripiprazole (Abilify®), and olanzapine (Zyprexa®), treat the negative symptoms of schizophrenia, leading to marked improvement in patients' quality of life (Lauriello, McEvoy, Rodriguez, Bossie, & Lasser, 2005; Worrel, Marken, Beckman, & Ruehter, 2000). Atypical neuroleptics target both dopamine and serotonin receptors (Kawanishi, Tachikawa, & Suzuki, 2000). They produce fewer side effects than standard neuroleptics, and patients taking them are less likely to develop tardive dyskinesia (Soares-Weiser & Fernandez, 2007). While antipsychotic drugs help some clients, they do not cure schizophrenia (Wolkin et al., 1989). Rather, they reduce and control many of the major symptoms so that patients can function. Most patients must continue to take them to keep the symptoms under control (Schooler et al., 1997).

---

biological therapy: A therapy based on the assumption that most mental disorders have physical causes; attempts to change or influence the biological mechanism involved (e.g., through drug therapy, ECT, or psychosurgery).

antipsychotic drugs: Drugs used to control severe psychotic symptoms, such as the delusions and hallucinations of schizophrenics; also known as *neuroleptics* or *major tranquilizers*.

Antidepressant Drugs

For what conditions are antidepressants prescribed?

Antidepressants work well as mood elevators for people who are severely depressed (Boren, Leventhal, & Pigott, 2009). **[LO 14.18]** They have also been helpful in the treatment of certain anxiety disorders, such as generalized anxiety disorder, panic disorder, and obsessive-compulsive disorder.

TRICYCLICS The first-generation antidepressants are known as the *tricyclics* (e.g., amitriptyline [Elavil®] and imipramine [Apo-imipramine, Tofranil®]; as well as clomipramine (Anafranil®), and desipramine (Norpramin®) (Nutt, 2000). **[LO 14.18]** The tricyclics work against depression by blocking the reuptake of norepinephrine and serotonin into the axon terminals, thus enhancing the action of these neurotransmitters in the synapses. **[LO 14.19]** But tricyclics can have unpleasant side effects, including sedation, dizziness, nervousness, fatigue, dry mouth, forgetfulness, and weight gain (Frazer, 1997). Progressive weight gain (an average of more than 20 pounds or about 9 kg) is the main reason people stop taking tricyclics, in spite of the relief these drugs provide from distressing psychological symptoms.

SELECTIVE SEROTONIN REUPTAKE INHIBITORS The second-generation antidepressants, the selective serotonin reuptake inhibitors (SSRIs), block the reuptake of the neurotransmitter serotonin, increasing its availability at the synapses in the brain (Nutt, 2000; Vetulani & Nalepa, 2000). **[LO 14.19]** Drugs in this class include fluoxetine (Prozac®), sertraline (Zoloft®), paroxetine (Paxil®), and citalopram (Celexa®). In general, SSRIs have fewer side effects (Nelson, 1997) and are safer in overdose than tricyclics (Thase & Kupfer, 1996). Fluoxetine is one of the most widely used SSRIs and is effective for less severe depression (Avenoso, 1997; Nelson, 1991). It is also effective in the treatment of obsessive-compulsive disorder, which has been associated with a serotonin imbalance (G. M. Goodwin, 1996; Rapoport, 1989). Similar outcomes have been obtained with sertraline and paroxetine.

MONOAMINE OXIDASE INHIBITORS Another class of first-generation antidepressants is the monoamine oxidase inhibitors (MAO inhibitors). **[LO 14.19]** By blocking the action of an enzyme that breaks down norepinephrine and serotonin in the synapses, MAO inhibitors increase the availability of norepinephrine and serotonin. These drugs, such as tranylcypromine (Parnate®) and phenelzine (Nardil®), are usually prescribed for depressed patients who do not respond to other antidepressants (Thase, Frank, Mallinger, Hammer, & Kupfer, 1992). **[LO 14.18]** They are also effective in treating panic disorder (Sheehan & Raj, 1988) and social phobia (R. D. Marshall, Schneier, Fallon, Feerick, & Liebowitz, 1994). But MAO inhibitors have many of the same unpleasant side effects as tricyclic antidepressants, and patients taking MAO inhibitors must avoid certain foods or run the risk of stroke.

Lithium: A Natural Salt That Evens Moods

How does lithium help patients with bipolar disorder?

Lithium, a naturally occurring salt, is considered a wonder drug for 40 to 50 percent of patients with bipolar disorder (Thase & Kupfer, 1996). **[LO 14.18]** It is said to begin to calm the manic state

within 5 to 10 days. This is a noteworthy accomplishment, in that the average episode, if untreated, lasts between three and four months. The proper maintenance dose of lithium will usually even out the moods of the patient and reduce the number and severity of episodes of both mania and depression (Prien et al., 1984; Teuting, Koslow, & Hirschfeld, 1981). Patients who discontinue lithium are 6.3 times more likely to have a recurrence (Suppes, Baldessarini, Faedda, & Tohen, 1991). Careful and continuous monitoring of lithium levels in the patient's system is absolutely necessary to guard against lithium poisoning and permanent damage to the nervous system (Schou, 1997).

The Minor Tranquilizers

The minor tranquilizers known as *benzodiazepines* include diazepam (Valium®), alprazolam (Xanax®), and chlordiazepoxide (Librax®). Used primarily to treat anxiety, benzodiazepines are prescribed more often than any other class of psychoactive drugs (Cloos & Ferreira, 2009) **[LO 14.18]**

Alprazolam is a fast-working, effective drug for treating panic disorder (J. R. T. Davidson, 1997; Verster & Volkerts, 2004) and has fewer side effects than antidepressants (Noyes et al., 1996). But there is a downside to alprazolam: many patients, after they are panic-free, experience moderate to severe withdrawal symptoms, including severe anxiety, if they stop taking the drug (Otto et al., 1993; Vester & Volkerts, 2004).

Some Problems with Drug Therapy

What are some of the problems with drug therapy?

So far, one might conclude that drug therapy is the simplest and possibly the most effective way of treating schizophrenia, depression, panic disorder, and obsessive-compulsive disorder. There are, however, a number of potential problems with the use of drugs. Beyond the drugs' unpleasant or dangerous side effects, it's important to note that drugs do not cure psychological disorders, so patients usually experience a relapse if they stop taking the drugs when their symptoms lift (Hollon et al., 2006). Antipsychotics and antidepressants have side effects that can be so unpleasant that many patients stop treatment before they have a reduction in symptoms.

The main problem with antidepressants is that they are relatively slow-acting. In addition, more often than not, depressed patients have to try several different antidepressants before finding one that is effective. A severely depressed patient needs at least two to six weeks to obtain relief, and 30 percent don't respond at all. This poses a risk for suicidal patients. If suicide is a danger, antidepressant drugs are not the treatment of choice (Keitner & Boschini, 2009).

ELECTROCONVULSIVE THERAPY: THE CONTROVERSY CONTINUES

For what purpose is electroconvulsive therapy (ECT) used, and what is its major side effect?

Antidepressants are not the only treatment that might be considered for depression. **Electroconvulsive therapy (ECT)** is sometimes used with severely depressed patients who are suicidal.

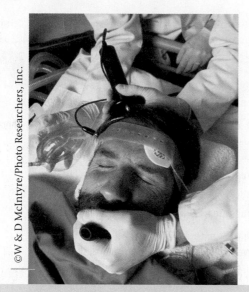

In electroconvulsive therapy, a mild electric current is passed through the brain for one to two seconds, causing a brief seizure.

©W & D McIntyre/Photo Researchers, Inc.

ECT has a bad reputation because it was misused and overused in the 1940s and 1950s. Nevertheless, when used appropriately, ECT is a highly effective treatment for major depression (Folkerts, 2000; Little, McFarlane, & Ducharme, 2002; A. I. Scott & Fraser, 2008). **[LO 14.20]**

How is ECT administered? For many years, ECT was performed by passing an electric current through both cerebral hemispheres, a procedure known as *bilateral ECT*. Today, electric current is administered to the right hemisphere only, and the procedure is called *unilateral ECT*. **[LO 14.20]** Research suggests that unilateral ECT is as effective as the more intense bilateral ECT, while producing fewer cognitive effects (Sackeim et al., 2000). Also, a patient undergoing ECT today is given anaesthesia, controlled oxygenation, and a muscle relaxant. Experts think that ECT changes the biochemical balance in the brain, resulting in a lifting of depression.

The Side Effects of ECT

Some psychiatrists and neurologists have spoken out and written books and articles against the use of ECT, arguing that the procedure causes pervasive brain damage and memory loss (Breggin, 1979; Friedberg, 1976, 1977; Grimm, 1976). But advocates of ECT say that claims of brain damage are based on animal studies in which dosages of ECT were much higher than those now used in human patients (Devanand, Dwork, Hutchinson, Bolwig, & Sackheim, 1994). No structural brain damage as a result of ECT has been revealed in studies in which MRI or CT scans were compared before and after a series of treatments (Devanand et al., 1994).

Even advocates of ECT acknowledge that there are side effects, the most disturbing of which is memory loss. The memory loss appears to result from a temporary disruption of memory consolidation that, in most cases, lasts for only a few weeks. Some patients have a spotty memory loss of events that happened before ECT (Sackeim et al., 1993; Squire, 1986). In a few patients, the memory loss may last longer than six months (Sackeim, 1992).

In Canada, several position papers have been presented to the Canadian Psychiatric Association supporting the selective use of ECT. Psychologists Murray Enns and Jeffrey Reiss (1992) at the University of Manitoba reviewed the pros and cons of the procedure and also concluded that, when used properly, ECT is a safe and effective treatment.

Toward the end of the twentieth century, a new brain-stimulation therapy known as *rapid transcranial magnetic stimulation (rTMS)* was developed. This magnetic therapy is not invasive in any way. Performed on patients who are not sedated, it causes no seizures or memory loss and has no known side effects. Its therapeutic value is similar to that of ECT, and it is much more acceptable to the public (Higgins & George, 2009).

PSYCHOSURGERY: CUTTING TO CURE

What is psychosurgery, and for what problems is it used?

An even more drastic procedure than ECT is **psychosurgery**—brain surgery performed strictly to alleviate serious psychological disorders, such as severe depression, severe anxiety, or obsessions, or to provide relief in some cases of unbearable chronic pain. **[LO 14.21]** Psychosurgery is not the same as brain surgery performed to correct a physical problem, such as a tumour or blood clot.

The first such surgical procedure for human patients was developed by Portuguese neurologist Egas Moniz in 1935 to treat severe phobias, anxiety, and obsessions. In his technique, the **lobotomy**, surgeons severed the frontal lobes and the deeper brain centres involved in emotion. No brain tissue was removed. At first the procedure was considered a tremendous contribution, and it won Moniz the Nobel Prize in Medicine in 1949. Not everyone considered it a contribution, however: one of Moniz's lobotomized patients curtailed the surgeon's activities by shooting him in the spine, leaving him paralyzed on one side.

Neurosurgeons performed tens of thousands of frontal lobotomies throughout the world from 1935 until 1955. Although the surgery was effective in calming many patients, it often left them in a severely deteriorated condition. Apathy, impaired intellect, loss of motivation, and a change in personality kept many from resuming a normal life.

antidepressants: Drugs that are prescribed to treat depression and some anxiety disorders.

electroconvulsive therapy (ECT): A treatment in which an electric current is passed though the brain, causing a seizure; usually reserved for the severely depressed who are either suicidal or unresponsive to other treatment.

psychosurgery: Brain surgery to treat some severe, persistent, and debilitating psychological disorders or severe chronic pain.

lobotomy: A psychosurgery technique in which the nerve fibres connecting the frontal lobes to the deeper brain centres are severed.

REMEMBER IT

Biomedical Therapies

1. Match the disorder with the drug or drug class most often used for its treatment.

_____ 1) panic disorder

_____ 2) schizophrenia

_____ 3) bipolar disorder

_____ 4) major depression

_____ 5) obsessive-compulsive disorder
    a. lithium
    b. antipsychotic drugs
    c. antidepressant drugs

2. Medication that relieves the symptoms of schizophrenia is thought to work by blocking the action of_____

a. serotonin. **c.** norepinephrine.

b. dopamine. **d.** epinephrine.

3. Which of the following statements concerning drug therapy for psychological disorders is false?
   a. It is often difficult to determine the proper dose.
   b. Drugs often have unpleasant side effects.
   c. Patients often relapse if they stop taking the drugs.
   d. Drugs are usually not very effective.

4. For which disorder is ECT typically used?
   a. severe depression **c.** anxiety disorders
   b. schizophrenia **d.** panic disorder

In the mid-1950s, when antipsychotic drugs came into use, psychosurgery virtually stopped. Modern psychosurgery procedures result in less intellectual impairment because, rather than using conventional surgery, surgeons deliver electric currents through electrodes to destroy a much smaller, more localized area of brain tissue. In one procedure, called a *cingulotomy*, electrodes are used to destroy the cingulum, a small bundle of nerves connecting the cortex to the emotional centers of the brain. Several procedures, including cingulotomy, have been helpful for some extreme cases of obsessive-compulsive disorder (Greist, 1992; Jenike et al., 1991; Lopes et al., 2004). **[LO 14.21]** But the results of psychosurgery are still not predictable, and the consequences—whether positive or negative—are irreversible. For these reasons, the treatment is considered experimental and absolutely a last resort (Feusner & Bystritsky, 2005; Glannon, 2006).

MODULE **14G** **THERAPIES AND THERAPISTS: MANY CHOICES**

LO 14.22 Compare the strengths and weaknesses of each therapy.
LO 14.23 Compare the training and skills that psychologists and psychiatrists offer for clients.
LO 14.24 Understand how culture and gender can impact on the effectiveness of therapy.

EVALUATING THE THERAPIES: DO THEY WORK?

If you look over the summaries of the various therapeutic approaches in *Review & Reflect 14.1*, you will notice that there are many similarities among them. Several, for example, focus on helping clients reflect on their own thoughts and/or emotions. Analyses of therapy sessions representing different perspectives suggest that there is a core set of techniques that therapists use

no matter which perspective they adopt, but these analyses also show that each therapeutic approach has elements that distinguish it from others (Gazzola & Stalikas, 2004; Trijsburg, Trent, & Semeniuk, 2004; Waldron & Helm, 2004).

But to what degree do the various therapies differ in effectiveness? In a classic study of therapeutic effectiveness, M. L. Smith, G. V. Glass, and T. I. Miller (1980) analyzed the results of 475 studies, which involved 25 000 patients. Their findings revealed that psychotherapy was better than no treatment, but that no one type of psychotherapy was more effective than another. **[LO 14.22]** A subsequent reanalysis of the same data by Hans Eysenck (1994), however, showed a slight advantage for behaviour therapies over other types. A study by Hollon and colleagues (2002) found that cognitive and interpersonal therapies had an advantage over psychodynamic approaches for depressed patients. **[LO 14.22]**

But how do the patients themselves rate the therapies? To answer this question, *Consumer Reports* ("Mental Health," 1995) conducted the largest survey to date on patient attitudes toward psychotherapy. Martin Seligman (1995, 1996), a consultant for the study, summarized its findings: **[LO 14.22]**

- Overall, patients believed that they benefited substantially from psychotherapy.

- Patients seemed equally satisfied with their therapy whether it was provided by a psychologist, a psychiatrist, or a social worker.

- Patients who were in therapy for more than six months did considerably better than the rest; generally, the longer patients stayed in therapy, the more they improved.

- Patients who took a drug such as Prozac® or Xanax® believed it helped them, but overall, psychotherapy alone seemed to work about as well as psychotherapy plus drugs.

Read *Review & Reflect 14.1*, which summarizes the five major approaches to therapy.

REVIEW & REFLECT 14.1 SUMMARY AND COMPARISON OF MAJOR APPROACHES TO THERAPY

Type of Therapy	Perceived Cause of Disorder	Goals of Therapy	Methods Used	Primary Disorders Treated
Psychoanalysis	Unconscious sexual and aggressive urges or conflicts; fixations; weak ego.	Help patient bring disturbing, repressed material to consciousness and work through unconscious conflicts; strengthen ego functions.	Psychoanalyst analyzes and interprets dreams, free associations, resistances, and transference.	General feelings of unhappiness; unresolved problems from childhood.
Person-centred	Blocking of normal tendency toward self-actualization; incongruence between real and desired self; overdependence on positive regard of others.	Increase self-acceptance and self-understanding; help patient become more inner-directed; increase congruence between real and desired self; enhance personal growth.	Therapist shows empathy and unconditional positive regard, and reflects client's expressed feelings back to client.	General feelings of unhappiness; problems with interpersonal genuineness.
Behaviour	Learning of maladaptive behaviours or failure to learn appropriate behaviours.	Extinguish maladaptive behaviours and replace with more adaptive ones; help patient acquire needed social skills.	Therapist uses methods based on classical and operant conditioning and modelling, which include systematic desensitization, flooding, exposure and response prevention, aversion therapy, and reinforcement.	Fears, phobias, panic disorder, obsessive-compulsive disorder, bad habits.
Cognitive	Irrational and negative assumptions and ideas about self and others.	Change faulty, irrational, and/or negative thinking.	Therapist helps client identify irrational and negative thinking and substitute rational thinking.	Depression, anxiety, panic disorder; general feelings of unhappiness.
Biological	Underlying physical disorder caused by structural or biochemical abnormality in the brain; genetic inheritance.	Eliminate or control biological cause of abnormal behaviour; restore balance of neurotransmitters.	Physician prescribes drugs such as antipsychotics, antidepressants, lithium, or tranquilizers; ECT, psychosurgery.	Schizophrenia, depression, bipolar disorder, anxiety disorders.

MENTAL HEALTH PROFESSIONALS: HOW DO THEY DIFFER?

What different types of mental health professionals conduct psychotherapy?

Who are mental health professionals, and for what problems are their services most appropriate?

For serious psychological disorders, a clinical psychologist or psychiatrist is the best source of help. A **clinical psychologist**, who usually has a Ph.D. in clinical psychology, specializes in assessing, treating, and/or researching psychological problems and behavioural disturbances. **[LO 14.23]** Clinical psychologists use various types of psychotherapy to treat a variety of psychological disorders and adjustment problems.

A **psychiatrist** is a medical doctor with a specialty in the diagnosis and treatment of mental disorders. **[LO 14.23]** Psychiatrists can prescribe drugs and other biological treatments; many also provide psychotherapy. It is important to

note that in Canada and the United States, there is a movement to allow psychologists with special training in psychopharmacology to prescribe drugs. A **psychoanalyst** is usually (not always) a psychiatrist with specialized training in psychoanalysis from a psychoanalytic institute.

Other trained professionals might also be able to assist clients with psychological problems such as substance abuse, marital or family problems, and adjustment disorders. For example, *counselling psychologists* usually have a doctorate in clinical or

---

clinical psychologist: A psychologist, usually with a Ph.D., trained in the diagnosis, treatment, and/or research of psychological and behavioural disorders.

psychiatrist: A medical doctor with a specialty in the diagnosis and treatment of mental disorders.

psychoanalyst (SY-ko-AN-ul-ist): A professional, usually a psychiatrist, with specialized training in psychoanalysis.

REMEMBER IT

Therapies and Therapists

1. What is true regarding the effectiveness of therapies?
   a. All are equally effective for any disorder.
   b. Specific therapies have proved effective in treating particular disorders.
   c. Insight therapies are consistently best.
   d. Therapy is no more effective than no treatment for emotional and behavioural disorders.

2. One must have a medical degree to become a _____
   a. clinical psychologist.
   b. psychoanalyst.
   c. psychiatrist.
   d. clinical psychologist, psychiatrist, or psychoanalyst.

3. Match the problem with the most appropriate therapy.
   _____ 1) eliminating fears, bad habits
   _____ 2) schizophrenia
   _____ 3) general unhappiness, interpersonal problems
   _____ 4) post-traumatic stress disorder
      a. behaviour therapy
      b. insight therapy
      c. drug therapy
      d. EMDR therapy

Answers: 1.b 2.c 3. (1).a (2).c (3).b (4).d

counselling psychology or a doctor of education degree with a major in counselling. *Counsellors* may have training such as a master's degree in psychology or counsellor education, but they also may have no training. Often employed by colleges and universities, counselling psychologists and counsellors help students with personal problems and/or test or counsel them in academic or vocational areas. *Social workers* usually have a master's degree in social work and some have specialized training in psychiatric problems, and may practise psychotherapy. Read *Apply It* to learn how to go about selecting a therapist.

THERAPY AND RACE, ETHNICITY, AND GENDER

Why is it important to consider cultural variables in the therapeutic setting?

There is a growing awareness of the need to consider cultural variables in diagnosing and treating psychological disorders (T. Field, 2009). In fact, the American Psychological Association (APA) published guidelines to help psychologists be more sensitive to cultural issues (APA, 2003). Similarly, many psychologists have expressed concern about the need for awareness of gender differences when practising psychotherapy (Addis & Mahalik, 2003; Gehart & Lyle, 2001). According to A. Kleinman and A. Cohen (1997), people experience and suffer from biological and psychological disorders within a cultural context in which the meaning of symptoms, outcomes, and responses to therapy may differ dramatically based on the culture and gender of the individual. **[LO 14.24]** When the cultures of the therapist and patient differ markedly, behaviour that is normal for the patient can be misinterpreted as abnormal by the therapist (Lewis-Fernández & Kleinman, 1994). Cultural values, social class, and non-verbal communication (i.e., gestures, facial expressions) that differ across cultures can all hinder effective counselling (Sue, 1994). Thus, many experts advocate for "culturally sensitive psychotherapy" and "gender-sensitive therapy," in which knowledge of clients' cultural backgrounds and/or gender guides the choice of therapeutic interventions (Gehart & Lyle, 2001; Kumpfer, Alvarado, Smith, & Ballamy, 2002). Attempts to frame best practices for culturally sensitive therapies are still unfolding (Cardemil, 2008; Helms, 2014). **[LO 14.24]**

For example, Rod McCormick of the University of British Columbia has advocated for the reintroduction of traditional healing practices to facilitate reconnection to cultural values and traditions and to treat Aboriginal clients within familiar contexts (2000; 2009). Review of outcomes where traditional healing practices have been introduced suggests that traditional healing circles and healing practices are desired (Wyrostok & Paulson, 2000) and successful (McCormick, 1997, 2000). As McCormick points out, for Aboriginal people, "connection to culture is treatment" (2000, p. 30).

APPLY IT

Choosing a Psychologist and a Therapy that Works for You

People are often embarrassed to seek professional help. Sometimes they are afraid of the therapy itself, or afraid that seeking help means there is something fundamentally wrong with them. There is no reason for such feelings. Going to a psychologist when you are feeling anxious or depressed is no different from going to a doctor when you are feeling sick. If you have a problem that has made you unhappy for a significant length of time, you should seek help—especially if you feel overwhelmed.

Just as you wouldn't select a doctor or lawyer at random, you shouldn't just go to any therapist who happens to be nearby. Bear in mind that in Canada there are no restrictions on the use of the title "therapist." Anyone can call themselves a therapist, but the term "psychologist" is restricted to individuals who are registered to practise and who have specific training and experience that prepares them to be able to deliver therapy. Before you select any psychologist, you should ask about his or her educational background, supervised experience, types of therapy practised, length of treatment, and fees. If you want to check whether a therapist is a psychologist, you can contact the local branch of the Canadian Mental Health Association, which will be listed in the white pages of the phone book, or you can go to http://www.cpa.ca/public/findingapsychologist, which outlines how to contact a Canadian clinical psychologist.

If you are not in crisis, take your time to choose a therapist. The person you choose should create an atmosphere of acceptance, trust, and empathy.

The first step in securing therapy for yourself involves contacting a psychologist (or other type of therapist) and arranging a brief consultation. In that meeting, you should find out about the treatments or therapies that can be provided to you, and also determine whether you feel comfortable with the therapist. If you find that you do not feel comfortable with the therapist or the treatments available, you should say so. Usually the therapist will be willing to recommend someone else.

Clinical psychologists in private practice receive fees for their services that are comparable to those received by doctors, dentists, and other professionals. Some health insurance plans cover those fees; others do not. If you have insurance that covers psychotherapy, check to make sure your policy covers the type of therapy you will be receiving. Also note any restrictions contained in the policy, such as limits on the number of sessions allowed.

Group therapy tends to be less expensive than individual therapy because the cost is shared among several people. You can also receive free or less expensive therapy at public facilities, such as community mental health centres.

You may be concerned about confidentiality, but you need not be. Confidentiality is a fundamental feature of therapy, however, to the client–therapist relationship. However, there are some limits that should be explained to you in your first interview.

What About E-Therapy?

At the beginning of this chapter you were introduced to the idea of online therapy. This form of therapy typically involves the exchange of email messages over a period of hours or days, but can also include video-conferencing and telephone sessions (Day & Schneider, 2002). In addition, therapists have begun experimenting with some virtual environments where therapists and clients manipulate avatars (graphic online identities) and settings to interact with each other and to create situations in which clients can practise the coping skills that they learn in either face-to-face or e-therapy (S. Cho et al., 2008; Gaggioli & Riva, 2007).

Researchers have found that e-therapy may be a helpful alternative to psychotherapy (M. Ainsworth, 2000; Postel, de Jong, & de Haan, 2005; D. Walker, 2000) for people who:

- are often away from home (travelling) or who have full schedules;
- cannot afford traditional therapy;
- live in rural areas and do not have access to mental health care;
- have disabilities that may impact their mobility;
- are too timid or embarrassed to make an appointment with a therapist; and

- are especially good at expressing their thoughts and feelings in writing.

It is important to be careful if considering e-therapy. Remember that the anonymity of the internet can allow imposters to pose as therapists. However, registered clinical psychologists who offer e-therapy are listed with governing bodies, just like those who meet face-to-face, and they must abide by the same standards. Limitations in communications (relying on mostly verbal exchanges) can reduce the effectiveness of treatment (Roan, 2000; D. Walker, 2000) because the therapist cannot use visual and auditory cues to determine when the person is becoming anxious or upset.

E-therapy is not appropriate for diagnosing and treating serious psychological disorders, such as schizophrenia or bipolar disorder (Manhal-Baugus, 2001), or for someone who is in the midst of a serious crisis.

If you decide to contact an e-therapist, bear this in mind: although e-therapy may be a good way to get started, if you have persistent problems, it would be wise in the long run to obtain traditional psychotherapy.

In situations involving a crisis, it is essential to get help immediately. In most communities you can call a hotline and receive counselling at any time, day or night. If the crisis is non-violent in nature, you can call a mental health centre or go to a hospital emergency room. If the crisis is more urgent—for example, if a friend is threatening to commit suicide—call the police. Whether you or someone else is experiencing a crisis or less immediate challenge, seeking therapy is an effective and important step in achieving mental health.

THINKING CRITICALLY

Evaluation

In your opinion, what are the major strengths and weaknesses of the following approaches to therapy: insight therapy, behaviour therapy, cognitive therapy, and drug therapy?

Point/Counterpoint

From what you have learned in this chapter, prepare a strong argument to support each of these positions:

a. Psychotherapy is generally superior to drug therapy in the treatment of psychological disorders.

b. Drug therapy is generally superior to psychotherapy in the treatment of psychological disorders.

Psychology in Your Life

What questions would you ask a therapist before beginning treatment?

SUMMARY & REVIEW

 INSIGHT THERAPIES

What are the four basic techniques of psychoanalysis, and how are they used to help disturbed patients?
The four basic techniques of psychoanalysis—free association, analysis of resistance, dream analysis, and analysis of transference—are used to uncover the repressed memories, impulses, and conflicts presumed to cause the patient's problems.

What is the role of the therapist in person-centred therapy?
Person-centred therapy is a non-directive therapy in which the therapist provides an atmosphere of unconditional positive regard. Clients are free to be themselves so that their natural tendency toward positive growth will be released.

What is the major emphasis in Gestalt therapy?
Gestalt therapy emphasizes the importance of clients fully experiencing, in the present moment, their feelings, thoughts, and actions, and then taking personal responsibility for their behaviour.

 RELATIONSHIP THERAPIES: THERAPIES EMPHASIZING INTERACTION WITH OTHERS

How do traditional and integrated behavioural couples therapies differ?
Traditional behavioural couples therapy focuses on identification and modification of behaviours that contribute to a couple's conflicts. Integrated behavioural couples therapy targets emotions as well as behaviours.

What are the goals of family therapy?
The goals of family therapy are to help family members reach agreement on certain changes that will help heal the wounds of the family unit, improve communication patterns, and create more understanding and harmony within the group.

What are some advantages of group therapy?
Group therapy can enhance a sense of belonging and provide an opportunity to receive feedback and emotional support from more than one person. In addition, it is often less expensive.

14C BEHAVIOUR THERAPIES: UNLEARNING THE OLD, LEARNING THE NEW

What is behaviour therapy?
Behaviour therapy is a treatment approach that employs the principles of operant conditioning, classical conditioning, and/or observational learning theory to replace inappropriate or maladaptive behaviours with more adaptive responses.

How do behaviour therapists modify behaviour using operant conditioning techniques?
Operant conditioning techniques involve the withholding of reinforcement to eliminate undesirable behaviours, as in time out, or the use of reinforcement to shape or increase the frequency of desirable behaviours, as in token economies.

What behaviour therapies are based on classical conditioning?
Behaviour therapies based on classical conditioning are systematic desensitization, flooding, exposure and response prevention, and aversion therapy.

How do therapists use systematic desensitization to rid people of fears?
Therapists using systematic desensitization train clients in deep muscle relaxation and then have them confront a series of graduated anxiety-producing situations, either real or imagined, until they can remain relaxed in the presence of even the most feared situation.

What is flooding?
With flooding, clients are exposed to the feared object or event (or asked to imagine it vividly) for an extended period until their anxiety decreases and they realize that none of the dreaded consequences come to pass.

How is exposure and response prevention used to treat people with obsessive-compulsive disorder?
As the name suggests, there are two components to this treatment type. First, clients are exposed to objects or situations they have been avoiding because they trigger obsessions and compulsive rituals. Second, patients agree to resist performing their compulsive rituals for progressively longer periods of time.

How does aversion therapy rid people of a harmful or undesirable behaviour?
Aversion therapy pairs the unwanted behaviour with an aversive stimulus until the bad habit becomes associated with pain or discomfort.

How does participant modelling help people overcome fears?
In participant modelling, an appropriate response is modelled in graduated steps and the client is asked to imitate each step with the encouragement and support of the therapist.

COGNITIVE THERAPIES: IT'S THE THOUGHT THAT COUNTS

What is the aim of rational-emotive therapy?
Rational-emotive therapy is a directive form of therapy designed to challenge and modify the client's irrational beliefs, which are believed to cause personal distress.

How does Beck's cognitive therapy help people overcome depression and anxiety disorders?
Beck's cognitive therapy helps people overcome depression and anxiety disorders by pointing out irrational thoughts that are causing them misery and by helping them learn other, more realistic ways of looking at themselves and their experience.

14E EYE MOVEMENT DESENSITIZATION AND REPROCESSING (EMDR)

What is EMDR?
EMDR is a method of psychotherapy whereby the patient thinks about a disturbing experience while visually tracking an external stimuli. This tracking produces controlled eye movements, which have been found to have a role in decreasing the memory's vividness and hence increasing the patient's cognitive flexibility.

14F THE BIOMEDICAL THERAPIES

What are the three main biological therapies?
The three main biological therapies are drug therapy, electroconvulsive therapy (ECT), and psychosurgery.

How do antipsychotic drugs help schizophrenic patients?
Antipsychotic drugs control the major symptoms of schizophrenia by inhibiting the activity of dopamine.

For what conditions are antidepressants prescribed?
Antidepressants are prescribed for depression, generalized anxiety disorder, panic disorder, and obsessive-compulsive disorder.

How does lithium help patients with bipolar disorder?
Lithium is used to control the symptoms in a manic episode and to even out the mood swings in bipolar disorder.

What are some problems with drug therapy?
Not all drugs are equally effective for all people, which means it may take some time for people to find a drug that works for them. Some drugs may produce unpleasant or dangerous side effects. Drugs do not cure psychological disorders, so patients usually experience a relapse if they stop taking the drugs when their symptoms lift.

For what purpose is electroconvulsive therapy (ECT) used, and what is its major side effect?
ECT is a treatment of last resort for people with severe depression. Its major side effect is some memory loss.

What is psychosurgery, and for what problems is it used?
Psychosurgery is brain surgery performed strictly to relieve some severe, persistent, and debilitating psychological disorders; it is considered experimental and highly controversial.

14G THERAPIES AND THERAPISTS: MANY CHOICES

What different types of mental health professionals conduct psychotherapy?
Professionals trained to conduct psychotherapy fall into the following categories: clinical psychologists, counselling psychologists, counsellors, psychiatrists, psychoanalysts, and psychiatric social workers.

Why is it important to consider cultural variables in the therapeutic setting?
People experience and suffer from biological and psychological disorders within a cultural context in which the meaning of symptoms, outcomes, and responses to therapy may differ dramatically based on the culture of the individual.

THERAPIES

MODULE 14A INSIGHT THERAPIES

Psychodynamic therapies try to resolve unconscious conflicts.

Freud's psychoanalysis attempts to uncover repressed memories and bring to consciousness unresolved conflicts. Four basic techniques are:
- **Free association:** Revealing thoughts without self-censorship.
- Analysis of **resistance:** Attempting to avoid embarrassing thoughts.
- **Dream analysis:** Analyzing symbolic meanings.
- Analysis of **transference:** Using the therapist as a parent substitute.

Traditional psychoanalysis:
Treatment involves seeing a therapist several times a week for years.

Brief psychodynamic therapy:
Treatment involves exploring specific issues, which means fewer visits to the therapist.

Humanistic therapy: Focuses on current experiences and encourages personal growth.

Rogers's person-centred therapy:
Helps people act in ways that are consistent with their true self. Rogers believes that people will grow toward self-actualization (realize their potential) if therapists have unconditional positive regard for clients, the therapists' feelings toward clients are genuine, and therapists have empathy with their clients.

Perls's Gestalt therapy: Emphasizes the importance of clients fully experiencing, in the present moment, their feelings, thoughts, and actions, and taking personal responsibility for their behaviour.

MODULE 14B RELATIONSHIP THERAPIES

Relationship-based therapies emphasize interaction with others.

Couples Therapy
Traditional behavioural couples therapy focuses on identification and modification of behaviours that contribute to a couple's conflicts. **Integrated behavioural couples therapy** targets emotions as well as behaviours.

Family Therapy: Parents and children enter therapy as a group.

Group Therapy: Several clients meet together with one or two therapists to solve a problem.

Psychodrama: One group member acts out a personal problem with the assistance of other members to gain insight into the problem.

Encounter groups: Try to promote personal growth through intense emotional encounters among group members.

Self-help groups: People with common problems meet to support and help one another, usually without the assistance of a professional therapist.

MODULE 14C BEHAVIOUR THERAPIES

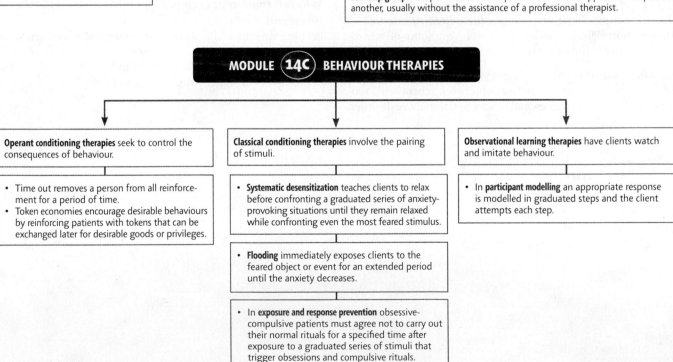

Operant conditioning therapies seek to control the consequences of behaviour.

- Time out removes a person from all reinforcement for a period of time.
- Token economies encourage desirable behaviours by reinforcing patients with tokens that can be exchanged later for desirable goods or privileges.

Classical conditioning therapies involve the pairing of stimuli.

- **Systematic desensitization** teaches clients to relax before confronting a graduated series of anxiety-provoking situations until they remain relaxed while confronting even the most feared stimulus.

- **Flooding** immediately exposes clients to the feared object or event for an extended period until the anxiety decreases.

- In **exposure and response prevention** obsessive-compulsive patients must agree not to carry out their normal rituals for a specified time after exposure to a graduated series of stimuli that trigger obsessions and compulsive rituals.

- **Aversion therapy** pairs undesirable behaviour with aversive stimuli until the behaviour becomes associated with pain and discomfort.

Observational learning therapies have clients watch and imitate behaviour.

- In **participant modelling** an appropriate response is modelled in graduated steps and the client attempts each step.

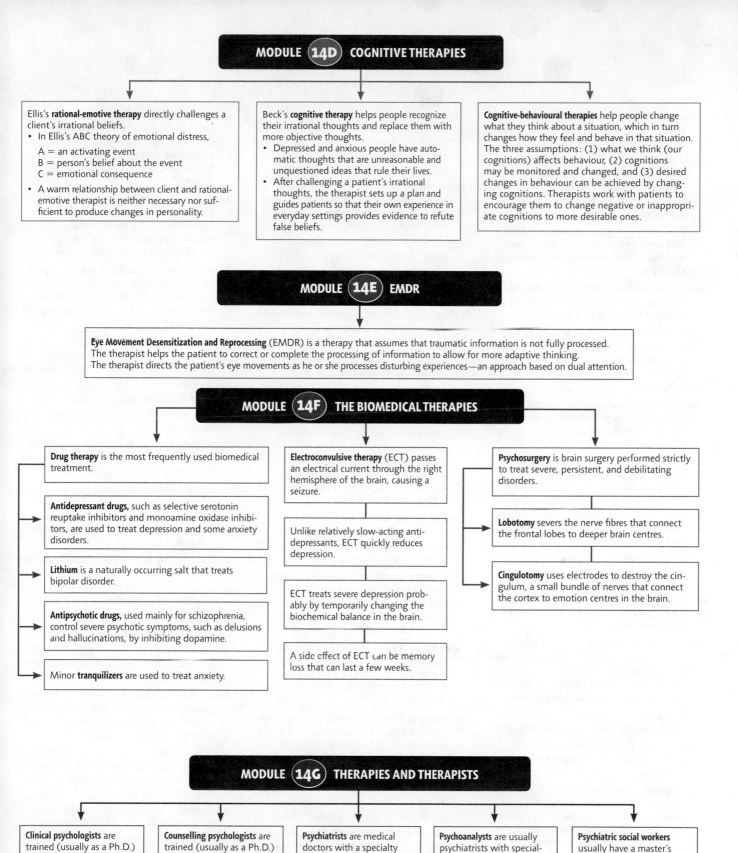

MODULE 14D COGNITIVE THERAPIES

Ellis's **rational-emotive therapy** directly challenges a client's irrational beliefs.
- In Ellis's ABC theory of emotional distress,

    A = an activating event
    B = person's belief about the event
    C = emotional consequence

- A warm relationship between client and rational-emotive therapist is neither necessary nor sufficient to produce changes in personality.

Beck's **cognitive therapy** helps people recognize their irrational thoughts and replace them with more objective thoughts.
- Depressed and anxious people have automatic thoughts that are unreasonable and unquestioned ideas that rule their lives.
- After challenging a patient's irrational thoughts, the therapist sets up a plan and guides patients so that their own experience in everyday settings provides evidence to refute false beliefs.

Cognitive-behavioural therapies help people change what they think about a situation, which in turn changes how they feel and behave in that situation. The three assumptions: (1) what we think (our cognitions) affects behaviour, (2) cognitions may be monitored and changed, and (3) desired changes in behaviour can be achieved by changing cognitions. Therapists work with patients to encourage them to change negative or inappropriate cognitions to more desirable ones.

MODULE 14E EMDR

Eye Movement Desensitization and Reprocessing (EMDR) is a therapy that assumes that traumatic information is not fully processed. The therapist helps the patient to correct or complete the processing of information to allow for more adaptive thinking. The therapist directs the patient's eye movements as he or she processes disturbing experiences—an approach based on dual attention.

MODULE 14F THE BIOMEDICAL THERAPIES

Drug therapy is the most frequently used biomedical treatment.

Antidepressant drugs, such as selective serotonin reuptake inhibitors and monoamine oxidase inhibitors, are used to treat depression and some anxiety disorders.

Lithium is a naturally occurring salt that treats bipolar disorder.

Antipsychotic drugs, used mainly for schizophrenia, control severe psychotic symptoms, such as delusions and hallucinations, by inhibiting dopamine.

Minor **tranquilizers** are used to treat anxiety.

Electroconvulsive therapy (ECT) passes an electrical current through the right hemisphere of the brain, causing a seizure.

Unlike relatively slow-acting antidepressants, ECT quickly reduces depression.

ECT treats severe depression probably by temporarily changing the biochemical balance in the brain.

A side effect of ECT can be memory loss that can last a few weeks.

Psychosurgery is brain surgery performed strictly to treat severe, persistent, and debilitating disorders.

Lobotomy severs the nerve fibres that connect the frontal lobes to deeper brain centres.

Cingulotomy uses electrodes to destroy the cingulum, a small bundle of nerves that connect the cortex to emotion centres in the brain.

MODULE 14G THERAPIES AND THERAPISTS

Clinical psychologists are trained (usually as a Ph.D.) in the diagnosis, treatment, or research of psychological and behavioural disorders.

Counselling psychologists are trained (usually as a Ph.D.) in clinical or counselling psychology. Counsellors usually have a master's degree in psychology or counsellor education.

Psychiatrists are medical doctors with a specialty in the diagnosis and treatment of mental disorders.

Psychoanalysts are usually psychiatrists with specialized training in psychoanalysis.

Psychiatric social workers usually have a master's degree in social work with specialized training in psychiatric problems.

GLOSSARY

absolute threshold: The minimum amount of sensory stimulation that can be detected 50 percent of the time.

accommodation: The changing in shape of the lens as it focuses objects on the retina; it becomes flatter for far objects and more spherical for near objects.

acetylcholine (ACh): A neurotransmitter that plays a role in learning, memory, and rapid eye movement (REM) sleep and causes the skeletal muscle fibres to contract.

action potential: The sudden reversal of the resting potential, a reversal that initiates the firing of a neuron.

actor–observer bias: The tendency of observers to make dispositional attributions for the behaviours of others but situational attributions for their own behaviours.

adolescent growth spurt: A period of rapid physical growth that peaks in girls at about age 12 and in boys at about age 14.

adoption study method: A method researchers use to study the relative effects of heredity and environment on behaviour and ability in children who are adopted shortly after birth, by comparing them with their biological and adoptive parents.

adrenal glands (ah-DREE-nal): A pair of endocrine glands that release hormones that prepare the body for emergencies and stressful situations, and also release small amounts of the sex hormones.

aerobic exercise (eh-RO-bik): Exercise involving the use of large muscle groups in continuous, repetitive action and requiring increased oxygen intake and increased breathing and heart rates.

afterimage: The visual sensation that remains after a stimulus is withdrawn.

aggression: The intentional infliction of physical or psychological harm on another.

agoraphobia (AG-or-uh-FO-bee-uh): An intense fear of being in a situation where immediate escape is not possible or help is not immediately available in case of incapacitating anxiety.

alarm stage: The first stage of the general adaptation syndrome, when there is emotional arousal and the defensive forces of the body are prepared for fight or flight.

alcohol: A central nervous system depressant.

algorithm: A systematic, step-by-step procedure, such as a mathematical formula, that guarantees a solution to a problem of a certain type if the algorithm is appropriate and executed properly.

alpha waves: The brainwaves of 8 to 12 cycles per second that occur when an individual is awake but deeply relaxed, usually with the eyes closed.

altered states of consciousness: Mental states other than ordinary waking consciousness, such as sleep, meditation, hypnosis, or a drug-induced state.

altruism: Behaviour aimed at helping another, requiring some self-sacrifice, and not designed for personal gain.

amnesia: A partial or complete loss of memory resulting from brain trauma or psychological trauma.

amphetamines: A class of central nervous system stimulants that increase arousal, relieve fatigue, and suppress appetite.

amplitude: Measured in decibels, the magnitude or intensity of a sound wave, determining the loudness of the sound; in vision, the magnitude or intensity of a light wave that affects the brightness of a stimulus.

amygdala (ah-MIG-da-la): A structure in the limbic system that plays an important role in emotion, particularly in response to aversive stimuli.

anal stage: Freud's second psychosexual stage (12 or 18 months to 3 years), in which the child derives sensual pleasure mainly from expelling and withholding feces.

analogy heuristic: A rule of thumb that applies a solution that solved a problem in the past to a current problem that shares many features with the past problem.

anchoring: Overestimation of the importance of a factor by focusing on it to the exclusion of other relevant factors.

anterograde amnesia: The inability to form long-term memories of events occurring after brain surgery or a brain injury, although memories formed before the trauma are usually intact.

antidepressants: Drugs that are prescribed to treat depression and some anxiety disorders.

antipsychotic drugs: Drugs used to control severe psychotic symptoms, such as the delusions and hallucinations of schizophrenics; also known as *neuroleptics* or *major tranquilizers*.

antisocial personality disorder: A disorder marked by lack of feeling for others; selfish, aggressive, irresponsible behaviour; and willingness to break the law, lie, cheat, or exploit others for personal gain.

anxiety: A generalized feeling of apprehension, fear, or tension that may be associated with a particular object or situation or may be free-floating, not associated with anything specific.

aphasia (uh-FAY-zyah): A loss or impairment of the ability to understand or communicate through the written or spoken word, resulting from damage to the brain.

apparent motion: Perceptions of motion that seem to be psychologically constructed in response to various kinds of stimuli.

applied research: Research conducted for the purpose of solving practical problems.

approach–approach conflict: A conflict arising from having to choose between desirable alternatives.

approach–avoidance conflict: A conflict arising when a choice has both desirable and undesirable features, so that you are both drawn to and repelled by the same choice.

archetype (AR-keh-type): Existing in the collective unconscious, an inherited tendency to respond in particular ways to universal human situations.

arousal: A state of alertness and mental and physical activation.

arousal theory: A theory suggesting that the aim of motivation is to maintain an optimal level of arousal.

assimilation: The process by which new objects, events, experiences, or pieces of information are incorporated into existing schemas.

association areas: Areas of the cerebral cortex that house memories and are involved in thought, perception, learning, and language.

attention: The process of sorting sensations and selecting some for further processing.

attitude: A relatively stable evaluation of a person, object, situation, or issue.

attributions: Inferences about the cause of our own or another's behaviour.

audience effects: The impact of passive spectators on performance.

audition: The sensation of hearing; the process of hearing.

authoritarian parents: Parents who make arbitrary rules, expect unquestioned obedience from their children, punish transgressions, and value obedience to authority.

authoritative parents: Parents who set high but realistic standards, reason with the child, enforce limits, and encourage open communication and independence.

autokinetic illusion: Apparent motion caused by the movement of the eyes rather than the movement of the objects being viewed.

automatic thoughts: Unreasonable and unquestioned ideas that rule a person's life and lead to depression and anxiety.

autonomy versus shame and doubt: Erikson's second psychosocial stage (ages one to three), when infants develop autonomy or shame depending on how parents react to their expression of will and their wish to do things for themselves.

availability heuristic: A cognitive rule of thumb that says that the probability of an event or the importance assigned to it is based on its availability in memory.

aversion therapy: A behaviour therapy used to rid clients of a harmful or socially undesirable behaviour by pairing it with a painful, sickening, or otherwise aversive stimulus until the behaviour becomes associated with pain and discomfort.

avoidance learning: Learning to avoid events or conditions associated with dreaded or aversive outcomes.

avoidance–avoidance conflict: A conflict arising from having to choose between equally undesirable alternatives.

axon (AK-sahn): The slender, tail-like extension of the neuron that transmits signals to the dendrites or cell body of other neurons or to the muscles, glands, or other parts of the body.

babbling: Vocalization of the basic speech sounds (phonemes), which begins between the ages of four and six months.

barbiturates: A class of addictive central nervous system depressants used as sedatives, sleeping pills, and anaesthetics; in overdose can cause coma or death.

basic emotions: Emotions that are found in all cultures (e.g., fear, anger, disgust, surprise, joy, happiness, sadness, distress), are reflected in the same facial expressions across cultures, and emerge in children according to their biological timetable.

basic research: Research conducted for the purpose of advancing knowledge rather than for its practical application.

basic trust versus basic mistrust: Erikson's first psychosocial stage (birth to 12 months), when infants develop trust or mistrust depending on the quality of care, love, and affection provided.

Beck's cognitive therapy: A brief cognitive therapy for depression and anxiety, designed to help people recognize their automatic thoughts and replace them with more objective thoughts.

behaviour modification: The systematic application of the learning principles of operant conditioning, classical conditioning, or observational learning to individuals or groups in order to eliminate undesirable behaviour and/or encourage desirable behaviour.

behaviour therapy: A treatment approach that employs the principles of operant conditioning, classical conditioning, and/or observational learning theory to eliminate inappropriate or maladaptive behaviours and replace them with more adaptive responses.

behavioural genetics: A field of research that investigates the relative effects of heredity and environment on behaviour and ability.

behaviourism: The school of psychology founded by John B. Watson that views observable, measurable behaviour as the appropriate subject matter for psychology and emphasizes the role of environment as a determinant of behaviour.

beta waves (BAY-tuh): The brainwaves of 13 or more cycles per second that occur when an individual is alert and mentally or physically active.

binocular depth cues: Depth cues that depend on two eyes working together; convergence and binocular disparity.

binocular disparity: A binocular depth cue resulting from differences between the two retinal images cast by objects at distances up to about six metres.

biological perspective: A perspective that emphasizes biological processes and heredity as the keys to understanding behaviour.

biological therapy: A therapy based on the assumption that most mental disorders have physical causes; attempts to change or influence the biological mechanism involved (e.g., through drug therapy, ECT, or psychosurgery).

biomedical model: A perspective that focuses on illness rather than health, explaining illness in terms of biological factors without regard to psychological and social factors.

biopsychosocial model: A perspective that focuses on health as well as illness, and holds that both are determined by a combination of biological, psychological, and social factors.

bipolar disorder: A disorder in which manic episodes alternate with periods of depression, usually with relatively normal periods in between.

bottom-up processing: Information processing in which individual components or bits of data are combined until a complete perception is formed.

brainstem: The structure that begins at the point where the spinal cord enlarges as it enters the brain; includes the medulla, the pons, and the reticular formation.

brightness: The dimension of visual sensation that is dependent on the intensity of light reflected from a surface and that corresponds to the amplitude of the light wave.

brightness constancy: The tendency to see objects as maintaining the same brightness regardless of differences in lighting conditions.

Broca's aphasia (BRO-kuz uh-FAY-zyah): An impairment in the ability to physically produce speech sounds or, in extreme cases, an inability to speak at all; caused by damage to Broca's area.

Broca's area (BRO-kuz): The area in the frontal lobe, usually in the left hemisphere, that controls production of the speech sounds.

bystander effect: As the number of bystanders at an emergency increases, the probability that the victim will receive help decreases, and help, if given, is likely to be delayed.

Cannon–Bard theory: The theory that physiological arousal and the feeling of emotion occur simultaneously after an emotion-provoking stimulus is relayed to the thalamus and the cerebral cortex.

cardinal trait: Allport's name for a personal quality that is so strong a part of a person's personality that he or she may become identified with that trait.

case study: An in-depth study of one or a few participants consisting of information gathered through observation, interviews, and perhaps psychological testing.

catatonic schizophrenia (KAT-uh-TON-ik): A type of schizophrenia identified in the *DSM-IV-TR*, characterized by extreme stillness or stupor and/or periods of great agitation and excitement; patients may assume an unusual posture and remain in it for long periods.

cell body: The part of the neuron that contains the nucleus and carries out the metabolic functions of the neuron.

central nervous system (CNS): The brain and the spinal cord.

central traits: Allport's name for the type of trait you would mention in writing a letter of recommendation.

centration: The child's tendency during the preoperational stage to focus on only one dimension of a stimulus and ignore the other dimensions.

cerebellum (sehr-uh-BELL-um): The brain structure that executes smooth, skilled body movements and regulates muscle tone and posture.

cerebral cortex (seh-REE-brul KOR-tex): The grey, convoluted covering of the cerebral hemispheres that is responsible for higher mental processes such as language, memory, and thinking.

cerebral hemispheres (seh-REE-brul): The right and left halves of the cerebrum, covered by the cerebral cortex and connected by the corpus callosum.

cerebrum (seh-REE-brum): The largest structure of the human brain, consisting of the two cerebral hemispheres connected by the corpus callosum and covered by the cerebral cortex.

chromosomes: Rod-shaped structures, found in the nuclei of body cells, that contain all the genes and carry all the hereditary information.

circadian rhythms (sur-KAY-dee-un): Within each 24-hour period, the regular fluctuations from high to low points of a bodily function, such as sleep/wakefulness.

classical conditioning: A process through which a response previously made only to a specific stimulus is made to another stimulus that has been paired repeatedly with the original stimulus.

clinical psychologist: A psychologist, usually with a Ph.D., trained in the diagnosis, treatment, and/or research of psychological and behavioural disorders.

co-action effects: The impact on performance caused by the presence of others engaged in the same task.

cocaine: A stimulant that produces a feeling of euphoria.

cochlea (KOK-lee-uh): The snail-shaped, fluid-filled organ in the inner ear that contains the hair cells (the sound receptors).

cognition: The mental processes involved in acquiring, storing, retrieving, and using information.

cognitive dissonance: The unpleasant state that can occur when people become aware of inconsistencies between their attitudes or between their attitudes and their behaviour.

cognitive processes (COG-nuh-tiv): Mental processes such as thinking, knowing, problem solving, and remembering.

cognitive psychology: A specialty that studies mental processes such as memory, problem solving, reasoning and decision making, language, perception, and other forms of cognition; often uses the information-processing approach.

cognitive therapies: Any therapies designed to change maladaptive thoughts and behaviour, based on the assumption that maladaptive behaviour can result from one's irrational thoughts, beliefs, and ideas.

cognitive-behavioural therapy (CBT): A therapy based on the belief that changing how a person thinks about a situation can result in changes in how a person feels and behaves in that situation, even if the situation itself does not change.

collective unconscious: In Jung's theory, the most inaccessible layer of the unconscious, which contains the universal experiences of humankind transmitted to each individual.

colour blindness: The inability to distinguish some or all colours in vision, resulting from a defect in the cones.

colour constancy: The tendency to see objects as maintaining about the same colour regardless of differences in lighting conditions.

compliance: Acting in accordance with the wishes, the suggestions, or the direct requests of another person.

compulsion: A persistent, irresistible, irrational urge to perform an act or ritual repeatedly.

concept: A label that represents a class or group of objects, people, or events sharing common characteristics or attributes.

concrete operations stage: Piaget's third stage of cognitive development (ages 7 to 11 or 12), during which a child acquires the concepts of reversibility and conservation and is able to apply logical thinking to concrete objects.

conditioned reflexes: Learned reflexes, as opposed to naturally occurring ones.

conditioned response (CR): A response that comes to be elicited by a conditioned stimulus as a result of its repeated pairing with an unconditioned stimulus.

conditioned stimulus (CS): A neutral stimulus that, after repeated pairing with an unconditioned stimulus, becomes associated with it and elicits a conditioned response.

conditions of worth: Conditions upon which the positive regard of others rests.

cones: The receptor cells in the retina that enable us to see colour and fine detail in adequate light but that do not function in dim light.

conformity: Changing or adopting a behaviour or an attitude to be consistent with the norms of a group or the expectations of others.

conscious (KON-shus): Those thoughts, feelings, sensations, and memories of which we are aware at any given moment.

consciousness: The continuous stream of thoughts, feelings, sensations, and perceptions of which we are aware from moment to moment.

conservation: The concept that a given quantity of matter remains the same despite rearrangement or a change in its appearance, as long as nothing has been added or taken away.

consolidation: The presumed process by which a permanent memory is formed; believed to involve the hippocampus.

consolidation failure: Any disruption in the consolidation process that prevents a permanent memory from forming.

consummate love: According to Sternberg's theory, the most complete form of love, consisting of three components—intimacy, passion, and commitment.

contact hypothesis: The notion that prejudice can be reduced through increased contact with members of different social groups.

continuous reinforcement: Reinforcement that is administered after every desired or correct response; the most effective method of conditioning a new response.

control group: In an experiment, a group that is similar to the experimental group and that is exposed to the same experimental environment but is not exposed to the independent variable; used for purposes of comparison.

conventional level: Kohlberg's second level of moral reasoning, in which right and wrong are based on the internalized standards of others; "right" is whatever helps or is approved of by others, or whatever is consistent with the laws of society.

convergence: A binocular depth cue in which the eyes turn inward as they focus on nearby objects—the closer an object, the greater the convergence.

conversion disorder: A somatic symptom disorder in which a loss of motor or sensory functioning in some part of the body has no physical cause but solves some psychological problem.

coping: Efforts through action and thought to deal with demands that are perceived as taxing or overwhelming.

cornea (KOR-nee-uh): The transparent covering of the coloured part of the eye that bends light rays inward through the pupil.

corpus callosum (KOR-pus kah-LO-sum): The thick band of nerve fibres that connects the two cerebral hemispheres and makes possible the transfer of information and the synchronization of activity between them.

correlation coefficient: A numerical value that indicates the strength and direction of the relationship between two variables; ranges from +1.00 (a perfect positive correlation) to −1.00 (a perfect negative correlation).

correlational method: A research method used to establish the relationship (correlation) between two characteristics, events, or behaviours.

crack: The most potent, inexpensive, and addictive form of cocaine, and the form that is smoked.

crash: The feelings of depression, exhaustion, irritability, and anxiety that occur following an amphetamine, a cocaine, or a crack high.

creativity: The ability to produce original, appropriate, and valuable ideas and/or solutions to problems.

critical periods: Periods that are so important to development that a harmful environmental influence can keep a bodily structure or behaviour from developing normally.

cross-sectional study: A type of developmental study in which researchers compare groups of individuals of different ages with respect to certain characteristics to determine age-related differences.

CT scan: A brain-scanning technique involving a rotating X-ray scanner and a high-speed computer analysis that produces slice-by-slice, cross-sectional images of the structure of the brain.

culture-fair intelligence test: An intelligence test designed to minimize cultural bias by using questions that will not penalize individuals whose culture or language differs from that of the urban middle or upper class.

decay theory: A theory of forgetting that holds that the memory trace, if not used, disappears with the passage of time.

decibels (dB) (DES-ih-bels): A unit of measurement of the intensity or loudness of sound based on the amplitude of the sound wave.

decision making: The process of considering alternatives and choosing among them.

declarative memory: The subsystem within long-term memory that stores facts, information, and personal life experiences; also called *explicit memory*.

deep structure: The underlying meaning of a sentence.

defence mechanism: An unconscious, irrational means used by the ego to defend against anxiety; involves self-deception and the distortion of reality.

delta waves: The slowest brainwaves, having a frequency of one to three cycles per second and associated with slow-wave (deep) sleep.

delusions: False beliefs, not generally shared by others in the culture, that cannot be changed despite strong evidence to the contrary.

delusions of grandeur: False beliefs that one is a famous person or that one has some great knowledge, ability, or authority.

delusions of persecution: An individual's false beliefs that a person or group is trying in some way to harm him or her.

dendrites (DEN-drytes): The branchlike extensions of a neuron that receive signals from other neurons.

denial: The act of refusing to consciously acknowledge the existence of a danger or a threatening condition.

dependent variable: The variable that is measured at the end of an experiment and that is presumed to vary as a result of manipulations of the independent variable.

depressants: Drugs that decrease activity in the central nervous system, slow down bodily functions, and reduce sensitivity to outside stimulation.

depth perception: The ability to see in three dimensions and to estimate distance.

descriptive research methods: Research methods that yield descriptions of behaviour rather than causal explanations.

developmental psychology: The study of how humans grow, develop, and change throughout the lifespan.

deviation score: A test score calculated by comparing an individual's score with the scores of others of the same age on whom the test's norms were formed.

diathesis–stress model: The idea that people with a constitutional predisposition (diathesis) toward a disorder, such as schizophrenia, may develop the disorder if they are subjected to sufficient environmental stress.

difference threshold: The smallest increase or decrease in a physical stimulus required to produce a difference in sensation that is noticeable 50 percent of the time (the just noticeable difference).

diffusion of responsibility: The feeling among bystanders at an emergency that the responsibility for helping is shared by the group, so that each individual feels less compelled to act than if he or she alone bore the total responsibility.

directive therapy: An approach to therapy in which the therapist takes an active role in determining the course of therapy sessions and provides answers and suggestions to the patient.

discrimination (*in social psychology*): Behaviour, usually negative, directed toward others based on their gender, religion, race, or membership in a particular group.

discrimination (*in learning theory*): The learned ability to distinguish between similar stimuli so that the conditioned response occurs only to the original conditioned stimulus but not to similar stimuli.

discriminative stimulus: A stimulus that signals whether a certain response or behaviour is likely to be followed by reward or punishment.

disorganized schizophrenia: The most serious type of schizophrenia identified in the DSM-IV-TR, marked by extreme social withdrawal, hallucinations, delusions, silliness, inappropriate laughter, grotesque mannerisms, and bizarre behaviour.

displacement (*in memory*): The event that occurs when short-term memory is holding its maximum and each new item entering short-term memory pushes out an existing item.

displacement (*in psychoanalytic theory*): Substitution of a less threatening object for the original object of an impulse; taking out frustrations on objects or people who are less threatening than those who provoked us.

display rules: Cultural rules that dictate how emotions should be expressed, and when and where their expression is appropriate.

dispositional attribution: Attribution of one's own or another's behaviour to some internal cause such as a personal trait, motive, or attitude; an internal attribution.

dissociative amnesia: A dissociative disorder in which there is a loss of memory for limited periods in one's life or for one's entire personal identity.

dissociative disorder: A disorder in which, under stress, one loses the integration of consciousness, identity, and memories of important personal events.

dissociative fugue: A disorder associated with dissociative amnesia in which one not only has a complete loss of memory for one's entire identity, but also travels away from home, and may assume a new identity.

dissociative identity disorder: A dissociative disorder in which two or more distinct personalities occur in the same individual, each taking over at different times; also called multiple personality.

divergent thinking: Producing one or more possible ideas, answers, or solutions to a problem rather than a single, correct response.

dominant gene: The gene that is expressed in the individual.

door-in-the-face technique: A strategy in which someone makes a large, unreasonable request with the expectation that the person will refuse but will then be more likely to respond favourably to a smaller request at a later time.

dopamine (DA) (DOE-pah-meen): A neurotransmitter that plays a role in learning, attention, movement, and reinforcement.

double-blind technique: An experimental procedure in which neither the participants nor the experimenters know who is in the experimental and control groups until the results have been gathered; a control for experimenter bias.

downers: A slang term for depressants.

drive: A state of tension or arousal brought about by an underlying need, which motivates one to engage in behaviour that will satisfy the need and reduce the tension.

drive-reduction theory: A theory of motivation suggesting that a need creates an unpleasant state of arousal or tension called a *drive*, which impels the organism to engage in behaviour that will satisfy the need and reduce tension.

drug tolerance: A condition in which the user becomes progressively less affected by the drug so that larger and larger doses are necessary to achieve or maintain the same effect.

DSM-5: The *Diagnostic and Statistical Manual of Mental Disorders* (fifth edition) describes about 300 mental disorders and the symptoms that must be present for diagnosing each disorder.

ecstasy (MDMA): A designer drug that is a hallucinogen-amphetamine and can produce permanent damage of the serotonin-releasing neurons.

ego (EE-go): In Freudian theory, the rational and largely conscious system of one's personality; operates according to the reality principle and tries to satisfy the demands of the id without violating moral values.

ego integrity versus despair: Erikson's eighth and final psychosocial stage, occurring during old age, when individuals look back on their lives with satisfaction and a sense of accomplishment or have major regrets about missed opportunities and mistakes.

eidetic imagery (eye-DET-ik): The ability to retain the image of a visual stimulus several minutes after it has been removed from view.

electroconvulsive therapy (ECT): A treatment in which an electric current is passed though the brain, causing a seizure; usually reserved for the severely depressed who are either suicidal or unresponsive to other treatment.

electroencephalogram (EEG) (ee-lek-tro-en-SEFF-uh-lo-gram): The record, made by an electroencephalograph, of an individual's brainwave activity.

elimination by aspects: A decision-making approach in which alternatives are evaluated against criteria that have been ranked according to importance.

embryo: The developing organism during the period (week 3 through week 8) when the major systems, organs, and structures of the body develop.

emotion: A feeling state involving physiological arousal, a cognitive appraisal of the situation arousing the state, and an outward expression of the state.

emotional intelligence: A type of intelligence that includes an awareness of—and an ability to manage—one's own emotions, as well as the ability to motivate oneself, to empathize, and to handle relationships successfully.

emotion-focused coping: A response aimed at reducing the emotional impact of the stressor.

encoding: Transforming information into a form that can be stored in short-term or long-term memory.

encoding failure: Forgetting resulting from material never having been put into long-term memory.

encounter group: Intense emotional group experiences designed to promote personal growth and self-knowledge; participants are encouraged to let down their defences and relate honestly and openly with one another.

endocrine system (EN-duh-krin): A system of ductless glands in various parts of the body that manufacture and secrete hormones into the bloodstream or lymph fluids, thus affecting cells in other parts of the body.

endorphins (en-DOOR-fins): Chemicals produced naturally by the brain that reduce pain and affect mood positively.

episodic memory (ep-ih-SOD-ik): The subpart of declarative memory that contains memories of personally experienced events.

evolutionary perspective: A perspective that focuses on how humans have evolved and adapted behaviours required for survival against various environmental pressures over the long course of evolution.

exemplars: The individual instances of a concept that we have stored in memory from our own experience.

exhaustion stage: The final stage of the general adaptation syndrome, occurring if the organism fails in its efforts to resist the stressor.

experimental group: In an experiment, the group of participants that is exposed to the independent variable or treatment.

experimental method: The research method whereby researchers randomly assign participants to groups and control all conditions other than one or more independent variables, which are then manipulated to determine their effect on some behaviour measured—the dependent variable in the experiment.

experimenter bias: A phenomenon that occurs when the researcher's preconceived notions in some way influence the participants' behaviour and/or the interpretation of experimental results.

exposure and response prevention: A behaviour therapy that exposes obsessive-compulsive disorder patients to objects or situations generating increasing anxiety; patients must agree not to carry out their normal rituals for a specified period of time after exposure.

extinction: The weakening and often eventual disappearance of a learned response (in classical conditioning, the conditioned response is weakened by repeated presentation of the conditioned stimulus without the unconditioned stimulus).

extraversion: The tendency to be outgoing, adaptable, and sociable.

extrinsic motivation: The desire to perform an act in order to gain a reward or to avoid an undesirable consequence.

facial-feedback hypothesis: The idea that the muscular movements involved in certain facial expressions trigger the corresponding emotions (for example, smiling makes us happy).

family therapy: Therapy involving an entire family, with the goal of helping family members reach agreement on changes that will help heal the family unit, improve communication problems, and create more understanding and harmony within the group.

fat cells: Numbering between 30 and 40 billion, cells that serve as storehouses for liquefied fat in the body; with weight loss, they decrease in size but not in number.

feature detectors: Neurons in the brain that respond only to specific visual patterns (e.g., lines or angles).

fetal alcohol spectrum disorder (FASD): A condition, caused by maternal alcohol intake during pregnancy, in which the baby is born mentally disabled, abnormally small, and with facial, organ, and limb abnormalities.

fetus: The developing organism during the period (week 9 until birth) when rapid growth and further development of the structures, organs, and systems of the body take place.

figure–ground: A principle of perceptual organization whereby the visual field is perceived in terms of an object (figure) standing out against a background (ground).

five-factor model: A trait theory that attempts to explain personality using five broad dimensions, each of which is composed of a constellation of personality traits.

fixation: Arrested development at a psychosexual stage occurring because of excessive gratification or frustration at that stage.

fixed-interval schedule: A schedule in which a reinforcer is administered following the first correct response after a fixed period of time has elapsed.

fixed-ratio schedule: A schedule in which a reinforcer is administered after a fixed number of non-reinforced correct responses.

flashback: The brief recurrence of effects a person has experienced while taking LSD or other hallucinogens, occurring suddenly and without warning at a later time.

flashbulb memory: An extremely vivid memory of the conditions surrounding one's first hearing of the news of a surprising, shocking, or highly emotional event.

flavour: The combined sensory experience of taste, smell, and touch.

flooding: A behavioural therapy used to treat phobias; clients are exposed to the feared object or event (or asked to imagine it vividly) for an extended period until their anxiety decreases.

foot-in-the-door technique: A strategy designed to secure a favourable response to a small request at first, with the aim of making the subject more likely to agree later to a larger request.

formal operations stage: Piaget's fourth and final stage, characterized by the ability to apply logical thinking to abstract, verbal, and hypothetical situations and to problems in the past, present, and future.

fovea (FO-vee-uh): A small area of the retina that provides the clearest and sharpest vision because it has the largest concentration of cones.

framing: The way information is presented so as to emphasize either a potential gain or a potential loss as the outcome.

fraternal (dizygotic) twins: Twins, no more alike genetically than ordinary siblings, who develop after two eggs are released during ovulation and are fertilized by two different sperm.

free association: A psychoanalytic technique used to explore the unconscious; patients reveal whatever thoughts or images come to mind.

frequency: Measured in the unit *hertz*, the number of sound waves or cycles per second, determining the pitch of the sound.

frequency theory: The theory that hair cell receptors vibrate the same number of times as the sounds that reach them, thereby accounting for the way variations in pitch are transmitted to the brain.

frontal lobes: The lobes that control voluntary body movements, speech production, and such functions as thinking, motivation, planning for the future, impulse control, and emotional responses.

frustration: Interference with the attainment of a goal or the blocking of an impulse.

frustration–aggression hypothesis: The hypothesis that frustration produces aggression.

functional fixedness: The failure to use familiar objects in novel ways to solve problems because of a tendency to view objects only in terms of their customary functions.

functionalism: An early school of psychology that was concerned with how mental processes help humans and animals adapt to their environments; developed as a reaction against structuralism.

fundamental attribution error: The tendency to overemphasize internal factors and underemphasize situational ones when explaining other people's behaviour.

***g* factor:** Spearman's term for a general intellectual ability that underlies all mental operations to some degree.

gate-control theory: The theory that the pain signals transmitted by slow-firing nerve fibres can be blocked at the spinal gate if fast-firing fibres get their message to the spinal cord first or if the brain itself inhibits the transmission of the pain messages.

gender dysphoria: Disorder characterized by a problem accepting one's identity as male or female.

general adaptation syndrome (GAS): The predictable sequence of reactions (the alarm, resistance, and exhaustion stages) that organisms show in response to stressors.

generalization: In classical conditioning, the tendency to make a conditioned response to a stimulus that is similar to the original conditioned stimulus; in operant conditioning, the tendency to make the learned response to a stimulus that is similar to the one for which it was originally reinforced.

generalized anxiety disorder: An anxiety disorder in which people experience excessive anxiety or worry that they find difficult to control.

generativity versus stagnation: Erikson's seventh psychosocial stage, occurring during middle age, when the individual becomes increasingly concerned with guiding and assisting the next generation rather than becoming self-absorbed and stagnating.

genes: Within the chromosomes, the segments of DNA that are the basic units for the transmission of hereditary traits.

genital stage: The last of Freud's psychosexual stages (from puberty on), in which for most people the focus of sexual energy gradually shifts to the opposite sex, culminating in the attainment of full adult sexuality.

Gestalt (geh-SHTALT): A German word roughly meaning "form" or "pattern."

Gestalt psychology (geh-SHTALT): The school of psychology that emphasizes that individuals perceive objects and patterns as whole units and that the perceived whole is more than just the sum of its parts.

Gestalt therapy (geh-SHTALT): A therapy originated by Fritz Perls that emphasizes the importance of clients fully experiencing, in the present moment, their feelings, thoughts, and actions and then taking responsibility for their feelings and behaviour.

glial cells (GLEE-ul): Cells that help to make the brain more efficient by holding the neurons together, removing waste products such as dead neurons, making the myelin coating for the axons, and nourishing tasks.

group polarization: The tendency of members of a group, after group discussion, to shift toward a more extreme position in whatever direction they were leaning initially.

group therapy: A form of therapy in which several clients (usually between 7 and 10) meet regularly with one or two therapists to resolve personal problems.

groupthink: The tendency for members of a very cohesive group to feel such pressure to maintain group solidarity and to reach agreement on an issue that they fail to adequately weigh available evidence or to consider objections and alternatives.

gustation: The sensation of taste.

habituation: A decrease in response or attention to a stimulus as an infant becomes accustomed to it.

hair cells: Sensory receptors for hearing, found in the cochlea.

hallucinations: Sensory perceptions in the absence of any external sensory stimulus; imaginary sensations.

hallucinogens (hal-LOO-sin-o-jenz): A category of drugs, sometimes called *psychedelics*, that alter perception and mood and can cause hallucinations.

halo effect: The tendency to attribute generally positive or negative traits to a person as a result of observing one major positive or negative trait; the tendency of raters to be excessively influenced in their overall evaluation of a person by one or a few favourable or unfavourable traits.

hardiness: A combination of three psychological qualities shared by people who can undergo high levels of stress yet remain healthy: commitment to one's personal goals, a sense of control over one's life, and a tendency to view change as a challenge rather than as a threat.

hassles: Little stressors that include the irritating demands and troubled relationships that are encountered daily and that, according to Lazarus, cause more stress than do major life changes.

health psychology: The field concerned with the psychological factors that contribute to health, illness, and response to illness.

heritability: An index of the degree to which a characteristic is estimated to be influenced by heredity.

heroin: A highly addictive, partly synthetic narcotic derived from morphine.

heuristics: Rules of thumb that are derived from experience and used in decision making and problem solving, even though there is no guarantee of their accuracy or usefulness.

hierarchy of needs: Maslow's theory of motivation, in which needs are arranged in order of urgency ranging from physiological needs to safety needs, belonging and love needs, esteem needs, and finally the need for self-actualization.

higher-order conditioning: Occurs when a neutral stimulus is paired with an existing conditioned stimulus, becomes associated with it, and gains the power to elicit the same conditioned response.

hippocampus (hip-po-CAM-pus): A structure in the limbic system that plays a central role in the formation of long-term memories.

homeostasis: The tendency of the body to maintain a balanced internal state with regard to body temperature, blood sugar, water, oxygen level, and so forth to ensure physical survival.

hormones: Substances manufactured and released in one part of the body that affect other parts of the body.

hue: The property of light commonly referred to as "colour" (red, blue, green, and so on), determined primarily by the wavelength of light reflected from a surface.

humanistic psychology: The school of psychology that focuses on the uniqueness of human beings and their capacity for choice, growth, and psychological health.

hypnosis: A trancelike state of concentrated, focused attention, heightened suggestibility, and diminished response to external stimuli.

hypothalamus (HY-po-THAL-uh-mus): A small but influential brain structure that controls the pituitary gland and regulates hunger, thirst, sexual behaviour, body temperature, our biological clock, and a wide variety of emotional behaviours.

hypothesis: A prediction about the relationship between two or more variables.

id: The unconscious system of the personality, which contains the life and death instincts and operates on the pleasure principle.

identical (monozygotic) twins: Twins with exactly the same genes, who develop after one egg is fertilized by one sperm and the zygote splits into two parts.

identity versus role confusion: Erikson's fifth psychosocial stage, when adolescents need to establish their own identity and to form values to live by; failure can lead to an identity crisis.

illness anxiety disorder: A disorder in which persons are preoccupied with their health and convinced they have some serious disorder despite reassurance from doctors to the contrary.

illusion: A false perception of actual stimuli involving a misperception of size, shape, or the relationship of one element to another.

imagery: Mental representation of a sensory experience—visual, auditory, gustatory, motor, olfactory, or tactile.

imaginary audience: A belief of adolescents that they are or will be the focus of attention in social situations and that others will be as critical or approving as they are of themselves.

inappropriate affect: A symptom common in schizophrenia in which an individual's behaviour (including facial expression, tone of voice, and gestures) does not reflect the emotion that would be expected under the circumstances—for example, a person laughs at a tragedy, cries at a joke.

inattentional blindness: The phenomenon in which we shift our focus from one object to another and, in the process, fail to notice changes in objects to which we are not directly paying attention.

incentive: An external stimulus that motivates behaviour (e.g., money, fame).

independent variables: In an experiment, the factors or conditions that the researcher manipulates (the treatment) in order to determine their effect on another behaviour or condition, known as the dependent variable.

industry versus inferiority: Erikson's fourth psychosocial stage (age six to puberty), when children develop a sense of industry or inferiority depending on how parents and teachers react to their efforts to undertake projects.

information-processing approach: An approach to the study of mental structures and processes that uses the computer as a model for human thinking.

in-group: A social group with a strong sense of togetherness and from which others are excluded.

initiative versus guilt: Erikson's third psychosocial stage (ages three to six), when children develop a sense of initiative or guilt depending on how parents react to their initiation of play, their motor activities, and their questions.

inner ear: The innermost portion of the ear, containing the cochlea, the vestibular sacs, and the semicircular canals.

insight therapies: Any type of psychotherapy based on the notion that psychological well-being depends on self-understanding.

insomnia: A sleep disorder characterized by difficulty falling or staying asleep, or by light, restless, or poor sleep; causes distress and impaired daytime functioning.

instinct: An inborn, unlearned, fixed pattern of behaviour that is characteristic of an entire species.

instinct theory: The notion that human behaviour is motivated by certain innate tendencies, or instincts, shared by all individuals.

integrated behavioural couples therapy (IBCT): A type of couples therapy that emphasizes both behaviour change and mutual acceptance.

intellectual disability: Evidenced by scores at least two standard deviations below the norm and by adaptive functioning severely deficient for one's age.

intelligence quotient (IQ): An index of intelligence originally derived by dividing mental age by chronological age and then multiplying by 100.

interference: The cause of memory loss that occurs when information or associations stored either before or after a given memory hinder our ability to remember it.

intimacy versus isolation: Erikson's sixth psychosocial stage, when the young adult must establish intimacy in a relationship in order to avoid feeling isolated and lonely.

intrinsic motivation: The desire to perform an act because it is satisfying or pleasurable in and of itself.

introversion: The tendency to focus inward.

intuition: Rapidly formed judgments based on "gut feelings" or "instincts."

inventory: A paper-and-pencil test with questions about a person's thoughts, feelings, and behaviours, which measures several dimensions of personality and can be scored according to a standard procedure.

James–Lange theory: The theory that emotional feelings result when we become aware of our physiological response to an emotion-provoking stimulus (in other words, we are afraid because we tremble).

just noticeable difference (JND): The smallest change in sensation that we are able to detect 50 percent of the time.

kinesthetic sense: The sense that provides information about the position of body parts and about body movement, detected by sensory receptors in the joints, ligaments, and muscles.

language: A means of communicating thoughts and feelings, using a system of socially shared but arbitrary symbols (sounds, signs, or written symbols) arranged according to rules of grammar.

latency period: The period following Freud's phallic stage (age five or six to puberty), in which the sex instinct is largely repressed and temporarily sublimated in school, sports, and play activities.

lateral hypothalamus (LH): The part of the hypothalamus that apparently acts as a feeding centre and, when activated, signals an animal to eat; when the LH is destroyed, the animal initially refuses to eat.

lateralization: The specialization of one of the cerebral hemispheres to handle a particular function.

Lazarus theory: The theory that an emotion-provoking stimulus triggers a cognitive appraisal, which is followed by the emotion and the physiological arousal.

learned helplessness: The learned response of resigning oneself passively to aversive conditions, rather than taking action to change, escape, or avoid them; learned through repeated exposure to inescapable or unavoidable aversive events.

learning: A relatively permanent change in behaviour, knowledge, capability, or attitude that is acquired through experience and cannot be attributed to illness, injury, or maturation.

left hemisphere: The hemisphere that controls the right side of the body, coordinates complex movements, and (in 95 percent of people) controls the production of speech and written language.

lens: The transparent structure behind the iris that changes in shape as it focuses images on the retina.

levels-of-processing model: A single-memory-system model in which retention depends on how deeply information is processed.

libido (lih-BEE-doe): Freud's name for the psychic, often sexual, energy that comes from the id and provides the energy for the entire personality.

limbic system: A group of structures in the brain, including the amygdala and hippocampus, that are collectively involved in emotion, memory, and motivation.

linguistic relativity hypothesis: The notion that the language a person speaks largely determines the nature of that person's thoughts.

lobotomy: A psychosurgery technique in which the nerve fibres connecting the frontal lobes to the deeper brain centres are severed.

locus of control: A concept used to explain how people account for what happens in their lives—people with an internal locus of control see themselves as primarily in control of their behaviour and its consequences; those with an external locus of control perceive what happens to be in the hands of fate, luck, or chance.

longitudinal study: A type of developmental study in which the same group of participants is followed and measured at different ages.

long-term memory (LTM): The relatively permanent memory system with a virtually unlimited capacity.

long-term potentiation: A long-lasting increase in the efficiency of neural transmission at the synapses.

low-ball technique: A strategy to gain compliance by making a very attractive initial offer to get a person to agree to an action and then making the terms less favourable.

low-birth-weight babies: Babies weighing less than 2.5 kilograms.

LSD: Lysergic acid diethylamide, a powerful hallucinogen with unpredictable effects ranging from perceptual changes and vivid hallucinations to states of panic and terror.

lucid dreams: Dreams during which the dreamer is aware of dreaming; the dreamer is often able to influence the content of a lucid dream while it is in progress.

mainstreaming: Educating students with intellectual disabilities in regular rather than special schools by placing them in regular classes for part of the day or having special classrooms in regular schools.

major depressive disorder: A disorder characterized by feelings of great sadness, despair, guilt, worthlessness, and hopelessness, and, in extreme cases, suicidal intentions.

manic episode (MAN-ik): A period of extreme elation, euphoria, and hyperactivity, often accompanied by delusions of grandeur and by hostility if activity is blocked.

marijuana: A hallucinogen with effects ranging from relaxation and giddiness to perceptual distortions and hallucinations.

massed practice: One long learning practice session as opposed to spacing the learning in shorter practice sessions over an extended period.

matching hypothesis: The notion that people tend to have spouses, lovers, or friends who are similar to themselves in social assets such as physical attractiveness.

means–end analysis: A heuristic problem-solving strategy in which the current position is compared with the desired goal, and a series of steps are formulated and taken to close the gap between them.

meditation: A group of techniques that involve focusing attention on an object, a word, one's breathing, or body movement in order to block out all distractions and achieve an altered state of consciousness.

medulla (muh-DUL-uh): The part of the brainstem that controls heartbeat, breathing, blood pressure, coughing, and swallowing.

menarche (men-AR-kee): The onset of menstruation.

menopause: The cessation of menstruation, occurring between ages 45 and 55 and signifying the end of reproductive capacity.

mental set: The tendency to apply a familiar strategy to the solution of a problem without carefully considering the special requirements of the problem.

mere-exposure effect: The tendency of people to develop a more positive evaluation of some person, object, or other stimulus with repeated exposure to it.

metabolic rate (meh-tuh-BALL-ik): The rate at which the body burns calories to produce energy.

microelectrode: An electrical wire so small that it can be used either to monitor the electrical activity of a single neuron or to stimulate activity within it.

microsleeps: Momentary lapses from wakefulness into sleep, usually occurring when one has been sleep-deprived.

middle ear: The portion of the ear containing the ossicles, which connect the eardrum to the oval window and amplify the vibrations as they travel to the inner ear.

Minnesota Multiphasic Personality Inventory–2 (MMPI–2): A revision of the most extensively researched and widely used personality test; used to screen and diagnose psychiatric problems and disorders.

minor tranquilizers: Central nervous system depressants that calm the user (e.g., Valium®, Librium®, Dalmane®, Xanax®).

model: The individual who demonstrates a behaviour or serves as an example in observational learning.

modelling: Another name for observational learning.

monocular depth cues (mah-NOK-yu-ler): Depth cues that can be perceived by only one eye.

morphemes: The smallest units of meaning in a language.

motivated forgetting: Forgetting through suppression or repression in order to protect oneself from material that is too painful, anxiety- or guilt-producing, or otherwise unpleasant.

motivation: The process that initiates, directs, and sustains behaviour to satisfy physiological or psychological needs.

motives: Needs or desires that energize and direct behaviour toward a goal.

motor cortex: The strip of tissue at the rear of the frontal lobes that controls voluntary body movement.

MRI: A diagnostic scanning technique that produces high-resolution images of the structures of the brain.

myelin sheath (MY-uh-lin): The white, fatty coating wrapped around some axons that acts as insulation and enables impulses to travel much faster.

narcolepsy (NAR-co-lep-see): A serious sleep disorder characterized by excessive daytime sleepiness and sudden, uncontrollable attacks of REM sleep.

narcotics: Derived from the opium poppy, a class of depressant drugs that have pain-relieving and calming effects.

naturalistic observation: A research method in which researchers observe and record behaviour without trying to influence or control it.

nature–nurture controversy: The debate concerning the relative influences of heredity and environment on development.

need for achievement: The need to accomplish something difficult and to perform at a high standard of excellence.

negative reinforcement: The termination of an unpleasant stimulus after a response in order to increase the probability that the response will be repeated.

neonates: Newborn infants up to one month old.

neurons (NEW-rons): A specialized cell that conducts impulses through the nervous system and contains three major parts—a cell body, dendrites, and an axon.

neurosis (new-RO-sis): An obsolete term for a disorder causing personal distress and some impairment in functioning, but not causing one to lose contact with reality or to violate important social norms.

neurotransmitters (NEW-ro-TRANS-miters): Chemicals that are released into the synaptic cleft from the axon terminal of the sending neuron, cross the synapse, and bind to appropriate receptors on the dendrites or cell body of the receiving neuron, influencing the cell either to fire or not to fire.

nightmares: Very frightening dreams occurring during REM sleep.

non-declarative memory: The subsystem within long-term memory that consists of skills acquired through repetitive practice, habits, and simple classically conditioned responses; also called *implicit memory*.

non-directive therapy: An approach in which the therapist acts to facilitate growth, giving understanding and support rather than proposing solutions, answering questions, or actively directing the course of therapy.

nonsense syllables: Consonant-vowel-consonant combinations that do not spell a word; used to control for the meaningfulness of the material.

norepinephrine (NE) (nor-eh-peh-NEF-rin): A neurotransmitter affecting eating and sleeping.

norms (*in testing*): Standards based on the range of test scores of a large group of people who are selected to provide the bases of comparison for those who will take the test later.

norms (*social*): The attitudes and standards of behaviour expected of members of a particular group.

NREM dreams: Mental activity occurring during NREM sleep that is more thoughtlike in quality than are REM dreams.

NREM sleep (NON-rem): Non-rapid eye movement sleep, consisting of the four sleep stages and characterized by slow, regular respiration and heart rate, an absence of rapid eye movement, and blood pressure and brain activity that are at a 24-hour low point.

obesity (o-BEE-sih-tee): Excessive fatness; a term applied to men whose body fat exceeds 20 percent of their weight and to women whose body fat exceeds 30 percent of their weight.

object permanence: The realization that objects continue to exist even when they are no longer perceived.

McAdams, D. P., & Pals, J. L. (2006). A new Big Five: Fundamental principles for an integrative science of personality. *American Psychologist, 61*(3), 204–217.

McCabe, R., & Gifford, S. (2009). Psychological treatment of panic disorder and agoraphobia. In M. Antony, & M. Stein (Eds.), *Oxford handbook of anxiety and related disorders* (pp. 308–320). New York: Oxford University Press.

McCabe, S. E., West, B. T., Teter, C. J., Ross-Durow, P., Young, A., & Boyd, C. J. (2011). Characteristics associated with the diversion of controlled medications among adolescents. *Drug and Alcohol Dependence, 118,* 452–458.

McCaffrey, T. (2012). Innovation relies on the obscure: A key to overcoming the classic problem of functional fixedness. *Psychological Science, 23*(3), 215–218.

McCartney, K., Harris, M. J., & Bernieri, F. (1990). Growing up and growing apart: A developmental meta-analysis of twin studies. *Psychological Bulletin, 107,* 226–237.

McClearn, G. E., Johansson, B., Berg, S., Pedersen, N. L., Ahern, F., Petrill, S. A., & Plomin, R. (1997). Substantial genetic influence on cognitive abilities in twins 80 or more years old. *Science, 276,* 1560–1563.

McClelland, D. C. (1958). Methods of measuring human motivation. In J. W. Atkinson (Ed.), *Motives in fantasy, action and society: A method of assessment and study*. Princeton, NJ: Van Nostrand.

McClelland, D. C. (1961). *The achieving society*. Princeton, NJ: Van Nostrand.

McClelland, D. C. (1985). *Human motivation*. New York: Cambridge University Press.

McClelland, D. C., Atkinson, J. W., Clark, R. W., & Lowell, E. L. (1953). *The achievement motive*. New York: Appleton-Century-Crofts.

McClelland, D. C., & Pilon, D. A. (1983). Sources of adult motives in patterns of parent behavior in early childhood. *Journal of Personality and Social Psychology, 44,* 564–574.

McClelland, J. L., McNaughton, B. L., & O'Reilly, R. C. (1995). Why there are complementary learning systems in the hippocampus and neocortex: Insights from the successes and failures of connectionist models of learning and memory. *Psychological Bulletin, 102,* 419–457.

McCormick, R. (1997). Healing through interdependence: The role of connecting in First Nations healing practices. *Canadian Journal of Counselling, 31*(3), 172–184.

McCormick, R. (2000). Aboriginal traditions in the treatment of substance abuse. *Canadian Journal of Counselling, 34*(1), 25–32.

McCormick, R. (2009). All my relations. In Canadian Institute for Health Information (CIHI) (Ed.), *Mentally healthy communities: Aboriginal perspectives* (pp. 3–8). Ottawa, ON: CIHI.

McCrady, B., Epstein, E., Cook, S., Jensen, N., & Hildebrandt, T. (2009). A randomized trial of individual and couple behavioral alcohol treatment for women. *Journal of consulting and Clinical Psychology, 77*(2), 243–256.

McCrae, C. S., Wilson, N, M., Lichstein, K. L., Durrence, H. H., Taylor, D. J., Riedel, B. W., & Bush, A. J. (2008). Self reported sleep, demographics, health and daytime functioning in young old and old old community-dwelling seniors. *Behavioral Sleep Medicine, 6,* 106–126.

McCrae, R. R. & Costa, P. T., Jr. (2008). Empirical and theoretical status of the five-factor model of personality traits. In G. Boye, G. Metthews, & D. Saklofske (Eds.), *The SAGE handbook of personality theory and assessment, Vol. 1: Personality theories and models* (pp. 273–297). Thousand Oaks, CA: Sage.

McCrae, R. R., & Terracciano, A. (2005). Universal features of personality traits from the observer's perspective: Data from 50 cultures. *Journal of Personality and Social Psychology, 88*(3), 547–561.

McDaniel, M. A., Anderson, D. C., Einstein, G. O., & O'Halloran, C. M. (1989). Modulation of environmental reinstatement effects through encoding strategies. *American Journal of Psychology, 102,* 523–548.

McDermott, J. (2014, January 21). Facebook losing its edge among college-aged adults. *Digiday*. Retrieved September 25, 2014, from http://digiday.com/platforms/social-platforms-college-kids-now-prefer/

McGee, A., & Skinner, M. (1987, June). Facial asymmetry and the attribution of personality traits. *British Journal of Social Psychology, 26*(2), 181–184.

McGorry, P. D., Purcell, R., Goldstone, S., & Amminger, G. P. (2011). Age of onset and timing of treatment for mental and substance use disorders: implications for preventive intervention strategies and models of care. *Current Opinion in Psychiatry, 24*(4), 301–306.

McGuire, W. J. (1969). The nature of attitudes and attitude change. In G. Lindzey & E. Aronson (Eds.), *Handbook of social psychology* (Vol. 3). Reading, MA: Addison-Wesley.

McGuire, W. J. (1985). Attitudes and attitude change. In G. Lindzey & E. Aronson (Ed.), *Handbook of social psychology* (Vol. 2, 3rd ed.). New York: Random House.

McKay, A. (2004) Adolescent sexual and reproductive sexual and reproductive health in Canada: A report card in 2004. *The Canadian Journal of Human Sexuality, 13*(2), 67–81.

McLean, C. P., Asnaani, A., Litz, B. T., & Hofmann, S. G. (2011). Gender differences in anxiety disorders: prevalence, course of illness, comorbidity and burden of illness. *Journal of psychiatric research, 45*(8), 1027–1035.

McNally, R. J., Lasko, N. B., Clancy, S. A., Macklin, M. L., Pitman, R. K., & Orr, S. P. (2004). Psychophysiological responding during script-driven imagery in people reporting abduction by space aliens. *Psychological Science, 15,* 493–497.

McNamara, P., McLaren, D., & Durso, K. (2007). Representation of the self in REM and NREM dreams. *Dreaming, 17,* 113–126.

McNeil, T. G., Cantor-Graae, E., & Weinberger, D. R. (2000). Relationship of obstetric complications and differences in size of brain structures in monozygotic twin pairs discordant for schizophrenia. *American Journal of Psychiatry, 157,* 203–212.

Mednick, S. A., & Mednick, M. T. (1967). *Examiner's manual, Remote Associates Test*. Boston: Houghton-Mifflin.

Medzerian, G. (1991). *Crack: Treating cocaine addiction*. Blue Ridge Summit, PA: Tab Books.

Mehlsen, M. (2005). The paradoxical life satisfaction of old age. *Psyke & Logos, 26,* 609–628.

Meichenbaum, D. (1985). *Stress inoculation training*. New York: Pergamon.

Meier, R. P. (1991). Language acquisition by deaf children. *American Scientist, 79*(1), 60–70.

Meijer, W. A., de Groot, R. H. M., van Gerven, P., van Boxtel, M. P. J., & Jolles, J. (2009). Level of processing and reaction time in young and middle-aged adults and the effect of education. *European Journal of Cognitive Psychology, 21,* 216–234

Meltzer, H. (1930). Individual differences in forgetting pleasant and unpleasant experiences. *Journal of Educational Psychology, 21,* 399–409.

Melzack, R., & Wall, P. D. (1965). Pain mechanisms: A new theory. *Science, 150,* 971–979.

Melzack, R., & Wall, P. D. (1983). *The challenge of pain*. New York: Basic Books.

Meschyan, G., & Hernandez, A. (2002). Is native-language decoding skill related to second-language learning? *Journal of Educational Psychology, 94,* 14–22.

Mesman, J., Oster, H., & Camras, L. (2012). Parental sensitivity to infant distress: what do discrete negative emotions have to do with it? *Attachment and Human Development, 14*(4), 337–348.

Meyer, B., Schermuly, C. C., & Kauffeld, S. (2015). That's not my place: The interacting effects of faultlines, subgroup size, and social competence on social loafing behaviour in work groups. *European Journal of Work and Organizational Psychology*, (ahead-of-print), 1–18.

Meyer, G. J., Finn, S. E., Eyde, L. D., Kay, G. G., Moreland, K. L., Dies, R. R., . . . Read, G. M. (2001). Psychological testing and psychological assessment: A review of evidence and issues. *American Psychologist, 56*(2), 128–165.

Meyer, G. J., Mihura, J. L., & Smith, B.L. (2005). The interclinician reliability of Rorschach interpretation in four data sets. *Journal of Personality Assessment, 84*(3), 296–314.

Meyer, P. (1972). If Hitler asked you to electrocute a stranger, would you? In R. Greenbaum & H. A. Tilker (Eds.), *The challenge of psychology* (pp. 456–465). Englewood Cliffs, NJ: Prentice-Hall.

Michaels, J. W., Bloomel, J. M., Brocato, R. M., Linkous, R. A., & Rowe, J. S. (1982). Social facilitation and inhibition in a natural setting. *Replications in Social Psychology, 2,* 21–24.

Middlebrooks, J. C., & Green, D. M. (1991). Sound localization by human listeners. *Annual Review of Psychology, 42,* 135–159.

Miles, R. (1999). A homeostatic switch. *Nature, 397,* 215–216.

Milgram, S. (1963). Behavioral study of obedience. *Journal of Abnormal and Social Psychology, 67,* 371–378.

Milgram, S. (1965). Liberating effects of group pressure. *Journal of Personality and Social Psychology, 1,* 127–134.

Miller, D. T. (1999). The norm of self-interest. *American Psychologist, 54*(12), 1053–1060.

Miller, D. T., & Turnbull, W. (1986). Expectancies and interpersonal processes. *Annual Review of Psychology, 37,* 233–256.

Miller, G. A. (1956). The magical number seven, plus or minus two: Some limits on our capacity for processing information. *Psychological Review, 63,* 81–97.

Miller, G. A., & Gildea, P. M. (1987). How children learn words. *Scientific American, 257,* 94–99.

Miller, I. J., & Reedy, F. E., Jr. (1990). Variations in human taste bud density and taste intensity perception. *Physiology & Behavior, 47,* 1213–1219.

Miller, J. G., Bersoff, D. M., & Harwood, R. L. (1990). Perceptions of social responsibilities in India and in the United States: Moral imperatives or personal decisions? *Journal of Personality and Social Psychology, 58,* 33–47.

Miller, L. (1988, February). The emotional brain. *Psychology Today,* 34–42.

Miller, N. E. (1941). The frustration-aggression hypothesis. *Psychological Review, 48,* 337–342.

Miller, S., & Maner, J. (2010). Scent of a Woman: Men's testosterone responses to olfactory ovulation cues. *Psychological Science, 21,* 276–283.

Milner, B. R. (1966). Amnesia following operation on the temporal lobes. In C. W. M. Whitty & O. L. Zangwill (Eds.), *Amnesia* (pp. 109–133). London: Butterworth.

Milner, B. (1970). Memory and the medial temporal regions of the brain. In K. H. Pribram & D. E. Broadbent (Eds.), *Biology of memory.* New York: Academic Press.

Milner, B., Corkin, S., & Teuber, H. L. (1968). Further analysis of the hippocampal amnesic syndrome: 14-year follow-up study of H. M. *Neuropsychologia, 6,* 215–234.

Milos, F., Spindler, A., Ruggiero, G., Klaghofer, R., & Schnyder, U. (2002). Comorbidity of obsessive-compulsive disorders and duration of eating disorders. *International Journal of Eating Disorders, 31,* 284–289.

Mineka, S., & Oehlberg, K. (2008). The relevance of recent developments in classical conditioning to understanding the etiology and maintenance of anxiety disorder. *Acta Psychologica, 127,* 567–580.

Miltner, W. H., Braun, C., Arnold, M., Witte, H., & Taub, E. (1999). Coherence of gamma band EEG activity as a basis for associative learning. *Nature, 397,* 434–436.

Mitelman, S. A., Shihabuddin, L., Brickman, A. M., Hazlett, E. A., & Buchsbaum, M. S. (2005). Volume of the cingulate and outcome in schizophrenia. *Schizophrenia Research, 72,* 91–108.

Mitler, M. M., Aldrich, M. S., Koob, G. F., & Zarcone, V. P. (1994). Narcolepsy and its treatment with stimulants. *Sleep, 17,* 352–371.

Mitsonis, C. I., Potagas, C., Zervas, I., & Sfagos, K. (2009). The effects of stressful life events on the course of multiple sclerosis: A review. *International Journal of Neuroscience, 119,* 315–335.

Modi, R. R., Camacho, M., & Valerio, J. (2014). Confusional arousals, sleep terrors, and sleepwalking. *Sleep Medicine Clinics, 9*(4), 537–551.

Moffitt, T., Arseneault, L., Belsky, D., Dickson, N., Hancox, R. J., Harrington, H., . . . Caspi, A. (2011). A gradient of childhood self-control predicts health, wealth, and public safety. *Proceedings of the National Academy of Sciences, 108,* 2693–2698.

Moldofsky, H., Gilbert, R., Lue, F. A., & MacLean, A. W. (1995). Sleep-related violence. *Sleep, 18,* 731–739.

Molloy, C., Conroy, R. M., Cotter, D. R., & Cannon, M. (2011). Is traumatic brain injury a risk factor for schizophrenia? A meta-analysis of case-controlled population-based studies. *Schizophrenia Bulletin, 37*(6), 1104–1110.

Monk, T. H. (1989). Circadian rhythms in subjective activation, mood, and performance efficiency. In M. H. Kryger, T. Roth, & W. C. Dement (Eds.), *Principles and practice of sleep medicine* (pp. 163–172). Philadelphia: W. B. Saunders.

Monk, T. H. (2012). Sleep and human performance. In C. M. Morin and C. A. Espie (Eds.), *The Oxford handbook of sleep and sleep disorders. Oxford library of psychology* (pp. 95–109). New York, NY: Oxford University Press.

Montagu, A. (1962). *The humanization of man.* Cleveland, OH: World.

Monteleone, P., Santonastaso, P., Tortorella, A., Favaro, A., Fabrazzo, M., Castaldo, E., . . . Maj, M. (2005). Serotonin transporter polymorphism and potential response to SSRIs in bulimia nervosa. *Molecular Psychiatry, 10,* 716–718.

Montgomery, G. H., David, D., Kangas, M., Green, S., Sucala, M., Bovbjerg, D. H., . . . & Schnur, J. B. (2014). Randomized controlled trial of a cognitive-behavioral therapy plus hypnosis intervention to control fatigue in patients undergoing radiotherapy for breast cancer. *Journal of Clinical Oncology, 32*(6), 557–563.

Moors, A., & Scherer, K. R. (2013). The role of appraisal in emotion. In M. D. Robinson, E. R. Watkins, & E. Harmon-Jones (Eds.), *Handbook of cognition and emotion* (pp. 131–155). New York: Guilford Press.

Moreno, J. L. (1959a). Concerning the origin of the terms group therapy and psychodrama. *American Journal of Psychiatry, 116,* 176–177.

Moreno, J. L. (1959b). Psychodrama. In S. Arieti et al. (Eds.), *American handbook of psychiatry* (Vol. 2). New York: Basic Books.

More women fill Canada's top business jobs. (2009, February 9). *HRM Guide.* Retrieved May 6, 2009, from http://www.hrmguide .net/canada/diversity/gender-equality.htm

Morgan, C. (1996). Odors as cues for the recall of words unrelated to odor. *Perceptual and Motor Skills, 83,* 1227–1234.

Morgan, C. D., & Murray, H. A. (1935). A method for investigating fantasies: The Thematic Apperception Test. *Archives of Neurology and Psychiatry, 34,* 289–306.

Morgan, C. D., & Murray, H. A. (1962). Thematic Apperception Test. In H. A. Murray et al. (Eds.), *Explorations in personality: A clinical and experimental study of fifty men of college age* (pp. 530–545). New York: Science Editions.

Morofushi, M., Shinohara, K., Funabashi, T., & Kimura, F. (2000). Positive relationship between menstrual synchrony and ability to smell 5alpha-androst-16-en-3alpha-ol. *Chemical Senses, 25,* 407–411.

Morofushi, M., Shinohara, K., & Kimura, F. (2001). Menstrual and circadian variations in time perceptions in healthy women and women with premenstrual syndrome. *Neuroscience Research, 41,* 339–344.

Morrison, M. A., Morrison, T. G., & Franklin, R. (2009). Modern and old-fashioned homonegativity among samples of Canadian and American university students, *Journal of Cross-Cultural Psychology, 40*(4), 523–542.

Morrison, T. L., Edwards, D. W., & Weissman, H. N. (1994). The MMPI and MMPI-2 as predictors of psychiatric diagnosis in an outpatient sample. *Journal of Personality Assessment, 62,* 17–30.

Morry, M. M., Kito, M., & Ortiz, L. (2011). The attraction-similarity model and dating couples: Projection, perceived similarity, and psychological benefits. *Personal Relationships, 18,* 125–143.

Moscovici, S., & Zavalloni, M. (1969). The group as a polarizer of attitudes. *Journal of Personality and Social Psychology, 12,* 125–135.

Moskowitz, D. S., & Fournier, M.A. (2015). The interplay of persons and situations: Retrospect and prospect. In M. Mikulincer, P. R. Shaver, M. L. Cooper, & R. J. Larsen (Eds.), *APA handbook of personality and social psychology, Volume 4: Personality processes and individual differences* (pp. 471–489). Washington, DC: American Psychological Association.

Mühlberger, A., Weik, A., Pauli, P., & Wiedemann, G. (2006). One-session virtual reality exposure treatment for fear of flying: 1-year follow-up and graduation flight accompaniment effects. *Psychotherapy Research, 16,* 26–40.

Muise, A., Christofides, E., & Desmarais, S. (2014). "Creeping" or just information seeking? Gender differences in partner monitoring in response to jealousy on Facebook. *Personal Relationships, 21*(1), 35–50.

Müller, M., Regenbogen, B., Sachse, J., Eich, F., Härtter, S., & Hiemke, C. (2006). Gender aspects in the clinical treatment of schizophrenic inpatients with amisulpride: A therapeutic drug monitoring study. *Pharmacopsychiatry, 39,* 41–46.

Mullins, H. M., Cortina, J. M., Drake, C. L., & Dalal, R. S. (2014). Sleepiness at work: A review and framework of how the physiology of sleepiness impacts the workplace. *Journal of Applied Psychology, 99*(6), 1096–1112.

Murdoch, J. (2005, May 10). Superstitious athletes. CBC Sports Online. Retrieved August 2, 2006, from http://www.cbc.ca/sports/columns-top10/superstition.html#1

Murray, D. (1995, July/August). Toward a science of desire. *The Sciences, 35,* 244–249.

Murray, D. (2009). Infectious diseases. In C. Rudolph, A. Rudolph, M. Hostetter, G. Lister, & N. Siegel (Eds.), *Rudolph's pediatrics* (22nd ed., pp. 867–1174). New York: McGraw-Hill.

Murray, H. (1938). *Explorations in personality*. New York: Oxford University Press.

Murray, H. A. (1965). Uses of the Thematic Apperception Test. In B. I. Murstein (Ed.), *Handbook of projective techniques* (pp. 425–432). New York: Basic Books.

Murray, J., Liotti, M., Ingmundson, P., Mayburg, H., Pu, Y., Zamarripa, F., . . . Fox, P. (2006). Children's brain activations while viewing televised violence revealed by fMRI. *Media Psychology, 8,* 24–37.

Mychasiuk, R., Gibb, R., & Kolb, B. (2012). Prenatal stress alters dendritic morphology and synaptic connectivity in the prefrontal cortex and hippocampus of developing offspring. *Synapse, 66*(4), 308–314. doi:10.1002/syn.21512

Myers, D. G., & Lamm, H. (1975). The polarizing effect of group discussion. *American Scientist, 63,* 297–303.

Naglieri, J. A., & Ronning, M. E. (2000). Comparison of White, African American, Hispanic, and Asian children on the Naglieri Nonverbal Ability Test. *Psychological Assessment, 12,* 328–334.

Nation, J. R., & Woods, D. J. (1980). Persistence: The role of partial reinforcement in psychotherapy. *Journal of Experimental Psychology: General, 109,* 175–207.

National Highway Transportation Safety Administration. (2010). *Traffic safety facts 2010—A compilation of motor vehicle crash data from the fatality analysis reporting system and the general estimates system (report No. DOT 811659) Washington, DC: U.S. Department of Transportation.* Available online at http://www-nrd.nhtsa.dot.gov/Pubs/811659.pdf

National Highway Transportation Safety Administration. (2013). *Traffic safety facts—Research note: Driver electronic device use in 2011* (Report No. DOT HS 811 719). Washington, DC: U.S. Department of Transportation.

National Institute of Mental Health. (2010). Suicide in the U.S.: Statistics and prevention. Retrieved May 16, 2012, from http://www.nimh.nih.gov/health/publications/suicide-in-the-us-statistics-and-prevention/index.shtml

National Institute of Neurological Disorders and Stroke (NINDS). (2014). *Brain basics: Understanding sleep.* Retrieved December 18, 2014, from: http://www.ninds.nih.gov/disorders/brain_basics/understanding_sleep.htm

National Institute on Drug Abuse. (2001). Ecstasy: What we know and don't know about MDMA: A scientific review. Retrieved May 21, 2006, from http://www.nida.nih.gov/Meetings/MDMA/MDMAExSummary.html

National Institutes of Health. (2005). National survey sharpens picture of major depression among U.S. adults. Retrieved June 1, 2009, from http://www.nih.gov/news/pr/oct2005/niaaa-03a.htm

National Reading Panel. (2000). *Teaching children to read: Reports of the subgroups.* Retrieved from http://www.nichd.nih.gov/publications/nrp/report.htm

National Sleep Foundation. (2006). Summary findings of the 2006 Sleep in America Poll. Retrieved May 26, 2006, from http://sleepdisorders.about.com/gi/dynamic/offsite.htm?zi=1/XJ&sdn=sleepdisorders&zu=http%3A%2F%2Fwww.sleepfoundation.rg%2F

Neil-Sztramko, S. E., Pahwa, M., Demers, P. A., & Gotay, C. C. (2014). Health-related interventions among night shift workers: a critical review of the literature. *Scandinavian Journal of Work, Environment & Health, 40*(6), 543–556.

Neimark, E. D. (1981). Confounding with cognitive style factors: An artifact explanation for the apparent nonuniversal incidence of formal operations. In I. Sigel, D. Brodzinsky, & R. Golinkoff (Eds.), *New directions in Piagetian research and theory*. Hillsdale, NJ: Erlbaum.

Neisser, U., & Harsch, N. (1992). Phantom flashbulbs: False recollections of hearing the news about *Challenger*. In E. Winograd & U. Neisser (Eds.), *Affect and accuracy in recall: Studies of "flashbulb" memories* (pp. 9–31). New York: Cambridge University Press.

Neisser, U., Boodoo, G., Bouchard, T., Boykin, A., Brody, N., Ceci, S., Halpern, D., Loehlin, J., Perloff, R., Sternberg, R., & Urbina, S. (1996). Intelligence: Knowns and unknowns. *American Psychologist, 51,* 77–101.

Neitz, M., & Neitz, J. (1995). Numbers and ratios of visual pigment genes for normal red-green color vision. *Science, 267,* 1013–1016.

Nelson, M. C., Gordon-Larsen, P., North, K. E., & Adair, L. S. (2006). Body mass index gain, fast food, and physical activity: Effects of shared environments over time. *Obesity, 14*(4), 701–709.

Nevsimalova, S., Prihodova, I., Kemlink, D., & Skibova, J. (2013). Childhood parasomnia—A disorder of sleep maturation? *European Journal of Paediatric Neurology, 17*(6), 615–619.

Niedenthal, P. M., & Brauer, M. (2012). Social functionality of human emotion. *Annual Review of Psychology, 63,* 259–285.

Nielsen, T. A., & Stenstrom, P. (2005). What are the memory sources of dreaming? *Nature,* 437, 1286–1289.

Nieto-Hernandez, R., Rubin, G., Cleare, A., Weinman, J., & Wessely, S. (2008). Can evidence change belief? Reported mobile phone sensitivity following individual feedback of an inability to discriminate active from sham signals. *Journal of Psychosomatic Research, 65,* 453–460.

Nelson, J. C. (1991). Current status of tricyclic antidepressants in psychiatry: Their pharmacology and clinical applications. *Journal of Clinical Psychiatry, 52,* 193–200.

Nelson, J. C. (1997). Safety and tolerability of the new antidepressants. *Journal of Clinical Psychiatry, 58*(6, Suppl.), 26–31.

Neugebauer, V., Li, W., Bird, G., & Han, J., (2004). The amygdala and persistent pain. *Neuroscientist, 10,* 221–234.

Neville, H., Bavelier, D., Corina, D., Rauschecker, J., Karni, A., Lalwani, A., . . . Turner, R. (1998). Cerebral organization for language in deaf and hearing subjects: Biological constraints and effects of experience. *Proceedings of the National Academy of Sciences, 95,* 922–929.

Nguyen, P. V., Abel, T., & Kandel, E. R. (1994). Requirement of a critical period of transcription for induction of a late phase of LTP. *Science, 265,* 1104–1107.

Nickerson, R. S., & Adams, M. J. (1979). Long-term memory for a common object. *Cognitive Psychology, 11,* 287–307.

Nielsen, T. A., Zadra, A. L., Simard, V., Saucier, S., Stenstrom, P., Smith, C., & Kuiken, D. (2003). The typical dreams of Canadian university students. *Dreaming, 13*(4), 211–235.

Nisbett, R. E., Aronson, J., Blair, C., Dickens, W., Flynn, J., Halpern, D. F., & Turkheimer, E. (2012). Intelligence: New findings and theoretical developments. *American Psychologist, 67,* 130–159. doi:10.1037=a0026699

Nisbett, R. E., & Wilson, T. D. (1977). The halo effect: Evidence for unconscious alteration of judgments. *Journal of Personality and Social Psychology, 35,* 250–256.

Nishida, M., Pearsall, J., Buckner, R., & Walker, M. (2008). REM sleep, prefrontal theta, and the consolidation of human emotional memory. *Cerebral Cortex, 19,* 1158–1166.

Nishiike, S., Nakagawa, S., Tonoike, M., Takeda, N., & Kubo, T. (2001). Information processing of visually-induced apparent self motion in the cortex of humans: Analysis with magnetoencephalography. *Acta Oto-laryngologica, 121,* 113–115.

Nishimura, H., Hashikawa, K., Doi, K., Iwaki, T., Watanabe, Y., Kusuoka, H., . . . Kubo, T. (1999). Sign language "heard" in the auditory cortex. *Nature, 397,* 116.

Nogrady, H., McConkey, K. M., & Perry, C. (1985). Enhancing visual memory: Trying hypnosis, trying imagination, and trying again. *Journal of Abnormal Psychology, 94,* 195–204.

Norman, W. (1963). Toward an adequate taxonomy of personality attributes: Replicated factor structure in peer nomination personality ratings. *Journal of Abnormal & Social Psychology, 66,* 574–583.

Noyes, R., Jr., Burrows, G. D., Reich, J. H., Judd, F. K., Garvey, M. J., Norman, T. R., . . . Marriott, P. (1996). Diazepam versus alprazolam for the treatment of panic disorder. *Journal of Clinical Psychiatry, 57,* 344–355.

Nutt, D. (2000). Treatment of depression and concomitant anxiety. *European Neuropsychopharmacology, 10*(Suppl. 4), S433–S437.

Nutt, D. J. (2007). Relationship of neurotransmitters to the symptoms of major depressive disorder. *The Journal of Clinical Psychiatry, 69,* 4–7.

Obhi, S. S. (2007). Evidence for feedback dependent conscious awareness of action. *Brain Research, 1161,* 88–94.

Obhi, S. S., Planetta, P. J., & Scantlebury J. (2009). On the signals underlying conscious awareness of action. *Cognition, 110*(1), 65–73.

O'Leary, K. D., & Smith, D. A. (1991). Marital interactions. *Annual Review of Psychology, 42,* 191–212.

Oliveira, M. (2014, February 19). 10 million Canadians use Facebook on mobiles daily. *The Globe and Mail.* Retrieved September 19, 2014, from http://www.theglobeandmail.com/technology/10-million-canadians-use-facebook-on-mobile-daily/article16976434/

Oliver, J. E. (1993). Intergenerational transmission of child abuse: Rates, research, and clinical implications. *American Journal of Psychiatry, 150,* 1315–1324.

Ong, A. D., Fuller-Rowell, T., & Burrow, A. L. (2009). Racial discrimination and the stress process. *Journal of Personality and Social Psychology, 96,* 1259–1271.

Organisation for Economic Co-operation and Development. (2011). *Society at a glance 2011: OECD social indicators.* Retrieved April 18, 2012, from http://www.oecd.org/els/socialpoliciesanddata/societyataglance2011-oecdsocialindicators.htm

Otto, M. W., Pollack, M. H., Sachs, G. S., Reiter, S. R., Meltzer-Brody, S., & Rosenbaum, J. F. (1993). Discontinuation of benzodiazepine treatment: Efficacy of cognitive-behavioral therapy for patients with panic disorder. *American Journal of Psychiatry, 150,* 1485–1490.

Overmeier, J. B., & Seligman, M. E. P. (1967). Effects of inescapable shock upon subsequent escape and avoidance responding. *Journal of Comparative and Physiological Psychology, 67,* 28–33.

Page, J., Snowden, J., Cheng, Y., Doss, A., Rosenstein, M., & Caughey, A. (2013). The risk of stillbirth and infant death by each additional week of expectant management stratified by maternal age. *American Journal of Obstetrics and Gynecology, 209*(375), 1–7.

Page-Gould, E., Mendoza-Denton, R., & Tropp, L. (2008). With a little help from my cross-group friend: Reducing anxiety in intergroup contexts through cross-group friendships. *Journal of Personality and Social Psychology, 95,* 1080–1094.

Pakkenberg, B., Pelvig, D., Marner, L., Bundgaard, M. J., Gundersen, H. J., Nyengaard, J. R., & Regeur, L. (2003). Aging and the human neocortex. *Experimental Gerontology, 38,* 95–99.

Papadopoulos, F., Ekbom, A., Brandt, L., & Ekselius, L. (2009). Excess mortality, causes of death and prognostic factors in anorexia nervosa. *British Journal of Psychiatry, 194,* 10–17.

Papalia, D., & Bielby, D. D. (1974). Cognitive functioning in middle and old age adults. *Human Development, 17,* 424–443.

Parada, M., Abdul-Ahad, F., Censi, S., Sparks, L., & Pfaus, J. G. (2011). Context alters the ability of clitoral stimulation to induce a sexually-conditioned partner preference in the rat. *Hormones and Behavior, 59*(4), 520–527. doi:10.1016/j.yhbeh.2011.02.001

Paraherakis, A., Charney, D., & Gill, K. (2001). Neuropsychological functioning in substance-dependent patients. *Substance Use & Misuse, 36,* 257–271.

Park, B., & Judd, C. M. (1990). Measures and models of perceived group variability. *Journal of Personality and Social Psychology, 59,* 173–191.

Park, K. A., & Waters, E. (1989). Security of attachment and pre-school friendships. *Child Development, 60,* 1076–1081.

Park, S. W., Bauer, J. J., & Arbuckle, N. B. (2009). Growth motivation attenuates the self-serving attribution. *Journal of Research in Personality, 43*(5), 914–917.

Parke, R. D. (1977). Some effects of punishment on children's behavior—revisited. In E. M. Hetherington, E. M. Ross, & R. D. Parke (Eds.), *Contemporary readings in child psychology.* New York: McGraw-Hill.

Parkin, A., & Mendelsohn, M. (2003, October). A new Canada: An identity shaped by diversity. Centre for Research on Information on Canada. Retrieved July 10, 2006, from http://www.cric.ca/pdf/cahiers/cricpapers_october2003.pdf

Parkinson, W. L., & Weingarten, H. P. (1990). Dissociative analysis of ventromedial hypothalamic obesity syndrome. *American Journal of Physiology, 259,* 829–835.

Parsons, T., & Rizzo, A. (2008). Affective outcomes of virtual reality exposure therapy for anxiety and specific phobias: A meta-analysis. *Journal of Behavior Therapy and Experimental Psychiatry, 39,* 250–261.

Partinen, M., Hublin, C., Kaprio, J. Koskenvuo, M., & Guilleminault, C. (1994). Twin studies in narcolepsy. *Sleep, 17,* S13–S16.

Pascual, A., & Guéguen, N. (2005). Foot-in-the-door and Door-in-the-face: A comparative meta-analytic study. *Psychological Reports, 96*(1), 122–128.

Pascual-Leone, A., & Torres, F. (1993). Plasticity of the sensorimotor cortex representation of the reading finger in Braille readers. *Brain, 116,* 39–52.

Pascual-Leone, A., Dhuna, A., Altafullah, I., & Anderson, D. C. (1990). Cocaine-induced seizures. *Neurology, 40,* 404–407.

Paul, G. L., & Lentz, R. J. (1977). *Psychosocial treatment of chronic mental patients.* Cambridge, MA: Harvard University Press.

Paulhus, D., Harms, P., Bruce, M., & Lysy, D. (2003). The over-claiming technique: Measuring self-enhancement independent of ability. *Journal of Personality & Social Psychology, 84,* 890–904.

Pauls, D. L., Abramovitch, A., Rauch, S. L., & Geller, D. A. (2014). Obsessive-compulsive disorder: an integrative genetic and neurobiological perspective. *Nature Reviews Neuroscience, 15*(6), 410–424.

Pause, B. M., and Krauel, K. (2000). Chemosensory event-related potentials (CSERP) as a key to the psychology of odors. *International Journal of Psychophysiology, 36,* 105–122.

Pavlov, I. P. (1960). *Conditioned reflexes: An investigation of the physiological activity of the cerebral cortex* (G. V. Anrep, Trans.). New York: Dover. (Original translation published 1927)

Pearlman, L. A., & Courtois, C. A. (2005). Clinical applications of the attachment framework: Relational treatment of complex trauma. *Journal of Traumatic Stress, 18*(5), 449–459.

Pedersen, D. M., & Wheeler, J. (1983). The Müller-Lyer illusion among Navajos. *Journal of Social Psychology, 121,* 3–6.

Pederson, D. R., Moran, G., Sitko, C., Campbell, K., Ghesquire, K., & Acton, H. (1990). Maternal sensitivity and the security of infant-mother attachment: A Q-sort study. *Child Development, 61,* 1974–1983.

Penfield, W. (1969). Consciousness, memory, and man's conditioned reflexes. In K. Pribram (Ed.), *On the biology of learning* (pp. 129–168). New York: Harcourt Brace Jovanovich.

Perls, F. S. (1969). *Gestalt therapy verbatim.* Lafayette, CA: Real People Press.

Perreault, S. (2013). Police-reported crime statistics in Canada, 2012. *Juristat* (Component of Statistics Canada catalogue no. 85 002-X. ISSN 1209-6393). Retrieved February 23, 2015 from http://www.statcan.gc.ca/pub/85-002-x/2013001/article/11854-eng.htm?fpv=269303

Perry, R., & Zeki, S. (2000). The neurology of saccades and covert shifts in spatial attention: An event-related fMRI study. *Brain, 123,* 2273–2288.

Pert, C. B., Snowman, A. M., & Snyder, S. H. (1974). Localization of opiate receptor binding in presynaptic membranes of rat brain. *Brain Research, 70,* 184–188.

Peters, M. (1995a). Does brain size matter? A reply to Rushton and Ankney. *Canadian Journal of Experimental Psychology, 49,* 570–576.

Peters, M. (1995b). Race differences in brain size: Things are not as clear as they seem to be. *American Psychologist, 50,* 947–948.

Peterson, L. R., & Peterson, M. J. (1959). Short-term retention of individual verbal items. *Journal of Experimental Psychology, 58,* 193–198.

Petit, A., Karila, L., Chalmin, F., & Lejoyeux, M. (2012). Methamphetamine addiction: A review of the literature. *Journal of Addiction Research and Therapy, S1.* Retrieved on March 24, 2012, from http://www.omicsonline.org/2155-6105/2155-6105-S1-006.pdf

Pettit, J. W., Hartley, C., Lewinsohn, P. M., Seeley, J. R., & Klein, D. N. (2013). Is liability to recurrent major depressive disorder present before first episode onset in adolescence or acquired after the initial episode? *Journal of Abnormal Psychology, 122*(2), 353.

Petitto, L. A., & Marentette, P. R. (1991). Babbling in the manual mode: Evidence for the ontogeny of language. *Science, 251,* 1493–1496.

Petrill, S. (2003). The development of intelligence: Behavioral genetic approaches. In R. Sternberg, J. Lautrey, & T. Lubart (Eds.), *Models of intelligence: International perspective* (pp. 81–90). Washington, DC: American Psychological Association.

Petry, N. (2002). Psychosocial treatments for pathological gambling: Current status and future directions. *Psychiatric Annals, 32,* 192–196.

Petry, N., Tedford, J., Austin, M., Nich, C., Carroll, K., & Rounsaville, B. (2004). Prize reinforcement contingency management for treating cocaine users: How low can we go, and with whom? *Addiction, 99,* 349–360.

Pett, M. A., & Johnson, M. J. M. (2005). Development and psychometric evaluation of the revised university student hassle scale. *Educational and Psychological Measurement, 65*(6), 984–1010.

Petty, R. E., & Wegener, D. T. (1998). Attitude change: Multiple roles for persuasion variables. In D. T. Gilbert, S. T. Fiske, & G. Lindzey (Eds.), *The handbook of social psychology* (4th ed., Vol. 1, pp. 323–390). New York: McGraw-Hill.

Pfaus, J., Erickson, K., & Talianakis, S. (2013). Somatosensory conditioning of sexual arousal and copulatory behavior in the male rat: A model of fetish development. *Physiology and Behavior, 122,* 1–7.

Pfaus, J. G. (2007). Models of sexual motivation. In Janssen E. (Ed.), *The Psychophysiology of Sex.* Bloomington: Indiana University Press.

Pfaus, J. G., Kippen, T., & Coria-Avila, G. (2003). What can animal models tell us about human sexual response? *Annual Review of Sex Research, 14,* 1–63.

Philip, P., Chaufton, C., Nobili, L., & Garbarino, S. (2014). Errors and accidents. In *Sleepiness and Human Impact Assessment* (pp. 81–92). Milan: Springer.

Piaget, J. (1960). *The child's conception of physical causality.* Patterson, NJ: Littlefield, Adams.

Piaget, J. (1963a). *The child's conception of the world.* Patterson, NJ: Littlefield, Adams.

Piaget, J. (1963b). *Psychology of intelligence.* Patterson, NJ: Littlefield, Adams.

Piaget, J. (1964). *Judgment and reasoning in the child.* Patterson, NJ: Littlefield, Adams.

Piaget, J., & Inhelder, B. (1969). *The psychology of the child*. New York: Basic Books.

Picard, A. (2009, March 27). Prescription sales rise by $1.2 billion, even as generics gain popularity. *The Globe and Mail*. Retrieved August 8, 2012, from http://www.theglobeandmail.com/life/prescription-sales-rise-by-12-billion-even-as-generics-gain-popularity/article1150403/

Pich, E. M., Pagliusi, S. R., Tessari, M., Talabot-Ayer, D., Van Huijsduijnen, R. H., & Chiamulera, C. (1997). Common neural substrates for the addictive properties of nicotine and cocaine. *Science, 275*, 83–86.

Pihl, R. O., Lau, M. L., & Assaad, J-M. (1997). Aggressive disposition, alcohol, and aggression. *Aggressive Behavior, 23*, 11–18.

Pillemer, D. B. (1990). Clarifying the flashbulb memory concept: Comment on McCloskey, Wible, and Cohen (1988). *Journal of Experimental Psychology: General, 119*, 92–96.

Pillow, D. R., Zautra, A. J., & Sandler, I. (1996). Major life events and minor stressors: Identifying mediational links in the stress process. *Journal of Personality and Social Psychology, 70*, 381–394.

Pinel, J. P. J. (2000). *Biopsychology* (4th ed.). Boston: Allyn & Bacon.

Plomin, R. (1989). Environment and genes: Determinants of behavior. *American Psychologist, 44*, 105–111.

Plomin, R., DeFries, J. C., Craig, I. W., & McGuffin, P. (2003). Behavioral genetics. In R. Plomin, J. C. DeFries, I. W. Craig, & P. McGuffin (Eds.), *Behavioral genetics in the postgenomic era* (pp. 3–15). Washington, DC: American Psychological Association.

Plomin, R., DeFries, J. C., & Fulker, D. W. (1988). *Nature and nurture during infancy and early childhood*. New York: Cambridge University Press.

Plomin, R., DeFries, J. C., Knopik, V. A., & Neiderhiser, J. M. (2013). *Behavioral Genetics* (6th ed.). Duffield, UK: Worth.

Plomin, R., Owen, M. J., & McGuffin, P. (1994). The genetic basis of complex human behaviors. *Science, 264*, 1733–1739.

Plomin, R., & Rende, R. (1991). Human behavioral genetics. *Annual Review of Psychology, 42*, 161–190.

Plummer, D., & Slane, S. (1996). Patterns of coping in racially stressful situations. *Journal of Black Psychology, 22*, 302–315.

Pollak, S., Messner, M., Kistler, D., & Cohn, J. (2009). Development of perceptual expertise in emotion recognition. *Cognition, 110*, 242–247.

Pomerleau, O. F., & Pomerleau, C. S. (1989). A biobehavioral perspective on smoking. In T. Ney & A. Gale (Eds.), *Smoking and human behavior* (pp. 69–93). New York: Wiley.

Porjesz, B., Rangaswamy, M., Kamarajan, C., Jones, K. A., Padmanabhapillai, A., & Begleiter, H. (2005). The utility of neurophysiological markers in the study of alcoholism. *Clinical Neurophysiology, 116*, 993–1018.

Porrino, L. J., & Lyons, D. (2000). Orbital and medial prefrontal cortex and psychostimulant abuse: Studies in animal models. *Cerebral Cortex, 10*, 326–333.

Porter, F. L., Porges, S. W., & Marshall, R. E. (1988). Newborn pain cries and vagal tone: Parallel changes in response to circum-cision. *Child Development, 59*, 495–505.

Posner, M. I. (1996, September). Attention and psychopathology. *Harvard Mental Health Letter, 13*(3), 5–6.

Postel, M., de Jong, C., & de Haan, H. (2005). Does e-therapy for problem drinking reach hidden populations? *American Journal of Psychiatry, 162*, 2393.

Postman, L., & Phillips, L. W. (1965). Short-term temporal changes in free recall. *Quarterly Journal of Experimental Psychology, 17*, 132–138.

Potts, N. L. S., Davidson, J. R. T., & Krishman, K. R. R. (1993). The role of nuclear magnetic resonance imaging in psychiatric research. *Journal of Clinical Psychiatry, 54*(12, Suppl.), 13–18.

Pouget, J. G., & Müller, D. J. (2014). Pharmacogenetics of antipsychotic treatment in schizophrenia. In Q. Yan (Ed.), *Pharmacogenomics in drug discovery and development* (pp. 557–587). Springer: New York.

Poulin, M. & Cohen Silver, R. (2008). World benevolence beliefs and well-being across the life span. *Psychology and Aging, 23*, 13–23.

Power, K. G., Sharp, D. M., Swanson, V., & Simpson, R. J. (2000). Therapist contact in cognitive behaviour therapy for panic disorder and agoraphobia in primary care. *Clinical Psychology & Psychotherapy, 7*, 37–46.

Pöysti, L., Rajalin, S., & Summala, H. (2005). Factors influencing the use of cellular (mobile) phone during driving and hazards while using it. *Accident Analysis & Prevention, 37*, 47–51.

Pozzulo, J. D., Dempsey, J., & Crescini, C. (2009). Preschoolers' person description and identification accuracy: A comparison of the simultaneous and elimination lineup procedures. *Journal of Applied Developmental Psychology, 30*(6), 667–676.

Pozzulo, J. D., & Lindsay, R. C. L. (1999). Elimination lineups: An improved identification procedure for child eyewitnesses. *Journal of Applied Psychology, 84*, 167–176.

Pratkanis, A. R. (1989). The cognitive representation of attitudes. In A. R. Pratkanis, S. J. Breckler, & A. G. Greenwald (Eds.), *Attitude structure and function* (pp. 71–93). Hillsdale, NJ: Erlbaum.

Premack, D. (1971). Language in chimpanzees. *Science, 172*, 808–822.

Premack, D. (1996). *Gavagai! Or the future history of the animal language controversy*. Cambridge, MA: MIT Press.

Premack, D., & Premack, A. J. (1983). *The mind of an ape*. New York: Norton.

Prescott, C. A., & Kendler, K. S. (1999). Genetic and environmental contributions to alcohol abuse and dependence in a population-based sample of male twins. *American Journal of Psychiatry, 148*, 52–56.

Pressman, S. D., & Cohen, S. (2005). Does positive affect influence health? *Psychological Bulletin, 131*, 925–971.

Price, D. D., Finniss, D. G., Benedetti, F. (2008). A comprehensive review of the placebo effect: Recent advances and current thought. *Annual Review of Psychology, 59*, 565–590. doi:10.1146/annurev.psych.59.113006.095941

Price, H. L., & Connolly, D. A. (2004). Event frequency and children's suggestibility: A study of cued recall responses. *Applied Cognitive Psychology, 18*, 809–821.

Price, H. L., & Connolly, D. A. (2007). Anxious and non-anxious children's recall of a repeated or unique event. *Journal of Experimental Child Psychology, 98*, 94–112.

Price, H. L. & Connolly, D. A. (2012). *Suggestibility effects persist after one year in children who experienced a single or repeated event*. Manuscript submitted for publication.

Price, H. L., & Connolly, D. A. (2013). Suggestibility effects persist after one year in children who experienced a single or repeated event. *Journal of Applied Research in Memory and Cognition. 3*, 89–94.

Price, M., Gros, D. F., Strachan, M., Ruggiero, K. J., & Acierno, R. (2012). Combat experiences, pre-deployment training, and outcome of exposure therapy for post-traumatic stress disorder in Operation Enduring Freedom/Operation Iraqi Freedom veterans. *Clinical Psychology and Psychotherapy*. Online preview retrieved on May 5, 2012, from http://onlinelibrary.wiley.com/doi/10.1002/cpp.1768/abstract

Prien, R. F., Kupfer, D. J., Mansky, P. A., Small, J. G., Tuason, V. B., Voss, C. B., & Johnson, W. E. (1984). Drug therapy in the prevention of recurrences in unipolar and bipolar affective disorders. *Archives of General Psychiatry, 41*, 1096–1104.

Prigerson, H. G., Bierhals, A. J., Kasl, S. V., Reynolds, C. F., III, Shear, M. K., Day, N., . . . Jacobs, S. (1997). Traumatic grief as a risk factor for mental and physical mortality. *American Journal of Psychiatry, 154,* 616–623.

Prinz, P. N., Vitiello, M. V., Raskind, M. A., & Thorpy, M. J. (1990). Geriatrics: Sleep disorders and aging. *New England Journal of Medicine, 323,* 520–526.

PROPEL Centre for Population Health Impact. (2012). *Tobacco use in Canada: Patterns and Trends* (2012 ed.). Waterloo, ON: University of Waterloo, 2012. Retrieved on March 25, 2012, from http://www.tobaccoreport.ca/2012/TobaccoUseinCanada_2012.pdf

Provine, R. R. (1996, January/February). Laughter. *American Scientist, 84,* 38–45.

Provins, K. (1997). Handedness and speech: A critical reappraisal of the role of genetic and environmental factors in the cerebral lateralization of function. *Psychological Review, 104,* 544–571.

Public Health Agency of Canada. (2005a). *Leading causes of death in Canada.* Retrieved from http://www.phac-aspc.gc.ca/publicat/lcd-pcd97/table1-eng.php

Public Health Agency of Canada. (2005b). *Leading causes of hospitalizations in Canada.* Retrieved from http://dsol-smed.phac-aspc.gc.ca/dsol-smed/is-sb/leadcauses/leading_causes_hosp_2005-eng.pdf

Public Health Agency of Canada. (2011). *Obesity in Canada.* Retrieved on April 9, 2012, from http://www.phac-aspc.gc.ca/hp-ps/hl-mvs/oic-oac/index-eng.php#toc

Public Health Agency of Canada. (2012a). *A report on mental illnesses in Canada.* Retrieved May 11, 2012, from http://www.phac-aspc.gc.ca/publicat/miic-mmac/index-eng.php

Public Health Agency of Canada. (2012b). *Physical activities tips for adults (18–64 years).* Retrieved March 1, 2015, from http://www.phac-aspc.gc.ca/hp-ps/hl-mvs/pa-ap/07paap-eng.php

Purves, D., Augustine, G., Fitzpatrick, D., Hall, W., LaMantia, A., & White, L. (Eds.). (2012). *Neuroscience* (5th ed., Chapter 6). Sunderland, MA: Sinnauer Associates.

Purves, D., Augustine, G. J., Fitzpatrick, D., Katz, L., LaMantia, A., McNamara, J., & Williams, S. (2001). Anatomical distribution of rods and cones. *Neuroscience* (2nd ed.). Sunderland (MA): Sinauer Associates. Retrieved from http://www.ncbi.nlm.nih.gov/books/NBK10848/

Pushkar, D., Etezadi, J., Andres, D., Arbuckle, T., Schwartzman, A. E., & Chaikelson, J. (1999). Models of intelligence in late life: Comment on Hultsch et al. *Psychology and Aging, 14,* 520–527.

Putnam, F. W. (1989). *Diagnosis and treatment of multiple personality disorder.* New York: Guilford Press.

Quadrel, M. J., Fischhoff, B., & Davis, W. (1993). Adolescent (in)vulnerability. *American Psychologist, 48,* 102–116.

Rabinowitz, J., Levine, S. Z., Garibaldi, G., Bugarski-Kirola, D., Berardo, C. G., & Kapur, S. (2012). Negative symptoms have greater impact on functioning than positive symptoms in schizophrenia: analysis of CATIE data. *Schizophrenia research, 137*(1), 147–150.

Rabinowitz, P. M. (2000). Noise-induced hearing loss. *American Family Physician, 61,* 1053.

Raffone, A., & Srinivasan, N. (2010). The exploration of meditation in the neuroscience of attention and consciousness. *Cognitive Processing, 11*(1), 1–7.

Rahe, R. J., Meyer, M., Smith, M., Kjaer, G., & Holmes, T. H. (1964). Social stress and illness onset. *Journal of Psychosomatic Research, 8,* 35–44.

Raichle, M. E. (1994). Visualizing the mind. *Scientific American, 270,* 58–64.

Rao, S. C., Rainer, G., & Miller, E. K. (1997). Integration of what and where in the primate prefrontal cortex. *Science, 276,* 821–824.

Rapoport, J. L. (1989). The biology of obsessions and compulsions. *Scientific American, 260,* 83–89.

Rapoport, J. L., Giedd, J. N., & Gogtay, N. (2012). Neurodevelopmental model of schizophrenia: Update 2012. *Molecular Psychiatry, 17*(12), 1228–1238.

Rawn, C. D., & Vohs, K. D. (2011). When people strive for self-harming goals: Sacrificing personal health for interpersonal success. In K. D. Vohs & R. F. Baumeister (Eds.), *Handbook of self-regulation* (pp. 374–389). NY: Guilford.

Ravindran, A. V., da Silva, T. L., Ravindran, L. N., Richter, M. A., & Rector, N. A. (2009). Obsessive-compulsive spectrum disorders: A review of the evidence-based treatments. *The Canadian Journal of Psychiatry, 54*(5), 331–343.

Ray, S., & Bates, M. (2006). Acute alcohol effects on repetition priming and word recognition memory with equivalent memory cues. *Brain and Cognition, 60,* 118–127.

Rea, M. S., Bierman, A., Figueiro, M. G., & Bullough, J. D. (2000). A new approach to understanding the impact of circadian disruption on human health. *Journal of Circadian Rhythms, 6, 7.*

Recupero, R., Harms, S., & Noble, J. (2008). Googling suicide: surfing for suicide information on the Internet. *Journal of Clinical Psychiatry, 69*(6), 878–888.

Rehm, J., Baliunas, D., Brochu, S., Fischer, B., Gnam, W., Patra, J., . . . Taylor, B. (2006). *The costs of substance abuse in Canada 2002.* Ottawa: Canadian Centre on Substance Abuse.

Rehm, J., Patra, J., & Popova, S. (2006). Alcohol-attributable mortality and potential years of life lost in Canada 2001: Implications for prevention and policy. *Addiction, 101,* 373–384.

Rescorla, R. A. (1967). Pavlovian conditioning and its proper control procedures. *Psychological Review, 74,* 71–80.

Rescorla, R. A. (1968). Probability of shock in the presence and absence of CS in fear conditioning. *Journal of Comparative and Physiological Psychology, 66,* 1–5.

Rescorla, R. A. (1988). Pavlovian conditioning: It's not what you think it is. *American Psychologist, 43,* 151–160.

Rescorla, R. A. (2008). Conditioning of stimuli with nonzero initial value. *Journal of Experimental Psychology: Animal Behavior Processes, 34,* 315–323.

Rescorla, R. A., & Wagner, A. R. (1972). A theory of Pavlovian conditioning: Variations in the effectiveness of reinforcement and nonreinforcement. In A. Black & W. F. Prokasy (Eds.), *Classical conditioning: II. Current research and theory.* New York: Appleton.

Restak, R. (1988). *The mind.* Toronto: Bantam.

Restak, R. (1993, September/October). Brain by design. *The Sciences,* 27–33.

Revicki, D. A., Travers, K., Wyrwich, K. W., Svedsäter, H., Locklear, J., Mattera, M. S., . . . & Montgomery, S. (2012). Humanistic and economic burden of generalized anxiety disorder in North America and Europe. *Journal of Affective Disorders, 140*(2), 103–112.

Rhéaume, J., & Ladouceur, R. (2000). Cognitive and behavioural treatments of checking behaviours: An examination of individual cognitive change. *Clinical Psychology & Psychotherapy, 7,* 118–127.

Rice, F. P. (1992). *Intimate relationships, marriages, and families.* Mountain View, CA: Mayfield.

Richter, W., Somorjai, R., Summers, R., Jarmasz, M., Ravi, S., Menon, J. S., . . . Kim, S. G. (2000). Motor area activity during mental rotation studies by time-resolved single-trial fMRI. *Journal of Cognitive Neuroscience, 12,* 310–320.

Riedel, G. (1996). Function of metabotropic glutamate receptors in learning and memory. *Trends in Neurosciences, 19,* 219–224.

Riemann, R., Volk, R., Müller, A., & Herzog, M. (2010). The influence of nocturnal alcohol ingestion on snoring. *European Archives of Oto-Rhino-Laryngology, 267*(7), 1147–1156.

Riley, B., & Kendler, K. S. (2005). Genetics of schizophrenia: Linkage and association studies. In K. S. Kendler and L. J. Eaves (Eds.), *Psychiatric genetics* (pp. 95–140). Review of psychiatry, 24, no. 1.. Washington, DC: American Psychiatric Publishing.

Roan, S. (2000, March 6). Cyber analysis. *L.A. Times.*

Roberts, B. W., & DelVechio, W. F. (2000). The rank-order consistency of personality traits from childhood to old age: A quantitative review of longitudinal studies. *Psychological Bulletin, 126,* 3–25.

Roberts, B. W., Kuncel, N., Shiner, R., Caspi, A., & Goldberg, L. (2007). The power of personality: The comparative validity of personality traits, socioeconomic status, and cognitive ability for predicting important life outcomes. *Perspectives on Psychological Science, 2,* 313–345.

Roberts, P., & Moseley, B. (1996, May/June). Fathers' time. *Psychology Today, 29,* 48–55, 81.

Robertson, G. L. (1983). Thirst and vasopressin function in normal and disordered states of water balance. *Journal of Laboratory and Clinical Medicine, 101,* 351–371.

Robertson, I. H., & Murre, J. M. (1999). Rehabilitation of brain damage: Brain plasticity and principles of guided recovery. *Psychological Bulletin, 125,* 544–575.

Robins, R. W., Gosling, S. D., & Craik, K. H. (1999). An empirical analysis of trends in psychology. *American Psychologists, 54,* 117–128.

Robles, T., Shaffer, V., Malarkey, W., & Kiecolt-Glaser, J. (2006). Positive behaviors during marital conflict: Influences of stress hormones. *Journal of Social and Personal Relationships, 23,* 305–325.

Rocha-Rego, V., Fiszman, A., Portugal, L., Pereira, M., de Oliveira, L., Mendlowicz, M., . . . Volchan, E. (2009). Is tonic immobility the core sign among conventional peritraumatic signs and symptoms listed for PTSD? *Journal of Affective Disorders, 115,* 269–273.

Roche, A. F., & Davila, G. H. (1972). Late adolescent growth in stature. *Pediatrics, 50,* 874–880.

Rodin, J. (1981). Current status of the internal-external hypothesis for obesity: What went wrong? *American Psychologist, 36,* 361–372.

Rodin, J. (1985). Insulin levels, hunger, and food intake: An example of feedback loops in body weight regulation. *Health Psychology, 4,* 1–24.

Rodin, J., & Salovey, P. (1989). Health psychology. *Annual Review of Psychology, 40,* 533–579.

Rodin, J., Slochower, J., & Fleming, B. (1977). The effects of degree of obesity, age of onset, and energy deficit on external responsiveness. *Journal of Comparative and Physiological Psychology, 91,* 586–597.

Rodin, J., Wack, J., Ferrannini, E., & DeFronzo, R. A. (1985). Effect of insulin and glucose on feeding behavior. *Metabolism, 34,* 826–831.

Roediger, H. L., III. (1991). They read an article? A commentary on the everyday memory controversy. *American Psychologist, 46,* 37–40.

Roediger, H. L., III, & McDermott, K. B. (1995). Creating false memories: Remembering words not presented in lists. *Journal of Experimental Psychology: Learning, Memory, and Cognition, 21,* 803–814.

Roehrich, L., & Kinder, B. N. (1991). Alcohol expectancies and male sexuality: Review and implications for sex therapy. *Journal of Sex and Marital Therapy, 17,* 45–54.

Rogers, C. R. (1951). *Client-centered therapy: Its current practice, implications, and theory.* Boston: Houghton Mifflin.

Rogers, C. R. (1959). A theory of therapy, personality, and interpersonal relationships, as developed in the client-centered framework. In S. Koch (Ed.), *Psychology: A study of a science, Vol. III. Formulations of the person and the social context* (pp. 184–256). New York: McGraw-Hill.

Rogers, C. R. (1961). *On becoming a person: A therapist's view of psychotherapy.* Boston: Houghton Mifflin.

Rogers, C. R. (1981). Notes on Rollo May. *Perspectives, 2*(1), 16.

Roid, G. H. (2003). *Stanford-Binet Intelligence Scales* (5th ed.). Itasca, IL: Riverside Publishing.

Rose, H., & Rose, S. (2010). *Alas Poor Darwin: Arguments Against Evolutionary Psychology.* New York: Random House.

Roorda, A., & Williams, D. R. (1999). The arrangement of the three cone classes in the living human eye. *Nature, 397,* 520–521.

Roos, P. A., & Gatta, M. L. (1999). The gender gap in earnings: Trends, explanations, and prospects. In G. N. Powell (Ed.), *Handbook of Gender and Work* (pp. 95–123). Thousand Oaks, CA: Sage.

Rosch, E. H. (1973). Natural categories. *Cognitive Psychology, 4,* 328–350.

Rosch, E. H. (1978). Principles of categorization. In E. H. Rosch & B. Lloyd (Eds.), *Cognition and categorization.* Hillsdale, NJ: Erlbaum.

Rose, H., & Rose, S. (Eds.). (2000). *Alas, poor Darwin: Arguments against evolutionary psychology.* London: Jonathan Cape.

Rose, J. (2006). Nicotine and nonnicotine factors in cigarette addiction. *Psychopharmacology, 184,* 274–285.

Rosen, L. D., Cheever, N. A., & Carrier, L. M. (2012). *iDisorder: Understanding our obsession with technology and overcoming its hold on us.* New York: Palgrave MacMillan.

Rosenthal, A. M. (1964). *Thirty-eight witnesses.* New York: McGraw-Hill.

Rosenvinge, J. H., Matinussen, M., & Ostensen, E. (2000). The comorbidity of eating disorders and personality disorders: A meta-analytic review of studies published between 1983 and 1998. *Eating and Weight Disorders: Studies on Anorexia, Bulimia, and Obesity, 5,* 52–61.

Rosenzweig, M. R. (1961). Auditory localization. *Scientific American, 205,* 132–142.

Ross, C. A. (2009). Errors of logic and scholarship concerning dissociative identity disorder. *Journal of Child Sexual Abuse, 18*(2), 221–231.

Ross, C. A., Norton, G. R., & Wozney, K. (1989). Multiple personality disorder: An analysis of 236 cases. *Canadian Journal of Psychiatry, 34,* 413–418.

Ross, L. (1977). The intuitive psychologist and his shortcomings: Distortions in the attribution process. In L. Berkowitz (Ed.), *Advances in experimental social psychology* (Vol. 10). New York: Academic Press.

Roth, T. (2012). Appropriate therapeutic selection for patients with shift work disorder. *Sleep Medicine, 13*(4), 335–341.

Roth-Hanania, R., Davidov, M., & Zahn-Waxler, C. (2011). Empathy development from 8 to 16 months: Early signs of concern for others. *Infant Behavior and Development, 34*(3), 447–458.

Rothbaum, B. O., Astin, M. C., & Marsteller, F. (2005). Prolonged exposure versus Eye Movement Desensitization and Reprocessing (EMDR) for PTSD rape victims. *Journal of Traumatic Stress, 18*(6), 607–616.

Rotter, J. B. (1966). Generalized expectancies for internal versus external control of reinforcement. *Psychological Monographs, 80*(1, Whole No. 609).

Rotter, J. B. (1971, June). External control and internal control. *Psychology Today,* 37–42, 58–59.

Rotter, J. B. (1990). Internal versus external control of reinforcement: A case history of a variable. *American Psychologist, 45,* 489–493.

Rotton, J., & Cohn, E. G. (2000). Violence is a curvilinear function of temperature in Dallas: A replication. *Journal of Personality and Social Psychology, 78,* 1074–1082.

Rotton, J., Frey, J., Barry, T., Milligan, M., & Fitzpatrick, M. (1979). The air pollution experience and physical aggression. *Journal of Applied Social Psychology, 9,* 397–412.

Rouch, I., Wild, P., Ansiau, D., & Marquié, J.-C. (2005). Shiftwork experience, age and cognitive performance. *Ergonomics, 48,* 1282–1293.

Rowe, D. (2003). Assessing genotype–environment interactions and correlations in the postgenomic era. In R. Plomin, J. DeFries, I. Craig, & P. McGuffin (Eds.), *Behavioral genetics in the postgenomic era* (pp. 71–86). Washington, DC: American Psychological Association.

Rozell, E. J., Pettijohn, C. E., & Parker, R. S. (2002). An empirical evaluation of emotional intelligence: The impact on management development. *Journal of Management Development, 21,* 272–289.

Rudman, L. A., Ashmore, R. D, & Gary, M. L. (2001). "Unlearning" automatic biases: The malleability of implicit prejudice and stereotypes. *Journal of Personality & Social Psychology, 81,* 856–868.

Ruggero, M. A. (1992). Responses to sound of the basilar membrane of the mammalian cochlea. *Current Opinion in Neurobiology, 2,* 449–456.

Ruggiero, J. S., & Redeker, N. S. (2013). Effects of napping on sleepiness and sleep-related performance deficits in night-shift workers: a systematic review. *Biological Research for Nursing,* 16(2), 134–42. doi:10.1177/1099800413476571

Ruiter, R. A., Kessels, L. T., Peters, G. J. Y., & Kok, G. (2014). Sixty years of fear appeal research: Current state of the evidence. *International Journal of Psychology,* 49(2), 63–70.

Rushton, J. P. (1991). Mongoloid-caucasoid differences in brain size from military samples. *Intelligence, 15,* 351–359.

Rushton, J. P. (1992). Contributions to the history of psychology: XC evolutionary biology and heritable traits (with reference to oriental-white-black differences). *Psychological Reports, 71,* 811–821.

Rushton, J. P., & Jensen, A. (2005). Thirty years of research on race differences in cognitive ability. *Psychology, Public Policy, and Law, 11,* 235–294.

Saad, L. (2011, November 28). To lose weight, Americans rely more on dieting than exercise. *Gallup Wellbeing.* Retrieved on April 1, 2012, from http://www.gallup.com/poll/150986/lose-weight-americans-rely-dieting-exercise.aspx

Sack, R. L. (2009). The pathophysiology of jet lag. *Travel Medicine and Infectious Disease,* 7(2), 102–110.

Sack, R. L., Auckley, D., Auger, R. R., Carskadon, M. A., Wright, K. P., Jr., Vitiello, M. V., & Zhdanova, I. V. (2007). Circadian rhythm sleep disorders: Part I, Basic principles, shift work and jet lag disorders. An American Academy of Sleep Medicine review. *Sleep, 30,* 1460–1483.

Sackeim, H. A. (1992). The cognitive effects of electroconvulsive therapy. In W. H. Moos, E. R. Gamzu, & L. J. Thal (Eds.), *Cognitive disorders: Pathophysiology and treatment.* New York: Marcel Dekker.

Sackeim, H. A., Prudic, J., Devanand, D. P., Kiersky, J. E., Fitzsimmons, L., Moody, B. J., . . . Settembrino, J. M. (1993). Effects of stimulus intensity and electrode placement on the efficacy and cognitive effects of electroconvulsive therapy. *New England Journal of Medicine, 328,* 839–846.

Sackeim, H. A., Prudic, J., Devanand, D. P., Nobler, M. S., Lisanby, S. H., Peyser, S., . . . Clark, J. (May 2000). A prospective, randomized, double-blind comparison of bilateral and right unilateral electroconvulsive therapy at different stimulus intensities. *Archives of General Psychiatry,* 57(5), 425–434.

Sadeh, A., Gruber, R., & Raviv, A. (2003). The effect of sleep restriction and extension on school-age children: What a difference an hour makes. *Child Development, 74,* 444–455.

Safdar, S., Friedmeier, W., Matsumoto, D., Yoo, S. H., Kwantes, C. T., Kakai, H., & Shigemasu, E. (2009). Variations of emotional display rules within and across cultures: A comparison between Canada, USA, and Japan. *Canadian Journal of Behavioural Science, 41,* 1–10.

Sakurai, T. (2013). Orexin deficiency and narcolepsy. *Current opinion in neurobiology,* 23(5), 760–766.

Salin-Pascual, R., Gerashchenko, D., Greco, M., Blanco-Centurion, C., & Shiromani, P. (2001). Hypothalamic regulation of sleep. *Neuropsychopharmacology, 25,* S21–S27.

Salisch, M. (2001). Children's emotional development: Challenges in their relationships to parents, peers, and friends. *International Journal of Behavioural Development, 25,* 310–319.

Salo, J., Niemelae, A., Joukamaa, M., & Koivukangas, J. (2002). Effect of brain tumour laterality on patients' perceived quality of life. *Journal of Neurology, Neurosurgery, & Psychiatry, 72,* 373–377.

Salovey, P., & Pizarro, D. (2003). The value of emotional intelligence. In R. Sternberg, J. Lautrey, & T. Lubart (Eds.), *Models of intelligence: International perspective* (pp. 263–278). Washington, DC: American Psychological Association.

Salthouse, T. (2009). When does age-related cognitive decline begin? *Neurobiology of Aging, 30,* 507–514.

Samra, R. A. (2010). Fats and satiety. In Jean-Pierre Montmayeur and Johannes le Coutre (Eds.), *Fat Detection: Taste, Texture and Post Ingestive Effects* (Chapter 15). Boca Raton, FL: CRC Press.

Sanbonmatsu, D. M., & Fazio, R. H. (1990). The role of attitudes in memory-based decision making. *Journal of Personality and Social Psychology, 59,* 614–622.

Sanes, J. N., & Donoghue, J. P. (2000). Plasticity and primary motor cortex. *Annual Review of Neuroscience, 23,* 393–415.

Santos, A., Pezawas, L., & Meyer-Lindenberg, A. (2014). Genetics and emotions. In K. N. Ochsner, & S. M. Kosslyn (Eds.), *The Oxford handbook of cognitive neuroscience, Vol. 2: The cutting edges. Oxford library of psychology,* (pp. 94–113). New York, NY: Oxford University Press.

Saper, C. B., Scammell, T. E., & Lu, J. (2005). Hypothalamic regulation of sleep and circadian rhythms. *Nature, 437,* 1257–1263.

Sapolsky, R. M., Romero, L. M., & Munck, A. U. (2000). How do glucocorticoids influence stress responses? Integrating permissive, suppressive, stimulatory, and preparative actions 1. *Endocrine Reviews,* 21(1), 55–89.

Sattler, J., & Dumont, R. (2004). *Assessment of children: WISC-IV and WPPSI-III supplement.* San Diego, CA: Jerome M. Sattler.

Saufley, W. H., Jr., Otaka, S. R., & Bavaresco, J. L. (1985). Context effects: Classroom tests and context independence. *Memory and Cognition, 13,* 522–528.

Sauter, D. A., McDonald, N. M., Gangi, D. N., & Messinger, D. S. (2014). Nonverbal expressions of positive emotions. In M. M. Tugade, M. N. Shiota, & L. D. Kirby (Eds.), *Handbook of positive emotions,* (Chapter 10). New York, NY: Guilford Press.

Savage, R., Abrami, P., Piquette, N., Wood, E., Deleveaux, G., Sangher-Sidhu, S. & Burgo, G. (2013). A (Pan-Canadian) Cluster randomized control effectiveness trial of the ABRACADABRA web-based literacy program, *Journal of Educational Psychology,* 105(2), 310–328.

Savage, R., Abrami, P. C., Piquette-Tomei, N., Wood, E., Deleveaux, G., & Sanghera-Sidhu, B. (2012). *A (pan-Canadian) cluster randomised control effectiveness trial of the ABRACADABRA web-based literacy program.* Manuscript under review.

Savage-Rumbaugh, E. S. (1986). *Ape language.* New York: Columbia University Press.

Savage-Rumbaugh, E. S. (1990). Language acquisition in a non-human species: Implications for the innateness debate. *Developmental Psychology, 26,* 599–620.

Savage-Rumbaugh, E. S., Sevcik, R. A., Brakke, K. E., & Rumbaugh, D. M. (1992). Symbols: Their communicative use, communication, and combination by bonobos (*Pan paniscus*). In L. P. Lipsitt & C. Rovee-Collier (Eds.), *Advances in infancy research* (Vol. 7, pp. 221–278). Norwood, NJ: Ablex.

Scarr, S. (1997). Why child care has little impact on most children's development. *Current Directions in Psychological Science, 6,* 143–147.

Scarr, S., Pakstis, A. J., Katz, S. H., & Barker, W. B.(1977). Absence of a relationship between degree of white ancestry and intellectual skills within a black population. *Human Genetics, 39,* 69–86.

Scarr, S., & Weinberg, R. A. (1976). IQ test performance of black children adopted by white families. *American Psychologist, 31,* 726–739.

Schab, F. R. (1990). Odors and the remembrance of things past. *Journal of Experimental Psychology: Learning, Memory, and Cognition, 16,* 648–655.

Schachter, D. L., Norman, K. A., & Koutstaal, W. (1998). The cognitive neuroscience of constructive memory. *Annual Review of Psychology, 49,* 289–318.

Schachter, S., & Singer, J. E. (1962). Cognitive, social, and physiological determinants of emotional state. *Psychological Review, 69,* 379–399.

Schaie, K. W. (2005). *Developmental influences on adult intelligence: The Seattle longitudinal study.* New York: Oxford University Press.

Scheier, M. F., Carver, C. S., & Bridge, M. W. (2001). Optimism, pessimism and psychological well-being. In E. C. Chang (Ed.), *Optimism and pessimism: Implications for theory, research, and practice* (pp. 189–217). Washington, DC: American Psychological Association.

Schenk, C. H., & Mahowald, M. W. (2000). Parasomnias: Managing bizarre sleep-related behavior disorders. *Post-graduate Medicine, 107,* 145–156.

Scherer, K. R., & Wallbott, H. G. (1994). Evidence for universality and cultural variation of differential emotion response patterning. *Journal of Personality and Social Psychology, 66,* 310–328.

Schieber, M. H., & Hibbard, L. S. (1993). How somatotopic is the motor cortex hand area? *Science, 261,* 489–492.

Schiff, M., & Lewontin, R. (1986). *Education and class: The irrelevance of IQ genetic studies.* Oxford: Clarendon.

Schiller, F. (1993). *Paul Broca: Explorer of the brain.* Oxford: Oxford University Press.

Schlaug, G., Jancke, L., Huang, Y., & Steinmetz, H. (1995). In vivo evidence of structural brain asymmetry in musicians. *Science, 267,* 699–700.

Schmitt, N., Fuchs, A., & Kirch, W. (2008). Mental health disorders and work-life balance. In A. Linos, & W. Kirch (Eds.), *Promoting health for working women* (pp. 117–136). New York: Springer.

Schneider, W., & Pressley, M. (1997). *Memory development between 2 and 20.* Hillsdale, NJ: Lawrence Erlbaum Associates.

Schooler, N. R., Keith, S. J., Severe, J. B., Matthews, S. M., Bellack, A. S., Glick, I. D., . . . Woerner, M. G. (1997). Relapse and rehospitalization during maintenance treatment of schizophrenia: The effects of dose reduction and family treatment. *Archives of General Psychiatry, 54,* 453–463.

Schou, M. (1997). Forty years of lithium treatment. *Archives of General Psychiatry, 54,* 9–13.

Schredl, M., & Reinhard, I. (2008). Gender differences in dream recall: A meta-analysis. *Journal of Sleep Research, 17*(2), 125–131.

Schreurs, B. G. (1989). Classical conditioning of model systems: A behavioral review. *Psychobiology, 17,* 145–155.

Schultz, W. (2006). Behavioral theories and the neurophysiology of reward. In S. Fiske, A. Kazdin, & D. Schacter (Eds.), *Annual Review of Psychology* (Vol. 57, pp. 87–116). Palo Alto, CA: Annual Reviews.

Schulz, R. A. (1991). Second language acquisition theories and teaching practice: How do they fit? *The Modern Language Journal, 75*(1), 17–25.

Schuman, E. M., & Madison, D. V. (1994). Locally distributed synaptic potentiation in the hippocampus. *Science, 263,* 532–536.

Schwartz, G. E. (1982). Testing the biopsychosocial model: The ultimate challenge facing behavioral medicine? *Journal of Consulting and Clinical Psychology, 50,* 1040–1052.

Scott, A. I., & Fraser, T. (2008). Decreased usage of electroconvulsive therapy: Implications. *British Journal of Psychiatry, 192,* 476.

Scott, J. (1996). Cognitive therapy of affective disorders: A review. *Journal of Affective Disorders, 37,* 1–11.

Scott, S. K., Young, A. W., Calder, A. J., Hellawell, D. J., Aggleton, J. P., & Johnson, M. (1997). Impaired auditory recognition of fear and anger following bilateral amygdala lesions. *Nature, 385,* 254–257.

Seara-Cardoso, A., & Viding, E. (2014). Functional neuroscience of psychopathic personality in adults. *Journal of Personality.* Online pre-release.

Segall, M. H., Campbell, D. T., & Herskovitz, M. J. (1966). *The influence of culture on visual perception.* Indianapolis, IA: Bobbs-Merrill.

Segall, R. (2000). Online shrinks: The inside story. *Psychology Today, 32*(3), 38–43.

Séguin, M., Renaud, J., Lesage, A., Robert, M., & Turecki, G. (2011). Youth and young adult suicide: A study of life trajectory. *Journal of Psychiatric Research, 45*(7), 863–870.

Sejnowski, T. (1997). The year of the dendrite. *Science, 275,* 178–79.

Self, M. W., & Zeki, S. (2005). The integration of colour and motion by the human visual brain. *Cerebral Cortex, 15,* 1270–1279.

Seligman, M. E. P. (1970). On the generality of the laws of learning. *Psychological Review, 77,* 406–418.

Seligman, M. E. P. (1972). Phobias and preparedness. In M. E. P. Seligman & J. L. Hager (Eds.), *Biological boundaries of learning.* Englewood Cliffs, NJ: Prentice Hall.

Seligman, M. E. P. (1990). *Learned optimism: How to change your mind and your life.* New York: Simon & Shuster.

Seligman, M. E. P. (1995). The effectiveness of psychotherapy: The *Consumer Reports* study. *American Psychologist, 50,* 965–974.

Seligman, M. E. P. (1996). Science as an ally of practice. *American Psychologist, 51,* 1072–1079.

Seligman, M. E. P., & Csikszentmihalyi, M. (2000). Positive psychology: An introduction. *American Psychologist, 55,* 5–14.

Selye, H. (1956). *The stress of life.* New York: McGraw-Hill.

Selye, H. (1974). *Stress without distress.* Philadelphia: Lippincott.

Serkh, K., & Forger, D. B. (2014). Optimal schedules of light exposure for rapidly correcting circadian misalignment. *PLoS computational Biology, 10*(4), e1003523.

Shah, M., & Jeffery, R. W. (1991). Is obesity due to overeating and inactivity, or to a defective metabolic rate? A review. *Annals of Behavioral Medicine, 13,* 73–81.

Shapiro, F. (1989). Eye movement desensitization: A new treatment for post-traumatic stress disorder. *Journal of Behavior Therapy and Experimental Psychiatry, 20,* 211–217.

Shapiro, F. (2001). *Eye movement desensitization and reprocessing: Basic principles, protocols and procedures* (2nd ed.). New York: The Guilford Press.

Shapiro, F., & Maxfield, L. (2002). Eye movement desensitization and reprocessing (EMDR): Information processing in the treatment of trauma. *Journal of Clinical Psychology, 58*, 933–948.

Sharma, S., & Sharma, M. (2010). Self, social identity and psychological well-being. *Psychological Studies, 55*(2), 118–136.

Shaw, J. S., III. (1996). Increases in eyewitness confidence resulting from postevent questioning. *Journal of Experimental Psychology: Applied, 2*, 126–146.

Shears, J., Robinson, J., & Emde, R. (2002). Fathering relationships and their associations with juvenile delinquency. *Infant Mental Health Journal, 23*, 79–87.

Sheehan, D. V., & Raj, A. B. (1988). Monoamine oxidase inhibitors. In C. G. Last & M. Hersen (Eds.), *Handbook of anxiety disorders* (pp. 478–506). New York: Pergamon Press.

Shepard, R. N., & Metzler, J. (1971). Mental rotation of three-dimensional objects. *Science, 171*, 701–703.

Sher, J. (2011). One-quarter of Canadian soldiers return from Afghanistan with mental-health problems. *The Globe and Mail.* Retrieved on May 5, 2012, from http://m.theglobeandmail.com/news/national/one-quarter-of-canadian-soldiers-return-from-afghanistan-with-mental-health-problems/article2040698/?service=mobile

Sherif, M. (1956). Experiments in group conflict. *Scientific American, 195*, 53–58.

Sherif, M. (1958). Superordinate goals in the reduction of intergroup conflict. *American Journal of Sociology, 63*, 349–358.

Sherif, M., & Sherif, C. W. (1967). The Robbers' Cave study. In J. F. Perez, R. C. Sprinthall, G. S. Grosser, & P. J. Anastasiou (Eds.), *General psychology: Selected readings* (pp. 411–421). Princeton, NJ: Van Nostrand.

Sherman, J. W., Kruschke, J. K., Sherman, S. J., Percy, E. J., Petrocelli, J. V., & Conrey, F. R. (2009). Attentional processes in stereo-type formation: A common model for category accentuation and illusory correlation. *Journal of Personality and Social Psychology, 96*, 305–323.

Sheth, K. (2005, July 28). Sleepwalking. Medline Plu. Retrieved July 28, 2006, from http://www.nlm.nih.gov/medlineplus/ency/article/000808.htm

Shiffrin, R. M. (1970). Forgetting: Trace erosion or retrieval failure? *Science, 168*, 1601–1603.

Shiffrin, R. M., & Atkinson, R. C. (1969). Storage and retrieval processes in long-term memory. *Psychological Review, 76*, 179–193.

Shimamura, A. P., Brerry, J. M., Mangela, J. A., Rusting, C. L., & Jurica, P. J. (1995). Memory and cognitive abilities in university professors: Evidence for successful aging. *Psychological Science, 6*, 271–277.

Shinar, D., Tractinsky, N., & Compton, R. (2005). Effects of practice, age, and task demands, on interference from a phone task while driving. *Accident Analysis & Prevention, 37*, 315–326.

Shorter, D., Domingo, C. B., & Kosten, T. R. (2014). Emerging drugs for the treatment of cocaine use disorder: A review of neurobiological targets and pharmacotherapy. *Expert Opinion on Emerging Drugs, 20*(1), 15–29.

Shulman, H. G. (1972). Semantic confusion errors in short-term memory. *Journal of Verbal Learning and Verbal Behavior, 11*, 221–227.

Siegel, S., Hinson, R. E., Krank, M. D., & McCully, J. (1982). Heroin "overdose" death: Contribution of drug-associated environmental cues. *Science, 216*, 436–437.

Siegler, R. S. (1991). *Children's thinking* (2nd ed.). Englewood Cliffs, NJ: Prentice-Hall.

Silberg, J. L. (2014). Dissociative disorders in children and adolescents. In M. Lewis and K. D. Rudolph (Eds.), *Handbook of Developmental Psychopathology* (pp. 761–775). New York: Springer US.

Simon, L., Greenberg, J., & Brehm, J. (1995). Trivialization: The forgotten mode of dissonance reduction. *Journal of Personality and Social Psychology, 68*, 247–260.

Simons, D. J., & Chabris, C. F. (1999). Gorillas in our midst: Sustained inattentional blindness for dynamic events. *Perception, 28*, 1059–1074.

Simons, D. J., & Rensink, R. (2005). Change blindness: Past, present, and future. *Trends in Cognitive Sciences, 9*, 16–20.

Singareddy, R., Vgontzas, A. N., Fernandez-Mendoza, J., Liao, D., Calhoun, S., Shaffer, M. L., & Bixler, E. O. (2012). Risk factors for incident chronic insomnia: a general population prospective study. *Sleep Medicine, 13*(4), 346–353.

Singh, B. R. (1991). Teaching methods for reducing prejudice and enhancing academic achievement for all children. *Educational Studies, 17*, 157–171.

Singh, D., & Singh, D. (2011). Shape and significance of feminine beauty: An evolutionary perspective. *Sex Roles, 64*(9–10), 723–731.

Sinha, R. (2013). The clinical neurobiology of drug craving. *Current opinion in neurobiology, 23*(4), 649–654.

Skinner, B. F. (1953). *Science and human behavior.* New York: Macmillan.

Skinner, B. F. (1957). *Verbal behavior.* New York: Appleton-Century-Crofts.

Skinner, B. F. (1988). The operant side of behavior therapy. *Journal of Behavior Therapy and Experimental Psychiatry, 19*, 171–179.

Skitka, L. J., & Sargis, E. G. (2006). The internet as a psychological laboratory. *Annual Review of Psychology, 57*, 529–555.

Slawinski, E. B., Hartel, D. M., & Kline, D. W. (1993). Self-reported hearing problems in daily life throughout adulthood. *Psychology and Aging, 8*, 552–561.

Slobin, D. (1972, July). Children and language: They learn the same all around the world. *Psychology Today*, 71–74, 82.

Smith, C., Jeneson, A., Frascino, J., Brock-Kirwan, C., Hopkins, R., & Squire, L. (2014). When recognition memory is independent of hippocampal function. *Proceedings of The National Academy of Sciences of the United States, 111*(27), 9935–9940.

Smith, C. T., De Houwer, J., & Nosek, B. A. (2013). Consider the source persuasion of implicit evaluations is moderated by source credibility. *Personality and Social Psychology Bulletin, 39*(2), 193–205.

Smith, M. L., Glass, G. V., & Miller, T. I. (1980). *The benefits of psychotherapy.* Baltimore, MD: Johns Hopkins University Press.

Smith, S., Handy, J., Angello, G., & Manzano, I. (2014) Effects of similarity on environmental context cueing, *Memory, 22*(5), 493–508.

Smoller, J. W., Block, S. R., & Young, M. M. (2009). Genetics of anxiety disorders: The complex road from DSM to DNA. *Depression and Anxiety, 26*, 965–975.

Snarey, J. R. (1985). Cross-cultural universality of social-moral development: A critical review of Kohlbergian research. *Psychological Bulletin, 97*, 202–232.

Snarey, J. R. (1995). In communitarian voice: The sociological expansion of Kohlbergian theory, research, and practice. In W. M. Kurtines & J. L. Gerwirtz (Eds.), *Moral development: An introduction* (pp. 109–134). Boston: Allyn & Bacon.

Snyder, D. K., Castellani, A. M., & Whisman, M. A. (2006). Current status and future directions in couple therapy. *Annual Review of Psychology, 57*, 317–344.

Snyder, S. H. (1984, November). Medicated minds. *Science, 84*, 141–142.

Soares-Weiser, K., & Fernandez, H. (2007). Tardive dyskinesia. *Seminars in Neurology, 27*, 159–69.

Soederberg Miller, L. (2009). Age differences in the effects of domain knowledge on reading efficiency. *Psychology and Aging, 24*, 63–74.

Soffer-Dudek, N., Shalev, H., Shiber, A., & Shahar, G. (2011). Role of severe psychopathology in sleep-related experiences: A pilot study. *Dreaming, 21*(2), 148–156.

Sohn, C. H., & Lam, R. W. (2005). Update on the biology of seasonal affective disorder. *CNS Spectrum, 10*, 635–646.

Sokolov, E. N. (2000). Perception and the conditioning reflex: Vector encoding. *International Journal of Psychophysiology, 35*, 197–217.

Soler, J., Pascual, J. C., Campins, J., Barrachina, J., Puigdemont, D., Alvarez, E., & Pérez, V. (2005). Double-blind, placebo-controlled study of dialectical behavior therapy plus olanzapine for borderline personality disorder. *American Journal of Psychiatry, 162*, 1221–1224.

Soler, H., Vinayak, P., & Quadagno, D. (2000). Biosocial aspects of domestic violence. *Psychoneuroendocrinology, 25*, 721–739.

Solomon, R. L. (1964). Punishment. *American Psychologist, 19*, 239–253.

Solso, R. (1991). *Cognitive psychology* (3rd ed.). Boston: Allyn & Bacon.

Son, L. (2004). Spacing one's study: Evidence for a metacognitive control strategy. *Journal of Experimental Psychology: Learning, Memory, and Cognition, 30*(3), 601–604.

Southwick, S. M., Gilmartin, R., Mcdonough, P., & Morrissey, P. (2006). Logotherapy as an adjunctive treatment for chronic combat-related PTSD: A meaning-based intervention. *American Journal of Psychotherapy, 60*, 161–174.

Spanos, N. (1991). A sociocognitive approach to hypnosis. In S. J. Lynn & J. R. Ruhe (Eds.), *Hypnosis theories: Current models and perspectives* (pp. 324–361). New York: Guilford Press.

Spearman, C. (1927). *The abilities of man*. New York: Macmillan.

Spencer, R. M. C., Zelaznik, H. N., Diedrichsen, J., & Ivry, R. B. (2003). Disrupted timing of discontinuous but not continuous movements by cerebellar lesions. *Science, 300*, 1437–1439.

Sperling, G. (1960). The information available in brief visual presentations. *Psychological Monographs: General and Applied, 74*(Whole No. 498), 1–29.

Sperry, R. W. (1964). The great cerebral commissure. *Scientific American, 210*, 42–52.

Sperry, R. W. (1966). Brain bisection and consciousness. In J. Eccles (Ed.), *Brain and conscious experience*. New York: Springer-Verlag.

Sperry, R. W. (1968). Hemisphere deconnection and unity in conscious experience. *American Psychologist, 23*, 723–733.

Spetch, M. L., Wilkie, D. M., & Pinel, J. P. J. (1981). Backward conditioning: A reevaluation of the empirical evidence. *Psychological Bulletin, 89*, 163–175.

Spiegel, D., Lewis-Fernández, R., Lanius, R., Vermetten, E., Simeon, D., & Friedman, M. (2013). Dissociative disorders in DSM-5. *Annual Review of Clinical Psychology, 9*, 299–326.

Spiers, H. J., Maguire, E. A., & Burgess, N. (2001). Hippocampal amnesia. *Neurocase, 7*, 357–382.

Spitz, R. A. (1946). Hospitalism: A follow-up report on investigation described in volume I, 1945. *The Psychoanalytic Study of the Child, 2*, 113–117.

Spitzer, M. W., & Semple, M. N. (1991). Interaural phase coding in auditory midbrain: Influence of dynamic stimulus features. *Science, 254*, 721–724.

Spooner, A., & Kellogg, W. N. (1947). The backward conditioning curve. *American Journal of Psychology, 60*, 321–334.

Springer, S. P., & Deutsch, G. (1985). *Left brain, right brain* (rev. ed.). New York: W. H. Freeman.

Squire, L. R. (1986). Memory functions as affected by electroconvulsive therapy. *Annals of the New York Academy of Sciences, 462*, 307–314.

Squire, L. R. (1992). Memory and the hippocampus: A synthesis from findings with rats, monkeys, and humans. *Psychological Review, 99*, 195–231.

Squire, L. R., Knowlton, B., & Musen, G. (1993). The structure and organization of memory. *Annual Review of Psychology, 44*, 453–495.

Stasik, S. M., Naragon-Gainey, K., Chmielewski, M., & Watson, D. (2012). Core OCD symptoms: Exploration of specificity and relations with psychopathology. *Journal of Anxiety Disorders, 26*(8), 859–870.

Statistics Canada. (2004, July 21). Health reports: Use of cannabis and other illicit drugs. *The Daily*. Retrieved May 29, 2006, from http://www.statcan.ca/Daily/English/040721/d040721a.htm

Statistics Canada. (2008). Role life balance and role overload of shift workers. *The Daily*. Retrieved March 2, 2009, from http://www.statcan.gc.ca/daily-quotidien/080827/dq080827d-eng.htm

Statistics Canada. (2009a). Average hourly wages of employees by selected characteristics and profession, unadjusted data, by province (monthly). Retrieved May 6, 2009, from http://www40.statcan.gc.ca/l01/cst01/labr69a-eng.htm

Statistics Canada. (2009b). Crimes by offences, by provinces and territories. Retrieved May 6, 2009, from http://www40.statcan.gc.ca/l01/cst01/legal04a-eng.htm

Statistics Canada. (2011a, January 19). Canadian Health Measures Survey: Physical activity of youth and adults. *The Daily*. Retrieved on April 5, 2012, from http://www.statcan.gc.ca/daily-quotidien/110119/dq110119b-eng.htm

Statistics Canada. (2011b). Overweight and obese adults (self-reported), 2010. Retrieved on April 1, 2012, from http://www.statcan.gc.ca/pub/82-625-x/2011001/article/11464-eng.htm

Statistics Canada. (2012a). Police-reported hate crimes, 2010. Retrieved on April 18, 2012, from http://www.statcan.gc.ca/daily-quotidien/120412/dq120412b-eng.htm

Statistics Canada. (2012b). Suicide. Retrieved May 16, 2012, from http://www.statcan.gc.ca/search-recherche/bb/info/3000019-eng.htm

Statistics Canada (2013). Police-reported crime statistics in Canada, 2013. Retrieved on June 18, 2015, from http://www.statcan.gc.ca/pub/85-002-x/2014001/article/14040-eng.htm

Statistics Canada (2014a). CANSIM, table 102-0551. Retrieved June 27, 2015, at http://www.statcan.gc.ca/tables-tableaux/sum-som/l01/cst01/hlth66d-eng.htm

Statistics Canada. (2014b). Canadian Forces Mental Health Survey, 2013. *The Daily*, Retrieved on February 24, 2015, from http://www.statcan.gc.ca/daily-quotidien/140811/dq140811a-eng.htm

Stead, L. F., Perera, R., Bullen, C., Mant, D., & Lancaster, T. (2008). Nicotine replacement therapy for smoking cessation. *The Cochrane Library*.

Steele, J., & Mays, S. (1995). Handedness and directional asymmetry in the long bones of the human upper limb. *International Journal of Osteoarchaeology, 5*, 39–49.

Steffens, A. B., Scheurink, A. J., & Luiten, P. G. (1988). Hypothalamic food intake regulating areas are involved in the homeostasis of blood glucose and plasma FFA levels. *Physiology and Behavior, 44*, 581–589.

Stein, L., Xue, B. G., & Belluzzi, J. D. (1993). Cellular targets of brain reinforcement systems. *Annals of the New York Academy of Sciences, 702*, 41–45.

Steinberg, L. (2005). Cognitive and affective development in adolescence. *Trends in Cognitive Science, 9*(2), 69–74.

Steinberg, L., Elman, J. D., & Mounts, N. S. (1989). Authoritative parenting, psychosocial maturity, and academic success among adolescents. *Child Development, 60*, 1424–1436.

Stephan, K. M., Fink, G. R., Passingham, R. E., Silbersweig, D., Ceballos-Baumann, A. O., Frith, C. D., & Frackowiak, R. S. J. (1995). Functional anatomy of the mental representation of upper extremity movements in healthy subjects. *Journal of Neurophysiology, 73,* 373–386.

Steptoe, A., & Kivimäki, M. (2012). Stress and cardiovascular disease. *Nature Reviews Cardiology, 9*(6), 360–370.

Stern, L. D. (1981). A review of theories of human amnesia. *Memory & Cognition, 9,* 247–262.

Stern, W. (1914). *The psychological methods of testing intelligence.* Baltimore: Warwick and York.

Sternberg, R. J. (1985). *Beyond IQ: A triarchic theory of human intelligence.* New York: Cambridge University Press.

Sternberg, R. J. (1986). A triangular theory of love. *Psychological Review, 93,* 119–135.

Sternberg, R. J. (1987). Liking versus loving: A comparative evaluation of theories. *Psychological Bulletin, 102,* 331–345.

Sternberg, R. J. (2006). A duplex theory of love. In R. Sternberg, & K. Weis (Eds.). *The new psychology of love.* New Haven, CT: Yale University Press.

Stewart, N. (2009). The cost of anchoring on credit-card minimum repayments. *Psychological Science, 20,* 39–41.

Stewart, T. L., Latu, I. M., Kawakami, K., & Myers, A. C. (2010). Consider the situation: Reducing automatic stereotyping through Situational Attribution Training. *Journal of Experimental Social Psychology, 46*(1), 221–225.

Stinson, D. A., Cameron, J. J., Wood, J. V., Gaucher, D., & Holmes, J. G. (2009). Deconstructing the "reign of error": Interpersonal warmth explains the self-fulfilling prophecy of anticipated acceptance. *Personality and Social Psychology Bulletin, 35*(9), 1165–1178.

Stores, G. (2009). Aspects of parasomnias in childhood and adolescence. *Archives of Disease in Childhood, 94*(1), 63–69.

Strack, F., Martin, L. L., & Stepper, S. (1988). Inhibiting and facilitating conditions of facial expressions: A nonobtrusive test of the facial feedback hypothesis. *Journal of Personality and Social Psychology, 54,* 768–777.

Strayer, D. L., & Drews, F. A. (2004). Profiles in driver distraction: Effects of cell phone conversations on younger and older drivers. *Human Factors, 46,* 640–649.

Stroebe, M., & Schut, H. (1999). The dual process model of coping with bereavement: Rationale and description. *Death Studies, 23,* 197–224.

Strome, M., & Vernick, D. (1989, April). Hearing loss and hearing aids. *Harvard Medical School Health Letter, 14,* 5–8.

Stromeyer, C. F., III. (1970, November). Eidetikers. *Psychology Today,* 76–80.

Stubbs, P. (2000). *Mental health care online.*

Stuss, D. T., Gow, C. A., & Hetherington, C. R. (1992). "No longer Gage": Frontal lobe dysfunction and emotional changes. *Journal of Consulting and Clinical Psychology, 60,* 349–359.

Suchecki, D., Tiba, P. A., & Machado, R. B. (2012). REM sleep rebound as an adaptive response to stressful situations. *Frontiers in Neurology, 3,* 41. doi:10.3389/fneur.2012.00041

Sue, D. (1994). *Counseling the culturally different: Theory and practice.* New York: Wiley.

Sugita, M., & Shiba, Y. (2005). Genetic tracing shows segregation of taste neuronal circuitries for bitter and sweet. *Science, 309,* 781–785.

Sullivan, A. M., Maerz, J. C., & Madison, D. M. (2002). Anti-predator response of red-backed salamanders (*Plethodon cinereus*) to chemical cues from garter snakes (*Thamnophis sirtalis*): Laboratory and field experiments. *Behavioral Ecology & Sociobiology, 51,* 227–233.

Sullivan, P. F., Neale, M. C., & Kendler, K. S. (2000). Genetic epidemiology of major depression: review and meta-analysis. *Genetic Epidemiology, 157*(10), 1552–1562.

Sulzer, D. (2011). How addictive drugs disrupt presynaptic dopamine neurotransmission. *Neuron, 69*(4), 628–649.

Sung, K. (2008). Serial and parallel attentive visual searches: Evidence from cumulative distribution functions of response times. *Journal of Experimental Psychology: Human Perception and Performance, 34,* 1372–1388.

Suppes, T., Baldessarini, R. J., Faedda, G. L., & Tohen, M. (1991). Risk of recurrence following discontinuation of lithium treatment in bipolar disorder. *Archives of General Psychiatry, 48,* 1082–1088.

Suthana, N., Ekstrom, A., Moshirsaviri, S., Knowlton, B., & Bookheimer, S. (2011). Dissociations within human hippocampal subregions during encoding and retrieval of spatial information. *Hippocampus, 21*(7), 694–701.

Swanson, A. (2015). The number of Fortune 500 companies lead by women is at an all-time high: 5 percent. *The Washington Post.* Retrieved on June 18, 2015, from http://www.washingtonpost.com/blogs/wonkblog/wp/2015/06/04/the-number-of-fortune-500-companies-led-by-women-is-at-an-all-time-high-5-percent/

Swartz, C. M., & Shorter, E. (2007). *Psychotic depression.* New York: Cambridge University Press.

Sweatt, J. D., & Kandel, E. R. (1989). Persistent and transcriptionally-dependent increase in protein phosphorylation in long-term facilitation of Aplysia sensory neurons. *Nature, 339,* 51–54.

Swedo, S. E., Leonard, L. H., Garvey, M., Mittleman, B., Allen, A. J., Perlmutter, S., . . . Dubbert, B. K. (2004). Pediatric autoimmune neuropsychiatric disorders associated with streptococcal infections: Clinical description of the first 50 cases. *Focus, 2,* 496–506.

Sweller, J., & Levine, M. (1982). Effects of goal specificity on means-end analysis and learning. *Journal of Experimental Psychology: Learning, Memory, and Cognition, 8,* 463–474.

Swets, J. A. (1992). The science of choosing the right decision threshold in high-stakes diagnostics. *American Psychologist, 47,* 522–532.

Swets, J. A. (1998). Separating discrimination and decision in detection, recognition, and matters of life and death. In D. Scarborough, S. Sternberg et al. (Eds.), *Methods, models and conceptual issues: An invitation to cognition sciences* (Vol. 4, pp. 635–702). Cambridge, MA: MIT Press.

Symister, P., & Friend, R. (2003). The influence of social support and problematic support on optimism and depression in chronic illness: A prospective study evaluating self-esteem as a mediator. *Health Psychology, 22,* 123–129.

Symons, C. S., & Johnson, B. T. (1997). The self-reference effect in memory: A meta-analysis. *Psychological Bulletin, 121*(3), 371–394.

Szeszko, P. R., Robinson, D. G., Ashtari, M., Vogel, J., Betensky, J., Sevy, S., . . . & Bilder, R. M. (2008). Clinical and neuropsychological correlates of white matter abnormalities in recent onset schizophrenia. *Neuropsychopharmacology, 33*(5), 976–984.

Szymanski, K., & Harkins, S. G. (1987). Social loafing and self-evaluation with a social standard. *Journal of Personality and Social Psychology, 53,* 891–897.

Taaffe, D. R., Irie, F., Masaki, K. H., Abbott, R. D., Petrovitch, H., Ross, G. W., & White, L. R. (2008). Physical activity, physical function, and incident dementia in elderly men: The Honolulu-Asia Aging Study. *Journal of Gerontology: Series A: Biological Sciences and Medical Sciences, 63A,* 529–535.

Tajfel, H. (1982). Social psychology of intergroup relations. *Annual Review of Psychology, 33,* 1–39.

Tamminga, C., & Vogel, M. (2005). Images in neuroscience: The cerebellum. *American Journal of Psychiatry, 162,* 1253.

Tanda, G., Pontieri, F. E., & Di Chiara, G. (1997). Cannabinoid and heroin activation of mesolimbic dopamine transmission by a common m opioid receptor mechanism. *Science, 276*, 2048–2050.

Tangney, R. (2008). An informal online learning community for student mental health at university: A preliminary investigation. *British Journal of Guidance and Counselling, 36*(1), 81–97.

Tanner, J. M. (1990). *Fetus into man* (2nd ed.). Cambridge MA: Harvard University Press.

Tashkin, D. (2006). No link between marijuana use and lung cancer. Paper presented at the 102nd International Conference of the American Thoracic Society, San Diego, May 19–24, 2006.

Tay, C., Ang, S., & Van Dyne, L. (2006). Personality, biographical characteristics, and job interview success: A longitudinal study of

Taylor, C., & Luce, K. (2003). Computer- and internet-based psychotherapy interventions. *Current Directions in Psychological Science, 12*, 18–22.

Taylor, L. S., Fiore, A. T., Mendelsohn, G. A., & Cheshire, C. (2011). "Out of my league": A real-world test of the matching hypothesis. *Personality and Social Psychology Bulletin, 37*(7), 942–954.

Taylor, S. E. (1991). *Health psychology* (2nd ed.). New York: McGraw-Hill.

Taylor, S. E. (2008). Current issues and new directions in *Psychology and Health*: Bringing basic and applied research together to address underlying mechanisms. *Psychology & Health, 23*, 131–134.

Taylor, S. E., & Brown, J. D. (1988). Illusion of well-being: A social psychological perspective on mental health. *Psychological Bulletin, 103*, 193–210.

Tchanturia, K., Liao, P. C., Uher, R., Lawrence, N., Treasure, J., & Campbell, I. C. (2007). An investigation of decision making in anorexia nervosa using the Iowa Gambling Task and skin conductance measurements. *Journal of the International Neuropsychological Society, 13*, 1–7.

Tefikow, S., Barth, J., Maichrowitz, S., Beelmann, A., Strauss, B., & Rosendahl, J. (2013). Efficacy of hypnosis in adults undergoing surgery or medical procedures: A meta-analysis of randomized controlled trials. *Clinical Psychology Review, 33*(5), 623–636.

Tel, H. (2013). Sleep quality and quality of life among the elderly people. *Neurology, Psychiatry and Brain Research, 19*(1), 48–52.

Tellegen, A., Lykken, D. T., Bouchard, T. J., Jr., Wilcox, K. J., Segal, N. L., & Rich, S. (1988). Personality similarity in twins reared apart and together. *Journal of Personality and Social Psychology, 54*, 1031–1039.

Teng, E., Stefanacci, L., Squire, L. R., & Zola, S. M. (2000). Contrasting effects on discrimination learning after hippocampal lesions and conjoint hippocampal-caudate lesions in monkeys. *Journal of Neuroscience, 20*, 3853–3863.

Terman, G. W., Shavit, Y., Lewis, J. W., Cannon, J. T., & Liebeskind, J. C. (1984). Intrinsic mechanisms of pain inhibition: Activation by stress. *Science, 226*, 1270–1277.

Terman, L. M., & Oden, M. H. (1947). *Genetic studies of genius, Vol. 4: The gifted child grows up*. Stanford, CA: Stanford University Press.

Terman, M., & Terman, J. S. (2005). Light therapy for seasonal and nonseasonal depression: Efficacy, protocol, safety, and side effects. *CNS Spectrum, 10*, 647–663.

Terracciano, A., McCrae, R. R., & Costa, P. T., Jr. (2010). Intra-individual Change in Personality Stability and Age. *Journal of Research in Personality, 44*(1), 31–37.

Terry, W. S. (1988). Everyday forgetting: Data from a diary study. *Psychological Reports, 62*, 299–303.

Teuting, P., Koslow, S. H., & Hirschfeld, R. M. A. (1981). Special report on depression research. Rockville, MD: U.S. Department of Health & Human Services.

Thase, M. E., Frank, E., Mallinger, A. G., Hammer, T., & Kupfer, D. J. (1992). Treatment of imipramine-resistant recurrent depression, III: Efficacy of monoamine oxidise inhibitors. *Journal of Clinical Psychiatry, 53*(1, Suppl.), 5–11.

Thase, M. E., & Kupfer, D. (1996). Recent developments in the pharmacotherapy of mood disorders. *Journal of Consulting and Clinical Psychology, 64*, 646–659.

Thoits, P. A. (2011). Mechanisms linking social ties and support to physical and mental health. *Journal of Health and Social Behavior, 52*(2), 145–161.

Thorsteinsson, E., & Brown, R. (2009). Mediators and moderators of the stressor-fatigue relationship in nonclinical samples. *Journal of Psychosomatic Research, 66*, 21–29.

Thurstone, L. L. (1938). *Primary mental abilities*. Chicago: University of Chicago Press.

Tidey, J. W., O'Neill, S. C., & Higgins, S. T. (2002, August). Contingent monetary reinforcement of smoking reductions, with and without transdermal nicotine, in outpatients with schizophrenia. *Experimental & Clinical Psychopharmacology, 10*(3), 241–247.

Tijdens, K.G., & Van Klaveren, M. (2012). *Frozen in time: Gender pay gap unchanged for 10 years*. Brussels: ITUC.

Tjepkema, M. (2005a). Adult obesity in Canada: Measured in heights and weights. *Nutrition: Findings from the Canadian Community Health Survey, no. 1*. Ottawa: Statistics Canada. Retrieved March 20, 2009, from http://www.statcan.gc.ca/pub/82-620-m/2005001/article/adults-adultes/8060-eng.htm

Tjepkema, M. (2005b). Insomnia. *Health reports, 17*(1), 9–25. Statistics Canada, Canadian Centre for Health Information. Retrieved August 4, 2012, from http://www.statcan.gc.ca/ads-annonces/82-003-x/pdf/4225221-eng.pdf

Tohen, M., Zarate Jr, C. A., Hennen, J., Khalsa, H. M. K., Strakowski, S. M., Gebre-Medhin, P., . . . & Baldessarini, R. J. (2003). The McLean-Harvard first-episode mania study: prediction of recovery and first recurrence. *American Journal of Psychiatry, 160*(12), 2099–2107.

Tomasello, M. (2000). First steps toward a usage-based theory of language acquisition. *Cognitive Linguistics, 11*(1/2), 61–82.

Tomkins, S. (1962). *Affect, imagery, and consciousness: The positive effects* (Vol. 1). New York: Springer.

Tomkins, S. (1963). *Affect, imagery, and consciousness: The negative effects* (Vol. 2). New York: Springer.

Tomko, J. K. & Munley, P. H. (2013). Predicting counselling psychologists' attitudes and clinical judgments with respect to older adults. *Aging and Mental Health, 17*(2), 233–241.

Topolinski, S., & Strack, F. (2009). The architecture of intuition: Fluency and affect determine intuitive judgments of semantic and visual coherence and judgments of grammaticality in artificial grammar learning. *Journal of Experimental Psychology: General, 138*, 39–63.

Tordoff, M. G. (1988). Sweeteners and appetite. In G. M. Williams (Ed.), *Sweeteners: Health effects* (pp. 53–60). Princeton, NJ: Princeton Scientific.

Torrey, E. F. (1983). *Surviving schizophrenia: A family manual*. New York: Harper & Row.

Toson, A. E. (2011). Impact of marijuana smoking on liver and sex hormones: Correlation with oxidative stress. *Nature and Science, 9*, 76–87.

Totterdell, P., & Kellett, S. (2008). Restructuring mood in cyclothymia using cognitive behavior therapy: An intensive time-sampling study. *Journal of Clinical Psychology, 64*, 501–518.

Traub, R., & Whittington, M. (2014). Delta rhythms: Models and physiology. In *Encyclopedia of Computational Neuroscience* (pp. 1–8). New York: Springer.

Tremblay, R. E. (2002, July). The development of human physical aggression: How important is early childhood? Paper presented at Johnson & Johnson Pediatric Institute Pediatric Roundtable, Rome.

Tremblay, R. E. (2003). Why socialization fails: The case of chronic physical aggression. In B. B. Lahey, T. E. Moffitt, & A. Caspi (Eds.), *The causes of conduct disorder and serious juvenile delinquency*. New York: Guilford Press.

Trijsburg, W. R., Trent, S. T., & Perry, C. J. (2004). An empirical study of the differences in interventions between psychodynamic therapy and cognitive-behavioural therapy for recurrent major depression. *Canadian Journal of Psychoanalysis, 12*, 325–345.

Triplett, N. (1898). The dynamogenic factors in pacemaking and competition. *American Journal of Psychology, 9*, 507–533.

Troglauer, T., Hels, T., & Christens, P. F. (2006). Extent and variations in mobile phone use among drivers of heavy vehicles in Denmark. *Accident Analysis & Prevention, 38*, 105–111.

Tulving, E. (1974). Cue-dependent forgetting. *American Scientist, 62*, 74–82.

Tulving, E. (1985). How many memory systems are there? *American Psychologist, 40*, 385–398.

Tulving, E. (1989). Remembering and knowing the past. *American Scientist, 77*, 361–367.

Tulving, E. (2002). Episodic memory: From mind to brain. *Annual Review of Psychology, 53*, 1–5.

Tulving, E., Schacter, D. L., McLachlan, D. R., & Moscovitch, M. (1988). Priming of semantic autobiographical knowledge: A case study of retrograde amnesia. *Brain and Cognition, 8*, 3–20.

Tulving, E., & Thompson, D. M. (1973). Encoding specificity and retrieval processes in episodic memory. *Psychological Review, 80*, 352–373.

Turecki, G., Ernst, C., Jollang, F., Labonté, B., & Mechawar, N. (2012). The neurodevelopmental origins of suicidal behavior. *Trends in Neuroscience, 35*(1), 14–23.

Turkheimer, E., & Waldron, M. (2000). Nonshared environment: A theoretical, methodological, and quantitative review. *Psychological Bulletin, 126*(1), 78.

Turner, J. C., Hogg, M. A., Oakes, P. J., Reicher, S. D., & Wetherell, M. S. (1987). *Rediscovering the social group: A self-categorization theory*. Oxford: Blackwell.

Turner, R., Hewstone, M., Voci, A., & Vonofakou, C. (2008). A test of extended intergroup contact hypothesis: The mediating role of intergroup anxiety, perceived ingroup and outgroup norms, and inclusion of the outgroup in the self. *Journal of Personality and Social Psychology, 95*, 843–860.

Tversky, A. (1972). Elimination by aspects: A theory of choice. *Psychological Review, 79*, 281–299.

Tversky, A., & Kahneman, D. (1974). Judgment under uncertainty: Heuristics and biases. *Science, 185*, 1124–1130.

Tyndale, R. F. (2003). Genetics of alcohol and tobacco use in humans. *Annals of Medicine, 3*, 94–121.

Uchino, B. N., & Birmingham, W. (2011). Stress and support processes. In B. N. Uchino and W. Birmingham (Eds.), *The handbook of stress science: Biology, psychology, and health* (pp. 111–121). New York: Springer.

Uhlhaas, P. J. (2011). The adolescent brain: implications for the understanding, pathophysiology, and treatment of schizophrenia. *Schizophrenia Bulletin, 37*(3), 480–483.

Uman, L. S., Chambers, C. T., McGrath, P. J., & Kisely, S. (2008). A systematic review of randomized controlled trials examining psychological interventions for needle-related procedural pain and distress in children and adolescents: An abbreviated Cochrone review. *Journal of Pediatric Psychology, 33*, 842–854.

Underwood, B. J. (1957). Interference and forgetting. *Psychological Review, 64*, 49–60.

Underwood, B. J. (1964). Forgetting. *Scientific American, 210*, 91–99.

University Health Network. (October 14, 2014). *From dark to light.* Toronto: University Health Network. Retrieved from http://www.uhn.ca/corporate/News/Pages/from_dark_to_light.aspx

University of Michigan Transportation Research Institute (UMTRI). (2012). Teen Driver Distraction Study Release available online at http://www.toyota.com/csrc/teen-driver-distraction-study-release.html

U.S. Food and Drug Administration. (2013). *How to evaluate health information on the Internet.* Retrieved March 1, 2015, from http://www.fda.gov/Drugs/ResourcesForYou/Consumers/BuyingUsingMedicineSafely/BuyingMedicinesOvertheInternet/ucm202863.htm

Vaillant, G. (2012). Lifting the field's "repression" of defenses. *American Journal of Psychiatry, 169*(9), 885–887.

Vaillant, G. E. (2000). Adaptive mental mechanisms: Their role in a positive psychology. *American Psychologist, 55*(1), 89–98.

Valtonen, H., Suominen, K., Haukka, J., Mantere, O., Arvilommi, P., Leppämäki, S., & Isometsä, E. (2009). Hopelessness across phases of bipolar I or II disorder: A prospective study. *Journal of Affective Disorders, 115*, 11–17.

Vandaelle, I. (2012, January, 17). Majority of Canadians support legalizing or decriminalizing marijuana, new poll suggests. *National Post.* Retrieved March 24, 2012, from http://news.nationalpost.com/2012/01/17/majority-of-canadians-support-legalizing-or-decriminalizing-marijuana-new-poll-suggests/

Vandell, D. L., & Mueller, E. C. (1980). Peer play and friendships during the first two years. In H. C. Foot, A. J. Chapman, & J. R. Smith (Eds.), *Friendship and social relations in children*. New York: Wiley.

van den Hout, M., & Merckelbach, H. (1991). Classical conditioning: Still going strong. *Behavioural Psychotherapy, 19*, 59–79.

Van der Elst, W., Van Boxtel, M. P. J., Van Breukelen, G. J. P., & Jolles, J. (2006). The Stroop color-word test: Influence of age, sex, and education; and normative data for a large sample across the adult age range. *Assessment, 13*, 62–79.

van der Kloet, D., Merckelbach, H., Giesbrecht, T., & Lynn, S. J. (2012). Fragmented sleep, fragmented mind. *Perspectives on Psychological Science, 7*(2), 159–175.

Van der Zee, K., Thijs, M., & Schakel, L. (2002). The relationship of emotional intelligence with academic intelligence and the Big Five. *European Journal of Personality, 16*, 103–125.

Vander Meer, R. K., & Alonso, L. E. (2002). Queen primer pheromone affects conspecific fire ant (*Solenopsis invicta*) aggression. *Behavioral Ecology & Sociobiology, 51*, 122–130.

van Dijk, A., Klompmakers, A., & Denys, D. (2008). Role of serotonin in obsessive-compulsive disorder. *Future Neurology, 3*, 589–603.

van Groen, T., Kadish, I., & Wyss, J. M. (2002). The role of the laterodorsal nucleus of the thalamus in spatial learning and memory in the rat. *Behavior and Brain Research, 136*, 329–337.

Van Lancker, D. R., Cummings, J. L., Kreiman, J., & Dobkin, B. H. (1988). Phonagnosia: A dissociation between familiar and unfamiliar voices. *Cortex, 24*, 195–209.

van Os, J., Kenis, G., & Rutten, B. P. (2010). The environment and schizophrenia. *Nature, 468*(7321), 203–212.

van Schoor, G., Bott, S. M., & Engels, R C.. (2008). Alcohol drinking in young adults: The predictive value of personality when peers come around. *European Addiction Research, 14*, 125–133.

Vargha-Khadem, F., Gadian, D. G., Watkins, K. E., Connelly, A., Van Paesschen, W., & Mishkin, M. (1997). Differential effects of early hippocampal pathology on episodic and semantic memory. *Science, 277*, 376–380.

Vasterling, J. J., Duke, L. M., Brailey, K., Constans, J. I., Allain, A. N., Jr., & Sutker, P. B. (2002). Attention, learning, and memory performances and intellectual resources in Vietnam veterans: PTSK and no disorder comparisons. *Neuropsychology, 16,* 5–14.

Veldhorst, M., Smeets, A., Soenen, S,. Hochstenbach-Waelen, A, Hursel, R., Dipvens, K., . . . Westerterp-Plantenga, M. (2008). Protein-induced satiety: Effects and mechanisms of different proteins. *Physiology & Behavior, 94,* 300–307.

Vermeersch, H., T'Sjoen, G., Kaufman, J.-M., & Vincke, J. (2008). The role of testosterone in aggressive and non-aggressive risk-taking in adolescent boys. *Hormones and Behavior, 53,* 463–471.

Verster, J., & Volkerts, E. (2004). Clinical pharmacology, clinical efficacy, and behavioral toxicity of alprazolam: A review of the literature. *CNS Drug Reviews, 10*(1), 45–76.

Vetter, C., Juda, M., & Roenneberg, T. (2012). The influence of internal time, time awake, and sleep duration on cognitive performance in shiftworkers. *Chronobiology international, 29*(8), 1127–1138.

Vetulani, J., & Nalepa, I. (2000). Antidepressants: Past, present and future. *European Journal of Pharmacology, 405,* 351–363.

Villani, S. (2001). Impact of media on children and adolescents: A 10-year review of the research. *Journal of the American Academy of Child & Adolescent Psychiatry, 40,* 392–401.

Vinokur, A., & Burnstein, E. (1978). Depolarization of attitudes in groups. *Journal of Personality and Social Psychology, 36,* 872–885.

Visser, P. S., & Mirabile, R. R. (2004). Attitudes in the social context: The impact of social network composition on individual-level attitude strength. *Journal of Personality and Social Psychology, 87,* 779–795.

Vogel, M., Braungardt, T., Meyer, W., & Schneider, W. (2012). The effects of shift work on physical and mental health. *Journal of Neural Transmission, 119*(10), 1121–1132.

Volkow, N. D., Wang, G.-J., Fowler, J. S., Logan, J., Gatley, S. J., Hitzemann, R., . . . Pappas, N. (1997). Decreased striatal dopaminergic responsiveness in detoxified cocaine-dependent subjects. *Nature, 386,* 830–833.

von Békésy, G. (1957). The ear. *Scientific American, 197,* 66–78.

von Mayrhauser, R. T. (1992). The mental testing community and validity: A prehistory. *American Psychologist, 47,* 244–253.

Votruba, S. B., Horvitz, M. A., & Schoeller, D. A. (2000). The role of exercise in the treatment of obesity. *Nutrition, 16,* 179–188.

Wachs, T. D., Gurkas, P., & Kontos, S. (2004). Predictors of preschool children's compliance behavior in early childhood classroom settings. *Journal of Applied Developmental Psychology, 25,* 439–457.

Wahba, M. A., & Bridwell, L. G. (1976). Maslow reconsidered: A review of research on the need hierarchy theory. *Organization Behavior and Human Performance, 15,* 212–240.

Wald, G. (1964). The receptors of human color vision. *Science, 145,* 1007–1017.

Wald, G., Brown, P. K., & Smith, P. H. (1954). Iodopsin. *Journal of General Physiology, 38,* 623–681.

Walder, D. J., Faraone, S. V., Glatt, S. J., Tsuang, M. T., & Seidman, L. J. (2014). Genetic liability, prenatal health, stress and family environment: Risk factors in the Harvard Adolescent Family High Risk for Schizophrenia Study. *Schizophrenia Research, 157*(1), 142–148.

Waldron, S., & Helm, F. (2004). Psychodynamic features of two cognitive-behavioural and one psychodynamic treatment compared using the analytic process scales. *Canadian Journal of Psychoanalysis, 12,* 346–368.

Walitzer, K. S., & Demen, K. H.(2004). Alcohol-focused spouse involvement and behavioral couples therapy: Evaluation of enhancements to drinking reduction treatment for male problem drinkers. *Journal of Consulting & Clinical Psychology, 72,* 944–955.

Walker, D. (2000). Online therapy? Not yet. *CBS News.* New York: CBS.

Walker, E., Kestler, L., Bollini, A., & Hochman, K. M. (2004). Schizophrenia: Etiology and course. *Annual Review of Psychology, 55,* 401–430.

Walker, E., Mittal, V., & Tessner, K. (2008). Stress and the hypothalamic pituitary adrenal axis in the developmental course of schizophrenia. *Annual Review of Clinical Psychology, 4,* 189–216.

Walker, L. (1989). A longitudinal study of moral reasoning. *Child Development, 60,* 157–166.

Walker, L., de Vries, B., & Trevethan, S. (1987). Moral stages and moral orientations in real life and hypothetical dilemmas. *Child Development, 58,* 842–858.

Walker, M., & Stickgold, R. (2006). Sleep, memory, and plasticity. In S. Fiske, A. Kazdin, & D. Schacter (Eds.) *Annual Review of Psychology: 57,* 139–166.

Wallach, H. (1985). Perceiving a stable environment. *Scientific American, 252,* 118–124.

Wallach, M. A., & Wallach, L. (1983). *Psychology's sanction for selfishness: The error of egoism in theory and therapy.* New York: W. H. Freeman.

Wang, S. H., & Morris, R. G. (2010). Hippocampal-neocortical interactions in memory formation, consolidation, and reconsolidation. *Annual Review of Psychology, 61,* 22.1–22.31.

Wang, X., & Perry, A. C. (2006). Metabolic and physiologic responses to video game play in 7- to 10-year-old boys. *Archives of Pediatric Adolescent Medicine, 160,* 411–415.

Wark, G. R., & Krebs, D. L. (1996). Gender and dilemma differences in real-life moral judgement. *Developmental Psychology, 32,* 220–230.

Warren, R. M. (1999). *Auditory perception: A new analysis and synthesis.* New York: Cambridge University Press.

Wasserman, E. A., & Miller, R. R. (1997). What's elementary about associative learning? *Annual Review of Psychology, 48,* 573–607.

Watamura, S. E., Donzella, B., Alwin, J., & Gunnar, M. R. (2003). Morning-to-afternoon increases in cortisol concentrations for infants and toddlers at childcare: Age differences and behavioral correlates. *Child Development, 74,* 1006–1020.

Watson, D. (2001). Dissociations of the night: Individual differences in sleep-related experiences and their relation to dissociation and schizotypy. *Journal of Abnormal Psychology, 110,* 526–535.

Watson, D., Beer, A., & McDade-Montez, E. (2014). The role of active assortment in spousal similarity. *Journal of personality, 82*(2), 116–129.

Watson, J. B., & Rayner, R. (1920). Conditioned emotional reactions. *Journal of Experimental Psychology, 3,* 1–14.

Waugh, N. C., & Norman, D. A. (1965). Primary memory. *Psychological Review, 72,* 89–104.

Weaver, M., & Schnoll, S. (2008). Hallucinogens and club drugs. In M. Galanter, & H. Kleber (Eds), *The American Psychiatric Publishing textbook of substance abuse* (4th ed., pp. 191–200). Arlington, VA: American Psychiatric Publishing.

Webb, W. B. (1995). The cost of sleep-related accidents: A reanalysis. *Sleep, 18,* 276–280.

Webb, T. L., & Sheeran, P. (2006). Does changing behavioral intentions engender behavior change? A meta-analysis of the experimental evidence. *Psychological Bulletin, 132*(2), 249–268.

Weber, R., Ritterfeld, U., & Mathiak, K. (2006). Does playing violent video games induce aggression? Empirical evidence of a functional magnetic resonance imaging study. *Media Psychology, 8,* 39–60.

Weeden, J., & Sabini, J. (2005). Physical attractiveness and health in Western societies: a review. *Psychological Bulletin, 131*(5), 635–653.

Weeks, D. L., & Anderson, L. P. (2000). The interaction of observational learning with overt practice: Effects on motor skill learning. *Acta Psychologia, 104,* 259–271.

Weigman, O., & van Schie, E. G. (1998). Video game playing and its relations with aggressive and prosocial behaviour. *British Journal of Social Psychology, 37*(Part 3), 367–378.

Weiner, B. (1972). *Theories of motivation: From mechanism to cognition.* Chicago: Rand McNally.

Weiner, B. (Ed.). (1974). *Achievement motivation and attribution theory.* Norristown, NJ: General Learning Press.

Weiner, B. (1985). "Spontaneous" causal thinking. *Psychological Bulletin, 97,* 74–84.

Weiner, I. B. (1997). Current status of the Rorschach Inkblot Method. *Journal of Personality Assessment, 68,* 5–19.

Weingartner, H., Adefris, W., Eich, J. E., & Murphy, D. L. (1976). Encoding-imagery specificity in alcohol state-dependent learning. *Journal of Experimental Psychology: Human Learning and Memory, 2,* 83–87.

Weinstein, S. (1968). Intensive and extensive aspects of tactile sensitivity as a function of body part, sex, and laterality. In D. R. Kenshalo (Ed.), *The skin senses.* Springfield, IL: Charles C. Thomas.

Weinstock, S. (1954). Resistance to extinction of a running response following partial reinforcement under widely spaced trials. *Journal of Comparative and Physiological Psychology, 47,* 318–322.

Weisberg, M. (2008). 50 years of hypnosis in medicine and clinical health psychology: A synthesis of cultural crosscurrents. *American Journal of Clinical Hypnosis, 51,* 13–27.

Weissman, M. M., Bland, R. C., Canino, G. J., Greenwald, S., Hwu, H.-G., Lee, C. K., . . . Yeh, E.-K. (1994). The cross national epidemiology of obsessive compulsive disorder. *Journal of Clinical Psychiatry, 55*(3, Suppl.), 5–10.

Wells, D. L., & Ott, C. A. (2011). The "new" marijuana. *Annals of Pharmacotherapy, 45*(3), 414–417.

Wesensten, N. J. (2014). Legitimacy of concerns about caffeine and energy drink consumption. *Nutrition Reviews, 72,* 78–86.

Wells, G. L. (1993). What do we know about eyewitness identification? *American Psychologist, 48,* 553–571.

Wertheimer, M. (1912). Experimental studies of the perception of movement. *Zeitschrift fur Psychologie, 61,* 161–265.

Wertheimer, M. (1958). Principles of perceptual organization. In D. C. Beardslee & M. Wertheimer (Eds.), *Readings in perception* (pp. 115–135). Princeton, NJ: Van Nostrand.

Wesensten, N. J., Belenky, G., Kautz, M. A., Thorne, D. R., Reichardt, R. M., & Balkin, T. J. (2002). Maintaining alertness and performance during sleep deprivation: Modafinil versus caffeine. *Psychopharmacology, 159*(3), 238–247.

Westen, D. (1998). The scientific legacy of Freud: Toward a psychonomically informed psychological science. *Psychological Bulletin, 124*(3), 333–371.

Westrin, A., & Lam, R. W. (2007). Seasonal affective disorder: A clinical update. *Annals of Clinical Psychiatry, 19*(4), 239–246.

Wetherell, J. L., Gatz, M., & Craske, M. G. (2003). Treatment of generalized anxiety disorder in older adults. *Journal of Consulting & Clinical Psychology, 71,* 31–40.

Wheeler, M. A., Stuss, D. T., & Tulving, E. (1997). Toward a theory of episodic memory: The frontal lobes and autonoetic consciousness. *Psychological Bulletin, 121*(3), 331–354.

Whisman, M. (2008). *Adapting cognitive therapy for depression: Managing complexity and comorbidity.* New York: Guilford Press.

Whitaker, D. J., & Miller, K. S. (2000). Parent-adolescent discussions about sex and condoms: Impact on peer influences of sexual risk behavior. *Journal of Adolescent Research, 15,* 251–272.

Whitehurst, G. J., Fischel, J. E., Caulfield, M. B., DeBaryshe, B. D., & Valdez-Menchaca, M. C. (1989). Assessment and treatment of early expressive language delay. In P. R. Zelazo & R. Barr (Eds.)., *Challenges to developmental paradigms: Implications for assessment and treatment* (pp. 113–135). Hillsdale, NJ: Erlbaum.

Whorf, B. L. (1956). Science and linguistics. In J. B. Carroll (Ed.), *Language, thought, and reality: Selected writings of Benjamin Lee Whorf.* Cambridge, MA: MIT Press.

Wickelgren, I. (1997). Getting a grasp on working memory. *Science, 275,* 1580–1582.

Wicker, A. W. (1969). Attitudes versus action: The relationship of verbal and overt behavioral responses to attitude objects. *Journal of Social Issues, 25,* 41–78.

Widom, C. S. (1989). Does violence beget violence? A critical examination of the literature. *Psychological Bulletin, 106,* 3–28.

Wigboldus, D. H., Dijksterhuis, A., & van Knippenberg, A. (2003). When stereotypes get in the way: Stereotypes obstruct stereotype-inconsistent trait inferences. *Journal of Personality and Social Psychology, 84,* 470–484.

Wigfield, A., & Eccles, A. (2000). Expectancy–value theory of achievement motivation. *Contemporary Educational Psychology, 25*(1), 68–81.

Wilbram, M., Kellett, S., & Beail, N. (2008). Compulsive hoarding: A qualitative investigation of partner and carer perspectives. *British Journal of Clinical Psychology, 47,* 59–73.

Wilford, M. M., Chan, J. C. K., & Tuhn, S. J. (2014). Retrieval enhances eyewitness suggestibility to misinformation in free and cued recall. *Journal of Experimental Psychology: Applied, 20*(1), 81–93. doi:http://dx.doi.org/10.1037/xap0000001

Williams, D. R., & Mohammed, S. A. (2009). Discrimination and racial disparities in health: Evidence and needed research. *Journal of Behavioral Medicine, 32,* 20–47.

Williams, K., Harkins, S. G., & Latané, B. (1981). Identifiability as a deterrent to social loafing: Two cheering experiments. *Journal of Personality and Social Psychology, 40,* 303–311.

Williams, K. D., & Karau, S. J. (1991). Social loafing and social compensation: The effects of expectations of co-worker performance. *Journal of Personality and Social Psychology, 61,* 570–581.

Willoughby, T., Good, M., Adachi, P.J.C., Hamza, C.A., & Tavernier, R. (2013). Examining the link between adolescent brain development and risk taking from a social-developmental perspective. *Brain and Cognition, 83*(3), 315–323.

Willoughby, T., Wood, E., McDermott, C., & McLaren, J. (2000). Enhancing learning through strategy instruction and group interaction: Is active generation of elaborations critical? *Applied Cognitive Psychology, 14,* 19–30.

Wilson, G., & Sysko, R. (2006). Cognitive-behavioral therapy for adolescents with bulimia nervosa. *European Eating Disorders Review, 14,* 8–16.

Wilson, F. R. (1998). *The hand: How its use shapes the brain, language, and human culture.* New York: Pantheon.

Wilson, M. A., & McNaughton, B. L. (1993). Dynamics of the hippocampal ensemble code for space. *Science, 261,* 1055–1058.

Winsler, A., & Naglieri, J. (2003). Overt and covert verbal problem-solving strategies: Developmental trends in use, awareness, and relations with task performance in children aged 5 to 17. *Child Development, 74,* 659–678.

Winston, A. S. (1996). The context of correctness: A comment on Rushton. *Journal of Social Distress and the Homeless, 5*(2), 231–250.

Wise, R. A., & Kiyatkin, E. A. (2011). Differentiating the rapid actions of cocaine. *Nature Reviews Neuroscience, 12*(8), 479–484.

Witelson, S. F. (1985). The brain connection: The corpus callosum is larger in left-handers. *Science, 229,* 665–668.

Witt, P. L., Brown, K. C., Roberts, J. B., Weisel, J., Sawyer, C. R., & Behnke, R. R. (2006). Somatic anxiety patterns of student speakers before, during, and after giving a public speech. *Southern Communication Journal, 71,* 87–100.

Witty, P. A., & Jenkins M. D. (1936). Intra-race testing and Negro intelligence. *Journal of Psychology, 1,* 188–191.

Wolkin, A., Barouche, F., Wolf, A. P., Rotrosen, J., Fowler, J. S., Shiue, C. Y., . . . Brodie, J. D. (1989). Dopamine blockade and clinical response: Evidence for two biological subgroups of schizophrenia. *American Journal of Psychiatry, 146,* 905–908.

Wolkove, N., Elkholy, O., Baltzan, M., & Palayew, M. (2007). Sleep and aging: 1: Sleep disorders commonly found in older people. *Canadian Medical Association Journal, 176*(9), 1299–1304.

Woloshyn, V., Willoughby, T., Wood, E., & Pressley, M. (1990). Elaborative interrogation facilitates adult learning of factual paragraphs. *Journal of Educational Psychology, 82,* 513–524.

Wolpe, J. (1958). *Psychotherapy by reciprocal inhibition.* Stanford, CA: Stanford University Press.

Wolpe, J. (1973). *The practice of behavior therapy* (2nd ed.). New York: Pergamon Press.

Wolters, C. A. (2003). Understanding procrastination from a self-regulated learning perspective. *Journal of Educational Psychology, 95*(1), 179–187.

Wong, I., McLeod, C. B., & Demers, B. (2011). Shift work trends and risk for worker injury in Canada. *Scandinavian Journal of Work Environment and Health, 37*(1), 54–61.

Wood, E., Pressley, M., & Winne, P. (1990). Elaborative interrogation effects on children's learning of factual content. *Journal of Educational Psychology, 82,* 741–748.

Wood, E., Woloshyn, V., & Willoughby, T. (1995). *Cognitive strategies for middle and high schools.* Cambridge, MA: Brookline Press.

Wood, J. M., Lilienfeld, S. O., & Garb, H. N. (2000). The Rorschach test in clinical diagnosis: A critical review with a backward look at Garfield (1947). *Journal of Clinical Psychology, 56*(3), 395–420.

Wood, J. M., Lilienfeld, S. O., Nezworski, M. T., Garb, H. N., Allen, K H., & Wildermuth, J. L. (2010). Validity of the Rorschach ink-blot scores for discriminating psychopaths from nonpsychopaths in forensic populations: A meta-analysis. *Psychological Assessment, 22*(2), 336–349.

Wood, W. J., & Conway, M. (2006). Subjective impact, meaning making, and current and recalled emotions for self-defining memories. *Journal of Personality, 75,* 811–846.

Woodman, G. F., & Luck, S. J. (2003). Serial deployment of attention during visual search. *Journal of Experimental Psychology: Human Perception and Performance, 29,* 121–138.

Woodruff-Pak, D. (2001). Eyeblink classical conditioning differentiates normal aging from Alzheimer's disease. *Integrative Physiological & Behavioral Science, 36,* 87–108.

Woolley, C. S., Weiland, N. G., McEwen, B. S., & Schwartzkroin, P. A. (1997). Estradiol increases the sensitivity of hippocampal CA1 pyramidal cells to NMDA receptor-mediated synaptic output: Correlation with dendritic spine density. *Journal of Neuroscience, 17,* 1848–1859.

World Health Organization (WHO). (2010). *Antiretroviral therapy for HIV infections in adults and adolescents: Recommendations for a public health approach.* Retrieved February 27, 2015, from http://whqlibdoc.who.int/publications/2010/9789241599764_eng.pdf

World Health Organization (2012). Suicide rates per 100,000 by country, year and sex. Retrieved May 16, 2012, from http://www.who.int/mental_health/prevention/suicide_rates/en/index.html

Worrel, J. A., Marken, P. A., Beckman, S. E., & Ruehter, V. L. (2000). Atypical antipsychotic agents: A critical review. *American Journal of Health System Pharmacology, 57,* 238–255.

Worthen, J. B., & Wood, V. V. (2001). Memory discrimination for self-performed and imagined acts: Bizarreness effects in false recognition. *Quarterly Journal of Experimental Psychology, 54A,* 49–67.

Wright Jr, K. P., McHill, A. W., Birks, B. R., Griffin, B. R., Rusterholz, T., & Chinoy, E. D. (2013). Entrainment of the human circadian clock to the natural light-dark cycle. *Current Biology, 23,* 1554–1558.

Wright, L. (2008, May 8). In the company of women. *Toronto Star.* Retrieved from http://www.thestar.com/Business/SmallBusiness/article/421959

Wright, M. J., & Myers, C. R. (1982). *History of academic psychology in Canada.* Toronto: C. J. Hogrefe.

Wright, S. C., Taylor, D. M., & Macarthur, J. (2000). Subtractive bilingualism and the survival of the Inuit language: Heritage-versus second-language education. *Journal of Educational Psychology, 92,* 63–84.

Wright, S. C., Taylor, D. M., & Moghaddam, F. (1990). Responding to membership in a disadvantaged group: From acceptance to collective protest. *Journal of Personality and Social Psychology, 58,* 994–1003.

Wyrobek, A. J., Eskenazi, B., Young, S., Arnheim, N., Tiemann-Boege, I., Jabs, E. W., . . . Evenson, D. (2006). Advancing age has differential effects on DNA damage, chromatin integrity, gene mutations, and aneuploidies. *Proceedings of the National Academies of Sciences, 103,* 9601–9606

Wyrostok, N. C., & Paulson, B. L. (2000). Traditional healing practices among First Nations students. *Canadian Journal of Counselling and Psychotherapy, 34*(1), 14–24.

Yackinous, C. A., & Guinard, J.-X. (2002, June). Relation between PROP (6-n-propylthiouracil) taster status, taste anatomy and dietary intake measures for young men and women. *Appetite, 38*(3), 201–209.

Yamada, T. (2009). The physiology of gastric motility and gastric emptying. In W. L. Hasler (Ed)., *Textbook of gastroenterology* (Chapter 10). New York: Wiley-Blackwell.

Yancey, J. R., Venables, N. C., Hicks, B. M., & Patrick, C. J. (2013). Evidence for a heritable brain basis to deviance-promoting deficits in self-control. *Journal of Criminal Justice, 41*(5), 309–317.

Yao, S., Fang, J., Zhu, X., & Zuroff, D. C. (2009). The depressive experiences questionnaire: Construct validity and prediction of depressive symptoms in a sample of Chinese undergraduates. *Depression and Anxiety, 26*(10), 930–937.

Yarmey, A. D., Yarmey, M. J., & Yarmey, A. L. (1996). Accuracy of eyewitness identification in showups and lineups. *Law and Human Behavior, 20*(4), 459–477.

Yerkes R. M., & Dodson, J. D. (1908). The relation of strength of stimulus to rapidity of habit-formation. *Journal of Comparative Neurology and Psychology, 18,* 459–482.

Yuille, J. C., & Tollestrup, P. A. (1992). A model of the diverse effects of emotion in eyewitness memory. In S. A. Christianson (Ed.), *The handbook of emotional learning: Research and theory.* Hillsdale, NJ: Erlbaum.

Zahr, N. M., Kaufman, K. L., & Harper, C. G. (2011). Clinical and pathological features of alcohol-related brain damage. *Nature Reviews Neurology, 7*(5), 284–294.

Zajonc, R. B. (1965). Social facilitation. *Science, 149,* 269–274.

Zajonc, R. B. (1968). Attitudinal effects of mere exposure. *Journal of Personality and Social Psychology, Monographs Supplement, 9*(Part 2), 1–27.

Zajonc, R. B. (1980). Feeling and thinking: Preferences need no inferences. *American Psychologist, 35,* 151–175.

Zajonc, R. B. (1984). On the primacy of affect. *American Psychologist, 39,* 117–123.

Zajonc, R. B. (1998). Emotions. In D. T. Gilbert, S. T. Fiske, et al. (Eds.), *The handbook of social psychology* (4th ed., pp. 591–632). Boston: McGraw-Hill.

Zajonc, R. B., & Sales, S. M. (1966). Social facilitation of dominant and subordinate responses. *Journal of Experimental Social Psychology, 2,* 160–168.

Zald, D.H., & Pardo, J.V. (2000). Functional neuroimaging of the olfactory system in humans. *International Journal of Psychophysiology, 36,* 165–181 .

Zanna, M. P., & Rempel, J. K. (1988). Attitudes and attitude change. *Annual Review of Psychology, 38,* 575–630.

Zarrindast, M-R. & Rezayof, A. (2004). Morphine state-dependent learning: sensitization and interactions with dopamine receptors. *European Journal of Pharmacology, 497,* 197–204.

Zatorre, R. J., Belin, P., & Penhune, V. B. (2002). Structure and function of the auditory cortex: Music and speech. *Trends in Cognitive Sciences, 6,* 37–46.

Zhang, X. L., Cohen, H. L., Porjesz, B., & Begleiter, H. (2001). Mismatch negativity in subjects at high risk for alcoholism. *Alcoholism: Clinical & Experimental Research, 25,* 330–337.

Zilbergeld, B. (1986, June). Psychabuse. *Science, 86,* 48–52.

Zimbardo, P. (1969). The human choice: Individuation, reason, and order versus deindividuation, impulse, and chaos. *Nebraska Symposium on Motivation, 17,* 237–307.

Zimbardo, P. G. (1972). Pathology of imprisonment. *Society, 9,* 4–8.

Zimbardo, P. G., Haney, C., & Banks, W. C. (1973, April 8). A Pirandellian prison. *The New York Times Magazine,* 38–60.

Zinbarg, R., & Griffith, J. (2008). Behavior therapy. In J. Lebow (Ed.), *Twenty-first century psychotherapies: Contemporary approaches to theory and practice* (pp. 8–42). Hoboken, NJ: Wiley.

Zola, S. M., Squire, L. R., Teng, E., Stefanacci, L., Buffalo, E. A., & Clark, R. E. (2000). Impaired recognition memory in monkeys after damage limited to the hippocampal region. *Journal of Neuroscience, 20,* 451–463.

Zubieta, J. K., Bueller, J. A., Jackson, L. R., Scott, D. J., Xu, Y., Koeppe, R. A., Nichols, T. E., & Stohler, C. S. (2005). Placebo effects mediated by endogenous opioid activity on μ-opioid receptors. *The Journal of Neuroscience, 25,* 7754–7762.

Zuckerman, M. (2014). Sensation seeking, impulsivity and the balance between behavioral approach and inhibition. *Personality and Individual Differences, 60*(Supplement), S4.

NAME INDEX

SUBJECT INDEX

Note: Page numbers followed by *f* and *t*, denote figure and table, respectively.